8th Edition

Criminal Procedure: A Case Approach

Judy Hails, J.D., LL.M.
California State University—Long Beach

THOMSON
WADSWORTH

Australia • Canada • Mexico • Singapore • Spain
United Kingdom • United States

ISBN: 1-928916-25-2
Library of Congress Catalog Number: 2003106878

Wadsworth/Thomson Learning
10 Davis Drive
Belmont CA 94002-3098
USA

For information about our products, contact us:
Thomson Learning Academic Resource Center
1-800-423-0563
http://www.wadsworth.com

Printed in the United States of America
10 9 8 7 6 5 4 3 2

Contents

Chapter 5

Chapter 6

Chapter 7

Chapter 8

Varying Expectations of Privacy: International Borders and Closed Containers 231

Chapter 9

Privilege against Self-Incrimination 261

Chapter 10

Chapter 14

Chapter 15

Preface

During the last 40 years, the United States Supreme Court has played a major role in shaping criminal procedure. Unfortunately, the Court's insistence on deciding "cases and controversies" has prevented it from taking a comprehensive approach to the subject. Instead, adjudication has been fragmented. Changes—some major, some minor—are made each year. Due to lack of congruence among the cases that have been accepted for review, as well as changing philosophies and personalities on the Court, the result has been a puzzle that does not fit together: Some pieces are missing and some of those that are present have edges that do not fit together.

Despite these problems, officers working in criminal justice must know how to apply the Court's holdings to the myriad of factual situations that confront them. This process of applying the established law to ever-changing scenarios requires both knowledge of what has already been decided and an understanding of the logic used by the Court. This book is designed to help the student develop both knowledge of the established law and the analytical skills needed for facing volatile situations in the field.

Each chapter begins with textual material explaining the current law on the topic, followed by "Key Supreme Court Cases." Cases have been selected for one of two reasons: The case is a landmark or the issue presented is one frequently encountered by law enforcement. Following these are "Other Supreme Court Cases," which include lesser-known cases or those dealing with more subtle issues. Lastly, each chapter ends with a quiz and hypothetical, factual situations for discussion. Each chapter goes from the concrete to the more nebulous aspects of criminal procedure. The cases serve two functions: They show how the law applies to specific facts; and they provide an opportunity to gain insight into the reasoning process used by the Supreme Court. The "Discussion Questions" offer readers an opportunity to apply what they have learned. Many of these questions have been designed to illustrate the "gray areas" that are not clearly covered by established law, thus providing students the opportunity to develop analytical skills.

Undergraduates studying criminal procedure are frequently confused by the way the Supreme Court cases are written. The procedural history of the case (sometimes a trail of decisions through three or four levels of the court system) can be complicated. Case decisions are often lengthy because the Court gives the history of the legal issues involved. Issues unrelated to criminal justice, such as whether the Supreme Court should hear the case, are often discussed. Opinions are often so full of citations and parenthetical references to old cases that it is difficult to determine the Court's reasoning in the case being read. Concurring decisions and dissents, although of great interest to legal scholars and law students, have no value as precedent.

This book presents the cases in a manner ideally suited for the undergraduate. Each case has been partially briefed to focus on the rationale for the Court's holding. The facts have been abstracted from the case and set out at the beginning of each case. The issue is also stated clearly in an easy-to-identify manner. The material presented under "Reasoning" is quoted from the opinion of the Court. The relevant elements of the Court's decision have been captured in as concise a manner as possible while still giving the flavor of the full opinion. Three asterisks (* * *) have been inserted to show that portions of the opinion were omitted. If the historical basis for the decision is given in an earlier case in the same chapter, it is not repeated. Absent are citations and parenthetical references to previous cases except where the case is actually discussed in the body of the decision. If the case being cited is in the chapter, the citation is not repeated. When a citation is given, only the official citation (United States Reports) is given to avoid unnecessary visual distraction and also because this is the Court's habit. Lastly, the disposition of the case is clearly noted so the student will understand the impact of the decision on the defendant.

This text includes fifteen chapters. Some classes will not be able to cover each in its entirety. The extra material is included to give the instructor the opportunity to tailor the course as desired. Some may want to focus on the "Key Supreme Court Cases" and others may decide to skip chapters that deal with topics that students will be less likely to confront in the field. The book is designed to maximize the instructor's ability to provide the student with a relevant understanding of criminal procedure and the judicial process.

JH

Table of Cases

Chapter 1

Criminal Procedure As a Constitutional Issue

Outline

The Bill of Rights is now over 200 years old. Those who have grown up in the last 35 years might assume that its protections have always governed how the criminal justice system operates. In fact, it was not until the 1960s that the United States Supreme Court became heavily involved in interpreting how the Bill of Rights applied to the actions of local law enforcement officers.

Every law enforcement officer has a duty to know the constitutional rights of criminal suspects. This will be a career-long learning process because the Court establishes new precedents and modifies old ones every year. It also requires an understanding of why the Court has decided cases the way it has because officers are constantly called upon to handle cases with facts that do not exactly match those in cases the Court has decided. To perform this analysis, the officer must know the spirit of the decisions as well as the specific holdings in the cases. This book is designed to teach officers the skills they will need; it states the current law and provides edited versions of Supreme Court opinions so that students can develop a feeling for the reasoning process used by the Court.

The vast majority of cases affecting criminal justice involve searches and seizures, confessions, and trial procedures. Also of importance are issues related to law enforcement's duty to protect suspects' First Amendment rights. Chapters of this book are devoted to these issues.

The use of force is a key issue and will be presented at the outset. At one time, the Court used a due process analysis, but current cases rely on the Fourth and Eighth Amendments. Two types of police actions are involved: (1) impermissible methods to recover evidence suspects have in their bodies; and (2) use of force to apprehend suspects.

Because the Bill of Rights was enacted expressly to restrain the federal government, the Supreme Court may not directly apply these protections to actions by state and local governments. Instead, it is done by interpreting the Due Process and Equal Protection Clauses of the Fourteenth Amendment. This has been done on an issue-by-issue basis and is referred to as "selective incorporation." Most, but not all, of the rights embodied in the first nine amendments have now been held to apply to state criminal justice systems in the same manner as to the federal system. For example, the Court has interpreted due process as prohibiting the introduction of coerced confessions (a violation of the Fifth Amendment Self-Incrimination Clause) in state courts; the requirement that felony charges be presented to a grand jury (also in the Fifth Amendment) has not been applied to the states.

1-1 Historical Development

The principle that "a man's home is his castle" existed in England long before the colonies were settled in America. It gave even the poorest peasants the right to exclude the King from their homes. The English Bill of Rights was enacted by Parliament in 1689, but the British freely used the "general warrant" in their American colonies. This warrant was a blank check for soldiers to search homes for whatever evidence they might find.

Many of the original states expressed disapproval of the "general warrant" by including a prohibition against unreasonable searches and seizures in their constitutions. When the U.S. Constitution was ratified, it did not contain any mention of the protections now in our Bill of Rights. Many of the states that ratified the Constitution did so on the condition that additional protections against the power of the federal government be included. The first ten amendments to the Constitution, known as the Bill of Rights, were added in 1791 only four years after the Constitution was ratified. Its wording has not been changed since then.

Even after the Bill of Rights was added to the U.S. Constitution there were few cases brought to the Supreme Court relating to criminal justice. The Supreme Court did decide cases related to actions of federal law enforcement agencies and the criminal prosecutions in federal courts. *Boyd v. United States,* decided in 1886, is one of the earliest examples of the Court applying one of the amendments in the Bill of Rights to the actions of federal agents.

In 1914, the Court decided *Weeks v. United States,* which required federal courts to exclude evidence seized illegally by federal agents. Once this precedent was established, the Court was forced to review numerous criminal cases to determine if the federal officers had violated constitutional rights. When the Court acts in this role of supervisor of the federal government or exercises its power to interpret federal statutes, the decisions have no direct impact on state and local agencies.

It was not until 1961 that the Court, in *Mapp v. Ohio,* required state courts to exclude evidence seized in violation of the Fourth Amendment. The authority to make this mandate to the states was found in the Due Process Clause of the Fourteenth Amendment. *Mapp* merely established the Exclusionary Rule—it did not answer the question of what the Fourth Amendment required. Later decisions also established Fifth Amendment protections of defendants in state courts.

In the nearly five decades between Weeks and *Mapp,* the Court had developed guidelines for federal agents. Much of the work had to be redone in order to decide which rules were of constitutional significance, and therefore applied to local law enforcement, and which rules applied only to federal officers. Additionally, many cases had to be decided that dealt with situations not frequently encountered by federal agents. Many novel problems are still undecided.

The procedures used by the Supreme Court have complicated the task for several reasons. First, the Court tries to decide as narrow an issue as possible in each case. The Court has never tried to make one comprehensive set of rules to cover searches and seizures or confessions. Second, the Court is continually changing the law. Sometimes it openly declares that an older case is no longer good precedent, as was done in 1963 when *Gideon v. Wainwright* reversed the 1942 case of *Betts v. Brady.* More commonly, a decision makes minor adjustments in an older case or declares that the older case can be distinguished on its facts. Third, as the individual members of the Court have changed, so has the tenor of the Court's decisions. The Warren Court of the 1960s viewed many issues differently than the Rehnquist Court of 1990. The result is law that resembles a jigsaw puzzle with some pieces missing and others that do not fit.

1-2 Impermissible Methods of Obtaining Evidence

Our society imposes certain boundaries that may not be crossed by the police in their search for criminals. The Supreme Court has said that police cannot use methods that "shock the conscience" or "offend the sense of justice." These concepts come directly from the Due Process Clause of the Fifth Amendment (for actions of federal agents) and the Fourteenth Amendment (for actions by state and local officers).

Rochin v. California is the landmark case in this area. Rochin attempted to swallow the evidence. The police responded by having his stomach pumped. The Court found that this procedure was very painful and could not be tolerated in a civilized society. The use of the "third degree" to obtain confessions is on a similar footing. Due process is violated when coercion is used during interrogation. The concept of due process is broader than the specific guarantees enumerated in the Bill of Rights.

Blood tests have also posed problems. The Court has balanced the need for the evidence that can be obtained in this manner against the invasion of a person's privacy. The relatively minor inconvenience of a blood test has been accepted in cases such as driving under the influence of alcohol, wherein it is desirable to perform laboratory tests. *Schmerber v. California* established the right to take blood samples without a warrant for this reason. The fact that the body rapidly absorbs alcohol was seen as creating an emergency exception to the warrant requirement. Most drivers would be sober before officers could obtain a search warrant. Even in these drunk driving cases there is still a limit on the amount of force that police can use to obtain the blood sample. Use of excessive force may render the evidence inadmissible.

Whenever blood is drawn by government employees for the use of law enforcement, the Fourth Amendment must be considered. In *Ferguson v. City of Charleston* (532 U.S. 67, 149 L.Ed. 2d 205, 121 S.Ct. 1281(2001)), the Court reviewed the actions of a state hospital's staff. Frustrated at the failure of their efforts to convince pregnant women to stop using drugs, the staff took blood samples and, without the knowledge of the women, turned the blood tests over to law enforcement. The medical staff's intent was to coerce the women into participating in substance abuse treatment but the result was that the women were arrested and prosecuted. The Court ruled that a state hospital's performance of diagnostic tests to obtain evidence of a patient's criminal conduct for law enforcement purposes was an unreasonable search that violated the Fourth Amendment rights of the women.

The Court has also considered the question of performing surgery on a suspect to obtain evidence. The case involved the prosecution's request to surgically remove a bullet lodged in the arm of a suspect who was shot during a robbery. The Court held that a search warrant or other court order based on probable cause must be obtained prior to performing the operation. Since the suspect will be in custody when this type of petition is filed, the defense has the right to present arguments at the time the prosecution asks the judge for the warrant.

The Court has established a balancing test heavily favoring the privacy of the individual. Surgical procedures that pose a threat to the suspect's health may not be done. The prosecution must show a compelling need for the evidence. If other witnesses who can supply the needed information, surgery is not considered a reasonable alternative.

1-3 Use of Physical Force

Methods used to make arrests are covered by the Fourth Amendment. Prior to 1985, the Court's analysis focused on whether there was probable cause to justify an arrest. In *Tennessee v. Garner*, the Court looked at the amount of force that could be used to detain a suspect. It found that it was unreasonable to use deadly force to apprehend a suspect if there was no immediate threat of death or life-threatening injury to the officer or others. The common law rule that permitted the use of deadly force to prevent the escape of a fleeing felon was held to be too broad.

In a later case, the Court explicitly stated that all claims that law enforcement officers have used excessive force in the course of arrest, investigatory stop, or other seizures of a citizen should be analyzed under the Fourth Amendment's reasonableness standard. This applies to the use of both deadly and nondeadly force. An officer's actions must show an objectively reasonable use of force; the officer's subjective opinion on how much force should be used is not considered. The standard is what a reasonable officer would do under the circumstances.

Police pursuits involve a different constitutional issue. While the right to stop a person is based on the Fourth Amendment, the Court held that actions taken by officers during a pursuit prior to detention or arrest are governed by due process. In this context, only deliberate acts intended to harm a person or interfere with his/her constitutional rights are actionable. Poor judgment and reckless driving during the pursuit, including failing to call off the chase when it became too dangerous, do not violate the suspect's due process rights.

1-4 Key Supreme Court Cases

1-4a *Rochin v. California:* 342 U.S. 165, 96 L.Ed. 183, 72 S.Ct. 205 (1952)

Facts: Three Los Angeles County deputy sheriffs went to Rochin's home on the morning of July 1, 1949 because they had information that he was selling narcotics. They entered the house through an open door and forced open the door to Rochin's bedroom. Rochin was sitting on the bed, partially dressed, and his wife was lying on the bed. The deputies saw two capsules on the nightstand beside the bed and said "Whose stuff is that?" Rochin grabbed the capsules and put them in his mouth. The deputies jumped him and unsuccessfully tried to remove the capsules from his mouth. Rochin was then arrested, handcuffed, and taken to a hospital. At the direction of the deputies, a doctor forced an emetic solution into Rochin's stomach through a tube. This caused vomiting. Two morphine capsules, which were the principal evidence against Rochin at trial, were found in the vomited matter. Rochin was convicted for possession of morphine.

Issue: Did pumping Rochin's stomach violate his due process rights?

Reasoning: "Regard for the requirements of the Due Process Clause 'inescapably imposes upon this Court an exercise of judgment upon the whole course of the proceedings [resulting in a conviction] in order to ascertain whether they offend those canons of decency and fairness which express the notions of justice of English-speaking people even toward those charged with the most heinous offenses.' These standards of justice are not authoritatively formulated anywhere as though they were specifics. Due process of law is a summarized constitutional guarantee of respect for those personal immunities which, as Mr. Justice Cardozo twice wrote for the Court, are 'so rooted in the traditions and conscience of our people as to be ranked as fundamental,' or are 'implicit in the concept of ordered liberty.'

*** "The vague contours of the Due Process Clause do not leave judges at large. We may not draw on our merely personal and private notions and disregard the limits that bind judges in their judicial function. Even though the concept of due process of law is not final and fixed, these limits are derived from considerations that are fused in the whole nature of our judicial process. These are considerations deeply rooted in reason and in the compelling traditions of the legal profession. The Due Process Clause places upon this Court the duty of exercising a judgment, within the narrow confines of judicial power, in reviewing State convictions, upon interests of society pushing in opposite directions.

*** "Applying these general considerations to the circumstances of the present case, we are compelled to conclude that the proceedings by which this conviction was obtained do more than offend some fastidious squeamishness or private sentimentalism about combatting crime too energetically. This is conduct that shocks the conscience. Illegally breaking into the privacy of the petitioner, the struggle to open his mouth and remove what was there, the forcible extraction of his stomach's contents—this course of proceeding by agents of government to obtain evidence is bound to offend even hardened sensibilities. They are methods too close to the rack and the screw to permit of constitutional differentiation.

"It has long since ceased to be true that due process of law is heedless of the means by which otherwise relevant and credible evidence is obtained. This was not true even before the series of recent cases enforced the constitutional principle that the States may not base convictions upon confessions, however much verified, obtained by coercion. These decisions are not arbitrary exceptions to the comprehensive right of States to fashion their own rules of evidence for criminal trials. They are not sports in our constitutional law but applications of a general principle. They are only instances of the general requirement that States in their prosecution respect certain decencies of civilized conduct. Due process of law, as a historic and generative principle, precludes defining, and thereby confining, these standards of conduct more precisely than to say that convictions cannot be brought about by methods that offend 'a sense of justice.' It would be a stultification of the responsibility which the course of constitutional history has cast upon this Court to hold that in order to convict a man the police cannot extract by force what is in his mind but can extract what is in his stomach."

Disposition: Conviction reversed; morphine capsules obtained by pumping Rochin's stomach are not admissible at trial.

1-4b *Schmerber v. California:* 384 U.S. 757, 16 L.Ed. 2d 908, 86 S.Ct. 1826 (1966)

Facts: Schmerber was arrested for driving under the influence of intoxicating liquor while he was at a hospital receiving treatment for injuries he suffered in an accident. At the direction of a police officer, a doctor drew a blood sample. Results of the blood alcohol test were admitted at Schmerber's trial. Schmerber was convicted of driving while under the influence of an intoxicating liquor.

Issue: Did the warrantless taking of a blood sample violate Schmerber's rights?

Reasoning: "*Breithaupt* was also a case in which police officers caused blood to be withdrawn from the driver of an automobile involved in an accident, and in which there was ample justification for the officer's conclusion that the driver was under the influence of alcohol. There, as here, the extraction was made by a physician in a simple, medically acceptable manner in a hospital environment. There, however, the driver was unconscious at the time the blood was withdrawn and hence had no opportunity to object to the procedure. We affirmed the conviction there resulting from the use of the test in evidence, holding that under such circumstances the withdrawal did not offend 'that "sense of justice" of which we spoke in *Rochin v. California.*' *Breithaupt* thus requires the rejection of petitioner's due process argument, and nothing in the circumstances of this case or in supervening events persuades us that this aspect of *Breithaupt* should be overruled.

*** "The values protected by the Fourth Amendment thus substantially overlap those the Fifth Amendment helps to protect. History and precedent have required that we today reject the claim that the Self-Incrimination Clause of the Fifth Amendment requires the human body in all circumstances to be held inviolate against state expeditions seeking evidence of crime. But if compulsory administration of a blood test does not implicate the Fifth Amendment, it plainly involves the broadly conceived reach of a search and seizure under the Fourth Amendment. That Amendment expressly provides that '[t]he right of the people to be secure in their persons, houses, papers, and effects, against unreasonable searches and seizures, shall not be violated.' *** It could not reasonably be argued, and indeed respondent does not argue, that the administration of the blood test in this case was free of the constrains of the Fourth Amendment. Such testing procedures plainly constitute searches of 'person,' and depend antecedently upon seizures of 'persons,' within the meaning of that Amendment.

*** "We begin with the assumption that once the privilege against self-incrimination has been found not to bar compelled intrusions into the body for blood to be analyzed for alcohol content, the Fourth Amendment's proper function is to constrain, not against all intrusions as such, but against intrusions which are not justified in the circumstances, or which are made in an improper manner. In other words, the questions we must decide in this case are whether the police were justified in requiring petitioner to submit to the blood test, and whether the means and procedures employed in taking his blood respected relevant Fourth Amendment standards of reasonableness.

*** "Whatever the validity of these considerations [right to make search incident of arrest] in general, they have little applicability with respect to searches involving intrusions beyond the body's surface. The interests in human dignity and privacy which the Fourth Amendment protects forbid any such intrusions on the mere chance that desired evidence might be obtained. In the absence of clear indication that in fact such evidence will be found, these fundamental human interests require law officers to suffer the risk that such evidence may disappear unless there is an immediate search.

"Although the facts which established probable cause to arrest in this case also suggested the required relevance and likely success of a test of petitioner's blood for alcohol, the question remains whether the arresting officer was permitted to draw these inferences himself, or was required instead to procure a warrant before proceedings with the test. Search warrants are ordinarily required for searches of dwellings, and, absent an emergency, no less could be required where intrusions into the human body are concerned. The requirement that a warrant be obtained is a requirement that the inferences to support the search 'be drawn by a neutral and detached magistrate instead of being judged by the officer engaged in the often competitive enterprise of ferreting out crime.' The importance of informed, detached and deliberate determinations of the issue whether or not to invade another's body in search of evidence of guilt is indisputable and great.

"The officer in the present case, however, might reasonably have believed that he was confronted with an emergency, in which the delay necessary to obtain a warrant, under the circumstances, threatened 'the destruction of evidence.' We are told that the percentage of alcohol in the blood begins to diminish shortly after drinking stops, as the body functions to eliminate it from the system. Particularly in a case such as this, where time had to be taken to bring the accused to a hospital and to investigate the scene of the accident, there was no time to seek out a magistrate and secure a warrant. Given these special facts, we conclude that the attempt to secure evidence of blood-alcohol content in this case was an appropriate incident to petitioner's arrest.

"Similarly, we are satisfied that the test chosen to measure petitioner's blood-alcohol level was a reasonable one. Extraction of blood samples for testing is a highly effective means of determining the degree to which a person is under the influence of alcohol. Such tests are a commonplace in these days of periodic physical examinations and experience with them teaches that the quantity of blood extracted is minimal, and that for most people the procedure involves virtually no risk, trauma, or pain. Petitioner is not one of the few who on grounds of fear, concern for health, or religious scruple might prefer some other means of testing, such as the 'breathalyzer' test petitioner refused. * * *

"Finally, the record shows that the test was performed in a reasonable manner. Petitioner's blood was taken by a physician in a hospital environment according to accepted medical practices. We are thus not presented with the serious questions which would arise if a search involving use of medical technique, even of the most rudimentary sort, were made by other than medical personnel or in other than a medical environment—for example, if it were administered by police in the privacy of the stationhouse. To tolerate searches under these conditions might be to invite an unjustified element of personal risk of infection.

"We thus conclude that the present record shows no violation of petitioner's right under the Fourth and Fourteenth Amendments to be free of unreasonable searches and seizures. It bears repeating, however, that we reach this judgment only on the facts of the present record. The integrity of an individual's person is a cherished value of our society. That we today hold that the Constitution does not forbid the States minor intrusions into an individual's body under stringently limited conditions in no way indicates that it permits more substantial intrusions, or intrusions under other conditions."

Disposition: Conviction affirmed; blood-alcohol test done on post-arrest blood sample drawn by medical personnel is admissible.

1-4c *Tennessee v. Garner:* 471 U.S. 1, 85 L.Ed. 2d 1, 105 S.Ct. 1694 (1985)

Facts: About 10:45 P.M. on October 3, 1974, Memphis Police Officers Hymon and Wright were dispatched to a prowler call. When they arrived, a woman was standing on her porch gesturing toward the adjacent house. She said "'they' were breaking in next door." Hymon went behind the house. He heard a door slam and saw someone run across the backyard. Garner fled, stopping at a six-foot-high chainlink fence at the edge of the yard. Light from Hymon's flashlight illuminated Garner's face and hands. There was no sign of a weapon. Hymon thought Garner was 17 or 18 years old and between 5′5″ and 5′7″ tall (he was actually 15 years old, 5′4″, and weighed 100–110 pounds). Hymon called "police, halt" and took a few steps forward as Garner began to climb over the fence. Hymon was convinced that Garner would evade capture if he made it over the fence, so he shot Garner. Garner died of one gunshot wound to the back of the head. Hymon was acting under a Tennessee law that stated "if, after notice of the intention to arrest the defendant, he either flee[s] or forcibly resist[s], the officer may use all the necessary means to effect the arrest." Garner's family filed a civil suit under the federal Civil Rights Act.

Issue: Can officers use deadly force to stop unarmed, fleeing felons?

Reasoning: "A police officer may arrest a person if he has probable cause to believe that person committed a crime. Petitioners and appellant argue that if this requirement is satisfied the Fourth Amendment has nothing to say about *how* that seizure is made. This submission ignores the many cases in which this Court, by balancing the extent of the intrusion against the need for it, has examined reasonableness of the manner in which a search or seizure is conducted. To determine the constitutionality of a seizure 'we must balance the nature and quality of the intrusion on the individual's Fourth Amendment interests against the importance of the governmental interests alleged to justify the intrusion.' * * * Because one of the factors is the extent of the intrusion, it is plain that reasonableness depends on not only when a seizure is made, but also how it is carried out. * * *

"The same balancing process applied in the cases cited above demonstrates that, notwithstanding probable cause to seize a suspect, an officer may not always do so by killing him. The intrusiveness of a seizure by means of deadly force is unmatched. The suspect's fundamental interest in his own life need not be elaborated upon. The use of deadly force also frustrates the interest of the individual, and of society, in judicial determination of guilt and punishment. Against these interests are ranged governmental interests in effective law enforcement. It is argued that overall violence will be reduced by encouraging the peaceful submission of suspects who know that they may be shot if they flee. Effectiveness in making arrests requires the resort to deadly force, or at least the meaningful threat thereof. * * *

"The use of deadly force to prevent the escape of all felony suspects, whatever the circumstances, is constitutionally unreasonable. It is not better that all felony suspects die than that they escape. Where the suspect poses no immediate threat to the officer and no threat to others, the harm resulting from failing to apprehend him does not justify the use of deadly force to do so. * * *

* * * "Where the officer has probable cause to believe that the suspect poses a threat of serious physical harm, either to the officer or to others, it is not constitutionally unreasonable to prevent escape by using deadly force. Thus, if the suspect threatens the officers with a weapon or there is probable cause to believe that he has committed a crime involving the infliction or threatened infliction of serious physical harm, deadly force may be used if necessary to prevent escape. * * *

* * * "It is true that this Court has often looked to the common law in evaluating the reasonableness, for Fourth Amendment purposes, of police activity. On the other hand, it 'has not simply frozen into constitutional law those law enforcement practices that existed at the time of the Fourth Amendment's passage.' Because of sweeping change in the legal and technological context, reliance on the common-law rule in this case would be a mistaken literalism that ignores the purpose of a historical inquiry.

"It has been pointed out many times that the common-law rule is best understood in light of the fact that it arose at a time when virtually all felonies were punishable by death. * * * Courts have also justified the common-law rule by emphasizing the relative dangerousness of felons.

"Neither of these justifications makes sense today. Almost all crimes formerly punishable by death no longer are or can be. And while in earlier times 'the gulf between the felonies and the minor offenses was broad and deep,' today the distinction is minor and often arbitrary. Many crimes classified as misdemeanors, or nonexistent, at common law are now felonies. These changes have undermined the concept, which was questionable to begin with, that use of deadly force against a fleeing felon is merely a speedier execution of someone who has already forfeited his life. They have also made the assumption that a 'felon' is more dangerous than a misdemeanant untenable. Indeed, numerous misdemeanors involve conduct more dangerous than many felonies.

"There is an additional reason why the common-law rule cannot be directly translated to the present day. The common-law rule developed at a time when weapons were rudimentary. Deadly force could be inflicted almost solely in a hand-to-hand struggle during which, necessarily, the safety of the arresting officer was at risk. Handguns were not carried by police officers until the latter half of the last century. Only then did it become possible to use deadly force from a distance as a means of apprehension. As a practical matter, the use of deadly force under the standard articulation of the common-law rule has an altogether different meaning—and harsher consequences—now than in past centuries.

*** "In evaluating the reasonableness of police procedures under the Fourth Amendment, we have also looked to prevailing rules in individual jurisdictions. The rules in the States are varied.

*** "It cannot be said that there is a constant or overwhelming trend away from the common law. In recent years, some States have reviewed their laws and expressly rejected abandonment of the common-law rule. Nonetheless, the long-term movement has been away from the rule that deadly force may be used against any fleeing felon, and that remains the rule in less than half the states.

"This trend is more evident and impressive when viewed in light of the policies adopted by the police departments themselves. Overwhelmingly, these are more restrictive than the common-law rule. *** A 1974 study reported that the police department regulations in a majority of the large cities of the United States allowed the firing of a weapon only when a felon presented a threat of death or serious bodily harm. Overall, only 7.5% of departmental and municipal policies explicitly permit the use of deadly force against any felon; 86.8% explicitly do not. ***

"Actual departmental policies are important for an additional reason. We would hesitate to declare a police practice of long standing 'unreasonable' if doing so would severely hamper effective law enforcement. But the indications are to the contrary. There has been no suggestion that crime has worsened in any way in jurisdictions that have adopted, by legislation or departmental policy, rules similar to that announced today. * * *

"While we agree that burglary is a serious crime, we cannot agree that it is so dangerous as automatically to justify the use of deadly force. The FBI classifies burglary as a 'property' rather than a 'violent' crime. Although the armed burglar would present a different situation, the fact that an unarmed suspect has broken into a dwelling at night does not automatically mean he is physically dangerous. * * * In fact, the available statistics demonstrate that burglaries only rarely involve physical violence. During the 10-year period from 1973–1982, only 3.8% of all burglaries involved violent crime."

Disposition: Statute is unconstitutional insofar as it gave Hymon authority to shoot an unarmed fleeing felon.

1-5 Other Supreme Court Cases

1-5a *Haynes v. Washington*: 373 U.S. 503, 10 L.Ed. 2d 513, 83 S.Ct. 1336 (1963)

Facts: On Thursday, December 19, 1957, Spokane police arrested Haynes for robbing a gasoline service station. He admitted the crime en route to the police station but was booked for "investigation." Shortly after arriving at the station at about 10 P.M., Haynes was questioned for about one-half hour by Lt. Wakeley. Haynes again admitted the crime. Haynes was then placed in a lineup and identified by witnesses as one of the robbers. During the evening Haynes made several specific requests to call an attorney and his wife. Police denied the requests and told Haynes that he could make a call if he confessed. Starting at about 9:30 A.M. the next morning, Haynes was questioned for about an hour and a half, this time by Detectives Peck and Cockburn. Haynes again was told that he could only call his wife if he made a confession. He made an oral confession and a written confession was transcribed. He was taken to the prosecutor's office, again denied permission to call his wife, and another statement was taken and transcribed. Haynes signed the first statement but refused to sign the second one. Later that same afternoon, Haynes had a preliminary hearing after which he was transferred to the county jail. Either the next Tuesday or Thursday he was returned to the prosecutor's office. Haynes refused to sign the second written statement because he still had not been allowed to call his wife to see about obtaining an attorney. He was held incommunicado either five or seven days (Haynes could not remember exact dates).

Issue: Did holding Haynes incommunicado as an interrogation tactic violate due process?

Reasoning: "The uncontroverted portions of the record thus disclose that the petitioner's written confession was obtained in an atmosphere of substantial coercion and inducement created by statements and actions of state authorities. We have only recently held again that a confession obtained by police through the use of threats is violative of due process and that 'the question in each case is whether the defendant's will was overborne at the time he confessed. In short, the true test of admissibility is that the confession is made freely, voluntarily and without compulsion or inducement of any sort.' And, of course, whether the confession was obtained by coercion or improper inducement can be determined only by an examination of all of the attendant circumstances. Haynes' undisputed testimony as to the making and signing of the challenged confession used against him at trial permits no doubt that it was obtained under a totality of circumstances evidencing an involuntary written admission of guilt.

*** "Confronted with the express threat of continued incommunicado detention and induced by the promise of communication with and access to family, Haynes understandably chose to make and sign the damning written statement; given the unfair and inherently coercive context in which made, that choice cannot be said to be the voluntary product of a free and unconstrained will, as required by the Fourteenth Amendment. ***

"In reaching the conclusion which we do, we are not unmindful of substantial independent evidence tending to demonstrate the guilt of the petitioner. As we said in *Rogers v. Richmond,* 365 U.S. 534: 'Indeed, in many of the cases in which the command of the Due Process Clause has compelled us to reverse state convictions involving the use of confessions obtained by impermissible methods, independent corroborating evidence left little doubt of the truth of what the defendant had confessed. Despite such verification, confessions were found to be the product of constitutionally impermissible methods in their inducement.'"

Disposition: Conviction reversed; coerced confession is inadmissible at trial.

1-5b *Winston v. Lee:* 470 U.S. 753, 84 L.Ed. 2d 662, 105 S.Ct. 1611 (1985)

Facts: At approximately 1:00 A.M. on July 18, 1982, Watkinson was closing his shop for the night. As he was locking the door, he observed someone armed with a gun coming toward him from across the street. When Watkinson drew his own gun, the other person (Lee) told him to freeze. Watkinson then fired at the other person, who returned his fire. Watkinson was hit in the legs. The other person, who appeared to be wounded in his left side, ran from the scene. About 20 minutes later, police found Lee about eight blocks away. He was suffering from a gunshot wound in his left chest and told the officers that he had been shot when two individuals attempted to rob him. Lee was taken to the same emergency room where Watkinson was waiting for treatment. Watkinson saw Lee and said, "that's the man who shot me." Lee was arrested and his story about being robbed was disproved. Police sought a court order to force Lee to undergo surgery to remove the bullet lodged under his left collarbone. X-rays later showed that the bullet was about one inch deep in muscular tissue and that general anesthesia would be required to remove it.

Issue: Can the government force surgical removal of evidence from the suspect's body?

Reasoning: "The reasonableness of surgical intrusion beneath the skin depends on a case-by-case approach, in which the individual's interests in privacy and security are weighted against society's interest in conducting the procedure. In a given case, the question whether the community's need for evidence outweighs the substantial privacy interests at stake is a delicate one admitting of few categorical answers. We believe that *Schmerber*, however, provides the appropriate framework for analysis for such cases.

"*Schmerber* recognized that the ordinary requirements of the Fourth Amendment would be the threshold requirements for conducting this kind of surgical search and seizure. We noted the importance of probable cause. And we pointed out: 'Search warrants are ordinarily required for searches of dwellings, and absent an emergency, no less could be required where intrusions into the human body are concerned. *** The importance of informed, detached and deliberate determinations of the issue whether or not to invade another's body in search of evidence of guilt is indisputable and great.'

"Beyond these standards, *Schmerber*'s inquiry considered a number of other factors in determining the 'reasonableness' of the blood test. A crucial factor in analyzing the magnitude of the intrusion in *Schmerber* is the extent to which the procedure may threaten the safety or health of the individual. * * *

"Another factor is the extent of intrusion upon the individual's dignitary interests in personal privacy and bodily integrity. * * *

"Weighed against these individual interests is the community's interest in fairly and accurately determining guilt or innocence. This interest is of course of great importance. * * *

"In weighing the various factors in this case, we therefore reach the same conclusion as the courts below. The operation sought will intrude substantially on respondent's protected interests. The medical risks of the operation, although apparently not extremely severe, are a subject of considerable dispute; the very uncertainty militates against finding the operation to be 'reasonable.' In addition, the intrusion on respondent's privacy interests entailed by the operation can only be characterized as severe. On the other hand, although the bullet may turn out to be useful to the Commonwealth in prosecuting respondent, the Commonwealth has failed to demonstrate a compelling need for it. We believe that in these circumstances the Commonwealth has failed to demonstrate that it would be 'reasonable' under the terms of the Fourth Amendment to search for evidence of this crime by means of the contemplated surgery."

Disposition: Prosecution cannot require Lee to undergo surgery to remove the bullet.

1-5c *Graham v. Connor:* 490 U.S. 386, 104 L.Ed. 2d 443, 109 S.Ct. 1865 (1989)

Facts: On November 12, 1984, Graham, a diabetic, felt the onset of an insulin reaction. He asked a friend to drive him to a nearby convenience store so he could purchase some orange juice to counteract the reaction. When Graham arrived at the store there were a number of people in line. Concerned about the delay, he left the store and asked his friend to drive him to a friend's house. Officer Connor, of the Charlotte, North Carolina Police Department, became suspicious after watching Graham's hasty entry to and exit from the store. He followed the car and stopped it about one-half mile from the store. The driver explained Graham's problem with an insulin reaction but the officer ordered both men out of the car while he determined what had happened at the store. While Officer Connor was at his patrol car calling for a backup unit, Graham got out of the car, ran around it twice, sat down on the curb and passed out. Several patrol cars arrived at the scene. An officer rolled Graham over on the sidewalk and handcuffed him tightly. Graham's pleas for some sugar to stop the insulin reaction were ignored. Graham was carried to his friend's car and placed face down on the hood. Graham regained consciousness and asked officers to check his wallet for a diabetic decal that he carried. Officers told him to "shut up" and shoved his face against the hood. Four officers grabbed Graham and threw him head-first into the police car. A friend of Graham brought some orange juice to the car, but the officers refused to let him have it. Finally, Officer Connor received a report that Graham had done nothing wrong in the store. Graham was driven home and released. Graham sustained a broken foot, cuts on his wrists, a bruised forehead, and an injured shoulder. He brought a civil suit under the federal Civil Rights Act.

Issue: What level of force can officers use when making investigatory stops?

Reasoning: "In addressing the excessive force claim brought under Section 1983, analysis begins by identifying the specific constitutional right allegedly infringed by the challenged application of force. In most instances, that will be either the Fourth Amendment's prohibition against unreasonable seizures of the person, or the Eighth Amendment's ban on cruel and unusual punishments, which are the two primary sources of constitutional protections against physically abusive governmental conduct. The validity of the claim must then be judged by reference to the specific constitutional standard which governs that right, rather than to some generalized 'excessive force' standard.

"Where, as here, the excessive force claim arises in the context of an arrest or investigatory stop of a free citizen, it is most properly characterized as one invoking the protections of the Fourth Amendment, which guarantees citizens the right 'to be secure in their *persons* *** against unreasonable *** seizures' of the person. *** Today we make explicit what was implicit in *Garner*'s analysis, and hold that *all* claims that law enforcement officers have used excessive force—deadly or not—in the course of an arrest, investigatory stop, or other 'seizure' of a free citizen would be analyzed under the Fourth Amendment and its 'reasonableness' standard, rather than under a 'substantive due process' approach. ***

*** "Our Fourth Amendment jurisprudence has long recognized that the right to make an arrest or investigatory stop necessarily carries with it the right to use some degree of physical coercion or threat thereof to effect it. Because 'the test of reasonableness under the Fourth Amendment is not capable of precise definition or mechanical application,' however, its proper application requires careful attention to the facts and circumstances of each particular case, including the severity of the crime at issue, whether the suspect poses an immediate threat to the safety of the officers or others, and whether he is actively resisting arrest or attempting to evade arrest by flight.

"The 'reasonableness' of a particular use of force must be judged from the perspective of a reasonable officer on the scene, rather than with the 20/20 vision of hindsight. * * * The calculus of reasonableness must embody allowance for the fact that police officers are often forced to make split-second judgments—in circumstances that are tense, uncertain, and rapidly evolving—about the amount of force that is necessary in a particular situation.

"As in other Fourth Amendment contexts, however, the 'reasonableness' inquiry in an excessive force case is an objective one: the question is whether the officers' actions are 'objectively reasonable' in light of the facts and circumstances confronting them, without regard to their underlying intent or motivation. * * * An officer's evil intentions will not make a Fourth Amendment violation out of an objectively reasonable use of force; nor will an officer's good intentions make an objectively unreasonable use of force constitutional."

Disposition: Case is sent back to the lower court for an evaluation of the facts under the Fourth Amendment standard.

1-5d *County of Sacramento v. Lewis:* 523 U.S. 833, 140 L.Ed. 2d 1043, 118 S.Ct. 1708 (1998)

Facts: After handling a call to break up a fight, Deputies Smith and Stapp saw a motorcycle approaching at high speed. It was operated by 18-year-old Brian Willard; 16-year-old Philip Lewis was a passenger. Neither boy had anything to do with the fight. Stapp turned on his overhead rotating lights, yelled to the boys to stop, and pulled his patrol car closer to Smith's in an attempt to pen the motorcycle in. Willard slowly maneuvered the cycle between the two police cars and sped off. Smith switched on his emergency lights and siren, made a quick turn, and began pursuit. The motorcycle wove in and out of oncoming traffic over a course of 1.3 miles in a residential neighborhood, forcing two cars and a bicycle to swerve off the road. Both the motorcycle and patrol car reached speeds up to 100 miles an hour, with Smith following as close as 100 feet. Willard tried to make a sharp left turn and tipped the motorcycle over; the patrol car skidded into Lewis at 40 miles an hour, propelling him some 70 feet down the road. Lewis was pronounced dead at the scene.

Issue: When does the operation of a police vehicle during a pursuit violate due process?

Reasoning: "[W]e hold that high-speed chases with no intent to harm suspects physically or to worsen their legal plight do not give rise to liability under the Fourteenth Amendment redressable by an action under § 1983 [Civil Rights Act].

*** "Smith was faced with a course of lawless behavior for which the police were not to blame. They had done nothing to cause Willard's high-speed driving in the first place, nothing to excuse his flouting of the commonly understood law enforcement authority to control traffic, and nothing (beyond a refusal to call off the chase) to encourage him to race through traffic at breakneck speed, forcing other drivers out of their travel lanes. Willard's outrageous behavior was practically instantaneous, and so was Smith's instinctive response. While prudence would have repressed the reaction, the officer's instinct was to do his job as a law enforcement officer, not to induce Willard's lawlessness or to terrorize, cause harm, or kill. Prudence, that is, was subject to countervailing enforcement considerations, and, while Smith exaggerated their demands, there is no reason to believe that they were tainted by an improper or malicious motive on his part.

"Regardless whether Smith's behavior offended the reasonableness held up by tort law or the balance struck in law enforcement's own codes of sound practice, it does not shock the conscience, and petitioners are not called upon to answer for it under § 1983."

Disposition: Case dismissed. Operation of a police vehicle during a pursuit violates due process only if the officer intends to injure the suspect or deprive him/her of constitutional rights.

Chapter Quiz

True/False

1. In 1791, the U. S. Supreme Court mandated that evidence obtained in violation of the Fourth Amendment be excluded from criminal trials.
2. The U. S. Supreme Court case of *Mapp v. Ohio* established the Exclusionary Rule that applies to the states.
3. When the U. S. Supreme Court decides a search and seizure case, it attempts to make a comprehensive set of rules that are easy for police officers to apply in the field.

4. Methods of obtaining evidence that shock the conscience and offend the sense of justice result in evidence that is not admissible in court due to a violation of due process.
5. The Fourth Amendment applies only to actions of police officers.
6. A court order is required to conduct surgery for the purpose of removing evidence from a defendant's body.
7. Drawing a blood sample as evidence in a driving under the influence case requires a search warrant.
8. The U.S. Supreme Court has interpreted the Fourth Amendment as allowing police officers to use deadly force only in life-threatening situations.
9. The use of nondeadly force is not covered by the Fourth Amendment.
10. During a police pursuit, only deliberate acts that are intended to harm a person or interfere with his/her constitutional rights violate due process.

Discussion Questions

1. Officer Smith observed John hand Dan a plastic bag in exchange for some money. Believing that a drug sale had just taken place, Officer Smith followed Dan. When he ordered Dan to stop, Dan raised his hand to his mouth and then appeared to be trying to swallow something. Officer Smith quickly put his hand on Dan's throat and attempted to stop him from swallowing. After a struggle to free himself, Dan jerked his head away and vomited. Capsules containing dangerous drugs were found in the material that Dan vomited. Does *Rochin v. California* prohibit the admission of these drugs in court? Explain.
2. Sam was arrested for murder. At the time, he appeared to be intoxicated. Officers thought that Sam might try to use intoxication as a defense so they rushed him to the emergency room and asked the doctor to take a blood sample to be used for a blood alcohol test. Sam became combative when the doctor appeared with the syringe. Two officers grabbed Sam's arm and held it out while a third officer applied a choke hold. Sam, who appeared to be on the verge of fainting, held his arm still while the doctor took the blood sample. Can the defense use *Rochin v. California* or *Schmerber v. California* as grounds for excluding the results of the blood alcohol test from court? Explain.
3. Adam stole $10 worth of merchandise from a convenience store. Officer Jones, who had just stopped by for coffee, saw Adam commit this misdemeanor. Adam started running when Officer Jones ordered him to stop. Officer Jones yelled, "Stop, or I will shoot!" Adam continued to run. Officer Jones then took careful aim for Adam's legs and shot him in the calf. Has Officer Jones violated Adam's Fourth Amendment rights *by using excessive force?* Explain.

Chapter

2

Warrant Requirements

Outline

The Fourth Amendment states:

> "The right of the people to be secure in their persons, houses, papers and effects, against unreasonable searches and seizures, shall not be violated, and no Warrants shall issue, but upon probable cause, supported by Oath or affirmation, and particularly describing the place to be searched, and the persons or things to be seized."

The Supreme Court has applied the "reasonable expectation of privacy" test developed in *Katz v. United States* (389 U.S. 347 (1967)) to determine what searches are unreasonable. Prior to considering how this test applies to police conduct, three basic concepts must be discussed: (1) search; (2) seizure; and (3) probable cause. *Black's Law Dictionary* (1990) is the primary source of definitions.

A *search* is defined as a probe or exploration for something that is concealed or hidden from the searcher; an invasion, a quest with some sort of force, either actual or constructive. Searching involves the act of looking for something that otherwise would not be seen. Only unreasonable searches are prohibited. The Supreme Court has spent a great deal of time deciding what is reasonable and what is not.

Seizure is defined as the act of taking possession of property; the term implies a taking or removal of something from the possession, actual or constructive, of another person or persons. Police seize evidence when they take it into their possession. When a person is seized, it is called an arrest. Even when there is no search—for example, if something was left out in the open where the police could see it—officers still must have the legal right to seize it.

Probable cause is defined as the group of facts that makes a reasonable person more certain than not that an event has occurred. In criminal cases, probable cause is required in three key situations: (1) determining if a crime was committed; (2) deciding which person committed the crime; and (3) establishing that evidence is at a specific location. The Fourth Amendment specifically requires that probable cause be shown in order to obtain a warrant.

While the Fourth Amendment specifically states that no warrant shall be issued unless there is probable cause, it does not say that all searches must be authorized by warrants. The Supreme Court has wrestled with the question of when warrants are required. The basic rule is that search warrants are required to obtain evidence for criminal cases unless the situation is covered by a recognized exception to the warrant requirement. They may be issued to search nearly any location including newsrooms and lawyers offices. Search warrants are also required in noncriminal situations, such as a check to see if a building's electrical wiring conforms with local codes, if no one will consent to the inspection.

2-1 Establishing Probable Cause

The warrant process was created to allow a neutral magistrate the opportunity to review the facts and decide if the police should be authorized to conduct a search or make an arrest. The Fourth Amendment further requires that the facts be stated under oath or affirmation. In most cases, the facts are written down and signed under penalty of perjury in a document called an *affidavit.*

The Supreme Court ruled that a warrant is valid only if a judge or magistrate determines that probable cause exists. *Aguilar's* "two-prong test" (*Aguilar v. Texas*, 378 U.S. 108 (1964)) requires the judge to have facts on two issues: (1) Has probable cause been established? and (2) How reliable is the information presented in the affidavit? *Illinois v. Gates* (462 U.S. 213 (1983)) altered the rule: Probable cause is considered after reviewing the totality of the circumstances. The reliability of the person providing the information is one factor considered, but it is examined in the context of the solid, factual information presented.

The affidavit must give enough information to establish probable cause. How this is done frequently depends on the source of the information. If the officer making the affidavit observed the facts firsthand, making the affidavit under oath is sufficient to establish reliability; the sole question is whether the facts are sufficient to show probable cause. Information provided by crime victims and eyewitnesses is usually assumed to be reliable unless there is a motive to lie. The more common problem with these types of informants is the quality of the information provided. For example, a victim who was in the presence of the suspect for a very brief time under poor lighting conditions probably will not be able to give a good description of the suspect. Other problems may develop, for example, if the eyewitness is very nearsighted or the victim became hysterical.

Informants who are themselves criminals create the biggest problem. Due to their past convictions or bad motives for incriminating the suspect, their credibility is suspect. Reliability must be established in the affidavit. The most common method used is to give specific examples of useful, accurate information the informant has given officers in the past. Another method is to verify the information provided in the present case. When this is done, the Supreme Court has insisted that the facts that were checked show criminal activity. Merely verifying facts such as addresses and telephone numbers is not enough.

Anonymous tips can be used to establish probable cause. The only way to establish reliability is by showing that the facts are given in great detail. When an anonymous informant is used, the affidavit should show that as many facts as possible were verified. The combination of facts from the anonymous informant and accompanying police investigation are evaluated to determine if probable cause has been established.

A distinction must be made between confidential and anonymous informants. A confidential informant gives a police officer information on the condition that the officer will not reveal the source of the information. The officer knows who the informant is but has agreed not to tell. This information, along with facts showing the reliability of the person who provided it, can be used in a warrant without giving the name of the informant. In both warrant and nonwarrant cases, the defendant may request the name of the informant before trial, but the judge will require the police to disclose it only if the identity of the informant is crucial to the defendant's case.

If a search warrant is requested, the judge must have detailed facts showing that items the officers have a legal right to seize are at a specific location. The warrant may be for the seizure of illegal drugs or other contraband, fruits of the crime, items used to commit the crime, or some other evidence that can be used in the case. The affidavit should include detailed information about the crime involved as well as an explanation of why the officers want to seize the items in question. The location of the items sought must be evaluated as part of the probable cause determination. Facts must be given as precisely as possible in the affidavit. The location must also appear on the face of the warrant.

Since the reason for requiring search warrants is to protect people's privacy, the search warrant must be worded so that the police are restricted to as small an area as possible. Street addresses are usually given, but the location should be described even more precisely when possible. For example, "the kitchen of the house at 4567 N. Main Street" is better than merely stating "4567 N. Main Street." Appellate courts generally uphold warrants that include a correct verbal description of the location even when the street address is wrong. An example of this would be, "the white house on the northeast corner of First and Spring."

Another problem unique to search warrants is the freshness of the information. If the facts are stale, there is no reliable indicator where the items to be seized are currently located. How long it takes facts to become stale depends on the type of case. In a drug case in which the dealer is known to do a high volume of business and change locations frequently, information two days old might be stale. If the case involves the use of stolen lumber at a construction site, the information is not likely to become stale if the stolen property is being incorporated into a building. No matter what the case is, the police should attempt to have information that is as current as possible to avoid rejection of the affidavit.

For an arrest warrant, facts must be given to establish every element of each crime listed in the warrant. Additional information must be included to show that the person named is the one who committed the crime(s). The physical description of the person to be arrested, along with his/her birthdate (if available) or approximate age, is usually required so the officers making the arrest can verify that they have the correct person.

2-2 Neutral Magistrate

The affidavit must be reviewed by a neutral judge or magistrate. This person must not be part of any law enforcement agency because all personnel in law enforcement agencies are considered to have a vested interest in apprehending criminals. The Supreme Court considered this to be a potential conflict of interest that could interfere with an objective review of the facts in the affidavit. Neutrality is also considered to be violated if the judge's salary is calculated on the basis of the number of warrants issued.

2-3 Execution of Warrants

The warrant directs a peace officer to take specific actions (search or make an arrest). The act of doing this is called the "execution of a warrant." Any peace officer with authority in the jurisdiction where the warrant is executed can participate. The officer executing the warrant is responsible for verifying that the warrant is "valid on its face." This means that the warrant appears to be correct and has not expired. Officers are not liable if the judge issued a warrant without probable cause unless they knew there was a problem with the warrant.

Sometimes it is necessary to contain the premises while the search warrant is being obtained. In *Illinois v. McArthur* (2001), the Supreme Court recognized a limited right to do this. It rested its decision on a combination of factors: The police had probable cause to believe contraband was in the house and had good reason to fear that it would be destroyed if the occupants were allowed access while the warrant was sought; due diligence was used to obtain a search warrant in a timely manner; and reasonable restrictions were placed on the individuals.

Prior to entering a residence, officers are required to announce their presence. This usually takes a four-step approach: (1) knock; (2) announce who is there and what is wanted ("Police. We have a search warrant."); (3) wait long enough for a cooperative person to come to the door; and (4) the officers may use force to enter if no one opens the door after a reasonable wait. In *Wilson v. Arkansas* (1995), the Supreme Court held that while the Fourth Amendment requires "knock and announce," it can be dispensed with if there is danger of physical violence, if the officers are in hot pursuit of an escaping suspect, or if there is danger that evidence will be destroyed. Reasonable suspicion is required to trigger one of these exceptions. The Supreme Court rejected blanket exceptions from "knock and announce" for drug cases.

When executing the warrant, officers must restrict their movement to locations listed in the warrant where they are reasonably likely to find the items specified. As a precautionary matter, officers may look in closets and other spaces immediately adjoining the place of the search or arrest from which an attack could be immediately launched. To search beyond that, however, there must be reasonable suspicion, based on articulable facts, that would warrant a reasonably prudent officer in believing that the area subject to the "protective sweep" harbors an individual who poses a danger to the officers at the scene. Anyone found on the premises may be detained in an area under the control of an officer to prevent destruction of evidence or assault on officers while executing the warrant. People may be thoroughly searched only if their search is specifically authorized by the warrant; merely being at the location where a search warrant is being executed is not grounds for searching a person. The right to a protective pat down for weapons applies while warrants are being executed if officers have reasonable suspicion that the person to be searched is armed.

If a large item such as a 24-cubic-foot refrigerator is to be seized, officers may not look in the bathroom medicine cabinet or other places that are obviously too small to conceal the refrigerator. If the warrant mentions the location of the evidence, such as the kitchen, officers may not search other rooms. While the courts have been quite strict in interpreting these requirements, they have also given officers the right to seize evidence they find in plain view while legally conducting the search. For example, if cocaine is found on the coffee table while officers are looking for a stolen television, the cocaine may be seized and appropriate charges filed.

The Fourth Amendment established the rule, based on the determination of a neutral magistrate that there was probable cause for the search, that police can invade the privacy of whoever lives at the address indicated on the search warrant. Traditionally, peace officers were the only people authorized to serve warrants. The Supreme Court sanctioned the practice of taking other people along when necessary. For example, if the police obtain a search warrant for a house where stolen property is believed to be hidden, the victim of the theft can accompany the police to help identify the stolen items. The Court refused, however, to allow newspaper reporters, camera crews from television stations, or other unnecessary people to go along with the police when they enter a private dwelling. The privacy interest of the residents outweighs the public interest in reporting the news and any possible deterrent to improper police conduct that could result from allowing the media to be present.

2-4 Administrative Warrants

There are many reasons to search a building that are not related to normal police activity. For example, inspectors may need to check for compliance with the fire and building codes. The Supreme Court has designed a modified warrant procedure for these situations.

The probable cause needed for this type of warrant is very different from that mandated for search warrants: There must be a reasonable legislative purpose behind the inspection program. The legislative purpose can be any legitimate government interest that requires periodic inspections. It can involve building codes, inspection of restaurants for health code violations, sanitation inspections for rodents and other pests, and inspections to determine if fire regulations are being complied with.

Most people are willing to permit inspectors to enter the premises and perform their duty. When admission is denied, a warrant can be used to complete the inspection. For example, if the fire department is authorized to inspect each building once every four years, the fact that one quadrant of the city is to be inspected this year is sufficient probable cause. There is no need to allege that a fire hazard exists at the address named in the warrant application.

Supreme Court cases establish exemptions from the administrative warrant requirement for heavily regulated businesses such as firearms dealers, establishments selling alcoholic beverages, junkyards that dismantle cars, and mines covered by the Federal Mine Safety and Health Act of 1977.

Fire inspections pose several interesting problems. While trying to put out a blaze or mopping up afterwards, fire fighters obviously do not need any type of warrant. Inspections that are primarily regulatory in nature require administrative warrants if consent to enter is denied. An administrative warrant is also required if there is suspicion of arson. Once investigators believe arson has occurred, they must obtain a regular search warrant to enter the structure. Burned-out structures may still have a protected privacy interest if the owners have tried to board them up or otherwise keep people out.

2-5 Key Supreme Court Cases

2-5a *Illinois v. Gates:* 462 U.S. 213, 76 L.Ed. 2d 527, 103 S.Ct. 2317 (1983)

Facts: Police in Bloomingdale, Illinois received an anonymous, handwritten letter on May 3, 1978 detailing Sue and Lance Gates' drug sales. It gave the location of their condominium and stated that the Gates' purchase most of their drugs in Florida; Sue drives the car to Florida where she leaves it to be loaded with drugs; Lance then flies to Florida and drives the car back while Sue flies back; Sue is driving to Florida on May 3 and Lance will fly down a few days later to drive the car back; when it returns the car will have drugs worth $100,000 in the trunk; and they presently have drugs worth over $100,000 in their basement. Detective Mader was assigned to investigate. He verified the address based on Lance's driver's license. The police confirmed the reservation to fly to Florida on May 5 and observed Lance boarding the plane and arriving in Florida. In Florida, he was seen entering a hotel room registered to Susan Gates. The next morning, Lance and a woman later identified as Mrs. Gates left the motel in a vehicle with Illinois license plates and drove northbound on the interstate. The car's license plates were registered to Gates. Driving time from West Palm Beach to Bloomingdale was estimated to be between 22–24 hours.

These facts and a copy of the anonymous letter were used to obtain a warrant to search Gates' residence and automobile. Police met Lance Gates and his wife when they returned to their home in Bloomingdale; they were driving the car in which they left West Palm Beach 22 hours earlier. A search of the car's trunk revealed 350 pounds of marijuana. Police found weapons, marijuana, and other contraband in the house. Evidence found during the execution of the search warrant was suppressed by the trial court.

Issue: Can information from an anonymous informant be used in an affidavit supporting a search warrant?

Reasoning: "The Illinois Supreme Court concluded—and we are inclined to agree—that, standing alone, the anonymous letter sent to the Bloomingdale Police Department would not provide the basis for a magistrate's determination that there was probable cause to believe contraband would be found in the Gate's car and home. The letter provides virtually nothing from which one might conclude that its author is either honest or his information reliable; likewise, the letter gives absolutely no indication of the basis for the writer's predictions regarding the Gates' criminal activities. * * *

"We agree with the Illinois Supreme Court that an informant's 'veracity,' 'reliability' and 'basis of knowledge' are all highly relevant in determining the value of his report. We do not agree, however, that these elements should be understood as entirely separate and independent requirements to be rigidly exacted in every case. * * * Rather, as detailed below, they should be understood simply as closely intertwined issues that may usefully illuminate the common sense, practical question whether there is 'probable cause' to believe that contraband or evidence is located in a particular place.

* * *"[W]e conclude that it is wiser to abandon the 'two-pronged test' established by our decisions in *Aguilar* and *Spinelli.* In its place we reaffirm the totality of the circumstances analysis that traditionally has informed probable cause determinations. The task of the issuing magistrate is simply to make a practical, common-sense decision whether, given all the circumstances set forth in the affidavit before him, including the 'veracity' and 'basis of knowledge' of persons supplying hearsay information, there is a fair probability that contraband or evidence of a crime will be found in a particular place. And the duty of a reviewing court is simply to ensure that the magistrate had a 'substantial basis for * * * concluding' that probable cause existed.

* * * "It is enough, for purposes of assessing probable cause, that 'corroboration through other sources of information reduced the chances of a reckless or prevaricating tale,' thus providing 'a substantial basis for crediting the hearsay.'

"Finally, the anonymous letter contained a range of details relating not just to easily obtained facts and conditions existing at the time of the tip, but to future actions of third parties ordinarily not easily predicted. The letter writer's accurate information as to the travel plans of each of the Gates was of a character likely obtained only from the Gates themselves, or from someone familiar with their not entirely ordinary travel plans. If the informant has access to accurate information of this type a magistrate could properly conclude that it was not unlikely that he also had access to reliable information of the Gates' alleged illegal activities. *** [P]robable cause does not demand the certainty we associate with formal trials. It is enough that there was a fair probability that the writer of the anonymous letter had obtained his entire story either from the Gates or someone they trusted. And corroboration of major portions of the letter's predictions provides just this probability."

Disposition: Conviction affirmed; the anonymous letter plus police corroboration provided probable cause for issuing the warrant to search Gates' home and vehicle.

2-5b *Ybarra v. Illinois:* 444 U.S. 85, 62 L.Ed. 2d 238, 100 S.Ct. 338 (1979)

Facts: On March 1, 1976, a Special Agent from the Illinois Bureau of Investigation obtained a warrant to search the Aurora Tap Tavern and Greg, the bartender, for evidence of possession of heroin, contraband, and other controlled substances. Seven or eight officers went to the tavern. When they entered, they announced that they were going to conduct a cursory search for weapons. Each of the 9 to 13 patrons in the tavern was patted down. Other officers conducted an extensive search of the premises. Ybarra was standing in front of the bar at a pinball machine when an officer patted him down. The officer felt "a cigarette pack with objects in it," but he did not remove the pack from Ybarra's pocket at that time. After all the patrons had been frisked, the officer returned to Ybarra and again searched him, this time retrieving the cigarette pack. Six tinfoil packets containing a brown powdery substance, later determined to be heroin, were found in the cigarette pack. Ybarra was convicted of possession of heroin.

Issue: Can officers search persons legitimately on the premises when executing a search warrant?

Reasoning: "There is no reason to suppose that, when the search warrant was issued on March 1, 1976, the authorities had probable cause to believe that any person found on the premises of the Aurora Tap Tavern, aside from 'Greg,' would be violating the law. The Complaint for Search Warrant did not allege that the bar was frequented by persons illegally purchasing drugs. It did not state that the informant had ever seen a patron of the tavern purchase drugs from 'Greg' or from any other person. Nowhere, in fact, did the complaint even mention the patrons of the Aurora Tap Tavern.

"Not only was probable cause to search Ybarra absent at the time the warrant was issued; it was still absent when the police executed the warrant. Upon entering the tavern, the police did not recognize Ybarra and had no reason to believe that he had committed, was committing or was about to commit any offense under state or federal law. Ybarra made no gestures indicative of criminal conduct, made no movements that might suggest an attempt to conceal contraband, and said nothing of a suspicious nature to the police officers. In short, the agents knew nothing in particular about Ybarra, except that he was present, along with several other customers, in the public tavern at a time when the police had reason to believe that the bartender would have heroin for sale.

"It is true that the police possessed a warrant based on probable cause to search the tavern in which Ybarra happened to be at the time the warrant was executed. But, a person's mere propinquity to others independently suspected of criminal activity does not, without more, give rise to probable cause to search that person. * * *

"Each patron who walked into the Aurora Tap Tavern on March 1, 1976, was clothed with constitutional protection against an unreasonable search or an unreasonable seizure. That individualized protection was separate and distinct from the Fourth and Fourteenth Amendment protection possessed by the proprietor of the tavern or by 'Greg.' Although the search warrant, issued upon probable cause, gave the officers authority to search the premises and to search 'Greg,' it gave them no authority whatever to invade the constitutional protections possessed individually by the tavern's customers.

* * * "The initial frisk of Ybarra was simply not supported by a reasonable belief that he was armed and presently dangerous, a belief which this Court has invariably held must form the predicate to a pat-down of a person for weapons. When the police entered the Aurora Tap Tavern on March 1, 1976, the lighting was sufficient for them to observe the customers. Upon seeing Ybarra, they neither recognized him as a person with a criminal history nor had any particular reason to believe that he might be inclined to assault them. Moreover, as police agent Johnson later testified, Ybarra, whose hands were empty, gave no indication of possessing a weapon, made no gestures or other actions indicative of an intent to commit an assault, and acted generally in a manner that was not threatening. * * * In short, the State is unable to articulate any specific fact that would have justified a police officer at the scene in even suspecting that Ybarra was armed and dangerous."

Disposition: Conviction reversed; heroin found in Ybarra's pocket is inadmissible because the warrant did not specifically authorize the search of patrons in the tavern.

2-5c *Camara v. Municipal Court:* 387 U.S. 523, 18 L.Ed. 2d 930, 87 S.Ct. 1727 (1967)

Facts: On November 6, 1963, an inspector of the Division of Housing Inspectors of the San Francisco Department of Public Health entered an apartment building to make a routine annual inspection for violations of the city's Housing Code. The building manager told the inspector that Camara was leasing the rear of the ground floor space for his personal residence. The inspector, claiming that the building use permit did not allow residential use of the ground floor, confronted Camara and demanded entrance to inspect the premises. Camara refused to allow the inspection without a warrant. Two days later, he again refused to allow an inspection. A citation was mailed to Camara demanding that he appear at the district attorney's office, but he failed to appear. A third attempt to make the inspection was futile. Camara was arrested for refusing to permit a lawful inspection. A pretrial appeal was filed in order to have the city ordinance permitting the warrantless inspection declared invalid.

Issue: Is a search warrant required to conduct a noncriminal inspection for code violations?

Reasoning: ***"[W]e hold that the administrative searches of the kind at issue here are significant intrusions upon the interests protected by the Fourth Amendment, that such searches when authorized and conducted without a warrant procedure lack the traditional safeguards which the Fourth Amendment guarantees to the individual, and that the reasons put forth in *Frank v. State of Maryland* [359 U.S. 360] and in other cases for upholding these warrantless searches are insufficient to justify so substantial a weakening of the Fourth Amendment's protections. Because of the nature of the municipal programs under consideration, however, these conclusions must be the beginning, not the end, of our inquiry. ***

"Unlike the search pursuant to a criminal investigation, the inspection programs at issue here are aimed at securing city-wide compliance with minimum physical standards for private property. The primary governmental interest at stake is to prevent even the unintentional development of conditions which are hazardous to public health and safety. Because fires and epidemics may ravage large urban areas, because unsightly conditions adversely affect the economic values of neighboring structures, numerous courts have upheld the police power of municipalities to impose and enforce such minimum standards even upon existing structures. In determining whether a particular inspection is reasonable—and thus in determining whether there is probable cause to issue a warrant for that inspection—the need for the inspection must be weighed in terms of these reasonable goals of code enforcement.

"There is unanimous agreement among those most familiar with this field that the only effective way to seek universal compliance with the minimum standards required by municipal codes is through routine periodic inspections of all structures. It is here that the probable cause debate is focused, for the agency's decision to conduct an area inspection is unavoidably based on its appraisal of conditions in the area as a whole, not on its knowledge of conditions in each particular building. * * *

"Having concluded that the area inspection is a 'reasonable' search of private property within the meaning of the Fourth Amendment, it is obvious that 'probable cause' to issue a warrant to inspect must exist if reasonable legislative or administrative standards for conducting an area inspection are satisfied with respect to a particular dwelling. Such standards, which will vary with the municipal program being enforced, may be based upon the passage of time, the nature of the building (for example, a multifamily apartment house), or the condition of the entire area, but they will not necessarily depend upon specific knowledge of the condition of the particular dwelling. It has been suggested that to vary the probable cause test from the standard applied in criminal cases would be to authorize a 'synthetic search warrant' and thereby to lessen the overall protections of the Fourth Amendment. But we do not agree. The warrant procedure is designed to guarantee that a decision to search private property is justified by a reasonable governmental interest. But reasonableness is still the ultimate standard. If a valid public interest justifies the intrusion contemplated, then there is probable cause to issue a suitably restricted search warrant. Such an approach neither endangers time-honored doctrines applicable to criminal investigations nor makes a nullity of the probable cause requirement in this area. It merely gives full recognition to the competing public and private interests here at stake and, in so doing, best fulfills the historic purpose behind the constitutional right to be free from unreasonable government invasion of privacy.

"Since our holding emphasizes the controlling standard of reasonableness, nothing we say today is intended to foreclose prompt inspections, even without a warrant, that the law has traditionally upheld in emergency situations. On the other hand, in the case of most routine area inspections, there is no compelling urgency to inspect at a particular time or on a particular day. Moreover, most citizens allow inspections of their property without a warrant. Thus, as a practical matter and in light of the Fourth Amendment's requirement that a warrant specify the property to be searched, it seems likely that warrants should normally be sought only after entry is refused unless there has been a citizen complaint or there is other satisfactory reasons for securing immediate entry."

Disposition: Charges against Camara for refusing to permit a warrantless inspection must be dismissed.

2-6 Other Supreme Court Cases

2-6a *New York v. P. J. Video:* 475 U.S. 868, 89 L.Ed. 2d 871, 106 S.Ct. 1610 (1986)

Facts: Police in Depew, New York obtained search warrants for the seizure of five videocassette movies from the defendant's adult video store. The warrant issued was based on affidavits in which officers described what they saw when they rented videocassettes from the defendant's store and viewed them.

Issue: What is the standard for issuing search warrants for allegedly obscene materials?

Reasoning: "We have long recognized that the seizure of films or books on the basis of their content implicates First Amendment concerns not raised by other kinds of seizures. For this reason, we have required that certain special conditions be met before such seizures may be carried out. In *Roaden v. Kentucky,* 413 U.S. 496 (1973), for example, we held that the police many not rely on the 'exigency' exception to the Fourth Amendment's warrant requirement in conducting a seizure of allegedly obscene materials, under circumstances where such a seizure would effectively constitute a 'prior restraint.' In *A Quantity of Books v. Kansas,* 378 U.S. 205 (1964), we had gone a step farther, ruling that the large-scale seizure of books or films constituting a 'prior restraint' must be preceded by an adversary hearing on the question of obscenity. In *Heller v. New York,* 413 U.S. 483 (1973), we emphasized that, even where a seizure of allegedly obscene materials would not constitute a 'prior restraint,' but instead would merely preserve evidence for trial, the seizure must be made pursuant to a warrant and there must be an opportunity for a prompt post-seizure judicial determination of obscenity. And in *Lee Art Theatre, Inc. v. Virginia,* 392 U.S. 636 (1968), we held that a warrant authorizing the seizure of materials presumptively protected by the First Amendment may not be issued based solely on the conclusory allegations of a police officer that the sought-after materials are obscene, but instead must be supported by affidavits setting forth specific facts in order that the issuing magistrate may 'focus searchingly on the question of obscenity.'

"The New York Court of Appeals construed our prior decisions in this area as standing for the additional proposition that an application for a warrant authorizing the seizure of books or films must be evaluated under a 'higher' standard of probable cause than that used in other areas of Fourth Amendment law. But we have never held or said that such a 'higher' standard is required by the First Amendment.* * *

* * *"We think, and accordingly hold, that an application for a warrant authorizing the seizure of materials presumptively protected by the First Amendment should be evaluated under the same standard of probable cause used to review warrant applications generally."

Disposition: Order dismissing charges reversed; the facts established probable cause to believe that the contents of the videocassettes were obscene.

2-6b *Mincey v. Arizona:* 437 U.S. 385, 57 L.Ed. 2d 290, 98 S.Ct. 2408 (1978)

Facts: On October 28, 1974, undercover police officer Barry Headricks purchased heroin from Mincey in his apartment. Later that afternoon, Headricks returned with nine other plain-clothes policemen and a deputy county attorney. Hodgman, a friend of Mincey, opened the door. Headricks slipped inside and moved quickly into the bedroom. Hodgman unsuccessfully attempted to slam the door before anyone else entered. Shots were heard from the bedroom. Officer Headricks emerged from the bedroom and collapsed on the floor. When officers entered the bedroom they found Mincey lying on the floor, wounded and semiconscious. They found a wounded young woman in a bedroom closet. One of Mincey's friends who was in the living room had been shot in the head. Headricks died a few hours later in the hospital.

Homicide detectives heard the call for medical assistance on their police radio and responded about 10 minutes after the shooting. They took charge of the crime scene and proceeded to gather evidence. Their search lasted four days and included an exhaustive search of nearly everything in the apartment. Between 200 to 300 objects were seized.

Issue: Is a search warrant required to search the scene of a homicide?

Reasoning: "The Fourth Amendment proscribes all unreasonable searches and seizures, and it is a cardinal principle that 'searches conducted outside the judicial process, without prior approval by judge or magistrate, are per se unreasonable under the Fourth Amendment—subject only to a few specifically established and well-delineated exceptions.' The Arizona Supreme Court did not hold that the search of the petitioner's apartment fell within any of the exceptions to the warrant requirement previously recognized by this Court, but rather that the search of a homicide scene should be recognized as an additional exception.

*** "The first contention is that the search of the petitioner's apartment did not invade any constitutionally protected right of privacy. *** [T]he State urges that by shooting Officer Headricks, Mincey forfeited any reasonable expectation of privacy in his apartment. *** [I]t suffices here to say that this reasoning would impermissibly convict the suspect even before the evidence against him was gathered. ***

"The State's second argument in support of Arizona's categorical exception to the warrant requirement is that a possible homicide presents an emergency situation demanding immediate action. We do not question the right of the police to respond to emergency situations. ***

"But a warrantless search must be 'strictly circumscribed by the exigencies which justify its initiation,' and it simply cannot be contended that this search was justified by any emergency threatening life or limb. All the persons in Mincey's apartment had been located before the investigating homicide officers arrived there and began their search. And a four-day search that included opening dresser drawers and ripping up carpets can hardly be rationalized in terms of the legitimate concerns that justify an emergency search.

"Third, the State points to the vital public interest in the prompt investigation of the extremely serious crime of murder. No one can doubt the importance of this goal. But the public interest in the investigation of other serious crimes is comparable. * * *

"Moreover, the mere fact that law enforcement may be more efficient can never by itself justify disregard of the Fourth Amendment. The investigation of crime would always be simplified if warrants were unnecessary. But the Fourth Amendment reflects the view of those who wrote the Bill of Rights that the privacy of a person's home and property may not be totally sacrificed in the name of maximum simplicity in enforcement of the criminal law.

*** "[W]e hold that the 'murder scene exception' created by the Arizona Supreme Court is inconsistent with the Fourth and Fourteenth Amendments—that the warrantless search of Mincey's apartment was not constitutionally permissible simply because a homicide had recently occurred there."

Disposition: Conviction reversed; evidence found during the warrantless search of Mincey's apartment is inadmissible.

2-6c *Thompson v. Louisiana:* 469 U.S. 17, 83 L.Ed. 2d 246, 105 S.Ct. 409 (1984)

Facts: On May 18, 1982, several deputies from the Jefferson Parish Sheriff's Department arrived at Thompson's home in response to a report by Mrs. Thompson's daughter that a homicide had occurred. The daughter told the deputies that her mother had shot her husband, taken an overdose of drugs, and then called the daughter requesting help. Deputies, who had been admitted to the house by the daughter, found Mr. Thompson dead and Mrs. Thompson unconscious from an apparent drug overdose. Mrs. Thompson was transported to the hospital and the crime scene was secured. About half an hour later, the homicide unit arrived to conduct the follow-up investigation. Officers entered the residence and began a general exploratory search for evidence of a crime. They examined each room of the house during the two-hour search and seized numerous items of evidence. The trial court suppressed part of the evidence seized during the search.

Issue: Did consent to enter the house to help the murder/suicide victims give homicide investigators the right to thoroughly search the entire house for evidence?

Reasoning: "Petitioner's attempt to get medical assistance does not evidence a diminished expectation of privacy on her part. To be sure, this action would have justified the authorities in seizing evidence under the plain view doctrine while they were in petitioner's house to offer her assistance. In addition, the same doctrine may justify seizure of evidence obtained in the limited 'victim-or-suspect' search discussed in Mincey. However, the evidence at issue here was not discovered in plain view while the police were assisting petitioner to the hospital, or was it discovered during the 'victim-or-suspect' search that had been completed by the time the homicide investigators arrived. Petitioner's call for help can hardly be seen as an invitation to the general public that would have converted her home into the sort of public place for which no warrant to search would be necessary."

Disposition: Suppression motion should have been granted for all evidence that was not in plain view.

2-6d *Zurcher v. Stanford Daily:* 436 U.S. 547, 56 L.Ed. 2d 525, 98 S.Ct. 1970 (1978)

Facts: On Friday, April 9, 1971, officers of the Palo Alto Police Department and the Santa Clara County Sheriff's Department responded to a call from the director of the Stanford University Hospital requesting the removal of a large group of demonstrators who had seized the hospital's administrative offices and occupied them for nearly 24 hours. The demonstrators refused to leave peacefully and barricaded the doors at both ends of a hall adjacent to the administrative offices. As police forced their way into one end of the hall, a group of demonstrators armed with sticks and clubs attached officers at the opposite end. Nine officers were injured, including one who was knocked to the floor and struck repeatedly on the head and another who suffered a broken shoulder. The police took no photographs and were able to identify only two of their attackers. One officer saw at least one person photographing the assault. The Sunday edition of the *Stanford Daily*, a student newspaper, carried articles and photographs about the violent confrontation. The following day the District Attorney secured a warrant to search the *Stanford Daily*'s offices for negatives, film, and pictures showing the events in question. The affidavit contained no allegations that *Stanford Daily* staff were in any way involved in unlawful acts at the demonstration. The newspaper offices were thoroughly searched but no evidence, other than the published photographs, was found.

The *Stanford Daily* brought a civil action seeking a declaratory judgment and an injunction against police searches of newspaper offices. The newspaper argued that a *subpoena duces tecum* should be used instead of a search warrant so that police would not be able to see and/or read confidential information in press files. A *subpoena duces tecum* is a subpoena for documents. It orders the person who is in possession of the documents to bring the documents to court.

Issue: Can a search warrant be issued to search premises controlled by innocent third parties for evidence?

Reasoning: "The critical element in a reasonable search is not that the owner of the property is suspected of crime but that there is reasonable cause to believe that the specific 'things' to be searched for and seized are located on the property in which entry is sought. * * *

* * * "Aware of the long struggle between Crown and press and desiring to curb unjustified official intrusions, the Framers took the enormously important step of subjecting searches to the test of reasonableness and to the general rule requiring search warrants issued by neutral magistrates. They nevertheless did not forbid warrants where the press was involved, did not require special showings that subpoenas would be impractical, and did not insist that the owner of the place to be searched, if connected with the press, must be shown to be implicated in the offense being investigated. Further, the prior cases do no more than insist that the courts apply the warrant requirement with particular exactitude when First Amendment interests would be endangered by the search. As we see it, no more than this is required where the warrant requested is for the seizure of criminal evidence reasonably believed to be on the premises occupied by a newspaper. Properly administered, the preconditions for a warrant—probable cause, specificity with respect to the place to be searched and the things to be seized, and overall reasonableness—should afford sufficient protection against the harms that are assertedly threatened by warrants for searching newspaper offices.

* * * "Of course, the Fourth Amendment does not prevent or advise against legislative or executive efforts to establish non-constitutional protections against possible abuses of the search warrant procedure, but we decline to reinterpret the Amendment to impose a general constitutional barrier against warrants to search newspaper premises, to require resort to subpoenas as a general rule, or to demand prior notice and hearing in connections with the issuance of search warrants."

Disposition: Search of the *Stanford Daily's* office was constitutional; court declines to impose different procedures when evidence is held by a newspaper.

2-6e *Franks v. Delaware:* 438 U.S. 154, 57 L.Ed. 2d 667, 98 S.Ct. 2674 (1978)

Facts: On Friday, March 5, 1976, Mrs. Bailey told police in Dover, Delaware that she had been confronted in her home earlier that morning by a man with a knife and that he had sexually assaulted her. She gave a detailed description of the assailant and the clothing that he wore at the time of the attack. The same day, Franks coincidentally was taken into custody for an assault on a 15-year-old girl named Brenda B. The assault had occurred six days earlier. Franks allegedly told Officer McClements, the youth officer accompanying him while he waited for a bail hearing, that he was surprised the bail hearing was "about Brenda B., I know her. I thought you said Bailey, I don't know her." The following Monday, Officer McClements mentioned the conversation to Detective Brooks, who was working on the Bailey case. The next day Detectives Brooks and Gray submitted an affidavit to a justice of the peace in Dover in support of a warrant to search Franks's apartment. The affidavit mentioned the previous conversation and detailed attempts to verify that Franks usually dressed in the manner described by the victim. When the warrant was executed, officers found clothing that matched that described by the victim and a knife similar to that used in the attack on Mrs. Bailey. At the suppression hearing, the defense offered to show that the two people listed in the affidavit as verifying Franks's normal mode of dress had not been interviewed by the detectives. The trial court refused to hear the motion to suppress. Franks was convicted.

Issue: Is a warrant valid if the affidavit contains misstatements of fact?

Reasoning: "* * * There is, of course, a presumption of validity with respect to the affidavit supporting the search warrant. To mandate an evidentiary hearing, the challenger's attack must be more than conclusory and must be supported by more than a mere desire to cross examine. There must be allegations of deliberate falsehood or of reckless disregard for the truth, and those allegations must be accompanied by an offer of proof. They should point out specifically the portion of the warrant affidavit that is claimed to be false; and they should be accompanied by a statement of supporting reasons. Affidavits or sworn or otherwise reliable statements of witnesses should be furnished, or their absence satisfactorily explained. Allegations of negligence or innocent mistake are insufficient. The deliberate falsity or reckless disregard whose impeachment is permitted today is only that of the affiant, not of any nongovernmental informant. Finally, if these requirements are met, and if, when material that is the subject of the alleged falsity or reckless disregard is set to one side, there remains sufficient content in the warrant affidavit to support a finding of probable cause, no hearing is required. On the other hand, if the remaining content is insufficient, the defendant is entitled, under the Fourth Amendment, to his hearing. Whether he will prevail at that hearing is, of course, another issue."

Disposition: Case remanded for hearing on sufficiency of affidavit; judge must review defendant's allegations to determine if probable cause was established by false statements that were deliberately or recklessly placed in the affidavit.

2-6f *Illinois v. McArthur:* 532 U.S. 326, 148 L.Ed. 2d 838, 121 S.Ct. 946 (2001)

Facts: Tera McArthur asked two police officers to accompany her to the trailer where she lived with her husband, Charles, to keep the peace while she removed her belongings. After collecting her possessions, she told Chief Love that he should check the trailer because "Chuck had dope in there." She added that she saw Chuck "slide some dope underneath the couch." Charles refused to give Love permission to conduct a search. Love sent Officer Skidis with Tera to get a search warrant and told Charles, who was on the porch, that he could not reenter the trailer unless a police officer accompanied him. During the two hours that followed, Charles entered the trailer two or three times to get cigarettes and make a phone call. Each time, Love stood just inside the door to observe what Charles did. After the warrant was obtained, police searched the trailer. Charles was convicted on two misdemeanors (unlawful possession of drug paraphernalia and unlawful possession of marijuana) based on discovery of a marijuana pipe, a box for marijuana, and a small amount of marijuana found under the sofa.

Issue: Is a police officer allowed to prevent a person from entering his/her own home while authorities seek a search warrant?

Reasoning: "We conclude that the restriction at issue was reasonable, and hence lawful, in light of the following circumstances, which we consider in combination. First, the police had probable cause to believe that McArthur's trailer home contained evidence of a crime and contraband, namely, unlawful drugs. * * * Second, the police had good reason to fear that, unless restrained, McArthur would destroy the drugs before they could return with a warrant. * * *

"Third, the police made reasonable efforts to reconcile their law enforcement needs with the demands of personal privacy. They neither searched the trailer nor arrested McArthur before obtaining a warrant. Rather, they imposed a significantly less restrictive restraint, preventing McArthur only from entering the trailer unaccompanied. They left his home and his belongings intact—until a neutral Magistrate, finding probable cause, issued a warrant.

"Fourth, the police imposed the restraint for a limited period of time, namely, two hours. As far as the record reveals, this time period was no longer than reasonably necessary for the police, acting with diligence, to onbtain a warrant. * * * Given the nature of the intrusion and the law enforcement interest at stake, this brief seizure of the premises was permissible."

Disposition: Conviction affirmed; the police officer had the right to prevent McArthur from entering his home unaccompanied during the two-hour period while the search warrant was being obtained.

2-6g *Wilson v. Arkansas:* 514 U.S. 927, 131 L.Ed. 2d 976, 115 S.Ct. 1914 (1995)

Facts: Police officers obtained warrants to search Wilson's home and to arrest both Wilson and Jacobs. Affidavits filed in support of the warrant stated details of the narcotics transactions in which Wilson sold marijuana and methamphetamine to an informant and that Jacobs had previously been convicted of arson and firebombing. Later that afternoon, police found the main door to petitioner's home open. While entering the residence without knocking, they identified themselves as police officers and stated that they had a warrant. Once inside the home, the officers seized marijuana, methamphetamine, valium, narcotics paraphernalia, a gun, and ammunition. Wilson was found in the bathroom flushing marijuana down the toilet. The trial court denied Wilson's motion to suppress evidence because the officers failed to "knock and announce" before entering her home. A jury convicted Wilson for delivery of marijuana and methamphetamine, possession of drug paraphernalia, and possession of marijuana.

Issue: Do officers serving a warrant have to "knock and announce" before entering a dwelling?

Reasoning: * * * "In evaluating the scope of this [Fourth Amendment] right, we have looked to the traditional protections against unreasonable searches and seizures afforded by the common law at the time of the framing. * * *

"Our own cases have acknowledged that the common-law principle of announcement is 'embedded in Anglo-American law,' but we have never squarely held that this principle is an element of the reasonableness inquiry under the Fourth Amendment. We now so hold. Given the long-standing common-law endorsement of the practice of announcement, we have little doubt that the framers of the Fourth Amendment thought that the method of an officer's entry into a dwelling was among the factors to be considered in assessing the reasonableness of a search or seizure. * * *

"Thus, because the common-law rule was justified in part by the belief that announcement generally would avoid 'the destruction or breaking of any house . . . by which great damage and inconvenience might ensue,' courts acknowledged that the presumption in favor of announcement would yield under circumstances presenting a threat of physical violence. Similarly, courts held that an officer may dispense with announcement in cases where a prisoner escapes from him and retreats to his dwelling. Proof of 'demand and refusal' was deemed unnecessary in such cases because it would be a 'senseless ceremony' to require an officer in pursuit of a recently escaped arrestee to make an announcement prior to breaking the door to retake him. Finally, courts have indicated that unannounced entry may be justified where police officers have reason to believe that evidence would likely be destroyed if advance notice were given.

"We need not attempt a comprehensive catalog of the relevant countervailing factors here. For now, we leave to the lower courts the task of determining the circumstances under which an unannounced entry is reasonable under the Fourth Amendment." * * *

Disposition: Case remanded to state court to determine if there were sufficient facts to justify entry of Wilson's home without prior announcement.

2-6h *Richards v. Wisconsin:* 520 U.S. 385, 137 L.Ed. 2d 615, 117 S.Ct. 1416 (1997)

Facts: Police officers in Madison, Wisconsin obtained a warrant to search Richards's hotel room for drugs and related paraphernalia. An officer dressed as a maintenance man knocked at Richards's door. Richards slammed the door when he saw a uniformed officer standing behind the "maintenance man." When officers gained entry by kicking the door and using a battering ram, they found Richards attempting to escape through a window. Officers found cash and cocaine in plastic bags hidden above the bathroom ceiling tiles.

Issue: Is there a blanket exception to the "knock-announce" rule in drug cases?

Reasoning: "[T]he fact that felony drug investigations may frequently present circumstances warranting a no-knock entry cannot remove from the neutral scrutiny of a reviewing court the reasonableness of the police decision not to knock and announce in a particular case. Instead, in each case, it is the duty of a court confronted with the question to determine whether the facts and circumstances of the particular entry justified dispensing with the knock-and-announce requirement.

"In order to justify a 'no-knock' entry, the police must have a reasonable suspicion that knocking and announcing their presence, under the particular circumstances, would be dangerous or futile, or that it would inhibit the effective investigation of the crime by, for example, allowing the destruction of evidence. This standard—as opposed to a probable cause requirement—strikes the appropriate balance between the legitimate law enforcement concerns at issue in the execution of search warrants and the individual privacy interest affected by no-knock entries."

Disposition: Conviction affirmed; there is no blanket exemption from knock and announce in drug cases but, under the facts of this case, the entry was legal because the officers had reasonable suspicion that Richards would destroy evidence.

2-6i *Michigan v. Summers:* 452 U.S. 692, 69 L.Ed. 2d 340, 101 S.Ct. 2587 (1981)

Facts: Summers descended the front stairs of his house and encountered Detroit police officers who were about to execute a warrant to search the house for narcotics. They requested his assistance in gaining entry and detained him while the search was conducted. They found narcotics in the basement. Summers was arrested after the police verified that the residence was his house. The search incident to the arrest revealed 8.5 grams of heroin in a envelope in his coat pocket.

Issue: Do the police have the authority to detain a resident of a house while executing a search warrant?

Reasoning: *** "If the evidence that a citizen's residence is harboring contraband is sufficient to persuade a judicial officer that an invasion of the citizen's privacy is justified, it is constitutionally reasonable to require that citizen to remain while the officers of the law execute a valid warrant to search his home. Thus, for Fourth Amendment purposes, we hold that a warrant to search for contraband founded on probable cause implicitly carries with it the limited authority to detain the occupants of the premises while a proper search is conducted.

"Because it was lawful to require respondent to reenter and to remain in the house until evidence establishing probable cause to arrest him was found, his arrest and the search incident thereto was constitutionally permissible."

Disposition: Conviction affirmed; police had the authority to detain Summers while executing the search warrant.

2-6j *Maryland v. Garrison:* 480 U.S. 79, 94 L.Ed. 2d 72, 107 S.Ct. 1013 (1987)

Facts: Baltimore police officers obtained and executed a warrant to search the person of Lawrence McWebb and the "premises known as 2036 Park Avenue, third-floor apartment." Police reasonably believed that there was only one apartment on the third floor of the building indicated but, in fact, it contained two apartments—McWebb's and Garrison's. Heroin was discovered in Garrison's apartment before the officers became aware that they were not in McWebb's apartment. Garrison was convicted under the Controlled Substance Act based on this evidence.

Issue: Is evidence admissible when found in good faith while executing a search warrant at a location not authorized in the warrant?

Reasoning: "Plainly, if the officers had known, or even if they should have known, that there were two separate dwelling units on the third floor of 2036 Park Avenue, they would have been obligated to exclude respondent's apartment from the scope of the requested warrant. But we must judge the constitutionality of their conduct in light of the information available to them at the time they acted. Those items of evidence that emerge after the warrant is issued have no bearing on whether or not a warrant was validly issued. Just as the discovery of contraband cannot validate a warrant invalid when issued, so is it equally clear that the discovery of facts demonstrating that a valid warrant was unnecessarily broad does not retroactively invalidate the warrant. The validity of the warrant must be assessed on the basis of the information that the officers disclosed, or had a duty to discover and to disclose, to the issuing magistrate. On the basis of that information, we agree with the conclusion of all three Maryland courts that the warrant, insofar as it authorized a search that turned out to be ambiguous in scope, was valid when it was issued.

*** "Under the reasoning in *Hill* [*Hill v. California,* 401 U.S. 797 (1971)], the validity of the search of respondent's apartment pursuant to a warrant authorizing the search of the entire third floor depends on whether the officers' failure to realize the overbreadth of the warrant was objectively understandable and reasonable. Here it unquestionably was. The objective facts available to the officers at the time suggests no distinction between McWebb's apartment and the third-floor premises."

Disposition: Conviction affirmed; evidence found while executing warrant at Garrison's apartment is admissible because the officers honestly believed the location was indicated in the warrant.

2-6k *New York v. Burger:* 482 U.S. 691, 96 L.Ed. 2d 601, 107 S.Ct. 2636 (1987)

Facts: Burger owned a junkyard in Brooklyn, New York, where he dismantled cars and sold their parts. His junkyard was surrounded by a high metal fence but there were no buildings. About noon on November 17, 1982, Officer Vega and four other plain-clothes officers entered the junkyard to conduct an inspection authorized by New York law. When asked for his license and "police book" listing the vehicles and parts in his possession, Burger replied that he had neither. The officers then announced their intention to conduct an inspection. Burger did not object. A check of VIN numbers of items found during the inspection showed that Burger was in possession of stolen property. Burger was convicted of possession of stolen property.

Issue: Was the warrantless inspection of the junkyard constitutional?

Reasoning: "The Court long has recognized that the Fourth Amendment's prohibition on unreasonable searches and seizures is applicable to commercial premises, as well as to private homes. An owner or operator of a business thus has an expectation of privacy in commercial property, which society is prepared to consider to be reasonable. This expectation exists not only with respects to traditional police searches conducted for the gathering of criminal evidence but also with respect to administrative inspections designed to enforce regulatory statutes. An expectation of privacy in commercial premises, however, is different from, and indeed less than, a similar expectation in an individual's home. This expectation is particularly attenuated in commercial property employed in 'closely regulated' industries. * * *

* * * "Indeed, in *Donovan v. Dewey* [452 U.S. 594 (1981)], we declined to limit our consideration to the length of time during which the business in question—stone quarries—had been subject to federal regulation. We pointed out that the doctrine is essentially defined by 'the pervasiveness and regularity of the federal regulation' and the effect of such regulation upon an owner's expectation of privacy. We observed, however, that 'the duration of a particular regulatory scheme' would remain an 'important factor' in deciding whether a warrantless inspection pursuant to the scheme is permissible.

* * * "This warrantless inspection, however, even in the context of a pervasively regulated business, will be deemed to be reasonable only so long as three criteria are met. First, there must be a 'substantial' government interest that informs the regulatory scheme pursuant to which the inspection is made. * * *

"Second, the warrantless inspection must be 'necessary to further [the] regulatory scheme.' * * *

"Finally, 'the statute's inspection program, in terms of the certainty and regularity of its application, [must] provid[e] a constitutionally adequate substitute for a warrant.' In other words, the regulatory statute must perform the two basic functions of a warrant: it must advise the owner of the commercial premises that the search is being made pursuant to the law and has a properly defined scope, and it must limit the discretion of the inspecting officers. To perform this function, the statute must be 'sufficiently comprehensive and defined that the owner of commercial property cannot help but be aware that his property will be subject to periodic inspections undertaken for specific purposes.' In addition, in defining how a statute limits the discretion of the inspectors, we have observed that it must be 'carefully limited in time, place, and scope.' * * *

* * * "[T]he Court of Appeals failed to recognize that a State can address a major social problem *both* by way of an administrative scheme *and* through penal sanctions. Administrative statutes and penal laws may have the same *ultimate* purpose of remedying the social problem, but they have different subsidiary purposes and prescribe different methods of addressing the problem. An administrative statute establishes how a particular business in a 'closely regulated' industry should be operated, setting forth rules to guide an operator's conduct of the business and allowing government officials to ensure that those rules are followed. Such a regulatory approach contrasts with that of the penal laws, a major emphasis of which is the punishment of individuals for specific acts of behavior.

* * * "Nor do we think that this administrative scheme is unconstitutional simply because, in the course of enforcing it, an inspecting officer may discover evidence of crimes, besides violation of the scheme itself. * * * The discovery of evidence of crimes in the course of an otherwise proper administrative inspection does not render that search illegal or the administrative scheme suspect.

"Finally, we fail to see any constitutional significance in the fact that police officers, rather than 'administrative' agents, are permitted to conduct the Section 415-a5 inspections. * * * So long as a regulatory scheme is properly administrative, it is not rendered illegal by the fact that the inspecting officer has the power to arrest individuals for violations other than those created by the scheme itself. In sum, we decline to impose upon the States the burden of requiring the enforcement of their regulatory statutes to be carried out by specialized agents."

Disposition: Conviction affirmed; stolen property found during inspection of junkyard is admissible at criminal trial.

2-6I *Michigan v. Clifford:* 464 U.S. 287, 78 L.Ed. 2d 477, 104 S.Ct. 641 (1984)

Facts: Fire erupted in the Cliffords' home while they were out of town on a camping trip. Fire units arrived at 5:42 A.M. and all fire and police units left the premises by 7:04 A.M. At 8:00 A.M., Lt. Beyer, a fire investigator with the arson section of the Detroit Fire Department, received instructions to investigate the suspected arson fire. He arrived at the house about 1:00 P.M. A work crew was on the scene boarding up the house and pumping water out of the basement. A neighbor told investigators that he had called Clifford and been instructed to ask the Cliffords' insurance agent to send a boarding crew out to secure the house. The neighbor also said that the Cliffords did not plan to return that day. Lt. Beyer observe a Coleman fuel can was observed in the driveway and took it as evidence. About 1:30 P.M., after the water had been pumped out of the basement, Lt. Beyer and his partner entered the house without consent or a warrant and began their investigation. They determined that the fire originated in the basement under the stairs. The entire basement had a strong odor of fuel. Lt. Beyer and his partner found two more Coleman fuel cans beneath the stairway and a crock pot with electrical wires leading to a timer. The timer was set to turn on at 3:45 A.M.; it had stopped between 4:00 and 4:30 A.M. An extensive, warrantless search of the entire house followed. Pictures and electrical appliances had been removed prior to the fire. Raymond and Emma Clifford were arrested and charged with arson. They filed a pretrial appeal of the trial court's refusal to suppress the evidence.

Issue: Can fire investigators enter burned-out buildings without a warrant?

Reasoning: *** "Privacy expectations will vary with the type of property, the amount of fire damage, the prior and continued use of the premises, and in some cases the owner's efforts to secure it against intruders. Some fires may be so devastating that no reasonable privacy interest remains in the ash and ruins, regardless of the owner's subjective expectations. The test essentially is an objective one: whether 'the expectation [is] one that society is prepared to recognize as "reasonable."' If reasonable privacy interests remain in the fire-damaged property, the warrant requirement applies, and any official entry must be made pursuant to a warrant in the absence of consent or exigent circumstances.

"A burning building of course creates an exigency that justifies a warrantless entry by fire officials to fight the blaze. Moreover, in *Tyler* [436 U.S. 499, 56 L.Ed. 2d 486, 98 S.Ct. 1942 (1978)] we held that once in the building, officials need no warrant to remain for 'a reasonable time to investigate the cause of the blaze after it has been extinguished.' Where, however, reasonable expectations of privacy remain in the fire-damaged property, additional investigations begun after the fire has been extinguished and fire and police officials have left the scene, generally must be made pursuant to a warrant or the identification of some new exigency.

"The aftermath of a fire often presents exigencies that will not tolerate the delay necessary to obtain a warrant or to secure the owner's consent to inspect fire-damaged premises. Because determining the cause and origin of a fire serves a compelling public interest, the warrant requirement does not apply in such cases.

"If a warrant is necessary, the object of the search determines the type of warrant required. If the primary object is to determine the cause and origin of a recent fire, an administrative warrant will suffice. To obtain such a warrant, fire officials need show only that a fire of undetermined origin has occurred on the premises, that the scope of the proposed search is reasonable and will not intrude unnecessarily on the fire victim's privacy, and that the search will be executed at a reasonable and convenient time.

"If the primary object of the search is to gather evidence of criminal activity, a criminal search warrant may be obtained only on a showing of probable cause to believe the relevant evidence will be found in the place to be searched. If evidence of criminal activity is discovered during the course of a valid administrative search, it may be seized under the 'plain view' doctrine. This evidence then may be used to establish probable cause to obtain a criminal search warrant. Fire officials may not, however, rely on this evidence to expand the scope of their administrative search without first making a successful showing of probable cause to an independent judicial officer.

*** "The Clifford home was a two-and-one-half story brick and frame residence. Although there was extensive damage to the lower interior structure, the exterior of the house and some of the upstairs rooms were largely undamaged by the fire, although there was some smoke damage. The firemen had broken out one of the doors and most of the windows in fighting the blaze. At the time Lt. Beyer and his partner arrived, the home was uninhabitable. But personal belongings remained, and the Cliffords had arranged to have the house secured against intrusion in their absence. Under these circumstances, and in light of the strong expectation of privacy associated with a home, we hold that the Cliffords retained reasonable privacy interests in their fire-damaged residence and that the post-fire investigation was subject to the warrant requirement. Thus, the warrantless and non-consensual searches of both the basement and the upstairs areas of the house would have been valid only if exigent circumstances had justified the object and the scope of each.

*** "At least where a homeowner has made a reasonable effort to secure his fire-damaged home after the blaze has been extinguished and the fire and police units have left the scene, we hold that a subsequent post-fire search must be conducted pursuant to a warrant, consent, or the identification of some new exigency. So long as the primary purpose is to ascertain the cause of the fire, an administrative warrant will suffice."

Disposition: Coleman fuel cans found inside the house are inadmissible because they were discovered while officers acted without a search warrant.

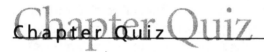

Chapter Quiz

True/False

1. Probable cause is satisfied if the officer believes that the person to be arrested committed the crime.
2. Only statements by individuals who have previously proven to be reliable can be used to establish probable cause
3. A search warrant cannot be based on stale information.
4. A search warrant can be issued by the court clerk.
5. A search warrant must give the accurate street address of the location to be searched.
6. Affidavits are used to provide the judge with facts in support of issuing the search warrant.
7. Anyone at the location may be searched at the time officers arrive to execute a search warrant.
8. Officers executing a search warrant are only allowed to enter rooms listed in the warrant to look for potential attackers.
9. If officers are properly executing a search warrant, any items they find in plain view will be admissible in evidence even though these items are not listed in the warrant.
10. An administrative warrant is needed only if criminal activity is involved.

Discussion Questions

1. Officer Nelson was investigating the robbery of the local bank. He submitted the following affidavit with his request for a warrant to search the storage space assigned to Tom's apartment:

> "I received an anonymous telephone call one hour after the robbery stating that Tom was the person who robbed the bank. The informant said that Tom had made a deposit at the bank earlier in the day and became irate when the teller refused to accept a check for $5,000 because she said it was forged. The informant also said that Tom went to Apartment 9 at 123 N. Main after the robbery and hid all of the cash taken in the robbery in the storage space adjacent to the apartment's carport and he locked it with a combination lock stolen from the local high school. I checked with the bank and verified that Tom made a deposit the morning of the robbery. The manager of the apartment building at 123 N. Main showed me the storage area in question. It is locked with a combination lock similar to those used for lockers in the local high school."

Should the judge grant Officer Nelson's request for a warrant to search the storage space adjacent to Apartment 9's carport? Explain.

2. Officer Hernandez was investigating the murder of Ms. Miller. He submitted the following affidavit in support of his request for a warrant to search Geoarge Smith's van:

> "I have talked to three people who saw Ms. Miller the day of her murder. Each stated that she complained that George, who drove a red VW van, had been stalking her. Mr. Jones, her neighbor, stated that he heard Ms. Miller scream about 4:00 P.M. and saw a red VW van drive away a few minutes later. Mr. Smith, who found the body at 4:30 P.M., said that he saw a red VW van with license number 123 ABC leaving the scene. A record check on 123 ABC shows that it is a red Toyota van registered to George Smith."

Should the judge issue a warrant to search George Smith's van? Explain.

3. Officer Curtis obtained a warrant to search Frank's house at 456 S. First Street for five, stolen 25-inch television sets. When Officer Curtis arrived, it appeared that no one was home so he let himself in by opening an unlocked door. During the course of the search, Officer Curtis found a diamond ring in a kitchen cupboard, which was later determined to be stolen. Is the ring admissible? Explain.

4. Officer Bensen responded to a call by neighbors that shots had been fired at the Richardson's house. When he arrived, he discovered the front door was partially open, so he went in. He found Mrs. Richardson dead on the living room floor. During a "protective sweep," Officer Bensen found Robert hiding in a closet in an upstairs bedroom. He then proceeded to conduct a detailed search of the house, which lasted four hours. Many pieces of evidence were found that led to the arrest of Robert, Mrs. Richardson's nephew who lived at the same address. Can Robert have the evidence suppressed because the police did not obtain a search warrant? Because officers failed to "knock and announce?" Because officers exceeded the permissible limits of a "protective sweep?" Explain.

Chapter 3

Field Interviews

Outline

Police officers frequently see individuals in suspicious situations but do not have probable cause to arrest them. In *Terry v. Ohio,* the Supreme Court recognized the necessity of stopping suspects briefly to investigate such situations. It also gave the officers the right to make limited searches for their personal safety.

3-1 When a Person May Be Stopped

Police frequently observe something that indicates the need for further investigation. Many times, the officer's initial observation does not provide sufficient information to make an arrest, but there is definitely something going on that needs to be checked out. Based on what they find, the police may either make an arrest or release the person involved.

The Supreme Court has agreed that the police should have the power to stop a suspect for brief questioning even though the facts do not indicate that there is probable cause to make an arrest. In *Terry v. Ohio,* the leading case, the Court said: "police may temporarily detain someone for questioning if there are specific articulable facts which lead a reasonable police officer to believe that criminal activity is occurring."

This standard, frequently called "reasonable suspicion," differs from the power to arrest in several ways. Reasonable suspicion does not require as many facts as are needed to make an arrest. Officers must be able to cite specific facts that cause them to believe criminal activity is occurring, but it is not necessary to identify a specific crime believed to be in progress. To make an arrest, the officer must believe that it is more probable than not that the suspect is committing a crime. Reasonable suspicion only requires that a reasonable officer believes that some criminal activity is occurring. An arrest is based on what a "reasonable person" would conclude; temporary detention can be based on what a "reasonable officer" would believe.

Any time an officer has the right to detain someone, the officer has the right to use force to prevent that person from leaving the scene. This applies to both temporary detentions and arrests. The force used must always be reasonable under the circumstances. Deadly force is justified only if a life (including the officer's life) is in danger. The Supreme Court set this standard in *Tennessee v. Garner,* a case that dealt with the right to use deadly force to make an arrest. The justification for the use of force is even less when officers are simply investigating to determine if a crime has occurred. Only a situation perceived as life threatening will ever justify using deadly force.

Even though the Court allowed the police to detain someone against his/her will without making an arrest, the police cannot stop a person any time they feel like it. An officer may stop someone on reasonable suspicion but not randomly, on mere suspicion, or based on a hunch. The officer must have specific facts that can be stated to justify each detention.

The courts have interpreted the temporary detention standard quite freely, permitting many police actions in this regard. A suspect's merely associating with other known criminals or loitering in a high-crime area, however, is not sufficient for police to make a stop. A suspect fleeing the scene as a police officer approaches may arouse reasonable suspicion and justify a brief detention.

While most temporary detentions are based on the police officer's firsthand observations, often someone else provides the information. The Supreme Court, in *Adams v. Williams,* indicated that the police may use facts supplied by others if there is sufficient reason to believe the informant is reliable.

The Supreme Court took this one step further in *Alabama v. White* (1990). This decision allowed information from an anonymous informant to be used to establish reasonable suspicion. Temporary detention is permissible if a totality-of-the-circumstances test indicates the tip, as corroborated by independent police work, provides reasonable suspicion of criminal activity. An uncorroborated, anonymous tip, however, is not sufficient reason to detain a person when the tipster merely describes the way a person is dressed and makes the bald allegation that the person is carrying a concealed gun.

3-2 Length of Detention

The Court has never set a specific time limit on temporary detentions. The length of time must allow the officer to conduct a brief investigation. How long that investigation may take varies with the circumstances. A 90-minute detention was ruled unreasonably long. Cases involving 20-minute stops have been upheld. The detention should last no longer than necessary to determine if the person stopped was actually involved in a crime. The important thing is that the police diligently pursue reasonable investigative techniques in order to decide if the suspect should be arrested.

3-3 When a Person May Be Searched

The Supreme Court, recognizing that it is frequently necessary to search a suspect in order to protect an officer, authorized protective searches during a temporary detention if the officer has a reasonable suspicion that the suspect is armed or dangerous. The officer may pat down the suspect's outer clothing for weapons. If the officer feels an object believed to be a weapon, the officer may reach into the suspect's clothing and remove it.

This limited search, frequently called a "frisk," is designed solely for the protection of the officer. There is no automatic right to search every person stopped. Officers must have a reasonable suspicion that the search is needed for their protection. If a person is stopped, for example, because there is reasonable suspicion that a violent crime has just been committed or is in progress, the right to search logically follows. If the situation involves a property crime, there may be no right to search.

3-4 Scope of Search

The scope of the search is limited to what is necessary to protect the officers. As previously indicated, in most cases this involves "patting down" the suspect for weapons. If an officer feels something believed to be a weapon, then the weapon may be removed from the suspect's clothing. Sometimes this search may be a bit broader. For example, in *Terry v. Ohio,* the suspects were wearing heavy coats because it was a cold winter day. The Court approved a search that included checking inner pockets in the suspects' coats.

When police, acting on reasonable suspicion, retrieve what is believed to be a weapon, it is a legal search. If, in fact, the object seized is not a weapon, whatever was seized will still be admissible. On the other hand, if the officer feels something in the suspect's pocket that does not resemble a weapon, there is no right to retrieve it even if there is strong suspicion that the suspect has drugs or evidence of a crime. If the police search with the intent to find evidence or contraband, the search violates the Fourth Amendment. Officers must keep in mind that the search authorized in *Terry* is limited to seizing weapons.

In 1993, the Supreme Court created a minor exception to this rule. It authorized the seizure of nonthreatening contraband, such as drugs, detected during an otherwise legal "pat down" for weapons if the officer can tell that the item is contraband without conducting an additional search. It extended "plain view" to "plain feel." The Court rejected a search in which the officer determined that a lump was cocaine by "squeezing, sliding and otherwise manipulating the contents of the defendant's pocket." These additional acts went beyond the normal "pat down" and violated the suspect's privacy.

3-5 Special Situations

3-5a Sobriety Checkpoints

One of the weapons in law enforcement's arsenal against drunk drivers is the sobriety checkpoint. Cars passing the checkpoint are stopped regardless of any individualized suspicion that a driver is under the influence of drugs or alcohol. A systematic process is required: All cars may be stopped or cars in a predetermined pattern, such as every fourth car, may be used. The Supreme Court approved this practice in *Michigan Department of State Police v. Sitz.* The Court applied a balancing test that weighed the state's interest in preventing drunk driving, and the extent that sobriety checkpoints advance this interest, against the degree of intrusion upon motorists. The state's interests were found to be great and the inconvenience minimal; therefore, the roadblocks do not violate the Fourth Amendment.

The Court was not willing to extend *Sitz* to checkpoints designed to detect illegal drugs. In *City of Indianapolis v. Edmond* (2000), the Court considered roadblocks that were clearly posted as a "NARCOTICS CHECKPOINT." An officer accompanied by a narcotics-detection dog walked around the outside of each stopped vehicle. Although officers checked driver's licenses and vehicle registrations and the city argued that interdiction of narcotics was in the interest of public safety, the Court focused on the primary purpose of the roadblock: making drug arrests. It found this to be no different from any other law enforcement effort to detect general criminal activity and refused to make an exception to the requirement that officers need particularized suspicion to stop a person or vehicle.

3-5b Wanted Flyers

The right to detain is not restricted to crimes in progress. Police may also stop someone on the basis of a wanted flyer. In these situations, the wanted flyer usually creates reasonable suspicion; additional details supplied by the law enforcement agency circulating the flyer establish probable cause for the arrest. The stop is valid only if the wanted flyer is based on reasonable suspicion. The Court approved this practice for felonies and has made no specific comments on its application to misdemeanors.

3-5c Car Stops

There is no special right to stop a car or other vehicle. The police do not have the right to randomly pull a car over to check registration or see if the driver has a valid license. Cars are frequently stopped, however, because of a suspected vehicle code violation. In *Pennsylvania v. Mimms* (1977), the Court recognized the right of a police officer to order the driver out of a vehicle when making a traffic stop. This rule was later extended so that an officer could order occupants to exit the car, but the Court did not rule on the officer's right to detain passengers once they alight from the vehicle. In *Knowles v. Iowa* (1998), the Supreme Court ruled that a thorough search of a car during a traffic stop in which no one was arrested violated the Fourth Amendment. The occupants and the interior of the car can be searched only if some other test is satisfied, such as a bulge in a person's pocket that creates a reasonable suspicion that the person has a gun or if the facts establish probable cause that illegal drugs are hidden in the car.

At other times there may be a reasonable suspicion that the occupants of a car are involved in criminal activity. These cars can be stopped under the authority to temporarily detain suspects. When this occurs, officers have the authority to conduct a search of the passenger compartment for weapons *if* there is an articulable and objectively reasonable belief that the suspect is dangerous and may gain immediate control of weapons. This right to look for weapons exists even if the officers have decided to release the suspects. The rationale for this is that when the suspects are released, they might return to the car and use the weapon against the officers.

3-5d Fingerprinting

Hayes v. Florida involved taking a suspect to the police station for fingerprinting. The Court ruled that, absent consent, this may not be done without probable cause to arrest, but that fingerprints may be taken at the scene.

3-5e Interrogation

Questioning during temporary detention does not require *Miranda* warnings, but the questioning must be done at the location where the detention occurred. *Dunaway v. New York* held that transportation to the station can only be done if the suspect consents or has been arrested.

3-5f School Searches

Searches by school officials are governed by standards similar to those that apply to temporary detentions. There must be a reasonable suspicion that a student has broken the law or violated a school regulation. These searches are not restricted to weapons. In *New Jersey v. T.L.O.*, the Supreme Court affirmed the search of a 14-year-old girl's purse for cigarettes.

3-5g Canine Searches

The Supreme Court has allowed customs agents to briefly detain luggage in order to have narcotics-detection dogs check it for drugs. *United States v. Place* held that agents must have a reasonable suspicion that the suitcase contains drugs. The luggage may not be opened prior to the canine inspection. Additionally, the detention must not be unreasonably long. The fact that a reliable, properly trained dog indicates drugs are present will establish probable cause. The closed container rule allows officers to seize the luggage while seeking a search warrant. No search is permissible without a search warrant unless some other exception to the warrant requirement applies.

3-5h Airport Detentions

Cases involving temporary detention of travelers at airports have relied either on *Terry* or on consent. The factual situations involved have been complex and it is hard to reconcile all of the decisions. If an officer approaches a suspect and asks to see airline tickets or requests that the suspect accompany the officer to another location, the decision is usually based on consent.

3-5i Profiling

Drug enforcement officers frequently rely on a drug courier profile, which includes such factors as traveling to/from a city known to be a major drug center, taking a long flight but returning after only a few hours, traveling with only carry-on luggage, attempts to be the last person off the airplane, or other furtive conduct. A match on a sufficient number of these factors establishes reasonable suspicion, but the Court has had trouble deciding how much evidence is necessary in these cases. Lengthy detentions have generally been found to violate the suspect's rights unless an arrest was made. The Court has not ruled on racial profiling or profiling of suspected terrorists.

3-5j Probationers and Parolees

A very common condition placed on probationers is that they submit to warantless searches by their probation officers. This has long been recognized as giving probation officers the right to conduct random searches. Recently the Supreme Court answered the question: Do police officers have the authority to search probationers? The Court held that these searches are legal if they are based on reasonable suspicion and are covered by the probation conditions. Similar rules would apply to parolees.

3-5k Government Employees

Unlike the workers in the private sector, government employees have Fourth Amendment protections against searches by their employers. The Court has held that workplace searches of, for example, desks and file cabinets, can be done if the search is reasonable under the circumstances. The same rule applies to investigations of on-the-job misconduct and noninvestigatory searches such as trying to locate a missing file. The Court did not state whether there must be suspicion focusing on a single individual in order to conduct this type of search.

Purses and briefcases do not come under this rule because they are personal property; the standard of suspicion used in nonworkplace searches would be used. Searches for nonjob-related reasons, such as crimes committed during off-duty hours, are also not covered by this rule.

3-6 Key Supreme Court Cases

3-6a *Terry v. Ohio:* 392 U.S. 1, 88 S.Ct. 1868, 20 L.Ed. 2d 889 (1968)

Facts: At about 2:30 P.M. on October 31, 1962, Officer McFadden, a police officer who had patrolled downtown Cleveland for 35 years, became suspicious of the activities of two men (Terry and Chilton) whom he had never seen before. He observed the two men on a corner. One would leave the other and walk past some stores. The man paused for a moment and looked in a store window, then walked on a short distance, turned around and walked back toward the corner, pausing once more to look in the same store window. He rejoined his companion at the corner and the two conferred briefly. Then the second man walked past the same store and looked in the window prior to returning to the corner. The two men repeated this ritual alternately five or six times. At one point, a third man approached and engaged the two men in a brief conversation. The men repeated their activity for about 10 minutes and then walked down the street together.

Officer McFadden had become thoroughly suspicious and believed the two men were "casing a job, a stick-up" and that the men might have a gun. He followed them and saw them stop to talk to the man who had previously approached them. Officer McFadden approached the three men, identified himself as a police officer, and asked for their names. When the men "mumbled something" in response to his inquiries, Officer McFadden grabbed Terry, spun him around so that they were facing the other two, with Terry between McFadden and the others, and patted down the outside of his clothing. The officer found a pistol in the left breast pocket of Terry's overcoat. He reached inside the pocket but was unable to retrieve the gun. He ordered all three men into a nearby store, removed Terry's overcoat, and retrieved a .38-caliber revolver from the pocket. He ordered all three men to face the wall with their hands up. He then patted down the other two men and discovered another revolver in the outer pocket of Chilton's overcoat. McFadden testified that he only patted the men down to see whether they had weapons and that he did not put his hands beneath the outer garments of either man until he felt their guns. All three men were transported to the police station, where Terry and Chilton were charged with carrying concealed weapons.

Issues:

1. Does an officer have the right to stop a person when there is no probable cause to make an arrest?
2. What right does an officer have to search a person who is stopped without probable cause to make an arrest?

Reasoning: "Our first task is to establish at what point in this encounter the Fourth Amendment becomes relevant. That is, we must decide whether and when Officer McFadden 'seized' Terry and whether and when he conducted a 'search.' There is some suggestion in the use of such terms as 'stop' and 'frisk' that such police conduct is outside the purview of the Fourth Amendment because neither action rises to the level of a 'search' or 'seizure' within the meaning of the Constitution. We emphatically reject this notion. It is quite plain that the Fourth Amendment governs 'seizures' of the person which do not eventuate in a trip to the station house and prosecution for crime—'arrests' in traditional terminology. It must be recognized that whenever a police officer accosts an individual and restrains his freedom to walk away, he has 'seized' that person. And it is nothing less than sheer torture of the English language to suggest that a careful exploration of the outer surface of a person's clothing all over his or her body in an attempt to find weapons is not a 'search.' Moreover, it is simply fantastic to urge that such a procedure performed in public by a policeman while the citizen stands helpless, perhaps facing a wall with his hands raised, is a 'petty indignity.' It is a serious intrusion upon the sanctity of the person, which may inflict great indignity and arouse strong resentment, and it is not to be undertaken lightly.

***

"Nevertheless, the notions which underlie both the warrant procedure and the requirement of probable cause remain fully relevant in this context. In order to assess the reasonableness of Officer McFadden's conduct as a general proposition, it is necessary 'first to focus upon the governmental interest which allegedly justifies official intrusion upon constitutionally protected interests of the private citizens,' for there is 'no ready test for determining reasonableness other than by balancing the need to search [or seize] against the invasion which the search [or seizure] entails.' And in justifying the particular intrusion the police officer must be able to point to specific and articulable facts which, taken together with rational inferences from those facts, reasonable warrant that intrusion. The scheme of the Fourth Amendment becomes meaningful only when it is assured that at some point the conduct of those charged with enforcing the laws can be subjected to the more detached, neutral scrutiny of a judge who must evaluate the reasonableness of a particular search or seizure in light of the particular circumstances. And in making that assessment it is imperative that the facts be judged against an objective standard: Would the facts available to the officer at the moment of the seizure or the search 'warrant a man of reasonable caution in the belief' that the action taken was appropriate? Anything less would invite intrusions upon constitutionally guaranteed rights based on nothing more substantial than inarticulate hunches, a result this Court has consistently refused to sanction. And simple 'good faith' on the part of the arresting officer is not enough." * * * If subjective good faith alone were the test, the protections of the Fourth Amendment would evaporate, and the people would be "secure in their persons, houses, papers and effects," only in the discretion of the police.

"Applying these principles to this case, we consider first the nature and extent of the governmental interests involved. One general interest is of course that of effective crime prevention and detection; it is this interest which underlies the recognition that a police officer may in appropriate circumstances and in an appropriate manner approach a person for purposes of investigating possible criminal behavior even though there is no probable cause to make an arrest. It was this legitimate investigative function Officer McFadden was discharging when he decided to approach petitioner and his companions. He had observed Terry, Chilton, and Katz go through a series of acts, each of them perhaps innocent in itself, but which taken together warranted further investigation. There is nothing unusual in two men standing together on a street corner, perhaps waiting for someone. Nor is there anything suspicious about people in such circumstances strolling up and down the street, singly or in pairs. Store windows, moreover, are made to be looked in. But the story is quite different where, as here, two men hover about a street corner for an extended period of time, at the end of which it becomes apparent that they are not waiting for anyone or anything; where these men pace alternately along an identical route, pausing to stare in the same store window roughly 24 times; where each completion of this route is followed immediately by a conference between the two men on the corner; where they are joined in one of these conferences by a third man who leaves swiftly; and where the two men finally follow the third and rejoin him a couple of blocks away. It would have been poor police work indeed for an officer of 30 years' experience in the detection of thievery from stores in this same neighborhood to have failed to investigate this behavior further.

"The crux of this case, however, is not the propriety of Officer McFadden's taking steps to investigate petitioner's suspicious behavior, but rather, whether there was justification for McFadden's invasion of Terry's personal security by searching him for weapons in the course of that investigation. We are now concerned with more than the governmental interest in investigating crime; in addition, there is the more immediate interest of the police officer in taking steps to assure himself that the person with whom he is dealing is not armed with a weapon that could unexpectedly and fatally be used against him. Certainly it would be unreasonable to require that police officers take unnecessary risks in the performance of their duties. American criminals have a long tradition of armed violence, and every year in this country many law enforcement officers are killed in the line of duty, and thousands more are wounded. Virtually all of these deaths and a substantial portion of the injuries are inflicted with guns and knives.

"In view of these facts, we cannot blind ourselves to the need for law enforcement officers to protect themselves and other prospective victims of violence in situations where they may lack probable cause for an arrest. When an officer is justified in believing that the individual whose suspicious behavior he is investigating at close range is armed and presently dangerous to the officer or to others, it would appear to be clearly unreasonable to deny the officer the power to take necessary measures to determine whether the person is in fact carrying a weapon and to neutralize the threat of physical harm.

"Our evaluation of the proper balance that has to be struck in this type of case leads us to conclude that there must be a narrowly drawn authority to permit a reasonable search for weapons for the protection of the police officer, where he has reason to believe that he is dealing with an armed and dangerous individual, regardless of whether he has probable cause to arrest the individual for a crime. The officer need not be absolutely certain that the individual is armed; the issue is whether a reasonable prudent man in the circumstances would be warranted in the belief that his safety or that of others was in danger. And in determining whether the officer acted reasonable in such circumstances, due weight must be given, not to his inchoate and unparticularized suspicion or 'hunch' but to the specific reasonable inferences which he is entitled to draw from the facts in light of his experience. * * *

* * * "Suffice it to note that such a search, unlike a search without a warrant incident to a lawful arrest, is not justified by any need to prevent the disappearance or destruction of evidence of crime. The sole justification of the search in the present situation is the protection of the police officer and others nearby, and it must therefore be confined in scope to an intrusion reasonably designed to discover guns, knives, clubs or other hidden instruments for the assault of the police officer.

"The scope of the search in this case presents no serious problem in light of these standards. Officer McFadden patted down the outer clothing of petitioner and his two companions. He did not place his hands in their pockets or under the outer surface of their garments until he had felt weapons, and then he merely reached for and removed the guns. He never did invade Katz' person beyond the outer surface of his clothes, since he discovered nothing in his pat-down which might have been a weapon. Officer McFadden confined his search strictly to what was minimally necessary to learn whether the men were armed and to disarm them once he discovered the weapons. He did not conduct a general exploratory search for whatever evidence of criminal activity he might find.

* * * "We merely hold today that where a police officer observed unusual conduct which leads him reasonably to conclude in light of his experience that criminal activity may be afoot and that the persons with whom he is dealing may be armed and presently dangerous, where in the course of investigating this behavior he identifies himself as a policeman and makes reasonable inquiries, and where nothing in the initial stages of the encounter serve to dispel his reasonable fear for his own or others' safety, he is entitled for the protection of himself and others in the area to conduct a carefully limited search of the outer clothing of such persons in an attempt to discover weapons which might be used to assault him."

Disposition: Conviction affirmed; the weapon found in Terry's pocket is admissible at trial because: (1) officers were allowed to stop Terry based on reasonable suspicion that criminal activity was afoot; (2) pat-down for weapons was permitted because the officer had a reasonable suspicion that Terry was armed.

3-6b *Alabama v. White:* 496 U.S. 325, 110 L.Ed. 2d 301, 110 S.Ct. 2412 (1990)

Facts: On April 22, 1987, at approximately 3:00 P.M., Corporal Davis received a telephone call from an anonymous person, stating: Vanessa

White would be leaving 235-C Lynwood Terrace Apartments at a particular time in a brown Plymouth station wagon with the right taillight lens broken; she would be going to Dobey's Motel; and she would have about an ounce of cocaine inside a brown attaché case. Corporal Davis and his partner proceeded to the Lynwood Terrace Apartments where they saw a brown Plymouth station wagon with a broken right taillight in the parking lot in front of the 235 building. They observed White leave the 235 building carrying nothing in her hands and watched her enter the station wagon. They followed the Plymouth as it took the most direct route to Dobey's Motel. When the vehicle reached the highway on which Dobey's Motel is located Corporal Reynolds requested a patrol unit to stop the Plymouth. It was stopped at approximately 4:18 P.M. before it reached Dobey's Motel. Corporal Davis asked White to step to the rear of her car and informed her that she had been stopped because she was suspected of carrying cocaine in her car. White gave Corporal Reynolds permission to look in the car; he found a locked brown attaché case in the car. The officer asked White for the combination to the lock and she gave it to him. The officer found marijuana in the attaché case and placed White under arrest. During booking at the station, officers found 3 milligrams of cocaine in White's purse.

Issue: Can reasonable suspicion to detain a person be based on an anonymous tip?

Reasoning: "*Illinois v. Gates* dealt with an anonymous tip in the probable cause context. The Court there abandoned the 'two-pronged test' of *Aguilar v. Texas* and *Spinelli v. United States* in favor of a 'totality of the circumstances' approach to determining whether an informant's tip establishes probable cause. Gates made clear, however, that those factors that had been considered critical under *Aguilar* and *Spinelli*—an informant's 'veracity,' 'reliability,' and 'basis of knowledge'—remain 'highly relevant in determining the value of his report.' These factors are also relevant in the reasonable suspicion context, although allowance must be made in applying them for the lesser showing required to meet that standard. * * *

"Reasonable suspicion is a less demanding standard than probable cause not only in the sense that reasonable suspicion can be established with information that is different in quantity or content than that required to establish probable cause, but also in the sense that reasonable suspicion can arise from information that is less reliable than that required to show probable cause. * * * Reasonable suspicion, like probable cause, is dependent upon both the content of information possessed by police and its degree of reliability. Both factors—quantity and quality—are considered in the 'totality of the circumstances—the whole picture,' that must be taken into account when evaluating whether there is reasonable suspicion. Thus, if a tip has a relatively low degree of reliability, more information will be required to establish the requisite quantum of suspicion than would be required if the tip were more reliable. The *Gates* Court applied its totality of the circumstances approach in this manner, taking into account the facts known to the officers from personal observation, and giving the anonymous tip the weight it deserved in light of its indicia of reliability as established through independent police work. The same approach applies in the reasonable suspicion context, the only difference being the level of suspicion that must be established. Contrary to the court below, we conclude that when the officers stopped respondent, the anonymous tip had been sufficiently corroborated to furnish reasonable suspicion that respondent was engaged in criminal activity and that the investigative stop therefore did not violate the Fourth Amendment. * * *

"The Court's opinion in *Gates* gave credit to the proposition that because an informant is shown to be right about some things, he is probably right about other facts that he has alleged, including the claim that the object of the tip is engaged in criminal activity. Thus, it is not unreasonable to conclude in this case that the independent corroboration by the police of significant aspects of the informer's predications imparted some degree of reliability to the other allegations made by the caller.

"We think it also important that, as in *Gates,* 'the anonymous [tip] contained a range of details relating not just to easily obtained facts and conditions existing at the time of the tip, but to future actions of third parties ordinarily not easily predicted.' The fact that the officers found a car precisely matching the caller's description in front of the 235 building is an example of the former. Anyone could have 'predicted' that fact because it was a condition presumably existing at the time of the call. What was important was the caller's ability to predict respondent's *future behavior,* because it demonstrated inside information—a special familiarity with respondent's affairs. The general public would have had no way of knowing that respondent would shortly leave the building, get in the described car, and drive the most direct route to Dobey's Motel. Because only a small number of people are generally privy to an individual's itinerary, it is reasonable for police to believe that a person with access to such information is likely to also have access to reliable information about that individual's illegal activities. When significant aspects of the caller's predictions were verified, there was reason to believe not only that the caller was honest but also that he was well informed, at least well enough to justify the stop.

"Although it is a close case, we conclude that under the totality of the circumstances the anonymous tip, as corroborated, exhibited sufficient indicia of reliability to justify the investigatory stop of respondent's car."

Disposition: Conviction affirmed; the stop of White's vehicle as a result of an anonymous tip was legal.

3-6c *Michigan v. Long:* 463 U.S. 1032, 77 L.Ed. 2d 1201, 103 S.Ct. 3469 (1983)

Facts: Deputies Howell and Lewis were on patrol in a rural area one evening when, shortly after midnight, they observed a speeding car that was driven erratically. The driver turned down a side road and the car swerved off into a shallow ditch. The officers stopped to investigate. Long, the only occupant in the car, met the officers at the rear of the car. He left the door on the driver's side of the vehicle open. Long appeared to be under the influence of something. He did not respond to requests for the vehicle registration; instead, he turned and walked toward the open car door. The officers followed Long and observed a large hunting knife on the floorboard of the driver's side of the car. They stopped Long's progress toward the car and subjected him to a pat-down for weapons. They found no weapons on his person. The officers stood at the rear of the car and shined flashlights into the car to check for weapons. They noticed something protruding from under the armrest of the front seat. Deputy Howell lifted the armrest and saw an open pouch that contained marijuana on the front seat. Long was arrested for possession of marijuana. A search of the passenger compartment did not reveal any more marijuana. Officers found approximately 75 pounds of marijuana when they opened the trunk after the car was impounded.

Issue: What parts of a car can be searched when the car is stopped on reasonable suspicion?

Reasoning: "Contrary to Long's view, *Terry* need not be read as restricting the preventative search to the person of the detained suspect.

"In two cases in which we applied *Terry* to specific factual situations, we recognized that investigative detentions involving suspects in vehicles are especially fraught with danger to police officers. In *Pennsylvania v. Mimms* we held that police may order persons out of an automobile during a stop for a traffic violation, and may frisk those persons for weapons if there is a reasonable belief that they are armed and dangerous. Our decision rested in part on the 'inordinate risk confronting an officer as he approaches a person seated in an automobile.' In *Adams v. Williams* we held that the police, acting on an informant's tip, may reach into the passenger compartment of an automobile to remove a gun from the driver's waistband even where the gun was not apparent to police from outside the car and the police knew of its existence only because of the tip. Again our decision rested in part on our view of the danger presented to police officers in 'traffic stop' and automobile situations.

"Finally, we have also expressly recognized that suspects may injure police officers and others by virtue of their access to weapons, even though they may not themselves be armed. *** In order to provide a 'workable rule' we held that articles inside the relatively narrow compass of the passenger compartment of an automobile are in fact generally, even if not inevitable, within 'the area into which an arrestee might reach in order to grab a weapon.' We also held that the police may examine the contents of any open or closed container found within the passenger compartment, 'for if the passenger compartment is within the reach of the arrestee, so will containers in it be within his reach.'

"Our past cases indicate then that protection of police and others can justify protective searches when police have a reasonable belief that the suspect poses a danger, that roadside encounters between police and suspects are especially hazardous, and that danger may arise from the possible presence of weapons in the area surrounding a suspect. These principles compel our conclusion that the search of the passenger compartment of an automobile, limited to those areas in which a weapon may be placed or hidden, is permissible if the police officer possesses a reasonable belief based on 'specific and articulable facts which, taken together with the rational inferences from those facts, reasonably warrant' the officer in believing that the suspect is dangerous and the suspect may gain immediate control of weapons. 'The issue is whether a reasonably prudent man in the circumstances would be warranted in the belief that his safety or that of others was in danger.' If a suspect is 'dangerous,' he is no less dangerous simply because he is not arrested. If, while conducting a legitimate *Terry* search of the interior of the automobile, the officer should, as here, discover contraband other than weapons, he clearly cannot be required to ignore the contraband and the Fourth Amendment does not require its suppression in such circumstances. ***

*** "Just as a *Terry* suspect on the street may, despite being under the brief control of a police officer, reach into his clothing and retrieve a weapon, so might a *Terry* suspect in Long's position break away from police control and retrieve a weapon from his automobile. In addition, if the suspect is not placed under arrest, he will be permitted to reenter his automobile, and he will then have access to any weapons inside. Or, as here, the suspect may be permitted to reenter the vehicle before the *Terry* investigation is over, and again, may have access to weapons. In any event, we stress that a *Terry* investigation, such as the one that occurred here, involves a police investigation 'at close range' when the officer remains particularly vulnerable in part *because* a full custodial arrest has not been effected, and the officer must make a 'quick decision as to how to protect himself and others from possible danger.' In such circumstances, we have not required that officers adopt alternate means to ensure their safety in order to avoid the intrusion involved in a *Terry* encounter."

Disposition: Conviction affirmed; marijuana found in Long's car is admissible at trial because there was reasonable suspicion that Long was dangerous and might retrieve a weapon from the car.

3-7 Other Supreme Court Cases

3-7a *Brown v. Texas:* 443 U.S. 47, 61 L.Ed. 2d 357, 99 S.Ct. 2637 (1979)

Facts: Officers observed Brown and another man walking in opposite directions away from one another in an alley. They believed that the two men had been together or were about to meet until the patrol car appeared. Brown was detained because he looked suspicious and was unknown to the officers. The area had a high incidence of drug traffic. Officers asked Brown to identify himself pursuant to a penal code section that required a person to give his name and address to an officer who had lawfully detained him. Brown refused and angrily asserted that officers had no right to stop him. Officers then frisked Brown and arrested him for failure to identify himself.

Issue: Did officers have the right to stop the suspect and demand identification?

Reasoning: "The flaw in the State's case is that none of the circumstances preceding the officers' detention of appellant justified a reasonable suspicion that he was involved in criminal conduct. Officer Venegas testified at appellant's trial that the situation in the alley 'looked suspicious' but he was unable to point to any facts supporting that conclusion. * * *

"In the absence of any basis for suspecting appellant of misconduct, the balance between the public interest and appellant's right to personal security and privacy tilts in favor of freedom from police interference. The Texas statute *** is designed to advance a weighty social objective in large metropolitan centers: prevention of crime. But even assuming that purpose is served to some degree by stopping and demanding identification from an individual without any specific basis for believing he is involved in criminal activity, the guarantees of the Fourth Amendment do not allow it."

Disposition: Conviction reversed; the stop of Brown was not based on reasonable suspicion.

3-7b *Illinois v. Wardlow:* 528 U.S. 119, 145 L.Ed. 2d 570, 120 S.Ct. 673 (2000)

Facts: Officers Nolan and Harvey were driving the last car of a four-car caravan converging on an area known for heavy narcotics trafficking. Officer Nolan observed Wardlow standing next to a building and holding an opaque bag. Wardlow looked in the direction of the officers and fled. The officers followed Wardlow, eventually cornering him. Officer Nolan immediately conducted a protective pat-down search. He felt a heavy, hard object that was shaped similar to the shape of a gun in the bag Wardlow was carrying. Officer Nolan seized the bag and discovered that it contained a .38-caliber handgun with five live rounds of ammunition. He justified this search based on his experience in the locale, where it was common for weapons to be near the vicinity of narcotics transactions. Wardlow was convicted for unlawful use of a weapon by a felon.

Issue: Did Wardlow's actions in fleeing from the approaching officers establish reasonable suspicion for a stop?

Reasoning: "Our cases have also recognized that nervous, evasive behavior is a pertinent factor in determining reasonable suspicion. Headlong flight—wherever it occurs—is the consummate act of evasion: It is not necessarily indicative of wrongdoing, but it is certainly suggestive of such. *** We conclude Officer Nolan was justified in suspecting that Wardlow was involved in criminal activity, and, therefore, in investigating further.

*** "Flight, by its very nature, is not 'going about one's business'; in fact, it is just the opposite. Allowing officers confronted with such flight to stop the fugitive and investigate further is quite consistent with the individual's right to go about his business or to stay put and remain silent in the face of police questioning."

Disposition: Conviction affirmed; the gun was seized lawfully.

3-7c *Michigan v. Chesternut:* 486 U.S. 567, 100 L.Ed. 2d 565, 108 S.Ct. 1975 (1988)

Facts: Four officers on routine patrol in a marked police car observed a car pull over to the curb. A man got out of the car and approached Chesternut, who was standing alone on the corner. When Chesternut saw the patrol car nearing the corner where he stood, he turned and began to run. Officers in the patrol car followed Chesternut and drove along beside him. The officers observed Chesternut pull a number of packets out of his pocket and throw them away. Officers stopped to examine what Chesternut had discarded and discovered pills believed to contain codeine. Chesternut was arrested for possession of narcotics.

Issue: Was the officer's action in following Chesternut an illegal detention?

Reasoning: "The test provides that the police can be said to have seized an individual 'only if, in view of all the circumstances surrounding the incident, a reasonable person would have believed that he was not free to leave.' * * *

"Applying the Court's test to the facts of this case, we conclude that respondent was not seized by the police before he discarded the packets containing the controlled substance. Although Officer Peltier referred to the police conduct as a 'chase,' and the magistrate who originally dismissed the complaint was impressed by this description, the characterization is not enough, standing alone, to implicate Fourth Amendment protections. * * * [T]he police conduct involved here would not have communicated to the reasonable person an attempt to capture or otherwise intrude upon respondent's freedom of movement. The record does not reflect that the police activated a siren or flashers; or that they commanded respondent to halt, or displayed any weapons; or that they operated the car in an aggressive manner to block respondent's course or otherwise control the direction or speed of his movement. * * * Without more, the police conduct here—a brief acceleration to catch up with respondent, followed by a short drive alongside him—was not 'so intimidating' that respondent could reasonably have believed that he was not free to disregard the police presence and go about his business. The police therefore were not required to have 'a particularized and objective basis for suspecting respondent of criminal activity.'"

Disposition: Conviction affirmed; the packets of codeine are admissible at trial because officers can follow a person in a public place even though they do not have reasonable suspicion to stop him/her.

3-7d *California v. Hodari D.:* 499 U.S. 621, 113 L.Ed. 2d 690, 111 S.Ct. 1547 (1991)

Facts: Late one evening in April 1988, Officers McColgin and Pertoso were on patrol in a high-crime area of Oakland, California. They were dressed in street clothes but wore jackets with "Police" embossed on both front and back. As they rounded the corner, they saw four or five youths huddled around a small, red car parked at the curb. The youths ran when they saw the officers' car approaching. Hodari and one companion ran west through an alley; the others fled south. The red car headed south at a high rate of speed. The officers were suspicious and gave chase. McColgin remained in the car and went south on 63rd Avenue; Pertoso went north along 63rd on foot, then west on Foothill, and turned south on 62nd Avenue. Hodari emerged from the alley onto 62nd and ran north. He looked over his shoulder as he ran and did not see Pertoso until the officer was almost upon him. When he saw the officer, he tossed away what appeared to be a small rock. A moment later, Pertoso tackled Hodari, handcuffed him, and radioed for assistance. Hodari was carrying $130 in cash; the rock he discarded was found to be crack cocaine.

Issue: Is a person "seized" within the meaning of the Fourth Amendment when an officer commands him to stop?

Reasoning: "The word 'seizure' [in the Fourth Amendment] readily bears the meaning of a laying on of hands or application of physical force to restrain movement, even when it is ultimately unsuccessful. *** It does not remotely apply, however, to the prospect of a policeman yelling 'Stop, in the name of the law!' at a fleeing form that continues to flee. That is no seizure. Nor can the result respondent wishes to achieve be produced—indirectly, as it were—by suggesting that Pertoso's uncomplied-with show of authority was a common-law arrest and then appealing to the principle that all common-law arrests are seizures. An arrest requires either physical force (as described above) or, where that is absent, *submission* to the assertion of authority.

"In sum, assuming that Pertoso's pursuit in the present case constituted a 'show of authority' enjoining Hodari to halt, since Hodari did not comply with that injunction he was not seized until he was tackled."

Disposition: Suppression motion properly denied; the rock cocaine Hodari threw away is admissible at trial because Hodari discarded it before he was detained by the officers.

3-7e *Adams v. Williams:* 407 U.S. 143, 32 L.Ed. 2d 612, 92 S.Ct. 1921 (1972)

Facts: Sgt. Connolly was alone on patrol at 2:15 A.M. when someone Sgt. Connolly knew approached his patrol car and informed him that an individual seated in a nearby car was carrying narcotics and had a gun at his waist. Sgt. Connolly called for assistance and then approached the vehicle to investigate. He tapped on the car window and asked Williams to open the door. Williams rolled down the window and Sgt. Connolly reached into the car and removed a fully loaded revolver from Williams's waistband. The gun had not been visible to Sgt. Connolly but was precisely where the informant indicated it would be. Williams was arrested for unlawful possession of the pistol. The search incident to Williams's arrest produced substantial quantities of heroin and other weapons.

Issue: Can an officer rely on hearsay to justify a temporary detention?

Reasoning: "[W]e believe that Sgt. Connolly acted justifiably in responding to his informant's tip. The informant was known to him personally and had provided him with information in the past. *** [W]e reject respondent's argument that reasonable cause for a stop and frisk can only be based on the officer's personal observation, rather than on information supplied by another. Informants' tips, like all other clues and evidence coming to a policeman on the scene, may vary greatly in their value and reliability. One simple rule will not cover every situation. Some tips, completely lacking in indicia of reliability, would either warrant no police response or require further investigation before a forcible stop of a suspect would be authorized. But in some situations—for example, when the victim of a street crime seeks immediate police aid and gives a description of his assailant, or when a credible informant warns of a specific impending crime—the subtleties of the hearsay rule should not thwart an appropriate police response."

Disposition: Conviction affirmed; the gun removed from William's waistband is admissible because an officer can use reliable hearsay when determining if there is reasonable suspicion a suspect is armed.

3-7f *Florida v. J. L.:* 529 U.S. 266, 146 L.Ed. 2d 254, 120 S.Ct. 1375 (2000)

Facts: Miami-Dade police received an anonymous call reporting that a young, black male, wearing a plaid shirt, was standing at a particular bus stop and carrying a gun. Police knew nothing about the informant. Two officers, who were instructed to respond, arrived at the bus stop a few minutes later and observed three black males "just hanging out." J. L. was wearing a plaid shirt. Apart from the tip, the officers had no reason to suspect any of the three of illegal conduct. One of the officers told J. L. to put his hands up on the bus stop and frisked him; a gun was found in his pocket. Officers also frisked the other individuals, but found nothing. J. L. was charged with carrying a concealed firearm without a license and possessing a firearm while under the age of 18.

Issue: Does an uncorroborated, anonymous tip provide sufficient justification for an officer to stop and frisk an individual?

Reasoning: "The anonymous call concerning J. L. provided no predictive information and therefore left the police without means to test the informant's knowledge or credibility. That the allegation about the gun turned out to be correct does not suggest that the officers, prior to the frisks, had a reasonable basis for suspecting J. L. of engaging in unlawful conduct. The reasonableness of official suspicion must be measured by what the officers knew before they conducted their search. All the police had to go on in this case was the bare report of an unknown, unaccountable informant who neither explained how he knew about the gun nor supplied any basis for believing he had inside information about J. L. * * *

"An accurate description of a subject's readily observable location and appearance is, of course, reliable in this limited sense: It will help the police correctly identify the person whom the tipster means to accuse. Such a tip, however, does not show that the tipster has knowledge of concealed criminal activity. The reasonable suspicion here at issue requires that a tip be reliable in its assertion of illegality, not just in its tendency to identify a determined person. * * *

* * * "Firearms are dangerous, and extraordinary dangers sometimes justify unusual precautions. ***But an automatic firearm exception to our established reliability analysis would rove too far. Such an exception would enable any person seeking to harass another to set in motion an intrusive, embarrassing police search of the targeted person simply by placing an anonymous call falsely reporting the target's unlawful carriage of a gun. * * *

* * * "We speak in today's decision only of cases in which the officer's authority to make the initial stop is at issue. In that context, we hold that an anonymous tip lacking indicia of reliability of the kind contemplated in *Adams* [*Adams v. Williams* 407 U.S. 143 (1972)] and *White* [*Alabama v. White* 496 U.S. 325 (1990)] does not justify a stop and frisk whenever and however it alleges the illegal possession of a firearm."

Disposition: Weapon suppressed; the officer could not base the *Terry* stop solely on information from anonymous informant who stated that J. L. was carrying a gun.

3-7g *United States v. Sharpe:* 470 U.S. 675, 84 L.Ed. 2d 605, 105 S.Ct. 1568 (1985)

Facts: A Drug Enforcement Administration agent patrolling in an unmarked car observed a pickup truck with a camper (driven by Savage) and a car (driven by Sharpe) driving in tandem. The agent became suspicious because the truck was riding low and did not bounce or sway appreciably when the truck drove over bumps or around curves. After following the vehicles for 20 miles, the agent decided to make an "investigative stop" and radioed the Highway Patrol for assistance. Officers turned on the patrol car's red lights to signal Savage and Sharpe to stop. While Sharpe pulled over, Savage cut between the cars, nearly hitting the patrol car, and continued down the highway. When officers stopped Savage they ordered him out of the pickup at gun point, patted him down, and detained him for 15 minutes until the DEA agent arrived. Savage refused to give the agent permission to search the truck. The agent put his nose close to the camper window and smelled marijuana. He then opened the camper with Savage's keys and observed 2,629 pounds of marijuana in burlap-wrapped bales. The agent placed Savage under arrest. The DEA agent returned to Sharpe and arrested him and Davis, a passenger in his car.

Issue: Was the 20-minute detention permissible under *Terry v. Ohio?*

Reasoning: "Obviously, if an investigative stop continues indefinitely, at some point it can no longer be justified as an investigative stop. But our cases impose no rigid time limitations on *Terry* stops.

"In assessing whether a detention is too long in duration to be justified as an investigative stop, we consider it appropriate to examine whether the police diligently pursued a means of investigation that was likely to confirm or dispel their suspicions quickly, during which time it was necessary to detain the defendant. A court making this assessment should take care to consider whether the police are acting in a swiftly developing situation, and in such cases the court should not indulge in unrealistic second-guessing.

"We reject the contention that a 20-minute stop is unreasonable when the police have acted diligently and a suspect's actions contribute to the added delay about which he complains."

Disposition: Conviction affirmed; the detention of Sharpe did not last too long.

3-7h *Minnesota v. Dickerson:* 508 U.S. 366, 124 L.Ed. 2d 334, 113 S.Ct. 2130 (1993)

Facts: On November 9, 1989, at about 8:15 P.M. two police officers were patrolling an area of Minneapolis' north side in a marked squad car. One officer saw Dickerson leave an apartment house and begin walking toward the police. Upon spotting the squad car and making eye contact with one of the officers, Dickerson abruptly halted and began walking in the opposite direction. The officer observed Dickerson turn and enter an alley on the other side of the apartment building. Suspicious of the evasive actions in an area known for cocaine traffic, the officers stopped Dickerson and did a pat-down. They found no weapons, but the officer conducting the search noticed a small lump in Dickerson's jacket pocket. The officer testified: "[A]s I pat-searched the front of his body, I felt a lump, a small lump, in the front pocket. I examined it with my fingers and it slid and it felt to be a lump of crack cocaine in cellophane." The officer reached into the pocket and retrieved a small plastic bag containing one-fifth of 1 gram of crack cocaine. Officers arrested Dickerson and charged him with possession of a controlled substance.

Issue: Was the officer allowed to retrieve the lump of cocaine as part of a *Terry* pat-down?

Reasoning: ***"The question presented today is whether police officers may seize nonthreatening contraband detected during a protective pat-down search of the sort permitted in *Terry*. We think the answer is clearly that they may, so long as the officer's search stays within the bounds marked by *Terry*. ***

"We think that this [Plain View] doctrine has an obvious application by analogy to cases in which an officer discovers contraband through the sense of touch during an otherwise lawful search. The rationale of the plain view doctrine is that if contraband is left in open view and is observed by a police officer from a lawful vantage point, there has been no invasion of a legitimate expectation of privacy and thus no 'search' within the meaning of the Fourth Amendment—or at least no search independent of the initial intrusion that gave the officers their vantage point. The warrantless seizure of contraband that presents itself in this manner is deemed justified by the realization that resort to a neutral magistrate under such circumstances would often be impracticable and would do little to promote the objectives of the Fourth Amendment. The same can be said of tactile discoveries of contraband. If a police officer lawfully pats down a suspect's outer clothing and feels an object whose contour or mass makes its identity immediately apparent, there has been no invasion of the suspect's privacy beyond that already authorized by the officer's search for weapons; if the object is contraband, its warrantless seizure would be justified by the same practical considerations that inhere in the plain view context. * * *

"... Regardless of whether the officer detects the contraband by sight or by touch, however, the Fourth Amendment's requirement that the officer have probable cause to believe that the item is contraband before seizing it ensures against excessively speculative seizures.... Accordingly, the suspect's privacy interests are not advanced by a categorical rule barring the seizure of contraband plainly detected through the sense of touch. * * *

"... Although the officer was lawfully in a position to feel the lump in respondent's pocket, because *Terry* entitled him to place his hands upon respondent's jacket, the court below determined that the incriminating character of the object was not immediately apparent to him. Rather, the officer determined that the item was contraband only after conducting a further search, one not authorized by *Terry* or by any other exception to the warrant requirement. Because this further search of respondent's pocket was constitutionally invalid, the seizure of the cocaine that followed is likewise unconstitutional."

Disposition: Conviction reversed; cocaine was not found legally because the officer continued to examine the contents of Dickerson's pocket after determining that there were no offensive weapons in the pocket.

3-7i *Michigan Department of State Police v. Sitz:* 496 U.S. 444, 110 L.Ed. 2d 412, 110 S.Ct. 2481 (1990)

Facts: A sobriety checkpoint was set up under Michigan Department of State Police guidelines. Police stopped all vehicles passing through the checkpoint and briefly examined the drivers for signs of intoxication. If officers detected intoxication, they directed the motorist out of the traffic flow and checked the motorist's driver's license and car registration. If warranted, they conducted a sobriety test and made an arrest, if appropriate. The average delay per vehicle was approximately 25 seconds. In the 1 hour and 15 minutes the checkpoint was in operation, 126 vehicles passed through it. Police detained two drivers for field sobriety testing and arrested one.

Issue: Does a sobriety checkpoint that stops cars without reasonable suspicion violate the Fourth Amendment?

Reasoning: "In sum, the balance of the State's interest in preventing drunken driving, the extent to which this system can reasonably be said to advance that interest, and the degree of intrusion upon individual motorists who are briefly stopped, weighs in favor of the state program. We therefore hold that it is consistent with the Fourth Amendment."

Disposition: Conviction affirmed; officers were allowed to stop Sitz's car at checkpoint.

3-7j *City of Indianapolis v. Edmond:* 531 U.S. 32, 148 L.Ed. 2d 333, 121 S.Ct. 447 (2000)

Facts: The City of Indianapolis operated vehicle checkpoints, usually during daylight hours, identified by lighted signs that read "NARCOTICS CHECKPOINT—MILE AHEAD, NARCOTICS K-9 IN USE, BE PREPARED TO STOP." Approximately 30 officers were stationed at each checkpoint. Officers stopped a predetermined number of vehicles; other traffic proceeded without interruption until all the cars had been processed or diverted for further investigation. At least one officer approached each vehicle, advised the driver that he or she was being stopped briefly at a drug checkpoint, and asked the driver to produce a license and registration. The officer also looked for signs of impairment and conducted an open-view examination of the vehicle from the outside. A narcotics-detection dog walked around the outside of each stopped vehicle. The average stop, when no further processing was required, lasted two to three minutes or less.

James Edmond and Joell Palmer were stopped at narcotics checkpoints and later filed a class action suit seeking an injunction prohibiting the City of Indianapolis from operating narcotics checkpoints.

Issue: Does the operation of a checkpoint for the purpose of detecting illegal drugs violate the Fourth Amendment?

Reasoning: "The primary purpose of the Indianapolis narcotics checkpoints is in the end to advance 'the general interest in crime control.' We decline to suspend the usual requirement of individualized suspicion where the police seek to employ a checkpoint primarily for the ordinary enterprise of investigating crimes. We cannot sanction stops justified only by the generalized and ever-present possibility that interrogation and inspection may reveal that any given motorist has committed some crime.

"Of course, there are circumstances that may justify a law enforcement checkpoint where the primary purpose would otherwise, but for some emergency, relate to ordinary crime control. For example, as the Court of Appeals noted, the Fourth Amendment would almost certainly permit an appropriately tailored roadblock set up to thwart an imminent terrorist attack or to catch a dangerous criminal who is likely to flee by way of a particular route. The exigencies created by these scenarios are far removed from the circumstances under which authorities might simply stop cars as a matter of course to see if there just happens to be a felon leaving the jurisdiction. While we do not limit the purposes that may justify a checkpoint program to any rigid set of categories, we decline to approve a program whose primary purpose is ultimately indistinguishable from the general interest in crime control."

Disposition: Injunction affirmed; Edmond and Palmer were entitled to an injunction prohibiting the City of Indianapolis from conducting narcotics roadblocks.

3-7k *United States v. Hensley:* 469 U.S. 221, 83 L.Ed. 2d 604, 105 S.Ct. 675 (1985)

Facts: Six days after a robbery, an informant gave police a written statement implicating Hensley as the driver of the getaway car. Police was immediately issued a "wanted flyer" to other police departments in the metropolitan area. Officers in a nearby town who had read the flyer saw Hensley, and believed that there was an outstanding warrant for his arrest. Officers stopped Hensley's car and ordered the occupants out of the car while the dispatcher tried to confirm the existence of the warrant. Officers recognized a passenger in the car as a convicted felon. When an officer approached the open passenger door, he observed the butt of a revolver protruding from underneath the passenger seat. The passenger was arrested. When a search of the car uncovered two more concealed handguns, Hensley was also arrested. State charges for possession of a weapon were dropped but Hensley was indicted on federal charges of being a felon in possession of firearms.

Issue: Did the stop based on the officer's recollection of the wanted flyer violate the Fourth Amendment?

Reasoning: "[I]f police have a reasonable suspicion, grounded in specific and articulable facts, that a person they encounter was involved in or is wanted in connection with a completed felony, then a *Terry* stop may be made to investigate that suspicion.

"We conclude that, if a flyer or bulletin has been issued on the basis of articulable facts supporting a reasonable suspicion that the wanted person has committed an offense, then reliance on the flyer or bulletin justifies a stop to check identification, to pose questions to the person, or to detain the person briefly while attempting to obtain further information. If the flyer has been issued in the absence of a reasonable suspicion, then a stop in the objective reliance upon it violates the Fourth Amendment. * * * It is the objective reading of the flyer or bulletin that determines whether other police officers can defensibly act in reliance on it. * * * Assuming the police make a *Terry* stop in objective reliance on a flyer or bulletin, we hold that the evidence uncovered in the course of the stop is admissible if the police who *issued* the flyer or bulletin possessed a reasonable suspicion justifying a stop, and if the stop that in fact occurred was not significantly more intrusive than would have been permitted the issuing department."

Disposition: Conviction affirmed; the wanted flyer provided reasonable suspicion to justify stopping Hensley.

3-71 *Delaware v. Prouse:* 440 U.S. 648, 59 L.Ed. 2d 660, 99 S.Ct. 1391 (1979)

Facts: A patrolman stopped a car for the purpose of checking the driver's license and vehicle registration. Prouse was a passenger in the car. The officer noticed no traffic or equipment violations. The patrolman smelled marijuana smoke as he walked up to the car and found marijuana in plain view. Prouse was indicted for illegal possession of a controlled substance.

Issue: Do random car stops to check the driver's license and registration violate the Fourth Amendment?

Reasoning: "We agree that the States have a vital interest in ensuring that only those qualified to do so are permitted to operate motor vehicles, that these vehicles are fit for safe operation, and hence that licensing, registration, and vehicle inspection requirements are being observed. * * * Given the alternative mechanisms available, * * * we are unconvinced that the incremental contribution to highway safety of the random spot check justifies the practices under the Fourth Amendment. * * *

"Accordingly, we hold that except in those situations in which there is at least articulable and reasonable suspicion that a motorist is unlicensed or that an automobile is not registered, or that either the vehicle or an occupant is otherwise subject to seizure for violation of law, stopping an automobile and detaining the driver in order to check his driver's license and the registration of the automobile are unreasonable under the Fourth Amendment."

Disposition: Conviction reversed; the car stop was not based on reasonable suspicion.

3-7m *Pennsylvania v. Mimms:* 434 U.S. 106, 54 L.Ed. 2d 331, 98 S.Ct. 330 (1977)

Facts: Police stopped Mimms for driving an automobile with an expired license plate. An officer approached the car and asked Mimms to step out of the car and produce his owner's card and operator's license. When Mimms exited the car, the officer noticed a large bulge under his jacket. Fearing for his safety, the officer immediately frisked Mimms and discovered a loaded .38-caliber revolver in his waistband. Police charged Mimms with carrying a concealed deadly weapon and unlawfully carrying a firearm without a license.

Issue: Does an officer need reasonable suspicion to justify ordering a person out of a vehicle during a routine traffic stop?

Reasoning: "We think it too plain for argument that the State's proffered justification—the safety of the officer—is both legitimate and weighty. *** We think this additional intrusion can only be described as *de minimis.* *** The police have already lawfully decided that the driver shall be briefly detained; the only question is whether he shall spend that period sitting in the driver's seat of his car or standing alongside it. *** What is at most a mere inconvenience cannot prevail when balanced against legitimate concerns for the officer's safety.

"There remains the second question of the propriety of the search once the bulge in the jacket was observed. *** [T]he answer is controlled by *Terry v. Ohio.* *** Under the standard enunciated in that case—whether 'the facts available to the officer at the moment of the seizure or the search "warrant a man of reasonable caution in the belief" that the action taken was appropriate'—there is little question the officer was justified."

Disposition: Conviction affirmed; the weapon seized from Mimms during the traffic stop is admissible because: (1) an officer may automatically order a person out of a vehicle during a traffic stop; and (2) a pat-down for weapons may be done during a traffic stop if there is reasonable suspicion the person is armed.

3-7n *Maryland v. Wilson:* 519 U.S. 408, 137 L.Ed. 2d 41, 117 S.Ct. 883 (1997)

Facts: Hughes, a Maryland State Trooper, observed a passenger car with no regular license tag traveling at 64 miles per hour in a 55-miles-per-hour zone. There was a torn piece of paper reading "Enterprise Rent-A-Car" dangling from the rear of the car. The car continued to travel for another mile and a half after Hughes activated his lights and siren and signaled the driver to pull over. During the pursuit, Hughes noticed that the two passengers turned to look at him several times; they repeatedly ducked out of sight and then reappeared. When Hughes approached the vehicle on foot, the driver alighted and met him halfway. The driver was trembling and appeared extremely nervous but produced a valid Connecticut driver's license; he returned to the car for the rental documents when instructed to do so. Hughes noticed that Wilson, the front-seat passenger, was sweating and appeared extremely nervous. Hugh's ordered Wilson out of the car while the driver was looking for the rental agreement. A quantity of crack cocaine fell to the ground as Wilson exited the car.

Issue: Can a passenger be ordered out of a car during a traffic stop?

Reasoning: "In summary, danger to an officer from a traffic stop is likely to be greater when there are passengers in addition to the driver in the stopped car. While there is not the same basis for ordering the passenger out of the car as there is for ordering the driver out, the additional intrusion on the passenger is minimal. We therefore hold that an officer making a traffic stop may order passengers to get out of the car pending completion of the stop."

Disposition: Conviction affirmed; the crack cocaine was seized legally because the officer had the right to order Wilson out of the car.

3-7o *Knowles v. Iowa:* 525 U.S. 113, 142 L.Ed. 2d 492, 119 S.Ct. 484 (1998)

Facts: Knowles was stopped in Newton, Iowa because he was clocked driving 43 mph. in a 25-mph. zone. The police officer issued Knowles a citation although, under Iowa law, he might have arrested him. The officer then conducted a full search of the car and found a bag of marijuana and a "pot pipe" under the driver's seat. Knowles was arrested for possession of a controlled substance.

Issue: Can a police officer routinely conduct a thorough search of a car when the driver is issued a traffic citation?

Reasoning: "This is not to say that the concern for officer safety is absent in the case of a routine traffic stop. It plainly is not. But while the concern for officer safety in this context may justify the 'minimal' additional intrusion of ordering a driver and passengers out of the car, it does not, by itself, justify the often considerably greater intrusion attending a full field-type search. . . . [O]fficers have other independent bases to search for weapons and protect themselves from danger. For example, they may order out of a vehicle both the driver and any passengers, perform a 'pat-down' of a driver and any passengers upon reasonable suspicion that they may be armed and dangerous, conduct a 'Terry pat-down' of the passenger compartment of a vehicle upon reasonable suspicion that an occupant is dangerous and may gain immediate control of a weapon, and even conduct a full search of the passenger compartment, including any containers therein, pursuant to a custodial arrest.

"In Robinson, we held that the authority to conduct a full field search as incident to an arrest was a 'bright-line rule,' which was based on the concern for officer safety and destruction or loss of evidence, but which did not depend in every case upon the existence of either concern. Here, we are asked to extend that 'bright-line rule' to a situation where the concern for officer safety is not present to the same extent, and the concern for destruction or loss of evidence is not present at all. We decline to do so."

Disposition: Conviction reversed; when an officer stops a car to issue a traffic citation, there is no automatic right to search the vehicle.

3-7p *Hayes v. Florida:* 470 U.S. 811, 84 L.Ed. 2d 705, 105 S.Ct. 1643 (1985)

Facts: Police were investigating a series of burglary-rapes. They found latent fingerprints believed to belong to the assailant on the doorknob of the bedroom of one of the victims. Police interviewed nearly 40 suspects who fit the general description of the assailant. Hayes was considered the principal suspect. Police went to Hayes's house without a warrant and spoke to him on his front porch. When he expressed reluctance to voluntarily go to the police station for fingerprinting, an investigator explained that he would be arrested. Hayes blurted out that he would rather go with the officer than be arrested. Officers took Hayes to the station where he was fingerprinted. Hayes was arrested after the prints were matched to those found at the crime scene.

Issue: Can the police take a suspect to the station for fingerprinting without consent or probable cause to arrest?

Reasoning: "Here, as in *Davis v. Mississippi*, there was no probable cause to arrest, no consent to the journey to the police station, and no judicial authorization for such a detention for fingerprinting purposes. * * * And our view continues to be that the line is crossed when the police, without probable cause or a warrant, forcibly remove a person from his home or other place in which he is entitled to be and transport him to the police station, where he is detained, although briefly, for investigative purposes. We adhere to the view that such seizures, at least where not under judicial supervision, are sufficiently like arrests to invoke the traditional rule that arrests may constitutionally be made only on probable cause.

"None of the foregoing implies that a brief detention in the field for the purpose of fingerprinting, where there is only reasonable suspicion not amounting to probable cause, is necessarily impermissible under the Fourth Amendment. * * *There is thus support in our cases for the view that the Fourth Amendment would permit seizures for the purpose of fingerprinting, if there is reasonable suspicion that the suspect has committed a criminal act, if there is a reasonable basis for believing that fingerprinting will establish or negate the suspect's connection with that crime, and if the procedure is carried out with dispatch. Of course, neither reasonable suspicion nor probable cause would suffice to permit the officers to make a warrantless entry into a person's house for the purpose of obtaining fingerprint identification. We also do not abandon the suggestion in *Davis* and *Dunaway* that under circumscribed procedures, the Fourth Amendment might permit the judiciary to authorize the seizure of a person on less than probable cause and his removal to the police station for the purpose of fingerprinting."

Disposition: Conviction reversed; Hayes could not be taken to the station for fingerprinting without being arrested.

3-7q *Berkemer v. McCarty:* 468 U.S. 420, 82 L.Ed. 2d 317, 104 S.Ct. 3138 (1984)

Facts: Ohio State Trooper Williams observed McCarty's car weaving in and out of a lane on Interstate Highway 270. He stopped the car and gave McCarty a field sobriety test prior to telling McCarty that he was under arrest. During the test, the trooper asked McCarty if he had been using intoxicants. He replied that he had consumed two beers and smoked several joints of marijuana a short time before.

Issue: Were McCarty's statements admissible even though he had not been given his *Miranda* rights?

Reasoning: "We conclude, in short, that respondent was not taken into custody for the purposes of *Miranda* until Williams arrested him. Consequently, the statements respondent made prior to that point were admissible against him."

Disposition: Conviction affirmed; McCarty's statements are admissible because *Miranda* warnings are not required prior to arrest.

3-7r *Dunaway v. New York:* 442 U.S. 200, 60 L.Ed. 2d 824, 99 S.Ct. 2248 (1979)

Facts: An informant implicated Dunaway in the killing of a pizza parlor proprietor during an attempted robbery. Police questioned the informant but there was not enough information to obtain an arrest warrant. Detectives asked patrol officers to pick up Dunaway and bring him to the station for questioning. Officers took him into custody at a neighbor's house. He was transported to the station, placed in an interrogation room, and given *Miranda* warnings. He waived his right to counsel and eventually made incriminating statements.

Issue: Can a person be transported to a police station for interrogation based on reasonable suspicion?

Reasoning: "[T]he detention of petitioner was in important respects indistinguishable from a traditional arrest. Petitioner was not questioned briefly where he was found. Instead, he was taken from a neighbor's home to a police car, transported to a police station, and placed in an interrogation room. He was never informed that he was 'free to go'; indeed, he would have been physically restrained if he had refused to accompany the officer or had tried to escape their custody. The application of the Fourth Amendment's requirement of probable cause does not depend on whether an intrusion of this magnitude is termed an 'arrest' under state law. The mere facts that petitioner was not told he was under arrest, was not 'booked,' and would not have had an arrest record if the interrogation had proved fruitless, while not insignificant for all purposes, obviously do not make petitioner's seizure even roughly analogous to the narrowly defined intrusions involved in *Terry* and its progeny.

"We accordingly hold that the Rochester police violated the Fourth and Fourteenth Amendments when, without probable cause, they seized petitioner and transported him to the police station for interrogation."

Disposition: Conviction reversed; Dunaway could not be taken to the station without being arrested.

3-7s *New Jersey v. T.L.O.:* 469 U.S. 325, 83 L.Ed. 2d 720, 105 S.Ct. 733 (1985)

Facts: A teacher discovered T.L.O., a 14-year-old high school freshman, and another girl smoking in the lavatory in violation of a school rule. Both girls were taken to the principal's office. T.L.O. denied smoking in the lavatory and claimed that she did not smoke at all. The vice-principal opened her purse without her permission and found a pack of cigarettes. The vice-principal also noticed cigarette rolling papers. He then searched the purse thoroughly and found a small amount of marijuana, a pipe, and a number of empty plastic bags along with a substantial quantity of money in $1 bills. He also found an index card that noted names of students who owed T.L.O. money and two letters implicating T.L.O. as a marijuana dealer. School officials turned the evidence over to the police. Delinquency proceedings were brought against T.L.O.

Issue: Do school officials need probable cause to search students and their possessions?

Reasoning: "In determining whether the search at issue in this case violated the Fourth Amendment, we are faced initially with the question whether that Amendment's prohibition on unreasonable searches and seizures applies to searches conducted by public school officials. We hold that it does.

*** "[T]he legality of a search of a student should depend simply on the reasonableness, under all the circumstances, of the search. . . . Under ordinary circumstances, a search of a student by a teacher or other school official will be 'justified at its inception' when there are reasonable grounds for suspecting that the search will turn up evidence that the student has violated or is violating either the law or the rules of the school. Such a search will be permissible in its scope when the measures adopted are reasonably related to the objectives of the search and not excessively intrusive in light of the age and sex of the student and the nature of the infraction. * * *

"Our review of the fact surrounding the search leads us to conclude that the search was in no sense unreasonable for Fourth Amendment purposes."

Disposition: Conviction affirmed; the vice-principal had the right to search T.L.O.'s purse because there was reasonable suspicion that she violated school rules.

3-7t *United States v. Place:* 462 U.S. 696, 77 L.Ed. 2d 110, 103 S.Ct. 2637 (1983)

Facts: Place's behavior aroused suspicions of law enforcement as he waited in line at Miami International Airport to purchase a ticket to LaGuardia Airport in New York. As Place proceeded to the gate for his flight, officers stopped him. Place complied with a request for identification and consented to a search of the two suitcases he had already checked. The luggage was not searched due to the fact the flight was about to depart. Further investigation showed that neither of the two addresses on the suitcase tags existed and the telephone number Place gave the airline belonged to a third address on the same street. DEA agents in New York were alerted. Place's behavior aroused the suspicion of DEA agents when he deplaned in New York. After he claimed his luggage, the agents approached him. Place told the agents that his luggage had been searched by police in Miami and refused to consent to the search of his luggage. Agents told Place his luggage was being taken to the federal courthouse where a search warrant would be sought, but he was free to go. Agents took the luggage to Kennedy Airport where a trained narcotics-sniffing dog reacted positively. Approximately 90 minutes had elapsed since the luggage was seized. The agents detained the luggage on Friday afternoon. They obtained a search warrant on Monday morning and found 1,125 grams of cocaine.

Issues:

1. Did the detention of the luggage so that a trained dog could sniff it violate the Fourth Amendment?
2. Did the length of the detention violate the suspect's Fourth Amendment rights?

Reasoning: "We have affirmed that a person possesses a privacy interest in the contents of personal luggage that is protected by the Fourth Amendment. A 'canine sniff' by a well-trained narcotics detection dog, however, does not require opening the luggage. * * * Thus, the manner in which the information is obtained through this investigative techniques is much less intrusive than a typical search. Moreover, the sniff discloses only the presence or absence of narcotics, a contraband item. * * * Therefore, we conclude that the particular course of investigation that the agents intended to pursue here—exposure of respondent's luggage, which was located in a public place, to a trained canine—did not constitute a 'search' within the meaning of the Fourth Amendment.

"There is no doubt that the agents made a 'seizure' of Place's luggage for purposes of the Fourth Amendment when, following his refusal to consent to a search, the agent told Place that he was going to take the luggage to a federal judge to secure issuance of a warrant. * * * [S]uch a seizure can effectively restrain the person since he is subjected to the possible disruption of his travel plans in order to remain with his luggage or to arrange for its return. Therefore, when the police seize luggage from the suspect's custody, we think the limitations applicable to investigative detentions of the person should define the permissible scope of an investigative detention of the person's luggage. * * *

"The length of the detention of respondent's luggage alone precludes the conclusion that the seizure was reasonable in the absence of probable cause. * * * Moreover, in assessing the effect of the length of the detention, we take into account whether the police diligently pursue their investigation."

Disposition: Conviction reversed; luggage may be detained for a trained dog to sniff if there is reasonable suspicion it contains illegal drugs. NOTE: Evidence was ruled inadmissible because officers detained Place's luggage too long before the canine search.

3-7u *Florida v. Rodriquez:* 469 U.S. 1, 83 L.Ed. 2d 165, 105 S.Ct. 308 (1984)

Facts: A narcotics officer observed Rodriguez, Blanco, and Ramirez behaving in an unusual manner when leaving the National Airlines ticket counter at Miami International Airport. The three men proceeded to the concourse. As they stood together on the escalator, Blanco noticed the officer and told the others, "Let's get out of here." He repeated this in a low voice. Each suspect quickly glanced at the officer. Rodriguez saw the officer and appeared to start running in place. The officer identified himself and asked to speak to the three men. Rodriguez agreed and they rejoined the other two, who had been stopped by another officer. Blanco gave the officers a name that did not match the one on the airline tickets. Rodriguez gave officers the key to his luggage so it could be searched. They found three bags of cocaine in the suit bag.

Issue: Was the detention based on reasonable suspicion?

Reasoning: "[D]etention for questioning in the case of an airport search is reviewed under the lesser standard enunciated in *Terry v. Ohio* and is permissible because of the 'public interest involved in the suppression of illegal transactions in drugs or of any other serious crime.'

"The initial contact between the officers and respondent, where they simply asked if he would step aside and talk with them, was clearly the sort of consensual encounter that implicates no Fourth Amendment interest. Assuming, without deciding, that after respondent agreed to talk with the police, moved over to where his cohorts and the other detective were standing, and ultimately granted permission to search his baggage, there was a 'seizure' for the purposes of the Fourth Amendment, we hold that any such seizure was justified by 'articulable suspicion.' "

Disposition: Conviction affirmed; officers had sufficient suspicion to justify stopping Rodriguez.

3-7v *United States v. Sokolow:* 490 U.S. 1, 104 L.Ed. 2d 1, 109 S.Ct. 1581 (1989)

Facts: Drug Enforcement Administration agents stopped Sokolow in Honolulu International Airport based on the following facts: He paid $2,100 for two airplane tickets from a roll of $20 bills; (2) he traveled under a name that did not match the name under which his telephone number was listed; (3) his original destination was Miami, a source city for illicit drugs; (4) he stayed in Miami for only 48 hours, even though a round-trip flight from Honolulu to Miami takes 20 hours; (5) he appeared nervous during his trip; and (6) he checked none of his luggage. Agents found 1,063 grams of cocaine in his carry-on luggage.

Issue: Can a drug courier profile be used to establish reasonable suspicion to detain a person?

Reasoning: "Any one of these factors is not by itself proof of any illegal conduct and is quite consistent with innocent travel. But we think taken together they amount to reasonable suspicion. * * * A court sitting to determine the existence of reasonable suspicion must require the agent to articulate the factors leading to that conclusion, but the fact that these factors may be set forth in a 'profile' does not somehow detract from their evidentiary significance as seen by a trained agent. * * * The reasonableness of the officer's decision to stop a suspect does not turn on the availability of less intrusive investigatory techniques."

Disposition: Conviction affirmed; the total facts available to officers, including the drug courier profile, provided reasonable suspicion to stop Sokolow.

3-7w *O'Connor v. Ortega:* 480 U.S. 709, 94 L.Ed. 2d 714, 107 S.Ct. 1492 (1987)

Facts: Dr. Ortega was Chief of Professional Education at Napa State Hospital for 17 years. His primary responsibility was training young physicians in psychiatric residency programs. In July 1981, hospital officials became concerned about possible improprieties in Dr. Ortega's management of the residency program. Dr. O'Connor, Executive Director of the hospital, was concerned that residents had been coerced to contribute funds for the purchase of a computer. Charges of sexual harassment and inappropriate disciplinary actions against residents were also involved. While Dr. Ortega was on administrative leave, a three-member investigative team—including a physician, an accountant, and a security officer—thoroughly searched Dr. Ortega's office. They entered the office a number of times and seized several items from Dr. Ortega's desk and file cabinets. Instead of making a formal inventory, the team merely placed all papers in Dr. Ortega's office in boxes and put the boxes in storage. Both personal items and state property were seized. Items taken during the search were used at a hearing regarding Dr. Ortega's dismissal. Dr. Ortega brought this suit under the Civil Rights Act alleging that his Fourth Amendment rights had been violated.

Issue: Do government employees have Fourth Amendment rights protecting the privacy of their desks and file cabinets?

Reasoning: * * * "Searches and seizures by government employers or supervisors of the private property of their employees, therefore, are subject to the restraints of the Fourth Amendment.

* * * "The workplace includes those areas and items that are related to work and are generally within the employer's control. At a hospital, for example, the hallways, cafeteria, offices, desks, and file cabinets, among other areas, are all part of the workplace. These areas remain part of the workplace context even if the employee has placed personal items in them, such as a photograph placed in a desk or a letter posted on an employee bulletin board.

* * * "Not everything that passes through the confines of the business address can be considered part of the workplace context, however.

* * * The appropriate standard for a workplace search does not necessarily apply to a piece of closed personal luggage, a handbag or a briefcase that happens to be within the employer's business address.

* * * "We hold, therefore, that public employer intrusions on the constitutionally protected privacy interests of government employees for

noninvestigatory, work-related purposes, as well as for investigations of work-related misconduct, should be judged by the standard of reasonableness under all the circumstances. Under this reasonableness standard, both the inception and the scope of the intrusion must be reasonable. * * *

"Ordinarily, a search of an employee's office by a supervisor will be 'justified at its inception' when there are reasonable grounds for suspecting that the search will turn up evidence that the employee is guilty of work-related misconduct, or that the search is necessary for a noninvestigatory work-related purpose such as to retrieve a needed file. Because the petitioners had an 'individualized suspicion' of misconduct by Dr. Ortega, we need not decide whether individualized suspicion is an essential element of the standard of reasonableness that we adopt today. The search will be permissible in its scope when 'the measures adopted are reasonably related to the objectives of the search and not excessively intrusive in light of * * * the nature of the [misconduct].'"

Disposition: Summary judgment in favor of the State reversed; government employee's office may be searched only if there is reasonable suspicion the search will disclose evidence that the employee is guilty of work-related misconduct or the search is for noninvestigatory, work-related purpose (i.e., retrieving a file).

Chapter Quiz

True/False

1. A police officer cannot detain a person against his/her will unless there is probable cause to arrest that person.
2. Reasonable suspicion is judged on the basis of what a reasonable police officer would believe to be true based on the facts then available.
3. Based on reasonable suspicion, a police officer may detain a person indefinitely for questioning.
4. A police office may search a detained person based on reasonable suspicion only if the officer has reasonable suspicion that the detainee is armed.
5. A police officer who is properly conducting the search authorized in *Terry v. Ohio* is allowed to do a pat-down only for weapons.
6. Stopping cars at a sobriety checkpoint can be done only if there is reasonable suspicion that the driver is intoxicated.
7. If a car is stopped and there is reasonable suspicion that it contains weapons, police officers may conduct a thorough search of the entire vehicle.

8. A suspect detained on the basis of reasonable suspicion may not be fingerprinted.
9. Prior to questioning a person detained based on reasonable suspicion, the officer must give the detainee a complete set of *Miranda* warnings.
10. Officers working at airports may rely on a drug courier profile and briefly detain possible couriers for questioning.

Discussion Questions

1. Officer Blackburn observed Tim slowly drive down the street looking at each garage late one night. When Tim passed a house with the lights off and the garage door open, he paused briefly and appeared to be writing something down. Tim went to the end of the street, made a U-turn, and parked in front of a house with an open garage. Officer Blackburn stopped Tim when he got out of his car and asked him what he was doing there. Before Tim could answer, Officer Blackburn patted him down and felt an object he believed to be a knife in a jacket pocket. When Officer Blackburn reached into the pocket, he found a large screw driver and a plastic bag containing marijuana. Was the stop of Tim legal under *Terry v. Ohio?* Was the seizure of the marijuana legal? Explain.
2. Officer Chin heard a broadcast on his police radio describing a suspect who had just fled the scene of an armed robbery. A short time later, he saw a pedestrian who matched the description. Chin stopped him and immediately patted him down. The officer found no weapons but did find money in a box in the suspect's pocket. The box was the same shape as the carrying case for a small pistol. Was the stop of the pedestrian legal under *Terry v. Ohio?* Was the seizure of the cash legal? Explain.
3. Officer Johnson was assigned to airport security. He watched Jerry meet Sue, who just arrived on a flight from Miami and had a connecting flight to New York. Jerry, who was carrying Sue's carry-on luggage, went into the rest room. When he returned, the carry-on luggage no longer bulged, but Jerry's pockets appeared to be full. Officer Johnson stopped Jerry and demanded an explanation for what was in his pockets. Jerry refused to answer. Officer Johnson then reached into Jerry's pocket and retrieved a gun. Was the stop of Jerry legal under *Terry v. Ohio?* Was the seizure of the gun legal? Explain.

Chapter 4

Arrest and Booking

Outline

In Fourth Amendment terms, an *arrest* is the seizure of a person. More commonly, it is thought of as taking a person into custody for committing a crime. Arrests, whether made with or without warrants, must be based on probable cause.

4-1 When an Arrest Warrant Is Required

At common law, and in most states today, an officer may arrest without a warrant if there is probable cause to believe the suspect has committed a felony. For misdemeanors, officers were traditionally allowed to arrest without a warrant only if the crime was committed in their presence. When the officer arrived at the scene after the crime was completed, the arrest had to be made by someone who witnessed it. Recent statutes, in some states, expand the rights of the police to make arrests for misdemeanors that are not committed in their presence.

A "citizen's arrest" occurs if an eyewitness makes the arrest at the scene. Another approach to the problem of misdemeanors not committed in an officer's presence is to have the victim and/or witnesses state the facts in an affidavit. The victim or the police can then go to the prosecutor. A judge will review the affidavit and, if probable cause has been established, issue an arrest warrant. This procedure can be used if it is not possible to make a "citizen's arrest" because the suspect left the scene. It is also used if the victim does not want to press charges at the time the crime occurred but later decides to pursue the case.

4-2 Establishing Probable Cause

Probable cause to arrest is established when a reasonable person is more certain than not that the person arrested committed the crime for which he/she was arrested. There must be probable cause to establish each element of the crime. This requires a higher level of certainty than the reasonable suspicion needed for a field interview, but it is a considerably lower level of proof than the beyond a reasonable doubt level used to convict. An officer may detain a person if there is probable cause that any crime has been committed; the fact that the officer subjectively made the stop as a pretext to investigate a different crime does not invalidate the arrest. For example, an officer may stop a car due to a traffic violation to see if the driver matches the description of a robbery suspect.

The states have broad discretion to authorize law enforcement officers to arrest based on probable cause. Allowing officers to make warrentless arrests for very minor crimes does not violate the Fourth Amendment. An officer who has probable cause to believe that a misdemeanor occurred does not need to consider the seriousness of the offense or whether an arrest is necessary to protect the public. For example, in *Atwater v. City of Lago Vista* (2001), the Supreme Court upheld a Texas statute that allowed officers to make full custody arrests of drivers who are not wearing a seat belt.

The arrest is valid if, at the time of the arrest, the officer had probable cause to believe the suspect committed the crime he/she was arrested for even if the prosecutor refuses to file charges. Neither does an acquittal of the defendant prove that the arrest was not based on probable cause.

4-3 Entering a Dwelling to Make an Arrest

While the Supreme Court repeatedly has stated that obtaining a warrant is the preferred procedure, it has never required the police to obtain arrest warrants merely because they have probable cause and there is no emergency requiring swift action. Neither is there a requirement that police arrest as soon as they believe they have enough evidence to establish probable cause.

Officers are required to obtain a warrant if the arrest is to be made in a home. An arrest warrant or a search warrant is required if officers enter the suspect's home looking for him/her. If someone else's home is to be entered, a search warrant is necessary. The Court based the rule on the right of people to privacy in their homes. An emergency exception to the rule applies if someone inside the house is calling for help, screaming, or apparently being attacked. If officers are in hot pursuit and the suspect runs into a house, the emergency exception also applies.

Prior to entering a dwelling, even with a warrant, officers are required to knock and announce their presence. As discussed in section 2-3, "Execution of Warrants," this requirement is waived if: (1) the officer was in hot pursuit of an escaping criminal, (2) there is immediate danger of violence to the officer, or (3) it appears that evidence will be destroyed if the officers take the time to comply.

Officers have the right to conduct a "protective sweep" to prevent ambush when they enter a house or apartment to make an arrest. In addition to searching the arrested person, they may do a cursory search of the immediate, surrounding area to make sure no one is hiding there. If they want to search further, they must have reasonable suspicion that someone is hiding in the area to be searched.

Although an arrest made in a home without an arrest warrant is unlawful, the Court has allowed statements made outside the home after the arrest to be used at trial. To qualify, there must be no coercion or violation of *Miranda.*

4-4 Scope of Search

Since 1914, the Supreme Court has repeatedly changed the rules on how far the police may search when they make an arrest. The basic rule, which has been in effect since *Chimel v. California* was decided in 1969, is that immediately following an arrest, officers may conduct a thorough search of the person arrested and the area under the arrestee's immediate control. The justification for the search is the arrest. Therefore, items found during the search may not be used to establish probable cause for the arrest.

The search must be done contemporaneously with the arrest. Only searches done at the scene immediately after the arrest qualify. Searches done later must be justified on some other grounds.

Unlike the protective search done during field interviews, there are no restrictions on the extent of the search conducted when the suspect is arrested and taken into custody. Only the area searched is restricted. Anywhere the person arrested could reach to obtain weapons or destroy evidence can be searched. This "arms' reach" rule is applied without considering the fact that the suspect is handcuffed. Anywhere he/she could reach, if not restrained, is included.

Officers are not restricted to places where they suspect evidence will be found; neither does the crime for which the suspect was arrested have any bearing on the extent of the search. Officers do not they need cause to believe weapons are within reach. They may open drawers, look under the sofa, or search anywhere else that is within arms' reach. Whatever is found on the person or under his/her immediate control is admissible.

Evidence does not have to be related to the crime for which the suspect was arrested.

Whether or not a custodial arrest is made is important. When the state law authorizes a custodial arrest, it shows the offense is sufficiently serious to justify a major invasion of the individual's privacy. Sometimes officers may be authorized to issue a citation and release the suspect on the spot—traffic stops are a typical example. This is a much smaller invasion of the suspect's privacy. Accordingly, intrusive searches are not permitted. If the suspect will be released at the scene, officers may not invade the suspect's privacy by doing a thorough search. The right to search is similar to what can be done during a field interview (i.e., a protective pat-down for weapons). Due to the fact that the officers are only with the offender briefly, their need to protect themselves is not the same as when the offender is taken into custody.

4-5 Search Incident to Arrest of a Person in a Car

Arrests frequently involve either the driver or a passenger of a car. In 1981, the Supreme Court held that the entire passenger compartment, including the glove box and console, may be searched incident to the custodial arrest of an occupant of a car. The search must be done at the time of the arrest, but the suspect may be removed from the car before the search. The Court authorized an extensive search of anything in the passenger compartment, including luggage and other parcels. The closed container rule does not apply. A search of other parts of the car, such as the trunk, requires some other justification.

4-6 Booking

Booking occurs when the person who has been arrested enters the jail or a holding facility. It also happens if a person reports directly to the jail to serve all or part of his/her sentence. Inmates who serve weekends or leave the facility daily on work furlough are subject to booking searches each time they re-enter the jail. Whether the person has been searched recently or not, the right to search at the time of booking is the same. It includes a thorough search of the person and any items in his/her possession at the time of booking.

The reason for allowing booking searches is to prevent weapons and contraband from entering the jail. Searches done at the time of booking are usually divided into two types: search of the person and search of property.

4-6a Search of the Person

The booking search is usually the most extensive search of the person that occurs. While both searches incident to arrest and booking searches allow thorough searches of the person, the booking situation provides the privacy necessary to do strip searches.

Because weapons and drugs can easily be hidden, strip searches and searches of body cavities are permitted. Reasonable attempts to preserve privacy, such as shielding the strip-search area from public view and having searches conducted by officers of the same sex as the suspect, are still required. Combative inmates who defy control by booking personnel or those who attempt to flee the booking area waive protection of their privacy.

In recent years, several states have restricted the right to conduct strip searches and body cavity searches. These new rules often follow a public outcry over how an average citizen, arrested for a very minor offense like violation of the leash law, was humiliated during a strip search.

4-6b Property Searches

At booking it is common to inventory and store all of the suspect's property, including clothing. Jail uniforms are frequently issued. This helps keep weapons and contraband out of the jail facility and also reduces problems in the jail caused by thefts.

The Supreme Court held that anything inmates have in their possession at the time of booking can be searched. The closed container rule does not apply. Inventorying property at the time of booking is seen as necessary to prevent theft by jail employees; it also reduces the number of inmates making unfounded reports of theft. Information found during the inventory is also useful in positively identifying the person being booked.

4-7 Probable Cause Hearing

Suspects who remain in custody pending trial are entitled to have a judge determine whether there is probable cause for the charges against them. This requirement is met when an arrest warrant is obtained. Defendants have a Fourth Amendment right to demand a Probable Cause Hearing in warrantless arrest cases unless they are released from custody within 48 hours.

The Probable Cause Hearing can be conducted in a variety of ways. At a minimum, a neutral magistrate must review sworn affidavits and determine that there is probable cause for at least one of the charges. Neither the defendant nor the defense attorney has the right to be present when the judge makes this determination. The delay between the arrest and the Probable Cause Hearing cannot be over 48 hours except in emergencies. Noncourt days, such as weekends, may not be routinely added to the 48-hour period. The Probable Cause Hearing can be combined with the arraignment as long as it meets this time line.

4-8 Key Supreme Court Cases

4-8a *Payton v. New York:* 445 U.S. 573, 63 L.Ed. 2d 639, 100 S.Ct. 1371 (1980)

Facts:

Case 1: On January 14, 1970, after intensive investigation, New York detectives had probable cause that Payton had murdered the manager of a gas station two days earlier. At about 7:30 A.M., six officers went to Payton's apartment intending to arrest him; they had not obtained a warrant. Officers could hear music coming from the apartment and saw that the lights were on, but no one responded to their knock on the metal door. About 30 minutes later, officers used crowbars to break open the door and enter the apartment. No one was there but officers found a 30-caliber shell casing in plain view. They seized the casing, which was later introduced into evidence at Payton's trial.

Case 2: Riddick was arrested in 1974 for two armed robberies committed in 1971. In January 1974, police learned Riddick's address but did not obtain an arrest warrant. On March 14, 1974, about noon, four officers knocked on the door of Riddick's residence. When a child opened the door, the officers could see Riddick sitting in bed covered by a sheet. The officers immediately entered and arrested Riddick. Search incident to the arrest revealed narcotics and related paraphernalia. Riddick was convicted on narcotics charges.

Issue: Can law enforcement officers legally enter a dwelling without a warrant to make an arrest?

Reasoning: "The simple language of the [Fourth] Amendment applies equally to seizures of persons and to seizures of property. Our analysis in this case may therefore properly commence with rules that have been well established in Fourth Amendment litigation involving tangible items. As the Court unanimously reiterated just a few years ago, the 'physical entry of the home is the chief evil against which the wording of the Fourth

Amendment is directed.' And we have long adhered to the view that the warrant procedure minimizes the danger of needless intrusion of that sort.

*** "But the critical point is that any differences in the intrusiveness of entries to search and entries to arrest are merely ones of degree rather than kind. The two intrusions share this fundamental characteristics: the breach of the entrance to an individual's home. The Fourth Amendment protects the individual's privacy in a variety of settings. In none is the zone of privacy more clearly defined than when bounded by the unambiguous physical dimensions of an individual's home—a zone that finds its roots in clear and specific constitutional terms: 'The right of the people to be secure in their *** houses *** shall not be violated.' That language unequivocally establishes the protection that '[a]t the very core [of the Fourth Amendment] stands the right of a man to retreat into his own home and there be free from unreasonable government intrusion.' In terms that apply equally to seizures of property and to seizures of persons, the Fourth Amendment has drawn a firm line at the entrance to the house. Absent exigent circumstances, that threshold may not reasonably be crossed without a warrant.

"A study of the common law on the question whether a constable had the authority to make warrantless arrests in the home on mere suspicion of a felony—as distinguished from an officer's right to arrest for a crime committed in his presence—reveals a surprising lack of judicial decisions and a deep divergence among scholars. ***

"Thus, our study of the relevant common law does not provide the same guidance that was present in *Watson.* Whereas the rule concerning the validity of an arrest in a public place was supported by cases directly in point and by the unanimous views of the commentators, we have found no direct authority supporting forcible entries into a home to make a routine arrest and the weight of the scholarly opinion is somewhat to the contrary. Indeed, the absence of any Seventeenth or Eighteenth Century English cases directly in point, together with the unequivocal endorsement of the tenet that 'a man's house is his castle,' strongly suggest that the prevailing practice was not to make such arrests except in hot pursuit or when authorized by a warrant. ***

"A longstanding, widespread practice is not immune from constitutional scrutiny. But neither is it to be lightly brushed aside. This is particularly so when the constitutional standard is as amorphous as the word 'reasonable,' and when custom and contemporary norms necessarily play such a large role in the constitutional analysis. In this case, although the weight of state-law authority is clear, there is by no means the kind of virtual unanimity on this question that was present in *United States v. Watson* with regard to warrantless arrest in public places. Only 24 of the 50 states currently sanction warrantless entries into the home to arrest, and there is an obvious declining trend. Further, the strength of the trend is greater than the numbers alone indicate. Seven state courts have recently held that warrantless home arrests violate their respective state constitutions. That is significant because by invoking a state constitutional provision, a state court immunizes its decision from review by this Court. This heightened degree of immutability underscores the depth of the principle underlying the result.

* * * "No congressional determination that warrantless entries into the home are 'reasonable' has been called to our attention. None of the federal statutes cited in the *Watson* opinion reflects any such legislative judgment. Thus, the support for the *Watson* holding finds no counterpart in this case.

* * * "The parties have argued at some length about the practical consequences of a warrant requirement as a precondition to a felony arrest in the home. In the absence of any evidence that effective law enforcement has suffered in those States that already have such a requirement, we are inclined to view such arguments with skepticism. More fundamentally, however, such arguments of policy must give way to a constitutional command that we consider to be unequivocal.

"Finally, we note the State's suggestion that only a search warrant based on probable cause to believe the suspect is at home at a given time can adequately protect the privacy interests at stake, and since such a warrant requirement is manifestly impractical, there need be no warrant of any kind. We find this ingenious argument unpersuasive. It is true that an arrest warrant requirement may afford less protection than a search warrant requirement, but it will suffice to interpose the magistrate's determination of probable cause between the zealous officer and the citizen. If there is sufficient evidence of a citizen's participation in a felony to persuade a judicial officer that his arrest is justified, it is constitutionally reasonable to require him to open his doors to the officers of the law. Thus, for Fourth Amendment purposes, an arrest warrant founded on probable cause implicitly carries with it the limited authority to enter a dwelling in which the suspect lives when there is reason to believe the suspect is within."

Disposition: Convictions reversed; the shell casing found in plain view in Payton's house and narcotics seized during search incident to Riddick's arrest are not admissible at trial because officers entered the dwellings to make an arrest in a nonemergency situation without a warrant.

4-8b *Chimel v. California:* 395 U.S. 752, 23 L.Ed. 2d 685, 89 S.Ct. 2034 (1969)

Facts: Late in the afternoon of September 13, 1965, three police officers arrived at Chimel's Santa Ana, California home with a warrant authorizing his arrest for the burglary of a coin shop. The officers knocked on the door, identified themselves to Chimel's wife, and waited inside until Chimel returned home from work. When Chimel entered the house, one of the officers handed him the arrest warrant and asked for permission to "look around." Chimel objected, but officers advised him that "on the basis of the lawful arrest," they would conduct a search. No search warrant had been issued.

The officers looked through the entire three-bedroom house, including the attic, the garage, and a small workshop. In some rooms, the search was relatively cursory. In the master bedroom and sewing room, however, the officers directed the petitioner's wife to open drawers and move contents of the drawers so that they might look for items taken during the burglary. After completing the search, they seized numerous items—primarily coins, but also several medals, tokens, and a few other objects. The entire search took between 45 minutes and an hour.

Issue: What is the scope of a search that is permissible incident to a lawful arrest?

Reasoning: "Only last Term in *Terry v. Ohio* we emphasized that 'the police must whenever practicable, obtain advance judicial approval of searches and seizures through the warrant procedure,' and that '[t]he scope of [a] search must be "strictly tied to and justified by" the circumstances which rendered its initiation permissible.' * * *

"A similar analysis underlies the 'search incident to arrest' principle, and marks its proper extent. When an arrest is made, it is reasonable for the arresting officer to search the person arrested in order to remove any weapons that the latter might seek to use in order to resist arrest or effect his escape. Otherwise, the officer's safety might well be endangered, and the arrest itself frustrated. In addition, it is entirely reasonable for the arresting officer to search for and seize any evidence on the arrestee's person in order to prevent its concealment or destruction. And the area into which an arrestee might reach in order to grab a weapon or evidentiary items must, of course, be governed by a like rule. A gun on a table or in a drawer in front of one who is arrested can be as dangerous to the arresting officer as one concealed in the clothing of the person arrested. There is amply justification therefore, for a search of the arrestee's person and the area 'within his immediate control'—construing that phrase to mean the area from within which he might gain possession of a weapon or destructible evidence.

"There is no comparable justification, however, for routinely searching any room other than that in which an arrest occurs—or, for that matter, for searching through all the desk drawers or other closed or concealed areas in that room itself. Such searches, in the absence of well-recognized exceptions, may be made only under the authority of a search warrant. The 'adherence to judicial process' mandated by the Fourth Amendment requires no less. * * *

"Application of sound Fourth Amendment principles to the facts of this case produce a clear result. The search here went far beyond the petitioner's person and the area from within which he might have obtained either a weapon or something that could have been used as evidence against him. There was not constitutional justification, in the absence of a search warrant, for extending the search beyond that area. The scope of the search was, therefore, 'unreasonable' under the Fourth and Fourteenth Amendments and the petitioner's conviction cannot stand."

Disposition: Conviction reversed; the evidence seized during the search of the house cannot be used at trial because officers went beyond the area under Chimel's immediate control.

4-8c *New York v. Belton:* 453 U.S. 454, 69 L.Ed. 2d 768, 101 S.Ct. 2860 (1981)

Facts: On April 9, 1978, Trooper Nicot, a New York State policeman driving an unmarked patrol car on the New York Expressway, was passed by a car traveling at an excessive rate of speed. Nicot chased and stopped the speeding car. There were four men (including Belton) in the car. The patrolman asked to see the driver's license and automobile registration and discovered that none of the men owned the vehicle or was related to its owner. While doing this, the officer smelled burnt marijuana and saw an envelope marked "Supergold" on the floor of the car. He ordered the men out of the car and placed them under arrest for possession of marijuana. During a search of the car, the officer found a black leather jacket belonging to Belton on the backseat. The officer unzipped one of the pockets and discovered cocaine. Belton was indicted for possession of a controlled substance and pled guilty to a lesser offense after a suppression motion was denied.

Issue: Does the search incident to an arrest legally include closed containers found in the passenger compartment of a car?

Reasoning: "[N]o straightforward rule has emerged from the litigated cases respecting the question involved here—the question of the proper scope of a search of the interior of an automobile incident to a lawful custodial arrest of its occupants. * * *

* * * "While the *Chimel* case established that a search incident to an arrest may not stray beyond the area within the immediate control of the arrestee, courts have found no workable definition of 'the area within the immediate control of the arrestee' when that area arguable includes the interior of an automobile and the arrestee is its recent occupant. Our reading of the cases suggests the generalization that articles inside the relatively narrow compass of the passenger compartment of an automobile are in fact generally, even if not inevitably, within 'the area into which an arrestee might reach in order to grab a weapon or evidentiary item.' In order to establish the workable rule this category of cases requires, we read *Chimel's* definition of the limits of the area that may be searched in light of that generalization. Accordingly, we hold that when a policeman has made a lawful custodial arrest of the occupant of an automobile, he may, as a contemporaneous incident of that arrest, search the passenger compartment of that automobile.

"It follows from this conclusion that the police may also examine the contents of any containers found within the passenger compartment, for if the passenger compartment is within reach of the arrestee, so also will containers in it be within his reach. Such a container may, of course, be searched whether it is open or closed, since the justification for the search is not that the arrestee has no privacy interest in the container, but that the lawful custodial arrest justifies the infringement of any privacy interest the arrestee may have. * * *

"It is true, of course, that these containers will sometimes be such that they could hold neither a weapon nor evidence of the criminal conduct for which the suspect was arrested. However, in *United States v. Robinson* the Court rejected the argument that such a container—there a 'crumpled up cigarette package'—located during a search of *Robinson* incident to his arrest could not be searched.

* * * "It is not questioned that the respondent was the subject of a lawful custodial arrest on a charge of possessing marijuana. The search of the respondent's jacket followed immediately upon that arrest. The jacket was located inside the passenger compartment of the car in which the respondent had been a passenger just before he was arrested. The jacket was thus within the area which we have concluded was 'within the arrestee's imme-

diate control' within the meaning of the *Chimel* case. The search of the jacket, therefore, was a search incident to a lawful custodial arrest, and it did not violate the Fourth and Fourteenth Amendments."

Disposition: Conviction affirmed; cocaine found in Belton's jacket pocket is admissible at trial because officers may thoroughly search a car (including closed containers) when a person in the car has been arrested.

4-8d *Illinois v. Lafayette:* 462 U.S. 640, 77 L.Ed. 65, 103 S.Ct. 2605 (1983)

Facts: Lafayette was arrested for disturbing the peace after an altercation with a theater manager. At the time, Lafayette was carrying a "purse-type shoulder bag." Police inventoried the shoulder bag during booking and 10 amphetamine pills inside a cigarette case. Illinois state courts suppressed the evidence found in the shoulder bag.

Issue: Does the Fourth Amendment allow police to search the personal effects of a lawfully arrested person during booking?

Reasoning: " *** [I]f an arrestee is taken to the police station, that is no more than a continuation of the custody inherent in the arrest status. Nonetheless, the factors justifying a search of the person and personal effects of an arrestee upon reaching a police station but prior to being placed in confinement are somewhat different from the factors justifying an immediate search at the time and place of arrest. ***

"At the station house, it is entirely proper for police to remove and list or inventory property found on the person or in the possession of an arrested person who is to be jailed. A range of governmental interests support an inventory process. It is not unheard of for persons employed in police activities to steal property taken from arrested persons; similarly, arrested person have been known to make false claims regarding what was taken from their possession at the station house. A standardized procedure for making a list or inventory as soon as reasonable after reaching the station house not only deters false claims but also inhibits theft or careless handling of articles taken from the arrested person. Arrested persons have also been known to injure themselves—or others—with belts, knives, drugs or other items on their person while being detained. Dangerous instrumentalities—such as razor blades, bombs, or weapons—can be concealed in innocent-looking articles taken from the arrestee's possession. The bare recital of these mundane realities justifies reasonable measures by police to limit these risks—either while the items are in police possession or at the time they are returned to the arrestee upon his release. Examining all the items removed from the arrestee's person or possession and listing or inventorying them is an entirely reasonable administrative procedure. It is immaterial whether the police actually fear any particular package or container; the need to protect against such risks arise independent of a particular officer's subjective concerns. Finally, inspection of an arrestee's personal property may assist the police in ascertaining or verifying his identity. In short, every consideration of orderly police administration benefiting both police and the public points toward the appropriateness of the examination of respondent's shoulder bag prior to his incarceration. * * *

"The reasonableness of any particular governmental activity does not necessarily or invariably turn on the existence of alternative 'less intrusive' means * * * We are hardly in a position to second-guess police departments as to what practical administrative method will best deter theft by and false claims against its employees and preserve the security of the station house. It is evident that a station house search of every item carried on or by a person who has lawfully been taken into custody by the police will amply serve the important and legitimate governmental interests involved. * * *

"Applying these principles, we hold that it is not 'unreasonable' for police, as part of the routine procedure incident to incarcerating an arrested person, to search any container or article in his possession, in accordance with established inventory procedures."

Disposition: Prosecution of case may proceed; amphetamines found in the shoulder bag are admissible at trial because officers may conduct a thorough search of everything a person has in his/her possession (including closed containers) when booked into jail.

4-8e *County of Riverside v. McLaughlin:* 500 U.S. 44, 114 L.Ed. 2d 49, 111 S.Ct. 1661 (1991)

Facts: This class action challenged the county's policy of combining probable cause determinations with arraignment. Under the County of Riverside's policy and California Penal Code Section 825, arraignments must be conducted without unnecessary delay and, in any event, within two days of arrest. This two-day requirement excludes weekends and holidays. Thus, an individual arrested without a warrant on Thursday could be held for as long as five days before receiving a probable cause determination; over Thanksgiving holiday, a seven-day delay is possible.

Issue: Does this delay of 48 hours plus weekends and holidays violate a defendant's right to a timely probable cause hearing?

Reasoning: * * * "Under *Gernstein* [*Gernstein v. Pugh* 420 U.S. 103 (1975)], warrantless arrests are permitted but persons arrested without a warrant must promptly be brought before a neutral magistrate for a judicial determination of probable cause. Significantly, the Court stopped short of holding that jurisdictions were constitutionally compelled to provide a probable cause hearing immediately upon taking a suspect into custody and completing booking procedures. We acknowledged the burden that proliferation of pretrial proceedings places on the criminal justice system and recognized that the interests of everyone involved, including those persons who are arrested, might be disserved by introducing further procedural complexity into an already intricate system. Accordingly, we left it to the individual States to integrate prompt probable cause determinations into their differing systems of pretrial procedures. * * *

"Given that *Gernstein* permits jurisdictions to incorporate probable cause determinations into other pretrial procedures, some delays are inevitable. For example, where, as in Riverside County, the probable cause determination is combined with arraignment, there will be delays caused by paperwork and logistical problems. Records will have to be reviewed, charging documents drafted, appearance of counsel arranged, and appropriate bail determined. On weekends, when the number of arrests is often higher and available resources tend to be limited, arraignments may be pushed back even further. In our view, the Fourth Amendment permits a reasonable postponement of a probable cause determination while the police cope with the everyday problems of processing suspects through an overly burdened criminal justice system. * * *

" . . . Taking into account the competing interests articulated in *Gernstein*, we believe that a jurisdiction that provides judicial determinations of probable cause within 48 hours of arrest will, as a general matter, comply with the promptness requirement of *Gernstein*. For this reason, such jurisdictions will be immune from systemic challenges.

" . . . Such a hearing may nonetheless violate *Gernstein* if the arrested individual can prove that his or her probable cause determination was delayed unreasonably. Examples of unreasonable delay are delays for the purpose of gathering additional evidence to justify the arrest, a delay motivated by ill will against the arrested individual, or delay for delay's sake. In evaluating whether the delay in a particular case is unreasonable, however, courts must allow a substantial degree of flexibility. Courts cannot ignore the often unavoidable delays in transporting arrested persons from one facility to another, handling late-night bookings where no magistrate is readily available, obtaining the presence of an arresting officer who may be busy processing other suspects or securing the premises of an arrest, and other practical realities.

"Where an arrested individual does not receive a probable cause determination within 48 hours, the calculus changes. In such a case, the arrested individual does not bear the burden of proving an unreasonable delay. Rather, the burden shifts to the government to demonstrate the existence of a bona fide emergency or other extraordinary circumstance. The fact that in a particular case it may take longer than 48 hours to consolidate pretrial proceedings does not qualify as an extraordinary circumstance. Nor, for that matter, do intervening weekends. A jurisdiction that chooses to offer combined proceedings must do so as soon as is reasonably feasible, but not later than 48 hours after arrest."

Disposition: Policy not upheld; county policy declared in violation of Fourth Amendment due to delays of over 48 hours between arrest and Probable Cause Hearing.

4-9 Other Supreme Court Cases

4-9a *Whren v. United States:* 517 U.S. 806, 135 L.Ed. 2d 89, 116 S.Ct. 1769 (1996)

Facts: Plain-clothes vice-squad officers of the District of Columbia Metropolitan Police Department were patrolling in a "high-drug area" in an unmarked car when their suspicions were aroused by a Pathfinder truck that remained at a stop sign for what they considered an unusually long time. The driver appeared to be looking down into the lap of the passenger. The Pathfinder turned suddenly to its right without signaling and sped off at an "unreasonable" speed when the police car made a U-turn in order to head back to the truck. The officers pursued the truck and overtook it at a red light. An officer exited and directed the driver of the Pathfinder to put his vehicle in park. When the officer walked to the driver's window, he immediately observed two, large plastic bags of what appeared to be crack cocaine in Whren's hands. Officers arrested both occupants of the truck and retrieved quantities of several types of illegal drugs from the vehicle.

Issue: Is a traffic stop valid if the officer's subjective intent is to check for illegal drugs?

Reasoning: "We think these cases [*United States v. Villamonte-Marquez* 462 U.S. 579 (1983), *United States v. Robinson* 414 U.S. 218 (1973), *Gustafson v. Florida* 414 U.S. 260 (1973), *Scott v. United States* 436 U.S. 128 (1978)] foreclose any argument that the constitutional reasonableness of traffic stops depends on the factual motivations of the individual officers involved. We of course agree with petitioners that the Constitution prohibits selective enforcement of the law based on considerations such as race. But the constitutional basis for objecting to intentionally discriminatory application of laws is the Equal Protection Clause, not the Fourth Amendment. Subjective intentions play no role in ordinary, probable-cause Fourth Amendment analysis.

***"Here the District Court found that the officers had probable cause to believe that petitioners had violated the traffic code. That rendered the stop reasonable under the Fourth Amendment, the evidence thereby discovered [is] admissible, ..."

Disposition: Conviction affirmed; as long as the officers had probable cause to make the stop, it did not matter that their subjective intent was to investigate a different crime.

4-9b *Whiteley v. Warden:* 401 U.S. 560, 28 L.Ed. 2d 306, 91 S.Ct. 1031 (1971)

Facts: On November 23, 1964, several businesses in Saratoga, Wyoming were broken into. Police issued arrest warrants about noon on November 24 for Whiteley and Daley for the burglary of the Rustic Bar. A statewide radio broadcast was put out asking officers to pick up the two suspects. Late that night, a Laramie patrolman, without a copy of the warrant but in reliance on the information in the radio bulletin, arrested Whiteley and his companion. The officer searched Whiteley's car and found incriminating evidence.

The arrest warrant was later determined to be invalid because insufficient facts were given in the affidavit to allow the magistrate to independently assess probable cause.

Issue: Is an arrest valid if is made in good-faith reliance on a radio broadcast stating that an arrest warrant has been issued?

Reasoning: "We do not, of course, question that the Laramie police were entitled to act on the strength of the radio bulletin. Certainly police officers in executing arrest warrants are entitled to assume that the officers requesting aid offered the magistrate the information requisite to support an independent judicial assessment of probable cause. Where, however, the contrary turns out to be true, an otherwise illegal arrest cannot be insulated from challenge by the decision of the instigating officer to rely on fellow officers to make the arrest.

"In sum, the complaint on which the warrant issued here clearly could not support a finding of probable cause by the issuing magistrate. The arresting officer was not himself possessed of any factual data tending to corroborate the informer's tip that Daley and Whiteley committed the crime. Therefore, petitioner's arrest violated his constitutional rights under the Fourth and Fourteenth Amendments; the evidence secured as an incident thereto should have been excluded from his trial."

Disposition: Conviction reversed; the arrest violated the Fourth Amendment. Incriminating evidence found in the car was inadmissible at trial because a radio broadcast that is not supported by probable cause cannot justify an arrest.

4-9c *Smith v. Ohio:* 494 U.S. 541, 108 L.Ed. 2d 464, 110 S.Ct. 1288 (1990)

Facts: Two plain-clothes officers for the Ashland Ohio Police Department approached Smith as he and a companion exited a private residence and entered the parking lot of a YMCA. Smith was gingerly carrying a brown-paper grocery bag. Neither officer knew Smith or his companion. One of the officers exited the unmarked police car and, without identifying himself, asked Smith to "come here a minute." Smith did not respond; he kept walking. When the officer identified himself, Smith threw the grocery sack on the hood of his car and turned to face the officer who was approaching him. The officer asked what the bag contained but Smith did not answer. The officer then pushed Smith's hand away, opened the bag, and discovered drug paraphernalia in the bag. Smith was arrested and convicted for drug abuse.

Issue: Can evidence found as part of a search incident to an arrest be used to establish probable cause for the arrest?

Reasoning: "No contention has been raised in this case that the officer's reaching for the bag involved a self-protective action necessary for the officer's safety. Although the Fourth Amendment may permit the detention for a brief period of property on the basis of only 'reasonable, articulable suspicion' that it contains contraband or evidence of criminal activity, it proscribes—except in certain well-defined circumstances—the search of that property unless accomplished pursuant to judicial warrant issued upon probable cause. That guarantee protects alike the 'traveler who carries a toothbrush and a few articles of clothing in a paper bag' and 'the sophisticated executive with the locked attaché case.' The Ohio Supreme Court upheld the warrantless search of petitioner's bag under the exception for searches incident to arrest. * * *

"That reasoning, however, 'justify[ing] the arrest by the search and at the same time * * * the search by the arrest,' just 'will not do.' As we have had occasion in the past to observe, '[i]t is axiomatic that an incident search may not precede an arrest and serve as part of its justification.' The exception for searches incident to arrest permits the police to search a lawfully arrested person and areas within his immediate control. Contrary to the Ohio Supreme Court's reasoning, it does not permit the police to search any citizen without a warrant or probably cause so long as an arrest immediately follows.

"The State does not defend the reasoning of the Ohio Supreme Court, but rather contends that petitioner abandoned the bag when he threw it on his car and turned to face Officer Thomas. That argument was unanimously rejected by the Ohio Supreme Court, and we have no reason to disturb its conclusion. As the state court properly recognized, a citizen who attempts to protect his private property from inspection, after throwing it on a car to respond to a police officer's inquiry, clearly has not abandoned that property."

Disposition: Conviction reversed; drug paraphernalia found in the grocery bag is not admissible at trial because evidence found during a search incident to arrest cannot be used to justify the arrest.

4-9d *Atwater v. City of Lago Vista:* 532 U.S. 318, 121 S.Ct. 1536, 149 L.Ed. 2d 549 (2001)

Facts: Gail Atwater was driving her pickup truck with her three-year-old son and five-year-old daughter in the front seat. None of them was wearing a seat belt—a misdemeanor under Texas law. Officer Turek pulled the vehicle over and rudely told Atwater that she was going to jail. She was handcuffed and taken to the local police station where the booking officer required her to remove her shoes, jewelry, and eyeglasses and to empty her pockets. Police took a "mug shot" and placed Atwater, alone, in a jail cell. About one hour later, she appeared before a magistrate and was released on $310 bond. She ultimately pleaded no contest and paid the maximum fine ($50). Later, Atwater filed a Civil Rights Act suit against the city claiming that her arrest violated the Fourth Amendment.

Issue: Does a full custody arrest for a minor offense violate the Fourth Amendment?

Reasoning: "[T]he first step here is to assess Atwater's claim that peace officers' authority to make warrantless arrests for misdemeanors was restricted at common law. . . . Although her historical argument is by no means insubstantial, it ultimately fails.

*** "An examination of specifically American evidence is to the same effect. Neither the history of the framing era nor subsequent legal development indicates that the Fourth Amendment was originally understood, or has traditionally been read, to embrace Atwater's position.

*** "Finally, both the legislative tradition of granting warrantless misdemeanor arrest authority and the judicial tradition of sustaining such statutes against constitutional attack are buttressed by legal commentary that, for more than a century now, has almost uniformly recognized the constitutionality of extending warrantless arrest power to misdemeanors without limitation to breach of the peace.

*** "Accordingly, we confirm today what our prior cases have intimated: the standard of probable cause 'applie[s] to all arrests, without the need to "balance" the interests and circumstances involved in particular situations.' If an officer has probable cause to believe that an individual has committed even a very minor criminal offense in his presence, he may, without violating the Fourth Amendment, arrest the offender.

*** "Atwater's arrest satisfied constitutional requirements. Turek was accordingly authorized (not required, but authorized) to make a custodial arrest without balancing costs and benefits or determining whether or not Atwater's arrest was in some sense necessary.

*** "Atwater's arrest was surely 'humiliating,' as she says in her brief, but it was no more 'harmful to . . . privacy or . . . physical interests' than the normal custodial arrest. *** The arrest and booking were inconvenient and embarrassing to Atwater, but not so extraordinary as to violate the Fourth Amendment."

Disposition: Suit dismissed; Atwater cannot collect civil damages based on her arrest because it did not violate the Fourth Amendment.

4-9e *Michigan v. DeFillipo:* 433 U.S. 31, 61 L.Ed. 2d 343, 99 S.Ct. 2627 (1979)

Facts: About 10:00 P.M. on September 14, 1976, Detroit police officers were dispatched to investigate two persons reportedly appearing to be intoxicated in an alley. When officers arrived, they observed a man and a woman in the process of lowering her slacks in the alley. She claimed she was about to relieve herself. When asked for identification, DeFillipo said he was Sgt. Mash of the Detroit Police Department. When again asked for identification, he stated that he either worked for or knew Sgt. Mash. DeFillipo did not appear intoxicated. The Detroit City Code gave officers the right to stop, question, and ask an individual for identification if there is reasonable cause to believe that the individual's behavior warrants further investigation. DeFillipo was arrested for failure to identify himself. Officers found marijuana and PCP in his shirt pockets during the search incident to the arrest. He was charged with possession of a controlled substance.

Due to his pretrial appeal, the section of the City Code that required persons stopped to provide identification was held unconstitutionally vague. The appellate court ordered the drug charges dismissed.

Issue: Is an arrest valid if it was made in good-faith reliance on an ordinance which is subsequently declared unconstitutional?

Reasoning: "It is not disputed that the Constitution permits an officer to arrest a suspect without a warrant if there is probable cause to believe that the suspect has committed or is committing an offense. The validity of the arrest does not depend on whether the suspect actually committed a crime; the mere fact that the suspect is later acquitted of the offense for which he is arrested is irrelevant to the validity of the arrest.

*** "The remaining question, then, is whether, in these circumstances, it can be said that the officer lacked probable cause to believe that the conduct he observed and the words spoken constituted a violation of law simply because he should have known the ordinance was invalid and would be judicially declared unconstitutional. The answer is clearly negative.

*** "Police are charged to enforce laws until and unless they are declared unconstitutional. The enactment of a law forecloses speculation by enforcement officers concerning its constitutionality—with the possible exception of a law so grossly and flagrantly unconstitutional that any person of reasonable prudence would be bound to see its flaws. Society will be ill served if its police officers took it upon themselves to determine which laws are and which are not constitutionally entitled to enforcement.

*** "The subsequently determined invalidity of the Detroit ordinance on vagueness grounds does not undermine the validity of the arrest made for violation of that ordinance and the evidence discovered in the search of respondent should not have been suppressed."

Disposition: Prosecutor may proceed to trial; marijuana and PCP found in the suspect's pocket are admissible at trial because officers relied in good faith on a statute believed to be constitutional when making the arrest.

4-9f *Minnesota v. Olson:* 495 U.S. 91, 109 L.Ed. 2d 85, 110 S.Ct. 1684 (1990)

Facts: Shortly after 6 A.M. on Saturday, July 18, 1987, a lone gunman robbed an Amoco gasoline station in Minneapolis and fatally shot the station manager. A police officer heard the police dispatcher's report and suspected Joseph Ecker. The officer and his partner drove immediately to Ecker's home, arriving about the same time as did an Oldsmobile. The Oldsmobile's driver took evasive action; the car spun out of control and came to a stop. Two men fled the car on foot. Ecker, who was later identified as the gunman, was captured shortly thereafter; the second man escaped. Police found a sack of money and the murder weapon in the abandoned Oldsmobile along with several items, including a letter addressed to Rob Olson. The next morning, a woman called the police and said that a man by the name of Rob drove the getaway car when the gas station manager was killed and that Rob planned to leave town by bus. She called several hours later to say that Rob had told his neighbors, Louanne and Julie, that he was the driver in the Amoco robbery. Detectives were dispatched to check on the women identified by the caller and learned that Rob had been staying in an upstairs duplex. That afternoon, a neighbor called police and informed them that Olson had returned to the duplex. Police surrounded the duplex. An officer called the woman who lived in the duplex and told her Rob should come out. A male voice was heard in the background saying "tell them I left." The woman told police Rob was gone. Police then entered the dwelling with guns drawn and without seeking permission to enter. They found Olson hiding in a closet. Olson was convicted of first-degree murder, three counts of armed robbery, and three counts of second-degree assault.

Issue: Can police enter the dwelling without a warrant to make an arrest of someone who does not live there?

Reasoning: "It was held in *Payton v. New York* that a suspect should not be arrested in his house without an arrest warrant, even though there is probable cause to arrest him. The purpose of the decision was not to protect the person of the suspect but to protect his home from entry in the absence of a magistrate's finding of probable cause. * * *

"To hold that an overnight guest has a legitimate expectation of privacy in his host's home merely recognizes the everyday expectations of privacy that we all share. Staying overnight in another's home is a longstanding social custom that serves functions recognized as valuable by society. We stay in others' homes when we travel to a strange city for business or pleasure, when we visit our parents, children, or more distant relatives out of town, when we are in between jobs or homes, or when we house-sit for a friend. We will all be hosts and we will all be guests many times in our lives. From either perspective, we think that society recognizes that a houseguest has a legitimate expectation of privacy in his host's home. * * *

"That the guest has a host who has ultimate control of the house is not inconsistent with the guest having a legitimate expectation of privacy. * * * The point is that hosts will more likely than not respect the privacy interests of their guests, who are entitled to a legitimate expectation of privacy despite the fact that they have no legal interest in the premises and do not have the legal authority to determine who may or may not enter the household. * * *

"Because respondent's expectation of privacy in the Bergstrom home was rooted in 'understandings that are recognized and permitted by society' it was legitimate, and respondent can claim the protection of the Fourth Amendment.

* * * "The Minnesota Supreme Court applied essentially the correct standard in determining whether exigent circumstances existed. The court observed that 'a warrantless intrusion may be justified by hot pursuit of a fleeing felon, or imminent destruction of evidence, or the need to prevent a suspect's escape, or the risk of danger to the police or to other persons inside or outside the dwelling.' The court also apparently thought that in the absence of hot pursuit there must be at least probable cause to believe that one or more of the other factors justifying the entry were present and that in assessing the risk of danger, the gravity of the crime and likelihood that the suspect is armed should be considered. Applying this standard, the state court determined that exigent circumstances did not exist.

"We are not inclined to disagree with this fact-specific application of the proper legal standard. The court pointed out that although a grave crime was involved, respondent 'was known not to be the murderer but thought to be the driver of the getaway car' and that the police had already recovered the murder weapon. 'The police knew that Louanne and Julie were with the suspect in the upstairs duplex with no suggestion of danger to them. Three or four Minneapolis police squads surrounded the house. The time was 3 P.M., Sunday. * * * It was evident the suspect was going nowhere. If he came out of the house he would have been promptly apprehended.' We do not disturb the state court's judgment that these facts do not add up to exigent circumstances."

Disposition: Conviction reversed; Olson's warrantless arrest in his friends' home violated the Fourth Amendment because the officers entered the house without consent or a search warrant.

4-9g *Steagald v. United States:* 451 U.S. 204, 68 L.Ed. 2d 38, 101 S.Ct. 1642 (1981)

Facts: In January 1978, a confidential informant in Detroit provided the Drug Enforcement Administration (DEA) with an Atlanta phone number where Ricky Lyons, a federal fugitive, could be reached during the next 24 hours. Police obtained an address that corresponded with the telephone number from Southern Bell Telephone Company. Records showed that a six-month-old arrest warrant was outstanding on Lyons. Two days later, 12 DEA agents from Atlanta drove to the address to search for Lyons. Gaultney and Steagald were observed outside the house. Officers approached them with guns drawn, frisked them, and demanded identification. When several agents went to the house, Gaultney's wife answered the door and told them she was alone in the house. Officers told her to put both hands against the wall and guarded her in that position while one agent searched the house. They did not find Lyons, but they did discover a substance believed to be cocaine. When he was informed of this the agent in charge sent someone to obtain a search warrant, and in the meantime, officers again searched the house. They found additional incriminating evidence. When the search warrant was executed, officers discovered 43 pounds of cocaine. Steagald, who also lived in the Gaultney's residence, was indicted and convicted on federal drug charges.

Issue: Can law enforcement officers search the home of a third party looking for a person for whom they have an arrest warrant?

Reasoning: "Thus, whether the arrest warrant issued in this case adequately safeguarded the interests protected by the Fourth Amendment depends upon what the warrant authorized the agents to do. To be sure, the warrant embodied a judicial finding that there was probable cause to believe that Ricky Lyons had committed a felony, and the warrant therefore authorized the officers to seize Lyons. However, the agents sought to do more than use the warrant to arrest Lyons in a public place or in his home; instead, they relied on the warrant as legal authority to enter the home of a third person based on their belief that Ricky Lyons might be a guest there. Regardless of how reasonable this belief might have been, it was never subjected to the detached scrutiny of a judicial officer. Thus, while the warrant in this case may have protected Lyons from an unreasonable seizure, it did absolutely nothing to protect petitioner's privacy interest in being free from an unreasonable invasion and search of his home. Instead, petitioner's only protection from an illegal entry and search was the agent's personal determination of probable cause. In the absence of exigent circumstances, we have consistently held that such judicially untested determinations are not reliable enough to justify an entry into a person's home to arrest him without a warrant, or a search of a home for objects in the absence of a search warrant. We see no reason to depart from this settled course when the search of a home is for a person rather than an object.

"A contrary conclusion—that the police, acting alone and in the absence of exigent circumstances, may decide when there is sufficient justification for searching the home of a third party for the subject of an arrest warrant—would create a significant potential for abuse. Armed solely with an arrest warrant for a single person, the police could search all the homes of that individual's friends and acquaintances. Moreover, an arrest warrant may serve as the pretext for entering a home in which the police have a suspicion, but not probable cause to believe, that illegal activity is taking place. The Government recognizes the potential for abuses, but contends that existing remedies—such as motions to suppress illegally procured evidence and damage actions for Fourth Amendment violations—provide adequate means of redress. We do not agree. * * *

"The Government also suggests that practical problems might arise if law enforcement officers are required to obtain a search warrant before entering the home of a third party to make an arrest. The basis of this concern is that persons, as opposed to objects, are inherently mobile, and thus officers seeking to effect an arrest may be forced to return to the magistrate several times as the subject of the arrest warrant moves from place to place. We are convinced, however, that a search warrant requirement will not significantly impede effective law enforcement efforts.

"First, the situations in which a search warrant will be necessary are few. As noted in *Payton v. New York* an arrest warrant alone will suffice to enter a suspect's own residence to effect his arrest. Furthermore, if probable cause exists, no warrant is required to apprehend a suspected felon in a public place. Thus, the subject of an arrest warrant can be readily seized before entering or after leaving the home of a third party. Finally, the exigent circumstances doctrine significantly limits the situations in which a search warrant would be needed. For example, a warrantless entry of a home would be justified if the police were in 'hot pursuit' of a fugitive. Thus, to the extent that searches for persons pose special problems, we believe that the exigent circumstances doctrine is adequate to accommodate legitimate law enforcement needs.

"Moreover, in those situations in which a search warrant is necessary, the inconvenience incurred by the police is simply not that significant. First, if the police know of the location of the felon when they obtain an arrest warrant, the additional burden of obtaining a search warrant at the same time is minuscule. The inconvenience of obtaining such a warrant does not increase significantly when an outstanding arrest warrant already exists. *** In routine search cases such as this, the short time required to obtain a search warrant from a magistrate will seldom hinder efforts to apprehend a felon. Finally, if a magistrate is not nearby, a telephonic search warrant can usually be obtained.

"Whatever practical problems remain, however, cannot outweigh the constitutional interests at stake. Any warrant requirement impedes to some extent the vigor with which the Government can seek to enforce its laws, yet the Fourth Amendment recognizes that this restraint is necessary in some cases to protect against unreasonable searches and seizures. We conclude that this is such a case. The additional burden imposed on the police by a warrant requirement is minimal. In contrast, the right protected—that of presumptively innocent people to be secure in their homes from unjustified, forcible intrusions by the Government—is weighty. Thus, in order to render the instant search reasonable under the Fourth Amendment a search warrant was required."

Disposition: Conviction reversed; cocaine discovered during the search of Gaultney's house was not admissible at trial because police need a search warrant to enter the house of a third party to make an arrest.

4-9h *United States v. Santana:* 427 U.S. 38, 49 L.Ed. 2d 300, 96 S.Ct. 2406 (1976)

Facts: On August 16, 1974, Michael Gilletti, an undercover officer with the Philadelphia Narcotics Squad, arranged a heroin "buy" from Patricia McCafferty. She directed Gilletti to drive to Santana's residence. McCafferty took marked money and went inside the house, stopping to speak to Alejandro, who was sitting on the front steps. McCafferty returned shortly with several glassine envelopes containing brownish-white powder. Gilletti then arrested McCafferty. He told her he was going back to Santana's house to search it. When asked where the money was, McCafferty said "Mom has the money." When several officers approached the house in their van, they saw Santana standing in the doorway with a brown paper bag in her hand. They pulled up to within 15 feet of Santana and got out of their van shouting "police" and displaying their identification. Santana retreated into the vestibule of her house. Officers followed through the open door. As she tried to pull away, the bag tilted and "two bundles of glazed paper packets with white powder" fell on the floor. Alejandro then tried to make off with the dropped envelopes but was forcible restrained. A search of Santana disclosed the marked money Gilletti had used to make the "buy." Alejandro and Santana successfully moved to have the heroin and money found during and after their arrests suppressed due to the warrantless entry into the house.

Issue: Is a warrant required to arrest someone standing in the open doorway of a house?

Reasoning: "In *United States v. Watson* we held that the warrantless arrest of an individual in a public place upon probable cause did not violate the Fourth Amendment. Thus the first question we must decide is whether, when the police first sought to arrest Santana, she was in a public place.

"While it may be true that under the common law of property the threshold of one's dwelling is 'private,' as is the yard surrounding the house, it is nonetheless clear that under the cases interpreting the Fourth Amendment Santana was in a 'public' place. She was not in an area where she had any expectation of privacy. * * * She was not merely visible to the public but was as exposed to public view, speech, hearing, and touch as if she had been standing completely outside her house. * * *

"The only remaining question is whether her act of retreating into her house could thwart an otherwise proper arrest. We hold that it could not. In *Warden v. Hayden* we recognized the right of police, who had probable cause to believe that an armed robber had entered a house a few minutes before, to make a warrantless entry to arrest the robber and to search for weapons. This case, involving a true 'hot pursuit,' is clearly governed by *Warden;* the need to act quickly here is even greater than in that case while the intrusion is much less. The District Court was correct in concluding that 'hot pursuit' means some sort of chase, but it need not be an extended hue and cry 'in and about the public streets.' The fact that the pursuit here ended almost as soon as it began did not render it any the less a 'hot pursuit' sufficient to justify the warrantless entry into Santana's house. Once Santana saw the police, there was likewise a realistic expectation that any delay would result in destruction of evidence. * * *

"We thus conclude that a suspect may not defeat an arrest which has been set in motion in a public place, and is therefore proper under *Watson,* by the expedient of escaping to a private place."

Disposition: Prosecutor may proceed with case; narcotics and money seized at the time of arrest may be used at trial because officers are not required to obtain a warrant in order to follow a suspect into a residence if he/she was in public view when officers started the pursuit.

4-9i *Vale v. Louisiana:* 399 U.S. 30, 26 L.Ed. 2d 409, 90 S.Ct. 1969 (1970)

Facts: On April 24, 1967, officers possessing two warrants for Vale's arrest set up surveillance on his mother's home. After approximately 15 minutes, the officers observed an individual in a green 1958 Chevrolet drive up and sound the horn; the car backed into a parking place and the horn sounded again. Members of the surveillance team know Vale and observed him coming out of the house. Vale walked up to the passenger side of the car and had a brief conversation with the driver; Vale then looked up and down the street prior to going back into the house. A few minutes later, he reappeared on the porch, cautiously looked up and down the street, and proceeded to the passenger side of the car and leaned through the window. The officers were convinced a narcotics sale had taken place. The officers drove toward Vale but when they reached within three car lengths of him, Vale noticed the officers and walked quickly toward the house. Officers called to Vale when he was on the front steps and told him that he was under arrest. After entering the front room, they made a cursory inspection to determine if anyone else was in the house. The search of the rear bedroom revealed a quantity of narcotics.

Issue: Can the interior of a house be searched as incident to an arrest made outside the house?

Reasoning: "A search may be incident to an arrest 'only if it is substantially contemporaneous with the arrest and is confined to the *immediate* vicinity of the arrest.' If a search of a house is to be upheld as incident to an arrest, that arrest must take place *inside* the house, not somewhere outside—whether two blocks away, twenty feet away, or on the sidewalk near the front steps.

*** "We decline to hold that an arrest on the street can provide its own 'exigent circumstances' so as to justify a warrantless search of the arrestee's house."

Disposition: Conviction reversed; narcotics found in the bedroom cannot be used at trial because officers who make an arrest outside a house are not allowed to extend the search incident to the arrest to areas inside the house.

4-9j *Welsh v. Wisconsin:* 466 U.S. 740, 80 L.Ed. 2d 732, 104 S.Ct. 2091 (1984)

Facts: About 9:00 P.M. on a rainy night, a witness saw a car being driven erratically. After changing speeds and veering from side to side, the driver swerved the car off the road and came to a stop in an open field. There was no damage to the car or injuries to the driver. The witness pulled up behind the car to prevent it from being driven on the road and called the police, but the driver of the vehicle walked away prior to their arrival. When officers arrived, they interviewed the witness who stated that the driver was either inebriated or very sick. A check of the vehicle's registration showed that Welsh, the owner, lived within walking distance of where the car had been abandoned. Police proceeded to Welsh's residence, gained entry, and went upstairs to Welsh's bedroom where they found him lying naked in bed. They arrested Welsh for operating a motor vehicle while under the influence of an intoxicant. Welsh refused to take a breathalyzer test at the police station. Wisconsin law at the time provided that a first offense for driving while intoxicated was a noncriminal violation subject to a maximum fine of $200; with a second or subsequent offense in the previous five years, the offense was a potential misdemeanor. Refusal to take breath, blood, or urine tests could subject the driver to revocation of operating privileges.

Issue: Does the Fourth Amendment allow an officer to enter a dwelling without a warrant to make an arrest for a noncriminal offense?

Reasoning: "It is axiomatic that 'the physical entry of the home is the chief evil against which the wording of the Fourth Amendment is directed.' *** Consistently with these long-recognized principles, the Court decided in *Payton v. New York* that warrantless felony arrests in the home are prohibited by the Fourth Amendment, absent probable cause and exigent circumstances. ***

"Our hesitation in finding exigent circumstances, especially when warrantless arrests in the home are at issue, is especially appropriate when the underlying offense for which there is probable cause to arrest is relatively minor. Before agents of the government may invade the sanctity of the home, the burden is on the government to demonstrate exigent circumstances that overcome the presumption of unreasonableness that attaches to all warrantless home entries. When the government's interest is only to arrest for a minor offense, that presumption of unreasonableness is difficult to rebut, and the government usually should be allowed to make such arrests only with a warrant issued upon probable cause by a neutral and detached magistrate. * * *

"We therefore conclude that the common sense approach utilized by most lower courts is required by the Fourth Amendment prohibition on 'unreasonable searches and seizures,' and hold that an important factor to be considered when determining whether any exigency exists is the gravity of the underlying offense for which the arrest is being made. Moreover, although no exigency is created simply because there is probable cause to believe that a serious crime has been committed, application of the exigent-circumstances exception in the context of a home entry should rarely be sanctioned when there is probable cause to believe that only a minor offense, such as the kind at issue in this case, has been committed.

* * * "The State of Wisconsin has chosen to classify the first offense for driving while intoxicated as a noncriminal, civil forfeiture offense for which no imprisonment is possible. This is the best indication of the state's interest in precipitating an arrest, and is one that can be easily identified both by the courts and by officers faced with a decision to arrest. Given this expression of the state's interest, a warrantless home arrest cannot be upheld simply because evidence of the petitioner's blood-alcohol level might have dissipated while the police obtained a warrant. To allow a warrantless home entry on these facts would be to approve unreasonable police behavior that the principles of the Fourth Amendment will not sanction."

Disposition: Conviction and suspension of driver's license reversed; entry into the house without a warrant to arrest for a noncriminal offense violated the Fourth Amendment.

4-9k *Maryland v. Buie:* 494 U.S. 325, 108 L.Ed. 2d 276, 110 S.Ct. 1093 (1990)

Facts: On February 3, 1986, two men committed an armed robbery of a Godfather's Pizza restaurant. One of the robbers was wearing a red running suit. Police obtained arrest warrants for Edward Buie and Lloyd Allen that same day. Police placed Buie's house under surveillance. Two days later, the police had a secretary call Buie's house to verify that he was home. Six or seven officers then proceeded to Buie's house. Once inside, the officers fanned out through the first and second floors. Corporal Rozar announced that he would "freeze" the basement so that no one could come up and surprise the officers. With his revolver drawn, Rozar twice shouted into the basement, ordering anyone down there to come out. When a voice asked who was calling, Rozar announced three times "this is the police, show me your hands." Eventually a pair of hands appeared and Buie emerged from the basement. He was arrested, searched, and handcuffed. Detective Frolich then entered the basement in case there was someone else down there. He seized a red running suit that was lying in plain view on a stack of clothing. Buie was convicted of robbery with a deadly weapon and using a handgun in the commission of a felony.

Issue: What level of justification is needed to enter a room after an arrest and search for other people who may be present?

Reasoning: "It is not disputed that until the point of Buie's arrest the police had the right, based on the authority of the arrest warrant, to search anywhere in the house that Buie might have been found, including the basement. * * * There is also no dispute that if Detective Frolich's entry into the basement was lawful, the seizure of the red running suit, which was in plain view and which the officer had probable cause to believe was evidence of a crime, was also lawful under the Fourth Amendment.

* * * "The *Terry* case is most instructive for present purposes. There we held that an on-the-street 'frisk' for weapons must be tested by the Fourth Amendment's general proscription against unreasonable searches because such a frisk involves 'an entire rubric of police conduct—necessarily swift action predicated upon the on-the-spot observations of the officer on the beat—which historically has not been, and as a practical matter could not be, subjected to the warrant procedure.' We stated that there is 'no ready test for determining reasonableness other than by balancing the need to search * * * against the invasion which the search * * * entails.' * * *

"In *Michigan v. Long* the principles of *Terry* were applied in the context of a roadside encounter: 'the search of the passenger compartment of an automobile, limited to those areas in which a weapon may be placed or hidden, is permissible if the police officer possesses a reasonable belief based on "specific and articulable facts which, taken together with the rational inferences from those facts, reasonably warrant the officer in believing that the suspect is dangerous and the suspect may gain immediate control of weapons." The Long Court expressly rejected the contention that *Terry* restricted preventative searches to the person of a detained suspect. * * *

"The ingredients to apply the balance struck in *Terry* and *Long* are present in this case. Possessing an arrest warrant and probable cause to believe Buie was in his home, the officers were entitled to enter and to search anywhere in the house in which Buie might be found. Once he was found, however, the search for him was over, and there was no longer that particular justification for entering any rooms that had not yet been searched.

"That Buie had an expectation of privacy in those remaining areas of his house, however, does not mean such rooms were immune from entry. In *Terry* and *Long* we were concerned with the immediate interest of the police officers in taking steps to assure themselves that the persons with whom they were dealing were not armed with or able to gain immediate control of a weapon that could unexpectedly and fatally be used against them. In the instant case, there is an analogous interest of the officers in taking steps to assure themselves that the house in which a suspect is being or has just been arrested is not harboring other persons who are dangerous and who could unexpectedly launch an attack. The risk of danger in the context of an arrest in the home is as great as, if not greater than, it is in an on-the-street or roadside investigatory encounter. A *Terry* or *Long* frisk occurs before a police-citizen confrontation has escalated to the point of arrest. A protective sweep, in contrast, occurs as an adjunct to the serious step of taking a person into custody for the purpose of prosecuting him for a crime. Moreover, unlike an encounter on the street or along a highway, an in-home arrest puts the officer at the disadvantage of being on his adversary's 'turf.' An ambush in a confined setting of unknown configuration is more to be feared than it is in open, more familiar surroundings. * * *

"We agree with the State, as did the court below, that a warrant was not required. We also hold that as an incident to the arrest the officers could, as a precautionary matter and without probable cause or reasonable suspicion, look in closets and other spaces immediately adjoining the place of arrest from which an attack could be immediately launched. Beyond that, however, we hold that there must be articulable facts which, taken together with the rational inferences from those facts, would warrant a reasonably prudent officer in believing that the area to be swept harbors an individual posing a danger to those on the arrest scene. * * *

"We should emphasize that such a protective sweep, aimed at protecting the arresting officers, if justified by the circumstances, is nevertheless not a full search of the premises, but may extend only to a cursory inspection of those spaces where a person may be found. The sweep lasts no longer than is necessary to dispel the reasonable suspicion of danger and in any event no longer than it takes to complete the arrest and depart the premises."

Disposition: Conviction affirmed; the red running suit is admissible at trial because officers had reasonable suspicion to go into the basement to look for someone hiding there who might attack them.

4-9I *New York v. Harris:* 495 U.S. 14, 109 L.Ed. 2d 13, 110 S.Ct. 1640 (1990)

Facts: On January 11, 1984, New York City police found Ms. Staton murdered in her apartment. Various facts gave the officers probable cause to believe that Harris had killed her. On January 16, three police officers went to Harris's apartment without a warrant to take him into custody. The police knocked on Harris's door and displayed their guns and badges; Harris admitted them. Officers read him the *Miranda* warnings and he made incriminating statements. Police then arrested Harris and took him to the station where he was again given *Miranda* warnings. Officers obtained a written, incriminating statement. The written statement was admitted at trial and Harris was convicted of second-degree murder.

Issue: Can post-arrest statements obtained at the police station after police gave the suspect *Miranda* warnings be used at trial if the officers entered the dwelling without a warrant to make an arrest?

Reasoning: "For present purposes, we accept the finding below that Harris did not consent to the police officers' entry into his home and the conclusion that the police had probable cause to arrest him. It is also evident, in light of *Payton,* that arresting Harris in his home without an arrest warrant violated the Fourth Amendment. But, as emphasized in earlier cases, 'we have declined to adopt a "*per se*" or "but for" rule that would make inadmissible any evidence, whether tangible or live-witness testimony, which somehow came to light through a chain of causation that began with an illegal arrest.' Rather, in this context, we have stated that '[t]he penalties visited upon the Government, and in turn upon the public, because its officers have violated the law must bear some relation to the purposes which the law is to serve.' In light of these principles, we decline to apply the exclusionary rule in this context because the rule in *Payton* was designed to protect the physical integrity of the home; it was not intended to grant criminal suspects, like Harris, protection for statements made outside their premises where the police have probable cause to arrest the suspect for committing a crime.

"*Payton* itself emphasized that our holding in that case stemmed from the 'overriding respect for the sanctity of the home that has been embedded in our traditions since the origins of the Republic.' Although it had long been settled that a warrantless arrest in a public place was permissible as long as the arresting officer had probable cause, *Payton* nevertheless drew a line at the entrance to the home. This special solicitude was necessary because 'physical entry of the home is the chief evil against which the wording of the Fourth Amendment is directed.' The arrest warrant was required to 'interpose the magistrate's determination of probable cause' to arrest before the officers could enter a house to effect an arrest.

"Nothing in the reasoning of the case suggests that an arrest in a home without a warrant but with probable cause somehow renders unlawful continued custody of the suspect once he is removed from the house. There could be no valid claim here that Harris was immune from prosecution because his person was the fruit of an illegal arrest. Nor is there any claim that the warrantless arrest required the police to release Harris or that Harris could not be immediately rearrested if momentarily released. Because the officers had probable cause to arrest Harris for a crime, Harris was not unlawfully in custody when he was removed to the station house, given *Miranda* warnings and allowed to talk. For Fourth Amendment purposes, the legal issue is the same as it would be had the police arrested Harris on his door step, illegally entered his home to search for evidence, and later interrogated Harris at the station house. Similarly, if the police had made a warrantless entry into Harris' home, not found him there, but arrested him on the street when he returned, a later statement made by him after proper warnings would no doubt be admissible. * * *

"We do not hold, as the dissent suggests, that a statement taken by the police while a suspect is in custody is always admissible as long as the suspect is in legal custody. Statements taken during legal custody would of course be inadmissible, for example if they were the product of coercion, if *Miranda* warnings were not given, or if there was a violation of the rule of *Edwards v. Arizona*.

"We hold that, where the police have probable cause to arrest a suspect, the exclusionary rule does not bar the State's use of a statement made by the defendant outside of his home, even though the statement is taken after an arrest made in the home in violation of *Payton*."

Disposition: Conviction affirmed; incriminating statements made by Harris at the police station can be used at trial. As long as there was probable cause to make the arrest, statements made outside the house after the arrest are admissible even though the entry to make the arrest was unconstitutional because the officers did not obtain a warrant.

4-9m *Washington v. Chrisman:* 455 U.S. 1, 70 L.Ed. 2d 778, 102 S.Ct. 812 (1982)

Facts: On the evening of January 21, 1978, Officer Daugherty of the Washington State University Police Department observed Overdahl, a student at the University who appeared to be under age 21, leave a dormitory carrying a half-gallon bottle of gin. The officer stopped him because state law prohibits possession of alcoholic beverages by persons under age 21. When asked for identification, Overdahl said his identification was in his dormitory room and asked if the officer would wait while he went to retrieve it. The officer replied that he would have to come with him. Overdahl replied "O.K." Chrisman, Overdahl's roommate, was in the room when they arrived. The officer remained in the open doorway while watching Chrisman and Overdahl. Chrisman, who was in the process of placing a small box in the room's medicine cabinet, became nervous at the sight of the officer. The officer noticed seeds and a small pipe lying on a desk less than 10 feet from where he was standing. Believing that the seeds were marijuana and the pipe was used to smoke marijuana, the officer entered the room and examined the pipe and seeds. Having confirmed his suspicions, the officer advised Overdahl and Chrisman of their *Miranda* rights. Both students waived their rights. When the officer asked if there were any other drugs in the room, Chrisman handed the officer the box he had been carrying earlier. It contained three small, plastic bags of marijuana and $112 in cash. The officer called for a backup. Police found more marijuana and LSD during a consensual search of the room. Chrisman was charged with possession of marijuana and possession of LSD. He was convicted on both counts.

Issue: Is an officer allowed to monitor the activities of a person after his/her arrest?

Reasoning: "The 'plain view' exception to the Fourth Amendment warrant requirement permits a law enforcement officer to seize what clearly is incriminating evidence or contraband when it is discovered in a place where the officer has a right to be. Here, the officer had placed Overdahl under lawful arrest, and therefore was authorized to accompany him to his room for the purpose of obtaining identification. The officer had a right to remain literally at Overdahl's elbow at all times; nothing in the Fourth Amendment is to the contrary.

* * * "The absence of an affirmative indication that an arrested person might have a weapon available or might attempt to escape does not diminish the arresting officer's authority to maintain custody over the arrested person. Nor is that authority altered by the nature of the offense for which the arrest was made.

* * * "We hold, therefore, that it is not 'unreasonable' under the Fourth Amendment for a police officer, as a matter of routine, to monitor the movements of an arrested person, as his judgment dictates, following the arrest. The officer's need to ensure his own safety—as well as the integrity of the arrest—is compelling. Such surveillance is not an impermissible invasion of the privacy or personal liberty of an individual who has been arrested."

Disposition: Conviction affirmed; marijuana and LSD found in the dormitory room are admissible at trial because the officer was entitled to keep Chrisman under visual surveillance at all times after making the arrest.

4-9n *United States v. Robinson:* 414 U.S. 218, 38 L.Ed. 2d 427, 94 S.Ct. 467 (1973)

Facts: On April 23, 1968, at approximately 11:00 P.M., Officer Jenks of the District of Columbia Metropolitan Police Department observed Robinson driving a 1965 Cadillac. Officer Jenks had checked Robinson's driver's license four days earlier and had reason to believe that Robinson was operating a motor vehicle after the revocation of his operator's permit. This offense carried a mandatory minimum jail term, a mandatory minimum fine, or both. Robinson stopped the car when Officer Jenks signaled for him to do so and was placed under arrest for "operating after revocation and obtaining a permit by misrepresentation." As part of the search incident to the arrest, Jenks searched Robinson and felt a hard object in a breast pocket and removed a "crumpled up cigarette package." Jenks could feel objects in the cigarette package that were not cigarettes. He then opened the package and found 14 gelatin capsules of white powder believed to be heroin. Robinson was tried and convicted for possession of heroin.

Issue: Can officers seize items that are not suspected of being weapons, contraband, or evidence of a crime during a search incident to a custodial arrest?

Reasoning: "The justification or reason for the authority to search incident to a lawful arrest rests quite as much on the need to disarm the suspect in order to take him into custody as it does on the need to preserve evidence on his person for later use at trial. The standards traditionally governing a search incident to lawful arrest are not, therefore, commuted to the stricter *Terry* standards by the absence of probable fruits or further evidence of the particular crime for which the arrest is made.

"Nor are we inclined, on the basis of what seems to us to be a rather speculative judgment, to qualify the breadth of the general authority to search incident to a lawful custodial arrest on an assumption that persons arrested for the offense of driving while their licenses have been revoked are less likely to possess dangerous weapons than are those arrested for other crimes. It is scarcely open to doubt that the danger to an officer is far greater in the case of the extended exposure which follows the taking of a suspect into custody and the transporting him to the police station than in the case of the relatively fleeting contact resulting from the typical *Terry*-type stop. This is an adequate basis for treating all custodial arrests alike for purposes of search justification.

*** "The authority to search the person incident to a lawful custodial arrest, while based upon the need to disarm and to discover evidence, does not depend on what a court may later decide was the probability in a particular arrest situation that weapons or evidence would in fact be found upon the person of the suspect. A custodial arrest of a suspect based on probable cause is a reasonable intrusion under the Fourth Amendment; that intrusion being lawful, a search incident to the arrest requires no additional justification. It is the fact of the lawful arrest which establishes the authority to search, and we hold that in the case of a lawful custodial arrest a full search of the person is not only an exception to the warrant requirement of the Fourth Amendment, but is also a 'reasonable' search under that Amendment.

*** "Since it is the fact of custodial arrest which gives rise to the authority to search, it is of no moment that Jenks did not indicate any subjective fear of the respondent or that he did not himself suspect that respondent was armed. Having in the course of a lawful search come upon the crumbled package of cigarettes, he was entitled to inspect it; and when his inspection revealed the heroin capsules, he was entitled to seize them as 'fruits, instrumentalities, or contraband' probative of criminal conduct."

Disposition: Conviction affirmed; heroin found in cigarette pack is admissible at trial because officers are entitled to do a complete search when making an arrest even though there is no reason to believe the suspect is armed.

4-9o *Gustafson v. Florida:* 414 U.S. 260, 38 L.Ed. 2d 456, 94 S.Ct. 488 (1973)

Facts: At approximately 2:00 A.M. on January 12, 1969, Lt. Smith observed Gustafson driving his car across the center line and back to the right side of the road three or four times. When occupants of the car observed Lt. Smith's patrol car, Gustafson drove the car across the highway and behind a grocery store and then headed south on another city street. When the car was stopped, Gustafson was unable to produce his driver's license, claiming he left it in his dormitory room in a nearby town. He was arrested and during the search incident to a valid custodial arrest the officer placed his hand into the left front coat pocket of the coat Gustafson was wearing and extracted a long chain and a cigarette box. The officer opened the cigarette box and found marijuana cigarettes. Gustafson was convicted for possession of marijuana.

Issue: Can officers seize items that are not suspected of being weapons, contraband, or evidence of a crime during a search incident to a custodial arrest?

Reasoning: "Though the officer here was not required to take the petitioner into custody by police regulations as he was in *Robinson*, and there did not exist a departmental policy establishing the conditions under which a full-scale body search should be conducted, we do not find these differences determinative of the constitutional issue. It is sufficient that the officer had probable cause to arrest the petitioner and that he lawfully effectuated the arrest and placed the petitioner in custody. In addition, as our decision in *Robinson* makes clear, the arguable absence of 'evidentiary' purpose for a search incident to a lawful arrest is not controlling. * * *

"We hold, therefore, that upon arresting petitioner for the offense of driving his automobile without a valid operator's license, and taking him into custody, Smith was entitled to make a full search of petitioner's person incident to that lawful arrest."

Disposition: Conviction affirmed; marijuana found in Gustafson's pocket is admissible at trial because officers are entitled to do a complete search whenever they make custodial arrests.

4-9p *United States v. Edwards:* 415 U.S. 800, 39 L.Ed. 2d 771, 94 S.Ct. 1234 (1974)

Facts: Edwards was lawfully arrested for attempting to break into the post office in Lebanon, Ohio, about 11:00 P.M. on May 31, 1970. Police took him to the local jail and placed him in a cell. Contemporaneously or shortly thereafter, investigation at the scene revealed that the attempted entry had been made through a wooden window that apparently had been pried up with a pry bar, leaving paint chips on the window sill and mesh screen. The next morning, police purchased trousers and a T-shirt for Edwards to substitute for the clothing he had been wearing. They took his clothing from him and held it as evidence. Examination of the clothing revealed paint chips matching the samples that had been taken from the window.

Issue: Can the suspect's clothing be taken after booking and examined for evidence?

Reasoning: "With or without probable cause, the authorities were entitled at that point [booking on May 31] not only to search Edwards' clothing but also to take it from him and keep it in official custody. There was testimony that this was the standard practice in this city. The police were also entitled to take from Edwards any evidence of the crime in his immediate possession, including his clothing. *** But it was late at night; no substitute clothing was available for Edwards to wear, and it would certainly have been unreasonable for the police to have stripped respondent of his clothing and left him exposed in his cell throughout the night. When the substitutes were purchased the next morning, the clothing he had been wearing at the time of arrest was taken from him and subjected to laboratory analysis. This was no more than taking from respondent the effects in his immediate possession that constituted evidence of crime. This was and is a normal incident of a custodial arrest, and reasonable delay in effectuating it does not change the fact that Edwards was no more imposed upon than he could have been at the time and place of the arrest or immediately upon arrival at the place of detention. The police did no more on June 1 than they were entitled to do incident to the usual custodial arrest and incarceration.

"Other closely related considerations sustain the examination of the clothing in this case. It must be remembered that on both May 31 and June 1 the police had lawful custody of Edwards and necessarily of the clothing he wore. When it became apparent that the articles of clothing were evidence of the crime for which Edwards was being held, the police were entitled to take, examine, and preserve them for use as evidence, just as they are normally permitted to seize evidence of crime when it is lawfully encountered. Surely, the clothes could have been brushed down and vacuumed while Edwards had them on in the cell, and it was similarly reasonable to take and examine them as the police did, particularly in view of the existence of probable cause linking the clothes to the crime. Indeed, it is difficult to perceive what is unreasonable about the police's examining and holding as evidence those personal effects of the accused that they already have in their lawful custody as the result of a lawful arrest.

"In upholding this search and seizure, we do not conclude that the Warrant Clause of the Fourth Amendment is never applicable to post-arrest seizures of the effects of an arrestee. But we do think that the Court of Appeals for the First Circuit captured the essence of situations like this when it said in *United States v. DeLeo,* 422 F.2d 487, 493 (1970): 'While the legal arrest of a person should not destroy the privacy of his premises, it does—for at least a reasonable time and to a reasonable extent — take his own privacy out of the realm of protection from police interests in weapons, means of escape, and evidence.'"

Disposition: Conviction affirmed; laboratory analysis of paint chips on Edwards's clothing is admissible at trial because anything in the suspect's possession at the time of booking can be used as evidence.

Chapter Quiz

True/False

1. To make a valid arrest, a police officer must have an arrest warrant except when there is an emergency that makes it impossible to contact a judge.
2. Probable cause to arrest is evaluated based on the totality of the circumstances that are known to the arresting officer at the time of the arrest.
3. An arrest warrant is required to enter the suspect's residence to make an arrest except in emergency situations.
4. A search warrant is required to enter a third party's home to arrest the suspect except in emergencies.
5. Incident to a custodial arrest, an officer may conduct a thorough search of the person being arrested and the area under that person's immediate control.
6. If a person is being arrested for a misdemeanor, the search incident to an arrest is restricted to a pat-down for weapons.
7. If a person is arrested while driving a car, the search incident to the arrest includes a thorough search of the passenger compartment of the car.
8. A person who is being given a traffic citation can be subjected to the same search as a person who is being arrested and taken into custody
9. A person may be legally searched when being booked only if he/she was not searched incident to the arrest.
10. A probable cause hearing must be held within 24 hours of arrest.

Discussion Questions

1. Officer Whitehouse was on patrol when he heard a loud argument at a nearby house. Then he heard a woman begin to cry as if she was in extreme pain. He went to the door and knocked. Suddenly everything was quiet. He forced open the door and began to search for the woman to see if she was badly injured. He found a woman lying in the corner and a man running out the back door. Officer Whitehouse arrested the man for battery. Was there probable cause to arrest? Was the arrest legal under *Payton v. New York?* Explain.
2. Officer Green was on patrol when he observed Bill grab an old lady's purse and run into a house. Officer Green followed immediately and arrested Bill in the living room. He walked through the rest of the house to make sure no one was hiding there who might attack him. While doing so, he discovered a stolen gun on the dresser in a back bedroom. He returned to the living room and searched it for weapons. The kitchen was nearby, so he also checked it to make sure there were no dangerous weapons there. He found cocaine on the kitchen table. Was the stolen gun legally discovered as part of a "protective sweep?" Is the cocaine admissible under *Chimel v. California?* Explain.
3. Officer Young was on patrol when he spotted a car driving at an excessive rate of speed. He stopped the car and was about to write a citation when he observed an illegal assault rifle on the front passenger seat. He arrested the driver and had him get out of the car. When he searched the car after a back-up officer had arrived, he found 3 ounces of heroin under the back seat. Is the heroin admissible under *New York v. Belton?* Explain.
4. Police arrested Ingrid for shoplifting and took her to the police station for booking. After filling out all the necessary forms, she was strip searched. Police examined her clothing and found narcotics concealed in the shoulder pads of her blouse. Are the narcotics admissible under *Illinois v. Lafayette?* Explain.

Chapter 5

Vehicle Searches

Outline

Cars are visible and highly regulated. The combination of their extensive exposure to public view, detailed licensing requirements, and safety inspections has resulted in a lesser expectation of privacy in vehicles than in homes. The mobility of vehicles is viewed as creating an urgency not present when evidence is found in buildings. For all of these reasons, the rules for searching vehicles are somewhat different than those for other locations.

Motor homes are usually treated like vehicles. Even though motor homes possess many of the characteristics of houses, they still have the ability to leave the scene. If, on the other hand, the motor home is hooked up to utilities or otherwise immobilized, it is treated like a house.

5-1 Searches of Vehicles Incident to Arrest

The search incident to a custodial arrest normally covers the person and area under his/her immediate control. If the occupant of a car is arrested, the search covers the person and the passenger compartment of the car. The entire passenger compartment is viewed as the area where the person may reach to obtain a weapon and/or destroy evidence or contraband. The search must be contemporaneous with the arrest, but the person arrested can be removed from the vehicle prior to the search.

Everything within the passenger compartment may be thoroughly searched. This includes items, such as briefcases, that would normally fall under the closed container rule. The glove compartment and console may be opened. Because both weapons and other evidence may be seized, areas too small to hide a gun or knife may be searched.

5-2 Searches of Vehicles Incident to Temporary Detention of Occupants

During a field interview, the passenger compartment of a vehicle may be searched for weapons. There are two prerequisites for this type of search: (1) There must have been specific, articulable facts that caused the officers to believe that at least one of the occupants of the vehicle was involved in criminal activity; and (2) there must be at least a reasonable suspicion that the suspect is dangerous and may gain immediate control of weapons.

While this type of vehicle search permits officers to search the entire passenger compartment, it is more limited than the search incident to a custodial arrest. Weapons are the only things officers are justified in looking for. This means that only areas large enough to conceal a weapon can be searched. Anything found while the officers are properly conducting this type of search is admissible under the Plain View Doctrine.

The search for weapons can be done while the suspects are out of the car if they will be permitted to return to it. This is allowed because on release, the suspect might immediately retrieve weapons from the car and attack the officer.

Noncustodial arrests, such as issuing traffic citations, also fall under this rule. In order to search a vehicle during this type of stop, officers must be able to state specific facts that caused them to suspect that weapons were present in the vehicle.

5-3 Probable Cause Searches of Vehicles

Primarily due to the mobility of cars and other vehicles, the Supreme Court has authorized searches without a warrant if the police have probable cause to believe evidence is in the vehicle. Recent cases make it clear that these searches do not require any type of emergency as justification. In fact, a probable cause search may be conducted after a car has been impounded for unrelated reasons.

The scope of a probable cause vehicle search is tied directly to the facts—for example, an officer saw someone run from the scene of a burglary, throw a bulging pillowcase into the backseat of a car, and then flee the scene on foot. There would be probable cause to believe evidence of the burglary may be in the backseat of the car. Based on this probable cause, the backseat may be immediately searched. These facts, however, do not provide any justification to search the trunk of the car.

Sometimes probable cause to search and probable cause to arrest overlap—for example, police observe two men run from the scene of a robbery, put something in a car, and drive away. They pursue the car because the occupants match the description of the robbers. There is probable cause to arrest the occupants and probable cause to search the car. On the other hand, sometimes there is probable cause to arrest but no probable cause to search the car. If an officer discovers that the driver of a car has an outstanding traffic warrant, there will be ample justification to arrest the driver but no probable cause to search the car.

There is no time limit on when a probable cause vehicle search must be done. The search can be done at the scene or later. Officers can tow the car to a storage yard, the police station, or some other convenient location before searching it.

The search of a vehicle based on probable cause can be as extensive as the one a judge could authorize if presented with an affidavit stating the facts known to the officers. Closed containers may be searched on the spot or removed from the location and searched later. Officers are not required to obtain a warrant before opening them. This applies to any item in the car as long as the officer has probable cause to search that item. For example, if there is probable cause to search for drugs, an officer may search a purse found on the seat of the car; it does not matter whether the purse belongs to the suspect or another person who is merely a passenger in the car.

Occasionally there is probable cause to believe the vehicle itself is contraband. When this occurs, the police have the authority to seize the car without a search warrant. An example would be a car declared contraband under a forfeiture law because it was used by a person selling drugs. There are two important prerequisites to taking this action:

1. There must be probable cause that the vehicle is subject to legal seizure.
2. The vehicle must be in a public place.

5-4 Inventories of Vehicles

Whenever a car is legally impounded, it may be inventoried. The reason for impounding the vehicle (involvement in a crime, illegal parking, etc.) has no bearing on the right to inventory. The Supreme Court based the right to conduct the inventory on the protection of both the owner of the vehicle and the police. The police protect the owner by accounting for everything that is present and removing valuable items. The police protect themselves against unfounded claims of theft because the inventory provides a detailed report stating exactly what was in the vehicle at the time it was taken into custody.

Any evidence found during the inventory is admissible. The primary question is whether the police were searching for evidence or conducting a legitimate inventory. In general, the courts are satisfied that an inventory was being conducted if the police systematically go over the entire car. The inventory is more likely to be considered a pretext to search if the officers stopped as soon as they found evidence. The Supreme Court held that opening closed containers during an inventory is permissible only if the officer's department has a policy providing guidelines for doing so.

5-5 Observing the Exterior of a Vehicle

The outside of a car parked in a public place falls under the Plain View Doctrine. What is seen may be used to establish probable cause for further action. For example, chipped paint on a car may indicate that it has been in a collision. If there is probable cause, samples may be taken either at the original location or later at the impound lot, and sent to a criminalistics laboratory for testing.

This rule also allows officers to look for vehicle identification numbers (VIN). Federal law requires a VIN to be on the dashboard and visible from the outside. If visibility is obstructed, officers may reach into the car and move whatever is blocking their view.

5-6 Searches of Vehicles for Noncriminal Purpose

Under some circumstances, cars may be searched if there is a legitimate reason for the search not related to the investigation of a crime. This is an exception to the search warrant requirement that has not been fully developed by the Supreme Court.

The noncriminal investigation search has been authorized by the Supreme Court in situations that can be considered as part of the "community caretaking function" of the police. The leading case involved searching an impounded car for a gun the driver had the legal right to possess. The search was considered justified because it was done to prevent vandals from stealing the gun and possibly using it to harm someone. Incriminating evidence discovered during such a search is admissible.

Cars may be seized and held for civil forfeiture proceedings because of their use in criminal activities. Police have the right to search these vehicles for their own protection.

5-7 Key Supreme Court Cases

5-7a *Preston v. United States:* 376 U.S. 364, 11 L.Ed. 2d 777, 84 S.Ct. 881 (1963)

Facts: At about 3:00 A.M., police in Newport, Kentucky received a telephone complaint that three men had been sitting in a parked car in a business district since 10:00 P.M. that evening. Four policemen immediately went to the scene and found Preston and two companions. The men gave evasive, unsatisfactory answers when asked why they were there. All three men admitted being unemployed and, among them, they had 25 cents. Police arrested the three men for vagrancy, searched for weapons, and took them to the police station. The car, which was not searched at the time of the arrest, was driven to the police station and then towed to a garage. After booking the three men, the police went to the garage and searched the car. They found two loaded revolvers in the glove compartment. Officers discovered caps, women's stockings (with mouth and eye holes), rope, pillow slips, an illegally manufactured license plate equipped to be snapped over another plate, and other items in the trunk. One of the men confessed that he and the others intended to rob a bank in a town about 50 miles away. The suspects were convicted on charges of conspiracy to rob a federally insured bank.

Issue: Can a car be searched as incident to an arrest if the search is not done at the scene of the arrest?

Reasoning: * * * "It is argued that the search and seizure was justified as incidental to a lawful arrest. Unquestionably, when a person is lawfully arrested, the police have the right, without a search warrant, to make a contemporaneous search of the person of the accused for weapons or for the fruits of or implements used to commit the crime. This right to search and seize without a search warrant extends to things under the accused's immediate control, and, to an extent depending on the circumstances of the case, to the place where he is arrested. The rule allowing contemporaneous searches is justified, for example, by the need to seize weapons and other things which might be used to assault an officer or effect an escape, as well as by the need to prevent the destruction of evidence of the crime—things which might easily happen where the weapon or evidence is on the accused's person or under his immediate control. But these justifications are absent where a search is remote in time or place from the arrest. * * *

* * * "The search of the car was not undertaken until petitioner and his companions had been arrested and taken in custody to the police station and the car had been towed to the garage. At this point there was no danger that any of the men arrested could have used any weapons in the car or could have destroyed any evidence of a crime—assuming that there are articles which can be the 'fruits' or 'implement' of the crime of vagrancy. Nor, since the men were under arrest at the police station and the car was in police custody at the garage, was there any danger that the car would be moved out of the locality or jurisdiction. We think that the search was too remote in time or place to have been made as incidental to

the arrest and conclude, therefore, that the search of the car without a warrant failed to meet the test of reasonableness under the Fourth Amendment, rendering the evidence obtained as a result of the search inadmissible."

Disposition: Conviction reversed; the search of car after it was towed to the garage was not contemporaneous with the arrest.

5-7b *Chambers v. Maroney:* 399 U.S. 42, 26 L.Ed. 2d 419, 90 S.Ct. 1975 (1970)

Facts: Two men carrying guns robbed a Gulf service station in North Braddock, Pennsylvania on the night of May 20, 1963. The robbers took the currency from the cash register and directed the service station attendant to place the coins in his right-hand glove. The gas station attendant stated that one of the robbers was wearing a green sweater and the other wore a trench coat. Two teenagers who had previously seen a blue, compact station wagon circling the block saw the station wagon speed away from a parking lot close to the Gulf station. Upon hearing of the robbery, they told the police that they had seen four men in the station wagon, one wearing a green sweater. Within an hour, two police officers who had heard the police radio broadcast, stopped a light-blue, compact station wagon carrying four men. Chambers was in the car and was wearing a green sweater. Officers found a trench coat in the car. The occupants of the car were arrested and the car driven to the police station. A thorough search of the car revealed two revolvers concealed in the dashboard, a right-hand glove containing change, and cards bearing the name of an attendant at a service station that had been robbed at gunpoint a week earlier. Police executed a search warrant at Chambers's home and discovered ammunition similar to that found in the car. Chambers was convicted for both robberies.

Issue: Can the police search a car without a warrant based on probable cause to believe that evidence of a crime is concealed in the car?

Reasoning: *** "In enforcing the Fourth Amendment's prohibition against unreasonable searches and seizures, the Court has insisted upon probable cause as a minimum requirement for a reasonable search permitted by the Constitution. As a general rule, it has also required the judgment of a magistrate on the probable cause issue and the issuance of a warrant before a search is made. Only in exigent circumstances will the judgment of the police as to probable cause serve as a sufficient authorization for a search. *Carroll* holds a search warrant unnecessary where there is probable cause to search an automobile stopped on the highway;

the car is movable, the occupants are alerted, and the car's contents may never be found again if a warrant must be obtained. Hence an immediate search is constitutionally permissible.

"Arguably, because of the preference for a magistrate's judgment, only the immobilization of the car should be permitted until a search warrant is obtained; arguably, only the 'lesser' intrusion is permissible until the magistrate authorizes the 'greater.' But which is the 'greater' and which the 'lesser' intrusion is itself a debatable question and the answer may depend on a variety of circumstances. For constitutional purposes, we see no difference between on the one hand seizing and holding a car before presenting the probable cause issue to a magistrate and on the other hand, carrying out an immediate search without a warrant. Given probable cause to search, either course is reasonable under the Fourth Amendment.

"On the facts before us, the blue station wagon could have been searched on the spot when it was stopped since there was probable cause to search and it was a fleeting target for a search. The probable cause factor still obtained at the station house, and so did the mobility of the car, unless the Fourth Amendment permits a warrantless seizure of the car and the denial of its use to anyone until a warrant is secured. In that event there is little to choose in terms of practical consequences between an immediate search without a warrant and the car's immobilization until a warrant is obtained. The same consequences may not follow where there is unforeseeable cause to search a house But as *Carroll* held, for the purpose of the Fourth Amendment there is a constitutional difference between houses and cars."

Disposition: Conviction affirmed; police had the right to search the car at the police station to the same extent they would if a judge had issued a warrant based on the facts available to them.

5-7c *South Dakota v. Opperman:* 428 U.S. 364, 49 L.Ed. 2d 1000, 96 S.Ct. 3092 (1976)

Facts: At about 3:00 A.M. on December 10, 1973, a Vermillion, South Dakota police officer issued an overtime parking ticket to Opperman's vehicle, which was parked illegally in a restricted zone in violation of a local ordinance that prohibited parking between 2:00 A.M and 6:00 A.M. A second overtime parking citation was issued at about 10:00 A.M. The car was then inspected and towed to the city impound lot. Officers saw a watch and other personal items in the car. They unlocked the car and inventoried the contents. They removed the personal items and marijuana found during the inventory for safe keeping. Opperman was convicted on possession of marijuana.

Issue: Can police inventory the contents of an impounded car if there is no probable cause that the car has been involved in criminal activity?

Reasoning: *** "When vehicles are impounded, local police departments generally follow a routine practice of securing and inventorying the automobile contents. These procedures developed in response to three distinct needs: the protection of the owner's property while it remains in police custody, the protection [of] the police against claims or disputes over lost or stolen property, and the protection of the police from potential danger. The practice has been viewed as essential to respond to incidents of theft or vandalism. In addition, police frequently attempt to determine whether a vehicle has been stolen and thereafter abandoned.

*** "In applying the reasonableness standard adopted by the Framers, this Court has consistently sustained police intrusions into automobiles impounded or otherwise in lawful police custody where the process is aimed at securing or protecting the car and its contents."

Disposition: Conviction affirmed; the evidence found during routine inventory of an impounded car is admissible in evidence.

5-8 Other Supreme Court Cases

5-8a *California v. Carney:* 471 U.S. 386, 85 L.Ed. 2d 406, 105 S.Ct. 2066 (1985)

Facts: DEA agents had uncorroborated information that a motor home was being used by someone who exchanged marijuana for sex. On May 31, 1979, DEA Agent Williams watched Carney, who was not then a suspect, approach a youth in downtown San Diego. The youth then accompanied Carney to a Dodge mini motor home parked in a nearby lot. All curtains in the motor home were then closed. The agent maintained surveillance for the hour and 15 minutes that the two remained inside the motor home. Agents followed the youth and stopped him after he left the motor home. He told the agents that he had received marijuana in exchange for sexual contact with Carney. At the agents' request, the youth returned to the motor home and knocked on the door. Carney stepped out. The agents identified themselves as law enforcement officers. Without consent, an agent entered the motor home and observed marijuana, plastic bags, and a scale. Carney was arrested. The agents took possession of the motor home and subsequently searched it at the police station. They found additional marijuana. Carney was convicted of possession of marijuana for sale.

Issue: Can officers conduct a probable cause search of a motor home without a warrant?

Reasoning: *** "While it is true that respondent's vehicle possessed some, if not many of the attributes of a home, it is equally clear that the vehicle falls clearly within the scope of the exception laid down in *Carroll* and applied in succeeding cases. Like the automobile in *Carroll*, respondent's motor home was readily mobile. Absent the prompt search and seizure, it could readily have been moved beyond the reach of the police. Furthermore, the vehicle was licensed to 'operate on public streets; [was] serviced in public places; *** and [was] subject to extensive regulation and inspection.' And the vehicle was so situation that an objective observer would conclude that it was being used not as a residence, but as a vehicle.

"Respondent urges us to distinguish his vehicle from other vehicles within the exception because it was capable of functioning as a home. *** We decline today to distinguish between 'worthy' and 'unworthy' vehicles which are either on the public roads and highways, or situated such that it is reasonable to conclude that the vehicle is not being used as a residence.

"Our application of the vehicle exception has never turned on the other uses to which a vehicle might be put. The exception has historically turned on the ready mobility of the vehicle, and on the presence of the vehicle in a setting that objectively indicates that the vehicle is being used for transportation. These two requirements for application of the exception ensure that law enforcement officials are not unnecessarily hamstrung in their efforts to detect and prosecute criminal activity, and that the legitimate privacy interests of the public are protected."

Disposition: Conviction affirmed; a motor home that is mobile can be searched under the same rules as other vehicles.

5-8b *New York v. Belton:* 453 U.S. 454, 69 L.Ed. 2d 768, 101 S.Ct. 2869 (1981)

Facts: On April 9, 1978, Trooper Nicot, a New York State policeman, stopped a driver for speeding. The car had four male occupants, including Belton, none of whom owned the vehicle or was related to its owner. Nicot smelled the odor of burnt marijuana and observed an envelope marked "Supergold" on the floor of the backseat. He directed the men to get out of the car and placed them under arrest for unlawful possession of marijuana. During a search of the car, Nicot found a black leather jacket belonging to Belton on the backseat. He unzipped one pocket of the jacket and discovered cocaine. Belton was charged with possession of cocaine. He pled guilty to a lesser offense but preserved his claim that the cocaine was seized unconstitutionally for appeal.

Issue: Can closed containers in a car be searched as incident to a legal arrest of an occupant of the car?

Reasoning: * * * "Our reading of the cases suggests the generalization that articles inside the relatively narrow compass of the passenger compartment of an automobile are in fact generally, even if not inevitably, within 'the area into which an arrestee might reach in order to grab a weapon or evidentiary item.' In order to establish a workable rule this category of cases requires, we read *Chimel's* definition of the limits of the area that may be searched in light of that generalization. Accordingly, we hold that when a policeman has made a lawful custodial arrest of the occupant of an automobile, he may, as a contemporaneous incident of that arrest, search the passenger compartment of that automobile.

"It follows from this conclusion that the police may also examine the contents of any containers found within the passenger compartment, for if the passenger compartment is within reach of the arrestee, so also will containers in it be within his reach. Such a container may, of course, be searched whether it is open or closed, since the justification for the search is not that the arrestee has no privacy interest in the container, but that the lawful custodial arrest justifies the infringement of any privacy interest the arrestee may have."

Disposition: Suppression motion was properly denied; an officer has the right to search a closed container in a vehicle as incident to arrest of a person in the vehicle.

5-8c *Michigan v. Long:* 463 U.S. 1032, 77 L.Ed. 2d 1201, 103 S.Ct. 3469 (1983)

Facts: Deputies Howell and Lewis were on patrol in a rural area one evening when, shortly after midnight, they observed a speeding car turn down a side road and swerve off into a shallow ditch. The officers stopped to investigate. Long, the only occupant in the car, met the officers at the rear of the car. Long appeared to be under the influence of something. He did not respond to requests for the vehicle registration; instead, he turned and walked toward the open car door. The officers followed Long and observed a large hunting knife on the floorboard of the driver's side of the car. Officers stopped Long and subjected him to a pat-down but found no weapons on his person. While the officers used flashlights to look for weapons in the car, they saw something protruding from under the armrest of the front seat. Deputy Howell lifted the armrest and saw an open pouch that contained marijuana on the front seat. Long was arrested for possession of marijuana. A search of the passenger compartment did not reveal any more marijuana. Police found approximately 75 pounds of marijuana when they opened the trunk after the car was impounded.

Issue: What parts of a car can be searched when the car is stopped on reasonable suspicion?

Reasoning: *** "Our past cases indicate then that protection of police and others can justify protective searches when police have a reasonable belief that the suspect poses a danger, that roadside encounters between police and suspects are especially hazardous, and that danger may arise from the possible presence of weapons in the area surrounding a suspect. These principles compel our conclusion that the search of the passenger compartment of an automobile, limited to those areas in which a weapon may be placed or hidden, is permissible if the police officer possesses a reasonable belief based on 'specific and articulable facts which, taken together with the rational inferences from those facts, reasonably warrant' the officer in believing that the suspect is dangerous and the suspect may gain immediate control of weapons. 'The issue is whether a reasonably prudent man in the circumstances would be warranted in the belief that his safety or that of others was in danger.' If a suspect is 'dangerous,' he is no less dangerous simply because he is not arrested. If, while conducting a legitimate *Terry* search of the interior of the automobile, the officer should, as here, discover contraband other than weapons, he clearly cannot be required to ignore the contraband and the Fourth Amendment does not require its suppression in such circumstances."

Disposition: Conviction affirmed; marijuana found in Long's car is admissible at trial because there was reasonable suspicion that he was dangerous and might obtain a weapon.

5-8d *Michigan v. Thomas:* 458 U.S. 259, 73 L.Ed. 2d 750, 102 S.Ct. 3079 (1982)

Facts: Officers stopped a car for the driver's failure to signal a left turn. Thomas, the car owner was in the front passenger seat; a 14-year-old was driving. As the police officers approached the vehicle, they saw Thomas bend forward so that his head was at or below the level of the dashboard. They observed an open bottle of malt liquor on the floorboard between Thomas's feet. Thomas was arrested for possession of an open intoxicant in a motor vehicle. The driver was issued a citation for not having a driver's license. Officers took Thomas and the driver to the patrol car and called a tow truck. Prior to towing the car, the officer, in compliance with department policy, searched the car and found two bags of marijuana in the unlocked glove compartment. Officers then searched the car more thoroughly and discovered a loaded .38-caliber revolver in an air vent under the dashboard. Thomas was convicted for possession of a concealed weapon.

Issue: Is the right to search a car based on probable cause dependent on there being exigent circumstances that indicate the search must be done immediately?

Reasoning: *** "In *Chambers v. Maroney* we held that when police officers have probable cause to believe there is contraband inside an automobile that has been stopped on the road, the officers may conduct a warrantless search of the vehicle, even after it has been impounded and is in police custody. We firmly reiterated this holding in *Texas v. White* (423 U.S. 67 (1975)). It is thus clear that the justification to conduct such a warrantless search does not vanish once the car has been immobilized; nor does it depend upon a reviewing court's assessment of the likelihood in each particular case that the car would have been driven away, or that its contents would have been tampered with, during the period required for the police to obtain a warrant.

"Here, the Court of Appeals recognized that the officers were justified in conducting an inventory search of the car's glove compartment, which led to the discovery of contraband. Without attempting to refute the State's contention that this discovery gave the officers probable cause to believe there was contraband elsewhere in the vehicle, the Court of Appeals held that the absence of 'exigent circumstances' precluded a warrantless search. This holding is plainly inconsistent with our decisions in *Chambers* and *Texas v. White*."

Disposition: Conviction affirmed; the probable cause search of the car was valid even though there was no showing of exigent circumstances.

5-8e *California v. Acevedo:* 500 U.S. 565, 114 L.Ed. 2d 619, 111 S.Ct. 1982 (1991)

Facts: On October 28, 1987, Officer Coleman of the Santa Ana Police Department received a telephone call from a DEA agent in Hawaii. The agent said he had a package containing marijuana that was to have been delivered to the Federal Express office in Santa Ana. He arranged to send Coleman the package, which was addressed to Daza in Santa Ana. Coleman verified the contents of the package when he received it and then took it to the Federal Express office. At about 10:30 A.M. on October 30, Coleman observed Daza claim the package and watched him carry it into his apartment. At 11:45 A.M., Daza left the apartment and dropped the box and the paper that had contained the marijuana into a trash bin. Coleman then left the scene to obtain a search warrant. At 12:05 P.M., officers saw St. George leave the apartment with a knapsack that appeared to be half full. Officers stopped St. George as he drove off; a search of the knapsack revealed 1-1/2 pounds of marijuana. Acevedo arrived at 12:30 P.M. and entered Daza's apartment. He reappeared about 10 minutes later carrying a brown paper bag that looked full, the size of one of the bags in the package from Hawaii. Acevedo put the paper bag in the trunk of his Honda and started to drive away. Fearing the loss of the evidence, officers in a marked police car stopped him. They found marijuana in the bag in the trunk. Acevedo was convicted on charges of possession of marijuana for sale.

Issue: Can an officer search a closed container found in a vehicle if there is probable cause to believe it contains contraband or evidence?

Reasoning: *** "To the extent that the *Chadwick-Sanders* rule protects privacy, its protection is minimal. Law enforcement officers may seize a container and hold it until they obtain a search warrant. 'Since the police, by hypothesis, have probable cause to seize the property, we can assume that a warrant will be routinely forthcoming in the overwhelming majority of cases.' And the police often will be able to search containers without a warrant, despite the *Chadwick-Sanders* rule, as a search incident to a lawful arrest.***

"Finally, the search of a paper bag intrudes far less on individual privacy than does the incursion sanctioned long ago in *Carroll*. In that case, prohibition agents slashed the upholstery on the automobile. This Court nonetheless found their search to be reasonable under the Fourth Amendment. If destroying the interior of an automobile is not unreasonable, we cannot conclude that looking inside a closed container is. In light of the minimal protection to privacy afforded by the *Chadwick-Sanders* rule, and our serious doubt whether that rule substantially serves privacy interests, we now hold that the Fourth Amendment does not compel separate treatment for an automobile search that extends only to a container within the vehicle.

*** "We conclude that it is better to adopt one clear-cut rule to govern automobile searches and eliminate the warrant requirement for closed containers set forth in *Sanders.*

*** "In other words, the police may search without a warrant if their search is supported by probable cause. The Court in *Ross* *** went on to note: 'Probable cause to believe that a container placed in the trunk of a taxi contains contraband or evidence does not justify a search of the entire cab.' We reaffirm that principle. ***

*** "We therefore interpret *Carroll* as providing one rule to govern all automobile searches. The police may search an automobile and the containers within it where they have probable cause to believe contraband or evidence is contained.

Disposition: Conviction affirmed; police may search closed containers in a vehicle without a warrant if there is probable cause to believe the vehicle contains contraband or evidence.

5-8f *United States v. Johns:* 469 U.S. 478, 83 L.Ed. 2d 890, 105 S.Ct. 881 (1985)

Facts: A U.S. Customs agent kept two trucks under surveillance as they traveled 100 miles to a remote, private airstrip near Bowie, Arizona, which is 50 miles from the Mexican border. A small aircraft landed shortly after the trucks arrived. The agent observed the trucks approaching the plane; the aircraft departed a short time later. Two Customs officers drove to within 30 yards of the two trucks and observed an individual at the rear of one truck covering the contents with a blanket. The officers ordered the suspects to lie on the ground. The officers smelled the odor of marijuana and observed packages in the trucks wrapped in dark-green plastic and sealed with tape. All the suspects at the scene were then arrested. Officers in aircraft followed the suspect's airplane back to Tucson and arrested additional suspects. After making the arrests at the airstrip, the Customs officers took the trucks back to DEA headquarters in Tucson. They removed the packages from the trucks and placed them in a DEA warehouse. Three days later, they opened some of the packages to obtain samples for laboratory testing. The trial court granted the defendant's suppression motion.

Issue: Is a search warrant necessary to open packages found during a probable cause search of a vehicle if the packages were not opened immediately?

Reasoning: *** "The warrantless search of the packages was not unreasonable merely because the Customs officers returned to Tucson and placed the packages in a DEA warehouse rather than immediately opening them. The practical effect of the opposite conclusion would only be to direct police officers to search immediately all containers that they discover in the course of a vehicle search. * * *

"We do not suggest that police officers may indefinitely retain possession of a vehicle and its contents before they complete a vehicle search. Nor do we foreclose the possibility that the owner of a vehicle or its contents might attempt to prove that delay in the completion of a vehicle search was unreasonable because it adversely affected a privacy or possessory interest. * * * Inasmuch as the Government was entitled to seize the packages and could have searched them immediately without a warrant, we conclude that the warrantless search three days after the packages were placed in the DEA warehouse was reasonable and consistent with our precedent involving searches of impounded vehicles."

Disposition: Suppression order granted in error; officers do not have to obtain a search warrant to open packages seized from a vehicle with probable cause merely because the search was not conducted at the time the vehicle was seized.

5-8g *Wyoming v. Houghton:* 526 U.S. 295, 143 L.Ed. 2d 408, 119 S.Ct. 1297 (1999)

Facts: A Wyoming Highway Patrol officer stopped a driver for speeding and driving with a faulty brake light. While questioning Young, the driver, the officer noticed a hypodermic syringe in his shirt pocket. When asked why he had a syringe, Young replied that he used it to take drugs.

The backup officers ordered the two female passengers out of the car and asked them for identification. Houghton falsely identified herself as "Sandra James" and stated that she did not have any identification. While searching the passenger compartment of the car for contraband, the officer found a purse that Houghton claimed as hers; in it he found a wallet containing Houghton's driver's license. Continuing his search of the purse, the officer found a brown pouch and a black wallet-type container. Houghton denied that the pouch was hers; it contained drug paraphernalia and a syringe with 60 ccs of methamphetamine. She admitted ownership of the black wallet, which contained drug paraphernalia and a syringe with 10 ccs of methamphetamine—an amount insufficient to support the felony conviction at issue in this case. At trial, Houghton claimed someone surreptitiously placed the brown pouch in her purse and she did not know it was there.

Issue: Can an officer search personal belongings of a vehicle's occupant(s) when conducting a probable cause search of a vehicle?

Reasoning: "When there is probable cause to search for contraband in a car, it is reasonable for police officers . . . to examine packages and containers without a showing of individualized probable cause for each one. A passenger's personal belongings, just like the driver's belongings or containers attached to the car like a glove compartment, are 'in' the car, and the officer has probable cause to search for contraband in the car.

*** "Effective law enforcement would be appreciably impaired without the ability to search a passenger's personal belongings when there is reason to believe contraband or evidence of criminal wrongdoing is hidden in the car. As in all car-search cases, the 'ready mobility' of an automobile creates a risk that the evidence or contraband will be permanently lost while a warrant is obtained. In addition, a car passenger—unlike the unwitting tavern patron in Ybarra—will often be engaged in a common enterprise with the driver and have the same interest in concealing the fruits or the evidence of their wrongdoing. ***

"To be sure, these factors favoring a search will not always be present, but the balancing of interests must be conducted with an eye to the generality of cases. To require that the investigating officer have positive reason to believe that the passenger and driver were engaged in a common enterprise, or positive reason to believe that the driver had time and occasion to conceal the item in the passenger's belongings, surreptitiously or with friendly permission, is to impose requirements so seldom met that a 'passenger's property' rule would dramatically reduce the ability to find and seize contraband and evidence of crime. *** When balancing the competing interests, our determinations of 'reasonableness' under the Fourth Amendment must take account of these practical realities. We think they militate in favor of the needs of law enforcement, and against a personal-privacy interest that is ordinarily weak."

Disposition: Conviction affirmed; police officers with probable cause to search a car may open items belonging to a passenger that are found in the car if the items are capable of concealing the object of the search.

5-8h *Colorado v. Bertine:* 479 U.S. 367, 93 L.Ed. 2d 739, 107 S.Ct. 738 (1987)

Facts: On February 10, 1984, a police officer in Boulder, Colorado arrested Bertine for driving under the influence of alcohol. Due to local police department policy, officers subjected Bertine's van to a detailed inventory prior to towing it to an impound lot. While conducting the inventory, the officer found a closed backpack directly behind the front seat and opened it. Inside it, he found a nylon bag containing a metal canister. When the officer opened the metal canister he found cocaine, methaqualone tablets, cocaine paraphernalia, and $700 in cash. In the outside zipper compartment of the backpack, he found $210 in cash in a sealed envelope. He then completed the inventory of the van and had it towed. Bertine was charged with driving under the influence of alcohol, unlawful possession of cocaine with intent to sell, and unlawful possession of methaqualone. The state appellate court ruled that the evidence found in the backpack must be suppressed.

Issue: Can an officer open closed containers during the inventory of an impounded vehicle?

Reasoning: *** "In the present case, as in *Opperman* and *Lafayette*, there was no showing that the police, who were following standardized procedures, acted in bad faith or for the sole purpose of investigation. In addition, the governmental interests justifying the inventory searches in *Opperman* and *Lafayette* are nearly the same as those which were obtained here. In each case, the police were potentially responsible for the property taken into their custody. By securing the property, the police protected the property from unauthorized interference. ***

*** "'The reasonableness of any particular government activity does not necessarily or invariably turn on the existence of alternative "less intrusive" means.' We conclude that here, as in *Lafayette*, reasonable police regulations relating to inventory procedures administered in good faith satisfy the Fourth Amendment, even though courts might as a matter of hindsight be able to devise equally reasonable rules requiring a different procedure.

"The Supreme Court of Colorado also thought it necessary to require that police, before inventorying a container, weigh the strength of the individual's privacy interest in the container against the possibility that the container might serve as a repository for dangerous or valuable items. We think that such a requirement is contrary to our decisions in *Opperman* and *Lafayette*, and by analogy to our decision in *United States v. Ross*."

Disposition: Suppression motion granted in error; police have the right to open closed containers during the inventory of a vehicle that is to be impounded.

5-8i *Cardwell v. Lewis:* 417 U.S. 583, 41 L.Ed. 2d 325, 94 S.Ct. 2464 (1974)

Facts: A murder investigation was focused on Lewis. The victim had been shot and his vehicle pushed over a cliff. Lewis's vehicle matched the description of the car seen near the crime scene and he had had body work done on his car recently. Several months later, police obtained an arrest warrant for Lewis and asked him to appear at the police station. After his arrest inside the police station, officers took his car keys and towed the car, which was parked in a nearby public parking lot. Technicians from the crime lab made tire impressions and took paint samples. Lewis was convicted on murder charges.

Issue: Can the police examine the exterior of a car based on probable cause for evidence without obtaining a search warrant?

Reasoning: *** "In the present case, nothing from the interior of the car and no personal effects, which the Fourth Amendment traditionally has been deemed to protect, were searched or seized and introduced in evidence. With the 'search' limited to the examination of the tire on the wheel and the taking of paint scrapings from the exterior of the vehicle left in the public parking lot, we fail to comprehend what expectation of privacy was infringed. *** Under circumstances such as these, where probable cause exists, a warrantless examination of the exterior of a car is not unreasonable under the Fourth and Fourteenth Amendments.

*** "Concluding, as we have, that the examination of the exterior of the vehicle upon probable cause was reasonable, we have yet to determine whether the prior impoundment of the automobile rendered that examination a violation of the Fourth and Fourteenth Amendments. We do not think that, because the police impounded the car prior to the examination, which they could have made on the spot, there is a constitutional barrier to the use of the evidence obtained thereby. Under the circumstances of this case, the seizure itself was not unreasonable.

*** "Respondent contends that here, unlike *Chambers,* probable cause to search the car existed for some time prior to arrest and that, therefore, there were no exigent circumstances. Assuming that probable cause previously existed, we know of no case or principle that suggests that the right to search on probable cause and the reasonableness of seizing a car under exigent circumstances are foreclosed if a warrant was not obtained at the first practicable moment."

Disposition: Conviction affirmed; evidence obtained from exterior of vehicle by police who had probable cause to search is admissible even though no search warrant had been obtained.

5-8j *New York v. Class:* 475 U.S. 106, 89 L.Ed. 2d 81, 106 S.Ct. 960 (1986)

Facts: On the afternoon of May 11, 1981, New York City police officers Meyer and McNamee stopped Class for driving above the speed limit in a car with a cracked windshield. There was no suspicion that the car was stolen, that it contained contraband, or that Class had committed any offense except two traffic violations. Class stopped the car as directed and got out of the car. Class gave Officer McNamee the vehicle's registration certificate and proof of insurance but stated truthfully that he had no driver's license. Officer Meyer opened the car door to look for the VIN, which was located in the left door jamb of vehicles manufactured prior to 1969. When he could not find the VIN, he reached into the car and moved some papers that were obscuring the area of the dashboard where the VIN is located on newer cars. While doing this he observed the handle of a gun protruding about 1 inch from underneath the driver's seat. Officers seized the gun was seized and promptly arrested Class. Class was convicted of criminal possession of a weapon in the third degree.

Issue: Do officers making traffic stops have the right to search for a VIN?

Reasoning: *** "The VIN consists of more than a dozen digits, unique to each vehicle and required on all cars and trucks. The VIN is roughly analogous to a serial number, but it can be deciphered to reveal not only the place of the automobile in the manufacturer's production run, but the make, model, engine type, and place of manufacture of the vehicle.

*** "In sum, because of the important role played by the VIN in the pervasive governmental regulation of the automobile and the efforts by the Federal Government to ensure that the VIN is placed in plain view, we hold that there was no reasonable expectation of privacy in the VIN.

"We think it makes no difference that the papers in respondent's car obscured the VIN from the plain view of the officer. We have recently emphasized that efforts to restrict access to an area do not generate a reasonable expectation of privacy where none would otherwise exist.

*** Here, where the object at issue is an identification number behind the transparent windshield of an automobile driven upon the public roads, we believe that the placement of the obscuring papers was insufficient to create a privacy interest in the VIN. The mere viewing of the formerly obscured VIN was not, therefore, a violation of the Fourth Amendment.

*** "The evidence that respondent sought to have suppressed was not the VIN, however, but a gun, the handle of which the officer saw from the interior of the car while reaching for the papers that covered the VIN. *** We agree with the New York Court of Appeals that the intrusion into that space constituted a 'search.'

*** "We hold that this search was sufficiently unintrusive to be constitutionally permissible in light of the lack of a reasonable expectation of privacy in the VIN and the fact that the officers observed respondent commit two traffic violations. ***

*** "We note that our holding today does not authorize police officers to enter a vehicle to obtain a dashboard-mounted VIN when the VIN is visible from outside the automobile. If the VIN is in the plain view of someone outside the vehicle, there is no justification for governmental intrusion into the passenger compartment to see it."

Disposition: Conviction affirmed; officers had the right to reach into the car in order to make the dashboard-mounted VIN visible.

5-8k *Cady v. Dombrowski:* 413 U.S. 433, 37 L.Ed. 2d 706, 93 S.Ct. 2523 (1973)

Facts: On September 9, 1969, Dombrowski, a Chicago police officer, drove to West Bend, Wisconsin after going to at least two taverns. Sometime the next morning, his car became disabled and he had it towed to his brother's farm in Fond du Lac County. His brother took him back to Chicago where he rented a car and went back to Wisconsin early the next morning. That day, Dombrowski drank heavily and was involved in a one-car traffic accident. A passer-by drove him to Kewaskum, where he called police. Police who drove Dombrowski back to the scene of the accident noticed that he appeared drunk and that he gave three different accounts of the accident. He was hospitalized overnight for observation because he lapsed into an unexplained coma. No weapon was observed on Dombrowski. The local police became concerned because they knew he was a Chicago police officer and thought Chicago officers were required to carry a gun at all times. Fearing injury to an innocent person, they searched his car in order to retrieve the gun before someone else found it at the unguarded impound lot where the car had been stored. During the search for the weapon, officers found bloody towels and other evidence of a murder. Dombrowski was convicted on murder charges.

Issue: Can evidence discovered in a car when it was searched for reasons unrelated to the investigation of a crime be admitted at a criminal trial?

Reasoning: *** "In *Harris* the justification for the initial intrusion into the vehicle was to safeguard the owner's property, and in *Cooper* it was to guarantee the safety of the custodians. Here the justification, while different, was as immediate and constitutionally reasonable as those in *Harris* and *Cooper:* concern for the safety of the general public who might be endangered if an intruder removed a revolver from the trunk of the vehicle. *** While perhaps in a metropolitan area the responsibility to the general public might have been discharged by the posting of a police guard during the night, what might be normal police procedure in such an area may be neither normal nor possible in Kewaskum, Wisconsin. The fact that the protection of the public might, in the abstract, have been accomplished by 'less intrusive' means does not, by itself, render the search unreasonable.

"The Court's previous recognition of the distinction between motor vehicles and dwelling places leads us to conclude that the type of caretaking 'search' conducted here of a vehicle that was neither in the custody nor on the premises of its owner, and that had been placed where it was by virtue of lawful police action, was not unreasonable solely because a warrant had not been obtained. *** Where, as here, the trunk of an automobile, which the officer reasonably believed to contain a gun, was vulnerable to intrusion by vandals, we hold that the search was not 'unreasonable' within the meaning of the Fourth and Fourteenth Amendments."

Disposition: Conviction affirmed; the search of the car for the protection of the public did not require a search warrant.

5-8l *Cooper v. California:* 386 U.S. 58, 17 L.Ed. 2d 730, 87 S.Ct. 788 (1967)

Facts: Cooper was arrested for selling heroin to a police informer. His car was impounded and held as evidence under a statute requiring the forfeiture of vehicles used to transport or conceal narcotics. About a week later, police searched the car and found a brown paper sack in the glove compartment. Evidence found in the bag was key in his conviction for sale of heroin.

Issue: Can police search a car without probable cause if it is held pending forfeiture proceedings and the search is done for their own protection?

Reasoning: *** "Here the officers seized petitioner's car because they were required to do so by state law. They seized it because of the crime for which they arrested petitioner. They seized it to impound it and they had to keep it until forfeiture proceedings were concluded. * * * The forfeiture of petitioner's car did not take place until over four months after it was lawfully seized. It would be unreasonable to hold that the police, having to retain the car in their custody for such a length of time, had no right, even for their own protection, to search it. It is no answer to say that the police could have obtained a search warrant, for '[t]he relevant test is not whether it is reasonable to procure a search warrant, but whether the search was reasonable.' Under the circumstances of this case, we cannot hold unreasonable under the Fourth Amendment the examination or search of a car validly held by officer for use as evidence in a forfeiture proceeding."

Disposition: Conviction affirmed; police have the right to search vehicles impounded and held while awaiting the outcome of forfeiture proceedings.

Chapter Quiz

True/False

1. The vehicle exception to the warrant requirement applies to all types of vehicles that are mobile.
2. If a person in a vehicle is arrested, the search incident to the arrest may include a thorough search of the entire car.
3. If a person in a vehicle is arrested, the search incident to the arrest may be done after the vehicle is taken to the impound lot.
4. There is no right to search vehicles during a stop based on reasonable suspicion.
5. When the passenger compartment of a vehicle is searched during a Terry stop, officers may do a thorough search of that area for weapons.
6. If there is probable cause to search a vehicle, the officer can conduct the search without obtaining a search warrant.
7. Searches of vehicles based on probable cause must be done at the location where the vehicle is stopped.
8. A vehicle that is impounded for reasons unrelated to a crime may not be inventoried.
9. The Plain View Doctrine governs the admissibility of evidence discovered on the outside of a car.
10. There is no right to search a car unless the car is believed to be involved in a crime.

Discussion Questions

1. Police stopped David because his car matched the description of a car seen speeding away from a drive-by shooting a few minutes earlier. An officer ordered David out of the car and questioned him. During the questioning, another officer searched the passenger compartment for weapons. Are drugs found hidden under a false bottom to the glove compartment admissible in court as part of a *search incident to an arrest?* As part of a *search incident to a temporary detention?* As part of a *probable cause search of the car?* Explain.
2. Scott's car was towed to a garage because it stalled in heavy traffic during rush hour. Scott said he would meet the tow-truck driver in 30 minutes but he did not show up. The police then impounded the car as an abandoned vehicle. They found a locked suitcase in the trunk during a routine inventory of the car. Officers opened the suitcase at the impound lot without a warrant and found cash, later traced to a bank robbery. Is the cash admissible as part of the *inventory of a vehicle?* Explain.
3. Police stopped Michelle for speeding. She was not released at the scene because she claimed she did not have any form of identification. Officers called a tow truck to take the car to an impound lot. Prior to the arrival of the tow truck, an officer searched her car. He found a driver's license and 10 stolen credit cards in the bottom of a purse he found on the floor behind the driver's seat. He stopped the search immediately and arrested Michelle on possession of stolen property. Are the credit cards admissible as part of a *search incident to an arrest?* As part of an *inventory of a vehicle?* Explain.

Chapter 6

Observations of Evidence Not Covered by Reasonable Expectation of Privacy

Outline

The Supreme Court has utilized the reasonable expectation of privacy test established in the 1967 case of *Katz v. United States* to determine if the protections of the Fourth Amendment apply to a given set of facts. Both an objective and a subjective expectation of privacy must exist. The subjective part of the analysis focuses on the efforts the person took to protect his/her own privacy. An objective expectation of privacy means there is a privacy interest that society is willing to protect. If the Court finds that either the subjective or objective expectation of privacy is missing, officers need neither probable cause nor a search warrant to conduct a search.

The most common situations in which there is no expectation of privacy are covered by the Plain View Doctrine and the Open Fields Doctrine. Abandoned property, by its very nature, is not constitutionally protected. Employee drug testing is a newly emerging area in which the Court has balanced the person's subjective expectation of privacy against society's willingness to accept that personalized belief as reasonable. Testing has been permitted for jobs impacting the public's safety.

Consent searches also exempt officers from the probable cause requirement. The Court has viewed them as not violating an expectation of privacy because a person, by consenting, has indicated that he/she does not have a subjective expectation of privacy at the time of the search.

6-1 Plain View Doctrine

The Plain View Doctrine is one of the most useful exceptions to the warrant requirement. It states that it is not an unreasonable search for officers who are legally on the premises to observe items left where they can be seen. Probable cause is needed to seize the objects observed in plain view.

The Plain View Doctrine has three key elements: (1) objects must be where officers can observe them; (2) officers must be legally at the location where the observation is made; and (3) probable cause must exist to seize the observed items.

6-1a The Observation

Objects in plain view do not require a search because they are not hidden. Under the Plain View Doctrine, officers are not allowed to move things to look for identifying markings or pick them up to examine them. This does not prevent officers from moving to a better vantage point to observe them—for example, walking around the room, stretching, or bending. Most courts also allow the use of flashlights and binoculars.

The Supreme Court rejected the argument that the observations must be inadvertent. The Plain View Doctrine applies even though the officers knew or suspected the presence of the items prior to going to the place to be searched—for example, officers believe a suspect is selling cocaine but cannot establish probable cause to support a search warrant for the cocaine. They do have sufficient information to obtain a search warrant for stolen property hidden in the suspect's apartment. While in the apartment executing the search warrant for stolen property, officers see cocaine just as they had hoped they would. The Plain View Doctrine applies to the observation of the cocaine as long as the officers had a valid search warrant and were legally executing it.

Officers may view what is in a public place and touch it in the same manner members of the public would be expected to touch it. For example, a passenger who places a piece of carry-on luggage in an overhead storage bin should expect that others might move it while stowing their own luggage. An officer's act of squeezing the carry-on to determine what is inside goes beyond what is reasonably expected.

High-tech devices are making it possible to observe things not visible to the naked eye. This was addressed in *Kyllo v. United States* (2001). At issue was the use of a thermal imaging device to detect infrared radiation in excess of what would normally be expected. Based on this information, plus a review of utility records and a tip from an informant, police obtained a warrant to search Kyllo's home. The Supreme Court ruled that use of a device that is not in general public use, to explore portions of the home that previously would have required physical intrusion, is a search and is presumptively unreasonable without a warrant.

6-1b Legally on Premises

For the Plain View Doctrine to operate, officers must be legally at the location where the observation is made. The most common situations involve making arrests, field interviews, car stops and executing search warrants. If an officer illegally entered a house, for example, nothing he/she observed inside qualifies for the Plain View Doctrine.

Aerial searches are an extension of this idea. The Supreme Court held that observations made from a police aircraft qualify for the Plain View Doctrine. The fact that the defendant built a fence around his backyard indicated a subjective expectation of privacy, but the Court found that this did not matter because the police observed the marijuana plants with the naked eye from navigable airspace. This case arose from police observations made from an aircraft chartered solely to view the suspected crop, so it is clear that the observation does not have to be made during routine patrol or from a frequently used flight path.

6-1c Probable Cause to Seize

The fact that an item is in plain view and the officers are legally present indicates that there is no unreasonable search. The final issue deals with the right to seize the item. To do this, there must be probable cause. Reasonable suspicion is not enough.

This probable cause requirement means the facts must indicate it is more likely than not that the item is evidence of a crime or contraband. Officers must make this decision without handling the item to look for clues such as serial numbers. If probable cause exists, the item can be seized on the spot without a warrant.

6-2 Open Fields Doctrine

Evidence found by officers in open areas that are not close to homes can be seized. This evidence is admissible even though the officers were trespassing at the time the seizure was made. This is known as the Open Fields Doctrine.

The Open Fields Doctrine relies heavily on history and the wording of the Fourth Amendment. Because farmland and other open spaces are not included in the "persons, houses, papers and effects" specified in the Fourth Amendment, they are not protected. Historical protection of the curtilage, or enclosed area immediately around a house, indicates that the Fourth Amendment was not intended to apply to open fields beyond the curtilage.

The Open Fields Doctrine has little use in the urban setting, but can be helpful in rural areas. It is very important in the search for clandestine marijuana cultivation. Open fields applies even though fences have been built and "No Trespassing" signs posted. Areas where there are no established roads can also be searched under this doctrine.

6-3 Abandoned Property

Seizing abandoned property is not an unreasonable search because there is neither an objective nor a subjective expectation of privacy. In most cases, the fact that the property has been abandoned clearly indicates that the owner no longer has any interest in it. This is clear when the property has been discarded in a public place.

A more difficult question arises when trash has been sealed in opaque plastic bags and left in a designated location for a garbage truck to pick up. While the opaque plastic may indicate a subjective expectation of privacy, the Supreme Court has ruled that there is no objective basis for this expectation: Strangers, scavengers, animals, and snoops are free to look through trash. The person throwing out the trash also has no authority to prevent the garbage collectors from rummaging through it or giving it to the police.

The final part of this analysis is determining when something has been abandoned. Dumping items in a trash can and littering the highway are pretty obvious examples of abandonment. A person who merely puts an item in a trash can inside a private home still has the right to retrieve it.

6-4 Consent Searches

A search done with the voluntary consent of a person with apparent authority over the area to be searched does not require probable cause or a search warrant. Three key points must be considered to determine if a search can be based on consent: (1) how the consent was obtained; (2) who can give consent; and (3) what can be searched based on the consent given.

6-4a Standard for Consent

Consent must be given voluntarily. The Supreme Court has specifically refused to require officers to warn suspects that they have a constitutional right to refuse to consent to a search. Each case must be analyzed on the totality of the circumstances that were present when the officers asked for permission to search.

Some factors clearly indicate that the consent is coerced. The consent is not voluntary if the police inform someone that there is a search warrant. Allowing the police to enter under these circumstances is considered to be merely acquiescing to authority. By stating they have a warrant, the police inform people that they do not have the right to refuse entry.

More commonly, the courts look at all of the facts present when the request for consent was made. If officers had their guns drawn, it is highly unlikely consent was voluntary. Other facts considered include the education and intelligence of the suspect, attempts by the police to intimidate the suspect, and whether the suspect already knew his/her rights. The fact that the suspect was in custody and had not been told he/she was "free to go" is considered but is not determinative. The Supreme Court has twice approved searches of passengers on busses when the officers entered the vehicle during a scheduled stop, asked passengers questions, and obtained consent to search a passenger and/or luggage.

6-4b Who Can Consent

Someone with apparent authority over the area to be searched must give consent. Officers may rely on reasonable appearances that a person lives in a house or owns a business.

Ownership, however, is not essential; in fact, the owner may not be able to consent. The key again is reasonable expectation of privacy. A landlord cannot consent to searches of a tenant's apartment, nor can hotel personnel grant permission to search a guest's room. Police cannot rely on consent from people whose personal privacy is not at stake.

If two people have equal rights to a location, either may consent to a search. This commonly applies to husband-wife and roommate situations. For example, either roommate may consent to a search of the kitchen, but if both have separate bedrooms, one may not consent to a search of the other's room. An occupant who is present may consent to a search even though police suspect the person who is absent would object.

The parent-child relationship is more complicated. Very young children do not have the authority to consent to police entering the house. Children generally do not have the right to consent to searches of their parent's room or other private areas of the house. A parent can give police consent to enter the house to search a child's room and possessions. Older children, however, may have their own privacy interests. Paying rent or the fact the parents recognize the child's right to exclude them from his/her room may indicate that a parent cannot give consent. Even if the parent can consent to police entering the room, a teenager may still have an expectation of privacy in locked containers kept in his/her room.

Some states make consent to searches a condition of probation or parole. The Supreme Court approved this practice because it is necessary to facilitate rehabilitation and deter criminal activity. The Court approved searches by probation officers based on "reasonable grounds" even though there was no probable cause. If a police officer conducts a search of a probationer, there must be at least reasonable suspicion that criminal conduct occurred.

6-4c Scope of the Search

The area to be searched and the length of time officers may search are governed by the person giving consent. The search may be stopped at any time without stating a reason for terminating the consent to search.

During a consent search, officers may pick up and examine items thoroughly unless the person giving consent objects. Plain view accompanies a consent search. Anything seen during the search may be seized if there is probable cause to tie it to a crime.

6-5 Employee and Student Drug Testing

As society's concern about drug abuse increased, employers began using pre-employment and in-service drug testing. Two cases involving these tests reached the Supreme Court in 1989. Both involved individuals whose jobs that were sensitive to public safety: railroad employees and U.S. Customs agents involved in drug interdiction or required to carry firearms. The Court balanced the personal interest in privacy against the public's need to be sure that these hazardous jobs were not performed by personnel who were substance abusers. It concluded that drug testing did not require probable cause, reasonable suspicion, or an administrative warrant. It must be noted, however, that the Court considered only two types of jobs directly impacting public safety; it did not authorize random drug tests of all employees. It also did not address the issue of drug testing by private sector employers not governed by government regulations requiring testing.

The Supreme Court also approved school districts' random drug testing policies for students who participate in extracurricular activities. The decisions hinge on two points: The right of schools, as guardians of their students, to impose necessary restrictions; and a showing that there was concern about drug usage at the school. The Court refused to require any type of individualized suspicion that the student tested was using drugs.

6-6 Key Supreme Court Cases

6-6a *Horton v. California:* 496 U.S. 128, 110 L.Ed. 2d 112, 110 S.Ct. 2301 (1990)

Facts: Two masked men with a machine gun and a "stun gun" robbed Wallaker when he returned home. They took cash and jewelry. Based on conversations during the robbery, Wallaker was able to identify Horton's distinctive voice. Sgt. LaRault obtained a search warrant for Horton's home to search for proceeds of the robbery, including three specifically described rings. The warrant application also sought permission to search for weapons but the magistrate did not grant this request. When the warrant was executed, police did not find any property stolen during the robbery, but they did find weapons, including an Uzi machine gun, a .38-caliber revolver, and two stun guns, in plain view and seized them. They also seized items of clothing connecting Horton with the robbery. Sgt. LaRault testified that he was searching for the rings but was also interested in finding other evidence connecting Horton to the robbery. Horton was convicted of robbery.

Issue: Must items be discovered inadvertently to qualify for the Plain View Doctrine?

Reasoning: "It is, of course, an essential predicate to any valid warrantless seizure of incriminating evidence that the officer did not violate the Fourth Amendment in arriving at the place from which the evidence could be plainly viewed. There are, moreover, two additional conditions that must be satisfied to justify the warrantless seizure. First, not only must the item be in plain view, its incriminating character must also be 'immediately apparent.' * * * Second, not only must the officer be lawfully located in a place from which the object can be plainly seen, but he or she must also have a lawful right of access to the object itself. * * * In all events, we are satisfied that the absence of inadvertence was not essential to the Court's rejection of the State's 'plain view' argument in Coolidge.

* * * "As we have already suggested, by hypothesis the seizure of an object in plain view does not involve an intrusion on privacy. If the interest in privacy has been invaded, the violation must have occurred before

the object came into plain view and there is no need for an inadvertence limitation on seizures to condemn it. The prohibition against general searches and general warrants serves primarily as a protection against unjustified intrusions on privacy. But reliance on privacy concerns that support that prohibition is misplaced when the inquiry concerns the scope of an exception that merely authorizes an officer with a lawful right of access to an item to seize it without a warrant.

"In this case the items seized from petitioner's home were discovered during a lawful search authorized by a valid warrant. When they were discovered, it was immediately apparent to the officer that they constituted incriminating evidence. He had probable cause, not only to obtain a warrant to search for the stolen property, but also to believe that the weapons and handguns had been used in the crime he was investigating. The search was authorized by the warrant, the seizure was authorized by the 'plain view' doctrine."

Disposition: Conviction affirmed; discovery of the guns in plain view while executing the search warrant was legal even though officers suspected the guns were in the house before they entered it.

6-6b *Oliver v. United States:* 466 U.S. 170, 80 L.Ed. 2d 214, 104 S.Ct. 1735 (1984)

Facts:

Case 1: Police officers received reports that Oliver was raising marijuana on his farm. They entered the farm by driving past Oliver's house to a locked gate with a "No Trespassing" sign. The officers walked around the gate and along the road for several hundred yards, passing a barn and a parked camper. Someone standing by the camper yelled to them, "No hunting is allowed, come back here." The officers shouted back that they were Kentucky State Police, but found no one when they returned to the camper. They resumed their investigation and found a field of marijuana over a mile from Oliver's house. Oliver was arrested and charged with manufacturing a controlled substance. The trial court suppressed evidence on Oliver's request at a pretrial suppression hearing.

Case 2: Police received an anonymous tip that marijuana was being grown in the woods behind Thornton's residence. Two police officers entered the woods by a path between two houses. They followed the path through the woods and found two fenced marijuana patches. When officers determined that the marijuana was on Thornton's property, they obtained a search warrant and seized the marijuana. Thornton was indicted but the trial court suppressed the marijuana.

Issue: Is evidence discovered while officers are trespassing admissible at trial?

Reasoning: *** "We conclude, as did the Court in deciding *Hester v. United States* [265 U.S. 57 (1924)], that the government's intrusion upon the open fields is not one of those 'unreasonable searches' proscribed by the text of the Fourth Amendment.

"This interpretation of the Fourth Amendment's language is consistent with the understanding of the right to privacy expressed in our Fourth Amendment jurisprudence. Since *Katz v. United States,* 389 U.S. 347 (1967), the touchstone of Amendment analysis has been the question whether a person has a 'constitutionally protected reasonable expectation of privacy.' The Amendment does not protect the merely subjective expectation of privacy, but only 'those expectations that society is prepared to recognize as "reasonable." '

"No single factor determines whether an individual legitimately may claim under the Fourth Amendment that a place should be free of government intrusion not authorized by warrant. In assessing the degree to which a search infringes upon individual privacy, the Court has given weight to such factors as the intention of the Framers of the Fourth Amendment, the uses to which the individual has put a location, and our *societal* understanding that certain areas deserve the most scrupulous protection from government invasions. These factors are equally relevant to determining whether the government's intrusion upon open fields without a warrant or probable cause violates reasonable expectations of privacy and is therefore a search proscribed by the Amendment.

"In this light, the rule of *Hester v. United States* that we reaffirm today, may be understood as providing that an individual may not legitimately demand privacy for activities conducted out of doors in fields, except in the area immediately surrounding the house. This rule is true to the conception of the right of privacy embodied in the Fourth Amendment.***

"In contrast, open fields do not provide the setting for those intimate activities that the Amendment is intended to shelter from government interference or surveillance. There is no societal interest in protecting the privacy of those activities, such as the cultivation of crops, that occur in open fields. Moreover, as a practical matter these lands usually are accessible to the public and the police in ways that a home, an office or commercial structure would not be. It is not generally true that fences or no trespassing signs effectively bar the public from viewing open fields in rural areas. *** For these reasons, the asserted expectation of privacy in open fields is not an expectation that 'society recognizes as reasonable.'

"The historical underpinnings of the 'open fields' doctrine also demonstrate that the doctrine is consistent with respect for 'reasonable expectations of privacy.' As Justice Holmes, writing for the Court, observed in *Hester*, the common law distinguished 'open fields' from the 'curtilage,' and land immediately surrounding and associated with the home. The distinction implies that only the curtilage, not the neighboring open fields, warrants the Fourth Amendment protections that attach to the home. At common law, the curtilage is the area to which extends the intimate activity associated with the 'sanctity of a man's home and the privacies of life,' and therefore has been considered part of home itself for Fourth Amendment purposes. Thus, courts have extended Fourth Amendment protection to the curtilage; and they have defined the curtilage, as did the common law, by reference to the factors that determine whether an individual reasonably may expect that an area immediately adjacent to the home will remain private. Conversely, the common law implies, as we reaffirm today, that no expectation of privacy legitimately attaches to open fields.

"We conclude, from the text of the Fourth Amendment and from the historical and contemporary understanding of its purposes, that an individual has no legitimate expectation that open fields will remain free from warrantless intrusion by government officers."

Disposition: Suppression orders reversed; marijuana found on Oliver's and Thornton's property may be admitted at trial even though the officers were trespassing at the time the evidence was discovered.

6-6c *California v. Greenwood:* 486 U.S. 35, 100 L.Ed. 2d 30, 108 S.Ct. 1625 (1988)

Facts: In early 1984, Investigator Jenny Stracner of the Laguna Beach Police Department learned that a criminal suspect had informed a federal drug enforcement agent that a truck filled with illegal drugs was en route to the address where Greenwood lived. A neighbor had also complained that numerous vehicles stopped at Greenwood's house late at night but stayed only a few minutes. Stracner put Greenwood's home under surveillance and observed several vehicles make brief stops at the house late at night. She also followed a truck from Greenwood's house to a residence that had previously been under investigation as a narcotics trafficking location. She asked the neighborhood's regular trash collector to pick up the plastic garbage bags in front of Greenwood's house and turn the bags over to her without mixing their contents with the garbage from other houses. The garbage truck driver did so. A search of Greenwood's rubbish disclosed items indicative of narcotics use. Information gleaned from the trash search was used in an affidavit for a search warrant. Cocaine and hashish were discovered when the search warrant was executed. Greenwood was arrested and posted bail. Complaints of narcotics trafficking continued. Investigator Robert Rahaeuser obtained Greenwood's trash from the garbage truck and discovered that it again contained evidence of narcotics use. Police obtained a second search warrant and discovered more evidence of narcotics trafficking when it was executed. Greenwood was arrested again. The Superior Court dismissed the charges based on a state court decision that held that warrantless trash searches violated the Fourth Amendment and the California Constitution.

Issue: Can items placed out for trash collection be legally searched without a search warrant?

Reasoning: "The warrantless search and seizure of the garbage bags left at the curb outside the Greenwood house would violate the Fourth Amendment only if respondents manifested a subjective expectation of privacy in their garbage that society accepts as objectively reasonable.

"Here, we conclude that respondents exposed their garbage to the public sufficiently to defeat their claim to Fourth Amendment protection. It is common knowledge that plastic garbage bags left on or at the side of a public street are readily accessible to animals, children, scavengers, snoops, and other members of the public. Moreover, respondents placed their refuse at the curb for the express purpose of conveying it to a third party, the trash collector, who might himself have sorted through respondents' trash or permitted others, such as the police to do so. Accordingly, having deposited their garbage 'in an area particularly suited for public inspection and, in a manner of speaking, public consumption, for the express purpose of having strangers take it,' respondents could have had no reasonable expectation of privacy in the inculpatory items that they discarded.

"Furthermore, as we have held, the police cannot reasonably be expected to avert their eyes from evidence of criminal activity that could have been observed by any member of the public.* * *

"Individual States may surely construe their own constitutions as imposing more stringent constraints on police conduct than does the Federal Constitution. We have never intimated, however, that whether or not a search is reasonable within the meaning of the Fourth Amendment depends on the law of the particular State in which the search occurs. We have emphasized instead that the Fourth Amendment analysis must turn on such factors as 'our societal understanding that certain areas deserve the most scrupulous protection from government invasion.' We have already concluded that society as a whole possesses no such understanding with regard to garbage left for collection at the side of a public street. Respondent's argument is no less than a suggestion that concepts of privacy under the laws of each State are to determine the reach of the Fourth Amendment. We do not accept this submission."

Disposition: Order of Superior Court dismissing drug charges against Greenwood is reversed; the evidence obtained by searching Greenwood's trash may be used at trial.

6-6d *Schneckloth v. Bustamonte:* 412 U.S. 218, 36 L.Ed. 2d 854, 93 S.Ct. 2041 (1973)

Facts: While on routine patrol in Sunnyvale, California at approximately 2:40 A.M., Officer James Rand stopped an automobile for having only one headlight and no license plate light. Six men were in the car. When the driver could not produce a driver's license, the officer asked if any of the others had identification. Joe Alcala, who claimed the car belonged to his brother, was the only one to produce a license. All six occupants climbed out of the car at the officer's request. After two additional officers arrived, Officer Rand asked Alcala if he could search the car. Alcala agreed. The officers did not threaten to arrest anyone and the general atmosphere was congenial when the consent was obtained. Alcala unlocked the trunk and opened the glove compartment. Officers found three stolen checks wadded up under the left rear seat. Bustamonte was convicted on charges of possession of a check with intent to defraud.

Issue: Do officers have to advise a suspect of the right to refuse to allow a search in order to obtain valid consent to conduct a search?

Reasoning: * * * "Just as was true with confessions, the requirement of a 'voluntary' consent reflects a fair accommodation of the constitutional requirements involved. In examining all the surrounding circumstances to determine if in fact the consent to search was coerced, account must be taken of subtly coercive police questions, as well as the possibly vulnerable subjective state of the person who consents. Those searches that are the product of police coercion can thus be filtered out without undermining the continuing validity of consent searches. * * *

"One alternative that would go far toward proving that the subject of a search did know he had a right to refuse consent would be to advise him of that right before eliciting his consent. That, however, is a suggestion that has been almost universally repudiated by both federal and state courts, and we think, rightly so. For it would be thoroughly impractical to impose on the normal consent search the detailed requirements of an effective warning. * * *

"The protections of the Fourth Amendment are of a wholly different order, and have nothing whatever to do with promoting the fair ascertainment of truth at a criminal trial. Rather, as Mr. Justice Frankfurter's opinion for the Court put it in *Wolf v. Colorado,* 338 U.S. 25, the Fourth Amendment protects the 'security of one's privacy against arbitrary intrusion by the police.'" * * *

"Nor can it even be said that a search, as opposed to an eventual trial, is somehow 'unfair' if a person consents to a search. While the Fourth and Fourteenth Amendments limit the circumstances under which the police can conduct a search, there is nothing constitutionally suspect in a person's voluntarily allowing a search. The actual conduct of the search may be precisely the same as if the police had obtained a warrant. And, unlike those constitutional guarantees that protect a defendant at trial, it cannot be said every reasonable presumption ought to be indulged against voluntary relinquishment. * * *

"Much of what has already been said disposes of the argument that the Court's decision in the *Miranda* case requires the conclusion that knowledge of a right to refuse is an indispensable element of a valid consent. The considerations that informed the Court's holding in *Miranda* are simply inapplicable in the present case. In *Miranda* the Court found that the techniques of police questioning and the nature of custodial surroundings produce an inherently coercive situation. The Court concluded that '[u]nless adequate protective devices are employed to dispel the compulsion inherent in custodial surroundings, no statement obtained from the defendant can truly be the product of his free choice.' * * *

"In this case, there is no evidence of any inherently coercive tactics—either from the nature of the police questioning or the environment in which it took place. Indeed, since consent searches will normally occur on a person's own familiar territory, the specter of incommunicado police interrogation in some remote station house is simply inapposite. There is no reason to believe, under circumstances such as are present here, that the response to a policeman's question is presumptively coerced; and there is, therefore, no reason to reject the traditional test for determining the voluntariness of a person's response. *Miranda,* of course, did not reach investigative questioning of a person not in custody, which is most directly analogous to the situation of a consent search, and it assuredly did not indicate that such questioning ought to be deemed inherently coercive.

"It is also argued that the failure to require the Government to establish knowledge as a prerequisite to a valid consent, will relegate the Fourth Amendment to the special province of 'the sophisticated, the knowledgeable and the privileged.' We cannot agree. The traditional definition of voluntariness we accept today has always taken into account evidence of minimal schooling, low intelligence, and the lack of any effective warnings to a person of his rights; and the voluntariness of any statement taken under those conditions has been carefully scrutinized to determine whether it was in fact voluntarily given.

"Our decision today is a narrow one. We hold only that when the subject of a search is not in custody and the State attempts to justify a search on the basis of his consent, the Fourth and Fourteenth Amendments require that it demonstrate that the consent was in fact voluntarily given, and not the result of duress or coercion, express or implied. Voluntariness is a question of fact to be determined from all the circumstances, and while the subject's knowledge of a right to refuse is a factor to be taken into account, the prosecution is not required to demonstrate such knowledge as a prerequisite to establishing a voluntary consent."

Disposition: Conviction affirmed; checks found during the search based on Alcala's voluntary consent are admissible at trial even though officers did not advise him that he had the right to refuse to consent to a search.

6-6e *National Treasury Employees Union v. Raab:* 489 U.S. 656, 103 L.Ed. 2d 685, 109 S.Ct. 1384 (1989)

Facts: In May 1986, the Commissioner of Customs implemented a program that made drug testing a condition of transfer or promotion to positions that met one of three criteria: (1) direct involvement in drug interdiction or enforcement of related laws; (2) carrying a firearm on duty; and (3) handling 'classified' material. When an employee qualifies for a position covered by the drug testing program, he/she is notified by letter of the selection decision and informed that placement is contingent upon successful completion of drug screening. An independent contractor conducts the test; same-sex monitors are present in the bathroom while the sample is obtained but the employee has the right to remain behind a partition. Two laboratory tests are used to detect the presence of marijuana, cocaine, opiates, amphetamines, and phencyclidine. Customs employees who test positive for drugs and can offer no satisfactory explanation are subject to dismissal from the Service but test results may not be used in criminal prosecution. The National Treasury Employees Union brought this suit challenging the right to conduct these tests.

Issue: Can employees about to be assigned to sensitive tasks be subjected to drug tests without probable cause?

Reasoning: "It is clear that the Customs Service's drug testing program is not designed to serve the ordinary needs of law enforcement. Test results may not be used in a criminal prosecution of the employee without the employee's consent. The purposes of the program are to deter drug use among those eligible for promotion to sensitive positions within the Service and to prevent the promotion of drug users to those positions. These substantial interests, no less than the Government's concern for safe rail transportation at issue in *Railway Labor Executives,* present a special need that may justify departure from the ordinary warrant and probable cause requirements.

*** "Under the Customs program, every employee who seeks a transfer to a covered position knows that he must take a drug test, and is likewise aware of the procedures the Service must follow in administering the test. *** Because the service does not make a discretionary determination to search based on a judgment that certain conditions are present, there are simply 'no special facts for a neutral magistrate to evaluate.'

*** "It is readily apparent that the Government has a compelling interest in ensuring that front-line interdiction personnel are physically fit, and have unimpeachable integrity and judgment. Indeed, the Government's interest here is at least as important as its interest in searching travelers entering the country. We have long held that travelers seeking to enter the country may be stopped and required to submit to a routine search without probable cause, or even founded suspicion, 'because of national self protection reasonably requiring one entering the country to identify himself as entitled to come in, and his belongings as effects which may be lawfully brought in.' This national interest in self protection could be irreparably damaged if those charged with safeguarding it were, because of their own drug use, unsympathetic to their mission of interdicting narcotics. *** The public interest demands effective measures to bar drug users from positions directly involving the interdiction of illegal drugs.

"The public interest likewise demands effective measures to prevent the promotion of drug users to positions that require the incumbent to carry a firearm, even if the incumbent is not engaged directly in the interdiction of drugs. Customs employees who may use deadly force plainly 'discharge duties fraught with such risks of injury to others that even a momentary lapse of attention can have disastrous consequences.' ***

"Against these valid public interests we must weight the interference with individual liberty that results from requiring these classes of employees to undergo a urine test. The interference with individual privacy that results from the collection of a urine sample for subsequent chemical analysis could be substantial in some circumstances. We have recognized, however, that the 'operational realities of the workplace' may render entirely reasonable certain work-related intrusions by supervisors and co-workers that might be viewed as unreasonable in other contexts. * * *

"We think Customs employees who are directly involved in the interdiction of illegal drugs or who are required to carry firearms in the line of duty likewise have a diminished expectation of privacy in respect to the intrusions occasioned by a urine test. Unlike most private citizens or government employees in general, employees involved in drug interdiction reasonably should expect effective inquiry into their fitness and probity. Much the same is true of employees who are required to carry firearms. Because successful performance of their duties depends uniquely on their judgment and dexterity, these employees cannot reasonably expect to keep from the Service personal information that bears directly on their fitness. While reasonable tests designed to elicit this information doubtless infringe some privacy expectations, we do not believe these expectations outweigh the Government's compelling interests in safety and in the integrity of our borders.

* * * "The mere circumstance that all but a few of the employees tested are entirely innocent of wrongdoing does not impugn the program's validity. * * * The Service's program is designed to prevent the promotion of drug users to sensitive positions as much as it is designed to detect those employees who use drugs. Where, as here, the possible harm against which the Government seeks to guard is substantial, the need to prevent its occurrence furnishes an ample justification for reasonable searches calculated to advance the Government's goal.

"We think petitioner's second argument—that the Service's testing program is ineffective because employees may attempt to deceive the test by a brief abstention before the test date, or by adulterating their urine specimens—overstates the case. * * * Thus, contrary to petitioners' suggestion, no employee reasonably can expect to deceive the test by the simple expedient of abstaining after the test date is assigned. Nor can he expect attempts at adulteration to succeed, in view of the precautions taken by the sample collector to ensure the integrity of the sample. In all the circumstances, we are persuaded that the program bears a close and substantial relation to the Service's goals of deterring drug users from seeking promotion to sensitive positions.

"In sum, we believe the Government has demonstrated that its compelling interests in safeguarding our borders and the public safety outweigh the privacy expectations of employees who seek to be promoted to positions that directly involve the interdiction of illegal drugs or that require the incumbent to carry a firearm. We hold that the testing of these employees is reasonable under the Fourth Amendment.

"We are unable, on the present record, to assess the reasonableness of the Government's testing program insofar as it covers employees who are required 'to handle classified material.' * * *

"It is not clear, however, whether the category defined by the Service's testing directive encompasses only those Customs employees likely to gain access to sensitive information. Employees who are tested under the Service's scheme include those holding such diverse positions as 'Accountant,' 'Accounting Technician,' 'Animal Caretaker,' 'Attorney (All),' 'Baggage Clerk,' 'Co-op Student (All),' * * *."

Disposition: Policy affirmed; drug testing prior to promotion to positions involving drug interdiction or the carrying of a firearm may be done without individualized suspicion.

6-7 Other Supreme Court Cases

6-7a *Arizona v. Hicks:* 480 U.S. 321, 94 L.Ed. 2d 347, 107 S.Ct. 1149 (1987)

Facts: On April 18, 1984, a bullet was fired through the floor of Hicks's apartment, striking and injuring a man in the apartment below. Police entered Hicks' apartment to search for the shooter, other victims, and weapons. They found and seized three weapons, including a sawed-off rifle and a stocking-cap mask. Officer Nelson noticed two sets of expensive stereo components that seemed out of place in the squalid and poorly furnished apartment. He moved the components to find their serial numbers. He ran the serial number on the turntable and learned that it had been taken in an armed robbery. He seized the turntable immediately. Some time later, a check of serial numbers on other items indicated that they were taken during the same robbery. Police obtained a search warrant to seize the remaining items. Hicks was indicted for robbery but the state court suppressed the evidence because the serial numbers had not been in plain view.

Issue: Are officers allowed to examine items in plain view to determine if they have evidentiary value?

Reasoning: "Officer Nelson's moving of the equipment, however, did constitute a 'search' separate and apart from the search for the shooter, victims and weapons that was the lawful objective of his entry into the apartment. Merely inspecting those parts of the turntable that came into view during the latter search would not have constituted an independent search, because it would have produced no additional invasion of respondent's privacy interest. But taking action, unrelated to the objectives of the authorized intrusion, which exposed to view concealed portions of the apartment or its contents, did produce a new invasion of respondent's privacy unjustified by the exigent circumstances that validated the entry. * * *

"The remaining question is whether the search was 'reasonable' under the Fourth Amendment.

*** "We now hold that probable cause is required [to seize items discovered in plain view]. To say otherwise would be to cut the 'plain view' doctrine loose from its theoretical and practical moorings. The theory of that doctrine consists of extending to nonpublic places such as the home, where searches and seizures without a warrant are presumptively unreasonable, the police's longstanding authority to make warrantless seizures in public places of such objects as weapons and contraband. And the practical justification for that extension is the desirability of sparing police, whose viewing of the object in the course of a lawful search is as legitimate as it would have been in a public place, the inconvenience and the risk—to themselves or to preservation of the evidence—of going to obtain a warrant. Dispensing with the need for a warrant is worlds apart from permitting a lesser standard of cause for the seizure than a warrant would require, i.e., the standard of probable cause. ***

*** "The same considerations preclude us from holding that, even though probable cause would have been necessary for a seizure, the search of objects in plain view that occurred here could be sustained on lesser grounds. A dwelling-place search, no less than a dwelling-place seizure, requires probable cause, and there is no reason in theory or practicality why application of the plain-view doctrine would supplant that requirement. *** In short, whether legal authority to move the equipment could be found only as an inevitable concomitant of the authority to seize it, or also as a consequence of some independent power to search certain objects in plain view, probable cause to believe the equipment was stolen was required."

Disposition: Suppression order affirmed; the stereo components are not admissible at trial because the officer had to move them to locate their serial numbers.

6-7b *Bond v. United States:* 529 U.S. 334, 146 L.Ed. 2d 365, 120 S.Ct. 1462 (2000)

Facts: Bond was a passenger on a Greyhound bus that left California headed for Little Rock, Arkansas. When the bus stopped at the Border Patrol checkpoint in Sierra Blanca, Texas, Agent Cantu boarded the bus. After reaching the back of the bus and satisfying himself that the passengers were lawfully in the United States, Agent Cantu began walking toward the front. Along the way, he squeezed the soft luggage that passengers had placed in the overhead storage space above the seats. When he squeezed a green canvas bag located above Bond's seat, he noticed it contained a "brick-like" object. Bond admitted that the bag was his and agreed to allow Agent Cantu to open it. The "brick" was composed of methamphetamine. Bond was convicted of conspiracy to possess, and possession with intent to distribute, methamphetamine.

Issue: Did Agent Cantu have the right to squeeze a bag that was in plain view?

Reasoning: "Our Fourth Amendment analysis embraces two questions. First, we ask whether the individual, by his conduct, has exhibited an actual expectation of privacy; that is, whether he has shown that 'he [sought] to preserve [something] as private.' Here, petitioner sought to preserve privacy by using an opaque bag and placing that bag directly above his seat. Second, we inquire whether the individual's expectation of privacy is "one that society is prepared to recognize as reasonable." When a bus passenger places a bag in an overhead bin, he expects that other passengers or bus employees may move it for one reason or another. Thus, a bus passenger clearly expects that his bag may be handled. He does not expect that other passengers or bus employees will, as a matter of course, feel the bag in an exploratory manner. But this is exactly what the agent did here. We therefore hold that the agent's physical manipulation of petitioner's bag violated the Fourth Amendment."

Disposition: Conviction reversed; Agent Cantu did not have authority to squeeze the luggage in the overhead bins in an exploratory manner.

6-7c *Kyllo v. United States:* 533 U.S. 27, 121 S.Ct. 2038, 150 L.Ed. 2d 94, (2001)

Facts: Agent Elliott of the U.S. Department of the Interior became suspicious that Kyllo was growing marijuana in his home. Elliot used a thermal imager to scan the triplex where Kyllo lived to determine whether the amount of heat emanating from Kyllo's home was consistent with the use of high-intensity lamps to grow plants. The scan took only a few minutes and was done from a car parked in front of Kyllo's home and also from the street in back of the house. The scan showed that the roof over the garage and a side wall of Kyllo's house were relatively hot compared to the rest of the home and substantially warmer than neighboring homes in the triplex. Agent Elliott concluded that Kyllo was using halide lights to grow marijuana in his house. Based on tips from informants, utility bills, and the thermal imaging, police obtained a warrant authorizing a search of Kyllo's home. They found over 100 marijuana plants.

Issue: Did the use of the thermal imaging device violate the Fourth Amendment?

Reasoning: "'At the very core' of the Fourth Amendment 'stands the right of a man to retreat into his own home and there be free from unreasonable governmental intrusion.' With few exceptions, the question whether a warrantless search of a home is reasonable and hence consitutional must be answered no.

*** "We think that obtaining by sense-enhancing technology any information regarding the interior of the home that could not otherwise have been obtained without physical 'intrusion into a constitutionally protected area' constitutes a search—at least where (as here) the technology in question is not in general public use. This assures preservation of that degree of privacy against government that existed when the Fourth Amendment was adopted. On the basis of this criterion, the information obtained by the thermal imager in this case was the product of a search *** and is presumptively unreasonable without a warrant."

Disposition: Evidence obtained by thermal imaging without a search warrant is not admissible; case is remanded to lower court to determine if, without reference to the illegally obtained information, there was probable cause to issue the warrant.

6-7d *Dow Chemical Company v. United States:* 476 U.S. 227, 90 L.Ed. 2d 226, 106 S.Ct. 1819 (1986)

Facts: Dow Chemical operates a 2,000-acre facility that manufactures chemicals at Midland, Michigan. The facility consists of numerous covered buildings with manufacturing equipment and piping conduits located between the buildings. Dow has elaborate perimeter security at the complex barring ground-level public views of these areas but has not covered the equipment and conduits between the buildings. It also investigates low-level flights by aircraft over the facility. In early 1978, enforcement officials of EPA made an on-site inspection with Dow's consent. The company denied a second request for an inspection. Instead of seeking an administrative warrant, EPA employed a commercial aerial photographer to take photographs of the facility while flying in navigable airspace at altitudes of 12,000, 3,000 and 1,200 feet using a standard, floor-mounted, precision aerial mapping camera. Dow brought suit in federal District Court alleging that the aerial photography violated its Fourth Amendment rights. Dow's motion for summary judgment was granted and EPA was permanently enjoined from taking aerial photographs of Dow's premises.

Issue: Did EPA's aerial photography violate Dow's constitutional rights?

Reasoning: "Dow nevertheless relies heavily on its claim that trade secret laws protect it from any aerial photography of this industrial complex by its competitors, and that this protection is relevant to our analysis of such photography under the Fourth Amendment. That such photography might be barred by state law with regard to competitors, however, is irrelevant to the questions presented here. State tort law governing unfair competition does not define the limits of the Fourth Amendment. The government is seeking these photographs in order to regulate, not to compete with, Dow. * * *

"We turn now to Dow's contention that taking aerial photographs constituted a search without a warrant, thereby violating Dow's rights under the Fourth Amendment. In making this contention, however, Dow concedes that a simple flyover with naked-eye observation, or the taking of a photograph from a nearby hillside overlooking such a facility, would give rise to no Fourth Amendment problem.

* * * "The intimate activities associated with family privacy and the home and its curtilage simply do not reach the outdoor areas or spaces between structures and buildings of a manufacturing plant.

* * * "It may well be, as the Government concedes, that surveillance of private property by using highly sophisticated surveillance equipment not generally available to the public, such as satellite technology, might be constitutionally proscribed absent a warrant. But the photographs here are not so revealing of intimate details as to raise constitutional concerns. Although they undoubtedly give EPA more detailed information than naked-eye views, they remain limited to an outline of the facility's buildings and equipment. The mere fact that human vision is enhanced somewhat, at least to the degree here, does not give rise to constitutional problems. * * *

" We conclude that the open areas of an industrial plant complex with numerous plant structures spread over an area of 2,000 acres are not analogous to the 'curtilage' of a dwelling for purpose of aerial surveillance; such an industrial complex is more comparable to an open field and as such it is open to the view and observation of persons in aircraft lawfully in the public airspace immediately above or sufficiently near the area for the reach of cameras."

Disposition: Summary judgment and injunction reversed; aerial photography of the industrial complex from navigable airspace does not violate the Fourth Amendment.

6-7e *Florida v. Riley:* 488 U.S. 445, 102 L.Ed. 2d 835, 109 S.Ct. 693 (1989)

Facts: Riley lived in a mobile home located on five acres of rural property. A greenhouse was located 10 to 20 feet behind the mobile home. Only two sides of the greenhouse were enclosed but the contents of the greenhouse were obscured from view by surrounding trees, shrubs, and the mobile home. The greenhouse was covered by corrugated roofing panels, but two panels covering 10 percent of the roof were missing. A wire fence surrounding the property was posted with "Do Not Enter" signs. An anonymous tipster to the Pasco County Sheriff's office stated that marijuana was being grown on Riley's property. After discovering that the contents of the greenhouse were not visible from the road, an investigator circled the property twice in a helicopter flying at 400 feet. The investigator, looking through the missing roof panels and the open sides of the greenhouse with his naked eye, identified what he believed to be marijuana plants. Officers obtained a search warrant and seized the marijuana. Riley was charged with possession of marijuana but the trial court granted a motion to suppress the evidence.

Issue: Do observations of buildings near a residence made from aircraft flying in navigable airspace violate the Fourth Amendment?

Reasoning: *** "In this case, as in *Ciraolo,* the property surveyed was within the curtilage of respondent's home. Riley no doubt intended and expected that his greenhouse would not be open to public inspection, and the precautions he took protected against ground-level observation. Because the sides and roof of his greenhouse were left partially open, however, what was growing in the greenhouse was subject to viewing from the air. Under the holding in *Ciraolo,* Riley could not reasonably have expected the contents of his greenhouse to be immune from examination by an officer seated in a fixed-wing aircraft flying in navigable airspace at an altitude of 1,000 feet or, as the Florida Supreme Court seemed to recognize, at an altitude of 500 feet, the lower limit of the navigable airspace for such aircraft. Here, the inspection was made from a helicopter, but as is the case with fixed-wing planes, 'private and commercial flight [by helicopter] in the public airways is routine' in this country, and there is no indication that such flights are unheard of in Pasco County, Florida. Riley could not reasonably have expected that his greenhouse was protected from public or official observation from a helicopter had it been flying within the navigable airspace for fixed-wing aircraft.

"Nor on the facts before us, does it make a difference for Fourth Amendment purposes that the helicopter was flying at 400 feet when the officer saw what was growing in the greenhouse through the partially open roof and sides of the structure. We would have a different case if flying at that altitude had been contrary to law or regulation. But helicopters are not bound by the lower limits of the navigable airspace allowed to other aircraft. Any member of the public could legally have been flying over Riley's property in a helicopter at the altitude of 400 feet and could have observed Riley's greenhouse. The police officer did no more. This is not to say that an inspection of the curtilage of a house from an aircraft will always pass muster under the Fourth Amendment simply because the plane is within the navigable airspace specified by law. But it is of obvious importance that the helicopter in this case *was not* violating the law, and there is nothing in the record or before us to suggest that helicopters flying at 400 feet are sufficiently rare in this country to lend substance to respondent's claim that he reasonably anticipated that his greenhouse would not be subject to observation from that altitude. Neither is there any intimation here that the helicopter interfered with respondent's normal use of the greenhouse or of other parts of the curtilage. As far as this record reveals, no intimate details connected with the use of the home or curtilage were observed, and there was no undue noise, and no wind, dust, or threat of injury. In these circumstances, there was no violation of the Fourth Amendment."

Disposition: Suppression order reversed; marijuana seen with the naked eye from the helicopter flying at 400 feet is admissible because there was no violation of the defendant's privacy.

6-7f *United States v. Dunn:* 480 U.S. 294, 94 L.Ed. 2d 326, 107 S.Ct. 1134 (1987)

Facts: In 1980, federal Drug Enforcement Administration (DEA) agents discovered that Carpenter had purchased large quantities of chemicals and equipment used in the manufacture of amphetamine and phenylacetone. DEA agents obtained a warrant from a state court for the installation of beepers (miniature electronic transmitter tracking devices) in several containers of items Carpenter had ordered. Agents followed the signal from one of the containers for about a week and traced it to Dunn's ranch. The ranch covered 198 acres and was enclosed by a perimeter fence. The house was about one-half mile from the public road. Several interior, barbed-wire fences also existed. The barns were in a fenced area with locked gates about 50 yards from the house. Aerial photographs of the ranch showed Carpenter's truck backed up to a barn behind the ranch house. Signals from two of the beepers were being transmitted from the ranch. Local officers and a DEA agent made a warrantless entry onto the ranch. After crossing two fences, they believed they smelled the odor of phenylacetic acid coming from one of the two barns. Officers only found empty boxes in the smaller barn. They climbed another barbed-wire fence and a wood fence to gain access to the second barn. Standing under the barn's overhang and using a flashlight, one agent saw what he thought was a phenylacetone laboratory, but he did not enter the barn. The officers left but returned twice the next day to verify what they had observed. DEA agents obtained a search warrant from a federal magistrate, which they executed on November 8. Officers arrested Dunn and seized chemicals and equipment as well as bags of amphetamines that were discovered in a closet in the ranch house. Dunn was convicted for conspiracy to manufacture phenylacetone and amphetamine and possession of amphetamine with intent to distribute.

Issue: Is evidence obtained while trespassing on private property in an area away from a dwelling admissible in court?

Reasoning: *** "Drawing upon the Court's own cases and the cumulative experience of the lower courts that have grappled with the task of defining the extent of a home's curtilage, we believe that curtilage questions should be resolved with particular reference to four factors: the proximity of the area claimed to be curtilage to the home, whether the area is included within an enclosure surrounding the home, the nature of the uses to which the area is put, and the steps taken by the resident to protect the area from observation by people passing by. We do not suggest that combining these factors produces a finely tuned formula that, when mechanically applied, yields a 'correct' answer to all extent-of-curtilage questions. Rather, these factors are useful analytical tools only to the degree that, in any given case, they bear upon the centrally relevant consideration—whether the area in question is so intimately tied to the home itself that it should be placed under the home's 'umbrella' of Fourth Amendment protections. Applying these factors to respondent's barn and to the area immediately surrounding it, we have little difficulty in concluding that this area lay outside the curtilage of the ranch house."

Disposition: Conviction affirmed; evidence discovered in Dunn's barn is admissible under the Open Fields Doctrine even though officers were trespassing.

6-7g *Bumper v. North Carolina:* 391 U.S. 543, 20 L.Ed. 2d 797, 88 S.Ct. 1788 (1968)

Facts: Bumper was a suspect in a rape case. Two days after the alleged rape, four officers went to the home of Mrs. Leath (Bumper's 66-year-old grandmother) and found her there with some young children. She met the officers at the front door. One of them announced, "I have a search warrant to search your house." Mrs. Leath responded "Go ahead" and opened the door. Officers found a rifle in the kitchen. At trial, the prosecution claimed that it was relying on consent to search and not on the existence of a search warrant. Bumper was convicted of rape.

Issue: Is consent to search valid if given after officers state that they have a warrant to search the premises?

Reasoning: "When a prosecutor seeks to rely upon consent to justify the lawfulness of a search, he has the burden of proving that the consent was, in fact, freely and voluntarily given. This burden cannot be discharged by showing no more than acquiescence to a claim of lawful authority. A search conducted in reliance upon a warrant cannot later be justified on the basis of consent if it turns out that the warrant was invalid. The result can be no different when it turns out that the State does not even attempt to rely upon the validity of the warrant, or fails to show that there was, in fact, any warrant at all.

"When a law enforcement officer claims authority to search a home under a warrant, he announces in effect that the occupant has no right to resist the search. The situation is instinct with coercion—albeit colorably lawful coercion. Where there is coercion there cannot be consent."

Disposition: Conviction reversed; the rifle seized in Bumper's grandmother's home is not admissible at trial because the consent obtained by telling a person that the officer has a search warrant is not considered voluntary.

6-7h *United States v. Drayton:* 536 U. S. ___, 153 L.Ed. 2d 242, 122 S.Ct. 2105 (2002)

Facts: On February 4, 1999, Drayton and Brown were traveling on a Greyhound bus en route from Ft. Lauderdale, Florida to Detroit, Michigan. The bus made a scheduled stop in Tallahassee, Florida. Three armed, plain-clothes Tallahassee police officers boarded the bus as part of a routine drug and weapons interdiction effort. One officer was stationed at the front of the bus, another at the back, and the third went from passenger to passenger, speaking to them individually about their travel plans. He also sought to match the passengers to the luggage in the overhead racks. The aisle was not blocked. The officer testified that he did not tell passengers of their right to refuse to talk to him, but if a passenger had declined or sought to leave, he/she would have been permitted to do so. Drayton and Brown were asked about their luggage and gave consent to search a green bag. The bag did not contain contraband. Officer Lang noted that both Drayton and Brown were wearing heavy jackets and baggy pants despite the warm weather. Brown gave consent to a search of his person, which revealed packages containing 483 grams of cocaine concealed on his thighs. He was arrested. The officer then asked Drayton for consent to search. Drayton lifted his hands about eight inches off his legs. A pat-down revealed packages, similar to those concealed on Brown, that contained 295 grams of cocaine.

Both were charged in federal court with conspiring to distribute cocaine and possession of cocaine with intent to distribute it. The U.S. District Court denied a motion to suppress the cocaine based on invalid consent to the pat-down searches. The U. S. Court of Appeals reversed.

Issue: Are officers required to inform passengers in a bus of their Fourth Amendment rights prior to asking for consent to search?

Reasoning: "Applying the *Bostick* framework (*Florida v. Bostick* 501 U.S. 429) to the facts of this particular case, we conclude that the police did not seize respondents when they boarded the bus and began questioning passengers. The officers gave the passengers no reason to believe that they were required to answer the officers' questions. When Officer Lang approached respondents, he did not brandish a weapon or make any intimidating movements. He left the aisle free so that respondents could exit. He spoke to passengers one by one and in a polite, quiet voice. Noting he said would suggest to a reasonable person that he or she was barred from leaving the bus or otherwise terminating the encounter.

*** "There was no application of force, no intimidating movement, no overwhelming show of force, no brandishing of weapons, no blocking of exits, no threat, no command, not even an authoritative tone of voice. It is beyond question that had this encounter occurred on the street, it would be constitutional. The fact that an encounter takes place on a bus does not on its own transform standard police questioning of citizens into an illegal seizure. Indeed, because many fellow passengers are present to witness officers' conduct, a reasonable person may feel even more secure in his or her decision not to cooperate with police on a bus than in other circumstances. *** The presence of a holstered firearm thus is unlikely to contribute to the coerciveness of the encounter absent active brandishing of the weapon.

*** " [T]he Court has repeated that the totality of the circumstances must control, without giving extra weight to the absence of this type of warning. Although Officer Lang did not inform respondents of their right to refuse the search, he did request permission to search, and the totality of the circumstances indicates that their consent was voluntary, so the searches were reasonable."

Disposition: Case sent back to district court for trial; the search of the passengers on the bus did not violate the Fourth Amendment and cocaine is admissible.

6-7i *Illinois v. Rodriquez:* 497 U.S. 177, 111 L.Ed. 2d 148, 110 S.Ct. 2793 (1990)

Facts: On July 26, 1985, police were summoned to the residence of Dorothy Jackson in Chicago. Gail Fischer, Ms. Jackson's daughter, met the officers there and showed signs of a severe beating. Fischer told the officers that Rodriguez had assaulted her earlier that day in his apartment. She stated that Rodriguez was currently asleep in his apartment. She consented to accompany officers to the apartment to unlock the door for them with her key so they could arrest Rodriguez. She referred to "our" apartment several times in the conversation and said that her clothes and furniture were there. Fischer unlocked the door and gave the officers permission to enter the apartment. Officers found drug paraphernalia and containers filled with white powder believed to be cocaine in plain view. In the bedroom, they found Rodriguez and two open attaché cases that contained additional containers of white powder. Rodriguez was charged with possession of a controlled substance with intent to deliver. His suppression motion was granted based on testimony that Fischer had moved out of the apartment almost a month before the search; she did not have authority to invite visitors into the apartment when Rodriguez was away; and the key she had used to unlock Rodriguez's door for the officers had been obtained without his knowledge.

Issue: Can police obtain consent to enter and/or search from a person they reasonably believe lives in a residence even though the facts later show that the person had no right to enter?

Reasoning: "We see no reason to depart from this general rule with respect to facts bearing upon the authority to consent to a search. Whether the basis for such authority exists is the sort of recurring factual question to which law enforcement officials must be expected to apply their judgment; and all the Fourth Amendment requires is that they answer it reasonably. The Constitution is no more violated when officers enter without a warrant because they reasonably (though erroneously) believe that the person who has consented to their entry is a resident of the premises, than it is violated when they enter without a warrant because they reasonably (though erroneously) believe they are in pursuit of a violent felon who is about to escape.

*** "As *Stoner* demonstrates, what we hold today does not suggest that law enforcement officers may always accept a person's invitation to enter premises. Even when the invitation is accompanied by an explicit assertion that the person lives there, the surrounding circumstances could conceivably be such that a reasonable person would doubt its truth and not act upon it without further inquiry. As with other factual determinations bearing upon search and seizure, determination of consent to enter must 'be judged against an objective standard: would the facts available to the officer at the moment *** "warrant a man of reasonable caution in the belief" that the consenting party had authority over the premises? If not, then warrantless entry without further inquiry is unlawful unless authority actually exists. But if so, the search is valid."

Disposition: Suppression order reversed; trial court must consider whether officers had a reasonable basis to believe that Fischer had the authority to consent to entry of Rodriguez's apartment.

6-7j *Stoner v. California:* 376 U.S. 483, 11 L.Ed. 2d 856, 84 S.Ct. 889 (1964)

Facts: On the night of October 25, 1960, the Budget Town Food Market in Monrovia, California was robbed by two men, one of whom was described by eyewitnesses as carrying a gun and wearing horn-rimmed glasses and a grey jacket. Stoner's checkbook was found in an adjacent parking lot. Two check stubs indicated payments to Mayfair Hotel in Pomona, California. Monrovia police contacted the Pomona Police Department and learned that Stoner had a criminal record. After viewing a photograph, two eyewitnesses identified Stoner as the man who carried the gun. Officers went to the Mayfair Hotel about 10:00 P.M. on October 27, without any type of warrant. They approached the night desk clerk and asked if Stoner lived at the hotel. The clerk informed them that Stoner lived there but was out at the time. The officers told the clerk that they were there to make an arrest for robbery and that they were concerned about the possibility of Stoner having weapons in his room. The clerk accompanied three officers to Stoner's room, unlocked the door, and said "Be my guest." During a thorough search of the room, officers found horn-rimmed glasses, a gray jacket, and a .45-caliber automatic pistol with a clip and several cartridges. Stoner was arrested two days later in Las Vegas. He was convicted of armed robbery.

Issue: Can a hotel clerk give valid consent to search a guest's room?

Reasoning: "It is important to bear in mind that it was the petitioner's constitutional right which was at stake here, and not the night clerk's nor the hotel's. It was a right, therefore, which only the petitioner could waive by word or deed, either directly or through an agent. It is true that the night clerk clearly and unambiguously consented to the search. But there is nothing in the record to indicate that the police had any basis whatsoever to believe that the night clerk had been authorized by the petitioner to permit the police to search the petitioner's room.

*** "In a closely analogous situation the Court has held that a search by police officers of a house occupied by a tenant invaded the tenant's constitutional right, even though the search was authorized by the owner of the house, who presumably had not only apparent but actual authority to enter the house for some purposes, such as to 'view waste.' The Court pointed out that the officers' purpose in entering was not to view waste but to search for distilling equipment, and concluded that to uphold such a search without a warrant would leave tenants' homes secure only in the discretion of their landlords.

"No less than a tenant of a house, or the occupant of a room in a boarding house, a guest in a hotel room is entitled to constitutional protection against unreasonable searches and seizures. That protection would disappear if it were left to depend upon the unfettered discretion of an employee of the hotel. It follows that this search without a warrant was unlawful."

Disposition: Conviction reversed; evidence found during the search of Stoner's hotel room with permission of the hotel clerk must be excluded from trial.

6-7k *Griffin v. Wisconsin:* 485 U.S. 868, 97 L.Ed. 2d 709, 107 S.Ct. 3164 (1987)

Facts: In September 1980, Griffin (who had a prior felony conviction) was convicted on charges of resisting arrest, disorderly conduct, and obstructing an officer. He was placed on probation. One of the conditions of probation was that he allow any probation officer to search his home without a warrant as long as the probation officer's supervisor approved and there were 'reasonable grounds' to believe contraband would be found. On April 5, 1983, a detective on the Beloit Police Department informed Lew, Griffin's probation officer's supervisor, that there might be guns in Griffin's apartment. Lew, accompanied by another probation officer and three plain-clothes policemen, went to Griffin's apartment. Griffin answered the door and Lew told him that they were going to search his apartment. During the search, the probation officers found a handgun. Griffin was convicted on possession of a firearm by a convicted felon.

Issue: Can a probationer be required to submit to warrantless searches of his/her residence?

Reasoning: "A State's operation of a probation system, like its operation of a school, government office or prison, or its supervision of a regulated industry, likewise presents 'special needs' beyond normal law enforcement that may justify departures from the usual warrant and probable cause requirements. *** To a greater or lesser degree, it is always true of probationers (as we have said it to be true of parolees) that they do not enjoy 'the absolute liberty to which every citizen is entitled, but only *** conditional liberty properly dependent on observance of special [probation] restrictions.'

"These restrictions are meant to assure that the probation serves as a period of genuine rehabilitation and that the community is not harmed by the probationer's being at large. These same goals require and justify the exercise of supervision to assure that the restrictions are in fact observed. Recent research suggests that more intensive supervision can reduce recidivism, and the importance of supervision has grown as probation has become an increasingly common sentence for those convicted of serious crimes. Supervision, then, is a 'special need' of the State permitting a degree of impingement upon privacy that would not be constitutional if applied to the public at large. That permissible degree is not unlimited, however, so we next turn to whether it has been exceeded here.

* * * "A warrant requirement would interfere to an appreciable degree with the probation system, setting up a magistrate rather than the probation officer as the judge of how close a supervision the probationer requires. Moreover, the delay inherent in obtaining a warrant would make it more difficult for probation officials to respond quickly to evidence of misconduct, and would reduce the deterrent effect that the possibility of expeditious searches would otherwise create.* * *

"In such circumstances it is both unrealistic and destructive of the whole object of the continuing probation relationship to insist upon the same degree of demonstrable reliability of particular items of supporting data, and upon the same degree of certainty of violation, as is required in other contexts. In some cases—especially those involving drugs or illegal weapons—the probation agency must be able to act based upon a lesser degree of certainty than the Fourth Amendment would otherwise require in order to intervene before a probationer does damage to himself or society. The agency, moreover, must be able to proceed on the basis of its entire experience with the probationer, and to assess probabilities in the light of its knowledge of his life, character and circumstances.

"To allow adequate play for such factors, we think it reasonable to permit information provided by a police officer, whether or not on the basis of first-hand knowledge, to support a probationer search. The same conclusion is suggested by the fact that the police may be unwilling to disclose their confidential sources to probation personnel. For the same reason, and also because it is the very assumption of the institution of probation that the probationer is in need of rehabilitation and is more likely than the ordinary citizen to violate the law, we think it enough if the information provided indicates, as it did here, only the likelihood ('had or might have guns') of facts justifying the search."

Disposition: Conviction affirmed; probation officers had the right to search Griffin's apartment based on the tip received from the police officer because one of the conditions of probation stated the probationer would submit to warrantless searches of his residence.

6-71 *United States v. Knights:* 534 U.S. 112, 151 L.Ed. 2d 497, 122 S.Ct. 587 (2001)

Facts: Knights was sentenced to summary probation for a drug offense; one of the conditions was that he submit to searches of his person, car, and residence at any time without a warrant or reasonable cause by any probation officer or law enforcement officer. Knights and Simoneau were suspects in a string of more than 30 recent acts of vandalism against Pacific Gas and Electric Company (PG&E). An arson causing $1.5 million in damage to PG&E property occurred three days after Knights was placed on probation. Immediately after the new attack, a detective drove by Knights's apartment and observed Simoneau carrying three cylindrical items believed to be pipe bombs. When the detective looked in Simoneau's parked truck, he observed a Molotov cocktail and explosive materials, a gasoline can, and two brass padlocks that fit the description of the ones removed during the last incident. The detective knew about the conditions of probation and decided to search Knights's apartment. He found detonation cord, ammunition, liquid chemicals, instruction manuals on chemistry and electrical circuitry, bolt cutters, telephone pole-climbing spurs, drug paraphernalia, and a brass padlock stamped "PG&E." Knights was charged in federal court with conspiracy to commit arson and a variety of other offenses. The District Court ruled the evidence must be suppressed because the search was not done for reasons related to the probation.

Issue: Can a police officer search a probationer without probable cause based on conditions of probation that grant the right to conduct searches?

Reasoning: "The judge who sentenced Knights to probation determined that it was necessary to condition the probation on Knights's acceptance of the search provision. It was reasonable to conclude that the search condition would further the two primary goals of probation—rehabilitation and protecting society from future criminal violations. The probation order clearly expressed the search condition and Knights was unambiguously informed of it. The probation condition thus significantly diminished Knights's reasonable expectation of privacy.

*** "The State has a dual concern with a probationer. On the one hand is the hope that he will successfully complete probation and be integrated back into the community. On the other is the concern, quite justified, that he will be more likely to engage in criminal conduct than an ordinary member of the community.... But we hold that ... [the State's] interest in apprehending violators of the criminal law, thereby protecting potential victims of criminal enterprise, may therefore justifiably focus on probationers in a way that it does not on the ordinary citizen.

*** "Although the Fourth Amendment ordinarily requires the degree of probability embodied in the term 'probable cause,' a lesser degree satisfies the Constitution when the balance of governmental and private interests makes such a standard reasonable. Those interests warrant a lesser than probable-cause standard here. When an officer has reasonable suspicion that a probationer subject to a search condition is engaged in criminal activity, there is enough likelihood that criminal conduct is occurring that an intrusion on the probationer's significantly diminished privacy interests is reasonable.

"The same circumstances that lead us to conclude that reasonable suspicion is constitutionally sufficient also render a warrant requirement unnecessary.

. . . "We therefore hold that the warrantless search of Knights, supported by reasonable suspicion and authorized by a condition of probation, was reasonable within the meaning of the Fourth Amendment."

Disposition: Case sent back to lower court to proceed to trial; the officer had the right to search Knights's apartment based on reasonable suspicion.

6-7m *Florida v. Jimeno:* 500 U.S. 248, 114 L.Ed. 2d 297, 111 S.Ct. 1801 (1991)

Facts: Officer Trujillo overheard Jimeno arranging what sounded like a drug transaction over a public telephone. He followed Jimeno's car and stopped him for making a right turn at a red light without stopping. The officer informed Jimeno that he had been stopped for the traffic infraction and that he had reason to believe that Jimeno was carrying narcotics in his car. Officer Trujillo asked for consent to search the car and explained that Jimeno did not have to give his permission. Jimeno stated that he had nothing to hide and consented to the search. Officer Trujillo opened the passenger door after Jimeno's wife exited the car and saw a folded, brown paper bag on the floorboard. He opened it and found a kilogram of cocaine. Both Jimenos were charged with possession of cocaine with intent to distribute. The trial court granted a motion to suppress the contents of the paper bag.

Issue: Does a general consent to search a car include the right to open closed containers the officers find during the search?

Reasoning: * * * "The scope of a search is generally defined by its expressed object. In this case, the terms of the search's authorization were simple. Respondent granted Officer Trujillo permission to search his car, and did not place any explicit limitations on the scope of the search. Trujillo had informed Jimeno that he believed Jimeno was carrying narcotics, and that he would be looking for narcotics in the car. We think that it was objectively reasonable for the police to conclude that the general consent to search respondents' car included consent to search containers within that car which might bear drugs. A reasonable person may be expected to know that narcotics are generally carried in some form of a container. * * * The authorization to search in this case, therefore, extended beyond the surfaces of the car's interior to the paper bag lying on the car's floor.

* * * "Respondents argue, and the Florida trial court agreed, that if the police wish to search closed containers within a car they must separately request permission to search each container. But we see no basis for adding this sort of superstructure to the Fourth Amendment's basic test of objective reasonableness."

Disposition: Suppression motion granted in error; consent to search a car includes consent to search any closed containers found.

6-7n *Skinner v. Railway Labor Executives' Association:* 489 U.S. 602, 103 L.Ed. 2d 639, 109 S.Ct. 1402 (1989)

Facts: In 1985, the Federal Railroad Administration (FRA) established new regulations covering alcohol and drug use by railroad employees. Subpart C requires the railroads to take all practicable steps to assure that all covered employees provide blood and urine samples immediately after major train accidents, impact accidents which result in either reportable injury or damage to railroad property of $50,000 or more, and accidents involving a fatality to any on-duty railroad employee. Employees must be advised of test results and given the opportunity to respond in writing before preparation of an investigative report. Subpart D of the FRA regulations also give railroads the right to require employees to submit to blood or urine tests after a reportable accident or incident if the supervisor has a "reasonable suspicion" that an employee's act or omission contributed to the occurrence or severity of the event; or when specific rule violations occur, including noncompliance with a signal and excessive speeding. Breath tests may be taken if a supervisor has a "reasonable suspicion" that an employee is under the influence of alcohol based on specific, personal observations concerning appearance, behavior, speech, or body odors of the employee. If impairment is suspected, a railroad may require urine tests, but only if two supervisors make the appropriate determination and suspect impairment due to a substance other than alcohol. Employees have the right to give blood samples, which are analyzed at independent laboratories if the tests are intended for use in disciplinary action. If an employee declines to give a blood sample, the railroad may presume impairment, absent persuasive evidence to the contrary. The Railway

Labor Executives' Association brought this suit seeking to enjoin the FRA's regulations.

Issue: Is probable cause required for an employer to conduct mandatory alcohol and drug testing of its employees?

Reasoning: "A railroad that complies with the provisions of Subpart C of the regulations does so by compulsion of sovereign authority, and the lawfulness of its acts is controlled by the Fourth Amendment. * * *

* * * "[W]e are unwilling to accept petitioners' submission that tests conducted by private railroads in reliance on Subpart D will be primarily the result of private initiative. The Government has removed all legal barriers to the testing authorized by Subpart D, and indeed has made plain not only its strong preference for testing, but also its desire to share the fruits of such intrusions. In addition, it has mandated that the railroads not bargain away the authority to perform tests granted by Subpart D. These are clear indices of the Government's encouragement, endorsement, and participation, and suffice to implicate the Fourth Amendment.

* * * "In light of our society's concern for the security of one's person, it is obvious that this physical intrusion, penetrating beneath the skin, infringes an expectation of privacy that society is prepared to recognize as reasonable. The ensuing chemical analysis of the sample to obtain physiological data is a further invasion of the tested employee's privacy interests. Much the same is true of the breath-testing procedures required under Subpart D of the regulations. Subjecting a person to a breathalyzer test, which generally requires the production of alveolar or 'deep lung' breath for chemical analysis implicates similar concerns about bodily integrity and, like the blood-alcohol test we considered in *Schmerber*, should also be deemed a search.

* * * "The Government's interest in regulating the conduct of railroad employees to ensure safety, like its supervision of probationers or regulated industries, or its operation of a government office, school, or prison, 'likewise presents "special needs" beyond normal law enforcement that may justify departures from the usual warrant and probable-cause requirements.' * * *

"The FRA has prescribed toxicological tests, not to assist in the prosecution of employees but rather 'to prevent accidents and casualties in railroad operations that result from impairment of employees by alcohol or drugs.' This governmental interest in ensuring the safety of the traveling public and of the employees themselves plainly justifies prohibiting covered employees from using alcohol or drugs on duty, or while subject to being called for duty. This interest also 'require[s] and justif[ies] the exercise of supervision to assure that the restrictions are in fact observed.' * * *

* * * "In sum, imposing a warrant requirement in the present context would add little to the assurances of certainty and regularity already afforded by the regulations, while significantly hindering, and in many cases frustrating, the objectives of the Government's testing program. We do not believe that a warrant is essential to render the intrusions here at issue reasonable under the Fourth Amendment.

* * * "In limited circumstances, where the privacy interests implicated by the search are minimal, and where an important governmental interest furthered by the intrusion would be placed in jeopardy by a requirement of individualized suspicion, a search may be reasonable despite the absence of such suspicion. We believe this is true of the intrusions in question here.

"By and large, intrusions on privacy under the FRA regulations are limited. To the extent transportation and like restrictions are necessary to procure the requisite blood, breath, and urine samples for testing, this interference alone is minimal given the employment context in which it takes place. * * *

* * * "*Schmerber* thus confirms 'society's judgment that blood tests do not constitute an unduly extensive imposition on an individual's privacy and bodily integrity.'

"The breath tests authorized by Subpart D of the regulations are even less intrusive than the blood tests prescribed by Subpart C. Unlike blood tests, breath tests do not require piercing the skin and may be conducted safely outside a hospital environment and with a minimum of inconvenience or embarrassment. Further, breath tests reveal the level of alcohol in the employee's bloodstream and nothing more. * * *

"A more difficult question is presented by urine tests. Like breath tests, urine tests are not invasive of the body and, under the regulations, may not be used as an occasion for inquiry into private facts unrelated to alcohol or drug use. We recognize, however, that the procedures for collecting the necessary samples, which require employees to perform an excretory function traditionally shielded by great privacy, raise concerns not implicated by blood or breath tests. While we would not characterize these additional privacy concerns as minimal in most contexts, we note that the regulations endeavor to reduce the intrusiveness of the collection process. The regulations do not require that samples be furnished under the direct observation of a monitor, despite the desirability of such a procedure to ensure the integrity of the sample. The sample is also collected in a medical environment, by personnel unrelated to the railroad employer, and is thus not unlike similar procedures encountered often in the context of a regular physical examination.

*** "We do not suggest, of course, that the interest in bodily security enjoyed by those employed in a regulated industry must always be considered minimal. *** Though some of the privacy interests implicated by the toxicological testing at issue reasonably might be viewed as significant in other contexts, logic and history show that a diminished expectation of privacy attaches to information relating to the physical condition of covered employees and to the reasonable means of procuring such information. We conclude, therefore, that the testing procedures contemplated by Subparts C and D pose only limited threats to the justifiable expectation of privacy of covered employees.

"By contrast, the government interest in testing without a showing of individualized suspicion is compelling. Employees subject to the tests discharge duties fraught with such risks of injury to others that even a momentary lapse of attention can have disastrous consequences. ***

*** "By ensuring that employees in safety-sensitive positions know they will be tested upon the occurrence of a triggering event, the timing of which no employee can predict with certainty, the regulations significantly increase the deterrent effect of the administrative penalties associated with the prohibited conduct, concomitantly increasing the likelihood that employees will forgo using drugs or alcohol while subject to being called for duty.

"A requirement of particularized suspicion of drug or alcohol use would seriously impede an employer's ability to obtain this information, despite its obvious importance. Experience confirms the Agency's judgment that the scene of a serious rail accident is chaotic. Investigators who arrive at the scene shortly after a major accident has occurred may find it difficult to determine which members of a train crew contributed to its occurrence. Obtaining evidence that might give rise to the suspicion that a particular employee is impaired, a difficult endeavor in the best of circumstances, is most impracticable in the aftermath of a serious accident. ***

*** "The court also failed to recognize that the FRA regulations are designed not only to discern impairment but also to deter it. Because the record indicates that blood and urine tests, taken together, are highly effective means of ascertaining on-the-job impairment and of deterring the use of drugs by railroad employees, we believe the Court of Appeals erred in concluding that the post-accident testing regulations are not reasonably related to the Government objectives that support them.

"We conclude that the compelling government interests served by the FRA's regulations would be significantly hindered if railroads were required to point to specific factors giving rise to a reasonable suspicion of impairment before testing a given employee. In view of our conclusion that, on the present record, the toxicological testing contemplated by the regulations is not an undue infringement on the justifiable expectations of privacy of covered employees, the Government's compelling interests outweigh privacy concerns."

Disposition: Policy upheld; alcohol and drug testing under the regulations in question may be done without suspicion that an employee to be tested is violating the regulation prohibiting employee use of alcohol or drugs on the job.

6-7o *Board of Education of Independent School District No. 92 of Pottawatomie County v. Earls:* 536 U.S. ___, 153 L.Ed. 2d 735, 122 S.Ct. 2559 (2002)

Facts: In the fall of 1998, the School District adopted the Student Activities Drug Testing Policy (Policy), which requires all middle and high school students to consent to drug testing in order to participate in any extracurricular activity. In practice, the Policy has been applied only to competitive extracurricular activities sanctioned by the Oklahoma Secondary Schools Activities Association, such as the Academic Team, Future Farmers of America, Future Homemakers of America, band, choir, pom pon, cheerleading, and athletics. Under the Policy, students are required to: (1) take a drug test before participating in an extracurricular activity, (2) submit to random drug testing while participating in that activity, and (3) agree to be tested at any time upon reasonable suspicion. Two students filed this suit claiming that the Policy violated their Fourth Amendment rights: Lindsay Earls was a member of the show choir, the marching band, the Academic Team, and the National Honor Society. Daniel James sought to participate in the Academic Team.

Issue: Does a public school policy that requires students who participate in extracurricular activities to submit to random drug testing violate the students' Fourth Amendment rights?

Reasoning: "While schoolchildren do not shed their constitutional rights when they enter the schoolhouse, 'Fourth Amendment rights . . . are different in public schools than elsewhere; the "reasonableness" inquiry cannot disregard the schools' custodial and tutelary responsibility for children.' In particular, a finding of individualized suspicion may not be necessary when a school conducts drug testing.

*** "This procedure [for collecting urine samples] is virtually identical to that reviewed in *Vernonia* (*Vernonia School District 47J v. Acton* 515 U.S. 646 (1995)), except that it additionally protects privacy by allowing male students to produce their samples behind a closed stall. Given that we considered the method of collection in *Vernonia* a 'negligible' intrusion, the method here is even less problematic.

"In addition, the Policy clearly requires that the test results be kept in confidential files separate from a student's other education records and released to school personnel only on a 'need to know' basis. ***

"Moreover, the test results are not turned over to any law enforcement authority. Nor do the test results here lead to the imposition of discipline or have any academic consequences. Rather, the only consequence of a failed drug test is to limit the student's privilege of participating in extracurricular activities. Indeed, a student may test positive for drugs twice and still be allowed to participate in extracurricular activities. ***

"Given the minimally intrusive nature of the sample collection and the limited uses to which the test results are put, we conclude that the invasion of students' privacy is not significant.

"Finally, this Court must consider the nature and immediacy of the government's concerns and the efficacy of the Policy in meeting them. This Court has already articulated in detail the importance of the governmental concern in preventing drug use by schoolchildren. ***

*** "[T]he need to prevent and deter the substantial harm of childhood drug use provides the necessary immediacy for a school testing policy. Indeed, it would make little sense to require a school district to wait for a substantial portion of its students to begin using drugs before it was allowed to institute a drug testing program designed to deter drug use.

"Given the nationwide epidemic of drug use, and the evidence of increased drug use in Tecumseh schools, it was entirely reasonable for the School District to enact this particular drug testing policy. ***

*** "In this context, the Fourth Amendment does not require a finding of individualized suspicion, and we decline to impose such a requirement on schools attempting to prevent and detect drug use by students."

Disposition: Court of Appeals ruling that the Policy is unconstitutional is reversed; School District may implement the Policy.

Chapter Quiz

True/False

1. The Plain View Doctrine applies only if the officer is legally at the location where the observation was made.
2. Under the Plain View Doctrine, an officer may seize an item only if it is contraband.
3. Under the Plain View Doctrine, an officer must have probable cause to seize an item.
4. The Open Fields Doctrine allows evidence to be admitted into court even if police officers were trespassing at the time the evidence was seized.
5. There is no Fourth Amendment prohibition on seizing abandoned property.
6. Valid consent may be obtained from any adult at the location.
7. The owner of a house can always provide valid consent for a search of that house.
8. A police officer must advise a person of his/her Fourth Amendment rights in order to obtain valid consent to conduct a search.
9. A consent search is limited to items in plain view.
10. School districts can impose random drug testing on high school athletes without violating the Fourth Amendment.

Discussion Questions

1. Officer Greenberg was executing a warrant that authorized the seizure of 10 stolen diamond rings believed to be located in Alice's apartment. He was carefully searching the dresser in the bedroom when he found a letter addressed to Alice. He picked it up to look under it and noticed that it was very heavy. He opened it and found counterfeit $20 bills. Is the counterfeit money admissible under the *Plain View Doctrine?* Explain.
2. Officer Freeman was investigating a complaint by neighbors that Jill was growing marijuana in her atrium. He asked the police helicopter to fly by the house and investigate. The helicopter hovered 100 feet above the house and showed its spotlight into the atrium. Officers did not observe marijuana but did see a stolen Rembrandt on the wall. Can the painting be admitted into evidence under the *Plain View Doctrine?* Explain

Chapter 7

Eavesdropping and Wiretapping

Outline

Eavesdropping has probably been done since people began keeping secrets from each other. Electronic surveillance, however, emerged only after the technology developed. Both involve the seizure of private conversations. The key distinction in Supreme Court cases in this area is whether the person making the comments knows a listener is present, not whether electronic equipment is used.

7-1 Eavesdropping and the Misplaced Reliance Doctrine

In situations in which the suspect knew someone was listening, the Supreme Court has placed the burden on the suspect to make sure that he/she can trust everyone who can hear what is said. This is called the Misplaced Reliance Doctrine. It applies whether or not tape recorders or radio transmitters are used. No warrant is required to obtain conversations that can be overheard by the police or their agents based on the misplaced reliance of the suspect.

The facts from two leading cases help explain this doctrine. When Jimmy Hoffa was on trial, in what is called the "*Test Fleet*" case, the Justice Department had another union official, named Partin, released from prison. Partin was instructed to join Hoffa's entourage and report back on Hoffa's out-of-court activities. No electronic monitoring equipment was used. Partin frequented Hoffa's hotel room and overheard conversations about plans to tamper with the jury. The *Test Fleet* case ended with a hung jury. Evidence supplied by Partin was used in a subsequent case in which Hoffa was charged with attempting to bribe jurors. The Supreme Court found this was a case of misplaced reliance. Hoffa knew Partin was present and took the risk that Partin might report jury tampering to the authorities. The fact that the Justice Department had planted Partin had no legal significance.

Federal narcotics agents used concealed radio transmitters in the *White* case. They recorded conversations in public places, restaurants, the defendant's home, and the informant's car. The informant also allowed an agent to hide in a kitchen closet and transmit conversations between the informant and the defendant. All of these recorded conversations were found admissible under the Misplaced Reliance Doctrine. White should have been more careful in deciding whom he could trust. This even applied to the agent in the closet. White should not have relied on his friend who allowed the agents to hide there.

7-2 Reasonable Expectation of Privacy Covers Conversations

Electronic surveillance has particularly troubled the Supreme Court because it has such a great potential for abuse. In both wiretap and bugging cases, the victim might be totally unaware the government is listening. Prior to 1967, electronic surveillance cases had focused on trespassing. Anything the police could accomplish without physically trespassing on the suspect's property was permitted. Sometimes this went to the extreme of measuring to see if a "spike mike" had gone more than halfway into a common wall between two apartments to determine if there had been a trespass.

In *Katz,* agents had probable cause to believe the suspect was using a telephone booth as part of an interstate gambling operation. The government placed listening device on the outside of the public telephone booth without committing a trespass. Even so, the Supreme Court held that the government had violated the Fourth Amendment. There was a reasonable expectation of privacy because Katz entered the telephone booth, closed the door, and kept his voice down. A warrant is required to install electronic listening devices that invade a person's reasonable expectation of privacy.

Statutes authorizing electronic surveillance warrants must provide more precise requirements than those needed for regular search warrants. A description of the offense under investigation and the types of conversations expected to be seized must be included. While the Court has never specifically stated a maximum time period, in *Berger v. New York* it found that two months was too long. Extensions of the original warrant must be based on a showing that probable cause exists for the continuance of the surveillance. Electronic monitoring must cease when the conversation sought has been obtained and the warrant must have a return.

No warrant is required for electronic devices that do not monitor audio messages or the content of messages sent by wire. Pen registers merely record the numbers dialed. The Court found no expectation of privacy in these numbers because the telephone company has access to them. Congress later enacted a law (18 U.S.C. 3121 et.seq.) that mandates officers to obtain court orders prior to installing pen registers. To obtain an order, officers must show the telephone numbers are relevant in an ongoing criminal investigation.

Transponders (sometimes called "bumper beepers") emit a radio signal that makes it possible to track a vehicle or other item without constantly keeping it under visual surveillance. The Court found the electronic device merely facilitates surveillance and does not invade a reasonable expectation of privacy. The Court drew the line, however, when the container holding the transmitter enters a suspect's home.

7-3 Title III of Omnibus Crime Control and Safe Streets Act

Immediately following *Katz* and *Berger*, Congress enacted the Omnibus Crime Control and Safe Streets Act of 1968. Title III was devoted to electronic surveillance. It made it a federal felony to willfully intercept any wire or oral communications by electronic or mechanical devices unless an electronic surveillance warrant has been obtained. Oral communications are covered if a person has both objective and subjective expectations of privacy.

Title III sets up detailed requirements to obtain electronic surveillance warrants. While this statute applies only to federal agents, it has much broader implications because many states have either authorized their officers to proceed under Title III or have used it as a basis for state statutes.

Title III allows electronic surveillance warrants to be issued only for specified crimes, most of which involve espionage, sabotage, treason, assassination of federal officials, organized crime, or drug trafficking. In addition to facts listed in the affidavit seeking a search warrant, the application for an electronic surveillance warrant must include a detailed description of the type of communication to be intercepted and the length of time the surveillance will be conducted. The application must give a full statement of other investigative procedures tried in the case and why it reasonably appears nonelectronic techniques will not work. If the application is for an extension of an existing warrant, the application must also give details of what has been obtained so far or give a reasonable explanation why nothing has been obtained to date.

The entire application for electronic surveillance warrants by federal officers must be approved by the Attorney General, or any Assistant Attorney General specially designated for this purpose, prior to submitting it to a judge. If a state empowers its officers to act under Title III, the screening is done by the principal prosecuting attorney of the county.

The electronic surveillance warrant must specify the identity of the person whose communications are to be intercepted, where the interception is to be done, and the types of communications to be intercepted. It may direct a common carrier, such as the telephone company, to cooperate with the agents executing the warrant. The maximum length of interception under a warrant is 30 days, although shorter periods are preferred.

There is an emergency exception that applies to conspiracies that threaten national security and organized crime activities that necessitate surveillance before a warrant can be obtained. There must be sufficient grounds to obtain a warrant before an emergency interception may be started. An application must be made for a warrant within 48 hours of the start of an emergency interception. If the application is denied, or if no application was made, the interception must stop immediately and anything obtained during the interception is inadmissible in court.

Title III sets up its own exclusionary rule. Illegally obtained conversations may not be used in any hearing, trial, or other proceeding before any court, grand jury, government agency, regulatory body, or legislative committee of the United States or of any of the states, counties, or cities. Anyone whose telephones or premises have been monitored, or anyone whose conversations were seized, has standing.

The Supreme Court has decided several cases regarding Title III. In *Dalia v. United States,* the Court found that the right to enter was a fundamental part of the right to use electronic devices. Re-entry to service the equipment and/or retrieve it at the end of the surveillance was included. No separate search warrant was required. Neither was it necessary to ask for authorization for covert entries when the original surveillance warrant was obtained.

Each person the government has probable cause to believe is involved in the crime and whose conversations are likely to be seized must be named in the warrant. Conversations of other people should only be monitored long enough to determine that there is no authorization to seize them. This does not make incriminating conversations inadmissible if police knew a person, such as the suspect's spouse, was likely to be using the telephone but had no reason to suspect that person's involvement in criminal activity. Each case is to be decided based on an objective review of the facts. The officer's subjective intent is not binding.

While Title III has an emergency provision that may be used in cases involving national security, the Supreme Court has narrowly interpreted its use; it does not give the President, Attorney General, or anyone else an exemption to Title III for wiretaps on "domestic dissidents." The Foreign Intelligence Surveillance Act (FISA)(50 U.S.C. 1801 et seq.) establishes procedures to obtain wiretap warrants in cases involving espionage by foreign governments and their agents. After the attacks on September 11, 2001, the Congress passed the USA PATRIOT ACT. Some of the provisions of this act amended FISA to facilitate conducting electronic surveillance on suspected terrorists.

7-4 Key Supreme Court Cases

7-4a *Hoffa v. United States:* 385 U.S. 293, 17 L.Ed. 2d 374, 87 S.Ct. 408 (1966)

Facts: Hoffa was on trial in Nashville, Tennessee for violating the Taft-Hartley Act. (This trial is referred to as the "*Test Fleet*" trial.) During this trial, Partin, a union official whom the government had released from prison because he knew Hoffa, served as a government informant. Partin made numerous trips to Nashville, where he was continually in the company of Hoffa. Partin made frequent reports to a federal agent regarding conversations between Hoffa and King related to attempts to bribe members of the *Test Fleet* jury. The *Test Fleet* case ended in a hung jury. Partin's reports were used in Hoffa's trial for endeavoring to bribe members of the jury. State and federal charges that were pending against Partin prior to the *Test Fleet* trial were either dropped or not actively pursued.

Issue: Can conversations overheard by a government informant intentionally placed in a criminal defendant's company be used at trial?

Reasoning: "It is contended that only by violating the petitioner's rights under the Fourth Amendment was Partin able to hear the petitioner's incriminating statements in the hotel suite, and that Partin's testimony was therefore inadmissible under the exclusionary rule of *Weeks v. United States.* The argument is that Partin's failure to disclose his role as a government informer vitiated the consent that the petitioner gave to Partin's repeated entries into the suite, and that by listening to the petitioner's statements Partin conducted an illegal 'search' for verbal evidence.

*** "In the present case, however, it is evident that no interest legitimately protected by the Fourth Amendment is involved. It is obvious that the petitioner was not relying on the security of his hotel suite when he made the incriminating statements to Partin or in Partin's presence. Partin did not enter the suite by force or by stealth. He was not a surreptitious eavesdropper. Partin was in the suite by invitation, and every conversation which he heard was either directed to him or knowingly carried on in his presence. The petitioner, in a word, was not relying on the security of the hotel room; he was relying upon his misplaced confidence that Partin would not reveal his wrongdoing. As counsel for the petitioner himself points out, some of the communications with Partin did not take place in the suite at all, but in the 'hall of the hotel,' in the 'Andrew Jackson Hotel lobby,' and 'at the courthouse.'

"Neither this Court nor any member of it has ever expressed the view that the Fourth Amendment protects a wrongdoer's misplaced belief that a person to whom he voluntarily confides his wrongdoing will not reveal it. Indeed, the Court unanimously rejected that very contention less than four years ago in *Lopez v. United States,* 373 U.S. 427. * * *

"Adhering to these views, we hold that no right protected by the Fourth Amendment was violated in the present case."

Disposition: Conviction affirmed; the statements Hoffa made in misplaced reliance on Partin's loyalty are admissible in court.

7-4b *Katz v. United States:* 389 U.S. 347, 19 L.Ed. 2d 576, 88 S.Ct. 507 (1967)

Facts: Katz used a public telephone booth to place calls from Los Angeles to Miami and Boston regarding wagering. At trial, the prosecution used tapes of Katz's side of conversations the FBI obtained by placing a listening device on the outside of the public telephone booth.

Issue: Do law enforcement officers need a warrant to intercept conversations from a public telephone booth?

Reasoning: * * * "But this effort to decide whether or not a given 'area,' viewed in the abstract, is 'constitutionally protected' deflects attention from the problem presented by this case. For the Fourth Amendment protects people, not places. What a person knowingly exposes to the public, even in his own home or office, is not a subject of Fourth Amendment protection. But what he seeks to preserve as private, even in an area accessible to the public, may be constitutionally protected.

"The Government stresses the fact that the telephone booth from which the petitioner made his calls was constructed partly of glass, so that he was as visible after he entered it as he would have been if he had remained outside. But what he sought to exclude when he entered the booth was not the intruding eye—it was the uninvited ear. He did not shed this right to do so simply because he made his calls from a place where he might be seen. No less than an individual in a business office, in a friend's apartment, or in a taxicab, a person in a telephone booth may rely upon the protection of the Fourth Amendment. One who occupies it, shuts the door behind him, and pays the toll that permits him to place a call is surely entitled to assume that the words he utters into the mouthpiece will not be broadcast to the world. To read the Constitution more narrowly is to ignore the vital role that the public telephone has come to play in private communication.

"The Government contends, however, that the activities of its agents in this case should not be tested by Fourth Amendment requirements, for the surveillance technique they employed involved no physical penetration of the telephone booth from which the petitioner placed his calls. It is true that the absence of such penetration was at one time thought to foreclose further Fourth Amendment inquiry for that Amendment was thought to limit only searches and seizures of tangible property. But the premises that property interests control the right of the Government to search and seize has been discredited. Thus, although a closely divided Court supposed in *Olmstead* [277 U.S. 438] that surveillance without any trespass and without the seizure of any material object fell outside the ambit of the Constitution, we have since departed from the narrow view on which that decision rested. Indeed, we have expressly held that the Fourth Amendment governs not only the seizure of tangible items, but extends as well to the recording of oral statements overheard without any 'technical trespass under * * * local property law.' [*Silverman v. United States* 365 U.S. 505]. Once this much is acknowledged, and once it is recognized that the Fourth Amendment protects people—and not simply 'areas'—against unreasonable searches and seizures it becomes clear that the reach of that Amendment cannot turn upon the presence or absence of a physical intrusion into any given enclosure.

"We conclude that the underpinnings of *Olmstead and Goldman* [316 U.S. 129] have been so eroded by our subsequent decisions that the 'trespass' doctrine there enunciated can no longer be regarded as controlling. The Government's activities in electronically listening to and recording the petitioner's words violated the privacy upon which he justifiably relied while using the telephone booth and thus constituted a 'search and seizure' within the meaning of the Fourth Amendment. The fact that the electronic device employed to achieve that end did not happen to penetrate the wall of the booth can have no constitutional significance.

* * * "The Government does not question these basic principles. Rather, it urges the creation of a new exception to cover this case. It argues that surveillance of a telephone booth should be exempt from the usual requirement of advanced authorization by a magistrate upon a showing of probable cause. We cannot agree."

Disposition: Conviction reversed; electronic monitoring of telephone conversations invades a reasonable expectation of privacy and requires prior judicial approval upon a showing of probable cause.

7-4c *Berger v. New York:* 388 U.S. 41, 18 L.Ed. 2d 1040, 87 S.Ct. 1873 (1967)

Facts: The District Attorney's office had received numerous complaints regarding payment of bribes by applicants for liquor licenses. Pansini, who asserted that his bar had been raided in reprisal for failure to pay a bribe for a liquor license, was equipped with a "minifon" recording device and sent for an interview with an employee of the New York State Liquor Authority. The employee advised Pansini that the price for a license was $10,000 and suggested that he contact Neyer, an attorney. Neyer told Pansini that he had worked for the Authority employee before and the employee was aware of the going rate on liquor licenses for downtown clubs. An eavesdropping order was obtained as provided by New York law. It permitted installation of a recording device in Neyer's office for 60 days. Leads obtained during the first 60 days were used to obtain a 60-day order for Steinman's office. After two weeks of eavesdropping, a conspiracy was uncovered involving the issuance of liquor licenses for the Playboy and Tenement clubs in New York City. Berger was indicted as a 'go-between' for the principal conspirators. Tapes of the intercepted conversations were played for the jury. Berger was convicted on two counts of conspiracy to bribe the Chairman of the New York State Liquor Authority.

Issues:

1. Can an electronic surveillance warrant be based on a minimal showing of probable cause?
2. Can an electronic surveillance warrant be issued for a 60-day period?

Reasoning: "The Fourth Amendment commands that a warrant issue not only upon probable cause supported by oath or affirmation, but also 'particularly describing the place to be searched, and the persons or things to be seized.' New York's statute lacks this particularization. It merely says that a warrant may issue on reasonable ground to believe that evidence of crime may be obtained by the eavesdrop. It lays down no requirement for particularity in the warrant as to what specific crime has been or is being committed, nor 'the place to be searched,' or 'the persons or things to be seized' as specifically required by the Fourth Amendment. The need for particularity and evidence of reliability in the showing required when judicial authorization of a search is sought is especially great in the case of eavesdropping. By its very nature eavesdropping involves an intrusion on privacy that is broad in scope. As was said in *Osborn v. United States,* 385 U.S. 323 (1966), the 'indiscriminate use of such devices in law enforcement raises grave constitutional questions under the Fourth and Fifth Amendments,' and imposes 'a heavier responsibility on this Court in its supervision of the fairness of procedures' * * *.

"We believe the statute here is equally offensive. First, as we have mentioned, eavesdropping is authorized without requiring belief that any particular offense has been or is being committed; nor that the 'property' sought, the conversations, be particularly described. The purpose of the probable-cause requirement of the Fourth Amendment, to keep the state out of constitutionally protected areas until it has reason to believe that a specific crime has been or is being committed, is thereby wholly aborted. Likewise, the statute's failure to describe with particularity the conversations sought gives the officer a roving commission to 'seize' any and all conversations. It is true that the statute requires the naming of 'the person or persons whose communications, conversations or discussions are to be overheard or recorded' * * *. But this does no more than identify the person whose constitutionally protected area is to be invaded rather than 'particularly describing' the communications, conversations, or discussions to be seized. As with general warrants this leaves too much to the discretion of the officer executing the order. Secondly, authorization of eavesdropping for a two-month period is the equivalent of a series of intrusions, searches, and seizures pursuant to a single showing of probable cause. Prompt execution is also avoided. During such a long and continuous (24 hours a day) period the conversations of any and all persons coming into the area covered by the device will be seized indiscriminately and without regard to their connection with the crime under investigation. Moreover, the statue permits, and there were authorized here, extensions of the original two-month period—presumably for two months each—on a mere showing that such extension is 'in the public interest.' Apparently the original grounds on which the eavesdrop order was initially issued also form the basis of the renewal. This we believe insufficient without a showing of present probable cause for the continuance of the eavesdrop. Third, the statute places no termination date on the eavesdrop once the conversation sought is seized. This is left entirely in the discretion of the officer. Finally, the statute's procedure, necessarily because its success depends on secrecy, has no requirement for notice as do conventional warrants, nor does it overcome the defect by requiring some showing of special facts. On the contrary, it permits uncontested entry without any showing of exigent circumstances. Such a showing of exigency, in order to avoid notice would appear more important in eavesdropping, with its inherent dangers, than that required when conventional procedures of search and seizure are utilized. Nor does the statute provide for a return on the warrant thereby leaving full discretion in the officer as to the use of seized conversations of innocent as well as guilty parties. In short, the statute's blanket grant of permission to eavesdrop is without adequate judicial supervision or protective procedures."

Disposition: Conviction reversed; the New York statute authorizing the eavesdropping did not require judicial determination of specific conversations justifying use of the electronic device; the warrant authorized eavesdropping for too long a period without renewed showing of probable cause.

7-5 Other Supreme Court Cases

7-5a *United States v. White:* 401 U.S. 745, 28 L.Ed. 2d 453, 91 S.Ct. 1122 (1971)

Facts: During an investigation of White for various narcotics offenses, Jackson, a government informant, had numerous conversations with White. On four occasions, the conversations took place in Jackson's home. Each of these conversations was overheard by an agent concealed, with Jackson's consent, in a kitchen closet, and by a second agent outside the house using a radio receiver. Four other conversations were overheard by use of radio equipment: one in White's home; one in a restaurant; and two in Jackson's car. Jackson did not testify at trial because the government was not able to locate him, but the agents testified to the content of the conversations. White was convicted.

Issue: Can government agents testify at trial concerning monitored radio transmissions of conversations between a criminal suspect and a government informant?

Reasoning: (Note: Plurality opinion) "Our problem is not what the privacy expectation of particular defendants in particular situations may be or the extent to which they may in fact have relied on the discretion of their companions. Very probably, individual defendants neither know nor suspect that their colleagues have gone or will go to the police or are carrying recorders or transmitters. Otherwise, conversation would cease and our problem with these encounters would be nonexistent or far different from those now before us. Our problem, in terms of the principles announced in Katz, is what expectations of privacy are constitutionally 'justifiable'—what expectations the Fourth Amendment will protect in the absence of a warrant. So far, the law permits the frustration of actual expectations of privacy by permitting authorities to use the testimony of those associates who for one reason or another have determined to turn to the police, as well as by authorizing the use of informants in the manner exemplified in Hoffa and Lewis. If the law gives no protection to the wrongdoer whose trusted accomplice is or becomes a police agent, neither should it protect him when that same agent has recorded or transmitted the conversations which are later offered in evidence to prove the State's case.

*** "No different result should obtain where, as in *On Lee* and the instant case, the informer disappears and is unavailable at trial; for the issue of whether specified events on a certain day violate the Fourth Amendment should not be determined by what later happens to the informer. His unavailability at trial and proffering the testimony of other agents may raise evidentiary problems or pose issues of prosecutorial misconduct with respect to the informer's disappearance, but they do not appear critical to deciding whether prior events invaded the defendant's Fourth Amendment rights."

Disposition: Conviction affirmed; trial testimony may be based on monitored radio transmissions of conversations between the defendant and a government informant even though the informant is unavailable to testify at trial.

7-5b *Smith v. Maryland:* 442 U.S. 735, 61 L.Ed. 2d 220, 99 S.Ct. 2577 (1979)

Facts: On March 5, 1976 in Baltimore, Maryland, Patricia McDonough was robbed. She gave the police a description of the robber and a 1975 Monte Carlo automobile she had observed near the crime scene. After the robbery, McDonough began receiving threatening and obscene phone calls from a man identifying himself as the robber. On one occasion, the caller asked her to step out on her front porch; when she did so she saw the 1975 Monte Carlo she described earlier. On March 16, police spotted a man who matched the robber's description driving a Monte Carlo in McDonough's neighborhood. By running the license number, police learned that the car was registered to Michael Smith. The next day, the police department had the telephone company install a pen register at its central offices to record the numbers dialed from Smith's telephone. They did not obtain a warrant for the pen register. The pen register showed that a call was made to McDonough from Smith's telephone on March 17. This information was used to obtain a search warrant for Smith's residence. During the execution of the warrant, police examined Smith's phone book and found McDonough's phone number found written in it. McDonough identified Smith in a lineup conducted after he was arrested. Smith's pretrial request to suppress the evidence found during the search was denied and Smith was convicted.

Issue: Is a warrant required to install a pen register?

Reasoning: "In applying the Katz analysis to this case, it is important to begin by specifying precisely the nature of the state activity that is challenged. The activity here took the form of installing and using a pen register. Since the pen register was installed on telephone company property at the telephone company's central offices, petitioner obviously cannot claim that his 'property' was invaded or that police intruded into a 'constitutionally protected area.' Petitioner's claim rather, is that, notwithstanding the absence of a trespass, the State, as did the Government in Katz, infringed a 'legitimate expectation of privacy' petitioner held. Yet a pen register differs significantly from the listening device employed in Katz, for pen registers do not acquire the contents of communications. *** Given a pen register's limited capabilities, therefore, petitioner's argument that its installation and use constituted a 'search' necessarily rests upon a claim that he had a 'legitimate expectation of privacy' regarding the numbers he dialed on his phone.

"This claim must be rejected. First, we doubt that people in general entertain any actual expectation of privacy in the numbers they dial. *** Telephone users, in sum, typically know that they must convey numerical information to the phone company; that the phone company has facilities for recording this information; and that the phone company does in fact record this information for a variety of legitimate business purposes. Although subjective expectations cannot be scientifically gauged, it is too much to believe that telephone subscribers, under these circumstances, harbor any general expectation that the numbers they dial will remain secret.

"Petitioner argues, however, that, whatever the expectations of telephone users in general, he demonstrated an expectation of privacy by his own conduct here, since he 'us[ed] the telephone *in his house* to the exclusion of all others.' But the site of the call is immaterial for purposes of analysis in this case. Although petitioner's conduct may have been calculated to keep the *contents* of his conversation private, his conduct was not and could not have been calculated to preserve the privacy of the number he dialed. Regardless of his location, petitioner had to convey that number to the telephone company in precisely the same way if he wished to complete his call. The fact that he dialed the number on his home phone rather than on some other phone could make no conceivable difference, nor could any subscriber rationally think that it would.

"Second, even if petitioner did harbor some subjective expectation that the phone numbers he dialed would remain private, this expectation is not 'one that society is prepared to recognize as "reasonable". This Court consistently has held that a person has no legitimate expectation of privacy in information he voluntarily turns over to third parties. ***

*** "We therefore conclude that petitioner in all probability entertained no actual expectation of privacy in the phone numbers he dialed, and that, even if he did, his expectation was not 'legitimate.' The installation and use of a pen register, consequently, was not a 'search' and no warrant was required."

Disposition: Conviction affirmed; no warrant is needed for a pen register.

7-5c *United States v. Knotts:* 460 U.S. 276, 75 L.Ed. 2d 55, 103 S.Ct. 1081 (1983)

Facts: 3M Company notified a narcotics investigator that Armstrong, a former 3M employee, had been stealing chemicals that could be used in manufacturing illicit drugs. Visual surveillance of Armstrong revealed that he had also been purchasing similar chemicals from Hawkins Chemical Company. Investigators observed that Armstrong delivered the purchases to Petschen. With permission of Hawkins Chemical Company, officers installed a beeper inside a five-gallon container for chloroform. Armstrong's next purchase was placed in this container. After Armstrong made his purchases, an officer followed his car using both visual surveillance and the beeper. Armstrong took the container to Petschen's house and transferred it to Petschen's car. Petschen made evasive maneuvers so the investigators relied on beeper signals rather than visual surveillance. Surveillance was continued from a helicopter with a monitoring device. Petschen was tracked to a cabin near Shell Lake, Wisconsin. Officers obtained a search warrant using information from the surveillance and other items. They discovered a fully operable lab to manufacture amphetamine and methamphetamine in the cabin. Knotts was convicted of conspiring to manufacture controlled substances.

Issue: Is a warrant needed to install a transmitting device to monitor the location of a vehicle?

Reasoning: "A person traveling in an automobile on public thoroughfares has no reasonable expectation of privacy in his movements from one place to another. When Petschen traveled over the public streets he voluntarily conveyed to anyone who wanted to look the fact that he was traveling over particular roads in a particular direction, the fact of whatever stops he made, and the fact of his final destination when he exited from public roads onto private property.

"Respondent Knotts, as the owner of the cabin and surrounding premises to which Petschen drove, undoubtedly had the traditional expectation of privacy within a dwelling place insofar as the cabin was concerned. ***

But no such expectation of privacy extended to the visual observation of Petschen's automobile arriving on his premises after leaving a public highway, nor to movements of objects such as the drum of chloroform outside the cabin in the 'open fields.'

*** "Admittedly, because of the failure of the visual surveillance, the beeper enabled the law enforcement officials in this case to ascertain the ultimate resting place of the chloroform when they would not have been able to do so had they relied solely on their naked eyes. But scientific enhancement of this sort raises no constitutional issues which visual surveillance would not also raise."

Disposition: Conviction affirmed; the use of a transmitting device to monitor movement of a five-gallon container in public places did not violate Knotts's Fourth Amendment rights.

7-5d *United States v. Karo:* 468 U.S. 705, 82 L.Ed. 2d 530, 104 S.Ct. 3296 (1984)

Facts: In August 1980, DEA Agent Rottinger learned that Karo, Horton, and Harley had ordered 50 gallons of ether, used to extract cocaine from clothing, from a government informant in Albuquerque, New Mexico. The government obtained a court order authorizing the installation and monitoring of a beeper in one of the cans of ether. Agents substituted their own container, which contained a beeper, for one of the original containers. All 10 cans were painted to give them the same appearance. Agents observed Karo picking up the ether and followed him to his house using visual and beeper surveillance. The beeper was in Karo's house for part of a day and then moved to Horton's house. Two days later, agents discovered that the ether had been moved; the beeper enabled them to trace it to Horton's father's residence. The next day, they traced the beeper to a commercial storage facility. Agents subpoenaed records of the storage company and learned that Horton had rented locker 143; they then confirmed that the beeper was in this locker. Using the beeper, agents traced the ether to another self-storage facility three days later. The owner of the facility gave permission for the DEA agents to install a closed-circuit video camera, which filmed Rhodes and an unidentified woman removing the cans from storage and loading them onto the rear bed of Horton's pickup truck. Using visual and beeper surveillance, agents tracked the cans to a residence in Taos. Information obtained through use of the beeper and visual surveillance was used to obtain a warrant to search the Taos residence. Cocaine and laboratory equipment were seized and Horton, Harley, Steele, and Roth were arrested. Karo, Horton, Harley, Steele, and Roth were indicted for conspiring to possess cocaine with intent to distribute. The District Court granted a pretrial motion to suppress the evidence seized from the Taos residence on the grounds that the warrant to install the beeper was invalid.

Issues:

1. Does installation of a transmitting device in a container with the consent of the original owner constitute a search or seizure within the meaning of the Fourth Amendment if the buyer is unaware of the transmitter?
2. Does monitoring a transmitting device located inside a private house fall under the Fourth Amendment when information is thus obtained that could not have been obtained through visual surveillance?

Reasoning: "It is clear that the actual placement of the beeper into the can violated no one's Fourth Amendment rights. The can into which the beeper was placed belonged at the time to the DEA, and by no stretch of the imagination could it be said that respondents then had a legitimate expectation of privacy in it. The ether and the original 10 cans, on the other hand, belonged to, and were in the possession of Muehlenweg, who had given his consent to any invasion of those items that occurred. Thus, even if there had been no substitution of cans and the agents had placed the beeper into one of the original 10 cans, Muehlenweg's consent was sufficient to validate the placement of the beeper in the can.

*** "We conclude that no Fourth Amendment interest of Karo or of any other respondent was infringed by the installation of the beeper. Rather, any impairment of their privacy interests that may have occurred was occasioned by the monitoring of the beeper.

*** "In this case, had a DEA agent thought it useful to enter the Taos residence to verify that the ether was actually in the house and had he done so surreptitiously and without a warrant, there is little doubt that he would have engaged in an unreasonable search within the meaning of the Fourth Amendment. For purposes of the Amendment, the result is the same where, without a warrant, the Government surreptitiously employs an electronic device to obtain information that it could not have obtained by observation from outside the curtilage of the house. The beeper tells the agent that a particular article is actually located at a particular time in the private residence and is in the possession of the person or persons whose residence is being surveilled. Even if visual surveillance has revealed that the article to which the beeper is attached has entered the house, the later monitoring not only verifies the officers' observations but also establishes that the article remains on the premises. * * *

* * * "We cannot accept the Government's contention that it should be completely free from the constraints of the Fourth Amendment to determine by means of an electronic device, without a warrant and without probable cause or reasonable suspicion, whether a particular article—or a person, for that matter—is in an individual's home at a particular time. Indiscriminate monitoring of property that has been withdrawn from public view would present far too serious a threat to privacy interests in the home to escape entirely some sort of Fourth Amendment oversight.

"We also reject the Government's contention that it should be able to monitor beepers in private residences without a warrant if there is the requisite justification in the facts for believing that a crime is being or will be committed and that monitoring the beeper wherever it goes is likely to produce evidence of criminal activity."

Disposition: Conviction affirmed; installation of the transmitter with the consent of the original owner was legal, but officers were not allowed to use information received by tracking the device inside a private dwelling.

7-5e *United States v. New York Telephone Co.:* 434 U.S. 159, 54 L.Ed. 2d 376, 98 S.Ct. 364 (1977)

Facts: On March 19, 1976, the FBI obtained a court order permitting the installation of pen registers on two telephone lines. The order directed New York Telephone to cooperate with the investigation. It also stated that New York Telephone should be compensated for its work at prevailing rates. New York Telephone agreed to show the FBI agents where the necessary wires were located but refused to lease the necessary lines to the FBI so that the pen register could be installed in an unobtrusive fashion. After a four-day investigation, FBI agents determined that there was no place in the neighborhood where the pen registers could be installed without alerting the suspects.

Issue: Must a telephone company cooperate with investigators by installing pen registers as authorized by a federal court order?

Reasoning: "We do not think that the Company was a third party so far removed from the underlying controversy that its assistance could not be permissible compelled. * * * Moreover, it can hardly be contended that the Company, a highly regulated public utility with a duty to serve the public, had a substantial interest in not providing assistance. Certainly the use of pen registers is by no means offensive to it. The Company concedes that it regularly employs such devices without court order for the purpose of checking billing operations, detecting fraud, and preventing violations of law. * * *

"Finally, we note, as the Court of Appeals recognized, that without the Company's assistance there is no conceivable way in which the surveillance authorized by the District Court could have been successfully accomplished. * * *

* * * "We are convinced that to prohibit the order challenged here would frustrate the clear indication by Congress that the pen register is a permissible law enforcement tool by enabling a public utility to thwart a judicial determination that its use is required to apprehend and prosecute successfully those employing the utility's facilities to conduct a criminal venture."

Disposition: Order is valid; federal courts have the authority to order telephone companies to cooperate with law enforcement in the installation of pen registers.

7-5f *Dalia v. United States:* 441 U.S. 238, 60 L.Ed. 2d 177, 99 S.Ct. 1682 (1979)

Facts: On March 14, 1973, the U.S. Justice Department obtained a Title III warrant authorizing it to install wiretaps on two telephones in Dalia's business for 20 days in order to investigate a conspiracy to steal goods being shipped in interstate commerce. At the end of the 20-day period, the department obtained another warrant that permitted the interception of telephone calls and all oral conversations taking place in Dalia's office. FBI agents entered the business at midnight on April 5 to install the listening devices and remained in the building for three hours; they re-entered the building on May 16 to remove the bug. Conversations relating to concealing and storing the contents of a tractor-trailer full of fabric worth $250,000 were intercepted. Dalia was convicted.

Issue: Does a Title III electronic surveillance warrant authorize covert entry into buildings to install and/or retrieve listening devices?

Reasoning: "Moreover, we find no basis for a constitutional rule proscribing all covert entries. It is well established that law officers constitutionally may break and enter to execute a search warrant where such entry is the only means by which the warrant effectively may be executed. Petitioner nonetheless argues that covert entries are unconstitutional for their lack of notice. This argument is frivolous. * * * We make explicit, therefore, what has long been implicit in our decisions dealing with this subject: The Fourth Amendment does not prohibit per se a covert entry performed for the purpose of installing otherwise legal electronic bugging equipment.

"Petitioner's second contention is that Congress has not given the courts statutory authority to approve covert entries for the purpose of installing electronic surveillance equipment, even if constitutionally it could have done so. * * *

* * * "In sum, we conclude that Congress clearly understood that it was conferring power upon the courts to authorize covert entries ancillary to their responsibility to review and approve surveillance applications under the statute. * * *

"Petitioner's final contention is that, if covert entries are to be authorized under Title III, the authorizing court must explicitly set forth its approval of such entries before the fact.

* * * "It would extend the warrant clause to the extreme to require that, whenever it is reasonably likely that Fourth Amendment rights may be affected in more than one way, the court must set forth precisely the procedures to be followed by the executing officers. Such an interpretation is unnecessary, as we have held—and the Government concedes—that the manner in which a warrant is executed is subject to later judicial review as to its reasonableness. More important, we would promote empty formalism were we to require magistrates to make explicit what unquestionably is implicit in bugging authorizations: that a covert entry, with its attendant interference with Fourth Amendment interests, may be necessary for the installation of the surveillance equipment. We conclude, therefore, that the Fourth Amendment does not require that a Title III electronic surveillance order include a specific authorization to enter covertly the premises described in the order."

Disposition: Conviction affirmed; permission to make necessary covert entries to install and retrieve electronic surveillance equipment was automatically included in the Title III warrant.

7-5g *United States v. Kahn:* 415 U.S. 143, 39 L.Ed. 2d 225, 94 S.Ct. 977 (1974)

Facts: On March 20, 1970, the U.S. Department of Justice obtained a court order under Title III to tap two telephones of Irving Kahn, a suspected bookmaker allegedly running a gambling operation out of his home. The order permitted the interception of conversations of Irving Kahn and "others as yet unknown." During the wiretaps it became apparent that Minnie Kahn (Irving's wife), who had not previously been a suspect, was also involved in the gambling operation. Both Irving and Minnie Kahn were indicted for using a facility in interstate commerce to promote, manage, and facilitate an illegal gambling business. The trial court granted a motion to suppress Minnie's conversations because she was not named in the intercept order.

Issue: Can conversations of a person who was not a criminal suspect at the time the Title III warrant was issued be used in court if the seized conversations indicate that that person is involved in criminal activity?

Reasoning: "We conclude, therefore, that Title III requires the naming of a person in the application or interception order only when the law enforcement authorities have probable cause to believe that that individual is 'committing the offense' for which the wiretap is sought. Since it is undisputed that the Government had no reason to suspect Minnie Kahn of complicity in the gambling business before the wire interception here began, it follows that under the statute she was among the class of persons 'as yet unknown' covered by Judge Campbell's order.

*** "The order signed by Judge Campbell in this case authorized the Government to 'intercept wire communications of Irving Kahn and others as yet unknown *** to and from two telephones, subscribed to by Irving Kahn.' The order does not refer to conversations between Irving Kahn and others; rather, it describes 'communications of Irving Kahn and others as yet unknown' to and from the target telephones. To read this language as requiring that Irving Kahn be a party to every intercepted conversation would not only involve a substantial feat of verbal gymnastics, but would also render the phrase 'and others as yet unknown' quite redundant, since Kahn perforce could not communicate except with others.

*** "Nothing in Title III requires that, despite the order's language, it must be read to exclude Minnie Kahn's communications. As already noted, 18 U.S.C. Section 2518 (1)(b)(iv) and 2518(4)(a) require identification of the person committing the offense only 'if known.' The clear implication of this language is that when there is probable cause to believe that a particular telephone is being used to commit an offense but no particular person is identifiable, a wire interception order may, nevertheless, properly issue under the statute. It necessarily follows that Congress could not have intended that the authority to intercept must be limited to those conversations *between* a party named in the order and others, since at least in some cases, the order might not name any specific party at all."

Disposition: Suppression order reversed; conversations of Minnie Kahn can be used at her trial because agents, when seeking the Title III warrant, had no reason to suspect that her conversations would relate to criminal activity.

7-5h *Scott v. United States:* 436 U.S. 128, 56 L.Ed. 2d 168, 98 S.Ct. 1717 (1978)

Facts: In January 1970, federal agents obtained a Title III wiretap authorization for a telephone registered to Geneva Jenkins. The warrant application named nine individuals who were participating in a conspiracy to import and distribute narcotics in the Washington, D.C. area. It alleged that Jenkins's telephone had been used in furtherance of this conspiracy, particularly by Thurmon who was living with Jenkins. The wiretap order authorized the interception of the conversations of Lee, Thurmon, and "other persons as may make use of the facilities." Agents were ordered to conduct the wiretap in a manner that would minimize the interception of communications that are not otherwise subject to interception. Agents intercepted virtually all conversations even though only 40 percent of them were related to narcotics. At the conclusion of the wiretap, 22 persons were arrested and 14 indicted. The trial court suppressed all intercepted conversations because the agents had not made an effort to minimize the wiretap.

Issue: Must conversations obtained during a legally authorized wiretap be suppressed because there was no good-faith attempt to minimize the intrusiveness of the interception?

Reasoning: "We have since held that the fact that the officer does not have the state of mind which is hypothecated by the reasons which provide the legal justification for the officer's action does not invalidate the action taken as long as the circumstances, viewed objectively, justify that action. * * *

"Petitioners do not appear, however, to rest their argument entirely on Fourth Amendment principles. Rather, they argue in effect that regardless of the search and seizure analysis conducted under the Fourth Amendment, the statute regulating wiretaps requires the agents to make good-faith efforts at minimization and the failure to make such efforts is itself a violation of the statute which requires suppression.

* * * "The statute does not forbid the interception of all nonrelevant conversations, but rather instructs the agents to conduct the surveillance in such a manner as to 'minimize' the interception of such conversations. Whether the agents have in fact conducted the wiretap in such a manner will depend on the facts and circumstances of each case.

"We agree with the Court of Appeals that blind reliance on the percentage of nonpertinent calls intercepted is not a sure guide to the correct answer. Such percentages may provide assistance, but there are surely cases, such as the one at bar, where the percentage of nonpertinent calls is relatively high and yet their interception was still reasonable. The reasons for this may be many. Many of the nonpertinent calls may have been very short. Others may have been onetime only calls. Still other calls may have been ambiguous in nature or involve guarded or coded language. In all these circumstances agents can hardly be expected to know that the calls are not pertinent prior to their termination.

"In determining whether the agents properly minimized it is also important to consider the circumstances of the wiretap. For example, when the investigation is focusing on what is thought to be a widespread conspiracy more extensive surveillance may be justified in an attempt to determine the precise scope of the enterprise. *** The type of use to which the telephone is normally put may also have some bearing on the extent of minimization required. For example, if the agents are permitted to tap a public telephone because one individual is thought to be placing bets over the phone, substantial doubts as to minimization may arise if the agents listen to every call which goes out over that phone regardless of who places the call. On the other hand, if the phone is located in the residence of a person who is thought to be the head of a major drug ring, a contrary conclusion may be indicated.

"Other factors may also play a significant part in a particular case. For example, it may be important to determine at exactly what point during the authorized period the interception was made. During the early stages of surveillance the agents may be forced to intercept all calls to establish categories of nonpertinent calls which will not be intercepted thereafter. Interception of those same types of calls might be unreasonable later on, however, once the nonpertinent categories have been established and it is clear that this particular conversation is of that type."

Disposition: Intercepted conversations are admissible at trial; a review of the intercepted calls shows that all but seven could reasonably have been intercepted under the warrant primarily due to their brief duration and that interception of the remaining calls was reasonable under the facts of the case.

7-5i *United States v. United States District Court, Eastern Michigan:* 407 U.S. 297, 32 L.Ed. 2d 752, 92 S.Ct. 2125 (1972)

Facts: Three defendants were charged with conspiracy to destroy government property. Plamondon was charged with the dynamite bombing of an office of the Central Intelligence Agency in Ann Arbor, Michigan. The government agents overheard conversations between Plamondon and others during wiretaps authorized by the Attorney General "to gather intelligence information deemed necessary to protect the nation from attempts of domestic organizations to attack and subvert the existing structure of the Government." The government claimed that these wiretaps were lawful even though done without judicial authorization based on the President's power to protect national security. There was no evidence that the defendants had either direct or indirect involvement with a foreign power. The District Court ordered the government to make full disclosure of the contents of the wiretaps to the defendants.

Issue: Is a warrant required to conduct wiretaps of domestic dissidents if the wiretap is done to protect national security?

Reasoning: "The Government relies on [18 U.S.C.] 2511(3). It argues that 'in excepting national security surveillance from the Act's warrant requirement Congress recognized the President's authority to conduct such surveillance without prior judicial approval.' * * *

"We think the language of Section 2511(3), as well as the legislative history of the statute, refutes this interpretation. The relevant language is that: 'Nothing contained in this chapter * * * shall limit the constitutional power of the President to take such measures as he deems necessary to protect * * *' against the dangers specified. At most, this is an implicit recognition that the President does have certain powers in the specified areas. Few would doubt this, as the section refers—among other things—to protection 'against actual or potential attack or other hostile acts of a foreign power.' But so far as the use of the President's electronic surveillance power is concerned, the language is essentially neutral.

* * * "In view of these and other interrelated provisions delineating permissible interceptions of particular criminal activity upon carefully specified conditions, it would have been incongruous for Congress to have legislated with respect to the important and complex area of national security in a single brief and nebulous paragraph. This would not comport with the sensitivity of the problem involved or with the extraordinary care Congress exercised in drafting other sections of the Act. We therefore think the conclusion inescapable that Congress only intended to make clear that the Act simply did not legislate with respect to national security surveillance.

* * * "These Fourth Amendment freedoms cannot properly be guaranteed if domestic security surveillance may be conducted solely within the discretion of the Executive Branch. The Fourth Amendment does not contemplate the executive officers of Government as neutral and disinterested magistrates. Their duty and responsibility are to enforce the

laws, to investigate, and to prosecute. But those charged with this investigative and prosecutorial duty should not be the sole judges of when to utilize constitutionally sensitive means in pursuing their tasks. The historical judgment, which the Fourth Amendment accepts, is that unreviewed executive discretion may yield too readily to pressure to obtain incriminating evidence and overlook potential invasions of privacy and protected speech.

*** "But we do not think a case has been made for the requested departure from Fourth Amendment standards. The circumstances described do not justify complete exemption of domestic security surveillance from prior judicial scrutiny. Official surveillance, whether its purpose be criminal investigation or ongoing intelligence gathering, risks infringement of constitutionally protected privacy of speech. Security surveillance are especially sensitive because of the inherent vagueness of the domestic security concept, the necessarily broad and continuing nature of intelligence gathering, and the temptation to utilize such surveillance to oversee political dissent. We recognize, as we have before, the constitutional basis of the President's domestic security role, but we think it must be exercised in a manner compatible with the Fourth Amendment. In this case we hold that this requires an appropriate prior warrant procedure.

*** "Moreover, we do not hold that the same type of standards and procedures prescribed by Title III are necessarily applicable to this case. We recognize that domestic security surveillance may involve different policy and practical considerations from the surveillance of 'ordinary crime.' The gathering of security intelligence is often long range and involves the interrelation of various sources and types of information. The exact targets of such surveillance may be more difficult to identify than in surveillance operations against many types of crime specified in Title III. Often, too, the emphasis of domestic intelligence gathering is on the prevention of unlawful activity or the enhancement of the Government's preparedness for some possible future crises or emergency. Thus, the focus of domestic surveillance may be less precise than that directed against more conventional types of crime."

Disposition: Suppression order affirmed; evidence obtained without a warrant while eavesdropping on domestic dissidents is not admissible at trial.

Chapter Quiz

True/False

1. All forms of eavesdropping done by government agents violate the Fourth Amendment.
2. The Misplaced Reliance Doctrine does not apply if electronic transmission devices are used.
3. The Misplaced Reliance Doctrine does not apply if the government recruits a person to be an informant.
4. A person has a reasonable expectation of privacy in things that are hidden from view but not in conversations.
5. Title III electronic surveillance warrants can authorize both wiretaps and electronic listening devices.
6. The process for obtaining a Title III electronic surveillance warrant is exactly the same as the process for obtaining a search warrant.
7. Title III electronic surveillance warrants are valid for a maximum of 30 days.
8. If a valid Title III electronic surveillance warrant has been obtained, conversations of the person(s) named in the application for the warrant will be admissible in court but all other conversations obtained during the execution of the warrant will be inadmissible.
9. The President of the United States has the authority to order wiretaps on anyone deemed to be a threat to the security of the United States.
10. The Foreign Intelligence Surveillance Act authorizes issuing electronic surveillance warrants in cases involving foreign terrorists.

Discussion Questions

1. Officer Long was assigned to narcotics and was investigating Mack for distributing PCP. Officer Long discovered that Paul, Mack's brother, was in jail on similar charges. He convinced Paul to wear a concealed microphone and try to talk Mack into quitting the drug business. The tape-recorded conversations included Mack's statement, "I'll never quit this business. It's too profitable. I have a big shipment coming in tomorrow." No warrant had been obtained for the concealed microphone. Is the conversation admissible under the *Misplaced Reliance Doctrine*? Explain.

2. Officer Miller was investigating an extortion plot. He consulted the high technology experts and discovered that he could place a very sensitive microphone in the living room of the house across the street from the suspect. By carefully aiming the receiver, he could hear all conversations occurring in the suspect's living room. Does Officer Miller need an *electronic surveillance warrant* to use this type of microphone? Explain.
3. Terry had a new anti-auto theft device installed in her car. If the car was stolen the police could activate the device and a transmitter would send radio signals so that the police could determine exactly where the car was located. Officer Goodwin suspected that Terry was selling drugs. By activating the anti-auto theft device he was able to track Terry to her supplier. From this vantage point he observed a drug transaction and arrested Terry. Should Officer Goodwin have obtained a *Title III* warrant before activating the transmitter? Explain

Chapter 8

Varying Expectations of Privacy: International Borders and Closed Containers

Outline

Due to the compelling interest in protecting the integrity of our national borders, the Supreme Court has said travelers entering the United States have a greatly decreased expectation of privacy at the borders. The Court has set separate standards for many activities of Border Patrol and Customs agents. In many situations, the probable cause requirement of the Fourth Amendment has been relaxed, and at a point of entry into the United States, it normally does not apply at all.

Closed containers, on the other hand, have been found to have a higher expectation of privacy than most other objects. While the Court started out in 1977 with very strict rules, the exceptions that later developed for vehicle searches and booking searches have diluted the impact of the decisions a great deal.

8-1 Searches at the U.S. Border

8-1a People Entering the United States at Border

People and physical items entering the United States may be routinely subjected to thorough searches without cause. This includes strip searches. To qualify for this unlimited right to search, the search must be done by Border Patrol or Customs agents at the border or a point of entry. The searches may be done randomly or on suspicion, however weak, that an undocumented alien is attempting to enter or something is being smuggled into the country.

The Supreme Court stopped short of allowing total discretion to search when it is suspected that a person is carrying narcotics or other contraband in his/her alimentary tract. These cases frequently involve couriers who swallow balloons containing narcotics. To detain a person for a rectal examination, x-ray, or to allow the foreign substances to be expelled from the body naturally, requires reasonable suspicion. Due to the nature of the examination, the time permitted for the detention will be longer than that normally permitted for a field interview. While the Court did not specifically address the issue, it appears logical that this standard would apply to all types of body cavity searches.

8-1b Mail Searches

The justifications for searching incoming mail are the same as those that allow searches of people entering the United States. Customs officers may open and search all mail entering the country without probable cause; reasonable suspicion is enough.

8-1c Boarding Vessels in Navigable Waters

The Supreme Court held that U.S. Customs agents may board vessels in waterways with easy access to the high seas. These stops may be done without any suspicion that the vessel is violating the law. The inspection statutes were designed to protect important government interests. Only random boardings can detect violations.

8-2 Border Patrol Checkpoints

No one rule applies to all Border Patrol activities. The right to detain people and search largely depends on the context of the encounter.

8-2a Fixed Checkpoints

Fixed border checkpoints are permanent Border Patrol stations on major highways entering the United States. They usually are well lighted with signs telling motorists of the upcoming checkpoint. Based on federal legislation, they can be located as far as 100 air miles from the international border. The Supreme Court specifically mentioned the higher levels of supervision that are present at fixed checkpoints as a reason to permit car stops on less cause than is required for other law enforcement activities.

Various levels of searches can occur at a fixed checkpoint. The least intrusive action is for officers to stand in the roadway and stop cars. No suspicion is needed to do this. Cars can be sent to a secondary area (usually a parking lot adjacent to the checkpoint that was constructed for this purpose) for further questioning of the occupants. While this requires some suspicion, the Court has allowed officers to consider a variety of factors, including the fact that the occupants look like foreign nationals. The "pat-down" for weapons authorized by *Terry v. Ohio* may be done if there is reasonable suspicion the person stopped is armed. Officers need probable cause to conduct a thorough search of the person or vehicle.

8-2b Roving Checkpoints

Roving checkpoints are also set up near the border, but they are temporary in nature. Typically, two or more carloads of officers select a spot on a highway near the border and set up a checkpoint. There are no warning signs to alert motorists to the fact that they are approaching a checkpoint. The image of a few officers working alone on a dark highway has caused the Supreme Court to cautiously limit the power to stop and search.

Officers need reasonable suspicion to stop a car and question the occupants about their citizenship; they need probable cause to search the vehicle. Officers at a roving checkpoint actually have no more power than any other police officer to make car stops conduct a search.

8-2c Stops Based on Reasonable Suspicion

In addition to working checkpoints, Border Patrol officers may patrol the border area. Inherent in this is the right to stop people and vehicles based on reasonable suspicion. The totality of the circumstances test is used to determine if the detention is valid. The Supreme Court pointed out that the legality of the stop could be based on the cumulative impact of a number of observations even though some of the actions observed may be subject to innocent interpretation.

8-2d Workplace Inspections

The Supreme Court upheld the right of Immigration and Naturalization Service agents to enter factories and other workplaces to check for undocumented aliens. Even though these workplace sweeps may involve blocking exits to temporarily detain everyone in the building, the Court found that they do not violate the Fourth Amendment.

8-3 Closed Containers That Require Search Warrants

In 1977, the Supreme Court ruled that there was a greater expectation of privacy in closed containers than in many other items. Since that time, several exceptions have been made to this rule. Distinctions have also been made between closed containers that are opened by police and those that are opened by other people and then turned over to the police.

The first two cases regarding closed containers involved luggage that a suspect was carrying immediately prior to being arrested. The Court took a two-step approach to the problem. Based on probable cause that the footlocker contained marijuana, police could seize it without a warrant. This was necessary to prevent it from being removed from the scene and the evidence destroyed. The officers were allowed to retain custody of it long enough to obtain a search warrant. Only after the warrant was obtained could officers search the footlocker.

8-4 Closed Containers That Do Not Require Search Warrants

Four clear exceptions to the closed container rule have emerged; three involve cars. When an occupant of a car is arrested, the entire passenger compartment may be searched. This includes opening closed containers. The Supreme Court also held that closed containers found during the inventory of a car may be opened. Closed containers may also be opened when a vehicle is searched based on probable cause to believe it contains evidence or contraband. In the latter case, items found may be opened without a warrant even though the container was held in police custody for several days between the seizure and the search of the container.

The fourth exception relates to booking searches. Any closed container in the possession of the person being booked may be searched. A routine inventory of everything taken from the arrestee may include what was inside closed containers.

A different rule relates to containers that have already been legally opened. Once legally opened, the expectation of privacy vanishes. A container may be reopened whether originally opened during a legal search by the police, or after it has been opened by someone else (such as a freight company) and turned over to authorities. This rule applies even though the package was resealed before being given to law enforcement authorities.

Sometimes officers intentionally reseal the package and maintain surveillance while the package is delivered to the addressee. This is called a "controlled delivery." Constant surveillance is crucial because the Court found that the recipient may develop a privacy interest in the contents if there is a substantial likelihood that he/she altered the contents of the package between the time it was delivered and when law enforcement officers seized it again.

8-5 Key Supreme Court Cases

8-5a *United States v. Martinez-Fuerte:* 428 U.S. 543, 49 L.Ed. 2d 1116, 96 S.Ct. 3074 (1976)

Facts: Interstate 5 is the principal highway between San Diego and Los Angeles; the San Clemente checkpoint is 66 road miles north of the Mexican border. Approximately one mile south of the checkpoint is a large sign with flashing yellow lights over the highway stating "ALL VEHICLES, STOP AHEAD, 1 MILE." One-quarter of a mile before the checkpoint there are two signs with flashing lights that state "WATCH FOR BRAKE LIGHTS." At the checkpoint there are two large signs with flashing red lights suspended over the highway that state "STOP HERE—U.S. OFFICERS." "Point" agents stand between two lanes of traffic and visually screen all northbound vehicles, which pass by at a very slow speed. In a small number of cases, the "point" agent concludes additional investigation is necessary and directs the car to a secondary inspection area where occupants are asked about their citizenship and immigration status. The average length of time spent on a secondary investigation is three to five minutes.

Martinez-Fuerte approached the San Clemente checkpoint driving a vehicle containing two female passengers who were illegal aliens. The car was directed to the secondary inspection area where Martinez-Fuerte was able to show that he was a lawful resident alien but the passengers admitted being present in the country unlawfully. The women had entered the United States at the San Ysidro port of entry using false papers and rendezvoused with Martinez-Fuerte in San Diego. Martinez-Fuerte was charged with two counts of transporting aliens.

Sifuentes was arrested at a similar checkpoint on U.S. Highway 77 near Sarita, Texas, which is about 90 miles north of Brownsville and 65 to 90 miles from the nearest point of entry from Mexico. All northbound motorists are usually stopped at this checkpoint except for those who are recognized as local inhabitants. Sifuentes drove up to the checkpoint without any visible passengers. When the agent approached the vehicle, he observed four passengers slumped down in their seats. Questioning revealed each passenger was an illegal alien who had met Sifuentes, a U.S. citizen, in the United States by prearrangement after swimming across the Rio Grande. Sifuentes was indicted on four counts of illegally transporting aliens.

Issues:

1. Can a vehicle be stopped for brief questioning of its occupants at a fixed checkpoint even though there is no reason to believe the occupants are illegal aliens?
2. What level of suspicion is needed to refer a vehicle to the secondary inspection area?

Reasoning: "We are concerned here with permanent checkpoints, the locations of which are chosen on the basis of a number of factors. The Border Patrol believes that to assure effectiveness, a checkpoint must be (i) distant enough from the border to avoid interference with traffic in populated areas near the border, (ii) close to the confluence of two or more significant roads leading away from the border, (iii) situated in terrain that restricts vehicle passage around the checkpoint, (iv) on a stretch of highway compatible with safe operation, and (v) beyond the 25-mile zone in which 'border passes' are valid.

"A requirement that stops on major routes inland always be based on reasonable suspicion would be impractical because the flow of traffic tends to be too heavy to allow the particularized study of a given car that would enable it to be identified as a possible carrier of illegal aliens. In particular, such a requirement would largely eliminate any deterrent to the conduct of well-disguised smuggling operations, even though smugglers are known to use these highways regularly.

"While the need to make routine checkpoint stops is great, the consequent intrusion on Fourth Amendment interests is quite limited. The stop does intrude to a limited extent on motorists' right to 'free passage without interruption,' and arguably on their right to personal security. But it involves only a brief detention of travelers during which '[a]ll that is required of the vehicle's occupants is a response to a brief question or two and possibly the production of a document evidencing a right to be in the United States.' Neither the vehicle or its occupants are searched, and visual inspection of the vehicle is limited to what can be seen without a search. This objective intrusion—the stop itself, the questioning, and the visual inspection—also existed in roving-patrol stops. But we view checkpoint stops in a different light because the subjective intrusion—the generating of concern or even fright on the part of lawful travelers—is appreciably less in the case of a checkpoint stop.* * *

"Routine checkpoint stops do not intrude similarly on the motoring public. First, the potential interference with legitimate traffic is minimal. Motorists using these highways are not taken by surprise as they know, or may obtain knowledge of, the location of the checkpoints and will not be stopped elsewhere. Second, checkpoint operations both appear to and actually involve less discretionary enforcement activity. The regularized manner in which established checkpoints are operated is visible evidence, reassuring to law-abiding motorists, that the stops are duly authorized and believed to serve the public interest. The location of a fixed checkpoint is not chosen by officers in the field, but by officials responsible for making overall decisions as to the most effective allocation of limited enforcement resources. We may assume that such officials will be unlikely to locate a checkpoint where it bears arbitrarily or oppressively on motorists as a class. And since field officers may stop only those cars passing the checkpoint, there is less room for abusive or harassing stops of individuals than there was in the case of roving-patrol stops. Moreover, a claim that a particular exercise of discretion in locating or operating a checkpoint is unreasonable is subject to post-stop judicial review.

* * * "Referrals are made for the sole purpose of conducting a routine and limited inquiry into residence status that cannot feasibly be made of every motorist where the traffic is heavy. The objective intrusion of the stop and inquiry thus remains minimal. Selective referral may involve some annoyance, but it remains true that the stops should not be frightening or offensive because of their public and relatively routine nature. Moreover, selective referrals—rather than questioning the occupants of every car—tend to advance some Fourth Amendment interests by minimizing the intrusion of the general motoring public.

* * * "And the reasonableness of the procedures followed in making these checkpoint stops makes the resulting intrusion on the interests of motorists minimal. On the other hand, the purpose of the stops is legitimate and in the public interest, and the need for this enforcement technique is demonstrated by the records in the cases before us. Accordingly, we hold that the stops and questioning at issue may be made in the absence of any individualized suspicion at reasonably located checkpoints.

"We further believe that it is constitutional to refer motorists selectively to the secondary inspection area at the San Clemente checkpoint on the basis of criteria that would not sustain a roving-patrol stop. Thus, even if it be assumed that such referrals are made largely on the basis of apparent Mexican ancestry, we perceive no constitutional violation. As the intrusion here is sufficiently minimal that no particularized reason need exist to justify it, we think it follows that the Border Patrol officers must have wide discretion in selecting the motorists to be diverted for the brief questioning involved.

* * * "[W]e hold that stops for brief questioning routinely conducted at permanent checkpoints are consistent with the Fourth Amendment and need not be authorized by warrant. The principal protection of Fourth Amendment rights at checkpoints lies in the appropriate limitations on the scope of the stop."

Disposition: Motions to suppress evidence should have been denied; vehicles may be briefly stopped at fixed checkpoints without suspicion; referral to secondary inspection area may be done based on any suspicion that immigration laws are being violated.

8-5b *California v. Acevedo:* 500 U.S. 565, 114 L.Ed. 2d 619, 111 S.Ct. 1982 (1991)

Facts: On October 28, 1987, Officer Coleman of the Santa Ana Police Department received a telephone call from a DEA agent in Hawaii. The agent said he had a package containing marijuana that was to have been delivered to the Federal Express office in Santa Ana. He arranged to send Coleman the package which was addressed to Daza in Santa Ana. Coleman verified the contents of the package, when he received it and then took it to the Federal Express office. At about 10:30 A.M. on October 30, Coleman observed Daza claim the package and watched him carry it into his apartment. At 11:45 A.M., Daza left the apartment and dropped the box and the paper that had contained the marijuana into a trash bin. Coleman then left the scene to obtain a search warrant. At 12:05 P.M., officers saw St. George leave the apartment with a knapsack that appeared to be half full. Officers stopped St. George as he drove off; a search of the knapsack revealed 1-1/2 pounds of marijuana. Acevedo arrived at 12:30 P.M. and entered Daza's apartment. He reappeared about 10 minutes later carrying a brown paper bag that looked full, the size of one of the bags in the package from Hawaii. Acevedo put the paper bag in the trunk of his Honda and started to drive away. Fearing the loss of the evidence, police in a marked car stopped him. They found marijuana in the bag in the trunk. Acevedo was convicted on charges of possession of marijuana for sale.

Issue: Can an officer search a closed container found in a vehicle if there is probable cause to believe that it contains contraband or evidence?

Reasoning: * * * "The Court had announced this separate rule, unique to luggage and other closed packages, bags, and containers, in *United States v.*

Chadwick, 433 U.S. 1 (1977). In *Chadwick*, federal narcotics agents had probable cause to believe that a 200-pound double-locked footlocker contained marijuana. The agents tracked the locker as the defendants removed it from a train and carried it through the station to a waiting car. As soon as the defendants lifted the locker into the trunk of the car, the agents arrested them, seized the locker, and searched it. In this Court, the United States did not contend that the locker's brief contact with the automobile's trunk sufficed to make the *Carroll* doctrine applicable. Rather, the United States urged that the search of movable luggage could be considered analogous to the search of an automobile.

"The Court rejected this argument because, it reasoned, a person expects more privacy in his luggage and personal effects than he does in his automobile. Moreover, it concluded that as 'may often not be the case when automobiles are seized,' secure storage facilities are usually available when the police seize luggage.

"In *Arkansas v. Sanders*, 442 U.S. 753 (1979), the Court extended *Chadwick*'s rule to apply to a suitcase actually being transported in the trunk of a car. * * * Although the Court had applied the *Carroll* doctrine to searches of integral parts of the automobile itself, (indeed, in *Carroll*, contraband whiskey was in the upholstery of the seats), it did not extend the doctrine to the warrantless search of personal luggage 'merely because it was located in an automobile lawfully stopped by the police.' Again, the *Sanders* majority stressed the heightened privacy expectation in personal luggage and concluded that the presence of luggage in an automobile did not diminish the owner's expectation of privacy in his personal items.

"In *Ross*, the Court endeavored to distinguish between *Carroll*, which governed the *Ross* automobile search, and *Chadwick*, which governed the *Sanders* automobile search. It held that the *Carroll* doctrine covered searches of automobiles when the police had probable cause to search an entire vehicle but that the *Chadwick* doctrine governed searches of luggage when the officers had probable cause to search only a container within the vehicle. Thus, in a *Ross* situation, the police could conduct a reasonable search under the Fourth Amendment without obtaining a warrant, whereas in a *Sanders* situation, the police had to obtain a warrant before they searched.

* * * "Thus, this Court in *Ross* took the critical step of saying that closed containers in cars could be searched without a warrant because of their presence within the automobile. Despite the protections that *Sanders* purported to extend to closed containers, the privacy interest in those closed containers yielded to the broad scope of an automobile search.

* * * "To the extent that the *Chadwick-Sanders* rule protects privacy, its protection is minimal. Law enforcement officers may seize a container and hold it until they obtain a search warrant. 'Since the police, by hypothesis, have probable cause to seize the property, we can assume that a warrant will be routinely forthcoming in the overwhelming majority of cases.' And the police often will be able to search containers without a warrant, despite the *Chadwick-Sanders* rule, as a search incident to a lawful arrest. * * *

"Finally, the search of a paper bag intrudes far less on individual privacy than does the incursion sanctioned long ago in *Carroll*. In that case, prohibition agents slashed the upholstery on the automobile. This Court nonetheless found their search to be reasonable under the Fourth Amendment. If destroying the interior of an automobile is not unreasonable, we cannot conclude that looking inside a closed container is. In light of the minimal protection to privacy afforded by the *Chadwick-Sanders* rule, and our serious doubt whether that rule substantially serves privacy interests, we now hold that the Fourth Amendment does not compel separate treatment for an automobile search that extends only to a container within the vehicle.

* * * "We therefore interpret *Carroll* as providing one rule to govern all automobile searches. The police may search an automobile and the containers within it where they have probable cause to believe contraband or evidence is contained."

Disposition: Conviction affirmed; the closed container rule does not apply to closed containers in a vehicle if there is probable cause to believe the vehicle contains contraband or evidence.

8-6 Other Supreme Court Cases

8-6a *United States v. Montoya de Hernandez:* 473 U.S. 531, 87 L.Ed. 2d 381, 105 S.Ct. 3304 (1985)

Facts: Montoya de Hernandez arrived at Los Angeles International Airport about midnight, March 5, 1983, on a direct flight from Bogotá, Colombia. A Customs agent reviewed her valid passport and noticed that she had made at least eight trips to either Miami or Los Angeles. During questioning, it was determined that Montoya de Hernandez did not speak English and had no family or friends in the United States. She claimed to have come to the United States to purchase goods for her husband's store in Bogotá. Montoya de Hernandez had $5,000, mostly in $50 bills, but did not have a billfold. She had no checks, way-bills, credit cards, or letters of credit. She had no hotel reservations or appointments with merchandise vendors but indicated that she intended to ride around Los Angeles in taxi cabs and purchase merchandise from stores such as JCPenny and K-Mart for her husband's store. Her one, small suitcase contained four changes of "cold-weather" clothing but she had no shoes other than the high heels she was wearing. Agents suspected that Montoya de Hernandez was a "balloon swallower" who was attempting to smuggle narcotics into this country in her alimentary canal.

Montoya de Hernandez consented to an x-ray of her abdomen but then told inspectors that she was pregnant. She initially consented to the x-ray but withdrew the consent when she learned she would be handcuffed en route to the hospital. She was given the option of returning to Colombia on the next available flight, agreeing to an x-ray, or remaining in detention until she produced a monitored bowel movement. She remained in the customs office, under observation, all night while attempts were made to place her on a flight. During this time, she refused food or drink and refused to go to the toilet. She exhibited symptoms of discomfort consistent with "heroic efforts to resist the usual calls of nature." At about 4:00 P.M., customs officials sought a court order authorizing a pregnancy test, an x-ray, and a rectal examination. The order was issued about midnight. The rectal exam revealed a balloon containing a foreign substance and Montoya de Hernandez was arrested. Over a period of the next four days, she passed 88 balloons containing 528 grams of 80 percent pure cocaine hydrochloride.

Issue: Was the detention justified based on reasonable suspicion that the suspect was smuggling drugs in her alimentary canal?

Reasoning: "Here the seizure of respondent took place at the international border. Since the founding of our Republic, Congress has granted the Executive plenary authority to conduct routine searches and seizures at the border, without probable cause or a warrant, in order to regulate the collection of duties and to prevent the introduction of contraband into this country. This Court has long recognized Congress' power to police entrants at the border. * * *

"Consistent, therefore, with Congress' power to protect the Nation by stopping and examining persons entering this country, the Fourth Amendment's balance of reasonableness is qualitatively different at the international border than in the interior. Routine searches of the person and effects of entrants are not subject to any requirement of reasonable suspicion, probable cause, or warrant, and first-class mail may be opened without a warrant on less than probable cause. * * *

"These cases reflect longstanding concern for the protection of the integrity of the border. This concern is, if anything, heightened by the veritable national crisis in law enforcement caused by smuggling of illicit narcotics, and in particular by the increasing utilization of alimentary canal smuggling. This desperate practice appears to be a relatively recent addition to the smugglers' repertoire of deceptive practices, and it also appears to be exceedingly difficult to detect. * * *

"Balanced against the sovereign's interest at the border are the Fourth Amendment rights of respondent. Having presented herself at the border for admission, and having subjected herself to the criminal enforcement powers of the Federal Government, respondent was entitled to be free from unreasonable search and seizure. But not only is the expectation of privacy less at the border than in the interior, but the Fourth Amendment balance between the interests of the Government and the privacy right of the individual is struck much more favorably to the Government at the border.

* * * "We hold that the detention of a traveler at the border, beyond the scope of a routine customs search and inspection, is justified at its inception if customs agents, considering all the facts surrounding the traveler and her trip, reasonably suspect that the traveler is smuggling contraband in her alimentary canal.

* * * "Under this standard officials at the border must have a 'particularized and objective basis for suspecting the particular person' of alimentary canal smuggling.

* * * "Respondent's detention was long, uncomfortable, indeed, humiliating; but both its length and its discomfort resulted solely from the method by which she chose to smuggle illicit drugs into this country. * * * Here, by analogy [to *Adams v. Williams*], in the presence of articulable suspicion of smuggling in her alimentary canal, the customs officers were not required by the Fourth Amendment to pass respondent and her 88 cocaine-filled balloons into the interior. Her detention for the period of time necessary to either verify or dispel the suspicion was not unreasonable."

Disposition: Conviction affirmed; Customs agents had reasonable suspicion that Montoya de Hernandez was smuggling narcotics in her alimentary tract and were justified in detaining her.

8-6b *United States v. Ramsey:* 431 U.S. 606, 52 L.Ed. 2d 617, 97 S.Ct. 1972 (1977)

Facts: A Customs officer in New York, without knowledge of the activities in Bangkok, spotted eight bulky envelopes in an incoming mail bag from Thailand. The envelopes, all apparently typed by the same typewriter and addressed to four different addresses in Washington, D.C., were opened because of their weight and the fact they felt like they contained something other than correspondence. DEA agents checked the contents and then resealed them for controlled delivery. DEA agents observed Kelly collect the envelopes from three different addresses and then rendezvous with Ramsey. He gave Ramsey a bag containing the six envelopes, which were filled with heroin, $1,100 in cash, and "cutting" material for the heroin. Both were arrested.

Issue: What level of suspicion is needed to open incoming first-class mail at the international border?

Reasoning: * * * "The border search exception is grounded in the recognized right of the sovereign to control, subject to substantive limitations imposed by the Constitution, who and what may enter the country. It is clear that there is nothing in the rationale behind the border search exception which suggests that the mode of entry will be critical. * * * Surely no different constitutional standard should apply simply because the envelopes were mailed, not carried. The critical fact is that the envelopes cross the border and enter this country, not that they are brought in by one mode of transportation rather than another. It is their entry into this country from without it that makes a resulting search 'reasonable.'

* * * "Nor do we agree that, under the circumstances presented by this case, First Amendment considerations dictate a full panoply of Fourth Amendment rights prior to the border search of mailed letters. There is, again, no reason to distinguish between letters mailed into the country, and letters carried on the traveler's person. More fundamentally, however, the existing system of border searches has not been shown to invade protected First Amendment rights, and hence there is no reason to think that the potential presence of correspondence makes the otherwise constitutionally reasonable search 'unreasonable.'

"The statute in question requires that there be 'reasonable cause to believe' the customs laws are being violated prior to the opening of envelopes. Applicable postal regulations flatly prohibit, under all circumstances, the reading of correspondence absent a search warrant. * * *

"We therefore conclude that the Fourth Amendment does not interdict the actions taken by Inspector Kallnischkies in opening and searching the eight envelopes."

Disposition: Conviction affirmed; the statute permitting incoming international mail to be opened and searched at the U.S. border based on reasonable suspicion is constitutional.

8-6c *United States v. Villamonte-Marquez:* 462 U.S. 579, 77 L.Ed. 2d 22, 103 S.Ct. 2573 (1983)

Facts: Near midday on March 6, 1980, customs officers and Louisiana state policemen were patrolling the Calcasieu River Ship Channel about 18 miles inland from the Gulf coast, when they sighted the Henry Morgan II, a 40-foot sailboat anchored facing east on the west side of the channel. The Calcasieu River Ship Channel connects the Gulf of Mexico with Lake Charles, Louisiana, a designated Customs Port of Entry. As the officers watched, a freighter moved north in the channel, creating a huge wake that rocked the Henry Morgan II violently from side to side. Officers on the patrol boat approached the sailboat and asked Hamparian, the only person on deck, if the sailboat and crew were all right. Hamparian shrugged his shoulders in an unresponsive manner. A Customs officer and a Louisiana State Police officer boarded the Henry Morgan II and asked to see the vessel's documentation. While examining the documents, Officer Wilkins smelled what he thought to be burning marijuana. Looking through an open hatch, he observed burlap-wrapped bales that proved to be marijuana. Villamonte-Marquez was on a sleeping bag atop the bales. The officers arrested Hamparian and Villamonte-Marquez and gave them Miranda warnings. A subsequent search revealed 5,800 pounds of marijuana stored in every conceivable place. The defendants were convicted of conspiring to import marijuana, importing marijuana, conspiring to possess marijuana with intent to distribute, and possession with intent to distribute.

Issue: What is the standard for boarding and searching vessels in navigable waters with access to the high seas?

Reasoning: * * * "We briefly recapitulate the reasons * * * which lead us to conclude that the Government's boarding of the Henry Morgan II did not violate the Fourth Amendment. In a lineal ancestor to the statute at issue here the First Congress clearly authorized the suspicionless boarding of vessels, reflecting its view that such boardings are not contrary to the Fourth Amendment; this gives the statute before us an impressive historical pedigree. Random stops without any articulable suspicion of vehicles away from the border are not permissible under the Fourth Amendment, but stops at fixed checkpoints or at roadblocks are. The nature of waterborne commerce in waters providing ready access to the open sea is sufficiently different from the nature of vehicular traffic on highways as to make possible alternatives to the sort of 'stop' made in this case less likely to accomplish the obviously essential governmental purpose involved. The system of prescribed outward markings used by States for vehicle registration is also significantly different than the system of external markings on vessels, and the extent and type of documentation required by federal law is a good deal more variable and more complex than are the state vehicle registration laws. The nature of the governmental interest in assuring compliance with documentation requirements, particularly in waters where the need to deter or apprehend smugglers is great, are substantial; the type of intrusion made in this case, while not minimal, is limited.

"All of these factors lead us to conclude that the action of the Customs officers in stopping and boarding the Henry Morgan II was 'reasonable,' and was therefore consistent with the Fourth Amendment."

Disposition: Convictions affirmed; the statute authorizing boarding vessels in navigable waters near the high seas without probable cause or reasonable suspicion does not violate the Fourth Amendment.

8-6d *United States v. Ortiz:* 422 U.S. 891, 45 L.Ed. 2d 623, 95 S.Ct. 2585 (1975)

Facts: On November 12, 1973, Border Patrol officers stopped Ortiz's car for a routine immigration search, without suspicion of illegal activity, at the fixed checkpoint on Highway 5 in San Clemente, California. Officers found three aliens concealed in the trunk. Ortiz was arrested on three counts of transporting aliens who were in the country illegally.

Issue: Must vehicle searches at fixed checkpoints be based on probable cause?

Reasoning: * * * "While the differences between a roving patrol and a checkpoint would be significant in determining the propriety of the stop, which is considerably less intrusive than a search, they do not appear to make any difference in the search itself. The greater regularity attending the stop does not mitigate the invasion of privacy that a search entails. Nor do checkpoint procedures significantly reduce the likelihood of embarrassment. Motorists whose cars are searched, unlike those who are only questioned, may not be reassured by seeing that the Border Patrol searches other cars as well. Where only a few are singled out for a search, as at San Clemente, motorists may find the searches especially offensive.

"Moreover, we are not persuaded that the checkpoint limits to any meaningful extent the officer's discretion to select cars for search. * * *

* * * "A search, even of an automobile, is a substantial invasion of privacy. To protect that privacy from official arbitrariness, the Court always has regarded probable cause as the minimum requirement for a lawful

search. We are not persuaded that the differences between roving patrols and traffic checkpoints justify dispensing in this case with the safeguards we required in *Almeida-Sanchez.* We therefore follow that decision and hold that at traffic checkpoints removed from the border and its functional equivalents, officers may not search private vehicles without consent or probable cause."

Disposition: Conviction reversed; officers at fixed checkpoint need consent or probable cause to search a vehicle.

8-6e *United States v. Brignoni-Ponce:* 422 U.S. 873, 45 L.Ed. 2d 607, 95 S.Ct. 2574 (1975)

Facts: On the evening of March 11, 1973, Brignoni-Ponce drove past the Border Patrol's San Clemente checkpoint, which was closed due to inclement weather. Two officers were observing northbound traffic from a patrol car parked at the side of the highway. The patrol car's headlights illuminated passing cars. The officers pursued Brignoni-Ponce's car because its three occupants appeared to be of Mexican descent. Officers questioned Brignoni-Ponce and the passengers and determined that the two passengers were aliens who had entered the country illegally. All three were arrested. Brignoni-Ponce was charged with transporting illegal immigrants. Note: This case is treated as a roving checkpoint case because the fixed checkpoint was closed at the time the stop was made.

Issue: Can a person be stopped at a roving checkpoint solely because of apparent Mexican ancestry?

Reasoning: * * * "In this case as well, because of the importance of the governmental interest at stake, the minimal intrusion of a brief stop, and the absence of practical alternatives for policing the border, we hold that when an officer's observations lead him reasonably to suspect that a particular vehicle may contain aliens who are illegally in the country, he may stop the car briefly and investigate the circumstances that provoke suspicion. As in *Terry,* the stop and inquiry must be 'reasonably related in scope to the justification for their initiation.' The officer may question the driver and passengers about their citizenship and immigration status, and he may ask them to explain suspicious circumstances, but any further detention or search must be based on consent or probable cause.* * *

"Any number of factors may be taken into account in deciding whether there is reasonable suspicion to stop a car in the border area. Officers may consider the characteristics of the area in which they encounter a vehicle. Its proximity to the border, the usual patterns of traffic on the particular road, and previous experience with alien traffic are all relevant. They also may consider information about recent illegal border crossings in the area. The driver's behavior may be relevant, as erratic driving or obvious attempts to evade officers can support a reasonable suspicion. Aspects of the vehicle itself may justify suspicion. For instance, officers say that certain station wagons, with large compartments for fold-down seats or spare tires, are frequently used for transporting concealed aliens. The vehicle may appear to be heavily loaded, it may have an extraordinary number of passengers, or the officers may observe persons trying to hide. The Government also points out that trained officers can recognize the characteristic appearance of persons who live in Mexico, relying on such factors as the mode of dress and haircut. In all situations the officer is entitled to asses the facts in light of his experience in detecting illegal entry and smuggling.

"In this case the officer relied on a single factor to justify stopping respondent's car: the apparent Mexican ancestry of the occupants. We cannot conclude that this furnished reasonable grounds to believe that the three occupants were aliens. At best the officers had only a fleeting glimpse of the persons in the moving car, illuminated by headlights. Even if they saw enough to think that the occupants were of Mexican descent, this factor alone would justify neither a reasonable belief that they were aliens, nor a reasonable belief that the car concealed other aliens who were illegally in the country. Large numbers of native-born and naturalized citizens have the physical characteristics identified with Mexican ancestry, and even in the border area a relatively small proportion of them are aliens. The likelihood that any given person of Mexican ancestry is an alien is high enough to make Mexican appearance a relevant factor, but standing alone it does not justify stopping all Mexican-Americans to ask if they are aliens."

Disposition: Conviction reversed; officers at roving checkpoints need reasonable suspicion to stop a vehicle.

8-6f *Almeida-Sanchez v. United States:* 413 U.S. 266, 37 L.Ed. 2d 596, 93 S.Ct. 2535 (1973)

Facts: At a roving checkpoint on State Highway 78 in California, the Border Patrol stopped Almeida-Sanchez, a Mexican citizen with a valid U.S. work permit, and thoroughly searched his car. Officers found a large quantity of marijuana. The stop occurred in an undeveloped region about 25 air miles north of the border and was done without a warrant, probable cause, or reasonable suspicion.

Issue: What level of suspicion is required to conduct a car search at a roving checkpoint?

Reasoning: * * * "Since neither this Court's automobile search decisions nor its administrative inspection decisions provide any support for the constitutionality of the stop and search in the present case, we are left simply with the statute that purports to authorize automobiles to be stopped and searched without a warrant and 'within a reasonable distance from any external boundary of the United States.' It is clear, of course, that no Act of Congress can authorize a violation of the Constitution. * * *

* * * "In the absence of probable cause or consent, that search violated the petitioner's Fourth Amendment right to be free of 'unreasonable searches and seizures.'"

Disposition: Conviction reversed; there must be either probable cause or consent to search an automobile at a roving checkpoint.

8-6g *Immigration and Naturalization Service v. Delgado:* 466 U.S. 210, 80 L.Ed. 2d 247, 104 S.Ct. 1758 (1984)

Facts: Based on a showing of probable cause that numerous illegal aliens were employed at Southern California Davis Pleating, INS obtained two warrants to survey the company's workforce Neither warrant identified any illegal alien by name. A third survey was conducted at Mr. Pleat, another garment factory. At the beginning of each survey, several agents positioned themselves near the buildings' exits, while other agents dispersed throughout the factory to question most, but not all, employees at their work stations. The armed agents displayed badges and carried walkie-talkies. At no time were weapons drawn. Agents moved systematically through the factory, approaching employees, identifying themselves, and asking a few questions relating to citizenship. If the employee gave a credible reply that he/she was a U.S. citizen, the questioning ended. If the employee gave an unsatisfactory response or admitted to being an alien, the employee was asked to produce immigration papers. Employees were free to walk around within the factory during the survey. Four employees, all of whom were either U.S. citizens or legal aliens, and their union representative, the International Ladies Garment Workers' Union, filed actions challenging the factory surveys as a violation of the Fourth Amendment and the Due Process Clause of the Fifth Amendment.

Issue: Did the "factory survey" amount to a detention that required individualized reasonable suspicion in order to detain and question employees?

Reasoning: * * * "We reject the claim that the entire work forces of the two factories were seized for the duration of the surveys when the INS placed agents near the exits of the factory sites. Ordinarily, when people are at work their freedom to move about has been meaningfully restricted, not by the actions of law enforcement officials, but by the workers' voluntary obligations to their employers. The record indicates that when these surveys were initiated, the employees were about their ordinary business, operating machinery and performing other job assignments. While the surveys did cause some disruption, including the efforts of some workers to hide, the record also indicates that workers were not prevented by the agents from moving about the factories.

"Respondents argue, however, that the stationing of agents near the factory doors showed the INS's intent to prevent people from leaving. But there is nothing in the record indicating that this is what the agents at the doors actually did. The obvious purpose of the agents' presence at the factory doors was to insure that all persons in the factories were questioned. The record indicates that the INS agents' conduct in this case consisted simply of questioning employees and arresting those they had probable cause to believe were unlawfully present in the factory. This conduct should have given respondents no reason to believe that they would be detained if they gave truthful answers to the questions put to them or if they simply refused to answer. If mere questioning does not constitute a seizure when it occurs inside the factory, it is no more a seizure when it occurs at the exits.

* * * "Likewise, the mere possibility that they would be questioned if they sought to leave the buildings should not have resulted in any reasonable apprehension by any of them that they would be seized or detained in any meaningful way. Since most workers could have had no reasonable fear that they would be detained upon leaving, we conclude that the work forces as a whole were not seized."

Disposition: Civil suit dismissed; brief questioning and the demand to produce immigration papers during the "factory survey" did not constitute a detention.

8-6h *New York v. Belton:* 453 U.S. 454, 69 L.Ed. 2d 768, 101 S.Ct. 2869 (1981)

Facts: On April 9, 1978, Trooper Nicot, a New York State policeman, was passed by another car traveling at an excessive rate of speed. Nicot stopped the car, which had four male occupants, including Belton. None of the occupants owned the vehicle or was related to its owner. Nicot smelled the odor of burnt marijuana and observed an envelope marked "Supergold" on the floor of the backseat. He directed the men to get out of the car and placed them under arrest for unlawful possession of marijuana. During a search of the car, Nicot found a black leather jacket belonging to Belton on the backseat. He unzipped one pocket of the jacket and discovered cocaine. Belton was charged with possession of cocaine. His motion to suppress the cocaine was denied.

Issue: Can closed containers found in a vehicle during a search incident to an arrest be opened without a warrant?

Reasoning: * * * "Our reading of the cases suggests the generalization that articles inside the relatively narrow compass of the passenger compartment of an automobile are in fact generally, even if not inevitably, within 'the area into which an arrestee might reach in order to grab a weapon or evidentiary item.' In order to establish a workable rule this category of cases requires, we read *Chimel's* definition of the limits of the area that may be searched in light of that generalization. Accordingly, we hold that when a policeman has made a lawful custodial arrest of the occupant of an automobile, he may, as a contemporaneous incident of that arrest, search the passenger compartment of that automobile.

"It follows from this conclusion that the police may also examine the contents of any containers found within the passenger compartment, for if the passenger compartment is within reach of the arrestee, so also will containers in it be within his reach. Such a container may, of course, be searched whether it is open or closed, since the justification for the search is not that the arrestee has no privacy interest in the container, but that the lawful custodial arrest justifies the infringement of any privacy interest the arrestee may have."

Disposition: Suppression motion was properly denied; an officer has the right to open a closed container in a vehicle as part of a search incident to arrest of a person in the vehicle.

8-6i *Colorado v. Bertine:* 479 U.S. 367, 93 L.Ed. 2d 739, 107 S.Ct. 738 (1987)

Facts: On February 10, 1984, a police officer in Boulder, Colorado arrested Bertine for driving under the influence of alcohol. Due to local police department policy, Bertine's van was subjected to a detailed inventory prior to being towed to an impound lot. While conducting the inventory, the officer found a closed backpack directly behind the front seat and opened it. Inside it he found a nylon bag containing a metal canister. When the officer opened the metal canister, he found cocaine, methaqualone tablets, cocaine paraphernalia, and $700 in cash. In the outside zipper compartment of the backpack, he found $210 in cash in a sealed envelope. He then completed the inventory of the van and had it towed. Bertine was charged with driving under the influence of alcohol, unlawful possession of cocaine with intent to sell, and unlawful possession of methaqualone. The state appellate court ruled that the evidence found in the backpack must be suppressed.

Issue: Can an officer open closed containers as part of taking inventory of an impounded vehicle?

Reasoning: * * * "In the present case, as in *Opperman* and *Lafayette*, there was no showing that the police, who were following standardized procedures, acted in bad faith or for the sole purpose of investigation. In addition, the governmental interests justifying the inventory searches in *Opperman* and *Lafayette* are nearly the same as those which obtain here. In each case, the police were potentially responsible for the property taken into their custody. By securing the property, the police protected the property from unauthorized interference. Knowledge of the precise nature of the property helped guard against claims of theft, vandalism, or negligence. Such knowledge also helped to avert any danger to police or others that may have been posed by the property.

* * * "But the security of the storage facility does not completely eliminate the need for inventorying; the police may still wish to protect themselves or the owners of the lot against false claims of theft or dangerous instrumentalities. And while giving Bertine an opportunity to make alternative arrangements would undoubtedly have been possible, we said in *Lafayette:* * * * 'The reasonableness of any particular government activity does not necessarily or invariably turn on the existence of alternative "less intrusive" means.' We conclude that here, as in *Lafayette*, reasonable police regulations relating to inventory procedures administered in good faith satisfy the Fourth Amendment, even though courts might as a matter of hindsight be able to devise equally reasonable rules requiring a different procedure.

"The Supreme Court of Colorado also thought it necessary to require that police, before inventorying a container, weigh the strength of the individual's privacy interest in the container against the possibility that the container might serve as a repository for dangerous or valuable items. We think that such a requirement is contrary to our decisions in *Opperman* and *Lafayette*, and by analogy to our decision in *United States v. Ross*."

Disposition: Suppression motion granted in error; police have the right to open closed containers during the inventory of a vehicle that is to be impounded.

8-6j *United States v. Johns:* 469 U.S. 478, 83 L.Ed. 2d 890, 105 S.Ct. 881 (1985)

Facts: A U.S. Customs agent observed two pickup trucks when he went to Duarte's residence in Tucson, Arizona, as part of a investigation of drug smuggling. The trucks were kept under surveillance as they traveled 100 miles to a remote private airstrip near Bowie, Arizona, which is 50 miles from the Mexican border. A small aircraft landed shortly after the trucks arrived. Agents observed trucks approaching the plane and the aircraft departing a short time later. Two Customs officers drove to within 30 yards of the two trucks and observed an individual at the rear of one truck covering the contents with a blanket. They ordered suspects to come out from behind the trucks and lie on the ground. The officers smelled the odor of marijuana and observed packages in the trucks wrapped in dark-green plastic and sealed with tape. All the suspects at the scene were then arrested. Officers in aircraft followed the suspect's airplane back to Tucson and arrested the remaining defendants. After making the arrests at the airstrip the Customs officers took the trucks back to DEA headquarters in Tucson. They removed the packages from the trucks and placed them in a DEA warehouse. Three days later, they opened some of the packages to obtain samples for laboratory testing. The trial court granted the defendant's suppression motion.

Issue: Is a search warrant necessary to open packages found during a probable cause search of a vehicle if the package was not opened immediately?

Reasoning: *** "The warrantless search of the packages was not unreasonable merely because the Customs officers returned to Tucson and placed the packages in a DEA warehouse rather than immediately opening them. The practical effect of the opposite conclusion would only be to direct police officers to search immediately all containers that they discover in the course of a vehicle search. This result would be of little benefit to the person whose property is searched, and where police officers are entitled to seize the container and continue to have probable cause to believe that it contains contraband, we do not think that delay in the execution of the warrantless search is necessarily unreasonable.

"We do not suggest that police officers may indefinitely retain possession of a vehicle and its contents before they complete a vehicle search.

Nor do we foreclose the possibility that the owner of a vehicle or its contents might attempt to prove that delay in the completion of a vehicle search was unreasonable because it adversely affected a privacy or possessory interest. We note that in this case there was probable cause to believe that the trucks contained contraband and there is no plausible argument that the object of the search could not have been concealed in the packages. * * * Inasmuch as the Government was entitled to seize the packages and could have searched them immediately without a warrant, we conclude that the warrantless search three days after the packages were placed in the DEA warehouse was reasonable and consistent with our precedent involving searches of impounded vehicles."

Disposition: Suppression order granted in error; officers do not have to obtain a search warrant to open packages seized from a vehicle with probable cause merely because the search was not conducted at the time the vehicle was seized.

8-6k *Illinois v. Lafayette:* 462 U.S. 640, 77 L.Ed. 65, 103 S.Ct. 2605 (1983)

Facts: Lafayette was arrested for disturbing the peace after an altercation with a theater manager. At the time, Lafayette was carrying a "purse-type shoulder bag." Officers inventoried the shoulder bag during booking and found 10 amphetamine pills inside a cigarette case. Illinois state courts suppressed the evidence found in the shoulder bag.

Issue: Does the Fourth Amendment allow police to search the personal effects of a lawfully arrested person during booking?

Reasoning: * * * "At the station house, it is entirely proper for police to remove and list or inventory property found on the person or in the possession of an arrested person who is to be jailed. A range of governmental interests support an inventory process. It is not unheard of for persons employed in police activities to steal property taken from arrested persons; similarly, arrested person have been known to make false claims regarding what was taken from their possession at the station house. A standardized procedure for making a list or inventory as soon as reasonable after reaching the station house not only deters false claims but also inhibits theft or careless handling of articles taken from the arrested person. Arrested persons have also been know to injure themselves—or others—with belts, knives, drugs or other items on their person while being detained. Dangerous instrumentalities—such as razor blades, bombs, or weapons—can be concealed in innocent-looking articles taken from the arrestee's possession. The bare recital of these mundane realities justifies reasonable measures by police to limit these risks—either while the items are in police possession or at the time they are returned to the arrestee upon his release. Examining all the items removed from the arrestee's person or possession and listing or inventorying them is an entirely reasonable administrative procedure. It is immaterial whether the police actually fear any particular package or container; the need to protect against such risks arise independent of a particular officer's subjective concerns. Finally, inspection of an arrestee's personal property may assist the police in ascertaining or verifying his identity. In short, every consideration of orderly police administration benefiting both police and the public points toward the appropriateness of the examination of respondent's shoulder bag prior to his incarceration. * * *

"Applying these principles, we hold that it is not 'unreasonable' for police, as part of the routine procedure incident to incarcerating an arrested person, to search any container or article in his possession, in accordance with established inventory procedures."

Disposition: Prosecution of case may proceed; amphetamines found in the shoulder bag during inventory at the time of booking are admissible at trial.

8-6l *United States v. Arvizu:* 534 U.S. 266, 151 L.Ed. 2d 740, 122 S.Ct. 744 (2002)

Facts: Sensors are located in Leslie Canyon Road, a northbound road rarely used except by ranchers and forest service personnel. Smugglers commonly try to avoid the main highway by using this road. About 2:15 P.M., Border Patrol Agent Stoddard received a radio report that the sensors had been activated. He thought this might indicate smugglers trying to circumvent the checkpoint on highway 191 during shift change. A few weeks before, he had stopped a minivan that was smuggling marijuana near this location. Stoddard observed a minivan approach his vehicle and dramatically reduce its speed. The minivan contained a man and a woman and three children. The driver appeared to have rigid posture and to pretend Agent Stoddard was not there. The knees of two children sitting in the backseat were very high, as if their feet were propped up on some cargo on the floor. Stoddard began following the car. Suddenly all of the children put their hands straight up and began waiving in an abnormal pattern. Although they never turned around, they continued waiving in this manner for nearly five minutes. As the minivan's driver approached Kuykendall Cutoff Road, he signaled to turn and then turned the turn signal off. The minivan abruptly turned at the intersection. Stoddard thought this was significant because this was the last place to turn that would allow the vehicle to avoid the checkpoint. The cutoff is a rough road normally used only by four-wheel-drive vehicles. Stoddard did not recognize the minivan as part of the normal traffic on the road and did not believe the family was on a picnic because there were no picnic grounds on this route. A radio check revealed that the minivan was registered to an address in Douglas, Arizona, that is four blocks from the border in an area notorious for alien and narcotics smuggling. Stoddard stopped the vehicle and obtained permission to look inside. A duffel bag containing marijuana was under the children's feet and another bag containing marijuana was behind the rear seat. A total of 128.85 pounds of marijuana valued at $99,080 was recovered. Arvizu was charged with possession of marijuana with intent to distribute. His motion to suppress the marijuana based on a lack of suspicion to stop his vehicle was denied by the U. S. District Court but the U. S. Court of Appeals reversed.

Issue: Did Agent Stoddard have enough facts to establish reasonable suspicion to stop the minivan?

Reasoning: "[W]e hold that Stoddard had reasonable suspicion to believe that respondent was engaged in illegal activity. It was reasonable for Stoddard to infer from his observations, his registration check, and his experience as a border patrol agent that respondent had set out from Douglas along a little-traveled route used by smugglers to avoid the 191 checkpoint. Stoddard's knowledge further supported a commonsense inference that respondent intended to pass through the area at a time when officers would be leaving their backroads patrols to change shifts. The likelihood that respondent and his family were on a picnic outing was diminished by the fact that the minivan had turned away from the known recreational areas accessible to the east of Rucker Canyon Road. Corroborating this inference was the fact that recreational areas farther to the north would have been easier to reach by taking 191, as opposed to the 40-to-50 mile trip on unpaved and primitive roads. The children's elevated knees suggested the existence of concealed cargo in the passenger compartment. Finally, for the reasons we have given, Stoddard's assessment of respondent's reactions upon seeing him and the children's mechanical-like waving, which continued for a full four to five minutes, were entitled to some weight.

*** "A determination that reasonable suspicion exists, however, need not rule out the possibility of innocent conduct. . . . Undoubtedly, each of these factors alone is susceptible to innocent explanation, and some factors are more probative than others. Taken together, we believe they suffice to form a particularized and objective basis for Stoddard's stopping the vehicle, making the stop reasonable within the meaning of the Fourth Amendment."

Disposition: The marijuana seized will be admissible at trial; the officer had reasonable suspicion to stop the vehicle.

8-6m *Illinois v. Andreas:* 463 U.S. 765, 77 L.Ed. 2d 1003, 103 S.Ct. 3319 (1983)

Facts: A large, locked metal container was shipped by air from Calcutta to Andreas in Chicago. Customs inspectors at O'Hare International Airport opened it and found marijuana concealed in a wooden table. DEA agents were informed of the find and performed chemical tests to verify that the substance was marijuana. Agents put the table back in the container and resealed it. A Chicago police inspector posing as a delivery truck driver entered Andreas's apartment building and announced that there was a package for him. Andreas came to the lobby and identified himself. In response to comments about the weight of the package, Andreas said that it "wasn't that heavy, that he had packaged it himself, that it only contained a table." At Andreas's request, the package was left in the hallway outside his apartment. About half an hour later, Andreas emerged from the apartment with the shipping container and was immediately arrested. Officers took the package to the police station and reopened it without a warrant. The marijuana was still inside the table. Andreas's motion to suppress the marijuana was granted by the trial court.

Issue: Was a search warrant required to open a package that had legally been opened by federal agents and then resealed?

Reasoning: *** "It is obvious that the privacy interest in the contents of a container diminishes with respect to a container that law enforcement authorities have already lawfully opened and found to contain illicit drugs. No protected privacy interest remains in contraband in a container once government officers lawfully have opened that container and identified its contents as illegal. The simple act of resealing the container to enable the police to make a controlled delivery does not operate to revive or restore the lawfully invaded privacy rights.

*** "A workable, objective standard that limits the risk of intrusion on legitimate privacy interests is whether there is a substantial likelihood that the contents of the container have been changed during the gap in surveillance. We hold that absent a substantial likelihood that the contents have been changed, there is no legitimate expectation of privacy in the contents of a container previously opened under lawful authority."

Disposition: Suppression motion granted in error; defendant had no privacy interest that required the obtaining of a search warrant in order to open the container that had been resealed and delivered to him after a lawful search.

8-6n *United States v. Jacobsen:* 466 U.S. 109, 80 L.Ed. 2d 85, 104 S.Ct. 1652 (1984)

Facts: Early in the morning of May 1, 1981, a Federal Express supervisor at the Minneapolis-St.Paul airport asked the office manager to look at a package that had been damaged by a forklift. Following company policy on insurance claims, they opened the ordinary cardboard box wrapped in brown paper to examine the contents. Inside, they found crumpled newspaper covering a tube about 10 inches long. The tube was made of silver duct tape. They cut open the tube and found four nested, zip-lock plastic bags. The innermost bag contained over 6 ounces of white powder. They notified Drug Enforcement Administration (DEA). The Federal Express employees returned the bags to the tube and put the tube back in the box before the DEA agents arrived. The first DEA agent to arrive reopened the box and subjected a small amount of the substance to chemical tests. It was determined to be cocaine. Using the results of the field test, the DEA obtained a search warrant for the address to which the box was to be delivered. Bradly Jacobsen and Donna Jacobsen were arrested when the search warrant was executed. They were convicted on charges of possession of an illegal substance with intent to distribute.

Issue: Can evidence found due to a search by a private person be examined without a search warrant?

Reasoning: "The initial invasions of respondents' package were occasioned by private action. Those invasions revealed that the package contained only one significant item, a suspicious looking tape tube. Cutting the end of the tube and extracting its contents revealed a suspicious looking plastic bag of white powder. Whether those invasions were accidental or deliberate, and whether they were reasonable or unreasonable, they did not violate the Fourth Amendment because of their private character.

"The additional invasion of respondents' privacy by the government agent must be tested by the degree to which they exceeded the scope of the private search. * * *

*** "Respondents could have no privacy interest in the contents of the package, since it remained unsealed and since the Federal Express employees had just examined the package and had, of their own accord, invited the federal agent to their offices for the express purpose of viewing its contents. The agent's viewing of what a private party had freely made available for his inspection did not violate the Fourth Amendment.

*** "While the agents' assertion of dominion and control over the package and its contents did constitute a 'seizure,' that seizure was not unreasonable. The fact that, prior to the field test, respondents' privacy interest in the contents of the package had been largely compromised, is highly relevant to the reasonableness of the agents' conduct in this respect. *** The package itself, which had previously been opened, remained unsealed, and the Federal Express employees had invited the agents to examine its contents. Under these circumstances, the package could no longer support any expectation of privacy. ***

"In sum, the federal agents did not infringe any constitutionally protected privacy interest that had not already been frustrated as the result of private conduct. To the extent that a protected possessory interest was infringed, the infringement was de minimis and constitutionally reasonable."

Disposition: Convictions affirmed; agents had the right to reopen the package Federal Express agents had given to them and conduct a field test to determine if substance was cocaine.

Chapter Quiz

True/False

1. Federal agents working at an international border (point of entry) do not need any specific justification to search people entering the United States.
2. First-class mail entering the United States can only be searched if there is probable cause to believe that it contains contraband.
3. The Coast Guard is allowed to board ships in navigable waterways near international waters and search them without even reasonable suspicion.
4. Border Patrol agents must have probable cause to stop cars at fixed checkpoints.
5. As long as they have a valid reason to stop a car at a fixed checkpoint, Border Patrol agents can search the car without any indication that criminal activity is occurring.
6. Border Patrol agents working at roving checkpoints need reasonable suspicion to stop a car.

7. Border Patrol agents working at roving checkpoints can search vehicles without probable cause.
8. Immigration and Naturalization Service agents may enter factories without consent of the owner to verify that individuals working there have the legal right to be in the United States.
9. Closed containers found in a car during the search incident to a valid arrest may be opened without a search warrant.
10. There is no need for the police to obtain a search warrant to view the contents of packages that were opened by private shipping companies and subsequently given to the police.

Discussion Questions

1. Agent Williams was working at the San Clemente Border Patrol checkpoint. He observed a car approaching the checkpoint very slowly. The rear of the car was nearly touching the road. He ordered the arriver to go to the secondary checkpoint and immediately forced open the trunk. He found stolen TVs in the trunk. Is this search at a *fixed checkpoint* legal? Explain.
2. Agent Adams was part of a team of Border Patrol officers who set up a temporary roadblock on a highway near the border. They stopped all cars passing their location heading away from the border. Pam refused to tell Agent Adams if she was a U.S. citizen. Agent Adams immediately forced Pam to get out of the car and searched the vehicle thoroughly. The agent found illegally imported computer components hidden in the door panels. Are the computer components admissible as part of a search at a *roving checkpoint?* Explain.
3. Sean was walking down the street carrying an attaché case when he was arrested on an old traffic warrant. He was taken to the jail and booked. Officers opened his attaché case without his consent and found illegally copied videotapes inside. Are the tapes admissible under an *exception* to the *closed container* rule? Explain.
4. Michelle was arrested for drunk driving while on her way to a Christmas party. Officers opened all of the gift-wrapped packages in the car as part of the inventory and discovered that each package contained designer clothing stolen during a recent burglary. Can the clothing be admitted under an *exception* to the *closed container rule?* Explain.

Chapter 9

Privilege against Self-Incrimination

Outline

The Self-Incrimination Clause of the Fifth Amendment protects a person from being compelled to give testimony that might be incriminating. This privilege does not apply to statements that could result in civil liability but would not raise the possibility that the person making the statement might be prosecuted for a crime. The Supreme Court also held that it does not protect a person if the only possible criminal repercussion is prosecution in a foreign country.

9-1 Types of Actions Covered by Fifth Amendment Privilege

The privilege against self-incrimination applies to statements (oral or written) whose content can be used in a criminal trial against the person making the statements. As with the Fourth Amendment, the actions of government agents are covered. This includes both law enforcement officers and people employed by the government in other capacities. Acts of people acting independently of the government are not covered.

The appropriate way to invoke the privilege against self-incrimination varies with the stage of the criminal justice system where it is used. Prior to arrest and during field interviews, any person may refuse to answer questions but the police have no duty to inform the suspect of the right to do so. If the suspect wants to seek advice from an attorney, it must be done at his/her own expense.

During custodial interrogations, the police must inform the suspect of his/her constitutional rights. In order to continue the questioning, a police must obtain knowing, intelligent, and voluntary waiver from the suspect. An indigent suspect has the right to counsel during questioning appointed at government expense, if desired.

9-2 When the Fifth Amendment Does Not Apply

Self-incrimination only applies if criminal charges can be based on the confession or admission. It does not apply in three situations that arise in criminal cases in which it is impossible to file charges: the statute of limitations has expired; the witness has been granted immunity; or the witness cannot be prosecuted due to double jeopardy. It must be noted that even in these cases, due process prevents police from using coercion to obtain confessions.

The Supreme Court has repeatedly held that the Fifth Amendment privilege against self-incrimination applies only to testimony. A statement, either written or oral, is testimonial if the person making it is responsible for its content. If a person makes a statement based on personal knowledge, it is testimonial; if the person merely repeats what he/she is told to say, the statement is not testimonial.

Laboratory testing of body fluids often provide incriminating evidence. For example, blood, urine, or breath tests can be used to establish intoxication; DNA tests of blood or semen can identify the perpetrator of a sexual assault. All of these tests rest on the same basis as far as the Fifth Amendment is concerned. While the results can be very incriminating, no privilege can be asserted as grounds for refusing to take the tests because they are not testimonial.

A person's appearance is also not testimonial evidence. The most commonly used identification procedure involves fingerprints. Visual identification by victims and witnesses to the crime also falls in this category. The suspect cannot invoke the Fifth Amendment as a reason to refuse to participate in any of these procedures.

Handwriting and voice exemplars are frequently used for identification purposes. Neither of these is testimonial because the suspect is told what to write or say. For this reason, the content of the exemplar is not an indication of guilt and cannot be incriminating.

9-3 *Miranda* Warnings

Miranda v. Arizona (1966) is one of the best-known Supreme Court cases. In *Dickerson v. United States* (2000), the Court reaffirmed its constitutional footing:

> * * * "*Miranda* has become embedded in routine police practice to the point where the warnings have become part of our national culture. * * * If anything, our subsequent cases have reduced the impact of the *Miranda* rule on legitimate law enforcement while reaffirming the decision's core ruling that unwarned statements may not be used as evidence in the prosecution's case in chief."
>
> * * * "[W]e conclude that *Miranda* announced a constitutional rule that Congress may not supersede legislatively. Following the rule of stare decisis, we decline to overrule *Miranda* ourselves." 530 U.S. 443, 444.

Confessions obtained in violation of *Miranda* are not admissible when offered by the prosecution to prove the defendant's guilt. They can be used to impeach a defendant who confesses to police and then makes contradictory statements while testifying at his/her trial.

Even after 30 years, many details surrounding the *Miranda* decision continue to cause confusion. To help clear up some of these problems, four key areas will be addressed: when *Miranda* warnings are required; what *Miranda* warnings are; how *Miranda* rights are waived; and what rules apply to sequential interrogations.

9-3a When *Miranda* Warnings Are Required

The key to giving *Miranda* warnings is custodial interrogation. The suspect must be in custody at the time and the police must be interrogating him/her.

Custody, for the purposes of *Miranda,* is the equivalent of a custodial arrest. It does not include traffic stops in which citations are issued and the violator is released at the scene. Field interviews based on reasonable suspicion, as authorized in *Terry v. Ohio,* are not covered. Neither are situations in which a suspect is being questioned at the police station but is not under arrest. An objective test is used: Did the officer convey, by words or actions, that the suspect is not free to leave? The officer's subjective intent to arrest the suspect is not important

It does not matter why the suspect is in custody. Warnings are required if a suspect is arrested for one crime and questioned regarding a different one. Questioning by a different law enforcement agency also requires the warnings. *Miranda* warnings are even required if the suspect is questioned in jail while serving time on a totally unrelated offense. An exception applies to prearraignment questioning by an undercover officer: No warnings are required if the suspect did not know he/she was talking to a law enforcement officer.

The Supreme Court has defined *interrogation* as the process of questioning, or its functional equivalent. Asking questions about a crime is clearly interrogation; so is requesting a narrative statement. The Court has also included indirect attempts to obtain information. For example, if two officers engage in a conversation with the intent of being overheard and eliciting a response, this is the functional equivalent of interrogation.

Questioning done by a private person whom the police did not authorize or condone does not require *Miranda* warnings, but under some circumstances *Miranda* warnings may be required prior to questioning by nonpolice personnel. The need for the warnings prior to a polygraph examination done at the request of a police officer is one illustration. Psychiatric examinations conducted on behalf of the prosecution, or ordered by the court, also require *Miranda* warnings.

Volunteered statements are admissible even though *Miranda* warnings were not given. As used in this context, "volunteered" means the suspect came forward on his/her own initiative and made a statement. Detailed questioning that follows the volunteered information is considered interrogation.

The courts recognize a minor exception to *Miranda* for the booking process. Questions related to name, address, person to notify in case of an emergency, date of birth, and a few other biographical facts are permitted without giving any warnings. *Miranda* applies if questioning at booking is extended to obtain information for a criminal investigation.

The Supreme Court recognized another for "public safety." Brief questioning at the time of arrest is permitted without giving *Miranda* warnings if it is done to obtain information to protect others from imminent harm. Asking where the suspect hid a gun would fit under this exception if the question was asked to prevent innocent people from being hurt.

9-3b Content of *Miranda* Warnings

Each officer must fully understand the *Miranda* warnings in order to explain them correctly. The Supreme Court has permitted paraphrasing but has been quite intolerant of misleading warnings. This includes answers to a suspect's questions about these rights.

Prior to custodial interrogation, the suspect must be warned:

1. You have the right to remain silent.
2. Anything you say can and will be used against you in a court of law.
3. You have the right to have an attorney present during questioning.
4. If you cannot afford an attorney, one will be appointed at no charge to assist you during questioning.

First, the right to remain silent includes the right to refrain from making both oral and written statements. Nodding the head "yes" or "no" is also covered. Agreeing to talk at the beginning of the interview does not mean the suspect has given up the right to stop the interrogation at any time.

Second, anything that the suspect says can be used against him/her in court. This includes all admissions that may be incriminating in any way, attempts to incriminate another person, and anything that can be used for impeachment. Attempts to talk to the police "off the record" indicate that the suspect does not understand the warnings.

Third, the suspect has the right to have an attorney present during questioning. Law enforcement officers cannot continue questioning a suspect after he/she has requested an attorney. The fact that an attorney will be appointed at arraignment is not enough. The police have two alternatives: give the suspect an attorney or stop questioning. Failure to provide an attorney violates the suspect's rights only if there is further questioning.

Lastly, if the suspect cannot afford an attorney, one will be provided at no cost to the suspect. The purpose of this warning is to inform the indigent suspect that a lack of money will not prevent him/her from having an attorney present during questioning. It is not the duty of the police to review the financial status of the suspect. If the suspect requests an attorney, the police should proceed in the same manner regardless of the suspect's apparent wealth (or lack thereof): Questioning must stop.

Merely reciting the Court's language is not enough. The warnings must be given so that the suspect understands them. The prosecution bears the burden of convincing the judge that the warnings were correctly explained to the suspect. This must be established by a preponderance of the evidence.

9-3c Waiver of *Miranda* Rights

Once *Miranda* warnings have been correctly given to a suspect who is in custody, the police may try to obtain a waiver of the suspect's rights. This must be a knowing, intelligent, and voluntary waiver.

To have a knowing waiver, the suspect must have been correctly advised of his/her rights. The courts have uniformly required that the police show that they have done this. It is not presumed that anyone knows the *Miranda* warnings.

"Intelligent," as used in this context, means that the person had the basic intelligence necessary to understand his/her rights. This may be in issue if a young juvenile is involved. It also comes up if the suspect is mentally retarded or extremely intoxicated (due either to alcohol or drugs). Only the most extreme cases qualify for suppression due to the lack of an intelligent waiver.

Voluntariness is somewhat hard to define in this context. The police cannot use coercion to obtain a waiver of *Miranda* rights. Physical force cannot be used to obtain a confession. A credible threat of physical violence makes a confession involuntary. This is true whether the person perceives the threat as coming from government agents or from another person. Deprivation of food and/or sleep for long periods is not allowed; neither are false promises of leniency, such as offers to drop charges or assurances that the suspect will get a light sentence if he/she confesses.

Absent one of these obviously coercive acts, the courts look at the totality of the circumstances. The key concept is that the police are not allowed to overbear the will of the suspect. This balances the acts of the police against the vulnerability of the defendant. What may be coercive when done to a naive teenager might be considered acceptable when applied to a street-wise ex-convict.

Police are permitted to tell lies and half-truths. The police do not have to tell the suspect all of the crimes being investigated; neither do they have to inform him/her that someone has arranged for an attorney to come to the jail to provide counsel.

Cases involving juveniles are considered on the totality of the circumstances. The clarity of the warnings given is very important. Other factors include the age and intelligence of the juvenile, prior contacts with the police, and other evidence of sophistication related to the criminal justice system. Police tactics that intimidate or coerce are carefully scrutinized. If juveniles ask to speak to their parents, the questioning must stop. The courts have treated this type of request as the equivalent of an adult demanding an attorney.

The last issue involving the waiver of *Miranda* rights is the procedure used to obtain the waiver. The Supreme Court has not set a protocol. Express waivers are preferred but, in one case, the Court found a valid waiver was implied by the suspect's conduct. The suspect had responded in the affirmative when asked if he understood his rights, but did not reply when asked if he wished to waive them. The indication that he understood the warnings, coupled with the fact that he answered the questions the police asked, was enough to convince the Court that a valid waiver had been obtained. In another case, the Court decided that an oral confession was admissible even though the suspect told police that he would talk to them but would not make a written confession without his attorney present.

Statements a suspect made during an interrogation can be used to impeach his/her testimony at trial; this includes any voluntary statement made during an interrogation that violated other aspects of *Miranda*. Coerced statements should not be used; if they are, the "harmless error rule" will be used to determine if the conviction should be reversed.

9-3d Subsequent Interrogations

It is not uncommon for the police to interrogate a suspect more than once. The procedures that should be followed at the second interrogation depend largely on what was done at the first. It is important to remember, though, that suspects can invoke the *Miranda* rights at any time: The fact they were waived once does not mean the suspect cannot refuse to talk or demand an attorney at any time after giving the waiver.

If the suspect waived his/her *Miranda* rights during the most recent interrogation session, the next interrogations can be conducted rather routinely. The Supreme Court has not required a new set of *Miranda* warnings every time questioning is resumed, but the warnings are needed if the suspect is not likely to remember his/her rights.

If the first confession was coerced, all subsequent confessions are inadmissible. On the other hand, if the first confession was voluntary but in violation of *Miranda,* subsequent confessions may be admissible if obtained following properly administered *Miranda* warnings. Each case is considered on its own merits. *Miranda* warnings given only seconds after obtaining the inadmissible confession will not be viewed as effective. A valid confession obtained several days after the suspect was released from custody will, more than likely, be admissible.

9-4 Questioning after Suspect Invokes the Right to Remain Silent

Interrogation must be stopped immediately if the suspect invokes the right to remain silent but does not request an attorney. This does not mean, however, that a police officer may never resume questioning.

The Supreme Court has insisted that the suspect's rights be scrupulously guarded. Police may not badger the suspect with frequent attempts to get the suspect to talk, but after a reasonable time they may ask the suspect if he/she would like to continue the interrogation. A new waiver of *Miranda* is mandatory prior to resuming questioning. Tactics that appear to harass the suspect are not tolerated. In the leading case, there was a two-hour gap between the interrogations. The second interview was conducted by different officers on a different floor of the police building and focused on a different crime.

9-5 Questioning after Suspect Requests an Attorney

Different rules apply if the suspect requested to speak to an attorney rather than merely demanding that the questioning stop. In these situations, the suspect not only must have an opportunity to speak with an attorney, but an attorney must be present at subsequent interrogation sessions unless the suspect voluntarily requests the interview. An objective test is used to determine if the suspect invoked the right to have an attorney present: Would a reasonable person have understood the suspect's statement to be an unequivocal request for an attorney? Officers are not required to ask a suspect to clarify an ambiguous request for counsel.

In 1988, the Supreme Court made it clear that the fact that the subsequent interrogation was about a different crime did not alter this rule. The Court clearly stated that it intended to follow the bright-line rule without exceptions. Having no knowledge of the prior request for an attorney is not an acceptable excuse.

9-6 Questioning after Arraignment

Questioning after arraignment may violate the right to counsel even if *Miranda* is not violated. The right to counsel attaches at the beginning of adversary court proceedings. This usually is at the arraignment unless some other proceeding, such as indictment by a Grand Jury, occurs first. From the time the right to counsel attaches, police violate the defendant's Sixth Amendment rights if they interview a suspect about the crimes charged without either an attorney present or a waiver of the right to counsel. This rule applies even if the interrogation did not take place in a custodial setting. The Court, in *Texas v. Cobb* (2001), applied the same test that is used for double jeopardy: If the defendant can claim double jeopardy if charged with the crime being discussed, the right to counsel covers both crimes and the suspect cannot be interrogated without an attorney present or a waiver of that right. If the crimes are related, but double jeopardy would not apply, the police may question the suspect without violating the right to counsel.

For interrogations that occur after arraignment or indictment, the key questions are: Was the accused made sufficiently aware of the right to have counsel present during questioning? Was the accused aware of the possible consequences of the decision to forgo the assistance of counsel? The Supreme Court has said that a knowing, intelligent, and voluntary waiver of *Miranda* satisfies these criteria.

The right to counsel guaranteed in *Miranda* and the right to counsel that starts with the arraignment are somewhat different but frequently overlap. If the suspect invoked the right to counsel under *Miranda*, that right applies to all questioning while the suspect is in custody regardless of the crime being investigated. This right can only be waived in the presence of an attorney. If the suspect did not invoke *Miranda's* right to counsel but has an attorney representing him/her in the court proceedings, the right to counsel applies only to the crimes charged. The suspect can waive the right to counsel without defense counsel present as long as it is a knowing, intelligent, and voluntary waiver. The *Miranda* warnings suffice for this purpose.

9-7 Key Supreme Court Cases

9-7a *Miranda v. Arizona:* 384 U.S. 436, 16 L.Ed. 2d 694, 86 S.Ct. 1602 (1966)

Facts:

Case 1: On March 13, 1963, police arrested Miranda at his home and took him to the Phoenix police station where a rape victim identified him as her assailant. Officers took him to an interrogation room in the detective bureau. After two hours of questioning, Miranda signed a written confession. At the top of the of the statement was a typed paragraph stating that the confession was made voluntarily, without threats or promises of immunity, and "with full knowledge of my legal rights, understanding any statement I make may be used against me." He had not been advised of his right to counsel. He was convicted on kidnap and rape charges.

Case 2: On October 14, 1960, New York police picked up Vignera in connection with a robbery. They took him first to 17th Detective Squad headquarters and then to 66th Detective Squad where he was questioned regarding the robbery. He made an oral confession. The store owner and a saleslady identified him as the robber. At 3:00 P.M., Vignera was formally arrested and then transported to the 70th Precinct "for detention." At 11:00 P.M., an assistant district attorney questioned him and made a transcript of the questions and answers. The transcript contained no statement of any warnings being given. Vignera was convicted of first-degree robbery.

Case 3: At about 9:45 P.M. on March 20, 1963, local police in Kansas City arrested Westover as a suspect in two robberies. Police then learned that Westover was wanted by the FBI on a felony charge in California. Kansas City police interrogated Westover on the night of his arrest and during most of the next morning. He denied any knowledge of criminal activities. At noon, three FBI agents continued the interrogation, focusing on the robbery of a savings and loan in Sacramento, California. After two-and-one-half hours, Westover signed separate confessions to each of the two robberies. A paragraph in each confession states that the agents advised Westover that he did not have to make a statement, that any statement he made could be used against him, and that he had the right to see an attorney. Westover was convicted for the robberies in California.

Case 4: Los Angeles police were investigating a series of purse-snatch robberies, one of which resulted in the victim's death. Stewart was pointed out to the police as the endorser of dividend checks taken in one of the robberies. Officers arrested Stewart, his wife, and three visitors at his home at about 7:15 P.M. on January 31, 1963. He consented to a search of his house, during which police found various items taken from five robbery victims. During the next five days, police interrogated Stewart nine different times. At the first interrogation session, he was confronted by an accusing witness; he was isolated during the other sessions. During the ninth session, Stewart admitted that he robbed the deceased robbery victim. Stewart was then arraigned and his wife and friends released from custody. Nothing in the record indicates whether Stewart was advised of his rights. He was convicted on robbery and first-degree murder charges.

Issue: What admonition of rights is required prior to custodial interrogation?

Reasoning: *** "Our holding will be spelled out with some specificity in the pages which follow but briefly stated it is this: The prosecution may not use statements, whether exculpatory or inculpatory, stemming from custodial interrogation of the defendant unless it demonstrates the use of procedural safeguards effective to secure the privilege against self-incrimination. By custodial interrogation, we mean questioning initiated by law enforcement officers after a person has been taken into custody or otherwise deprived of his freedom of action in any significant way. As for the procedural safeguards to be employed, unless other fully effective means are devised to inform accused persons of their right of silence and to assure a continuous opportunity to exercise it, the following measures are required. Prior to any questioning, the person must be warned that he has a right to remain silent, that any statement he does make may be used as evidence against him, and that he has a right to the presence of an attorney, either retained or appointed. The defendant may waive effectuation of these rights, provided the waiver is made voluntarily, knowingly and intelligently. If, however, he indicates in any manner and at any stage of the process that he wishes to consult with an attorney before speaking there can be no questioning. Likewise, if the individual is alone and indicates in any manner that he does not wish to be interrogated, the police many not question him. The mere fact that he may have answered some questions or volunteered some statements on his own does not deprive him of the right to refrain from answering any further inquiries until he has consulted with an attorney and thereafter consents to be questioned.

*** "We have concluded that without proper safeguards the process of in-custody interrogation of persons suspected or accused of crime contains inherently compelling pressures which work to undermine the individual's will to resist and to compel him to speak where he would not otherwise do so freely. In order to combat these pressures and to permit a full opportunity to exercise the privilege against self-incrimination, the accused must be adequately and effectively apprised of his rights and the exercise of those rights must be fully honored.

*** "At the outset, if a person in custody is to be subjected to interrogation, he must first be informed in clear and unequivocal terms that he has the right to remain silent. For those unaware of the privilege, the warning is needed simply to make them aware of it—the threshold requirement for an intelligent decision as to its exercise. More important, such a warning is an absolute prerequisite in overcoming the inherent pressures of the interrogation atmosphere. ***

*** "The warning of the right to remain silent must be accompanied by the explanation that anything said can and will be used against the individual in court. This warning is needed in order to make him aware not only of the privilege, but also of the consequences of forgoing it. It is only through an awareness of these consequences that there can be any assurance of real understanding and intelligent exercise of the privilege. Moreover, this warning may serve to make the individual more acutely aware that he is faced with a phase of the adversary system—that he is not in the presence of persons acting solely in his interest.

*** "An individual need not make a pre-interrogation request for a lawyer. While such request affirmatively secures his right to have one, his failure to ask for a lawyer does not constitute a waiver. No effective waiver of the right to counsel during interrogation can be recognized unless specifically made after the warnings we here delineate have been given. ***

"Accordingly we hold that an individual held for interrogation must be clearly informed that he has the right to consult with a lawyer and to have the lawyer with him during interrogation under the system for protecting the privilege we delineate today. As with the warnings of the right to remain silent and that anything stated can be used in evidence against him, this warning is an absolute prerequisite to interrogation. No amount of circumstantial evidence that the person may have been aware of this right will suffice to stand in its stead. ***

"If an individual indicates that he wishes the assistance of counsel before any interrogation occurs, the authorities cannot rationally ignore or deny his request on the basis that the individual does not have or cannot afford a retained attorney. The financial ability of the individual has no relationship to the scope of the rights involved here. The privilege against self-incrimination secured by the Constitution applies to all individuals. The need for counsel in order to protect the privilege exists for the indigent as well as the affluent. In fact, were we to limit these constitutional rights to those who can retain an attorney, our decisions today would be of little significance. * * *

"In order fully to apprise a person interrogated of the extent of his rights under this system then, it is necessary to warn him not only that he has the right to consult with an attorney, but also that if he is indigent a lawyer will be appointed to represent him. * * * As with the warnings of the right to remain silent and of the general right to counsel, only by effective and express explanation to the indigent of this right can there be assurance that he was truly in a position to exercise it.

"Once warnings have been given, the subsequent procedure is clear. If the individual indicates in any manner, at any time prior to or during questioning, that he wishes to remain silent, the interrogation must cease. * * * Without the right to cut off questioning, the setting of in-custody interrogation operates on the individual to overcome free choice in producing a statement after the privilege has been once invoked. If the individual states that he wants an attorney, the interrogation must cease until an attorney is present. At that time, the individual must have an opportunity to confer with the attorney and to have him present during any subsequent questioning. * * *

"This does not mean, as some have suggested, that each police station must have a 'station house lawyer' present at all times to advise prisoners. It does mean, however, that if police propose to interrogate a person they must make known to him that he is entitled to a lawyer and that if he cannot afford one, a lawyer will be provided for him prior to any interrogation. If authorities conclude that they will not provide counsel during a reasonable period of time in which investigation in the field is carried out, they may do so without violating the person's Fifth Amendment privilege so long as they do not question him during that time.

"If the interrogation continues without the presence of an attorney and a statement is taken, a heavy burden rests on the Government to demonstrate that the defendant knowingly and intelligently waived his privilege against self-incrimination and his right to retained or appointed counsel. * * *

"An express statement that the individual is willing to make a statement and does not want an attorney followed closely by a statement could constitute a waiver. But a valid waiver will not be presumed simply from the silence of the accused after warnings are given or simply from the fact that a confession was in fact eventually obtained.

* * * "Moreover, where in-custody interrogation is involved, there is no room for the contention that the privilege is waived if the individual

answers some questions or gives some information on his own prior to invoking his right to remain silent when interrogated.

"Whatever the testimony of the authorities as to waiver of rights by an accused, the fact of lengthy interrogation or incommunicado incarceration before a statement is made is strong evidence that the accused did not validly waive his rights. * * *

* * * "The warnings required and the waiver necessary in accordance with our opinion today are, in the absence of a fully effective equivalent, prerequisites to the admissibility of any statement made by a defendant. No distinction can be drawn between statements which are direct confessions and statements which amount to 'admissions' of part or all of an offense. * * * Similarly, for precisely the same reason, no distinction may be drawn between inculpatory statements and statements alleged to be merely 'exculpatory.' * * * In fact, statements merely intended to be exculpatory by the defendant are often used to impeach his testimony at trial or to demonstrate untruths in the statement given under interrogation and thus to prove guilt by implication. These statements are incriminating in any meaningful sense of the word and may not be used without the full warnings and effective waiver required for any other statement. * * *

* * * "There is no requirement that the police stop a person who enters a police station and states that he wishes to confess to a crime, or a person who calls the police to offer a confession or any other statement he desires to make. Volunteered statements of any kind are not barred by the Fifth Amendment and their admissibility is not affected by our holding today."

Disposition: Convictions reversed; prior to custodial interrogation suspects must be warned of the right to remain silent, that anything said can be used against them, and that they have the right to have an attorney (retained or appointed) present during questioning.

9-7b *Brewer v. Williams:* 430 U.S. 387, 51 L.Ed. 2d 424, 97 S.Ct. 1232 (1977)

Facts: Pamela Powers disappeared from the YMCA in Des Moines, Iowa on December 24, 1968. Williams, a recent escapee from a mental hospital who resided at the YMCA, was seen leaving the building with a bundle of clothing wrapped in a blanket at about the time of the girl's disappearance. A witness said that he saw two skinny, white legs sticking out of the bundle. On December 26, Williams surrendered to Davenport Police and was given *Miranda* warnings. He was allowed to converse with his lawyer, who was located in Des Moines, on the telephone. Officers assured the lawyer that they would not interrogate Williams until after the two had an opportunity to talk in Des Moines. Williams was arraigned on the arrest warrant. Prior to leaving the courtroom, he conferred with an attorney and was advised not to make any statements until he reached Des Moines and consulted his lawyer there. Officers denied the lawyer permission to ride with Williams but gave assurances that Williams would be allowed to confer with the Des Moines lawyer prior to questioning. At no time during the 160-mile trip did Williams express a willingness to be interrogated in the absence of an attorney but he did state several times that he would make a statement after consulting with his lawyer. Detective Leaming, who knew that Williams was a former mental patient and that he was deeply religious, had a long conversation with Williams. At one point he said: "I want to give you something to think about while we're traveling down the road. * * * Number one, I want you to observe the weather conditions, it's raining, it's sleeting, it's freezing, driving is very treacherous, visibility is poor, it's going to be dark early this evening. They are predicting several inches of snow for tonight, and I feel that you yourself are the only person that knows where this little girl's body is, that you yourself have only been there once, and if you get a snow on top of it you yourself may be unable to find it. And, since we will be going right past the area on the way into Des Moines, I feel that we could stop and locate the body, that the parents of this little girl should be entitled to a Christian burial for the little girl who was snatched away from them on Christmas [E]ve and murdered. And I feel we should stop and locate it on the way in rather than waiting until morning and trying to come back out after a snow storm and possibly not being able to find it at all." After responding to a question by Williams, Detective Leaming continued: "I do not want you to answer me. I don't want to discuss it any further. Just think about it as we're riding down the road." Williams ultimately led the officers to the girl's body. He was convicted of murder.

Issue: Did indirect questioning conducted after the suspect's arraignment violate his right to counsel?

Reasoning: * * * "There can be no doubt in the present case that judicial proceedings had been initiated against Williams before the start of the automobile ride from Davenport to Des Moines. A warrant had been issued for his arrest, he had been arraigned on that warrant before a judge in a Davenport courtroom, and he had been committed by the court to confinement in jail. * * *

"There can be no serious doubt, either, that Detective Leaming deliberately and designedly set out to elicit information from Williams just as surely as—and perhaps more effectively than—if he had formally interrogated him. * * *

*** "That the incriminating statements were elicited surreptitiously in the *Massiah* case, and otherwise here, is constitutionally irrelevant. Rather, the clear rule of *Massiah* is that once adversary proceedings have commenced against an individual, he has a right to legal representation when the government interrogates him. It thus requires no wooden or technical application of the *Massiah* doctrine to conclude that Williams was entitled to the assistance of counsel guaranteed to him by the Sixth and Fourteenth Amendments.

*** "It is true that Williams had been informed of and appeared to understand his right to counsel. But waiver requires not merely comprehension but relinquishment, and Williams' consistent reliance upon the advise of counsel in dealing with the authorities refutes any suggestion that he waived that right. ***

"Despite Williams' express and implicit assertions of his right to counsel, Detective Leaming proceeded to elicit incriminating statements from Williams. Leaming did not preface this effort by telling Williams that he had a right to the presence of a lawyer, and made no effort at all to ascertain whether Williams wished to relinquish that right. The circumstances of record in this case thus provide no reasonable basis for finding that Williams waived his right to the assistance of counsel."

Disposition: Conviction reversed; questioning of the defendant, whether direct or indirect, after the initiation of court proceedings without a waiver of the right to counsel violated the defendant's Sixth Amendment rights.

9-7c *Michigan v. Mosley:* 423 U.S. 96, 46 L.Ed. 2d 313, 96 S.Ct. 321 (1975)

Facts: Mosley was arrested in Detroit in the early afternoon of April 8, 1971 in connection with two recent robberies. He was taken to the Robbery, Breaking and Entering Bureau located on the fourth floor of the departmental headquarters building. He was advised of his *Miranda* rights and indicated that he did not want to answer any questions. Mosley was then returned to his cell. Shortly after 6:00 P.M., a detective from Homicide Bureau took Mosley to his fifth floor office for questioning about a fatal shooting during a holdup attempt that was unrelated to the robberies he had been questioned about earlier. A new set of *Miranda* warnings was administered. Mosley indicated he understood his rights and at first denied any involvement in the murder. After being told that another person had confessed and implicated him as the "shooter," Mosley made a statement that implicated himself in the homicide. Mosley was convicted of first-degree murder.

Issue: Can the police initiate another interrogation session after a suspect has invoked the right to remain silent?

Reasoning: *** "A reasonable and faithful interpretation of the *Miranda* opinion must rest on the intention of the Court in that case to adopt 'fully effective means *** to notify the person of his right of silence and to assure that the exercise of the right will be scrupulously honored *** .' The critical safeguard identified in the passage at issue is a person's 'right to cut off questioning.' Through the exercise of his option to terminate questioning he can control the time at which questioning occurs, the subjects discussed, and the duration of the interrogation. The requirement that law enforcement authorities must respect a person's exercise of that option counteracts the coercive pressure of the custodial setting. We therefore conclude that the admissibility of statements obtained after the person in custody has decided to remain silent depends under *Miranda* on whether his 'right to cut off questioning' was 'scrupulously honored.'

*** "This is not a case, therefore, where the police failed to honor a decision of a person in custody to cut off questioning, either by refusing to discontinue the interrogation upon request or by persisting in repeated efforts to wear down his resistance and make him change his mind. In contrast to such practices, the police here immediately ceased the interrogation, resumed questioning only after the passage of a significant period of time and the provision of a fresh set of warnings, and restricted the second interrogation to a crime that had not been a subject of the earlier interrogation."

Disposition: Conviction affirmed; interrogation may be resumed after a suspect invokes the right to remain silent if his/her right to cut off questioning has been scrupulously guarded and a valid waiver of the right to remain silent has been obtained.

9-7d *Edwards v. Arizona:* 451 U.S. 477, 68 L.Ed. 2d 378, 101 S.Ct. 1880 (1981)

Facts: On January 19, 1976, police issued an arrest warrant for Edwards for robbery, burglary, and first-degree murder. Officers arrested him later the same day at his home and took him to the police station. Edwards initially waived his *Miranda* rights. After being told another suspect had been arrested and implicated him, Edwards denied involvement and gave a taped statement presenting an alibi. He then sought to "make a deal." The interrogating officer told him that he did not have the authority to make deals and provided Edwards with the telephone number of the county attorney. Edwards made a call but hung up after a few moments.

He then said, "I want an attorney before making a deal." Officers stopped the questioning at this point and took Edwards to the county jail. At about 9:15 the next morning, two detectives came to the county jail and asked to see Edwards. Edwards told the guard that he did not want to talk to anyone. The guard replied that "he had" to talk and then took him to meet the detectives who identified themselves and gave him his *Miranda* rights. Edwards said he was willing to talk but first he wanted to hear the alleged accomplices taped statement that incriminated him. After listening to the statement, he said he would make a statement but the detectives could not tape-record it. The detectives told him that the fact that the statement was recorded was irrelevant because they could testify in court to what was said. Edwards again said he would talk so long as no tape recording was made. By his statement, he implicated himself in the crime. Edwards was convicted.

Issue: Can police officers institute custodial interrogation after a person has invoked *Miranda* rights by demanding an attorney?

Reasoning: *** "It is reasonably clear under our cases that waivers of counsel must not only be voluntary, but constitute a knowing and intelligent relinquishment or abandonment of a known right or privilege, a matter which depends in each case 'upon the particular facts and circumstances surrounding that case, including the background, experience and conduct of the accused.'

*** "[A]lthough we have held that after initially being advised of his *Miranda* rights, the accused may himself validly waive his rights and respond to interrogation, the Court has strongly indicated that additional safeguards are necessary when the accused asks for counsel; and we now hold that when an accused has invoked his right to have counsel present during custodial interrogation, a valid waiver of that right cannot be established by showing only that he responded to further police-initiated custodial interrogation even if he has been advised of his rights. We further hold that an accused, such as Edwards, having expressed his desire to deal with the police only through counsel, is not subject to further interrogation by the authorities until counsel has been made available to him, unless the accused himself initiates further communication, exchanges or conversations with the police.

*** "In concluding that the fruits of the interrogation initiated by the police on January 20 could not be used against Edwards, we do not hold or imply that Edwards was powerless to countermand his election or that the authorities could in no event use any incriminating statements made by Edwards prior to his having access to counsel. Had Edwards initiated the meeting on January 20, nothing in the Fifth and Fourteenth Amendments would prohibit the police from merely listening to his voluntary, volunteered statements and using them against him at the trial. The Fifth Amendment right identified in *Miranda* is the right to have counsel present at any custodial interrogation. Absent such interrogation, there would have been no infringement of the right that Edwards invoked and there would be no occasion to determine whether there had been a valid waiver."

Disposition: Conviction reversed; once the suspect has been advised of his/her *Miranda* rights and requested an attorney, officers cannot initiate additional interrogation until the suspect has had an opportunity to consult with an attorney.

9-8 Other Supreme Court Cases

9-8a *Stansbury v. California:* 511 U.S. 318, 128 L.Ed. 2d 293, 114 S.Ct. 1526 (1994)

Facts: Ten-year old Robyn Jackson disappeared from a playground in Baldwin Park, California at about 6:30 P.M. on September 28, 1982. Early the next morning, about 10 miles away in Pasadena, Andrew Zimmerman observed a large man emerge from a turquoise, American sedan and throw something into a nearby flood-control channel. Zimmerman called the police, who came to the scene and discovered Robyn's body. There was evidence that she had been raped; the cause of death was asphyxia complicated by blunt-force trauma to the head. Lt. Johnston, a homicide detective investigating the case, learned from witnesses that Robyn had talked to two ice cream truck drivers, one being Stansbury, the afternoon of her disappearance. Johnston considered the other driver the leading suspect, but sent officers to ask both to come to the station for questioning as possible witnesses to the crime. At the station, Johnston questioned Stansbury about his activities on the day in question. Stansbury told officers that he spoke with the victim about 6:00 P.M., returned to his home about 9:00 P.M. after work, and that he left home about midnight in his housemate's turquoise, American-made car. The description of the car aroused Lt. Johnston's suspicion because it matched the description given by Zimmerman. During further questioning, Stansbury admitted to having prior convictions for rape, kidnapping, and child molestation. Lt. Johnston terminated the interview. Another officer administered *Miranda* warnings; Stansbury requested an attorney and declined to make further statements. At trial, Stansbury was convicted of first-degree murder and other crimes; the penalty was fixed at death.

Issue: Is the suspect in custody for purposes of *Miranda* if the officer has formed the subjective intent to arrest the suspect?

Reasoning: *** "An officer's obligation to administer *Miranda* warnings attaches, however, 'only where there has been such a restriction on a person's freedom as to render him "in custody."' In determining whether an individual was in custody, a court must examine all of the circumstances surrounding the interrogation, but 'the ultimate inquiry is simply whether there [was] a "formal arrest or restraint on freedom of movement" of the degree associated with a formal arrest.'

"Our decisions make clear that the initial determination of custody depends on the objective circumstances of the interrogation, not on the subjective views harbored by either the interrogating officer or the person being questioned. In *Beckwith v. United States*, 425 U.S. 341 (1976), for example, the defendant, without being advised of his *Miranda* rights, made incriminating statements to Government agents during an interview in a private home. . . . We. . . explain[ed] that it 'was the compulsive aspect of custodial interrogation, and not the strength or content of the government's suspicions at the time the questioning was conducted, which led the Court to impose the *Miranda* requirements with respect to custodial questioning.' As a result, we concluded that the defendant was not entitled to *Miranda* warnings: 'Although the "focus" of an investigation may indeed have been on Beckwith at the time of the interview . . . , he hardly found himself in the custodial situation described by the *Miranda* Court as the basis for its holding.'

"*Berkemer v. McCarty*, 468 U.S. 420 (1984), reaffirmed the conclusions reached in Beckwith. . . . We decided that the motorist was not in custody for purposes of *Miranda* even though the traffic officer 'apparently decided as soon as [the motorist] stepped out of his car that [the motorist] would be taken into custody and charged with a traffic offense.' The reason, we explained, was that the officer 'never communicated his intention to' the motorist during the relevant questioning. The lack of communication was crucial, for under *Miranda* '[a] policeman's unarticulated plan has no bearing on the question whether a suspect was "in custody" at a particular time'; rather, 'the only relevant inquiry is how a reasonable man in the suspect's shoes would have understood his situation.' ***

"It is well settled, then, that a police officer's subjective view that the individual under questioning is a suspect, if undisclosed, does not bear upon the question whether the individual is in custody for purposes of *Miranda.* The same principle obtains if an officer's undisclosed assessment is that the person being questioned is not a suspect. In either instance, one cannot expect the person under interrogation to probe the officer's innermost thoughts. Save as they are communicated or otherwise manifested to the person being questioned, an officer's evolving but unarticulated suspicions do not affect the objective circumstances of an interrogation or interview, and thus cannot affect the *Miranda* custody inquiry. * * *

"An officer's knowledge or beliefs may bear upon the custody issue if they are conveyed, by word or deed, to the individual being questioned. Those beliefs are relevant only to the extent they would affect how a reasonable person in the position of the individual being questioned would gauge the breadth of his or her '"freedom of action."' Even a clear statement from an officer that the person under interrogation is a prime suspect is not, in itself, dispositive of the custody issue, for some suspects are free to come and go until the police decide to make an arrest. The weight and pertinence of any communications regarding the officer's degree of suspicion will depend upon the facts and circumstances of the particular case. In sum, an officer's views concerning the nature of an interrogation, or beliefs concerning the potential culpability of the individual being questioned, may be one among many factors that bear upon the assessment whether that individual was in custody, but only if the officer's views or beliefs were somehow manifested to the individual under interrogation and would have affected how a reasonable person in that position would perceive his or her freedom to leave. (Of course, instances may arise in which the officer's undisclosed views are relevant in testing the credibility of his or her account of what happened during an interrogation; but it is the objective surroundings, and not any undisclosed views, that control the *Miranda* custody inquiry.)"

Disposition: Case remanded to state court to determine whether the subjective facts indicate the suspect was in custody at the time statement was made.

9-8b *Oregon v. Mathiason:* 429 U.S. 492, 50 L.Ed. 2d 714, 97 S.Ct. 711 (1977)

Facts: Mathiason, a parolee, was the only suspect in a burglary. An officer went to his house several times but no one was home. He left his card with a note asking Mathiason to call him. Finally, they met at the station, shook hands, and went to an office. The door of the office was closed during the subsequent interview regarding the burglary. The officer falsely told Mathiason that his fingerprints had been found at the scene. Five minutes had elapsed from the time he entered the office and to when he admitted taking the property. He was then advised of his *Miranda* rights and a confession. Mathiason was not arrested until a later date. He was convicted of first-degree burglary.

Issue: Are *Miranda* warnings required prior to interrogations conducted inside a police station if the suspect is not under arrest?

Reasoning: *** "In the present case, however, there is no indication that the questioning took place in a context where respondent's freedom to depart was restricted in any way. He came voluntarily to the police station, where he was immediately informed that he was not under arrest. At the close of a 1/2-hour interview respondent did in fact leave the police station without being arrested. It is clear from these facts that Mathiason was not in custody 'or otherwise deprived of his freedom of action in any significant way.'

*** "But police officers are not required to administer *Miranda* warnings to everyone whom they question. Nor is the requirement of warnings to be imposed simply because the questioning takes place in the station house, or because the questioned person is one whom the police suspect. *Miranda* warnings are required only where there has been such a restriction on a person's freedom as to render him 'in custody.' "

Disposition: Conviction affirmed; *Miranda* warnings are not required when a suspect who is not under arrest is questioned even if the questioning takes place in the police station.

9-8c *Minnesota v. Murphy:* 465 U.S. 420, 79 L.Ed. 2d 409, 104 S.Ct. 1136 (1984)

Facts: In 1974, Murphy was twice questioned by Minneapolis police regarding the rape and murder of a teenage girl. In 1980, he pled guilty to false imprisonment as a reduced charge for an unrelated, criminal sex crime. He was given three years' probation and a suspended prison sentence. As a term of probation he was to attend a treatment program for sexual offenders at Alpha House. In September 1981, an Alpha House counselor informed Murphy's probation officer that Murphy had confessed to the 1974 rape-murder. The probation officer determined that the police should have the information and wrote to Murphy asking him to come and discuss a treatment plan for the remainder of his probation. When Murphy met with the probation officer, he was told what Alpha

House had said and that it evinced his continued need for treatment. Murphy became angry at the breach of his confidence and stated that he "felt like calling a lawyer." The probation officer replied that he would have to deal with that problem outside the office because their immediate concern was the connection between his conviction and the rape-murder. During the subsequent interview, Murphy denied the crime for which he had been convicted but admitted the rape-murder. The probation officer advised Murphy to turn himself in but he did not do so. Two days later, the probation officer obtained an arrest and detention order. Murphy was convicted on the murder charge.

Issue: Does a probation officer have to give *Miranda* warnings prior to noncustodial questioning of a probationer about criminal activity?

Reasoning: *** "Under the narrower standard appropriate in the *Miranda* context, it is clear that Murphy was not 'in custody' for the purposes of receiving *Miranda* protection since there was no 'formal arrest or restraint on freedom of movement' of the degree associated with a formal arrest.

*** "Since Murphy was not physically restrained and could have left the office, any compulsion he might have felt from the possibility that terminating the meeting would have led to revocation of probation was not comparable to the pressure on a suspect who is painfully aware that he literally cannot escape a persistent custodial interrogation.

*** "Murphy was informed that he was required to be truthful with his probation officer in all matters and that failure to do so could result in revocation of probation. *** Such compulsion, however, is indistinguishable from that felt by any witness who is required to appear and give testimony, and, as we have already made clear, it is insufficient to excuse Murphy's failure to exercise the privilege in a timely manner."

Disposition: Conviction affirmed; *Miranda* warnings are not required prior to noncustodial interrogation by a probation officer.

9-8d *Berkemer v. McCarty:* 468 U.S. 420, 82 L.Ed. 2d 317, 104 S.Ct. 3138 (1984)

Facts: On the evening of March 31, 1980, Trooper Williams observed McCarty's car weaving in and out of a lane of traffic. He followed the car for two miles and then stopped it. When McCarty exited the vehicle as requested, Williams noticed that McCarty was having trouble standing. Williams decided to charge McCarty with a traffic offense and had him perform a field sobriety test, which he failed. In response to questions regarding consumption of intoxicants, McCarty said he had consumed two beers and smoked several joints of marijuana. McCarty was then formally arrested and transported to the county jail. Intoxilyzer tests showed no alcohol in his blood. Williams then resumed questioning in order to obtain information for his report regarding whether McCarty had been drinking and if the marijuana had been treated with angel dust or PCP. McCarty had not been given any *Miranda* warnings. McCarty pled "no contest" to misdemeanor charges of driving under the influence.

Issue: Are *Miranda* warnings required at the scene of a noncustodial arrest such as the issuing of a traffic citation?

Reasoning: *** "[T]he usual traffic stop is more analogous to a so-called 'Terry stop' than to a formal arrest. *** The comparatively nonthreatening character of detentions of this sort explains the absence of any suggestion in our opinions that Terry stops are subject to the dictates of *Miranda*. The similarly noncoercive aspect of ordinary traffic stops prompts us to hold that persons temporarily detained pursuant to such stops are not 'in custody' for the purposes of *Miranda*."

Disposition: Conviction affirmed; McCarty did not have to be warned of his *Miranda* rights prior to his formal arrest.

9-8e *Orozco v. Texas:* 394 U.S. 324, 22 L.Ed. 2d 311, 89 S.Ct. 1095 (1969)

Facts: Orozco became involved in an altercation outside a restaurant, apparently over the fact that another man spoke to his female companion. Orozco shot the victim after the man beat him and called him racially insulting names. Four officers went to his boarding house about 4:00 A.M. They considered Orozco to be under arrest as soon as they verified his name. He was then asked if he had been at the restaurant and if he had a gun. He told officers that the gun was inside a washing machine in a back room of the boarding house. Tests showed that this gun was the one that had fired the fatal shot. Orozco was convicted of murder without malice.

Issue: Do the *Miranda* warnings need to be given prior to questioning that is not conducted inside a police facility?

Reasoning: *** "It is true that the Court did say in *Miranda* that 'compulsion to speak in the isolated setting of the police station may well be greater than in courts or other official investigations, where there are other impartial observers to guard against intimidation or trickery.' But the opinion iterated and reiterated the absolute necessity for officers interrogating people 'in custody' to give the described warnings. According to the officer's testimony, petitioner was under arrest and not free to leave when he was questioned in his bedroom in the early hours of the morning. The *Miranda* opinion declared that the warnings were required when the person being interrogated was 'in custody at the station *or otherwise deprived of his freedom of action significant in any way.*' "

Disposition: Conviction reversed; *Miranda* warnings are required any time a person is under custodial arrest.

9-8f *Illinois v. Perkins:* 496 U.S. 292 110 L.Ed. 2d 243, 110 S.Ct. 2394 (1990)

Facts: In March 1986, police learned from Carlton, an informant, that Perkins had confessed to a previously unsolved murder that occurred in November 1984. The informant and an undercover officer, who posed as escapees from a work release program arrested in the course of a burglary, were placed in Perkins's cellblock. The undercover officer told Perkins that he "wasn't going to do any more time," and suggested the three of them escape. Perkins replied that the jail was "rinky-dink" and they could "break out." The trio met in Perkins's cell late at night to refine their plan. Perkins claimed his girlfriend could smuggle in a pistol. Carlton said, "Hey, I'm not a murderer, I'm a burglar. That's your guys' profession." The undercover officer said he would be responsible for any murder that occurred and then asked Perkins if he had ever "done" anybody. Perkins said that he had, and then gave a detailed description of the murder. Perkins's motion to suppress the statement was granted because no *Miranda* warnings had been given.

Issue: Are *Miranda* warnings required prior to questioning by an undercover officer posing as an inmate?

Reasoning: *** "We reject the argument that *Miranda* warnings are required whenever a suspect is in custody in a technical sense and converses with someone who happens to be a government agent. Questioning by captors, who appear to control the suspect's fate, may create mutually reinforcing pressures that the Court has assumed will weaken the suspect's will, but where a suspect does not know that he is conversing with a government agent, these pressures do not exist. ***

"*Miranda* forbids coercion, not mere strategic deception by taking advantage of a suspect's misplaced trust in one he supposes to be a fellow prisoner. *** Ploys to mislead a suspect or lull him into a false sense of security that do not rise to the level of compulsion or coercion to speak are not within *Miranda's* concerns."

Disposition: Suppression motion was granted in error; *Miranda* warnings are not required when the suspect is not aware that he/she is speaking to a government agent.

9-8g *Rhode Island v. Innis:* 446 U.S. 291, 64 L.Ed. 2d 297, 100 S.Ct. 1682 (1980)

Facts: On the night of January 12, 1975, a taxicab driver disappeared after being dispatched to pick up a customer. Four days later, his body was discovered in a shallow grave. He died from a shotgun blast to the back of his head. Just after midnight on January 17, another taxi driver called police and said that he had just been robbed by a man with a sawed-off shotgun. He reported where he dropped the man off and identified a picture of Innis as his assailant. About 4:30 A.M., Patrolman Lovell observed Innis standing in the street and arrested him. *Miranda* warnings were administered but no conversations took place at that time. The warnings were given two more times by other officers arriving at the scene. Innis stated that he understood his rights but wanted to talk to his lawyer. Three officers were ordered to transport Innis to the central police station and directed not to question him. While en route to the station, one of the patrolmen initiated a conversation with another officer regarding the missing shotgun and said that there was a school for handicapped children located nearby and "God forbid one of them might find the weapon with shells and hurt themselves." The other officer concurred. Innis then interrupted the conversation, stating that the officers should turn the car around so he could show them where the gun was located. When they returned to the scene, another set of *Miranda* warnings was given prior to allowing Innis to lead them to the hidden gun. Innis was convicted for kidnap, robbery, and murder.

Issue: Was the officers' conversation conducted in the suspect's presence the functional equivalent of interrogation?

Reasoning: *** "We conclude that the *Miranda* safeguards come into play whenever a person in custody is subjected to either express questioning or its functional equivalent. That is to say, the term 'interrogation' under *Miranda* refers not only to express questioning, but also to any words or actions on the part of the police (other than those normally attendant to arrest and custody) that the police should know are reasonably likely to elicit an incriminating response from the suspect. The latter portion of this definition focuses primarily upon the perceptions of the suspect, rather than the intent of the police. *** A practice that the police should know is reasonably likely to evoke an incriminating response from a suspect thus amounts to interrogation. But, since the police surely cannot be held accountable for the unforeseeable results of their words or actions, the definition of interrogation can extend only to words or actions on the part of police officers that they *should have known* were reasonably likely to elicit an incriminating response."

Disposition: Conviction affirmed; the conversation between the patrolmen was not the functional equivalent of interrogation because there is no showing that they knew or should have known that their comments were likely to elicit a response from the suspect.

9-8h *Estelle v. Smith:* 451 U.S. 454, 68 L.Ed. 2d 359, 101 S.Ct. 1866 (1981)

Facts: On December 28, 1973, Smith was indicted for a murder occurring during the robbery of a grocery store. After the state announced its intention of seeking the death penalty, a judge ordered the State's Attorney to arrange a psychiatric examination of Smith by Dr. Grigson to determine Smith's competence to stand trial. Dr. Grigson interviewed Smith for approximately 90 minutes and concluded that he was competent to stand trial. During the penalty phase of the trial, Dr. Grigson testified that Smith was a "very severe sociopath" whose condition would only get worse and that he would continue his previous behavior if returned to society. Smith was convicted and sentenced to death.

Issue: Must a defendant be advised of the *Miranda* rights prior to court-ordered psychiatric examinations?

Reasoning: *** "Dr. Grigson's prognosis as to future dangerousness rested on statements respondent made, and remarks he omitted, in reciting the details of the crime. The Fifth Amendment privilege, therefore, is directly involved here because the State used as evidence against respondent the substance of his disclosures during the pretrial psychiatric examination.

*** "The considerations calling for the accused to be warned prior to custodial interrogation apply with no less force to the pretrial psychiatric examination at issue here. *** When Dr. Grigson went beyond simply reporting to the court on the issue of competence and testified for the prosecution at the penalty phase on the crucial issue of respondent's future dangerousness, his role changed and became essentially like that of an agent of the State recounting unwarned statements made in a post-arrest custodial setting. * * *

"A criminal defendant, who neither initiates a psychiatric evaluation nor attempts to introduce any psychiatric evidence, may not be compelled to respond to a psychiatrist if his statements can be used against him at a capital sentencing proceeding. Because respondent did not voluntarily consent to the pretrial psychiatric examination after being informed of his right to remain silent and the possible use of his statements, the State could not rely on what he said to Dr. Grigson to establish his future dangerousness. If, upon being adequately warned, respondent had indicated that he would not answer Dr. Grigson's questions, the validly ordered competency examination nevertheless could have proceed upon the condition that the results would be applied solely for that purpose.

* * * "Here, respondent's Sixth Amendment right to counsel clearly had attached when Dr. Grigson examined him at the Dallas County Jail, and their interview proved to be a 'critical stage' of the aggregate proceedings against respondent. Defense counsel, however, were not notified in advance that the psychiatric examination would encompass the issue of their client's future dangerousness, and respondent was denied the assistance of his attorneys in making the significant decision of whether to submit to the examination and to what end the psychiatrist's findings could be employed."

Disposition: Death sentence reversed; the prosecution's use of a court-ordered psychiatric exam at penalty phase was in error because the defendant's Fifth and Sixth Amendment rights had been violated because he did not receive *Miranda* warnings prior to the interviews.

9-8i *New York v. Quarles:* 467 U.S. 649, 81 L.Ed. 2d 550, 104 S.Ct. 2626 (1984)

Facts: On September 11, 1980 at approximately 12:30 A.M., Officers Kraft and Scarring were on patrol in Queens when a woman approached their car and told them that she had just been raped. She told the officers that the man had just entered the A & P supermarket located nearby and that he was carrying a gun. Officer Kraft entered the store and spotted Quarles, who matched the description given by the victim, approaching a check-out counter. Upon seeing the officer, Quarles turned and ran toward the rear of the store. Officer Kraft pursued him with a drawn gun but briefly lost sight of him when he turned a corner at the end of an aisle. When the officer regained sight of Quarles, he ordered him to stop and put his hands over his head. By this time more officers had arrived at the scene. Officer Kraft was the first to reach Quarles. He frisked him and discovered he was wearing an empty shoulder holster. After handcuffing him, Officer Kraft asked Quarles where the gun was. Quarles nodded in the direction of some empty cartons and said "the gun is over there." A loaded .38-caliber revolver was retrieved from one of the cartons. Quarles was formally arrested and given *Miranda* rights, which he waived. Quarles admitted owning the gun and was charged with criminal possession of a weapon.

Issue: Can statements obtained in violation of *Miranda* be used in court if they were obtained in order to protect public safety in an emergency?

Reasoning: *** "We hold that on these facts there is a 'public safety' exception to the requirement that *Miranda* warnings be given before a suspect's answers may be admitted into evidence, and that the availability of that exception does not depend upon the motivation of the individual officers involved. ***

"Whatever the motivation of individual officers in such a situation, we do not believe that the doctrinal underpinnings of *Miranda* require that it be applied in all its rigor to a situation in which police officers ask questions reasonably prompted by a concern for the public safety. ***

*** "Here, had *Miranda* warnings deterred Quarles from responding to Officer Kraft's question about the whereabouts of the gun, the cost would have been something more than merely the failure to obtain evidence useful in convicting Quarles. Officer Kraft needed an answer to his question not simply to make his case against Quarles but to insure that further danger to the public did not result from the concealment of the gun in a public area.

"We conclude that the need for answers to questions in a situation posing a threat to the public safety outweighs the need for the prophylactic rule protecting the Fifth Amendment's privilege against self-incrimination."

Disposition: Conviction affirmed; the gun found in response to Officer Kraft's question is admissible because the question was asked in order to protect the public from injury.

9-8j *California v. Prysock:* 453 U.S. 355, 69 L.Ed. 2d 696, 101 S.Ct. 2806 (1981)

Facts: On January 30, 1978, Prysock and a codefendant were arrested for a murder that had occurred earlier that day. Prysock, who was a minor, initially invoked his *Miranda* rights but after conversations with his parents, decided to talk to police. He was then re-advised of his rights in the following fashion: "You have the right to remain silent. This means you don't have to talk to me at all unless you so desire. If you give up your right to remain silent, anything you say can and will be used as evidence against you in a court of law. You have the right to talk to a lawyer before you are questioned, have him present with you while you are being questioned, and all during the questioning. You also, being a juvenile, have the right to have your parents present. You have the right to have a lawyer appointed to represent you at no cost to yourself." The mother then asked if Prysock could still have an attorney at a later time if he gave a statement now without one. She was assured that her son would have an attorney when he went to court and that "he could have one at this time if he wished one." Statements made after this conversation were admitted at trial. Prysock was convicted of first-degree murder.

Issue: Do *Miranda* warnings have to be in language nearly identical to that used in the original *Miranda* opinion?

Reasoning: *** "This Court has never indicated that the 'rigidity' of *Miranda* extends to the precise formulation of the warnings given a criminal defendant. This Court and others have stressed as one virtue of *Miranda* the fact that the giving of the warnings obviates the need for a case-by-case inquiry into the actual voluntariness of the admissions of the accused. Nothing in these observations suggests any desirable rigidity in the form of the required warnings.

"Quite the contrary, *Miranda* itself indicated that no talismanic incantation was required to satisfy its strictures. The Court in that case stated that '[t]he warnings required and the waiver necessary in accordance with our opinion today are, *in the absence of a fully effective equivalent,* prerequisites to the admission of any statement made by a defendant.'"

Disposition: Conviction affirmed; *Miranda* warnings must convey the intended content of the Court but do not have to mirror its language.

9-8k *Duckworth v. Eagan:* 492 U.S. 195, 106 L.Ed. 2d 166, 109 S.Ct. 2875 (1989)

Facts: Late on May 16, 1982, Eagan contacted a police officer he knew to report that he had seen the naked body of a dead woman lying on a Lake Michigan beach. He denied any involvement in criminal activity. He took several Chicago police officers to the beach where the found the woman alive and crying for help. When she saw Eagan she said, "Why did you stab me?" Eagan told the police that he had been with the woman earlier when several men attacked them and abducted the woman. Hammond, Indiana police questioned him at about 11:00 A.M. and read a *Miranda* waiver form to him, which said, in part, "You have a right to talk to a lawyer for advice before we ask you any questions, and to have him with you during questioning. You have this right to the advice and presence of a lawyer even if you cannot afford to hire one. We have no way of giving you a lawyer, but one will be appointed for you, if you wish, if and when you go to court." Eagan waived his rights. After a second interview, he confessed to stabbing the woman because she refused to have sex with him. Eagan was convicted of attempted murder.

Issue: Was the *Miranda* waiver valid even though it indicated that appointed counsel would not be available until the suspect went to court?

Reasoning: * * * "First, this instruction accurately described the procedure for the appointment of counsel in Indiana. * * * We think it must be relatively commonplace for a suspect, after receiving *Miranda* warnings, to ask *when* he will obtain counsel. The 'if and when you go to court' advice simply anticipates that question. Second, *Miranda* does not require that attorneys be producible on call, but only that the suspect be informed, as here, that he has the right to an attorney before and during questioning, and that an attorney would be appointed for him if he could not afford one. * * *

* * * "[W]e hold that the initial warnings given to respondent, in their totality, satisfied *Miranda,* and therefore that his first statement denying his involvement in the crime, as well as the knife and the clothing were all properly admitted into evidence."

Disposition: Conviction affirmed; the *Miranda* warnings stating that the suspect had the right to counsel but that counsel would not be appointed until the first court appearance satisfied *Miranda.*

9-8l *Arizona v. Fulminante:* 499 U.S. 279, 113 L.Ed. 2d 302, 111 S.Ct. 1246 (1991)

Facts: Fulminante was a suspect in the rape-murder of his 11-year-old stepdaughter but was not arrested. He moved to another state and was later convicted on federal charges of possession of a firearm by a felon. In prison, he became friends with Sarivola, a paid FBI informant who masqueraded as an organized crime figure. Sarivola heard rumors that Fulminante was suspected of killing a child and raised the issue in several conversations. Fulminante repeatedly denied involvement but gave conflicting accounts of the circumstances surrounding the girl's death.

Sarivola passed the information on to the FBI. Sarivola told Fulminante he knew he was "starting to get some tough treatment and what-not" from other inmates because of the rumors. He offered to protect Fulminante from his fellow inmates, but only if Fulminante told him about the killing. Fulminante confessed to Sarivola. He was later convicted for the girl's murder and sentenced to death.

Issue: Is a confession made under a perceived threat of violence by third parties voluntary?

Reasoning: * * * "Although the question is a close one, we agree with the Arizona Supreme Court's conclusion that Fulminante's confession was coerced. The Arizona Supreme Court found a credible threat of physical violence unless Fulminante confessed. Our cases have made clear that a finding of coercion need not depend upon actual violence by a government agent; a credible threat is sufficient. As we have said, 'coercion can be mental as well as physical, and . . . the blood of the accused is not the only hallmark of an unconstitutional inquisition.' As in *Payne [Payne v. Arkansas,* 356 U.S. 560 (1958)], where the Court found that a confession was coerced because the interrogating police officer had promised that if the accused confessed, the officer would protect the accused from an angry mob outside the jailhouse door, so too here, the Arizona Supreme Court found that it was fear of physical violence, absent protection from his friend (and Government agent) Sarivola, which motivated Fulminante to confess. Accepting the Arizona court's finding, . . . that there was a credible threat of physical violence, we agree with its conclusion that Fulminante's will was overborne in such a way as to render his confession the product of coercion."

Disposition: Confession inadmissible; it was obtained by coercion.

9-8m *Colorado v. Connelly:* 479 U.S. 157, 93 L.Ed. 2d 473, 107 S.Ct. 515 (1986)

Facts: On August 18, 1983, Connelly approached Officer Anderson and, without any prompting, stated that he had murdered someone and wanted to talk about it. Officer Anderson immediately gave him the *Miranda* warnings. Connelly said he understood the warnings but still wanted to talk. In response to questions, Connelly denied drinking or using drugs but admitted that he had been a patient in several mental hospitals. After again being advised that he did not have to talk, Connelly stated that it was "all right" and that he wanted to talk because his conscience was bothering him. Homicide detectives arrived and again advised Connelly of his rights. Connelly claimed that he had come from Boston to confess to a murder that occurred in Denver in November 1982. Connelly took the officers to the scene of the crime and pointed out the exact location of the murder. The next morning when being interviewed by a public defender, Connelly became visibly disoriented and began giving confused answers to questions. He was evaluated at the state hospital and initially declared incompetent to stand trial. By March 1984, the doctors decided he had sufficiently recovered. At a suppression hearing, a psychiatrist from the state hospital testified that Connelly was suffering from chronic schizophrenia and was in a psychotic state the day before he confessed. At that time, he believed the "voice of God" told him to either come to Denver and confess or commit suicide. The psychiatrist believed that Connelly had experienced "command hallucinations" that interfered with his "volitional abilities" to make rational choices. This condition did not interfere with his cognitive abilities and he was able to understand his *Miranda* rights. The trial court suppressed the confession as "involuntary."

Issue: Did the suspect's mental state make his *Miranda* waiver invalid because it was involuntary?

Reasoning: * * * "We hold that coercive police activity is a necessary predicate to the finding that a confession is not 'voluntary' within the meaning of the Due Process Clause of the Fourteenth Amendment. We also conclude that the taking of respondent's statements, and their admission into evidence, constitute no violation of that Clause.

* * * "*Miranda* protects defendants against government coercion leading them to surrender rights protected by the Fifth Amendment; it goes no further than that. Respondent's perception of coercion flowing from the 'voice of God,' however important or significant such a perception may be in other disciplines, is a matter to which the United States Constitution does not speak."

Disposition: Suppression motion granted in error; the confession is admissible because the police did not exert coercion.

9-8n *Moran v. Burbine:* 475 U.S. 412, 89 L.Ed. 2d 410, 106 S.Ct. 1135 (1986)

Facts: Burbine was arrested in Cranston, Rhode Island for burglary. He refused to waive his *Miranda* rights. At about 7:00 P.M., officers from Providence, Rhode Island arrived at the station to question him about a murder. At about 7:45 P.M., Burbine's sister (who did not know about the murder charge) telephoned the Public Defender's office, which already represented Burbine on unrelated charges, seeking legal assistance for Burbine on the burglary charge. An attorney from the Public Defender's Office called the detective division and explained that she would represent Burbine; the police told her they would not question him or put him in a lineup. She was not informed that Providence officers were at the station to question Burbine about the murder. Burbine was not told of the efforts to obtain counsel for him or that the attorney had telephoned. Less than an hour later, the first of several interrogation sessions began. *Miranda* warnings were given prior to each session. Burbine signed three separate waiver forms indicating that he understood his right to have counsel present and indicating that he did not want an attorney called or appointed for him. Eventually, Burbine signed three written statements fully admitting the murder. He was convicted of murder in the first degree.

Issue: Does the fact that the police did not inform the suspect (who had not asked for an attorney) that his family had arranged for an attorney to represent him invalidate a subsequent confession?

Reasoning: *** "Nor do we believe that the level of the police's culpability in failing to inform respondent of the telephone call has any bearing on the validity of the waiver. *** But whether intentional or inadvertent, the state of mind of the police is irrelevant to the question of the intelligence and voluntariness of respondent's election to abandon his rights. Although highly inappropriate, even deliberate deception of an attorney could not possibly affect a suspect's decision to waive his *Miranda* rights unless he were at least aware of the incident. Nor was the failure to inform respondent of the telephone call the kind of 'trick[ery]' that can vitiate the validity of a waiver. Granting that the 'deliberate or reckless' withholding of information is objectionable as a matter of ethics, such conduct is only relevant to the constitutional validity of a waiver if it deprives a defendant of knowledge essential to his ability to understand the nature of his rights and the consequences of abandoning them. Because respondent's voluntary decision to speak was made with full awareness and comprehension of all the information *Miranda* requires the police to convey, the waivers were valid."

Disposition: Conviction affirmed; prior to arraignment or indictment, a *Miranda* waiver is valid even though police do not inform the suspect that an attorney had been retained for him/her.

9-8o *Colorado v. Spring:* 479 U.S. 364, 93 L.Ed. 2d 954, 107 S.Ct. 851 (1987)

Facts: In February 1979, Spring and a companion shot and killed Walker during a hunting trip in Colorado. Shortly thereafter, an informant told agents of the Bureau of Alcohol, Tobacco, and Firearms (ATF) that Spring was engaged in interstate transportation of stolen firearms. The informant also said Spring had told him about killing Walker. At that time, Walker's body had not been found and no missing person's report had been made about him. ATF set up an undercover operation to purchase firearms from Spring and arrested him in Kansas City, Missouri during an undercover purchase. Spring was advised of his *Miranda* rights at the scene of the arrest and again at the Kansas City ATF office. Spring waived his rights. ATF agents first questioned Spring about the firearms transaction and then asked about his criminal record. He was asked if he had ever shot anyone and admitted that he had, but he denied ever being in Colorado. Two months later, Colorado officers visited Connelly in jail where he was awaiting trial on the firearms charges. Spring waived his *Miranda* rights and indicated that he wanted to get the killing "off his chest." He confessed during a 90-minute interview. A written statement was prepared that Spring edited. Spring was convicted of first-degree murder.

Issue: Is a waiver of *Miranda* invalid if the suspect was not aware of the possible subjects of the questioning?

Reasoning: *** "There also is no doubt that Spring's waiver of his Fifth Amendment privilege was knowingly and intelligently made: that is, that Spring understood that he had the right to remain silent and that anything he said could be used as evidence against him. The Constitution does not require that a criminal suspect know and understand every possible consequence of a waiver of the Fifth Amendment privilege. ***

*** " '[W]e have never read the Constitution to require that the police supply a suspect with a flow of information to help him calibrate his self-interest in deciding whether to speak or stand by his rights.' Here, the additional information could affect only the wisdom of a *Miranda* waiver, not its essentially voluntary and knowing nature. Accordingly, the failure of the law enforcement officials to inform Spring of the subject matter of the interrogation could not affect Spring's decision to waive his Fifth Amendment privilege in a constitutionally significant manner."

Disposition: Conviction affirmed; officers do not have to inform a suspect of all topics the interrogation will cover in order to obtain a valid *Miranda* waiver.

9-8p *North Carolina v. Butler:* 441 U.S. 369, 60 L.Ed. 2d 286, 99 S.Ct. 1755 (1979)

Facts: Butler and Lee robbed a gas station in Goldsboro in December 1976 and shot the station attendant as he was attempting to escape. The attendant was paralyzed but survived and testified at trial. Butler was arrested by FBI agents in the Bronx, New York, based on a fugitive warrant. Agent Martinez fully advised Butler of his *Miranda* rights and then took Butler to the FBI office in New Rochelle. Agents determined that Butler had an 11th-grade education and was literate. Butler was then given an "Advise of Rights" form, which he read. When asked if he understood his rights, he replied that he did but he refused to sign the waiver at the bottom of the form. He was told that he need neither speak nor sign the form, but that the agents would like him to talk to them. Butler replied, "I will talk to you but I am not signing any form." He then made incriminating statements. At no time did Butler request a lawyer or attempt to terminate the interview. Butler was convicted for the armed robbery, kidnapping, and felonious assault.

Issue: Does the waiver of *Miranda* rights have to be made explicitly in order to be valid?

Reasoning: *** "An express written or oral statement of waiver of the right to remain silent or of the right to counsel is usually strong proof of the validity of that waiver, but is not inevitably either necessary or sufficient to establish waiver. The question is not one of form, but rather whether the defendant in fact knowingly and voluntarily waived the rights delineated in the *Miranda* case. As was unequivocally said in *Miranda*, mere silence is not enough. That does not mean that the defendant's silence, coupled with an understanding of his rights and a course of conduct indicating waiver, may never support a conclusion that a defendant has waived his rights. The courts must presume that a defendant did not waive his rights; the prosecution's burden is great; but in at least some cases waiver can be clearly inferred from the actions and words of the person interrogated."

Disposition: Conviction affirmed; a waiver of *Miranda* rights can be inferred from the suspect's conduct after officers have verified that he/she understands his/her rights.

9-8q *Connecticut v. Barrett:* 479 U.S. 523, 93 L.Ed. 2d 920, 107 S.Ct. 828 (1987)

Facts: In the early morning of October 24, 1980, Barrett was transported to Wallingford, Connecticut where he was a suspect in a sexual assault. Barrett was given *Miranda* warnings, acknowledged that he understood them, and stated that "he would not give the police any written statements without consulting his attorney but he had no problem in talking about the incident." Thirty minutes later, he made a similar statement to a different officer when another set of *Miranda* warnings was given. He gave an oral statement admitting his involvement in the crime. A second interview was conducted because the tape recorder used by the police during the first interrogation had failed. He waived his *Miranda* rights in a similar fashion and again made incriminating statements. He was convicted.

Issue: Is a lawyer required at an interview if a suspect waives *Miranda* by saying he is willing to make oral but not written statements without consulting with an attorney?

Reasoning: *** "It is undisputed that Barrett desired the presence of counsel before making a written statement. Had the police obtained such a statement without meeting the wavier standards of *Edwards,* it would clearly be inadmissible. Barrett's limited requests for counsel, however, were accompanied by affirmative announcements of this willingness to speak with the authorities. The fact that officials took the opportunity provided by Barrett to obtain an oral confession is quite consistent with the Fifth Amendment. *Miranda* gives the defendant a right to choose between speech and silence, and Barrett chose to speak.

*** "We also reject the contention that the distinction drawn by Barrett between oral and written statements indicates an understanding of the consequences so incomplete that we should deem his limited invocation of the right to counsel effective for all purposes."

Disposition: Conviction affirmed; the statement that he would make oral, but not written, statement without a lawyer present did not invoke the right to counsel for oral interviews.

9-8r *Smith v. Illinois:* 469 U.S. 91, 83 L.Ed. 2d 488, 105 S.Ct. 490 (1984)

Facts: Shortly after his arrest, two police detectives took Smith, who was 18 years old, to an interrogation room for questioning. During the administration of the *Miranda* warnings, Smith was asked if he understood that he had the right to have a lawyer present when he was being questioned. He replied, "Uh, yeah. I'd like to do that." The following dialogue took place after the detective went on to explain that a lawyer would be appointed if Smith could not afford one:

> Detective: "If you want a lawyer and you're unable to pay for one a lawyer will be appointed to represent you free of cost, do you understand that?"
>
> Smith: "Okay."
>
> Detective: "Do you wish to talk to me at this time without a lawyer being present?"
>
> Smith: "Yeah and no, uh, I don't know what's what, really."
>
> Detective: "Well. You either have to talk to me this time without a lawyer being present and if you do agree to talk with me without a lawyer being present you can stop at any time you want to."
>
> Smith: "All right. I'll talk to you then."

Smith then admitted knowledge of the planned robbery but denied participating in it. After considerable probing, Smith confessed to committing the robbery but later returned to his earlier story. Smith was convicted for armed robbery.

Issue: Did Smith invoke his right to counsel?

Reasoning: *** "Neither the State nor the courts below, for example, have pointed to anything Smith previously had said that might have cast doubt on the meaning of his statement 'I'd like to do that' upon learning that he had the right to his counsel's presence. Nor have they pointed to anything inherent in the nature of Smith's actual request for counsel that reasonably would have suggested equivocation. ***

*** "Our decision is a narrow one. We do not decide the circumstances in which an accused's request for counsel may be characterized as ambiguous or equivocal as a result of events preceding the request or of nuances inherent in the request itself, nor do we decide the consequences of such ambiguity or equivocation. We hold only that, under the clear logical force of settle precedent, an accused's post-request responses to further interrogation may not be used to cast retrospective doubt on the clarity of the initial request itself. Such subsequent statements are relevant only to the distinct question of waiver."

Disposition: Conviction reversed; when the initial request for counsel is unambiguous, further questioning regarding the request for assistance violates the suspect's rights.

9-8s *Oregon v. Elstad:* 470 U.S. 298, 84 L.Ed. 2d 222, 105 S.Ct. 1285 (1985)

Facts: In December 1981, a home was burglarized and $150,000 worth of art objects and furnishings taken. A witness implicated Elstad, an 18-year-old neighbor and friend of the owner's teenage son. Officers went to Elstad's home with a warrant and arrested him. While in the living room, Elstad engaged in a brief conversation with the officer during which he admitted being present during the burglary. About an hour later at the police station, Elstad was advised of his *Miranda* rights for the first time. He waived his rights and made a full statement, which was then typed. He reviewed the statement and signed it. Elstad was convicted of burglary in the first degree.

Issue: Does lack of administering *Miranda* warnings prior to one interrogation make a confession obtained at a later interrogation session, in which *Miranda* was properly administered, inadmissible?

Reasoning: *** "It is an unwarranted extension of *Miranda* to hold that a simple failure to administer the warnings, unaccompanied by any actual coercion or other circumstances calculated to undermine the suspect's ability to exercise his free will so taints the investigatory process that a subsequent voluntary and informed waiver is ineffective for some indeterminate period. Though *Miranda* requires that the unwarned admission must be suppressed, the admissibility of any subsequent statement should turn in these circumstances solely on whether it is knowingly and voluntarily made.

*** "We must conclude that absent deliberate coercive or improper tactics in obtaining the initial statement, the mere fact that a suspect has made an unwarned admission does not warrant a presumption of compulsion. A subsequent administration of *Miranda* warnings to a suspect who has given a voluntary but unwarned statement ordinarily should suffice to remove the conditions that precluded admission of the earlier statement. ***

*** "We hold today that a suspect who has once responded to unwarned yet uncoercive questioning is not thereby disabled from waiving his rights and confessing after he has been given the requisite *Miranda* warnings."

Disposition: Conviction affirmed; a statement made after a valid *Miranda* waiver is admissible even though officers obtained a prior, uncoerced statement in violation of *Miranda*.

9-8t *Davis v. United States:* 512 U.S. 452, 129 L.Ed. 2d 362, 114 S.Ct. 2350 (1994)

Facts: Davis and Shackleford were shooting pool and betting on games at a club on a Navy base. Shackleford, who refused to pay a $30 bet, was beaten to death with a pool cue after the club closed. Naval Investigative Service agents handling the case interviewed Davis and advised him of his *Miranda* rights as required by the Uniform Code of Military Justice. Davis waived his rights. About an hour and a half into the interview he said, "Maybe I should talk to a lawyer." The agents then told Davis that they would stop the interview if he wanted a lawyer. Davis said, "No, I'm not asking for a lawyer." The interview continued for another hour before Davis invoked the right to counsel. Davis was convicted of unpremeditated murder.

Issue: Must questioning stop when a suspect makes an equivocal statement about wanting a lawyer?

Reasoning: *** "If the suspect effectively waives his right to counsel after receiving the *Miranda* warnings, law enforcement officers are free to question him. But if a suspect requests counsel at any time during the interview, he is not subject to further questioning until a lawyer has been made available or the suspect himself reinitiates conversation. . . .

"The applicability of the '"rigid" prophylactic rule' of *Edwards* requires courts to 'determine whether the accused *actually invoked* his right to counsel.' (emphasis added by Court) To avoid difficulties of proof and to provide guidance to officers conducting interrogations, this is an objective inquiry. Invocation of the *Miranda* right to counsel 'requires, at a minimum, some statement that can reasonably be construed to be an expression of a desire for the assistance of an attorney.' But if a suspect makes a reference to an attorney that is ambiguous or equivocal in that a reasonable officer in light of the circumstances would have understood only that the suspect *might* be invoking the right to counsel, our precedents do not require the cessation of questioning. ***

"We recognize that requiring a clear assertion of the right to counsel might disadvantage some suspects who—because of fear, intimidation, lack of linguistic skills, or a variety of other reasons—will not clearly articulate their right to counsel although they actually want to have a lawyer present. But the primary protection afforded suspects subject to custodial interrogation is the *Miranda* warnings themselves. '[F]ull comprehension of the rights to remain silent and request an attorney [is] sufficient to dispel whatever coercion is inherent in the interrogation process.' A suspect who knowingly and voluntarily waives his right to counsel after having that right explained to him has indicated his willingness to deal with the police unassisted. Although *Edwards* provides an additional protection—if a suspect subsequently requests an attorney, questioning must cease—it is one that must be affirmatively invoked by the suspect. * * *

"Of course, when a suspect makes an ambiguous or equivocal statement it will often be good police practice for the interviewing officers to clarify whether or not he actually wants an attorney. That was the procedure followed by the NIS agents in this case. Clarifying questions help protect the rights of the suspect by ensuring that he gets an attorney if he wants one, and will minimize the chance of a confession being suppressed due to subsequent judicial second-guessing as to the meaning of the suspect's statement regarding counsel. But we decline to adopt a rule requiring officers to ask clarifying questions. If the suspect's statement is not an unambiguous or unequivocal request for counsel, the officers have no obligation to stop questioning him." * * *

Disposition: Conviction affirmed; officers are not required to clarify a suspect's equivocal or ambiguous request for an attorney.

9-8u *Arizona v. Roberson:* 486 U.S. 675, 100 L.Ed. 2d 704, 108 S.Ct. 2093 (1988)

Facts: On April 16, 1985, Roberson was arrested at the scene of a burglary and immediately advised of his *Miranda* rights. He replied that he "wanted a lawyer before answering any questions." The conversation was recorded in the arresting officer's report. On April 19, while still in custody, an officer who was not aware of the previous request for counsel interrogated Roberson about a burglary that had occurred on April 15. Roberson made incriminating statements concerning that burglary. The trail judge suppressed these statements.

Issue: Can officers interrogate a suspect for any reason after the suspect has requested counsel in response to *Miranda* warnings?

Reasoning: * * * "Roberson's unwillingness to answer any questions without the advice of counsel, without limiting his request for counsel, indicated that he did not feel sufficiently comfortable with the pressures of custodial interrogation to answer questions without an attorney. This discomfort is precisely the state of mind that *Edwards* presumes to persist unless the suspect himself initiates further conversation about the investigation; unless he otherwise states, there is no reason to assume that a suspect's state of mind is in any way investigation specific.

* * * "Whether a contemplated reinterrogation concerns the same or a different offense, or whether the same or different law enforcement authorities are involved in the second investigation, the same need to determine whether the suspect has requested counsel exists. The police department's failure to honor that request cannot be justified by the lack of diligence of a particular officer."

Disposition: Suppression order correctly granted; when a suspect requests an attorney, law enforcement may not initiate new interrogation sessions about the original crime or a different crime.

9-8v *Minnick v. Mississippi:* 498 U.S. 146, 112 L.Ed. 2d 489, 111 S.Ct. 486 (1990)

Facts: Minnick and Dyess escaped from a county jail in Mississippi. The following day, they broke into a mobile home in search of weapons but were interrupted when the owner, accompanied by a friend and an infant, arrived home. The two adults who had intruded on the burglary were killed. Two women who arrived at the mobile home were bound and left at the scene. The fugitives fled to Mexico where they fought. Minnick then went to California alone. On Friday, August 22, 1986, he was arrested on a Mississippi murder warrant and held in the San Diego County Jail. The next day two, FBI agents came to the jail to interview him. Minnick refused to go to the interview but was told he had to "go down or else." He refused to sign a *Miranda* waiver form and said he would not answer "very many" questions. He then made statements blaming Dyess for the killings and claimed that he acted under threat of his own life. The agents reminded him that he did not have to answer questions without a lawyer present. Minnick replied, "Come back Monday when I have a lawyer," and promised to make a more complete statement then. An appointed attorney met with Minnick after the FBI interview and again on two or three other occasions. On Monday, a deputy from Clarke County, Mississippi came to the jail to question Minnick. Again the jailers told Minnick that he "could not refuse." He again refused to sign a *Miranda* waiver. He then told the deputy about the escape and the killings, placing blame on Dyess. Minnick was convicted on two counts of murder.

Issue: Is a confession obtained after giving *Miranda* warnings admissible if the suspect is in custody and has previously requested to speak to an attorney?

Reasoning: *** "In our view, a fair reading of *Edwards* and subsequent cases demonstrates that we have interpreted the rule to bar police-initiated interrogation unless the accused has counsel with him at the time of questioning. Whatever the ambiguities of our earlier cases on this point, we now hold that when counsel is requested, interrogation must cease, and officials may not re-initiate interrogation without counsel present, whether or not the accused has consulted with his attorney.

"We consider our ruling to be an appropriate and necessary application of the *Edwards* rule. A single consultation with an attorney does not remove the suspect from persistent attempts by officials to persuade him to waive his rights, or from the coercive pressures that accompany custody and that may increase as custody is prolonged.

*** "*Edwards* does not foreclose finding a waiver of Fifth Amendment protections after counsel has been requested, provided the accused has initiated the conversation or discussions with the authorities; but that is not the case before us."

Disposition: Conviction reversed; once a suspect has invoked *Miranda* by requesting an attorney, police may not initiate questioning unless the suspect has an attorney present during questioning.

9-8w *McNeil v. Wisconsin:* 501 U.S. 171, 115 L.Ed. 2d 158, 111 S.Ct. 2204 (1991)

Facts: McNeil was arrested in Omaha, Nebraska, on a warrant charging him with armed robbery in West Allis, Wisconsin. Shortly after arrest, two Milwaukee County deputy sheriffs advised him of his *Miranda* rights. McNeil refused to answer questions but did not request an attorney. He was arraigned and bail was set in Milwaukee County on the robbery charge. An attorney from the Wisconsin Public Defender's Office was appointed to represent him during the initial appearance. Later that evening, a detective investigating a murder, an attempted murder, and an armed burglary in Caledonia, Wisconsin, visited McNeil at the jail and advised him of his *Miranda* rights. McNeil signed a waiver form and did not deny involvement in the case. Two days later, the detective returned, obtained a new *Miranda* waiver, and McNeil admitted involvement in the crime.

Issue: Can police interview a suspect without an attorney present if the suspect has invoked the right to counsel at arraignment?

Reasoning: *** "In *Edwards v. Arizona,* 451 U.S. 477 (1981), we established a second layer of prophylaxis for the *Miranda* right to counsel: Once a suspect asserts the right, not only must the current interrogation cease, but he may not be approached for further interrogation 'until counsel has been made available to him,'—which means, we have most recently held, that counsel must be present. If the police do subsequently initiate an encounter in the absence of counsel (assuming there has been no break in custody), the suspect's statements are presumed involuntary and therefore inadmissible as substantive evidence at trial, even where the suspect executes a waiver and his statements would be considered voluntary under traditional standards. This is 'designed to prevent police from badgering a defendant into waiving his previously asserted *Miranda* rights.' The *Edwards* rule, moreover, is *not* offense-specific: Once a suspect invokes the *Miranda* right to counsel for interrogation regarding one offense, he may not be reapproached regarding *any* offense unless counsel is present.***

. . . "The purpose of the Sixth Amendment counsel guarantee—and hence the purpose of invoking it—is to 'protec[t] the unaided layman at critical confrontations' with his 'expert adversary,' the government after 'the adverse positions of government and defendant have solidified' with respect to a particular alleged crime. The purpose of the *Miranda-Edwards* guarantee, on the other hand—and hence the purpose of invoking it—is to protect a quite different interest: the suspect's 'desire to deal with the police only through counsel.' *** [T]he *likelihood* that a suspect would wish counsel to be present is not the test for applicability of *Edwards*. The rule of that case applies only when the suspect 'ha[s] *expressed*' his wish for the particular sort of lawyerly assistance that is the subject of *Miranda*. It requires, at a minimum, some statement that can reasonably be construed to be expression of a desire for the assistance of an attorney *in dealing with custodial interrogation by the police*. Requesting the assistance of an attorney at a bail hearing does not bear that construction."

Disposition: Conviction affirmed; a post-arraignment confession with a valid *Miranda* waiver of the right to counsel is admissible as long as defendant has not invoked the right to counsel under *Miranda* during custodial interrogation.

9-8x *Massiah v. United States:* 377 U.S. 201, 12 L.Ed. 2d 246, 84 S.Ct. 1199 (1964)

Facts: In 1958, Massiah, a merchant seaman, was a member of the crew of the S.S. Santa Maria. In April, Customs agents received a tip that Massiah was going to transport narcotics from South America to the United States aboard that ship. Customs agents searched the Santa Maria upon arrival in New York and found approximately 3-1/2 pounds of cocaine. They also discovered other information connecting Massiah to the cocaine. Massiah was arrested and promptly arraigned; an indictment followed. In July, a superseding indictment was returned charging Massiah and Colson with the original offense and charging Colson with conspiracy and importing narcotics for sale. Massiah, who had retained a lawyer, entered a plea of not guilty and was released. A few days later, Colson decided to cooperate with the government agents in their investigation of Massiah's on-going activities. Agent Murphy, with Colson's consent, installed a radio transmitter under the front seat of Colson's car. Agent Murphy was equipped with a receiver so that he could overhear the conversations from a distance. On the evening of November 19, 1959, Colson and Massiah had a lengthy conversation while sitting in Colson's car, which was parked on a New York street. By prearrangement with Colson, Murphy monitored the conversations from a car that was parked out-of-sight down the street. Incriminating statements made during this conversation were introduced at trial. Massiah was convicted of several narcotics-related offenses.

Issue: Do noncustodial interrogations conducted after arraignment, with neither counsel present nor a waiver of counsel, violate the defendant's Sixth Amendment rights?

Reasoning: *** "We do not question that in this case, as in many cases, it was entirely proper to continue an investigation of the suspected criminal activities of the defendant and his alleged confederates, even though the defendant had already been indicted. All that we hold is that the defendant's own incriminating statements, obtained by federal agents under the circumstances here disclosed, could not constitutionally be used by the prosecution as evidence against him at his trial."

Disposition: Conviction reversed; post-indictment statements obtained without a waiver of counsel or having counsel present violate the defendant's Sixth Amendment rights.

9-8y *Texas v. Cobb:* 532 U.S. 162, 149 L.Ed. 2d 321, 121 S.Ct. 1335 (2001)

Facts: The Walker County Sheriff's Office received a report that the home of Lindsey Owings had been burglarized and his wife Margaret and their 16-month-old daughter Kori Rae were missing. Cobb, who lived across the street from the burglarized house, was questioned and released. Cobb later confessed to the burglary and an attorney was appointed to represent him on the burglary charge. Investigators received permission from the attorney and questioned Cobb on two occasions regarding the disappearance of the woman and baby; Cobb continued to deny involvement. In November 1995, while Cobb was free on bond in the burglary case, his father contacted the Walker County Sheriff's Office and reported that Cobb had confessed to the killings. After Cobb was arrested on a murder warrant, he waived his *Miranda* rights and confessed to the two murders. He later led investigators to the location where he had buried the victims' bodies. Cobb was convicted of capital murder and sentenced to death.

Issue: Were investigators allowed to question Cobb about the murders without an attorney present while he was represented by counsel on the burglary charge?

Reasoning: "Although it is clear that the Sixth Amendment right to counsel attaches only to charged offenses, we have recognized in other contexts that the definition of an 'offense' is not necessarily limited to the four corners of a charging instrument. In *Blockburger v. United States* 284 U.S. 299 (1932), we explained that 'where the same act or transaction constitutes a violation of two distinct statutory provisions, the test to be applied to determine whether there are two offenses or only one, is whether each provision requires proof of a fact which the other does not.' We have since applied the *Blockburger* test to delineate the scope of the Fifth Amendment's Double Jeopardy Clause, which prevents multiple or successive prosecutions for the 'same offense.' We see no constitutional difference between the meaning of the term 'offense' in the contexts of double jeopardy and of the right to counsel. Accordingly, we hold that when the Sixth Amendment right to counsel attaches, it does encompass offenses that, even if not formally charged, would be considered the same offense under the *Blockburger* test.

* * * "It remains only to apply these principles to the facts at hand. At the time he confessed to Odessa police, respondent had been indicted for burglary of the Owings residence, but he had not been charged in the murders of Margaret and Kori Rae. As defined by Texas law, burglary and capital murder are not the same offense under *Blockburger*. Accordingly, the Sixth Amendment right to counsel did not bar police from interrogating respondent regarding the murders, and respondent's confession was therefore admissible."

Disposition: Murder conviction affirmed; police had the right to question Cobb without an attorney present about the murder after he waived *Miranda* because his attorney was not representing him on the charge under investigation.

9-8z *United States v. Henry:* 447 U.S. 264, 65 L.Ed. 2d 115, 100 S.Ct. 2183 (1980)

Facts: On November 12, 1972, Nichols, an inmate in the Norfolk City jail who had previously been a confidential informant for the FBI, contacted government agents. Nichols stated that he was housed in the same cell-block with Henry. Agents told Nichols to be alert to any statements made by federal prisoners but not to initiate any conversations or question them. Nichols was later paid for reporting a conversation in which Henry told about the robbery of the Janaf bank. Henry was convicted of bank robbery.

Issue: Does post-indictment questioning by a government informant while an inmate is in jail awaiting trial violated the inmate's Sixth Amendment rights?

Reasoning: *** "The question here is whether under the facts of this case, a government agent 'deliberately elicited' incriminating statements from Henry within the meaning of *Massiah*. Three factors are important. First, Nichols was acting under instructions as a paid informant for the government; second Nichols was ostensibly no more than a fellow inmate of Henry; and third, Henry was in custody and under indictment at the time he was engaged in conversation by Nichols.

*** "Even if the agent's statement is accepted that he did not intend that Nichols would take affirmative steps to secure incriminating information, he must have known that such propinquity likely would lead to that result.

*** "It is quite a different matter when the government uses undercover agents to obtain incriminating statements from persons not in custody but suspected of criminal activity prior to the time charges are filed. *** But the Fourth and Fifth Amendment claims made in those cases are not relevant to the inquiry under the Sixth Amendment here—whether the government has interfered with the right to counsel of the accused by 'deliberately eliciting' incriminating statements. ***

*** "By intentionally creating a situation likely to induce Henry to make incriminating statements without the assistance of counsel, the government violated Henry's Sixth Amendment right to counsel."

Disposition: Conviction reversed; using an inmate informant after the suspect has been indicted violates his Sixth Amendment right to counsel.

9-8aa *Patterson v. Illinois:* 487 U.S. 285, 101 L.Ed. 2d 261, 108 S.Ct. 2389 (1988)

Facts: Before dawn on August 21, 1983, Patterson and other members of the "Vice Lords" street gang became involved in a fight with their rival, the "Black Mobsters." Some time later, Jackson, a former Black Mobster, went to the home where the Vice Lords had fled. Patterson and three other Vice Lords beat Jackson severely, drove him to the end of a nearby street, and left him face down in a puddle of water. Police later discovered Jackson dead at this location. Patterson was arrested a few hours later and given his *Miranda* rights. He volunteered to answer questions and gave a statement about the initial fight but denied knowing anything about Jackson's death. On August 23, Patterson and two other gang members were indicted for Jackson's death. Prior to transportation from the holding cell to the Cook County jail, Patterson asked who had been indicted. When he learned that one of the participants had not been indicted he said, "Why wasn't he indicted, he did everything?" Patterson explained that there was a witness who could support his version of the incident. The officer then interrupted Patterson and handed him a *Miranda* waiver form and read the warnings aloud. Patterson initialed the warnings and then made a lengthy statement. He made a second confession later that day. Patterson was convicted of murder.

Issue: Did post-indictment questioning, following a *Miranda* waiver but without an attorney present, deprive Patterson of his right to counsel?

Reasoning: *** "The fact that petitioner's Sixth Amendment right came into existence with his indictment, i.e., that he had such a right at the time of his questioning, does not distinguish him from the pre-indictment interrogatee whose right to counsel is in existence and available for his exercise while he is questioned. Had petitioner indicated he wanted the assistance of counsel, the authorities' interview with him would have stopped, and further questioning would have been forbidden (unless petitioner called for such a meeting). *** Preserving the integrity of an accused's choice to communicate with police only through counsel is the essence of *Edwards* and its progeny—not barring an accused from making an *initial* election as to whether he will face the State's officers during questioning with the aid of counsel, or go it alone. If an accused 'knowingly and intelligently' pursues the latter course, we see no reason why the uncounseled statements he then makes must be excluded at his trial.

*** "As a general matter, then, an accused who is admonished with the warnings prescribed by this Court in *Miranda* has been sufficiently apprised of the nature of his Sixth Amendment rights, and of the consequences of abandoning those rights, so that his waiver on this basis will be considered a knowing and intelligent one."

Disposition: Conviction affirmed; where there had been no prior request for an attorney, *Miranda* warnings are adequate to advise an indicted defendant of his/her right to counsel prior to questioning.

Chapter Quiz

True/False

1. A person cannot invoke the Fifth Amendment as a reason to refuse to give a blood sample for DNA testing.
2. *Miranda* warnings must be given at the time a person is arrested.
3. *Miranda* warnings must be given prior to all interrogations.
4. *Miranda* warnings can be given only in the exact words provided by the Supreme Court.
5. A waiver of the *Miranda* rights is valid only if it was knowingly, intelligently, and voluntarily made.
6. Once a suspect invokes his/her *Miranda* rights, he/she may never be questioned again about the crime under discussion when the rights were invoked.
7. Police officers may attempt to question a person after he/she invoked the *Miranda* right to remain silent if there has been a sufficient time lapse to indicate the suspect's rights will be scrupulously honored.
8. If a suspect waives his/her *Miranda* rights at the beginning of an interrogation, the suspect retains the right to invoke those rights at anytime.
9. Once a person has been given *Miranda* warnings and demanded an attorney, questioning can be resumed at the request of the police only if there is an attorney present.
10. Once a suspect has been arraigned, he/she can be questioned about the crimes that have been charged only if there is an attorney present or the suspect waives the right to have an attorney present

Discussion Questions

1. Michael was the prime suspect in a murder. Three police detectives cornered him at his office and began rapidly asking him questions. Michael was frightened and confessed after the officers said they would not leave until he told them why the victim was shot. Can Michael have his statements suppressed because he was not given his *Miranda* rights? Explain.
2. Sandy was convicted of driving under the influence of alcohol and sentenced to spend 30 days at a secure detoxification center. Ten days after Sandy began serving her sentence, the police went to the detoxification center to question her about the accident because the other driver had just died of injuries suffered in the collision. Do the police need to give *Miranda* warnings prior to this questioning? Explain.
3. Sean was arrested for burglary and taken to an interrogation room. When he was given his *Miranda* warnings, he absolutely refused to waive his right to counsel. Questioning immediately stopped and he was taken to the booking area. The booking officer asked the routine questions and then started to inventory everything he found in Sean's pockets. He found several merchant deposit slips from the local bank and said "Where did you get these?" Sean replied, "Oh, John must have left those at my house after we did the bank job last week." Can Sean have this statement suppressed as a violation of his *Miranda* rights? Explain.
4. Bill was arrested for a bank robbery. A police officer started to question him without giving him any warnings but quit a few minutes later because a high-priority call came in. Later that afternoon, another officer took Bill to an interrogation room and gave him his *Miranda* rights. Bill said that he did not mind talking for a few minutes but he wanted to talk to his lawyer before he confessed. In the conversation that followed, Bill admitted being at the scene of the crime. Can Bill have this statement suppressed because his rights were violated? Explain.
5. George was indicted for extortion but was never taken into custody because the judge believed there was no danger of his fleeing the county. The following week, a police officer saw George at a restaurant. He casually stopped by the table and began to talk to George. During the conversation, George admitted that he had received money from the victim but claimed that it was a gift. Can this statement be admitted at trial? Explain

Chapter 10

Identification Procedures

Outline

Three basic procedures are used to allow victims or eyewitnesses to identify the person who committed a crime: lineup, showup, and photographic lineup. Fourth, Fifth, Sixth, and Fourteenth Amendment rights must be considered.

10-1 Definitions

A **lineup** is a procedure in which the victim or an eyewitness is asked to view a group of people and select the person who committed the crime.

A **showup** is a much simpler procedure. One suspect is shown to the person who is to make the identification. This can be done in the field or at a police facility.

A **photographic lineup** involves showing pictures. The suspect does not need to be in custody when this is done. It may involve handing the witness a few carefully selected photographs or allowing him/her to look through mug books.

10-2 Fourth Amendment Rights

There is no special exception to the Fourth Amendment that allows police to detain a suspect solely to conduct a lineup or a showup. A suspect may be detained briefly based on reasonable suspicion and a showup conducted at the scene of this detention; the suspect may not be transported to the station under these circumstances.

Probable cause to arrest is necessary to transport the suspect to the police station. Once there, either a lineup or a showup may be conducted for any crime in which the person arrested is suspected of participating.

10-3 Fifth Amendment Rights

Being identified by an eyewitness is very incriminating, but the privilege not to incriminate oneself applies only to testimonial communications. The Supreme Court held that a legally arrested suspect has no Fifth Amendment right to refuse to participate in a lineup. The suspect can be required to walk, take a particular stance, wear clothing or disguises, or make gestures observed during the commission of the crime. While none of these procedures violates the Fifth Amendment, due process demands fundamental fairness. Any special effects that are used on one person in a lineup must be applied to all of the participants.

Voice exemplars are not covered by the Fifth Amendment. Although they require the suspect to speak, he/she is told what to say. Therefore, the content of the speech is not incriminating. For this reason, the participants in a lineup or a showup can be required to repeat what the witness claims the criminal said during the commission of the crime.

10-4 Sixth Amendment Rights

The defendant has the right to have counsel present during in-court identification procedures. This applies whenever a witness is asked if the person who committed the crime is present in the courtroom. It does not matter whether the identification is made before, during, or after the court hearing; it applies if done formally while the witness is testifying or informally while court is in recess.

The suspect has a right to counsel during a lineup *only after* adversary court proceedings have begun; the same is true for showups. Adversary proceedings usually begin with arraignment or indictment. On the other hand, there is no right to counsel during an identification procedure if the suspect is not present. Photographic lineups can be done without either the suspect or an attorney present whether the pictures are shown before or after arraignment.

10-5 Due Process Rights

The Fourteenth Amendment's Due Process Clause ensures that the justice systems in the 50 states are based on fundamental fairness. Similar Fifth Amendment protections apply to cases in federal courts. In the area of identification procedures, this means that the police must not use unnecessarily suggestive techniques. If there is a substantial likelihood of mistaken identification, the evidence will not be admissible in court.

10-5a Lineups and Photographic Lineups

Lineups and photographic lineups have many of the same problems. Nothing in the way these procedures are conducted should point to one individual. One of the first rules is that there must be a good selection of individuals with similar characteristics. Five to seven individuals are adequate. Each person in the lineup must match the general description of the perpetrator of the crime. The goal is to have participants who are sufficiently similar so there is no clue as to which one is the suspect. Anything that makes the suspect stand out is unduly suggestive.

Additional problems arise if the same witness views more than one lineup, photographic lineup, or showup. The fact that the witness sees one suspect twice may cause him/her to draw the inference that the person who was in both lineups is the one the police believe committed the crime. This is unduly suggestive.

Care must be taken to prevent witnesses from drawing their conclusions based on the way the identification procedures were conducted, rather than their memory of the crime scene. The officers conducting the lineup or photographic lineup must be careful not to indicate by words or gestures which participant is believed to be the criminal. Each person in a lineup must be asked to do and say the same things. Equal time should be devoted to each participant. Each witness must make an independent decision. Witnesses should not be allowed to discuss their choices with each other.

10-5b Showups

Many of the protections against unduly suggestive lineups do not apply to showups because usually only one person is shown to the witness. Some rules govern both types of identification procedures: Police should not coach the witnesses and witnesses must arrive at their conclusions independently.

In showup cases, the United States Supreme Court has focused on the reliability of the identification. Factors considered include the opportunity of the witness to view the suspect at the time of the crime (including lighting and the length of time the witness was with the suspect); the degree of attention the witness paid to the suspect while the crime was in progress; the level of certainty of the witness; the accuracy of a prior description of the suspect; prior inaccurate identifications made by the witness; and the length of time between showup and crime.

This approach was also applied to a case in which only one photograph was shown for identification purposes. While the Court found this procedure was suggestive, the conviction was upheld because the totality of the circumstances indicated that the procedure did not corrupt the witness.

10-6 Use of Identification Testimony at Trial

Testimony in the jury's presence regarding an identification procedure that violated the defendant's right to counsel is grounds for automatic reversal of a conviction. The Harmless Error Rule applies to the prosecution's introduction of evidence about identification procedures that violated other constitutional rights. If the defense challenges the constitutional validity of the process, a hearing must be held without the jury present prior to any witnesses testifying about the events at the lineup, showup, or photographic lineup in question.

The Fruit of the Poison Tree Doctrine has been applied to in-court identifications that followed improper pretrial procedures. If the in-court testimony is not influenced by the unconstitutional procedure, the witness may testify about the crime scene and make an in-court identification of the defendant. The prosecutor cannot ask questions about the improperly conducted lineup or other procedure, but the defense can bring up the issue on cross-examination.

10-7 Key Supreme Court Cases

10-7a *United States v. Wade:* 388 U.S. 218, 18 L.Ed. 2d 1149, 87 S.Ct. 1926 (1967)

Facts: A man entered a bank in Eustace, Texas, on September 21, 1964, wearing a small strip of tape on each side of his face. He pointed a gun at the teller and vice president and forced them to fill a pillowcase with the bank's money. The robber fled with an accomplice in a stolen car that was waiting outside. Wade was indicted for the robbery six months later and arrested about a week after that. Fifteen days after counsel was appointed to represent him, an FBI agent put Wade in a lineup without informing Wade's attorney. Each person in the lineup wore strips of tape on his face and was required to say, "Put the money in the bag." Both bank employees picked Wade out of the lineup and identified him again at trial. Wade was convicted.

Issue: Does a suspect have the right to have an attorney present during a lineup?

Reasoning: *** "Neither the lineup itself nor anything shown by this record that Wade was required to do in the lineup violated his privilege against self-incrimination. *** "We have no doubt that compelling the accused merely to exhibit his person for observation by a prosecution witness prior to trial involves no compulsion of the accused to give evidence having testimonial significance. It is compulsion of the accused to exhibit his physical characteristics, not compulsion to disclose any knowledge he might have. *** Similarly, compelling Wade to speak within hearing distance of the witnesses, even to utter words purportedly uttered by the robber, was not compulsion to utter statements of a 'testimonial' nature; he was required to use his voice as an identifying physical characteristic, not to speak his guilt. * * *

* * * "In sum, the principle of *Powell v. Alabama* and succeeding cases requires that we scrutinize *any* pretrial confrontation of the accused to determine whether the presence of his counsel is necessary to preserve the defendant's basic right to a fair trial as affected by his right meaningfully to cross-examine the witnesses against him and to have effective assistance of counsel at the trial itself. It calls upon us to analyze whether potential substantial prejudice to defendant's rights inheres in the particular confrontation and the ability of counsel to help avoid that prejudice.

* * * "The identification of strangers is proverbially untrustworthy. * * * A major factor contributing to the high incidence of miscarriage of justice from mistaken identification has been the degree of suggestion inherent in the manner in which the prosecution presents the subject to witnesses for pretrial identification. * * *

* * * "Since it appears that there is grave potential for prejudice, intentional or not, in the pretrial lineup, which may not be capable of reconstruction at trial, and since presence of counsel itself can often avert prejudice and assure a meaningful confrontation at trial, there can be little doubt that for Wade the post-indictment lineup was a critical stage of the prosecution at which he was 'as much entitled to such aid [of counsel] * * * as at the trial itself.' Thus both Wade and his counsel should have been notified of the impending lineup, and counsel's presence should have been a requisite to conduct of the lineup, absent an 'intelligent waiver.' * * *

* * * "We come now to the question whether the denial of Wade's motion to strike the courtroom identification by the bank witnesses at trial because of the absence of his counsel at the lineup required, as the Court of Appeals held, the grant of a new trial at which such evidence is to be excluded. * * *

* * * "We think it follows that the proper test to be applied in these situations is that quoted in *Wong Sun v. United States*, '[W]hether, granting establishment of the primary illegality, the evidence to which instant objection is made has been come at by exploitation of that illegality or instead by means sufficiently distinguishable to be purged of the primary taint.' Application of this test in the present context requires consideration of various factors; for example, the prior opportunity to observe the alleged criminal act, the existence of any discrepancy between any pre-lineup description and the defendant's actual description, any identification prior to lineup of another person, the identification by picture of the defendant prior to the lineup, failure to identify the defendant on a prior

occasion, and the lapse of time between the alleged act and the lineup identification. It is also relevant to consider those facts which, despite the absence of counsel, are disclosed concerning the conduct of the lineup."

Disposition: Conviction reversed; the defendant has the right to have counsel present at a post-indictment lineup.

10-7b *United States v. Ash:* 413 U.S. 300, 37 L.Ed. 2d 619, 93 S.Ct. 2568 (1973)

Facts: On August 26, 1965, a man wearing a stocking mask and brandishing a gun entered a bank in Washington, D.C. Seconds later, a second man, also wearing a stocking mask, entered and scooped money from the tellers' drawers into a bag and left. The gunman followed. An informant told authorities that he had discussed the robbery with Ash. In February 1966, an FBI agent showed five mug shots of men generally matching Ash's description to four witnesses. All made uncertain identifications of Ash's picture. Ash was indicted on April 1, 1966. During final preparation for the trial, which was set for May 1968, the prosecutor showed five mug shots to the same four witnesses to determine whether they would be able to make in-court identifications. Three of the four again selected Ash's picture. At trial, three witnesses identified Ash but each was unwilling to state that he/she was certain. A fourth witness, who had been outside the bank and saw the robbers after they removed their masks, made a positive identification. Ash was convicted.

Issue: Does the defendant have the right to have an attorney present during a post-indictment photographic lineup?

Reasoning: *** "Throughout this expansion of the counsel guarantee to trial-like confrontations, the function of the lawyer has remained essentially the same as his function at trial. In all cases considered by the Court, counsel has continued to act as a spokesman for, or advisor to, the accused. The accused's right to the 'Assistance of Counsel' has meant just that, namely, the right of the accused to have counsel acting as his assistant. ***

"The function of counsel in rendering 'Assistance' continued at the lineup under consideration in *Wade* and its companion cases. Although the accused was not confronted there with legal questions, the lineup offered opportunities for prosecuting authorities to take advantage of the accused. Counsel was seen by the Court as being more sensitive to, and aware of, suggestive influences than the accused himself, and as better able to reconstruct the events at trial. Counsel present at lineup would be able to remove disabilities of the accused in precisely the same fashion that counsel compensated for the disabilities of the layman at trial. * * *

* * * "The structure of *Wade*, viewed in light of the careful limitation of the Court's language to 'confrontations,' makes it clear that lack of scientific precision and inability to reconstruct an event are not the tests for requiring counsel in the first instance. These are, instead, the tests to determine whether confrontation with counsel at trial can serve as a substitute for counsel at the pretrial confrontation. If accurate reconstruction is possible, the risks inherent in any confrontation still remain, but the opportunity to cure defects at trial causes the confrontation to cease to be 'critical.' * * *

* * * "A substantial departure from the historical test would be necessary if the Sixth Amendment were interpreted to give Ash a right to counsel at the photographic identification in this case. Since the accused himself is not present at the time of the photographic display, and asserts no right to be present, no possibility arises that the accused might be misled by his lack of familiarity with the law or overpowered by his professional adversary. Similarly, the counsel guarantee would not be used to produce equality in a trial-like adversary confrontation. * * *

* * * "We are not persuaded that the risks inherent in the use of photographic displays are so pernicious that an extraordinary system of safeguards is required.

"We hold, then, that the Sixth Amendment does not grant the right to counsel at photographic displays conducted by the Government for the purpose of allowing a witness to attempt an identification of the offender."

Disposition: Conviction affirmed; a defendant has no Sixth Amendment right to have an attorney present during a photographic lineup.

10-7c *Neil v. Biggers:* 409 U.S. 188, 34 L.Ed. 2d 401, 93 S.Ct. 375 (1972)

Facts: On the evening of January 22, 1965, a youth with a butcher knife grabbed the victim from behind while she stood in the doorway to her unlit kitchen and threw her to the floor. Light from the bedroom enabled her to see his face. When she screamed, her 12-year-old daughter came out of the bedroom and also began to scream. The assailant directed the victim to tell the daughter to shutup or he would kill both of them. The daughter stopped screaming. He then walked the victim at knifepoint about two blocks along a railroad track, took her into a woods, and raped her. There was a full moon shining brightly and the victim was able to observe her assailant's face for about 15 minutes. The victim gave the police "only a very general description" of the attacker. During the next seven months, police asked the victim to view suspects (in lineups, showups, and photographic lineups) but she never selected one of them as her assailant. On August 17, they asked her to come to the station to view Biggers, who was being detained on another charge. The police checked the city jail and juvenile hall but could not find other men with sufficiently similar characteristics to form a lineup. Two detectives walked the suspect past the victim. At her request, he repeated the words said on the night of the rape. The victim later testified that she had no doubt that Biggers was her assailant. Biggers was convicted of rape.

Issue: Under what circumstances do showups meet due process requirements?

Reasoning: * * * "Some general guidelines emerge from these cases as to the relationship between suggestiveness and misidentification. It is, first of all, apparent that the primary evil to be avoided is 'a very substantial likelihood of irreparable misidentification.' While the phrase was coined as a standard for determining whether an in-court identification would be admissible in the wake of a suggestive out-of-court identification, with the deletion of 'irreparable' it serves equally well as a standard for the admissibility of testimony concerning the out-of-court identification itself. It is the likelihood of misidentification which violates a defendant's right to due process, and it is this which was the basis of the exclusion of evidence in *Foster.* Suggestive confrontations are disapproved because they increase the likelihood of misidentification, and unnecessarily suggestive ones are condemned for the further reason that the increased chance of misidentification is gratuitous. But as *Stovall* makes clear, the admission of evidence of a showup without more does not violate due process.

"We turn, then, to the central question, whether under the 'totality of the circumstances' the identification was reliable even though the confrontation procedure was suggestive. As indicated by our cases, the factors to be considered in evaluating the likelihood of misidentification include the opportunity of the witness to view the criminal at the time of the crime, the witness' degree of attention, the accuracy of the witness' prior description of the criminal, the level of certainty demonstrated by the witness at the confrontation and the length of time between the crime and the confrontation."

Disposition: Conviction affirmed; a showup does not violate due process if, based on the totality of the circumstances, the victim is able to make a reliable identification.

10-8 Other Supreme Court Cases

10-8a *Gilbert v. California:* 388 U.S. 263, 18 L.Ed. 2d 1178, 87 S.Ct. 1951 (1967)

Facts: The Mutual Savings and Loan in Alhambra, California was robbed and a police officer killed during the robbery. FBI agents arrested Gilbert in Philadelphia and herefused to answer questions without his attorney present. He later answered another agent's questions about a robbery in Philadelphia and gave handwriting exemplars that were matched with the demand note used in the California robbery. Sixteen days after indictment, Gilbert was placed in a lineup without notice to his attorney. The lineup was conducted on the stage of an auditorium with bright lights that prevented those in the lineup from seeing the audience. Over 100 people were in the audience, each an eyewitness to a robbery charged to Gilbert. Nine witnesses who identified Gilbert at the lineup testified at trial about the lineup and identified him in the courtroom. Gilbert was convicted.

Issues:

1. Did obtaining handwriting exemplars violate the suspect's Fifth Amendment Rights?
2. Did in-court testimony of witnesses who identified the suspect at a lineup held without counsel present violate the suspect's Sixth Amendment rights?

Reasoning: *** "The taking of the exemplars did not violate petitioner's Fifth Amendment privilege against self-incrimination. The privilege reaches only compulsion of 'an accused's communications, whatever form they might take, and the compulsion of responses which are also communications.' *** One's voice and handwriting are, of course, means of communication. It by no means follows, however, that every compulsion of an accused to use his voice or write compels a communication within the cover of the privilege. A mere handwriting exemplar, in contrast to the content of what is written, like the voice or body itself, is an identifying physical characteristics outside its protection. ***

"The taking of the exemplars was not a 'critical' stage of the criminal proceedings entitling petitioner to the assistance of counsel. *** [T]here is minimal risk that the absence of counsel might derogate from his right to a fair trial. ***

*** "The admission of the in-court identifications without first determining that they were not tainted by the illegal lineup but were of independent origin was constitutional error. *** Gilbert is therefore entitled only to a vacation of his conviction pending the holding of such proceedings as the California Supreme Court may deem appropriate to afford the State the opportunity to establish that the in-court identification had an independent source, or that their introduction in evidence was in any event harmless error.

"Quite different considerations are involved as to the admission of the testimony of the manager of the apartment house at the guilt phase and of the eight witnesses at the penalty stage that they identified Gilbert at the lineup. That testimony is the direct result of the illegal lineup 'come at by exploitation of [the primary] illegality.' The State is therefore not entitled to an opportunity to show that that testimony had an independent source. Only a *per se* exclusionary rule as to such testimony can be an effective sanction to assure that law enforcement authorities will respect the accused's constitutional right to the presence of his counsel at the critical lineup."

Disposition: Conviction reversed; (1) there is no Fifth Amendment right to refuse to give a handwriting exemplar; (2) testimony regarding a post-indictment lineup conducted without the defendant's attorney present violates the Sixth Amendment.

10-8b *Moore v. Illinois:* 434 U.S. 220, 54 L.Ed. 2d 424, 98 S.Ct. 458 (1977)

Facts: Shortly after noon on December 14, 1967, the victim awoke from a nap to find a man holding a knife standing in the doorway to her bedroom. The man threw her face-down on the bed and choked her until she was quiet. He covered her face with a bandanna, partially undressed her, and committed sodomy and rape. When he left, he took her guitar and flute with him. The victim, who only saw her assailant's face for about 15 seconds, thought the man was the same one who had made offensive remarks to her in a neighborhood bar the night before. She gave the police a notebook she found next to her bed after the attack. The victim looked at 200 mug shots; she selected about 30 that resembled her attacker. Later, she looked at a group of 10 pictures and she picked two or three (one of which was Moore). A letter found in the notebook led investigators to suspect Moore. He was arrested on December 20 and held overnight pending a preliminary hearing to determine whether he should be bound over to the Grand Jury. The next morning, a police officer accompanied the victim to the hearing. The officer told her she was going to view a suspect and she should identify him if she could. Moore was called before the bench and the judge informed him of the charges. The victim was then called before the bench and the state's attorney asked her if she saw her assailant in the courtroom. She pointed at Moore, who was not represented by counsel at that time. At trial, the victim testified about the identification at the preliminary hearing and again identified Moore as her assailant. Moore presented an alibi defense. He was convicted.

Issue: Does the defendant have the right to have counsel present during in-court identifications?

Reasoning: *** "It is difficult to imagine a more suggestive manner in which to present a suspect to a witness for their critical first confrontation that was employed in this case. The victim, who had seen her assailant for only 10 to 15 seconds, was asked to make her identification after she was told that she was going to view a suspect, after she was told his name and heard it called as he was led before the bench, and after she heard the prosecutor recite the evidence believed to implicate petitioner. Had petitioner been represented by counsel, some or all of this suggestiveness could have been avoided.

*** "Here, as in those [*Wade* and *Gilbert*] cases, petitioner's Sixth Amendment rights were violated by a corporeal identification conducted after the initiation of adversary judicial criminal proceedings and in the absence of counsel. *** *Gilbert* held that the prosecution cannot buttress its case-in-chief by introducing evidence of a pretrial identification made in violation of the accused's Sixth Amendment rights, even if it can prove that the pretrial identification had an independent source. That testimony is the direct result of the illegal lineup 'come at by exploitation of [the primary] illegality' and the prosecution is 'therefore not entitled to show that the testimony had an independent source.'"

Disposition: Conviction reversed; in-court identification in the absence of defense counsel violated the defendant's Sixth Amendment rights.

10-8c *Kirby v. Illinois:* 406 U.S. 682, 32 L.Ed. 2d 411, 92 S.Ct. 1877 (1972)

Facts: On February 21, 1968, Shard reported to Chicago police that two men had robbed him the previous day, taking his wallet, traveler's checks, and social security card. The next day, officers stopped Kirby and Bean and asked them for identification. Kirby produced a wallet containing Shard's traveler's checks and social security card. Officers found other items taken from Shard in Bean's possession and took Kirby and Bean to the police station. When Shard entered the room, he immediately identified them as the robbers. Six weeks later, Kirby and Bean were indicted for the robbery and counsel was appointed. Both Kirby and Bean were convicted.

Issue: Does a suspect have the right to have counsel present at a preindictment identification procedure?

Reasoning: *** "Less than a year after *Wade* and *Gilbert* were decided, the Court explained the rule of those decisions as follows: 'The rationale of those cases was that an accused is entitled to counsel at any "critical stage of the *prosecution*," and that a post-indictment lineup is such a "critical stage." ' We decline to depart from that rationale today by imposing a *per se* exclusionary rule upon testimony concerning an identification that took place long before the commencement of any prosecution whatever.

*** "When a person has not been formally charged with a criminal offense, *Stovall* strikes the appropriate constitutional balance between the right of a suspect to be protected from prejudicial procedures and the interest of society in the prompt and purposeful investigation of an unsolved crime."

Disposition: Conviction affirmed; there is no right to have counsel present at a pre-indictment identification procedure.

10-8d *Foster v. California:* 394 U.S. 440, 22 L.Ed. 2d 402, 89 S.Ct. 1127 (1969)

Facts: The day after the armed robbery of a Western Union office, Clay, one of the robbers, surrendered to the police and implicated Foster, whom he claimed entered the office, and Grice, who allegedly waited in the car. The only eyewitness was Joseph David, the Western Union manager. Foster was placed in a three-man lineup. He was the tallest by nearly six inches and wore a jacket similar to the one David described seeing on one of the robbers. David could not make a positive identification. He said he thought Foster might be the robber but he was not sure. David asked to speak to Foster. Foster was brought to the room and seated across the table from David. Even after this one-on-one confrontation, David could not make a positive identification. About a week later, the police arranged for David to view another lineup. Of the five men in the lineup, Foster was the only one who had been in the first lineup. David positively identified Foster as the robber. He also made an in-court identification. David's identification of Foster and the testimony of the alleged accomplice were the only evidence against Foster. He was convicted.

Issue: When do lineup procedures violate due process?

Reasoning: *** "[W]e recognized that, judged by the 'totality of the circumstances,' the conduct of identification procedures may be 'so unnecessarily suggestive and conducive to irreparable mistaken identification' as to be a denial of due process of law.

"Judged by that standard, this case presents a compelling example of unfair lineup procedures. In the first lineup arranged by the police, petitioner stood out from the other two men by the contrast of his height and by the fact that he was wearing a leather jacket similar to that worn by the robber. When this did not lead to positive identification, the police permitted a one-to-one confrontation between petitioner and the witness. This Court pointed out in *Stovall* that '[t]he practice of showing suspects singly to persons for the purpose of identification, and not as part of a lineup, has been widely condemned.' Even after this the witness's identification of petitioner was tentative. So some days later another lineup was arranged. Petitioner was the only person in this lineup who had also participated in the first lineup. This finally produced a definite identification.

"The suggestive elements in this identification procedure made it all but inevitable that David would identify petitioner whether or not he was in fact 'the man.' In effect, the police repeatedly said to the witness, 'This is the man.' This procedure so undermined the reliability of the eyewitness identification as to violate due process."

Disposition: Conviction reversed; procedures used in both lineups and the showup were so unduly suggestive that they violated due process.

10-8e *Stovall v. Denno:* 388 U.S. 293, 18 L.Ed. 2d 1199, 87 S.Ct. 1967 (1967)

Facts: Dr. Paul Behrendt was stabbed to death in the kitchen of his home in Garden City, Long Island, about midnight on August 23, 1961. His wife, also a physician, followed her husband into the kitchen and jumped at his attacker. She was knocked to the floor and stabbed 11 times. Police found a shirt on the kitchen floor with keys in the pocket. The keys were traced to Stovall. He was arrested the day after the attack and promptly arraigned. A continuance was obtained until he could retain counsel. Dr. Behrendt had been hospitalized immediately after the attack and underwent major surgery to save her life. Immediately after the initial arraignment, the police contacted her surgeon and obtained permission to bring Stovall to Dr. Behrendt's hospital room for a showup. Stovall was handcuffed to an officer and accompanied by two members of the district attorney's staff. He was the only Negro in the room. The victim made an identification after

Stovall gave a voice exemplar. The showup occurred before Stovall was able to retain counsel. He was convicted of murder.

Issue: Does a one-person showup violate due process?

Reasoning: *** "The practice of showing suspects singly to persons for the purpose of identification, and not as part of a lineup, has been widely condemned. However, a claimed violation of due process of law in the conduct of a confrontation depends on the totality of the circumstances surrounding it, and the record in the present case reveals that the showing of Stovall to Mrs. Behrendt in an immediate hospital confrontation was imperative. *** 'Here was the only person in the world who could possibly exonerate Stovall. *** No one knew how long Mrs. Behrendt might live. Faced with the responsibility of identifying the attacker, with the need for immediate action and with the knowledge that Mrs. Behrendt could not visit the jail, the police followed the only feasible procedure and took Stovall to the hospital room. Under the circumstances, the usual police station lineup *** was out of the question.'" Note: The Court did not reach the question of whether the showup violated the Sixth Amendment right to counsel.

Disposition: Conviction affirmed; based on the totality of the circumstances the showup did not violate due process.

10-8f *Manson v. Brathwaite:* 432 U.S. 98, 53 L.Ed. 2d 140, 97 S.Ct. 2243 (1977)

Facts: Well before sunset on May 5, 1970, Connecticut State Trooper Glover, as part of an undercover narcotics investigation, went to a house in Hartford with Brown, an informant, for the purpose of purchasing narcotics from "Dickie Boy" Cicero, who lived on the third floor. When a man answered the door, Brown identified himself and Glover asked for "two things" of narcotics. The man held out his hand and Glover gave him two $10 bills. The door closed. Soon the man returned and handed Glover two glassine bags, which were later determined to contain heroin. Glover was at the door nearly seven minutes and was able to see into the apartment by ample natural light coming through a window in the hallway. He stood within two feet of the person who sold the narcotics. After the purchase, Glover and Brown drove to headquarters. Glover described the transaction to two other narcotics officers. Based on the description given, one of the officers suspected Brathwaite was the seller. He obtained a photograph of Brathwaite and left it in Glover's office. Two days later, Glover, when alone, viewed the photograph for the first time and identified Brathwaite as the man who sold him the heroin. Brathwaite was arrested nearly three months later while visiting the woman who lived in the apartment where the original transaction took place. He was convicted on possession and sale of heroin.

Issue: Was the viewing of a single photograph so unduly suggestive that testimony regarding it had to be excluded from trial?

Reasoning: *** "The standard, after all, is that of fairness as required by the Due Process Clause of the Fourteenth Amendment. *Stovall,* with its reference to 'the totality of the circumstances,' and *Biggers,* with its continuing stress on the same totality, did not, singly or together, establish a strict exclusionary rule or new standard of due process. ***

"We therefore conclude that reliability is the linchpin in determining the admissibility of identification testimony for both pre- and post-*Stovall* confrontations. The factors to be considered are set out in *Biggers.* ***

"These indicators of Glover's ability to make an accurate identification are hardly outweighed by the corrupting effect of the challenged identification itself. Although identifications arising from single-photograph displays may be viewed in general with suspicion, we find in the instant case little pressure on the witness to acquiesce in the suggestion that such a display entails. D'Onofrio had left the photograph at Glover's office and was not present when Glover first viewed it two days after the event. There thus was little urgency and Glover could view the photograph at his leisure. And since Glover examined the photograph alone, there was no coercive pressure to make an identification arising from the presence of another. The identification was made in circumstances allowing care and reflection.

*** "Surely, we cannot say that under all the circumstances of this case there is 'a very substantial likelihood of irreparable misidentification.' Short of that point, such evidence is for the jury to weigh. We are content to rely upon the good sense and judgement of American juries, for evidence with some element of untrustworthiness is customary grist for the jury mill. Juries are not so susceptible that they cannot measure intelligently the weight of identification testimony that has some questionable feature."

Disposition: Conviction affirmed; identification of a single photograph is admissible in this case due to the reliability of Glover's identification and the lack of coercion.

Chapter Quiz

True/False

1. Police can transport a suspect to the police station in order to conduct a lineup only if there is probable cause to arrest the suspect.
2. A showup can be conducted in the field if there is reasonable suspicion to detain the suspect for identification.
3. The suspect can invoke the Fifth Amendment privilege against self-incrimination as legal grounds to refuse to participate in a lineup.
4. An indigent suspect has a Sixth Amendment right to appointed counsel at all lineups.
5. A suspect never has a Sixth Amendment right to appointed counsel at a showup.
6. If a witness attends a lineup that was not conducted properly, that witness will not be allowed to make an identification of the suspect during the trial.
7. There should be a minimum of five to seven people who are similar in appearance in a lineup.
8. Police are allowed to help the witnesses who are attempting to make identifications at a lineup.
9. Witnesses may confer at a lineup to make sure they are selecting the correct person.
10. Showups are prohibited because they violate due process.

Discussion Questions

1. Jim was charged with robbery after being picked out of a lineup. The victim had described the robber as "a tall guy wearing a baseball uniform with the name JIM on the back." Six men were placed in a lineup. Their ages ranged from 18 to 40. All were about six feet tall but their weights ranged from 150 to 250 pounds. Each wore the uniform of a different major league baseball team but all had the name JIM on the back. Did this lineup violate Jim's *due process* rights? Explain.
2. Tom caught a glimpse of a burglar fleeing his home and immediately called the police. Sam was stopped running from the scene. Tom was taken to the corner where the police were detaining Sam. An officer said, "We just stopped this guy. Is he the one that you saw running from your house?" Tom was not sure. The officer then opened a box Sam was carrying and pulled out items stolen from Tom's house. Tom then said, "Yes, that must be the guy I saw." Did this showup violate Sam's *due process* rights? Explain.

3. Jane was in jail awaiting trial for grand theft auto because she could not make bail. She was told to participate in a lineup as an "extra." Much to the officer's surprise, the witness picked Jane instead of the woman the police had arrested for the burglary they were investigating. A check of fingerprints indicated that Jane had been at the scene of the burglary. She was then charged with the burglary. Did participation in the lineup violate Jane's Sixth Amendment *right to counsel?* Explain.

Chapter 11

Right to Counsel

Outline

The Sixth Amendment guarantees a person's right to the assistance of coun sel in his/her defense in a criminal proceeding. As we have seen in chapters 9 and 10, the Supreme Court has held that there is a right to have counsel present during custodial interrogation and also during post-arraignment identification procedures conducted in the suspect's presence. This chapter will explore the other reaches of the right to counsel.

11-1 When Must Counsel Be Provided?

In nearly all proceedings in a criminal case, a suspect has the right to have an attorney present. This means that a person may hire an attorney (called "retained" counsel). In some situations, the Supreme Court has interpreted the right to counsel to mean that the government must provide counsel without charge (called "appointed" counsel) for those who cannot afford to retain an attorney.

Gideon v. Wainwright, the landmark case, in which the Supreme Court declared that indigents have the right to appointed counsel at trial, involved a felony. In later cases the Court more carefully delineated when the right to appointed counsel applies: A person cannot be jailed for a conviction unless he/she was represented by counsel or made a valid waiver of this right. A suspended sentence that could result in a jail or prison sentence cannot be imposed unless the defendant was afforded the right to counsel. Probation, fines, and other noncustody sentences can be imposed if there was no defense counsel.

The right to appointed counsel attaches when the formal criminal proceedings commence. In federal courts, this occurs at the return of an indictment. The defendant has the right to counsel starting with the first court appearing on the indictment. State laws vary. If proceedings are begun by indictment, the right to counsel matches the federal procedures. If charges are filed without an indictment, the right to counsel begins when the defendant makes his/her first court appearance.

All trial and pretrial court hearings are covered. Counsel must also be provided at sentencing hearings. While most sentencing hearings will be held shortly after the verdict is returned, sometimes the defendant is placed on probation and sentence is imposed only if probation is violated. An indigent has the right to appointed counsel at these delayed sentencing hearings, too. If the defendant has already been sentenced, there is no automatic right to counsel at hearings held to revoke probation or parole; each case is judged on its facts. Counsel must be appointed if the case is too complex for the defendant to handle alone or if the defendant is unable to represent him/herself due to illiteracy, low intelligence, or other factors.

Some defendants wish to represent themselves (called *in propria persona* and commonly referred to as *pro per* or *pro se*). The Supreme Court strongly discouraged self-representation but said that defendants who knowingly and intelligently waive the right to trial counsel may act as their own attorneys. In order to make this waiver, the defendant must be mentally competent to stand trial. The right to self-representation cannot be based on the defendant correctly answering questions regarding legal procedures. The defendant who acts as his/her own attorney cannot appeal on grounds of ineffective representation. The Supreme Court refused to extend the right of self-representation to the first appeal. States have the right to mandate that appellants be represented by licensed attorneys; if the defendant, is indigent the state must provide this attorney free of charge.

The Supreme Court held that there is a right to appointed counsel for the first appeal. Subsequent discretionary appeals, whether to state or federal courts, are not automatically covered. Neither are other post-conviction proceedings.

Only criminal proceedings are covered by the Sixth Amendment. There is no automatic right to appointed counsel when proceeding under *habeas corpus* because it is considered a civil proceeding. Suits under the federal Civil Rights Act (42 U.S.C. 1983) are also not covered.

Inmates frequently wish to file legal challenges to their convictions after the first direct appeal when the right to appointed counsel has been exhausted. The Supreme Court held that such inmates must be provided with some form of assistance. This can be accomplished in a variety of ways: making legal assistance available in custodial facilities (paralegals, law school interns, or lawyers) or allowing inmates to help each other ("jail-house lawyers"). Law libraries must also be provided if "jail-house lawyers" are the only assistance available. Jail and prison administrators retain the right to make reasonable regulations that apply to "jail-house lawyers." There are no special First Amendment rights in this respect beyond those granted to other inmates.

11-2 Who Is Entitled to Free Counsel?

Indigence is the term most often used to describe those who have the right to appointed counsel. This implies that a person does not have the financial resources to hire an attorney. A number of factors must be taken into account: income, number of dependents, and likely cost of hiring counsel.

In minor misdemeanor cases, such as petty theft, the cost of counsel is relatively low; therefore, there will be fewer cases justifying appointed counsel. On the other hand, the price of representation in a homicide case is very high and a much greater percentage of defendants will qualify for free attorneys.

The fact that a person retains private counsel at the beginning of a case does not indicate that there never will be an attorney appointed in the case. A person may run out of money and qualify for appointed counsel after the case has begun. It is fairly common to have retained counsel at trial and appointed counsel on appeal.

The Supreme Court has permitted the states to try to recoup the cost of appointing counsel. Payment of these costs can be made a condition of probation but a person cannot be sent to jail for failure to pay them if there is a *bona fide* reason such as inability to work due to illness.

11-3 Representing More Than One Defendant

Co-defendants frequently have opposing interests—the best defense is to try to place as much blame as possible on the other defendant. For this reason, it is frequently a conflict of interests for one attorney to represent more than one defendant in a case. If an attorney asserts that two clients should not be represented by the same lawyer, the judge is normally required to see that the defendants have separate attorneys. Defendants who appeal their conviction on the basis of a conflict of interest must establish: (1) The judge knew, or should have known, about the potential conflict of interest, and (2) the conflict of interest adversely affected the attorney's performance.

Defendants are usually allowed to waive the conflict and use the same attorney. The judge has the authority to refuse to accept such a waiver if the integrity of the trial or sentencing hearing will be jeopardized.

11-4 Services That Must Accompany Appointment of Counsel

Appointing an attorney is frequently not enough. Many other costs accompany the defense of a criminal defendant. Filing fees must be waived in order to permit indigents to appeal. Necessary transcripts, whether of the preliminary hearing or the trial, must also be provided at no charge.

No clear ruling has been made on the use of expert witnesses. The Court has ruled that the defense is entitled to a psychiatrist in capital cases if insanity is likely to be a key issue.

11-5 Counsel's Right to Withdraw

An attorney may wish to withdraw from a case, or a defendant seek to have a new attorney appointed, for a variety of reasons. One common one is the inability to agree on trial strategy. The judge has the discretion to appoint a new attorney when necessary. Requests for new counsel may be denied if the judge believes that they are a stalling tactic. If a new attorney is appointed, that attorney must be given adequate time to prepare for trial.

An appointed appellate attorney may review the case and decide that there are no meritorious issues. States cannot allow the appeal to be dropped solely on the appointed attorney's bald assertion that the case is frivolous, but they have leeway to develop procedures to handle these cases. In *Anders v. California* [386 U.S. 738 (1967)], the Supreme Court suggested that counsel be required to file a brief stating every arguable issue. More recently, in *Smith v. Robbins* [528 U.S. 259 (2000)], the Court approved a procedure requiring counsel to file a brief summarizing the case (with specific references to the trial transcripts) and request the appellate court to independently review the record. The attorney remains available to provide additional briefs for the case if requested to do so by the appellate court. It was also mandatory for the attorney to give a copy of the brief to the client along with an explanation of the procedures for the client to file a supplemental brief.

11-6 How the Competency of Counsel Is Judged

The right to counsel is meaningful only if the attorney acts with at least the skill of an attorney of average ability acting under similar circumstances. This applies to both retained and appointed counsel. The constitutional test is twofold: (1) Counsel was not functioning effectively; and (2) counsel's errors were so serious that they deprived the defendant of a fair trial. Most errors do not meet this test. To have a conviction reversed, the defendant must be able to show a reasonable probability that, except for counsel's errors, the outcome of the trial would have been different. The same standard is applied to actions of counsel that adversely affect the sentence. On the other hand, the state's actions must be reasonable; for example, a defendant whose appeal was dismissed due to a technical error of the appellate attorney had the right to have the appeal reinstated.

11-7 Key Supreme Court Cases

11-7a *Gideon v. Wainwright:* 372 U.S. 335, 9 L.Ed. 2d 799, 83 S.Ct. 792 (1963)

Facts: Gideon was charged with a felony for entering a poolroom with intent to commit a misdemeanor. He appeared in court without a lawyer because he could not afford one. At trial, his request that the court appoint an attorney for him was denied. He "conducted his defense about as well as could be expected for a layman": He made an opening statement; cross-examined witnesses; presented witnesses in his own defense; declined to testify himself; and made a short closing argument. The jury convicted him.

Issue: Does an indigent person have the right to appointed counsel at trial?

Reasoning: * * * "We accept *Betts v. Brady's* assumption, based as it was on our prior cases, that a provision of the Bill of Rights which is 'fundamental and essential to a fair trial' is made obligatory upon the States by the Fourteenth Amendment. We think the Court in Betts was wrong, however, in concluding that the Sixth Amendment's guarantee of counsel is not one of these fundamental rights. * * *

* * * "Not only these precedents [*Powell v. Alabama*, 287 U.S. 45 (1932); *Johnson v. Zerbst*, 304 U.S. 458 (1938); *Avery v. Alabama*, 308 U.S. 444 (1940); *Smith v. O'Grady*, 312 U.S. 329 (1941)] but also reason and reflection require us to recognize that in our adversary system of criminal justice, any person haled into court, who is too poor to hire a lawyer, cannot be assured a fair trial unless counsel is provided for him. This seems to us to be an obvious truth. Governments, both state and federal, quite properly spend vast sums of money to establish machinery to try defendants accused of crime. Lawyers to prosecute are everywhere deemed essential to protect the public's interest in an orderly society. Similarly, there are few defendants charged with crime, few indeed, who fail to hire the best lawyers they can get to prepare and present their defenses. That government hires lawyers to prosecute and defendants who have the money hire lawyers to defend are the strongest indications of the widespread belief that lawyers in criminal courts are necessities, not luxuries. The right of one charged with crime to counsel may not be deemed fundamental and essential to fair trial in some countries, but it is in ours. From the very begin-

ning, our state and national constitutions and laws have laid great emphasis on procedural and substantive safeguards designed to assure fair trials before impartial tribunals in which every defendant stands equal before the law. This noble ideal cannot be realized if the poor man charged with crime has to face his accusers without a lawyer to assist him. A defendant's need for a lawyer is nowhere better stated than in the moving words of Mr. Justice Sutherland in *Powell v. Alabama:* *** 'The right to be heard would be, in many cases, of little avail if it did not comprehend the right to be heard by counsel. Even the intelligent and educated layman has small and sometimes no skill in the science of law. If charged with crime, he is incapable, generally, of determining for himself whether the indictment is good or bad. He is unfamiliar with the rules of evidence. Left without the aid of counsel he may be put on trial without a proper charge, and convicted upon incompetent evidence, or evidence irrelevant to the issue or otherwise inadmissible. He lacks both the skill and knowledge to adequately prepare his defense, even though he have a perfect one. He requires the guiding hand of counsel at every step in the proceedings against him. Without it, though he be not guilty, he faces the danger of conviction because he does not know how to establish his innocence.' "

Disposition: Conviction reversed; an indigent person cannot be tried for a felony unless counsel is appointed to handle the case.

11-7b *Scott v. Illinois:* 440 U.S. 367, 59 L.Ed. 2d 383, 99 S.Ct. 1158 (1979)

Facts: Scott was convicted and fined $50 for shoplifting merchandise valued at less than $150 at a bench trial at which he did not have an attorney. Under Illinois law, the maximum penalty for this offense was a $500 fine, up to one year in jail, or both.

Issue: When is the state required to appoint an attorney for an indigent?

Reasoning: *** "Although the intentions of the *Argersinger* [*v. Hamlin* 407 U.S. 25 (1972)] Court are not unmistakably clear from its opinion, we conclude today that *Argersinger* did indeed delimit the constitutional right to appointed counsel in state criminal proceedings. Even were the matter res nova, we believe that the central premise of *Argersinger*—that actual imprisonment is a penalty different in kind from fines or the mere threat of imprisonment—is eminently sound and warrants adoption of actual imprisonment as the line defining the constitutional right to appointment of counsel. *Argersinger* has proved reasonably workable, whereas any extension would create confusion and impose unpredictable, but necessarily substantial, costs on 50 quite diverse States. We therefore hold that the Sixth and Fourteenth Amendments to the United States Constitution require only that no indigent criminal defendant be sentenced to a term of imprisonment unless the State has afforded him the right to assistance of appointed counsel in his defense."

Disposition: Conviction affirmed; no appointed counsel is required when the defendant is not sentenced to a term of incarceration.

11-7c *Douglas v. California:* 372 U.S. 353, 9 L.Ed. 2d 811, 83 S.Ct. 814 (1963)

Facts: Meyes and Douglas were tried jointly for 13 felonies. They were represented by a single public defender who unsuccessfully moved for a continuance at the beginning of trial in order to better prepare for the complicated case. A motion for separate counsel for each defendant was also denied. Meyes and Douglas then dismissed the public defender and represented themselves at trial. They were convicted on all 13 counts and sentenced to prison. They were denied the assistance of counsel on appeal even though the record plainly shows that they were indigents. The California Court of Appeals stated that it had "gone through" the record and come to the conclusion that "no good whatever could be served by appointment of counsel."

Issue: Are indigent defendants entitled to appointed appellate counsel?

Reasoning: "In *Griffin v. Illinois* [351 U.S. 12 (1955)] we held that a State may not grant appellate review in such a way as to discriminate against some convicted defendants on account of their poverty. There, as in *Draper v. Washington* [372 U.S. 487 (1963)], the right to a free transcript on appeal was in issue. Here the issue is whether or not an indigent shall be denied the assistance of counsel on appeal. In either case the evil is the same: discrimination against the indigent. For there can be no equal justice where the kind of an appeal a man enjoys 'depends on the amount of money he has.' ***

*** "We are dealing only with the first appeal, granted as a matter of right to rich and poor alike from a criminal conviction *** . But it is appropriate to observe that a State can, consistently with the Fourteenth Amendment, provide for difference so long as the result does not amount to a denial of due process or an 'invidious discrimination.' Absolute equality is not required; lines can be and are drawn and we often sustain them. But where the merits of the one and only appeal an indigent has as of right are decided without benefit of counsel, we think an unconstitutional line has been drawn between rich and poor.

"When an indigent is forced to run this gauntlet of a preliminary showing of merit, the right to appeal does not comport with fair procedure. *** The present case, where counsel was denied petitioners on appeal, shows that the discrimination is not between 'possibly good and obviously bad cases,' but between cases where the rich man can require the court to listen to argument of counsel before deciding on the merits, but a poor man cannot. There is lacking that equality demanded by the Fourteenth Amendment where the rich man, who appeals as of right, enjoys the benefit of counsel's examination into the record, research of the law, and marshalling of arguments on his behalf, while the indigent, already burdened by a preliminary determination that his case is without merit, is forced to shift for himself. The indigent, where the record is unclear or the errors are hidden, has only the right to a meaningless ritual, while the rich man has a meaningful appeal."

Disposition: Case reversed; counsel must be appointed for an indigent on the first appeal.

11-8 Other Supreme Court Cases

11-8a *Gagnon v. Scarpelli:* 411 U.S. 778, 36 L.Ed. 2d 656, 93 S.Ct. 1756 (1973)

Facts: In July 1965, Scarpelli pleaded guilty to armed robbery in Wisconsin and was sentenced to 15 years' imprisonment. The sentence was suspended and he was placed on probation for seven years. He was allowed to reside in Illinois where he would be supervised by the Adult Probation Department of Cook County. On August 6, 1965, he was arrested when caught in the process of burglarizing a house. He waived his *Miranda* rights and confessed. Probation was revoked on September 1, 1965, without a hearing and Scarpelli was sent to Wisconsin to serve his 15-year sentence.

Issues:

1. What due process rights does a probationer have in revocation proceedings?
2. Does a probationer have a right to counsel at a revocation hearing?

Reasoning: *** "Probation revocation, like parole revocation, is not a stage of a criminal prosecution, but does result in a loss of liberty.

Accordingly, we hold that a probationer, like a parolee, is entitled to a preliminary and a final revocation hearing, under the conditions specified in *Morrissey v. Brewer* [408 U.S. 471 (1972)].

*** "At the preliminary hearing, a probationer or parolee is entitled to notice of the alleged violations of probation or parole, an opportunity to appear and to present evidence in his own behalf, a conditional right to confront adverse witnesses, an independent decisionmaker, and a written report of the hearing. ***

*** "It is neither possible nor prudent to attempt to formulate a precise and detailed set of guidelines to be followed in determining when the providing of counsel is necessary to meet the applicable due process requirements. The facts and circumstances in preliminary and final hearings are susceptible of almost infinite variation, and a considerable discretion must be allowed the responsible agency in making the decision. Presumptively, it may be said that counsel should be provided in cases where, after being informed of his right to request counsel, the probationer or parolee makes such a request, based on a timely and colorable claim (i) that he has not committed the alleged violation of the conditions upon which he is at liberty; or (ii) that, even if the violation is a matter of public record or is uncontested, there are substantial reasons which justify or mitigate the violation and make revocation inappropriate, and that the reasons are complex or otherwise difficult to develop or present. In passing on a request for the appointment of counsel, the responsible agency also should consider, especially in doubtful cases, whether the probationer appears to be capable of speaking effectively for himself. In every case in which a request for counsel at a preliminary or final hearing is refused, the grounds for refusal should be stated succinctly in the record."

Disposition: Case remanded so state can conduct revocation hearing; the probationer must be afforded a two-tier hearing; counsel must be provided if the charges are contested or if there are substantial reasons why the defendant needs assistance.

11-8b *Faretta v. California*: 422 U.S. 806, 45 L.Ed. 2d 562, 95 S.Ct. 2525 (1975)

Facts: Faretta was charged with grand theft. At the arraignment, the judge appointed a public defender to represent him. Well before the trial date, Faretta ask permission to represent himself. The judge determined that Faretta had once represented himself in a criminal case, had a high school education, and did not want to be represented by a public defender because he believed the public defender had too heavy of a caseload. Faretta was initially allowed to represent himself but before trial, the judge held a hearing during which he asked very specific questions about the hearsay rule and state law governing challenging jurors during *voir dire*. The judge ruled that there had not been an intelligent and knowing waiver of the right to assistance of counsel and that Faretta had no constitutional right to represent himself. Faretta's request to act as co-counsel was denied as were his attempts to make motions on his own. Faretta was found guilty as charged.

Issue: Does a criminal defendant have a constitutional right to act as his/her own attorney?

Reasoning: *** "[I]t is one thing to hold that every defendant, rich or poor, has the right to the assistance of counsel, and quite another to say that a State may compel a defendant to accept a lawyer he does not want. The value of state-appointed counsel was not unappreciated by the Founders, yet the notion of compulsory counsel was utterly foreign to them. And whatever else may be said of those who wrote the Bill of Rights, surely there can be no doubt that they understood the inestimable worth of free choice.

"It is undeniable that in most criminal prosecutions defendants could better defend with counsel's guidance than by their own unskilled efforts. But where the defendant will not voluntarily accept representation by counsel, the potential advantage of a lawyer's training and experience can be realized, if at all, only imperfectly. To force a lawyer on a defendant can only lead him to believe that the law contrives against him. Moreover, it is not inconceivable that in some rare instances, the defendant might in fact present his case more effectively by conducting his own defense. Personal liberties are not rooted in the law of averages. The right to defend is personal. The defendant, and not his lawyer or the State, will bear the personal consequences of a conviction. It is the defendant, therefore, who must be free personally to decide whether in his particular case counsel is to his advantage. And although he may conduct his own defense ultimately to his own detriment, his choice must be honored out of 'that respect for the individual which is the lifeblood of the law.'

"When an accused manages his own defense, he relinquishes, as a purely factual matter, many of the traditional benefits associated with the right to counsel. For this reason, in order to represent himself, the accused must 'knowingly and intelligently' forgo those relinquished benefits. Although a defendant need not himself have the skill and experience of a lawyer in order competently and intelligently to choose self-representation, he should be made aware of the dangers and disadvantages of self-representation, so that the record will establish that 'he knows what he is doing and his choice is made with eyes open.'

*** "We need make no assessment of how well or poorly Faretta had mastered the intricacies of the hearsay rule and the California code provisions that govern challenges of potential jurors on *voir dire*. For his technical legal knowledge, as such, was not relevant to an assessment of his knowing exercise of the right to defend himself."

Disposition: Conviction reversed; a defendant has the right to represent him/herself as long as there is a knowing and intelligent waiver of the right to counsel.

11-8c *Ross v. Moffitt:* 417 U.S. 600, 41 L.Ed. 2d 341, 94 S.Ct. 2437 (1974)

Facts: In two separate cases, Moffitt pled guilty to charges of forgery and uttering a forged instrument. He took an unsuccessful appeal to the North Carolina Court of Appeals in one case. Due to his indigency, he was represented at trial and on appeal by appointed counsel. Moffitt then sought to invoke the discretionary review procedures of the North Carolina Supreme Court. The state refused to appoint counsel for this appeal. In the other case, he was given appointed counsel for a writ of certiorari but the North Carolina Supreme Court denied the writ. He then requested counsel so that he could appeal to the United States Supreme Court. This request was denied.

Issue: Does the state have a duty to appoint counsel for indigents who wish to appeal to higher courts after the first appeal?

Reasoning: *** "We do not believe that the Due Process Clause requires North Carolina to provide respondent with counsel on his discretionary appeal to the State Supreme Court. ***

*** "The defendant needs an attorney on appeal not as a shield to protect him against being 'haled into court' by the State and stripped of his presumption of innocence, but rather as a sword to upset the prior determination of guilt. This difference is significant for, while no one would agree that the State may simply dispense with the trial stage of proceedings without a criminal defendant's consent, it is clear that the State need not provide any appeal at all. The fact that an appeal has been provided does not automatically mean that a State then acts unfairly by refusing to provide counsel to indigent defendants at every stage of the way. Unfairness results only if indigents are singled out by the State and denied meaningful access to the appellate system because of their poverty. That question is more profitably considered under an equal protection analysis.

*** "We do not believe that it can be said, therefore, that a defendant in respondent's circumstances is denied meaningful access to the North Carolina Supreme Court simply because the State does not appoint counsel to aid him in seeking review in that court. At that stage he will have, at the very least, a transcript or other record of trial proceedings, a brief on his behalf in the Court of Appeals setting forth his claims of error, and in many cases an opinion by the Court of Appeals disposing of his case. These materials, supplemented by whatever submission respondent may make *per se*, would appear to provide the Supreme Court of North Carolina with an adequate basis for its decision to grant or deny review.

"We are fortified in this conclusion by our understanding of the function served by discretionary review in the North Carolina Supreme Court. The critical issue in that court, as we perceive it, is not whether there has been 'a correct adjudication of guilt' in every individual case, but rather whether 'the subject matter of the appeal has significant public interest,' whether 'the cause involves legal principles of major significance to the jurisprudence of the State,' or whether the decision below is in probable conflict with a decision of the Supreme Court. The Supreme Court may deny certiorari even though it believes that the decision of the Court of Appeals was incorrect since a decision which appears incorrect may nevertheless fail to satisfy any of the criteria discussed above. ***

*** "Much of the discussion in the preceding section is equally relevant to the question of whether a State must provide counsel for a defendant seeking review of his conviction in this Court. North Carolina will have provided counsel for a convicted defendant's only appeal as of right, and the brief prepared by the counsel together with one and perhaps two North Carolina appellate opinions will be available to this Court in order that it may decide whether or not to grant certiorari. This Court's review, much like that of the Supreme Court of North Carolina, is discretionary and depends on numerous factors other than the perceived correctness of the judgment we are asked to review."

Disposition: Convictions affirmed; defendant does not have a right to have counsel appointed to handle discretionary appeals to either the State's highest court or the United States Supreme Court.

11-8d *Pennsylvania v. Finley:* 481 U.S. 551, 95 L.Ed. 2d 539, 107 S.Ct. 1990 (1987)

Facts: Finley was convicted of second-degree murder in 1975 and sentenced to life in prison. The conviction was unanimously affirmed by the Pennsylvania Supreme Court. She then proceeded *pro se* for relief from the trial court under the Pennsylvania Post Conviction Hearing Act (similar to *habeas corpus*). The court denied the relief. This action was reversed on appeal because Finley had not been given appointed counsel. An attorney was appointed on remand. This attorney reviewed the file and notified the court that there was no arguable basis for collateral relief. The court also reviewed the file and determined that there were no nonfrivolous issues. The attorney's motion to withdraw from the case was granted and the petition for post-conviction relief was dismissed.

Issue: Does an indigent defendant have a right to appointed counsel for post-conviction proceedings?

Reasoning: *** "We think that since a defendant has no federal constitutional right to counsel when pursuing a discretionary appeal on direct review of his conviction, *a fortiori*, he has no such right when attacking a conviction that has long since become final upon exhaustion of the appellate process.

*** "We also conclude that the equal protection guarantee of the Fourteenth Amendment does not require the appointment of an attorney for an indigent appellant just because an affluent defendant may retain one. ***

* * * "We think that the analysis that we followed in Ross forecloses respondent's constitutional claim. The procedures followed by respondent's *habeas* counsel fully comported with fundamental fairness. Post-conviction relief is even further removed from the criminal trial than is discretionary direct review. It is not part of the criminal proceeding itself, and it is in fact considered to be civil in nature. It is a collateral attack that normally occurs only after the defendant has failed to secure relief through direct review of his conviction. States have no obligation to provide this avenue of relief, and when they do, the fundamental fairness mandated by the Due Process Clause does not require that the State supply a lawyer as well."

Disposition: Dismissal of post-conviction action affirmed; the defendant does not have the right to appointed counsel when seeking post-conviction relief.

11-8e *Johnson v. Avery:* 393 U.S. 483, 21 L.Ed. 2d 718, 89 S.Ct. 747 (1969)

Facts: Johnson was serving a life sentence in the Tennessee State Penitentiary. He was transferred to maximum security because he violated a prison regulation that prohibited one inmate from advising or assisting another inmate on legal matters.

Issue: Can inmates be prohibited from assisting each other our legal matters?

Reasoning: * * * "Since the basic purpose of the writ [of *habeas corpus*] is to enable those unlawfully incarcerated to obtain their freedom, it is fundamental that access of prisoners to the courts for the purpose of presenting their complaints may not be denied or obstructed. * * *

* * * "There can be no doubt that Tennessee could not constitutionally adopt and enforce a rule forbidding illiterate or poorly educated prisoners to file *habeas corpus* petitions. Here Tennessee has adopted a rule which, in the absence of any other source of assistance for such prisoners, effectively does just that. * * *

* * * "It has not been held that there is any general obligation of the courts, state or federal, to appoint counsel for prisoners who indicate, without more, that they wish to seek post-conviction relief. Accordingly, the initial burden of presenting a claim to post-conviction relief usually rests upon the indigent prisoner himself with such help as he can obtain within the prison walls or the prison system. In the case of all except those who are able to help themselves—usually a few old hands or exceptionally gifted prisoners—the prisoner is, in effect, denied access to the courts unless such help is available.

* * * "Even in the absence of such alternatives [public defenders, senior law students, volunteer members of the State Bar], the State may impose reasonable restrictions and restraints upon the acknowledged propensity of prisoners to abuse both the giving and the seeking of assistance in the preparation of applications for relief: for example, by limitations on the time and location of such activities and the imposition of punishment for giving or receipt of consideration in connection with such activities. But unless and until the State provides some reasonable alternative to assist inmates in the preparation of petitions for post-conviction relief, it may not validly enforce a regulation such as that here in issue, barring inmates from furnishing such assistance to other prisoners."

Disposition: Inmate's petition granted; absent other forms of legal assistance, a prison cannot prohibit "jail-house lawyers" from assisting other inmates.

11-8f *Wheat v. United States:* 486 U.S. 153, 100 L.Ed. 2d 140, 108 S.Ct. 1692 (1988)

Facts: Wheat and numerous co-defendants were charged with a far-flung drug distribution conspiracy that involved the transportation of thousands of pounds of marijuana from Mexico over a period of several years. Iredale represented two co-defendants: One pled guilty and was likely to be a prosecution witness against Wheat; the other entered a plea that had not yet been accepted by the judge. Two days before trial, Iredale notified the court that he would be representing Wheat but the government registered substantial concern about the possibility of a conflict of interests raised by this joint representation. The judge heard detailed arguments on this issue and then denied the substitution. Wheat proceeded to trial with his original attorney and was convicted.

Issue: Is a judge required to permit joint representation if the parties agree to waive any claims of conflict of interest?

Reasoning: *** "Thus, while the right to select and be represented by one's preferred attorney is comprehended by the Sixth Amendment, the essential aim of the Amendment is to guarantee an effective advocate for each criminal defendant rather than to ensure that a defendant will inexorably be represented by the lawyer whom he prefers.

*** "In previous cases, we have recognized that multiple representation of criminal defendants engenders special dangers of which a court must be aware. While 'permitting a single attorney to represent codefendants *** is not *per se* violative of constitutional guarantees of effective assistance of counsel,' a court confronted with and alerted to possible conflicts of interest must take adequate steps to ascertain whether the conflict warrants separate counsel. As we said in *Holloway* [*Holloway v. Arkansas,* 435 U.S. 475 (1978)], 'Joint representation of conflicting interests is suspect because of what it tends to prevent the attorney from doing. *** [A] conflict may *** prevent an attorney from challenging the admission of evidence prejudicial to one client but perhaps favorable to another, or from arguing at the sentencing hearing the relative involvement and culpability of his clients in order to minimize the culpability of one by emphasizing that of another.'

"Petitioner insists that the provision of waivers by all affected defendants cures any problems created by the multiple representation. But no such flat rule can be deduced from the Sixth Amendment presumption in favor of counsel of choice. Federal courts have an independent interest in ensuring that criminal trials are conducted within the ethical standards of the profession and that legal proceedings appear fair to all who observe them. *** Not only the interest of a criminal defendant but the institutional interest in the rendition of just verdicts in criminal cases may be jeopardized by unregulated multiple representation.

*** "The District Court must recognize a presumption in favor of petitioner's counsel of choice, but that presumption may be overcome not only by a demonstration of actual conflict but by a showing of a serious potential for conflict. The evaluation of the facts and circumstances of each case under this standard must be left primarily to the informed judgment of the trial court."

Disposition: Conviction affirmed; a judge has the right to refuse to allow one attorney to represent two or more defendants if the judge believes there is serious potential for a conflict of interest.

11-8g *Mayer v. City of Chicago:* 404 U.S. 189, 30 L.Ed. 2d 372, 92 S.Ct. 410 (1971)

Facts: Mayer was convicted of nonfelony charges of disorderly conduct and interference with a police officer in violation of a city ordinance. He was fined $250 for each offense. The maximum penalty for this charge was $500. He requested a free transcript of the proceedings so that he could appeal on insufficiency of the evidence and prejudicial prosecutorial misconduct. His request was denied because he had not been convicted of a felony.

Issue: When does an indigent have the right to a free transcript to be used on appeal?

Reasoning: *** "*Griffin v. Illinois* [351 U.S. 12 (1955)] is the watershed of our transcript decisions. We held there that '[d]estitute defendants must be afforded as adequate appellate review as defendants who have money enough to buy transcripts.' This holding rested on the 'constitutional guaranties of due process and equal protection both [of which] call for procedures in criminal trials which allow no invidious discriminations between persons and different groups of persons.' We said that '[p]lainly the ability to pay costs in advance bears no rational relationship to a defendant's guilt or innocence,' *** and concluded '[t]here can be no equal justice where the kind of trial a man gets depends on the amount of money he has.' *** In terms of a trial record, this means that the State must afford the indigent a 'record of sufficient completeness' to permit proper consideration of [his] claims.

*** "We emphasize, however, that the State must provide a full verbatim record where that is necessary to assure the indigent as effective an appeal as would be available to the defendant with resources to pay his own way. Moreover, where the grounds of appeal, as in this case, make out a colorable need for a complete transcript, the burden is on the State to show that only a portion of the transcript or an 'alternative' will suffice for an effective appeal on those grounds. ***

*** "The size of the defendant's pocketbook bears no more relationship to his guilt or innocence in a nonfelony than in a felony case. The distinction drawn by Rule 607(b) is, therefore, an 'unreasonable distinction' proscribed by the Fourteenth Amendment. ***

*** "Griffin does not represent a balance between the needs of the accused and the interests of society; its principle is a flat prohibition against pricing indigent defendants out of as effective an appeal as would be available to others able to pay their own way. The invidiousness of the discrimination that exists when criminal procedures are made available only to those who can pay is not erased by any differences in the sentences that may be imposed. The State's fiscal interest is, therefore, irrelevant."

Disposition: Denial of transcript reversed; an indigent person convicted of a crime has the right to a free transcript regardless of the level of the offense (felony, misdemeanor, or petty offense) or the sentence.

11-8h *Penson v. Ohio:* 488 U.S. 75, 102 L.Ed. 2d 300, 109 S.Ct. 346 (1988)

Facts: Penson and two co-defendants were found guilty of several serious crimes. Penson's appointed appellate counsel filed a document captioned "Certificate of Meritless Appeal and Motion," which stated: "Appellant's attorney respectfully certifies to the Court that he has carefully reviewed the within record on appeal, that he has found no errors requiring reversal, modification and/or vacation of appellant's jury trial convictions and/or the trial court's sentence *** and that he will not file a meritless appeal in this matter." The document then moved that the attorney be permitted to withdraw as Penson's attorney of record and relieved of the duty to pursue the appeal. The Court of Appeals granted the attorney's motion and gave Penson 30 days in which to file an appellate brief. The court granted Penson's requests for continuances but refused to appoint a new attorney. No brief was ever filed addressing the merits of the case. The Court of Appeals later reviewed the case and noted that the attorney's certificate stating that the case was meritless was "highly questionable" and found several "arguable claims." It concluded that plain error had been committed in the jury instructions on one count. This count was reversed but the other counts were affirmed and the court concluded that the petitioner "suffered no prejudice" as a result of "counsel's failure to give a more conscientious examination of the record" because the court had thoroughly examined the record and received the benefit of arguments advanced by counsel for Penson's co-defendants.

Issue: Should the court have appointed new counsel after allowing the initial appellate counsel to withdraw?

Reasoning: *** "[I]n *Anders v. California* [386 U.S. 738 (1967)] we held that a criminal appellant may not be denied representation on appeal based on appointed counsel's bare assertion that he or she is of the opinion that there is no merit to the appeal.

"The *Anders* opinion did, however, recognize that in some circumstances counsel may withdraw without denying the indigent appellant fair representation provided that certain safeguards are observed: Appointed counsel is first required to conduct 'a conscientious examination' of the case. If he or she is then of the opinion that the case is wholly frivolous, counsel may request leave to withdraw. The request 'must, however, be accompanied by a brief referring to anything in the record that might arguably support the appeal.' Once the appellate court receives this brief, it must then itself conduct 'a full examination of all the proceeding[s] to decide whether the case is wholly frivolous.' Only after this separate inquiry, and only after the appellate court finds no nonfrivolous issue for appeal, may the court proceed to consider the appeal on the merits without the assistance of counsel. On the other hand, if the court disagrees with counsel—as the Ohio Court of Appeals did in this case—and concludes that there are nonfrivolous issues for appeal, 'it must, prior to decision, afford the indigent the assistance of counsel to argue the appeal.'

*** "Most significantly, the Ohio court erred by failing to appoint new counsel to represent petitioner after it had determined that the record supported 'several arguable claims.' As *Anders* unambiguously provides, 'if [the appellate court] finds any of the legal points arguable on their merits (and therefore not frivolous) it must, prior to decision, afford the indigent the assistance of counsel, to argue the appeal.' ***

*** "Finally, it is important to emphasize that the denial of counsel in this case left petitioner completely without representation during the appellate court's actual decisional process. This is quite different from a case in which it is claimed that counsel's performance was ineffective. *** Because the fundamental importance of the assistance of counsel does not cease as the prosecutorial process moves from the trial to the appellate stage, the presumption of prejudice must extend as well to the denial of counsel on appeal."

Disposition: Appellate decision affirming conviction reversed; defendant has the right to appointed appellate counsel if there are any arguably non-frivolous issues in the case.

11-8i *Strickland v. Washington:* 466 U.S. 668, 80 L.Ed. 2d 674, 104 S.Ct. 2052 (1984)

Facts: During a 10-day period in September 1976, Washington planned and committed three groups of crimes including three brutal stabbing murders, torture, kidnapping, severe assaults, attempted murders, attempted extortion, and theft. He voluntary surrendered and made a lengthy statement after his accomplices were arrested. An experienced criminal lawyer was appointed to represent him. The attorney actively pursued pretrial motions and discovery, but curtailed his efforts after learning that Washington, against the specific advice of his attorney, had confessed to the first two murders. By the trial date, Washington had been charged with three counts of first-degree capital murder as well as numerous other felonies. Washington waived his right to a jury trial and, again acting against counsel's advice, pled guilty to all charges. He also rejected counsel's advice to request an advisory jury at the penalty phase of the capital cases. In preparation for the sentencing hearing, the attorney discussed the case with Washington and telephoned Washington's wife and mother. He did not follow up his unsuccessful efforts to meet them, nor did he otherwise seek character witnesses or request a psychiatric examination. He decided not to present evidence of Washington's character or emotional state, apparently out of a sense of hopelessness about trying to overcome the effect of respondent's confessions of the gruesome crimes. He chose instead to rely on the plea colloquy for evidence about Washington's background and emotional stress in order to prevent cross-examination on this topic. He also excluded other evidence he believed to be damaging. He did not request a presentencing report for fear that it would reveal the true extent of the defendant's criminal history. The trial judge found numerous aggravating circumstances and no facts in mitigation. Washington was given a death sentence for each murder count.

Issue: What is the standard for effective representation by counsel at trial?

Reasoning: * * * "That a person who happens to be a lawyer is present at trial alongside the accused, however, is not enough to satisfy the constitutional command. The Sixth Amendment recognized the right to the assistance of counsel because it envisions counsel's playing a role that is critical to the ability of the adversarial system to produce just results. An accused is entitled to be assisted by an attorney, whether retained or appointed, who plays the role necessary to ensure that the trial is fair.

* * * "The benchmark for judging any claim of ineffectiveness must be whether counsel's conduct so undermined the proper functioning of the adversarial process that the trial cannot be relied on as having produced a just result.

* * * "When a convicted defendant complains of the ineffectiveness of counsel's assistance, the defendant must show that counsel's representation fell below an objective standard of reasonableness.

"More specific guidelines are not appropriate. The Sixth Amendment refers simply to 'counsel,' not specifying particular requirements of effective assistance. It relies instead on the legal profession's maintenance of standards sufficient to justify the law's presumption that counsel will fulfill the role in the adversary process that the Amendment envisions. The proper measure of attorney performance remains simply reasonableness under prevailing professional norms.

* * * "An error by counsel, even if professionally unreasonable, does not warrant setting aside the judgment of a criminal proceeding if the error had no effect on the judgment. The purpose of the Sixth Amendment guarantee of counsel is to ensure that a defendant has the assistance necessary to justify reliance on the outcome of the proceeding. Accordingly, any deficiencies in counsel's performance must be prejudicial to the defense in order to constitute ineffective assistance under the Constitution.

* * * "When a defendant challenges a conviction, the question is whether there is a reasonable probability that, absent the errors, the factfinder would have had a reasonable doubt respecting guilt. When a defendant challenges a death sentence such as the one at issue in this case, the question is whether there is a reasonable probability that, absent the errors, the sentencer—including an appellate court, to the extent it independently reweighs the evidence—would have concluded that the balance of aggravating and mitigating circumstances did not warrant death.

"In making this determination, the court hearing an ineffectiveness claim must consider the totality of the evidence before the judge or jury.

*** Moreover, a verdict or conclusion only weakly supported by the record is more likely to have been affected by errors than one with overwhelming record support. Taking the unaffected findings as a given, and taking due account of the effect of the errors on the remaining findings, a court making the prejudice inquiry must ask if the defendant has met the burden of showing that the decision reached would reasonably likely have been different absent the errors.

"A number of practical considerations are important for the application of the standards we have outlined. Most important, in adjudicating a claim of actual ineffectiveness of counsel, a court should keep in mind that the principles we have stated do not establish mechanical rules. Although those principles should guide the process of decision, the ultimate focus of inquiry must be on the fundamental fairness of the proceeding whose result is being challenged. In every case the court should be concerned with whether, despite the strong presumption of reliability, the result of the particular proceeding is unreliable because of a breakdown in the adversarial process that our system counts on to produce just results.

*** "The principles governing ineffectiveness claims should apply in federal collateral proceedings as they do on direct appeal or in motions for a new trial.

*** "Finally, in a federal *habeas* challenge to a state criminal judgment, a state court conclusion that counsel rendered effective assistance is not a finding of fact binding on the federal court to the extent stated by 28 USC 2254(d)."

Disposition: Sentence affirmed; a defendant has the right to have a conviction reversed due to ineffective assistance of counsel only if the attorney's conduct fell below the standard for a reasonable attorney under the circumstances and the errors committed were likely to have affected the outcome of the case.

11-8j *Evitts v. Lucey:* 469 U.S. 387, 83 L.Ed. 2d 821, 105 S.Ct. 830 (1985)

Facts: Lucey was found guilty of trafficking in controlled substances. His retained counsel filed a timely notice of appeal but failed to file a mandatory "statement of appeal" when he filed his brief with the appellate court. The Court of Appeals granted the state's motion to dismiss for failure to file the statement as required. Defense motion to reconsider the dismissal was summarily denied. The action of the Court of Appeals was affirmed by the Supreme Court of Kentucky. Lucey then sought federal *habeas corpus* relief on the grounds that he had been denied effective assistance of counsel. During the next seven years, Lucey unsuccessfully tried every method open to her to have the case heard on its merits.

Issue: Can the state dismiss a defendant's first appeal due to a technical error by the appellate attorney?

Reasoning: *** "In bringing an appeal as of right from his conviction, a criminal defendant is attempting to demonstrate that the conviction, and the consequent drastic loss of liberty, is unlawful. To prosecute the appeal, a criminal appellant must face an adversary proceeding that—like a trial—is governed by intricate rules that to a layperson would be hopelessly forbidding. An unrepresented appellant—like an unrepresented defendant at trial—is unable to protect the vital interests at stake. To be sure, respondent did have nominal representation when he brought this appeal. But nominal representation on an appeal as of right—like nominal representation at trial—does not suffice to render the proceedings constitutionally adequate; a party whose counsel is unable to provide effective representation is in no better position than one who has no counsel at all.

"A first appeal as of right therefore is not adjudicated in accord with due process of law if the appellant does not have the effective assistance of an attorney. ***

*** "[A] State may certainly enforce a vital procedural rule by imposing sanctions against the attorney, rather than against the client. Such a course may well be more effective than the alternative of refusing to decide the merits of an appeal and will reduce the possibility that a defendant who was powerless to obey the rules will serve a term of years in jail on an unlawful conviction."

Disposition: Dismissal of appeal reversed; a defendant's first appeal cannot be dismissed due to the incompetency of appellate counsel.

Chapter Quiz

True/False

1. Everyone, regardless of wealth, has the right to have an attorney appointed and provided by the government if charged with a crime.
2. A person cannot be sentenced to serve time in jail if he/she did not have an attorney because he/she could not afford to hire one.
3. Indigent defendants have the right to have a government-appointed attorney handle all of their appeals.

4. The right to a government-appointed attorney includes sufficient funds to hire any expert the defense attorney believes is necessary to prepare a strong defense.
5. An attorney can never represent more than one defendant in the same criminal case.
6. A mentally competent individual has the right to represent him/herself at trial.
7. Anyone who appeals a criminal case to the U. S. Supreme Court has a Sixth Amendment right to have an attorney appointed to handle the case.
8. Inmates do not have the right to have an attorney represent them if they file *habeas corpus* suits.
9. The government is not required to pay for attorneys for inmates who file cases under the federal Civil Rights Act.
10. A defendant has the automatic right to have his/her conviction reversed if it is shown that the defense attorney who handled the trial had legal skills substantially below the norm for the local community.

Discussion Questions

1. John was arrested for robbery. He requested an attorney at his arraignment but the judge denied the request because a large amount cash was taken in the robbery and had not been recovered. John went to trial without a lawyer and was convicted. Was John's right to counsel violated? Explain.
2. Mary was charged with burglary. Her public defender asked for a continuance at the preliminary hearing because he was currently defending another client in a trial. The judge allowed the preliminary hearing to proceed without a defense attorney but assured Mary that she would have an attorney at trial. Did this violate Mary's right to counsel? Explain.
3. Sam was charged with murder. A public defender was appointed but Sam demanded to act as his own attorney because he was too paranoid to trust the public defender. The judge allowed Sam to go *pro per* without even holding a hearing to determine if Sam had any knowledge of the law. Sam was convicted. Was Sam's right to counsel violated? Explain.
4. Tim was convicted on two counts of embezzlement. His request for an appellate attorney was granted but the attorney who was appointed was too busy to file a brief on time. The appellate court dismissed the case after the third continuance. Did this violate Tim's right to counsel? Explain

Chapter 12

Other Issues Related to Criminal Trials

Outline

The Sixth Amendment contains a variety of protections related to criminal trials. In addition to the right to counsel, it also covers a defendant's right to a speedy trial, a trial by jury, and confrontation of witnesses. The exclusion of jurors due to race or gender involves the Equal Protection Clause. Discovery, another process relevant to the trial, is considered a due process right. This chapter also covers the Fifth Amendment protection against double jeopardy and Eighth Amendment issues related to sentencing.

12-1 Speedy Trial

A defendant's right to a speedy trial is explicitly stated in the Sixth Amendment. Like most other guarantees in the Bill of Rights, there are no specific guidelines given. The Supreme Court has interpreted the right to a speedy trial to mean that the defendant may not be unduly prejudiced by a delay between the time when charges are filed and when the trial begins. If the defendant is held in custody, the period starts when the arrest is made.

The Court has identified four factors to be considered: length of delay, reasons for the delay, defendant's assertion of the right to a speedy trial, and prejudice to the defendant. No one factor will establish the case, but it is rare that a defendant who has not made repeated motions to avoid continuances will be able to show a constitutional violation.

State and federal statutes impose more specific rights to a speedy trial. For example, in some states a person held in custody on felony charges has a right to a trial within 90 days. The Supreme Court does not consider these statutes when analyzing violations of the Sixth Amendment right to speedy trial.

12-2 Discovery

Discovery is the right to obtain information in the possession of the other side. Most discovery issues are governed by local statute but the Supreme Court has found a few instances that involve constitutional issues.

The prosecution has a duty to reveal exculpatory information in its possession to the defense prior to trial. While the defense normally must request specific items from the prosecution (for example, all statements made by eyewitnesses), the Court held that there is a duty to disclose information known to be material to the defense even if no request was made. The duty to disclose applies to all information in police files whether or not the prosecutor is aware of its existence. There is no corresponding duty for a prosecutor seeking an indictment to disclose exculpatory information to the Grand Jury. Neither is there a duty to disclose this type of evidence prior to the defendant entering a guilty plea.

A different situation comes up when the defense wants to run independent tests on physical evidence. Such tests are normally allowed if the item is being held as evidence, but the police have no duty to preserve evidence solely for the purpose of allowing independent testing.

Some states have procedural rules that require the defendant to give the prosecution notice that an alibi defense will be used. The Supreme Court found that these rules do not violate the defendant's rights. A similar rule applies to requirements that both sides file a list naming the witnesses they intend to call at trial. The defense does not, however, have to reveal its plans to call the defendant to testify.

12-3 Right to a Jury Trial

The jury has been a part of the criminal justice system since common law. The Supreme Court's review of the jury's history indicates that a defendant does not have the right to demand trial without a jury; therefore, a jury will hear a case if either the prosecution or the defense requests one.

Congress gave defendants tried in federal courts the right to a jury trial if the offense carries a sentence of more than six months in prison. Application of the Sixth Amendment right to trial by jury to the states resulted in a similar rule: The defendant has a right to a jury trial only if charged with at least one offense that has a potential sentence of more than six months in custody. The Court reviewed Nevada's drunk driving law and found that no jury was required even though the sentence included both six months in jail and other no-prison penalties. The analysis pointed out that drunk driving is not considered such a serious offense by society that it should trigger the right to a jury trial. The Court refused, however, to categorically state that there could never be a situation in which the gravity of the crime would mandate a jury even though the sentence was less than six months.

American juries have historically been composed of 12 people who must reach a unanimous verdict. Statutes still mandate this for criminal cases held in federal courts. The Supreme Court determined that this tradition has no constitutional significance. Juries as small as six members, but no smaller, meet constitutional muster. Twelve-member juries need not be unanimous; verdicts of 10–2 and 9–3 have been approved by the Supreme Court in states where the legislature enacted appropriate laws. Six-member juries, however, must reach unanimous verdicts.

12-4 Jury Selection

A jury should represent a cross section of society. Exclusions from jury duty cannot be based on race or gender. The process used to call citizens to jury duty must provide a jury pool representing the community's racial composition. Women cannot be excluded from jury duty nor can they be allowed to withdraw their names from consideration for reasons different from those afforded men.

The Supreme Court has held that peremptory challenges cannot be used by either the prosecution or the defense to exclude people on account of race or gender. For example, if it can be shown that the prosecution systematically used peremptory challenges to exclude African-Americans, the conviction must be reversed whatever the race of the defendant. Use of peremptory challenges in a racially discriminatory manner by the defense is also prohibited. Excluding Hispanic jurors because the prosecutor believes the jurors would rely on their knowledge of Spanish, rather than the translation provided by the official interpreter, does not raise a question of racial discrimination.

Jurors may be questioned regarding their racial prejudices if it appears that the case will raise issues of racism. More is required than a mere showing that the victim and defendant are of different races, except in death penalty cases, where the defendant always has the right to have prospective jurors informed of the race of the victim and questioned regarding their personal racial prejudices.

Jurors are supposed to base their decisions solely on the evidence presented at trial and the law contained in the jury instructions. Pretrial publicity can make it very difficult to find jurors who do not already have preconceived notions on the case. Prospective jurors who have already formed an opinion on the defendant's guilt can be excluded for cause. As seen in chapter 13, judges can impose "gag orders" before trial to restrict the flow of information to the media. Other alternatives include a change of venue and continuances until the furor over the case has subsided.

Death penalty cases present a unique problem because some people oppose capital punishment for moral reasons. Prospective jurors may be asked whether their personal opinions on the death penalty would interfere with their ability to review the facts and apply the law. Anyone who feels compelled to vote against the death penalty under all circumstances may be challenged for cause. The fact that the person has qualms about imposition of capital punishment, but will not categorically refuse to vote for it, is not grounds to remove the prospective juror with a challenge for cause; the prosecution may, however, decide to use a peremptory challenge.

12-5 Confrontation and Cross-Examination

The Sixth Amendment gives defendants the right to confront the witnesses who make allegations against them. Under normal conditions, this means that the witness is called to testify in open court and is subject to cross-examination by the defense. This right to cross-examination is considered to be fundamental to the truth-seeking process, but the right is not absolute. A disruptive defendant can be barred from the courtroom.

There are times when it is impossible to have a witness testify in court; for example, the person may have died or cannot be located. The hearsay rule contains exceptions to cover the most frequent situations. The Supreme Court has recognized that the Confrontation Clause is not violated when the prosecution relies on a traditional exception to the Hearsay Rule that is based on the inherent reliability of the statement. The Court has specifically recognized the following exceptions: prior testimony under oath, spontaneous declarations, and statements made for purpose of medical treatment. Newly created exceptions, however, must bear some indicia of trustworthiness and it must be shown that the declarant is unavailable to testify at trial.

Impeachment is considered an important part of the truth-seeking process. The defendant must be given ample opportunity during cross-examination to show possible bias of a witness. One Supreme Court case held that a state's interest in the confidentiality of juvenile convictions must yield to the defendant's right to show that a juvenile witness might slant the truth due to being on probation. Another case upheld a rape suspect's right to cross-examine the accusing witness about her relevant sexual history despite the possibility that the facts involved might engender racial bias.

Confessions by co-defendants raise two separate problems. First, a co-defendant's confession is frequently self-serving. For this reason, such statements must be shown to be reliable in order to be admissible and the jury must be cautioned about possible motivations to alter the truth.

The second problem with co-defendant statements involves the Confrontation Clause. Due to the co-defendant's Fifth Amendment right to refuse to testify, the defendant does not have the right to call a co-defendant to testify unless that person is willing to take the stand. Several solutions have been suggested for this problem. If the defendants are tried separately, the defendant who has already been convicted (or acquitted) can no longer claim the Fifth Amendment privilege; therefore he/she could be forced to take the witness stand. Unfortunately, this approach is costly (at least twice as many trials will be needed) and very time consuming (the second trial cannot start until appeals of the first conviction are complete). Another approach used when the person making the statement does not testify is to edit (redact) the confession so that it makes no reference to defendant(s) other than the one making the confession. Attempts to redact a confession by merely inserting the word "deleted," blanks, or another symbol in place of the name of the co-defendant are not sufficient because the identity of the person whose name has been deleted will be obvious to the jurors. While redacting may work in some cases, the resulting statement may be totally meaningless in others. If neither separate trials or redacting is practical, the prosecution may have to go to trial without using the co-defendant's confession.

The Supreme Court has been faced with two cases dealing with the defendant's right to confront his/her accuser face-to-face. Both cases involved abused children. The use of closed circuit-television, wherein the child was not present in the same room as the defendant but was otherwise subjected to cross-examination in view of the jury, was found to satisfy the Sixth Amendment. Placing a screen in the courtroom so that the witness could not see the defendant from the witness stand was found to violate the defendant's rights. The key difference between these cases was that the Court upheld the state law that required the judge to make an individualized determination that the child would suffer psychological trauma from testifying in the presence of the defendant; the conviction that was reversed involved a rule that permitted the screen to be used in all cases in which young children testify.

12-6 Double Jeopardy

The double jeopardy protection of the Fifth Amendment has been applied to both state and federal prosecutions since *Benton v. Maryland* [395 U.S. 784 (1969)]. The basic idea behind double jeopardy is that the government should not be allowed to harass citizens by repeatedly subjecting them to prosecution for the same thing. In its most common form, this means that once a defendant has been either acquitted or convicted, there can be no additional prosecution on the same charge(s). A person is considered to be acquitted when a jury returns a verdict of acquittal; a trial judge grants a motion for an acquittal; a judge grants the defendant's motion for a demur at the end of the prosecution's case in chief; or a judge rules as a *matter of law* that the prosecution has failed to establish a case. A similar rule applies if the conviction is reversed on appeal on the grounds of insufficient evidence. Retrial after a conviction is reversed on appeal for other reasons does not violate double jeopardy.

Sometimes the trial judge grants a defense motion to set aside a conviction. The prosecution can appeal this ruling without violating double jeopardy if a successful appeal would reinstate a general finding of guilt. The defendant may claim a violation of double jeopardy if further proceedings would be required after the appeal to develop facts regarding guilt or innocence.

Trials that end without a determination of guilt or innocence can usually be retried. "Hung jury" cases have followed this rule since 1824. Cases declared a "mistrial" due to misconduct by prosecutor, defense attorney, or judge can also be retried except when the prosecution's misconduct was intentionally done to goad the defense into requesting a new trial.

Multiple convictions based on the same actions violate double jeopardy. A defendant cannot be convicted for a crime and its lesser included offense. This applies when every element of the lesser offense is included in the definition of the greater crime. If each offense contains at least one element not contained in the other, conviction for both does not violate double jeopardy. For double jeopardy purposes, the substantive crime is not a lesser included offense in a conspiracy. For example, robbery is not a lesser included offense in a conspiracy to commit that robbery.

Acquittal at the first trial on either the crime or a lesser included offense bars a second trial on the remaining charge; for example, theft of the cash taken during a robbery is a lesser included offense to the robbery. If the defendant is convicted for the robbery, the theft charges cannot be refiled; if the jury returns a verdict for the theft, the robbery charges cannot be refiled. The same is true if the jury acquits: Acquittal on the robbery bars refiling the theft charges; acquittal on the theft bars refiling the robbery charges.

Double jeopardy does not prevent multiple charges wherein the offenses are prosecuted by separate sovereigns. This doctrine recognizes separate sovereignty between the federal government and the states; two or more different states; and the federal government and Native American nations. For example, in a case in which the defendant hired men to kidnap his wife in Alabama and she was killed in Georgia, the Court held that double jeopardy did not prevent convictions for murder in both states. Municipalities are seen as deriving their power from the state; therefore, prosecution under state law and a local ordinance for the same acts violates double jeopardy.

Imposition of the death penalty in cases in which the sentence is imposed after a bifurcated trial is covered by double jeopardy. Unlike other sentencing hearings, the prosecution presents evidence and the trier of fact is required to determine if aggravating circumstances are present that justify the death penalty. If not, life imprisonment is imposed. Due to this trial-like proceeding with the prosecution bearing the burden of proof, the Supreme Court held that a life sentence implies acquittal on the death penalty allegation. If a conviction is reversed after life imprisonment is imposed, the death penalty cannot be sought when the case is tried a second time. Double jeopardy has not been applied to sentencing in other cases.

12-7 Civil Forfeiture Proceedings

Civil forfeiture laws, first popular during Prohibition, have become common in recent years. The purpose of these laws is to seize the profits of a crime. They frequently give the government the authority to seize cash and sell items used during a crime as well as assets purchased with money generated by a criminal enterprise. Conviction on related criminal charges is not a prerequisite to forfeiture under the laws of some states.

Seizure of cars subject to forfeiture may be done without a warrant if the vehicle is found in a public place. For example, in *Florida v. White* [526 U.S. 559, 143 L.Ed. 2d 748, 119 S.Ct. 1555 (1999)], the Court held that a search warrant was not required to seize a car used during drug sales; the officer's observation of the car while it was being used for a purpose specified in the statute established probable cause that the vehicle was contraband.

The Supreme Court has consistently held that civil forfeiture cases do not violate double jeopardy even though the defendant was convicted and fined for the same criminal activity. Property may be subject to forfeiture even though it is co-owned by an innocent third party. Normally, the defendant will be notified that a forfeiture suit has been filed. If the items involved are portable and could be spirited out of the jurisdiction, the government may seize them pending the outcome of the civil proceedings. Most forfeiture laws require the government to establish the connection between the assets and the crime by a preponderance of the evidence; some statutes require a higher level of proof.

While forfeiture laws do not violate double jeopardy, the Supreme Court recently indicated that the Excessive Fine Clause of the Eighth Amendment is implicated in some cases. At issue was the case of a man who attempted to transport money out of the United States without completing the required declaration. The criminal penalty for violation of the reporting law included a maximum fine of $5,000. The portion of the law that enabled the government to seek forfeiture of all of the cash involved—in this case, $357,144 that was in no other way related to a crime—was found to be an excessive fine. The Court held that there was no justification for seizure of the money other than to impose a criminal penalty; therefore, the totally disproportionate nature of the forfeiture compared to the fine resulted in a violation of the Eighth Amendment.

12-8 Sentencing

12-8a Death Penalty

Beginning with *Furman v. Georgia* [408 U.S. 238 (1972)] and *Gregg v. Georgia* [428 U.S. 153 (1976)], the Supreme Court has attempted to provide standards for constitutional death penalty procedures. The goal is to provide carefully drafted statutes that ensure guidance for the jury so that the death penalty will not be imposed capriciously or arbitrarily. Two basic concepts are key to the Court's analysis: (1) The statute must clearly set forth the standard for determining when the death penalty is merited (aggravating circumstances); and (2) the defense has the right to have any mitigating circumstances it deems relevant considered.

The Court has placed two specific limits on death penalty legislation regarding age and mental capacity. While it has approved laws allowing the execution of minors, it has refused to endorse state laws that allow capital punishment for persons under the age of 16 at the time the crime was committed. It has also prohibited executions of inmates who are mentally retarded. The Court refrained from defining the degree of retardation that qualifies for this rule; it left it to the state legislatures to consult mental health experts and enact appropriate standards.

Statutes must specify the types of murder cases eligible for the death penalty (frequently called "special circumstances"). Mandatory death penalties, even for the killing of a peace officer, are prohibited because the jury must be allowed to consider mitigating circumstances. State statutes, aided by interpretation by the state's highest court and appropriate jury instructions, must clearly define aggravating circumstances. Merely authorizing the death penalty for murders that are "heinous, atrocious, or cruel" is inadequate; more specific guidelines must be given to the jury. The death penalty is not reserved for people who personally inflict the wounds that result in death. The Supreme Court declared that the death penalty may also be imposed on co-defendants who show reckless disregard of human life by knowingly engaging in criminal activities known to carry a grave risk of death to others.

The defendant must be given notice before trial that the death penalty will be sought and is entitled to a jury trial on the question of whether he/she is guilty of a killing under special circumstances. A second hearing, frequently called the *penalty phase*, is held to hear evidence on aggravating and mitigating circumstances and determine if the death penalty should be imposed. Unless the defendant waives the right to a jury, the decision on whether or not the death penalty should be imposed must be made by the jury.

The jury (or judge in a bench trial) must determine if the prosecution proved at least one of the statutory aggravating circumstances beyond a reasonable doubt. Then it must weigh the aggravating circumstance(s) against any mitigating circumstances introduced by the defense. The jury cannot be required to unanimously agree on one mitigating factor before weighing all of the evidence. Where the defendant proffers mitigating evidence relevant to moral culpability, as opposed to the facts of the case, the jurors must be given a special instruction informing them how to consider it. An example of this situation would be a defendant who introduces evidence of his/her severe mental retardation as a mitigating factor.

The jury must also be instructed on the lesser included punishment of life imprisonment. The Court found that this is important because a jury faced with only two choices (death or acquittal) may make arbitrary decisions. Forcing this type of choice violates due process. The defendant also has the right to have the jury instructed that if the defendant is sentenced to life in prison, he/she will not be eligible for parole.

While the jury must be adequately instructed on aggravating and mitigating circumstances, the defendant does not have the constitutional right to have an appellate court do a "proportionality review." This type of review compares the facts in the case under appeal with other murder cases and determines that the death penalty was being imposed in factually similar cases.

Death penalty cases in which the sentence is imposed after a bifurcated trial pose different double jeopardy issues. Each phase of the trial results in a separate verdict. The guilty verdict will stand even if the jury cannot reach a verdict at the penalty phase. Unlike most other sentencing hearings, the prosecution presents evidence at the penalty phase and the jury must render a verdict. The trier of fact is required to determine if aggravating circumstances are present that justify the death penalty: The death penalty is imposed if jurors unanimously agree that aggravating circumstances are present; a unanimous finding of no aggravating circumstances results in life imprisonment. If the jurors are not unanimous, many states allow the prosecution to present the penalty issues to another jury. Due to this trial-like proceeding, with the prosecution bearing the burden of proof, the Supreme Court held that a unanimous vote for a life sentence implies acquittal on the death penalty allegation. If a conviction is reversed after jurors unanimously voted for life imprisonment, the death penalty cannot be sought when the case is tried a second time.

12-8b Other Sentencing Issues

It is well known that all elements of a crime must be established beyond a reasonable doubt. In *Apprendi v. New Jersey* [530 U.S. 466, 147 L.Ed. 2d 435, 120 S.Ct. 2348 (2000)], the Court required that any fact that increases the penalty for a crime beyond the prescribed statutory maximum, other than prior convictions, must be submitted to a jury and proved beyond a reasonable doubt. This applies to enhancements and other sentencing factors such as inflicting serious injuries, use of a weapon, victimization of an elderly person, etc.

Solem v. Helm [463 U.S. 277 (1983)] held the Eighth Amendment prohibited life imprisonment without possibility of parole under a South Dakota statute for recidivists even though the defendant had six prior convictions for nonviolent felonies. The Court found life without parole to be disproportionate to the gravity of the offense and punishment imposed on other criminals in the same state who committed much more serious crimes. Only one other state treated recidivists as harshly.

The Supreme Court recently considered a "three strikes" case from a state that uses a bifurcated trial—a guilt phase on the charges and a penalty phase to determine if life in prison should be imposed due to the recidivist law. It held that double jeopardy did not prevent a new penalty phase before a different jury when there was a conviction at the guilt phase of the trial but a hung jury when imposition of the recidivism law was considered.

Although the Supreme Court held that the Eighth Amendment requires that the punishment be proportionate to the crime, sentences except death and life without possibility of parole have been left to the judgment of state legislatures in all but a few cases; for example, two consecutive, 20-year prison terms and two fines of $10,000 were held not excessive for possession and distribution of 9 ounces of marijuana; life with the possibility of parole under a recidivism statute was upheld for a man with three separate felony convictions—all involved property crimes and netted a total of $229.11. In noncapital cases, the sentences enacted by the legislature do not have to be proportionate to other crimes of equivalent severity. Mandatory sentences can be imposed without consideration of mitigating circumstances.

Robinson v. California [370 U.S. 660 (1962)] held that making it a crime to be a narcotics addict violated the Eighth Amendment. The Court recognized narcotics addiction as an illness and held that making it a crime would be in the same category as making mental illness criminal. While this case prohibits status offenses, it does not prevent addicts from being punished for possession of narcotics or other criminal acts.

The Federal Sentencing Guidelines, and rules from several states, permit an enhancement to the sentence if the defendant committed perjury during the trial. The Supreme Court held that this does not violate a defendant's right to testify at trial. It found the false testimony relevant to the sentencing decision because it reflects on a defendant's criminal history, willingness to accept the commands of the law, the authority of the court, and on the defendant's character in general.

12-9 Other Due Process Issues

A variety of due process issues apply to criminal trials. Several have been addressed by recent Supreme Court decisions.

12-9a Competency to Stand Trial

A trial meets minimum due process requirements only if the defendant has the mental capacity to understand the trial process and assist in the defense by rationally communicating with his/her attorney. If the defendant's mental capacity appears questionable, there will usually be a separate hearing on competency to stand trial. States may require proof of incompetence by a preponderance of the evidence in order to stop the trial. Higher levels of proof are unacceptable because the result would be that defendants who probably are incompetent may be required to stand trial. Since this is a due process issue, the judge is required to monitor the competency of the defendant; the issue is not lost if the defense fails to raise it.

12-9b Intoxication and Insanity As Defenses

Unlike the competency issue, the states are allowed to create defenses, such as "not guilty by reason of insanity" and intoxication, that relate to mental capacity. These defenses are not of constitutional dimension. States may abolish their use without violating the defendant's rights as long as there is no *ex post facto* application of laws terminating them.

12-9c Sexually Violent Predator Laws

Many professionals in the therapeutic community doubt that a person with a history of making numerous sexual assaults can be cured. This led to efforts to keep sexually violent predators in custody after serving their sentences. The Supreme Court declared that this type of law does not violate due process as long as there are strong procedural protections. The statute before the Court required a hearing at the end of the prison sentence. It mandated proof beyond a reasonable doubt that the person had a history of sexually violent behavior and presently has a mental condition that creates a likelihood that the conduct will reoccur in the future if the person is not incapacitated. If the jury unanimously decides that the inmate is a violent sexual predator, the defendant is transferred to a secure mental hospital after release from prison; confinement may continue as long as there is proof that, due to this mental condition, it would be difficult (if not impossible) for the defendant to control his/her dangerous behavior. To date, the Court has explicitly expressed no opinion on whether courts are restricted to considering the defendant's emotional state or whether they can also consider volitional, emotional, and cognitive impairments.

12-9d Assisted Suicide

In 1997, the Supreme Court considered two challenges to laws that made it a crime to assist a mentally competent person who wants to commit suicide. It ruled that terminally ill patients who wish to die do not have a due process right to the assistance of a doctor who is willing to help them. Equal protection arguments, based on the fact many states give patients the right to refuse "heroic means" to prolong life, also failed to convince the Court that there is a right to have members of the medical profession assist when a person has decided to commit suicide.

12-10 Key Supreme Court Cases

12-10a *Barker v. Wingo:* 407 U.S. 514, 33 L.Ed. 2d 101, 92 S.Ct. 2182 (1972)

Facts: In July 1958, Barker and Manning were arrested for the tire iron murder of an elderly couple. They were indicted on September 15, counsel was appointed, and trial was set for October 21. The Commonwealth of Kentucky considered the case against Manning stronger and did not want to go to trial against Barker until after Manning was convicted so that Manning could be called to testify against Barker. Manning's first trial ended in a hung jury; the second and third trials ended in convictions that were reversed on appeal; the fourth trial ended in another hung jury. The Commonwealth then tried Manning in separate trials for each count of murder and won convictions. The last (sixth) trial ended in December 1962.

After 10 months in jail, Barker was able to post bail and remained free on bond until trial. Barker made no objection to the first 11 continuances. In February 1962, when the twelfth continuance was sought, a defense motion was filed that unsuccessfully tried to dismiss the case. The defense did not oppose the next two continuances. The case was set for trial on March 19, 1963, but this date was later changed due to illness of the chief investigator. Barker unsuccessfully objected to this continuance, as he did the next. A defense motion to dismiss for lack of a speedy trial was denied on October 9, 1963, and the case went to trial. Manning was the chief prosecution witness; Barker was convicted.

Issue: Was the right to a speedy trial violated by the five-year delay between indictment and trial?

Reasoning: * * * "The approach we accept is a balancing test, in which the conduct of both the prosecution and the defendant are weighed.

"A balancing test necessarily compels courts to approach speedy-trial cases on an *ad hoc* basis. We can do little more than identify some of the factors which courts should assess in determining whether a particular defendant has been deprived of his right. * * * [W]e identify four such factors: Length of delay, the reasons for the delay, the defendant's assertion of his right, and prejudice to the defendant.

"The length of the delay is to some extent a triggering mechanism. Until there is some delay which is presumptively prejudicial, there is no necessity for inquiry into the other factors that go into the balance. Nevertheless because of the imprecision of the right to speedy trial, the length of delay that will provoke such an inquiry is necessarily dependent upon the peculiar circumstances of the case. * * *

"Closely related to length of delay is the reason the government assigns to justify the delay. Here, too, different weights should be assigned to different reasons. A deliberate attempt to delay the trial in order to hamper the defense should be weighed heavily against the government. A more neutral reason such as negligence or overcrowded courts should be weighed less heavily but nevertheless should be considered since the ultimate responsibility for such circumstances must rest with the government rather than with the defendant. Finally, a valid reason, such as a missing witness, should serve to justify appropriate delay.

*** "Whether and how a defendant asserts his right is closely related to the other factors we have mentioned. *** The defendant's assertion of his speedy trial right, then, is entitled to strong evidentiary weight in determining whether the right is being deprived. We emphasize that failure to assert the right will make it difficult for a defendant to prove that he was denied a speedy trial.

"A fourth factor is prejudice to the defendant. *** This Court has identified three such interests: (i) to prevent oppressive pretrial incarceration; (ii) to minimize anxiety and concern of the accused; and (iii) to limit the possibility that the defense will be impaired. Of these, the most serious is the last, because the inability of a defendant adequately to prepare his case skews the fairness of the entire system. If witnesses die or disappear during a delay, the prejudice is obvious. There is also prejudice if defense witnesses are unable to recall accurately events of the distant past. ***

*** "We regard none of the four factors identified above as either a necessary or sufficient condition to the finding of a deprivation of the right of speedy trial. Rather, they are related factors and must be considered together with such other circumstances as may be relevant. In sum, these factors have no talismanic qualities; courts must still engage in a difficult and sensitive balancing process."

Disposition: Conviction affirmed; the five-year delay was excessive but the defendant could show no prejudice in the form of missing witnesses and he failed to make demands for a speedy trial during most of the delay.

12-10b *United States v. Agurs:* 427 U.S. 97, 49 L.Ed. 2d 342, 96 S.Ct. 2392 (1976)

Facts: Agurs and Sewell registered at a cheap motel as husband and wife. About 15 minutes later, motel employees heard Agurs call for help. They forced entry into the room and found Sewell on top of Agurs. Both were struggling for possession of a bowie knife. She was holding the knife; his bleeding hand grasped the blade and appeared to be trying to jam the blade into her chest. Motel employees separated the two and called police. Sewell was dead on arrival at the hospital. Agurs left before the police arrived but surrendered to police the following day. She had no cuts or bruises except for needle marks on her upper arm. An autopsy disclosed that Sewell had several deep stab wounds in his chest and abdomen, and a number of slashes on his arms and hands, characterized as "defensive wounds." Agurs's sole defense was that Sewell had initially attacked her and she acted in self defense. In addition to her screams for help and the fact that he was found on top of her, evidence showed that Sewell was in possession of two knives at the time and was a violence-prone person. Agurs was convicted. Three months later the defense filed a motion for a new trial based on the fact that the prosecutor had failed to inform the defense that Sewell had a prior criminal record, evidence that would have supported her contention that he had a violent character.

Issue: Under what circumstances is the prosecution required to provide information for the defense that has not been specifically requested?

Reasoning: *** "The rule in *Brady v. Maryland,* 373 U.S. 83 (1963), arguably applies to three quite different situations. Each involves the discovery, after trial, of information which had been known to the prosecution but unknown to the defense.

"In the first situation, *** the undisclosed evidence demonstrates that the prosecution's case includes perjured testimony and that the prosecution knew, or should have known, of the perjury. *** In those cases the Court has applied a strict standard of materiality, not just because they involve prosecutorial misconduct, but more importantly because they involve a corruption of the truth-seeking function of the trial process. ***

"The second situation, illustrated by the *Brady* case itself, is characterized by a pretrial request for specific evidence. In that case defense counsel had requested the extrajudicial statements made by Brady's accomplice, one Boblit. This Court held that the suppression of one of Boblit's statements deprived Brady of due process, noting specifically that the statement had been requested and that it was 'material.' A fair analysis of the holding in *Brady* indicates that implicit in the requirement of materiality is a concern that the suppressed evidence might have affected the outcome of the trial.

*** "In many cases, however, exculpatory information in the possession of the prosecutor may be unknown to defense counsel. In such a situation he may make no request at all, or possibly ask for 'all *Brady* material' or for 'anything exculpatory.' Such a request really gives the prosecutor no better notice than if no request is made. If there is a duty to respond to a general request of that kind, it must derive from the obviously exculpatory character of certain evidence in the hands of the prosecutor. But if the evidence is so clearly supportive of a claim of innocence that it gives the prosecution notice of a duty to produce, that duty should equally arise even if no request is made. *** We conclude that there is no significant difference between cases in which there has been merely a general request for exculpatory matter and cases, like the one we must now decide, in which there has been no request at all. The third situation in which the *Brady* rule arguably applies, typified by this case, therefore embraces the case in which only a general request for '*Brady* material' has been made.

*** "Nor do we believe the constitutional obligation is measured by the moral culpability, or the willfulness, of the prosecutor. If evidence highly probative of innocence is in his file, he should be presumed to recognize its significance even if he has actually overlooked it. ***

*** "It necessarily follows that if the omitted evidence creates a reasonable doubt that did not otherwise exist, constitutional error has been committed. This means that the omission must be evaluated in the context of the entire record. If there is no reasonable doubt about guilt whether or not the additional evidence is considered, there is no justification for a new trial. On the other hand, if the verdict is already of questionable validity, additional evidence of relatively minor importance might be sufficient to create a reasonable doubt."

Disposition: Conviction affirmed; the prosecutor has the duty to give information to the defense, even without a request, if it is obvious that the information has exculpatory value. In this case, evidence involved was not material.

12-10c *Burch v. Louisiana:* 441 U.S. 130, 60 L.Ed. 2d 96, 99 S.Ct. 1623 (1979)

Facts: Burch was charged with two counts of exhibition of obscene motion pictures. The trial was held before a six-person jury, which voted 5 to 1 to convict. This constituted a conviction under Louisiana law.

Issue: Does a nonunanimous jury verdict violate the constitutional right to trial by jury?

Reasoning: *** "[I]n *Apodaca v. Oregon,* 406 U.S. 404 (1972), we upheld a state statute providing that only 10 members of a 12-person jury need concur to render a verdict in certain noncapital cases. In terms of the role of the jury as a safeguard against oppression, the plurality opinion perceived no difference between those juries required to act unanimously and those permitted to act by votes of 10 to 2. Nor was unanimity viewed by the plurality as contributing materially to the exercise of the jury's common-sense judgment or as a necessary precondition to effective application of the requirement that jury panels represent a fair cross-section of the community.

*** "We thus have held that the Constitution permits juries of less than 12 members, but that it requires at least six. And we have approved the use of certain nonunanimous verdicts in cases involving 12-person juries. ***

*** "[M]uch the same reasons that led us in *Ballew* [*Ballew v. Georgia,* 435 U.S. 223 (1978)] to decide that use of a five-member jury threatened the fairness of the proceeding and the proper role of the jury, lead us to conclude now that conviction for a nonpetty offense by only five members of a six-person jury presents a similar threat to preservation of the substance of the jury trial guarantee and justifies our requiring verdicts rendered by six-person juries to be unanimous. We are buttressed in this view by the current jury practices of the several States. It appears that of those States that utilizes six-member juries in trials of nonpetty offenses, only two, including Louisiana, also allow nonunanimous verdicts. We think that this near-uniform judgement of the Nation provides a useful guide in delimiting the line between those jury practices that are constitutionally permissible and those that are not."

Disposition: Conviction reversed; nonunanimous verdicts are constitutional for 12-member juries but when jury size is reduced to six, the verdict must be unanimous.

12-10d *Sheppard v. Maxwell:* 384 U.S. 333, 16 L.Ed. 2d 600, 86 S.Ct. 1507 (1966)

Facts: On July 4, 1954, Marilyn Sheppard, the defendant's pregnant wife, was bludgeoned to death in the upstairs bedroom of their lakeshore home in a suburb of Cleveland. The case received massive publicity both before and during trial. During the trial, a table running the width of the courtroom was set up for the press inside the bar. It reached within three feet of the jury box. Approximately 20 members of the media were assigned seats at this table and others were in the spectator section of the courtroom. The media were allowed to use all the rooms of the floor of the courthouse where the trial was held. Private telephone lines and telegraphic equipment were installed. A local station set up broadcasting facilities in the room next to the jury room. Inflammatory articles were published throughout the trial. Sheppard was convicted.

Issue: Does extensive media coverage violate the defendant's right to a fair trial?

Reasoning: *** "The carnival atmosphere at trial could easily have been avoided since the courtroom and courthouse premises are subject to the control of the court. As we stressed in *Estes* [*Estes v. Texas,* 381 U.S. 532 (1965)], the presence of the press at judicial proceedings must be limited when it is apparent that the accused might otherwise be prejudiced or disadvantaged. *** The number of reporters in the courtroom itself could have been limited at the first sign that their presence would disrupt the trial. They certainly should not have been placed inside the bar. Furthermore, the judge should have more closely regulated the conduct of newsmen in the courtroom. ***

"Secondly, the court should have insulated the witnesses. All the newspapers and radio stations apparently interviewed prospective witnesses at will, and in many instances disclosed their testimony. *** Although the witnesses were barred from the courtroom during the trial the full verbatim testimony was available to them in the press. This completely nullified the judge's imposition of the rule.

"Thirdly, the court should have made some effort to control the release of leads, information, and gossip to the press by police officers, witnesses, and the counsel for both sides. Much of the information thus disclosed was inaccurate, leading to groundless rumors and confusion. ***

*** "More specifically, the trial court might well have proscribed extrajudicial statements by any lawyer, party, witness, or court official which divulged prejudicial matters. *** Being advised of the great public interest in the case, the mass coverage of the press, and the potential prejudicial impact of publicity, the court could also have requested the appropriate city and county officials to promulgate a regulation with respect to dissemination of information about the case by their employees. In addition, reporters who wrote or broadcast prejudicial stories, could have been warned as to the impropriety of publishing material not introduced in the proceedings. ***

*** "Due process requires that the accused receive a trial by an impartial jury free from outside influences. Given the pervasiveness of modern communications and the difficulty of effacing prejudicial publicity from the minds of the jurors, the trial courts must take strong measures to ensure that the balance is never weighed against the accused. *** But where there is a reasonable likelihood that prejudicial news prior to trial will prevent a fair trial, the judge should continue the case until the threat abates, or transfer it to another county not so permeated with publicity. In addition, sequestration of the jury was something the judge should have raised sua sponte with counsel. If publicity during the proceedings threatens the fairness of the trial, a new trial should be ordered. But we must remember that reversals are but palliative; the cure lies in those remedial measures that will prevent the prejudice at its inception."

Disposition: Conviction reversed; the judge has a duty to control the case so that media publicity does not interfere with the defendant's right to a fair trial.

12-10e *Richardson v. Marsh:* 481 U.S. 200, 95 L.Ed. 2d 176, 107 S.Ct. 1702 (1987)

Facts: Marsh, Williams, and Martin were charged with assaulting Knighton during a robbery and murdering Knighton's four-year-old son and her aunt. Martin was a fugitive at the time of the trial. Knighton testified at length at trial. Williams's confession was also admitted. It had been redacted to omit all references to Marsh—the edited form gave no indication that anyone other than Martin and Williams participated in the crime. The jury was admonished not to use the confession against Marsh. Williams did not testify. Marsh testified that she had no prior knowledge of Williams's and Martin's plan to commit a robbery or that they were armed; she had gone to the victim's house to obtain a loan; once Martin pulled a gun to rob the victim Marsh claimed she was too afraid to do anything to escape or stop the robbery. During closing arguments, the prosecutor admonished the jury not to use Williams's confession against Marsh but also linked Marsh to activity described in the confession. The judge also instructed the jurors not to use the confession against Marsh. Marsh was convicted on two counts of felony murder and one of assault with intent to commit murder.

Issue: Under what circumstances can the out-of-court confession of a nontestifying co-defendant be used at trial?

Reasoning: *** "Ordinarily, a witness whose testimony is introduced at a joint trial is not considered to be a witness 'against' a defendant if the jury is instructed to consider that testimony only against a co-defendant. *** In *Bruton* [*Bruton v. United States,* 391 U.S. 123 (1968)], however, we recognized a narrow exception to this principle: We held that a defendant is deprived of his Sixth Amendment right of confrontation when the facially incriminating confession of a nontestifying co-defendant is introduced at their joint trial, even if the jury is instructed to consider the confession only against the co-defendant. ***

"There is an important distinction between this case and *Bruton,* which causes it to fall outside the narrow exception we have created. In *Bruton,* the codefendant's confession 'expressly implicat[ed]' the defendant as his accomplice. Thus, at the time that confession was introduced there was not the slightest doubt that it would prove 'powerfully incriminating.' By contrast, in this case the confession was not incriminating on its face, and became so only when linked with evidence introduced later at trial (the defendant's own testimony).

"Where the necessity of such linkage is involved, it is a less valid generalization that the jury will not likely obey the instruction to disregard the evidence. Specific testimony that 'the defendant helped me commit the crime' is more vivid than inferential incrimination, and hence more difficult to thrust out of mind. *** In short, while it may not always be simple for the members of a jury to obey the instruction that they disregard an incriminating inference, there does not exist the overwhelming probability of their inability to do so that is the foundation of *Bruton's* exception to the general rule.

"Even more significantly, evidence requiring linkage differs from evidence incriminating on its face in the practical effect which application of the *Bruton* exception would produce. If limited to facially incriminating confessions, *Bruton* can be complied with by redaction—a possibility suggested in that opinion itself. If extended to confessions incriminating by connection, not only is that not possible, but it is not even possible to predict the admissibility of a confession in advance of trial. ***

*** "It would impair both the efficiency and the fairness of the criminal justice system to require, in all these cases of joint crimes where incriminating statements exist, that prosecutors bring separate proceedings, presenting the same evidence again and again, requiring victims and witnesses to repeat the inconvenience (and sometimes trauma) of testify, and randomly favoring the last-tried defendants who have the advantage of knowing the prosecution's case beforehand. Joint trials generally serve the interests of justice by avoiding inconsistent verdicts and enabling more accurate assessment of relative culpability—advantages which sometimes operate to the defendant's benefit. Even apart from these tactical considerations, joint trials generally serve the interests of justice by avoiding the scandal and inequity of inconsistent verdicts. The other way of assuring compliance with an expansive *Bruton* rule would be to forgo use of codefendant confessions. That price also is too high, since confessions 'are more than merely "desirable"; they are essential to society's compelling interest in finding, convicting, and punishing those who violate the law.'

*** "We hold that the Confrontation Clause is not violated by the admission of a nontestifying codefendant's confession with proper limiting instruction when, as here, the confession is redacted to eliminate not only the defendant's name, but any reference to her existence."

Disposition: The lower court properly admitted the co-defendant's redacted confession; such statements can be used in court if they are edited so that the other defendant's name is not used and there is no reference to his/her participation in the crime.

NOTE: The court stated that the prosecutor's use of the confession in closing arguments to tie Marsh to the crime was impermissible and directed the lower court to determine whether Marsh's failure to object removed the issue from consideration on *habeas corpus.*

12-10f *Illinois v. Vitale:* 447 U.S. 410, 65 L.Ed. 2d 228, 100 S.Ct. 2260 (1980)

Facts: On November 24, 1974, an automobile driven by respondent John Vitale, a juvenile, struck two small children. One of the children died almost immediately; the other died the following day. A police officer at the scene of the accident issued a traffic citation charging Vitale with failing to reduce speed to avoid an accident in violation of § 11-601(a) of the Illinois Vehicle Code. On December 23, 1974, Vitale appeared in the Circuit Court of Cook County and entered a plea of not guilty to the charge of failing to reduce speed. After a trial without a jury, Vitale was convicted and sentenced to pay a fine of $15. On the following day, a petition for adjudication of wardship was filed in the juvenile division of the Circuit Court of Cook County, charging Vitale with two counts of involuntary manslaughter. The petition, which was signed by the police officer who issued the traffic citation, alleged that Vitale "without lawful justification while recklessly driving a motor vehicle caused the death of" the two children killed in the November 24, 1974 accident. The trail judge dismissed the charges based on double jeopardy.

Issue: Can a defendant be convicted of an offense if a guilty plea has already been accepted for a lesser offense?

Reasoning: *** "The Double Jeopardy Clause of the Fifth Amendment provides that no person shall 'be subject for the same offense to be twice put in jeopardy of life or limb.' This constitutional guarantee is applicable to the States through the Due Process Clause of the Fourteenth Amendment, and it applies not only in traditional criminal proceedings but also in the kind of juvenile proceedings Vitale faced.

"The constitutional prohibition of double jeopardy has been held to consist of three separate guarantees; (1) 'it protects against a second prosecution for the same offense after acquittal. [(2)] it protects against a second prosecution for the same offense after conviction. [(3)] And it protects against multiple punishments for the same offense.' . . . The sole question before us is whether the offense of failing to reduce speed to avoid an accident is the 'same offense' for double jeopardy purposes as the manslaughter charges brought against Vitale.

"In *Brown v. Ohio*, 432 U.S. 161 (1977), we stated the principal test for determining whether two offenses are the same for purposes of barring successive prosecutions. Quoting from *Blockburger v. United States*, 284 U.S. 299 (1932), which in turn relied on *Gavieres v. United States*, 220 U.S. 338 (1911), we held that:

> 'The applicable rule is that where the same act or transaction constitutes a violation of two distinct statutory provisions, the test to be applied to determine whether there are two offenses or only one, is whether each provision requires proof of a fact which the other does not.'

We recognized that the *Blockburger* test focuses on the proof necessary to prove the statutory elements of each offense, rather than on the actual evidence to be presented at trial. Thus we stated that if "each statute requires proof of an additional fact which the other does not," the offenses are not the same under the *Blockburger* test.

***. . . "The point is that if manslaughter by automobile does not always entail proof of a failure to slow, then the two offenses are not the 'same' under the *Blockburger* test. The mere possibility that the State will seek to rely on all the ingredients necessarily included in the traffic offense to establish an element of its manslaughter case would not be sufficient to bar the latter prosecution.

"If, as a matter of Illinois law, a careless failure to slow is always a necessary element of manslaughter by automobile, then the two offenses are the 'same' under *Blockburger* and Vitale's trial on the latter charge would constitute double jeopardy under *Brown v. Ohio*. In any event, it may be that to sustain its manslaughter case the State may find it necessary to prove a failure to slow or to rely on conduct necessarily involving such failure; it may concede as much prior to trial. In that case, because Vitale has already been convicted for conduct that is a necessary element of the more serious crime for which he has been charged, his claim of double jeopardy would be substantial under Brown and our later decision in *Harris v. Oklahoma*, 433 U.S. 682 (1977).

"In *Harris*, we held, without dissent, that a defendant's conviction for felony murder based on a killing in the course of an armed robbery barred a subsequent prosecution against the same defendant for the robbery. The Oklahoma felony murder statute on its face did not require proof of a robbery to establish felony murder; other felonies could underlie a felony-murder prosecution. But for the purposes of the Double Jeopardy Clause, we did not consider the crime generally described as felony murder as a separate offense distinct from its various elements. Rather, we treated a killing in the course of a robbery as itself a separate statutory offense, and the robbery as a species of lesser-included offense. The State conceded that the robbery for which petitioner had been indicted was in fact the underlying felony, all elements of which had been proved in the murder prosecution. We held the subsequent robbery prosecution barred under the Double Jeopardy Clause, since under *In re Nielsen,* 131 U.S. 176 (1889), a person who has been convicted of a crime having several elements included in it may not subsequently be tried for a lesser-included offense—an offense consisting solely of one or more of the elements of the crime for which he has already been convicted. Under *Brown,* the reverse is also true; a conviction on a lesser-included offense bars subsequent trial on the greater offense.

"By analogy, if in the pending manslaughter prosecution Illinois relies on and proves a failure to slow to avoid an accident as the reckless act necessary to prove manslaughter, Vitale would have a substantial claim of double jeopardy under the Fifth and Fourteenth Amendments of the United States Constitution."

Disposition: Charges reinstated; double jeopardy is not violated by convictions for both lesser and more serious crimes if all elements of the lesser crime are not included in the definition of the greater offense.

12-10g *Maynard v. Cartwright:* 486 U.S. 356, 100 L.Ed. 2d 372, 108 S.Ct. 1853 (1988)

Facts: On May 4, 1982, Charma Riddle encountered Cartwright in her home. She struggled for the gun he was holding and was shot twice in the legs. Cartwright, a disgruntled ex-employee, then went to the living room and shot and killed Hugh Riddle. Mrs. Riddle dragged herself down the hall to a bedroom and tried to use the telephone. Cartwright entered the bedroom, slit her throat, stabbed her twice with a hunting knife the Riddles had given him for Christmas, and then left the house. Mrs. Riddle survived and called the police. Cartwright was convicted of murder and the jury voted to impose the death penalty based on two statutory aggravating circumstances: knowingly creating a great risk of death to more than one person and murder that was "especially heinous, atrocious, or cruel."

Issue: Is "especially heinous, atrocious, or cruel" capital murder unconstitutionally vague under the Eighth Amendment?

Reasoning: *** "Claims of vagueness directed at aggravating circumstances defined in capital punishment statutes are analyzed under the Eighth Amendment and characteristically assert that the challenged provision fails adequately to inform juries what they must find to impose the death penalty and as a result leaves them and appellate courts with the kind of open-ended discretion which was held invalid in *Furman v. Georgia* 408 U.S. 238 (1972).

"*Furman* held that Georgia's then-standardless capital punishment statute was being applied in an arbitrary and capricious manner; there was no principled means provided to distinguish those that received the penalty from those that did not. Since *Furman*, our cases have insisted that the channeling and limiting of the sentencer's discretion in imposing the death penalty is a fundamental constitutional requirement for sufficiently minimizing the risk of wholly arbitrary and capricious action.

"*Godfrey v. Georgia*, 446 U.S. 420 (1980), which is very relevant here, applied this central tenet of Eighth Amendment law. The aggravating circumstance at issue there permitted a person to be sentenced to death if the offense 'was outrageously or wantonly vile, horrible or inhuman in that it involved torture, depravity of mind, or an aggravated battery to the victim.' The jury had been instructed in the words of the statute, but its verdict recited only that the murder was 'outrageously or wantonly vile, horrible or inhuman.' *** Although the Georgia Supreme Court in other cases had spoken in terms of the presence or absence of these factors, it did not do so in the decision under review, and this Court held that such an application of the aggravating circumstance was unconstitutional, saying:

> 'In the case before us, the Georgia Supreme Court has affirmed a sentence of death based upon no more than a finding that the offense was "outrageously or wantonly vile, horrible and inhuman." There is nothing in these few words, standing alone, that implies any inherent restraint on the arbitrary and capricious infliction of the death sentence. A person of ordinary sensibility could fairly characterize almost every murder as "outrageously or wantonly vile, horrible and inhuman." Such a view may, in fact, have been one to which the members of the jury in this case subscribed. If so, their preconceptions were not dispelled by the trial judge's sentencing instructions. These gave the jury no guidance concerning the meaning of any of [the aggravating circumstance's] terms. In fact, the jury's interpretation of [that circumstance] can only be the subject of sheer speculation.'

"The affirmance of the death sentence by the Georgia Supreme Court was held to be insufficient to cure the jury's unchanneled discretion because that court failed to apply its previously recognized limiting construction of the aggravating circumstances. This Court concluded that, as a result of the vague construction applied, there was 'no principled way to distinguish this case, in which the death penalty was imposed, from the many cases in which it was not.' It plainly rejected the submission that a particular set of facts surrounding a murder, however shocking they might be, were enough themselves, and without some narrowing principle to apply to those facts, to warrant the imposition of the death penalty.

"We think the Court of Appeals was quite right in holding that *Godfrey* controls this case. First, the language of the Oklahoma aggravating circumstance at issue—'especially heinous, atrocious, or cruel'—gave no more guidance than the 'outrageously or wantonly vile, horrible or inhuman' language that the jury returned in its verdict in *Godfrey*. The State's contention that the addition of the word 'especially' somehow guides the jury's discretion, even if the term 'heinous,' does not, is untenable. To say that something is 'especially heinous' merely suggests that the individual jurors should determine that the murder is more than just 'heinous,' whatever that means and an ordinary person could honestly believe that every unjustified, intentional taking of human life is 'especially heinous.' Likewise, in *Godfrey* the addition of 'outrageously or wantonly' to the term 'vile' did not limit the overbreadth of the aggravating factor.

"Second, the conclusion of the Oklahoma court that the events recited by it 'adequately supported the jury's finding' was indistinguishable from the action of the Georgia court in *Godfrey*, which failed to cure the unfettered discretion of the jury and to satisfy the commands of the Eighth Amendment. The Oklahoma court relied on the facts that Cartwright had a motive of getting even with the victims, that he lay in wait for them, that the murder victim heard the blast that wounded his wife, that he again brutally attacked the surviving wife, that he attempted to conceal his deeds, and that he attempted to steal the victims' belongings. Its conclusion that on these facts the jury's verdict that the murder was especially heinous, atrocious, or cruel was supportable did not cure the constitutional infirmity of the aggravating circumstances."

Disposition: Death penalty reversed; a statute that permits "especially heinous, atrocious, or cruel" to be used as an aggravating circumstance, without further defining how these terms are to be applied, is unconstitutional.

12-11 Other Supreme Court Cases

12-11a *Dillingham v. United States:* 423 U.S. 64, 46 L.Ed. 2d 205, 96 S.Ct. 303 (1975)

Facts: Dillingham was arrested and held in custody for 22 months before being indicted on federal auto theft charges. There was an additional 12-month delay between indictment and trial. Dillingham's motion to dismiss for denial of a speedy trial was denied.

Issue: Does preindictment delay violate the right to a speedy trial if the accused is kept in custody during the delay?

Reasoning: *** "The Court [in *United States v. Marion*, 404 U.S. 307 (1971)] held: 'On its face, the protection of the [Sixth] Amendment is activated only when a criminal prosecution has begun and extends only to those persons who have been "accused" in the course of that prosecution. These provisions would seem to afford no protection to those not yet accused, nor would they seem to require the Government to discover, investigate, and accuse any person within any particular period of time.' In contrast, the Government constituted petitioner an 'accused' when it arrested him and thereby commenced its prosecution of him."

Disposition: Motion to dismiss denied in error; a person can challenge preindictment delay as a violation of the Sixth Amendment right to a speedy trial only if he/she is held in custody during the delay.

12-11b *Doggett v. United States:* 505 U.S. 647, 120 L.Ed. 2d 520, 112 S.Ct. 2686 (1992)

Facts: On February 22, 1980, Doggett was indicted for conspiracy to distribute cocaine. Police made an attempt to arrest him on March 18, 1980 at his parents' home in Raleigh, North Carolina. His mother told the officers that he was in Colombia. His name was inserted in NCIC and the Treasury Enforcement Communication System (TECS) network to help customs agents apprehend him if he entered the country. The TECS entry expired six months later and his name vanished from the system. In July 1981, when it was learned that Doggett was under arrest on drug charges in Panama, a request was made that he be expelled, but he was instead released. He returned to the United States through a customs check at New York City on September 25, 1982, but was not detained. Since that time, he settled in Virginia and lived openly under his own name and stayed within the law. DEA learned that Doggett was in Colombia in 1985 and assumed he would settle there. Doggett was located when, in 1988, the marshal's service ran a credit check on several thousand people subject to outstanding arrest warrants. He was arrested on September 5, 1988. He moved to dismiss the indictment for failure of a speedy trial.

Issue: Can the passage of time, without showing of prejudice, be grounds for dismissing an indictment for failure to provide a speedy trial?

Reasoning: *** "Although negligence is obviously to be weighed more lightly than a deliberate intent to harm the accused's defense, it still falls on the wrong side of the divide between acceptable and unacceptable reasons for delaying a criminal prosecution once it has begun. And such is the nature of the prejudice presumed that the weight we assign to official negligence compounds over time as the presumption of evidentiary prejudice grows. Thus, our toleration of such negligence varies inversely with its protractedness, and its consequent threat to the fairness of the accused's trial. Condoning prolonged and unjustifiable delays in the prosecution would both penalize many defendants for the state's fault and simply encourage the government to gamble with the interests of criminal suspects assigned a low prosecutorial priority. The Government, indeed, can hardly complain too loudly, for persistent neglect to conclude a criminal prosecution indicates an uncommonly feeble interest in bringing an accused to justice; the more weight the Government attaches to securing a conviction, the harder it will try to get it.

"To be sure, to warrant granting relief, negligence unaccompanied by particularized trial prejudice must have lasted longer than negligence demonstrably causing such prejudice. But even so, the Government's egregious persistence in failing to prosecute Doggett is clearly sufficient. The lag between Doggett's indictment and arrest was 8-1/2 years, and he would have faced trial 6 years earlier than he did except for the Government's inexcusable oversight. The portion of the delay attributable to the Government's negligence far exceeds the threshold needed to state a speedy trial claim; indeed, we have called shorter delays 'extraordinary.' When the Government's negligence thus causes delay six times as long as that generally sufficient to trigger judicial review, and when the presumption of prejudice, albeit unspecified, is neither extenuated, as by the defendant's acquiescence, nor persuasively rebutted, the defendant is entitled to relief."

Disposition: Indictment dismissed; negligence in failing to apprehend the defendant for an extended period of time after indictment violates the right to speedy trial.

12-11c *United States v. Loud Hawk:* 474 U.S. 302, 88 L.Ed. 2d 640, 106 S.Ct. 648 (1986)

Facts: On November 14, 1975, Oregon state troopers, acting on a tip from the FBI, stopped two vehicles to search for federal fugitives. Subsequent searches of the vehicles disclosed 350 pounds of dynamite, six partially assembled time bombs, 2,600 rounds of ammunition, 150 blasting caps, nine empty hand grenades, and miscellaneous firearms. State troopers destroyed the dynamite without realizing it had evidentiary value. Loud Hawk, KaMook Banks, Dennis Banks, and Render were indicted in December 1975 for transportation of an unregistered destructive device and unlawful possession of firearms. A defense motion to dismiss the charges related to destructive devices was granted on March 31, 1976 because the dynamite had been destroyed. Six months after the original indictment, the remaining charges were dismissed with prejudice when the government responded "Not ready" when the case was called for trial. The government appealed and obtained a favorable ruling on March 12, 1980. The case was returned to District Court where the defendants were re-indicted. All filed motions for dismissal on grounds of vindicative prosecution. On August 8, 1980, KaMook Banks's charges were dismissed and the remaining defendants, who were free on their own recognizance, appealed. This appeal, which the government won, was decided on July 29, 1982 and *certiorari* was denied on January 10, 1983. The case was returned to the trial court and on May 20, 1983, it was dismissed on grounds of violation of the right to speedy trial.

Issue: Is the right to a speedy trial violated by pretrial appeals?

Reasoning: *** "Under *Barker* [*Barker v. Wingo*, 407 U.S. 514 (1972)], delays in bringing the case to trial caused by the Government's interlocutory appeal may be weighed in determining whether a defendant has suffered a violation of his right to a speedy trial. It is clear in this case, however, that respondents have failed to show a reason for according these delays any effective weight towards their speedy trial claims. There is no showing of bad faith or dilatory purpose on the Government's part. The Government's position in each of the appeals was strong, and the reversals by the Court of Appeals are *prima facie* evidence of the reasonableness of the Government's action. Moreover, despite the seriousness of the charged offenses, the District Court chose not to subject the respondents to any actual restraints pending the outcome of the appeals.

"The only remaining question is the weight to be attributed to delays caused by respondents' interlocutory appeals. In that limited class of cases where a pretrial appeal by the defendant is appropriate, delays from such an appeal ordinarily will not weigh in favor of a defendant's speedy trial claims."

Disposition: Dismissal reversed; time spent on good-faith, interlocutory appeals does not violate the right to a speedy trial.

12-11d *Arizona v. Youngblood:* 488 U.S. 51, 102 L.Ed. 2d 281, 109 S.Ct. 333 (1988)

Facts: On October 29, 1983, 10-year-old David L. attended a church service with his mother. About 9:30 P.M., he left the service and went to a carnival behind the church, where he was abducted by a middle-aged man. He was driven to a secluded area near a ravine and molested. The abductor then took him to a sparsely furnished house where he sodomized the boy five times. He returned the boy to the carnival after threatening to kill him if he told anyone about the attack. When the boy returned home, his mother took him to the hospital where he was treated for rectal injuries. A sexual assault kit, provided by the Tucson Police Department, was used to collect evidence. The physician used a Q-tip-like swab to collect samples from the boy's rectum and mouth. Clothing taken from the victim was kept as evidence but not refrigerated. A police criminologist examined the evidence obtained with the sexual assault kit and verified that a sexual assault had occurred. Blood grouping tests conducted later on the swabs and clothing failed to produce usable evidence. The victim picked Youngblood out of a lineup. At trial, the defense claimed mistaken identification and asserted that if the evidence had been properly handled, laboratory tests would have shown that Youngblood was not the perpetrator. He was convicted as charged.

Issue: Do the police have a constitutional duty to obtain evidence for examination by defense experts?

Reasoning: *** "The Due Process Clause of the Fourteenth Amendment, as interpreted in *Brady* [*Brady v. Maryland,* 373 U.S. 83 (1963)], makes the good or bad faith of the State irrelevant when the State fails to disclose to the defendant material exculpatory evidence. But we think the Due Process Clause requires a different result when we deal with the failure of the State to preserve evidentiary material of which no more can be said than that it could have been subjected to tests, the results of which might have exonerated the defendant. Part of the reasoning for the difference in treatment is found in the observation made by the Court in *Trombetta* [*California v. Trombetta,* 467 U.S. 479 (1984)], that '[w]henever potentially exculpatory evidence is permanently lost, courts face the treacherous task of divining the import of materials whose contents are unknown and, very often, disputed.' Part of it stems from our unwillingness to read the 'fundamental fairness' requirement of the Due Process Clause as imposing on the police an undifferentiated and absolute duty to retain and to preserve all material that might be of conceivable evidentiary significance in a particular prosecution. We think that requiring a defendant to show bad faith on the part of the police both limits the extent of the police's obligation to preserve evidence to reasonable bounds and confines it to that class of cases where the interests of justice most clearly require it, those cases in which the police themselves by their conduct indicate that the evidence could form a basis for exonerating the defendant. We therefore hold that unless a criminal defendant can show bad faith on the part of the police, failure to preserve potentially useful evidence does not constitute a denial of due process of law."

Disposition: Conviction affirmed; due process is violated by failure to preserve evidence for testing only if the police did so in bad faith.

12-11e *Taylor v. Illinois:* 484 U.S. 400, 98 L.Ed. 2d 798, 108 S.Ct. 646 (1988)

Facts: Bridges and Travis were in a 20-minute argument. About an hour later, several friends of Travis, including Taylor, had a violent encounter with Bridges. Bridges's brother came to his aid near the end of the attack. At least three members of Taylor's group carried pipes and clubs, which they used to beat Bridges. Twenty to thirty bystanders witnessed the dispute: Some said Taylor had a gun and shot Bridges in the back as he attempted to flee; others claimed it was Bridges's brother who had the gun. Well in advance of trial, the prosecutor filed a discovery motion requesting a list of defense witnesses. The defense submitted a list with names of two people who eventually did testify and two who were not called. On the first day of the trial, the list was amended to include two other people, neither of whom was actually called. On the second day of trial, after the two principal prosecution witnesses had testified, the defense made an oral motion to amend the witness list again. The defense claimed that it had just learned of two more potential witnesses who had probably seen the "entire incident." A hearing was held outside the presence of the jury and one of the new witnesses testified. During cross-examination, the prosecution showed that the new witness was not an eyewitness to the shooting and had first met the defendant over a year after the incident. The trial judge concluded that the appropriate sanction for violation of proper discovery procedures was to exclude the testimony of the witness. Taylor was convicted of attempted murder.

Issue: Does the exclusion of a witness as punishment for violating discovery procedures violate the Compulsory Process Clause of the Sixth Amendment?

Reasoning: *** "The defendant's right to compulsory process is itself designed to vindicate the principle that the 'ends of criminal justice would be defeated if judgments were to be founded on a partial or speculative presentation of the facts.' Rules that provide for pretrial discovery of an opponent's witnesses serve the same high purpose. Discovery, like cross-examination, minimizes the risk that a judgment will be predicated on incomplete, misleading, or even deliberately fabricated testimony. The 'State's interest in protecting itself against an eleventh hour defense' is merely one component of the broader public interest in a full and truthful disclosure of critical facts.

*** "A trial judge may certainly insist on an explanation for a party's failure to comply with a request to identify his or her witnesses in advance of trial. If that explanation reveals that the omission was willful and motivated by a desire to obtain a tactical advantage that would minimize the effectiveness of cross-examination and the ability to adduce rebuttal evidence, it would be entirely consistent with the purposes of the Confrontation Clause simply to exclude the witness' testimony."

Disposition: Conviction affirmed; the witness who was left off the witness list during discovery can be precluded from testifying at trial if the judge finds that the omission was done intentionally for the purpose of preventing effective cross-examination.

12-11f *Williams v. Florida:* 399 U.S. 78, 26 L.Ed. 2d 446, 90 S.Ct. 1893 (1970)

Facts: Williams filed a "Motion for a Protective Order" seeking to be relieved from compliance with a state rule requiring defendants, on written demand by the prosecutor, to give notice in advance of trial if an alibi defense will be used. Under this rule, the defense must furnish the prosecution with information on the place where the defendant claims to have been and the names and addresses of alibi witnesses that may be called to testify at trial. The prosecution is required to give the defense the names of any witnesses it intends to call to disprove the alibi. Williams declared his intent to claim an alibi but sought exemption from supplying further information due to Fifth and Fourteenth Amendment protection from self-incrimination. The motion was denied. Williams informed the prosecution the alibi would be that he and his wife were at the apartment of Mr. and Mrs. Scotty during the time the robbery was committed. He provided Mrs. Scotty's address. The prosecution took Mrs. Scotty's deposition prior to the trial and used it at trial to impeach her. Mrs. Scotty insisted the trial testimony was correct and the earlier statement regarding dates and times was inaccurate. Williams was convicted.

Issue: Does a state law that requires pretrial disclosure of particulars of an alibi defense violate the privilege against self-incrimination?

Reasoning: *** "We need not linger over the suggestion that the discovery permitted the State against petitioner in this case deprived him of 'due process' or a 'fair trial.' Florida law provides for liberal discovery by the defendant against the State, and the notice-of-alibi rule is itself carefully hedged with reciprocal duties requiring state disclosure to the defendant. Given the ease with which an alibi can be fabricated, the State's interest in protecting itself against an eleventh-hour defense is both obvious and legitimate. ***

*** "We conclude, however, as has apparently every other court that has considered the issue, that the privilege against self-incrimination is not violated by a requirement that the defendant give notice of an alibi defense and disclose his alibi witnesses.

"Nothing in such a rule requires the defendant to rely on an alibi or prevents him from abandoning the defense; these matters are left to his unfettered choice."

Disposition: Conviction affirmed; requiring a defendant to disclose information on an alibi defense prior to trial does not violate the Fifth, Sixth, or Fourteenth Amendment.

12-11g *Singer v. United States:* 380 U.S. 24, 13 L.Ed. 2d 630, 85 S.Ct. 783 (1965)

Facts: Singer was charged in federal court with 30 infractions of the mail fraud statute due to his efforts to dupe amateur songwriters into sending him money for marketing their songs. He demanded a trial without a jury. The trial court was willing to approve the request but the prosecutor was not. A jury convicted Singer on 29 of the 30 counts.

Issue: Does a criminal defendant have the right to demand trial without a jury?

Reasoning: *** "We can find no evidence that the common law recognized that defendants had the right to choose between court and jury trial. Although instances of waiver of jury trial can be found in certain of the colonies prior to the adoption of the Constitution, they were isolated instances occurring pursuant to colonial 'constitutions' and statutes and were clear departures from the common law. There is no indication that the colonist considered the ability to waive a jury trial to be of equal importance to the right to demand one. ***

*** "A defendant's only constitutional right concerning the method of trial is to an impartial trial by jury. We find no constitutional impediment to condition a waiver of this right on the consent of the prosecuting attorney and the trial judge when, if either refuses to consent, the result is simply that the defendant is subject to an impartial trial by jury—the very thing that the Constitution guarantees him. The Constitution recognizes an adversary system as the proper method of determining guilt, and the Government, as a litigant, has a legitimate interest in seeing that cases in which it believes a conviction is warranted are tried before the tribunal which the Constitution regards as most likely to produce a fair result."

Disposition: Conviction affirmed; the defendant does not have the right to waive a jury trial if the prosecution demands one.

12-11h *Blanton v. City of North Las Vegas, Nevada:* 489 U.S. 538, 103 L.Ed. 2d 550, 109 S.Ct. 1289 (1989)

Facts: Blanton was charged with driving under the influence of alcohol (DUI) under a Nevada law that makes the offense punishable by a maximum of six months' imprisonment or 48 hours of community service work dressed in distinctive garb that identifies him as a DUI offender; fines ranging from $200 to $1,000; automatic loss of driver's license for 90 days; and mandatory attendance at an alcohol abuse education course. Blanton's request for trial by jury was denied.

Issue: When does a criminal defendant have the right to a trial by jury?

Reasoning: *** "It has long been settled 'that there is a category of petty crimes or offenses which is not subject to the Sixth Amendment jury trial provision.' In determining whether a particular offense should be categorized as 'petty,' our early decisions focused on the nature of the offense and on whether it was triable by a jury at common law. In recent years, however, we have sought more 'objective indications of the seriousness with which society regards the offense.' '[W]e have found the most relevant such criteria is the severity of the maximum authorized penalty.' ***

"In using the word 'penalty,' we do not refer solely to the maximum prison term authorized for a particular offense. A legislature's view of the seriousness of an offense also is reflected in the other penalties that it attaches to the offense. We thus examine 'whether the length of the authorized prison term or the *seriousness of other punishment* is enough in itself to require a jury trial.' Primary emphasis, however, must be placed on the maximum authorized period of incarceration. Penalties such as probation or a fine may engender 'a significant infringement of personal freedom,' but they cannot approximate in severity the loss of liberty that a prison term entails. ***

"Following this approach, our decision in *Baldwin* [*Baldwin v. New York*, 399 U.S. 66 (1970)] established that a defendant is entitled to a jury trial whenever the offense for which he is charged carries a maximum authorized prison term of greater than six months. ***

"Although we did not hold in *Baldwin* that an offense carrying a maximum prison term of six months or less automatically qualifies as a 'petty' offense, and decline to do so today, we do find it appropriate to presume for purposes of the Sixth Amendment that society views such an offense as 'petty.' A defendant is entitled to jury trial in such circumstances only if he can demonstrate that any additional statutory penalties, viewed in conjunction with the maximum authorized period of incarceration, are so severe that they clearly reflect a legislative determination that the offense in question is a 'serious' one. ***

"Applying these principles here, it is apparent that petitioners are not entitled to a jury trial. The maximum authorized prison sentence for first-time DUI offenders does not exceed six months. A presumption therefore exists that the Nevada legislature views DUI as a 'petty' offense for purposes of the Sixth Amendment. Considering the additional statutory penalties as well, we do not believe that the Nevada Legislature has clearly indicated that DUI is a 'serious' offense."

Disposition: Conviction affirmed; the right to a jury trial attaches only to cases with maximum sentences of more than six months; in special cases, factors other than the length of sentence may indicate that the offense is considered serious.

12-11i *Ballew v. Georgia:* 435 U.S. 223, 55 L.Ed. 2d 234, 98 S.Ct. 1029 (1978)

Facts: In November 1973, Ballew was the cashier at the Paris Adult Theatre in Atlanta. He was charged with two misdemeanors for distributing obscene material and was convicted by a five-person jury.

Issue: Does a jury with only five members satisfy the constitutional guarantee of trial by jury?

Reasoning: *** "In *Williams v. Florida*, 339 U.S. 78 (1970), the Court reaffirmed that the 'purpose of the jury trial, *** is to prevent oppression by the Government. "Providing an accused with the right to be tried by a jury of his peers gave him an inestimable safeguard against the corrupt or overzealous prosecutor and against the compliant, biased, or eccentric judge." This purpose is attained by the participation of the community in determinations of guilt and by the application of the common sense of laymen who, as jurors, consider the case.'

"*Williams* held that these functions and this purpose could be fulfilled by a jury of six members. As the Court's opinion in that case explained at some length, common law juries included 12 members by historical accident, 'unrelated to the great purposes which gave rise to the jury in the first place.' *** Rather than requiring 12 members, then, the Sixth Amendment mandated a jury only of sufficient size to promote group deliberation, to insulate members from outside intimidation, and to provide a representative cross-section of the community. ***

*** "While we adhere to, and reaffirm our holding in *Williams v. Florida*, these studies, most of which have been made since *Williams*, was decided in 1970, lead us to conclude that the purpose and functioning of the jury in a criminal trial is seriously impaired, and to a constitutional degree, by a reduction in size to below six members. We readily admit that we do not pretend to discern a clear line between six members and five. But the assembled data raise substantial doubt about the reliability and appropriate representation of panels smaller than six. Because of the fundamental importance of the jury trial to the American system of criminal justice, any further reduction that promotes inaccurate and possibly biased decision making, that causes untoward differences in verdicts, and that prevents juries from truly representing their communities, attains constitutional significance.

*** "[G]eorgia argues that its use of five-member juries does not violate the Sixth and Fourteenth Amendments because they are used only in misdemeanor cases. *** We cannot conclude that there is less need for the imposition and the direction of the common sense of the community in this case than when the State has chosen to label an offense a felony."

Disposition: Conviction reversed; a jury of less than six members does not satisfy the constitutional right to trial by jury.

12-11j *Duren v. Missouri:* 439 U.S. 357, 58 L.Ed. 2d 579, 99 S.Ct. 664 (1979)

Facts: Duren was indicted for first-degree murder and first-degree robbery. He made a pretrial motion to quash the jury panel for failure to have a cross section of the community because Missouri law granted women an automatic exemption from jury service if they requested it. At a hearing on the motion, it was shown that the jury-selection process in Jackson County began with the annual mailing of questionnaires to persons randomly selected from voter registration lists. The questionnaires contained lists of occupations and other categories that either disqualified a person from jury duty or qualified a person for exemption from service. One paragraph stated: "TO WOMEN" "Any woman who elects not to serve will fill out this paragraph and mail this questionnaire to the jury commissioner at once." A similar paragraph was addressed "TO MEN OVER 65 YEARS OF AGE." Those not exempt at this phase were mailed summonses if their names were drawn for jury duty. Similar instructions were printed on the summonses. In practice, a woman who did not return the summons or failed to appear for jury duty when so directed was treated as if she had claimed the exemption. The 1970 census showed 54 percent of adult inhabitants of Jackson County were women. A review of eight months in 1975 and 1976 showed that only 26.7 percent of the persons summoned for jury duty were women and only 14.5 percent who actually appeared for jury duty were women.

Issue: Can women be excluded from jury duty using different procedures than are used for men?

Reasoning: *** "In order to establish a *prima facie* violation of the fair-cross-section requirement, the defendant must show (1) that the group alleged to be excluded is a 'distinctive' group in the community; (2) that the representation of this group in venires from which juries are selected is not fair and reasonable in relation to the number of such persons in the community; and (3) that this under-representation is due to systematic exclusion of the group in the jury-selection process.

"With respect to the first part of the *prima facie* test, *Taylor* [*v. Louisiana*, 419 U.S. 522 (1975)] without doubt established that women 'are sufficiently numerous and distinct from men' such that 'if they are systematically eliminated from the jury panels, the Sixth Amendment's fair-cross-section requirement cannot be satisfied.'

"The second prong of the *prima facie* case was established by petitioner's statistical presentation. Initially, the defendant must demonstrate the percentage of the community made up of the group alleged to be under-represented, for this is the conceptual benchmark of the Sixth Amendment fair-cross-section requirement. * * *

* * * "The demonstration of a *prima facie* fair-cross-section violation by the defendant is not the end of the inquiry into whether a constitutional violation has occurred. * * * Rather, it requires that a significant state interest be manifestly and primarily advanced by those aspects of the jury-selection process, such as exemption criteria, that result in the disproportionate exclusion of a distinctive group.

* * * "However, once the defendant has made a *prima facie* showing of an infringement of his constitutional right to a jury drawn from a fair cross section of the community, it is the State that bears the burden of justifying this infringement by showing attainment of a fair cross section to be incompatible with a significant state interest. * * * The record contains no such proof, and mere suggestion or assertion of that effect are insufficient.

* * * "[C]ounsel for respondent ventured that the only state interest advanced by the exemption is safeguarding the important role played by women in home and family life. But exempting all women because of the preclusive domestic responsibility of some women is insufficient justification for their disproportionate exclusion on jury venires. * * *

* * * "We recognize that a State may have an important interest in assuring that those members of the family responsible for the care of children are available to do so. All exemptions appropriately tailored to this interest would, we think, survive a fair-cross-section challenge. We stress, however, that the constitutional guarantee to a jury drawn from a fair cross section of the community requires that States exercise proper caution in exempting broad categories of persons from jury service. Although most occupational and other reasonable exemptions may inevitably involve some degree of over- or under-inclusiveness, any category expressly limited to a group in the community of sufficient magnitude and distinctiveness so as to be within the cross-section requirements—such as women—runs the danger of resulting in under-representation sufficient to constitute a *prima facie* violation of that constitutional requirement. We also repeat the observation made in *Taylor* that it is unlikely that reasonable exemptions, such as those based on special hardship, incapacity, or community needs, 'would pose substantial threats that the remaining pool of jurors would not be representative of the community.'"

Disposition: Conviction reversed; a system that provides women as automatic exemption to jury service violates the fair-cross-section requirement of the Sixth Amendment.

12-11k *Ristanino v. Ross:* 424 U.S. 589, 47 L.Ed. 2d 258, 96 S.Ct. 1017 (1976)

Facts: Ross was tried in a Massachusetts court with two other Negroes for armed robbery, assault and battery by means of a deadly weapon, and assault and battery with intent to commit murder. The victim was a white man employed by Boston University as a uniformed security guard. Motions to have prospective jurors questioned during *voir dire* regarding racial prejudice were denied. All defendants were convicted.

Issue: When does a defendant have the right to ask questions of prospective jurors during *voir dire* regarding their racial prejudices?

Reasoning: *** "In *Ham* [*Ham v. South Carolina,* 409 U.S. 524 (1973)], however, we recognized that some cases may present circumstances in which an impermissible threat to the fair trial guaranteed by due process is posed by a trial court's refusal to question prospective jurors specifically about racial prejudice during *voir dire.* ***

"By its terms *Ham* did not announce a requirement of universal applicability. Rather, it reflected an assessment of whether under all of the circumstances presented there was a constitutionally significant likelihood that, absent questioning about racial prejudice, the jurors would not be as 'indifferent as [they stand] unsworne.'

*** "The mere fact that the victim of the crimes alleged was a white man and the defendants were Negroes was less likely to distort the trial than were the special factors involved in *Ham.* *** The circumstances thus did not suggest a significant likelihood that racial prejudice might infect Ross' trial."

Disposition: Conviction affirmed; prospective jurors can be questioned regarding their racial prejudices in noncapital cases only if the facts of the case are likely to inflame pre-existing racial prejudices.

12-11l *Turner v. Murray:* 476 U.S. 28, 90 L.Ed. 2d 27, 106 S.Ct. 1683 (1986)

Facts: Turner entered a jewelry store in Franklin, Virginia armed with a sawed-off shotgun. He ordered Smith, the proprietor, to put jewelry and money from the cash register into some jewelry bags. Smith complied but triggered a silent alarm. Turner surprised the officer responding to the alarm and disarmed him. When Turner heard another police siren, he shot Smith in the head; he later fired two more shots into Smith's chest for "snitching." Defense counsel asked the judge to use the following question during *voir dire* of the jury: "The defendant, Willie Lloyd Turner, is a member of the Negro race. The victim, W. Jack Smith, Jr., was a white Caucasian. Will these facts prejudice you against Willie Lloyd Turner or affect your ability to render a fair and impartial verdict based solely on the evidence?" The judge denied the request. Turner was convicted and sentenced to death.

Issue: In a capital case, does the defendant charged with an interracial crime have the right to have jurors questioned regarding potential racial prejudice?

Reasoning: *** "We hold that a capital defendant accused of an interracial crime is entitled to have prospective jurors informed of the race of the victim and questioned on the issue of racial bias. The rule we propose is minimally intrusive; as in other cases involving 'special circumstances,' the trial judge retains discretion as to the form and number of questions on the subject, including the decision whether to question the venire individually or collectively. Also, a defendant cannot complain of a judge's failure to question the venire on racial prejudice unless the defendant has specifically requested such an inquiry."

Disposition: Conviction reversed; in capital cases, the defendant has the right, if an appropriate request is made, to have jurors informed of the race of the victim and to question jurors regarding racial prejudice.

12-11m *Wainwright v. Witt:* 469 U.S. 412, 83 L.Ed. 2d 841, 105 S.Ct. 844 (1985)

Facts: Witt, who was 30 years old, and a younger accomplice were hunting with bows and arrows in a wooded area near a trail often used by children. When an 11-year-old boy rode by on his bicycle, the accomplice hit him on the head with a star bit from a drill. Witt and the accomplice then gagged the victim, placed him in the trunk of Witt's car, and drove to a deserted grove. When they opened the trunk, they discovered the boy had died from suffocation due to the gag. They performed various sexual and violent acts on the body and then buried it. Witt was convicted of first-degree murder in Florida and sentenced to death.

Issue: In a death penalty case, can jurors be excluded due to their opposition to capital penalty?

Reasoning: *** "*Witherspoon* [*Witherspoon v. Illinois,* 391 U.S. 510 (1968)] is best understood in the context of its facts. The case involved the capital sentencing procedures for the State of Illinois. *** Pursuant to this statute, nearly half of the veniremen at Witherspoon's trial were excused for cause because they 'expressed qualms about capital punishment.' This Court held that under this procedure the jury obtained would not be the impartial jury required by the Sixth Amendment, but rather a jury 'uncommonly willing to condemn a man to die.' It concluded 'that a sentence of death cannot be carried out if the jury that imposed or recommended it was chosen by excluding veniremen for cause simply because they voiced general objections to the death penalty or expressed conscientious or religious scruples against its infliction.'

*** "We therefore take this opportunity to clarify our decision in *Witherspoon,* and to reaffirm the above-quoted standard from *Adams* [*Adams v. Texas* 448 U.S. 38 (1980)] as the proper standard for determining when a prospective juror may be excluded for cause because of his or her views on capital punishment. That standard is whether the juror's views would 'prevent or substantially impair the performance of his duties as a juror in accordance with his instructions and his oath.' We note that, in addition to dispensing with *Witherspoon's* reference to 'automatic' decision making, this standard likewise does not require a juror's bias be proved with 'unmistakable clarity.' This is because determinations of juror bias cannot be reduced to question-and-answer sessions which obtain results in the manner of a catechism. What common sense should have realized experience has proved: Many veniremen simply cannot be asked enough questions to reach the point where their bias has been made 'unmistakably clear'; these veniremen may not know how they will react when faced with imposing the death sentence, or may be unable to articulate, or may wish to hide their true feelings. Despite this lack of clarity in the printed record, however, there will be situations where the trial judge is left with the definite impression that a prospective juror would be unable to faithfully and impartially apply the law."

Disposition: Conviction affirmed; a prospective juror can be excluded for cause in a capital case if his/her views would 'prevent or substantially impair the performance of his duties as a juror in accordance with his instructions and his oath.'

12-11n *Illinois v. Allen:* 397 U.S. 337, 25 L.Ed. 2d 353, 90 S.Ct. 1057 (1970)

Facts: Allen entered a tavern and, after ordering a drink, took $200 from the bartender at gunpoint. He refused appointed counsel and requested to represent himself. The judge granted the motion on grounds that Allen accept a court-appointed attorney to "sit in and protect the record for you." During jury selection, Allen began arguing with the judge in a most abusive and disrespectful manner. In desperation, the judge asked appointed counsel to continue examining the jurors. Allen continued to argue and terminated his remarks by saying, "When I go out for lunchtime, you're [the judge] going to be a corpse here." Allen then tore the file from the appointed counsel's hands and threw the papers on the floor. The judge admonished him that he would be removed from the courtroom if there was one more outburst. Allen replied, "There's not going to be no trial, either. I'm going to sit here and you're going to talk and you can bring your shackles out and straight jacket and put them on me and tape my mouth, but it will do no good because there's not going to be no trial." After more abusive remarks, the judge ordered the trial to proceed without Allen present. Allen complained about the fairness of the trial and was allowed to return to the courtroom if he behaved himself. Once again he was disruptive and stated that he would prevent the trial by talking throughout the proceedings. He was removed a second time. He was allowed to return while the defense witnesses testified. He was convicted.

Issue: Does the defendant have a constitutional right to be present during trial?

Reasoning: *** "It is essential to the proper administration of criminal justice that dignity, order, and decorum be the hallmarks of all court proceedings in our country. The flagrant disregard in the courtroom of elementary standards of proper conduct should not and cannot be tolerated. We believe trial judges confronted with disruptive, contumacious, stubbornly defiant defendants must be given sufficient discretion to meet the circumstances of each case. No one formula for maintaining the appropriate courtroom atmosphere will be best in all situations. We think there are at least three constitutionally permissible ways for a trial judge to handle an obstreperous defendant like Allen: (1) bind and gag him thereby keeping him present; (2) cite him for contempt; (3) take him out of the courtroom until he promises to conduct himself properly."

Disposition: Conviction affirmed; a disruptive defendant can be removed from the courtroom and his trial allowed to continue without him/her present.

12-11o *Ohio v. Roberts:* 448 U.S. 56, 65 L.Ed. 2d 597, 100 S.Ct. 2531 (1980)

Facts: Roberts was arrested for forgery and possession of stolen credit cards. Mr. Isaacs, the victim, testified at the preliminary hearing. The defense called Anita, the daughter of the victim, to testify that she had allowed Roberts to use her apartment. Defense counsel unsuccessfully tried to get Anita to admit that she gave Roberts the checks and credit cards without telling him that she did not have permission to use them. Five unsuccessful attempts were made to subpoena Anita to testify at trial. At trial, Roberts testified that Anita had given him the checkbook and credit cards with the understanding that he could use them. The prosecution used the transcript of Anita's testimony at the preliminary hearing to rebut Roberts's testimony. Mrs. Isaacs testified that she knew of no way to reach her daughter Anita. Roberts was convicted on all counts.

Issue: Is the Confrontation Clause violated by introduction at trial of the transcript of preliminary hearing testimony of an unavailable witness?

Reasoning: *** "In sum, when a hearsay declarant is not present for cross-examination at trial, the Confrontation Clause normally requires a showing that he is unavailable. Even then, his statement is admissible only if it bears adequate 'indicia of reliability.' Reliability can be inferred without more in a case where the evidence falls within a firmly rooted hearsay exception. In other cases, the evidence must be excluded, at least absent a showing of particularized guarantees of trustworthiness.

*** "[W]e perceive no reason to resolve the reliability issue differently here than the Court did in *Green* [*California v. Green,* 399 U.S. 149 (1970)]. 'Since there was an adequate opportunity to cross-examine [the witness], and counsel *** availed himself of that opportunity, the transcript *** bore sufficient "indicia of reliability" and afforded "the trier of fact a satisfactory basis for evaluating the truth of the prior statement." '

*** "The basic litmus of Sixth Amendment unavailability is established: '[A] witness is not 'unavailable' for purposes of *** the exception to the confrontation requirement unless the prosecutorial authorities have made a *good-faith effort* to obtain his presence at trial.' ***

*** "The law does not require a futile act. Thus, if no possibility of procuring the witness exists (as, for example, the witness' intervening death), 'good faith' demands nothing of the prosecution. But if there is a possibility, albeit remote, that affirmative measures might produce the declarant, the obligation of good faith may demand their effectuation. 'The lengths to which the prosecution must go to produce a witness *** is a question of reasonableness.' The ultimate question is whether the witness is unavailable despite good-faith efforts undertaken prior to trial to locate and present that witness. As with other evidentiary proponents, the prosecution bears the burden of establishing this predicate."

Disposition: Conviction affirmed; a transcript of the preliminary hearing can be used at trial when a witness is unavailable; there has been an opportunity for the defense to question the witness at the preliminary hearing; and a good-faith effort has been made to subpoena the witness for trial.

12-11p *White v. Illinois:* 502 U.S. 346, 116 L.Ed. 2d 848, 112 S.Ct. 736 (1992)

Facts: In the early morning hours of April 16, 1988, S.G.'s baby-sitter was awakened by S.G.'s screams. The baby-sitter ran to the four-year-old's bedroom and saw White leaving the room. She recognized White because he was a friend of S.G.'s mother. The baby-sitter asked S.G. what had happened. S.G. told her White put his hand over her mouth, choked her, threatened to whip her if she screamed, and then "touched her in the wrong places." She explained this by pointing to her vaginal area. S.G.'s mother returned home about 30 minutes later and was told essentially the same thing and that White had "put his mouth on her front part." S.G. had bruises and red marks on her neck that had not been there previously. The police were called. The officer who questioned S.G. was told the same story. Four hours after the attack, S.G. was taken to the hospital and examined by an emergency room nurse and then by a doctor. At trial, the mother, the baby-sitter, a police officer, a nurse and a doctor testified. S.G. was taken into the courtroom twice to be called as a witness but she apparently experienced emotional difficulty each time and left without testifying. S.G. was never declared to be unavailable as a witness. White was convicted.

Issue: Does the use of hearsay violate the Confrontation Clause if it is admitted when the witness is available but does not testify?

Reasoning: *** "*Roberts* [*Ohio v. Roberts,* 448 U.S. 56 (1980)] stands for the proposition that unavailability analysis is a necessary part of the Confrontation Clause inquiry only when the challenged out-of-court statements were made in the course of a prior judicial proceeding.

*** "We note first that the evidentiary rationale for permitting hearsay testimony regarding spontaneous declarations and statements made in the course of receiving medical care is that such out-of-court declarations are made in contexts that provide substantial guarantees of their trustworthiness. *** A statement that has been offered in a moment of excitement—without the opportunity to reflect on the consequences of one's exclamation—may justifiably carry more weight with the trier of fact than a similar statement offered in the relative calm of the courtroom. Similarly, a statement made in the course of procuring medical services, where the declarant knows that a false statement may cause misdiagnosis or mistreatment, carries special guarantees of credibility that a trier of fact may not think replicated by courtroom testimony. * * *

* * * "We therefore think it is clear that the out-of-court statements admitted in this case had substantial probative value, value that could not be duplicated simply by the declarant later testifying in court. To exclude such probative statements under the strictures of the Confrontation Clause would be the height of wrong-headedness, given that the Confrontation Clause has as a basic purpose the promotion of the 'integrity of the factfinding process.' And as we have also noted, a statement that qualifies for admission under a 'firmly rooted' hearsay exception is so trustworthy that adversarial testing can be expected to add little to its reliability. Given the evidentiary value of such statements, their reliability, and that establishing a generally applicable unavailability rule would have few practical benefits while imposing pointless litigation costs, we see no reason to treat the out-of-court statements in this case differently from those we found admissible in *Inadi* [*United States v. Inadi,* 475 U.S. 387 (1986)]. * * *

* * * "*Coy* [*Coy v. Iowa,* 487 U.S. 1012 (1988)] and *Craig* [*Maryland v. Craig,* 497 U.S. 836 (1990)] involved only the question of what *in-court* procedures are constitutionally required to guarantee a defendant's confrontation right once a witness is testifying. Such a question is quite separate from that of what requirements the Confrontation Clause imposes as a predicate for the introduction of out-of-court declarations. * * * There is thus no basis for importing the 'necessity requirement' announced in those cases into the much different context of out-of-court declarations admitted under established exceptions to the hearsay rule."

Disposition: Conviction affirmed; statements of the victim that are covered by spontaneous declaration and medical treatment exceptions to the Hearsay Rule may be admitted without showing unavailability of witness.

12-11q *Olden v. Kentucky:* 488 U.S. 227, 102 L.Ed. 2d 513, 109 S.Ct. 480 (1988)

Facts: Olden and Harris, both of whom are black, were indicted for kidnapping, rape, and forcible sodomy. Starla Matthews, a young white woman, alleged that she and a female friend stopped in J.R.'s, a "boot-legging joint" serving a predominantly black clientele, to use the rest room. Both drank beer; the two became separated. Olden later approached Matthews and told her that her friend had left and was involved in a traffic accident. She left the bar with Olden and Harris to find out what happened to her friend. They drove her to another location, threatened her with a knife, and then raped and sodomized her. They then took her to a dump where other men joined the group and she was again raped. At her request, she was dropped off in the vicinity of the house of Russell, Olden's half-brother. Cross-examination focused on inconsistencies with former statements. Olden and Harris used the defense of consent. Olden wanted to introduce the following facts at trial: Matthews and Russell, both of whom were married at the time, had been having an extramarital affair; by the time of the trial they were living together. Olden alleged that Matthews concocted the rape story to protect her relationship with Russell. Olden and Harris were convicted.

Issue: Can the state prohibit introduction of information regarding the prior sexual conduct of the victim in a rape trial?

Reasoning: *** "In the instant case, petitioner has consistently asserted that he and Matthews engaged in consensual sexual acts and that Matthews—out of fear of jeopardizing her relationship with Russell—lied when she told Russell she had been raped and has continued to lie since. It is plain to us that '[a] reasonable jury might have received a significantly different impression of [the witness'] credibility had [defense counsel] been permitted to pursue his proposed line of cross-examination.'

*** "While a trial court may, of course, impose reasonable limits on defense counsel's inquiry into the potential bias of a prosecution witness, to take account of such factors as 'harassment, prejudice, confusion of the issues, the witness' safety, or interrogation that [would be] repetitive or only marginally relevant,' the limitation here was beyond reason. Speculation as to the effect of jurors' racial biases cannot justify exclusion of cross-examination with such strong potential to demonstrate the falsity of Matthews' testimony.

"In *Delaware v. Van Arsdall* [475 U.S. 673 (1986)] we held that 'the constitutionally improper denial of a defendant's opportunity to impeach a witness for bias, like other Confrontation Clause errors, is subject to *Chapman* [*Chapman v. California,* 386 U.S.18 (1967)] harmless-error analysis.'"

Disposition: Conviction reversed; the defendant has the right to introduce highly relevant information on the victim's sexual history.

12-11r *United States v. Owens:* 484 U.S. 554, 98 L.Ed. 2d 951, 108 S.Ct. 838 (1988)

Facts: On April 12, 1982, Foster, a correctional counselor at the federal prison in Lompoc, California, was attacked and brutally beaten with a metal pipe. A skull fracture resulted in his memory being severely impaired. When first interviewed by a FBI agent on April 19, Foster was unable to remember the name of his attacker. On May 5, he was interviewed again and was able to describe his assailant and pick Owens's picture out of a photographic lineup. At trial, Foster described the attack and the identification he made on May 5. On cross-examination, Foster admitted he did not remember seeing his assailant. He could not recall any of his visitors during his month-long hospitalization except for the FBI agent. He could not recall if anyone had suggested to him that Owens was his attacker. The defense attorney was unable to refresh Foster's recollection of events occurring in the hospital, including Foster's statement that someone other than Owens had committed the assault. Owens was convicted.

Issue: Does the inability of the witness at trial to recall the basis for a pretrial identification violate the defendant's Sixth Amendment right to confront the accuser?

Reasoning: *** "[T]he Confrontation Clause guarantees only 'an *opportunity* for effective cross-examination, not cross-examination that is effective in whatever way, and to whatever extent, the defense might wish.' As *Fensterer* [474 U.S. 15 (1985)] demonstrates, that opportunity is not denied when a witness testifies as to his current belief but is unable to recollect the reason for that belief. It is sufficient that the defendant has the opportunity to bring out such matters as the witness's bias, his lack of care and attentiveness, his poor eyesight, and even (what is often a prime objective of cross-examination) the very fact that he has a bad memory. If the ability to inquire into these matters suffices to establish the constitutionally requisite opportunity for cross-examination when a witness testifies as to his current belief, the basis for which he cannot recall, we see no reason why it should not suffice when the witness's past belief is introduced and he is unable to recollect the reason for that past belief. In both cases the foundation for the belief (current or past) cannot effectively be elicited, but other means of impugning the belief are available."

Disposition: Conviction affirmed; a witness's lack of memory while testifying at trial does not violate the Confrontation Clause.

12-11s *Davis v. Alaska:* 415 U.S. 308, 39 L.Ed. 2d 347, 94 S.Ct. 1105 (1974)

Facts: A safe taken during a burglary of the Polar Bar in Anchorage was found the day after the burglary. Green told police that he saw two Negro men standing alongside a late-model, metallic-blue Chevrolet sedan near where the safe was discovered. Green later made an identification of Davis in a photographic lineup. Davis unsuccessfully sought to introduce evidence that Green, a juvenile, was on probation at the time and therefore may have been biased in his identification of Davis. Davis was convicted.

Issue: Can the fact that a juvenile is on probation be used to impeach?

Reasoning: *** "The claim of bias which the defense sought to develop was admissible to afford a basis for an inference of undue pressure because of Green's vulnerable status as a probationer, as well as of Green's possible concern that he might be a suspect in the investigation.

*** "The State's policy interest in protecting the confidentiality of a juvenile offender's record cannot require yielding of so vital a constitutional right as the effective cross-examination for bias of an adverse witness. The State could have protected Green from exposure of his juvenile adjudication in these circumstances by refraining from using him to make out its case; the State cannot, consistent with the right of confrontation, require the petitioner to bear the full burden of vindication of the State's interest in the secrecy of juvenile criminal records."

Disposition: Conviction reversed; the defense has the right to cross-examine both adult and juvenile witnesses regarding their criminal records.

12-11t *Lee v. Illinois:* 476 U.S. 530, 90 L.Ed. 2d 514, 106 S.Ct. 2056 (1986)

Facts: Police called Lee to the police station to identify a badly burned body, later determined to be her aunt, who was discovered in an apartment house complex where she lived. Lee began to cry and the police questioned her; she confessed that she and her boyfriend, Thomas, had stabbed her aunt and a friend to death. Thomas was interviewed but invoked his *Miranda* right to remain silent. Since both Lee and Thomas had asked to speak to each other, the police allowed them to meet. Lee told Thomas, "They know about the whole thing, don't you love me Edwin, didn't you in fact say *** that we wouldn't let one or the other take the rap alone *** ." Thomas then made a confession. Lee and

Thomas were tried jointly without a jury. Both the prosecution and the defense relied heavily on the confessions at trial. Lee was convicted.

Issue: Must a co-defendant's confession be shown to be reliable in order to have it admitted at trial?

Reasoning: *** "Our cases recognize that this truthfinding function of the Confrontation Clause is uniquely threatened when an accomplice's confession is sought to be introduced against a criminal defendant without the benefit of cross-examination. As has been noted, such a confession 'is hearsay, subject to all the dangers of inaccuracy which characterize hearsay generally. *** More than this, however, the post-arrest statements of a co-defendant have traditionally been viewed with special suspicion. Due to his strong motivation to implicate the defendant and to exonerate himself, a co-defendant's statements about what the defendant said or did are less credible than ordinary hearsay evidence.'

*** "But a confession is not necessarily rendered reliable simply because some of the facts it contains 'interlock' with the facts in the defendant's statement. The true danger inherent in this type of hearsay is, in fact, its selective reliability. As we have consistently recognized, a co-defendant's confession is presumptively unreliable as to the passages detailing the defendant's conduct or culpability because those passages may well be the product of the co-defendant's desire to shift or spread blame, curry favor, avenge himself, or divert attention to another. If those portions of the co-defendant's purportedly 'interlocking' statement which bear to any significant degree on the defendant's participation in the crime are not thoroughly substantiated by the defendant's own confession, the admission of the statement poses too serious a threat to the accuracy of the verdict to be countenanced by the Sixth Amendment. In other words, when the discrepancies between the statements are not insignificant, the co-defendant's confession may not be admitted."

Disposition: Conviction reversed; a conviction cannot be based on the confession of a co-defendant when there was no opportunity to cross-examine and the statement has not been shown to be reliable.

12-11u *Powers v. Ohio:* 499 U.S. 400, 113 L.Ed. 2d 411, 111 S.Ct. 1364 (1991)

Facts: Powers, a white man, was indicted on two counts of aggravated murder and one count of attempted aggravated murder. Powers unsuccessfully objected to the prosecutor's exercise of seven peremptory challenges to remove blacks from the jury. He was convicted.

Issue: Can peremptory challenges be used to exclude prospective jurors based on their race?

Reasoning: *** "Invoking the Equal Protection Clause and federal statutory law, and relying upon well-established principles of standing, we hold that a criminal defendant may object to race-based exclusions of jurors affected through peremptory challenges whether or not the defendant and the excluded juror share the same race.

*** "The Equal Protection Clause guarantees the defendant that the State will not exclude members of his race from the jury venire on account of race, or on the false assumption that members of his race as a group are not qualified to serve as jurors. Although a defendant has no right to a 'petit jury composed in whole or in part of persons of [the defendant's] own race,' he or she does have the right to be tried by a jury whose members are selected by nondiscriminatory criteria.

*** "In *Batson* [*Batson v. Kentucky* [476 U.S. 79 (1986)] we held that a defendant can raise an equal protection challenge to the use of peremptories at his own trial by showing that the prosecutor used them for the purpose of excluding members of the defendant's race.

*** "The purpose of the jury system is to impress upon the criminal defendant and the community as a whole that a verdict of conviction or acquittal is given in accordance with the law by persons who are fair. The verdict will not be accepted or understood in these terms if the jury is chosen by unlawful means at the outset. Upon these considerations, we find that a criminal defendant suffers a real injury when a prosecutor excludes jurors at his or her own trial on account of race."

Disposition: Conviction reversed; use of peremptory challenges to exclude a juror because of race violates equal protection regardless of the race of the defendant.

12-11v *Maryland v. Craig:* 497 U.S. 836, 111 L.Ed. 2d 666, 110 S.Ct. 3157 (1990)

Facts: Craig was charged with sexually abusing a six-year-old girl who had attended prekindergarten and kindergarten at a center he owned and operated. At trial, the victim and three other children were permitted to testify via one-way, closed-circuit television. Under the procedure authorized by Maryland statutes, the child witness, the prosecutor, and defense counsel are televised from one room; the judge, the jury, and the defendant (who remains in electronic communication with his attorney) remain in the courtroom and watch a video monitor. The witness cannot see the defendant. Craig was convicted.

Issue: Does the use of closed-circuit television violate the defendant's right to confrontation of the witnesses?

Reasoning: * * * "Maryland's statutory procedure, when invoked, prevents a child witness from seeing the defendant as he or she testifies against the defendant at trial. We find it significant, however, that Maryland's procedure preserves all of the other elements of the confrontation right: The child witness must be competent to testify and must testify under oath; the defendant retains full opportunity for contemporaneous cross-examination and the judge, jury, and defendant are able to view (albeit by video monitor) the demeanor (and body) of the witness as he or she testifies. * * *

* * * "We likewise conclude today that a State's interest in the physical and psychological well-being of child abuse victims may be sufficiently important to outweigh, at least in some cases, a defendant's right to face his or her accusers in court. That a significant majority of States has enacted statutes to protect child witnesses from the trauma of giving testimony in child abuse cases attests to the widespread belief in the importance of such a public policy. * * *

* * * "The requisite finding of necessity must, of course, be a case-specific one: The trial court must hear evidence and determine whether the use of one-way closed circuit television procedure is necessary to protect the welfare of the particular child witness who seeks to testify. Denial of face-to-face confrontation is not needed to further the state interest in protecting the child witness from trauma unless it is the presence of the defendant that causes the trauma. In other words, if the state interest were merely the interest in protecting child witnesses from courtroom trauma generally, denial of face-to-face confrontation would be unnecessary because the child could be permitted to testify in less intimidating surroundings, albeit with the defendant present. Finally, the trial court must find that the emotional distress suffered by the child witness in the presence of the defendant is more than *de minimis*, i.e., more than 'mere nervousness or excitement or some reluctance to testify.' * * *

* * * "We conclude that where necessary to protect a child witness from trauma that would be caused by testifying in the physical presence of the defendant, at least where such trauma would impair the child's ability to communicate, the Confrontation Clause does not prohibit use of a procedure that, despite the absence of face-to-face confrontation, ensures the reliability of the evidence by subjecting it to rigorous adversarial testing and thereby preserves the essence of effective confrontation."

Disposition: Conviction affirmed; a child witness may be allowed to testify by one-way, closed-circuit television if necessary to reduce the trauma of being in the defendant's presence, as long as other procedural safeguards of the adversarial process are retained.

12-11w *Bennis v. Michigan:* 516 U.S. 442, 134 L.Ed. 2d 68, 116 S.Ct. 994 (1996)

Facts: Mr. Bennis engaged in sexual activity with a prostitute while in the family car. A Michigan court ordered the car forfeited as a public nuisance without allowing Mrs. Bennis to claim an offset for her interest in the car even though she had no knowledge of her husband's activity prior to his arrest. Mrs. Bennis filed a Civil Rights Act suit.

Issue: Is a civil forfeiture law constitutional if it does not provide for an offset for an innocent owner's financial interest in property used by another during criminal activity?

Reasoning: "We conclude today, as we concluded 75 years ago, that the cases authorizing actions of the kind at issue are 'too firmly fixed in the punitive and remedial jurisprudence of the country to be now displaced.' The State here sought to deter illegal activity that contributes to neighborhood deterioration and unsafe streets. The Bennis automobile, it is conceded, facilitated and was used in criminal activity."

Disposition: The car was forfeited to the state; Mrs. Bennis received no reimbursement.

12-11x *Atkins v. Virginia:* 536 U.S. ___, 153 L.Ed. 2d 335, 122 S.Ct. 2242 (2002)

Facts: At about midnight, Atkins and Jones, armed with a semi-automatic handgun, abducted Eric Nesbitt, robbed him of his money, drove him to an ATM, and forced him to withdraw cash. They then took him to an isolated location where they shot him eight times and killed him. Atkins was charged with capital murder and convicted. At the sentencing hearing, testimony revealed that Atkins had an IQ of 59 and had committed at least four prior robberies. The jury sentenced Atkins to death.

Issue: Does execution of mentally retarded defendants convicted of capital murder violate the Eighth Amendment?

Reasoning: "A claim that punishment is excessive is judged not by the standards that prevailed in 1685 when Lord Jeffreys presided over the

'Bloody Assizes' or when the Bill of Rights was adopted, but rather by those that currently prevail. ***

*** "Given the well-known fact that anticrime legislation is far more popular than legislation providing protections for persons guilty of violent crime, the large number of States prohibiting the execution of mentally retarded persons (and the complete absence of States passing legislation reinstating the power to conduct such executions) provides powerful evidence that today our society views mentally retarded offenders as categorically less culpable than the average criminal. The evidence carries even greater force when it is noted that the legislatures that have addressed the issue have voted overwhelmingly in favor of the prohibition. Moreover, even in those States that allow the execution of mentally retarded offenders, the practice is uncommon. *** And it appears that even among those States that regularly execute offenders and that have no prohibition with regard to the mentally retarded, only five have executed offenders possessing a known IQ less than 70 since we decided *Penry* (*Penry v. Lynaugh,* 492 U.S. 302 (1989)). The practice, therefore, has become truly unusual, and it is fair to say that a national consensus has developed against it.

"To the extent there is serious disagreement about the execution of mentally retarded offenders, it is in determining which offenders are in fact retarded. In this case, for instance, the Commonwealth of Virginia disputes that Atkins suffers from mental retardation. Not all people who claim to be mentally retarded will be so impaired as to fall within the range of mentally retarded offenders about whom there is a national consenses. As was our approach . . . with regard to insanity, 'we leave to the State[s] the task of developing appropriate ways to enforce the constitutional restrictions upon its execution of sentences.'

*** "Our independent evaluation of the issue reveals no reason to disagree with the judgment of 'the legislatures that have recently addressed the matter' and concluded that death is not a suitable punishment for a mentally retarded criminal. We are not persuaded that the execution of mentally retarded criminals will measurably advance the deterrent or the retributive purpose of the death penalty. Construing and applying the Eight Amendment in the light of our 'evolving standards of decency,' we therefore conclude that such punishment is excessive and that the Constitution 'places a substantive restriction on the State's power to take the life' of a mentally retarded offender."

Disposition: Case is remanded to Virginia for determination whether Atkins was mentally retarded; if it is determined that he is retarded, he cannot be executed.

12-11y *Eddings v. Oklahoma:* 455 U.S. 104, 71 L.Ed. 2d 1, 102 S.Ct. 869 (1982)

Facts: On April 4, 1977, Eddings, a 16-year-old, and several companions ran away from their homes in Missouri. When stopped after momentarily losing control of the car, Eddings shot and killed the police officer who approached the car. At the penalty phase of the capital trial, Eddings presented substantial evidence of his troubled youth including abusive physical punishment by his father. The trial judge ruled the court was not permitted to consider the fact of Eddings's violent background.

Issue: Can the state restrict what types of mitigating evidence the defense can present in a death penalty case?

Reasoning: *** "Beginning with *Furman* [*Furman v. Georgia,* 408 U.S. 238 (1972)], the Court has attempted to provide standards for a constitutional death penalty that would serve both goals of measured, consistent application and fairness to the accused. Thus, in *Gregg v. Georgia,* 428 U.S. 153, the plurality held that the danger of an arbitrary and capricious death penalty could be met 'by a carefully drafted statute that ensures that the sentencing authority is given adequate information and guidance.' By its requirement that the jury find one of the aggravating circumstances listed in the death penalty statute, and by its direction to the jury to consider 'any mitigating circumstances,' the Georgia statute properly confined and directed the jury's attention to the circumstances of the particular crime and to 'the characteristics of the person who committed the crime.' ***

"Similarly, in *Woodson v. North Carolina,* 428 U.S. 280 (1976), the plurality held that mandatory death sentencing was not a permissible response to the problem of arbitrary jury discretion. As the history of capital punishment had shown, such an approach to the problem of discretion could not succeed while the Eighth Amendment required that the individual be given his due: 'the fundamental respect for humanity underlying the Eighth Amendment *** requires consideration of the character and record of the individual offender and the circumstances of the particular offense as a constitutionally indispensable part of the process of inflicting the penalty of death.'

*** "By holding that the sentencer in capital cases must be permitted to consider any relevant mitigating factors, the rule in *Lockett* [*Lockett v. Ohio,* 438 U.S. 586 (1978)] recognizes that a consistency produced by ignoring individual differences is a false consistency."

Disposition: Death penalty reversed; the state cannot limit mitigating factors that the defense may introduce for consideration by the judge and/or jury.

12-11z *Tison v. Arizona:* 481 U.S. 137, 95 L.Ed. 2d 127, 107 S.Ct. 1676 (1987)

Facts: Three Tison brothers planned and assisted their father in an escape from prison where he was serving a life sentence for killing a guard. Greenwalt, a cellmate who was also a convicted murderer, joined in the escape. After the car intended for use in the escape blew two tires, the group flagged down a car occupied by four members of a family. After sending the sons to obtain water to leave with the family members who would be abandoned in the desert, Tison and Greenwalt killed the entire family with repeated shotgun blasts. The father died of exposure in the desert; Greenwalt and the two brothers who were captured alive were tried and sentenced to death.

Issue: Can the death penalty be imposed on a person who did not personally kill?

Reasoning: *** "In *Enmund v. Florida* [458 U.S. 782 (1982)], this court reversed the death sentence of a defendant convicted under Florida's felony-murder rule. Enmund was the driver of a 'getaway' car in an armed robbery of a dwelling. ***

*** "[T]he Court undertook its own proportionality analysis. Armed robbery is a serious offense, but one for which the penalty of death is plainly excessive; the imposition of the death penalty for robbery, therefore, violates the Eighth and Fourteenth Amendments' proscription 'against all punishments which by their excessive length or severity are greatly disproportionate to the offenses, charged.' Furthermore, the Court found that Enmund's degree of participation in the murders was so tangential that it could not be said to justify a sentence of death. ***

*** "A critical facet of the individualized determination of culpability required in capital cases is the mental state with which the defendant commits the crime. Deeply ingrained in our legal tradition is the idea that the more purposeful is the criminal conduct, the more serious is the offense, and, therefore, the more severely it ought to be punished. ***

"A narrow focus on the question of whether or not a given defendant 'intended to kill,' however, is a highly unsatisfactory means of definitively distinguishing the most culpable and dangerous of murderers. Many who intend to, and do, kill are not criminally liable at all—those who act in self-defense or with other justification or excuse. Other intentional homicides, though criminal, are often felt undeserving of the death penalty—those that are the result of provocation. On the other hand, some nonintentional murderers may be among the most dangerous and inhumane of all—the person who tortures another not caring whether the victim lives or dies, or the robber who shoots someone in the course of the robbery, utterly indifferent to the fact that the desire to rob may have the unintended consequence of killing the victim as well as taking the victim's property. This reckless indifference to the value of human life may be every bit as shocking to the moral sense as an 'intent to kill.' * * * Enmund held that when 'intent to kill' results in its logical though not inevitable consequence—the taking of human life—the Eighth Amendment permits the State to exact the death penalty after a careful weighing of the aggravating and mitigating circumstances. Similarly, we hold that the reckless disregard for human life implicit in knowingly engaging in criminal activities known to carry a grave risk of death represents a highly culpable mental state, a mental state that may be taken into account in making a capital sentencing judgment when that conduct causes its natural, though also not inevitable, lethal result."

Disposition: Death penalty affirmed; the death penalty can be imposed on a co-felon who did not do the killing personally if the co-felon showed a reckless disregard for human life by knowingly engaging in criminal activity known to carry a grave risk of death.

12-11aa *Ring v. Arizona:* 536 U.S. ___, 153 L.Ed. 2d 556, 122 S.Ct. 2428 (2002)

Facts: A Wells Fargo armored van stopped at Dillard's department store in Glendale, Arizona. A courier left the van to pick up money inside the store. When he returned, the van and its driver were gone. The van was located later that day. The driver was inside, dead due to one gunshot wound to the head. More than $562,000 in cash and $271,000 in checks were missing from the van. Ring, along with two others, was arrested for the robbery and murder. The jury deadlocked on the premeditated murder charge against Ring, but convicted him of felony murder in the course of a robbery. The facts presented to the jury never established that Ring was at the scene of the robbery. Between Ring's trial and sentencing hearing, Greenham, one of the participants in the robbery, entered a guilty plea to second-degree murder and armed robbery. Greenham testified at Ring's sentencing hearing that the three men had planned the robbery for weeks and that Ring was the leader in laying out tactics. He also testified that Ring fired the fatal shot. At the end of the sentencing, hearing the judge entered a "Special Verdict," sentencing Ring to death. The judge found that the penalty was justified because Ring was the actual killer or a major participant in the armed robbery.

Issue: In a death penalty case, can the aggravating circumstances be found by the judge or must they be determined by the jury?

Reasoning: "The dispositive question, *** 'is one not of form, but of effect.' If a State makes an increase in a defendant's authorized punishment contingent on the finding of a fact, that fact—no matter how the State labels it—must be found by a jury beyond a reasonable doubt. A defendant may not be 'expose[d] *** to a penalty *exceeding* the maximum he would receive if punished according to the facts reflected in the jury verdict alone.'

*** "[W]e overrule *Walton* [*Walton v. Arizona,* 497 U.S. 639 (1990)] to the extent that it allows a sentencing judge, sitting without a jury, to find an aggravating circumstance necessary for imposition of the death penalty. *** The right to trial by jury guaranteed by the Sixth Amendment would be senselessly diminished if it encompassed the factfinding necessary to increase a defendant's sentence by two years [*Apprendi* (*Apprendi v. New Jersey*) 530 U.S. 466 (2000)], but not the factfinding necessary to put him to death. We hold that the Sixth Amendment applies to both."

Disposition: Case is remanded to Arizona courts for sentencing; the death penalty cannot be imposed on Ring.

12-11ab *Harmelin v. Michigan:* 501 U.S. 957, 115 L.Ed. 2d 836, 111 S.Ct. 2680 (1991)

Facts: Harmelin was convicted of possessing 672 grams of cocaine and sentenced to a mandatory term of life in prison without the possibility of parole. Harmelin contends his sentence is "cruel and unusual" for two reasons: It is significantly disproportionate to the crime he committed, and the judge was statutorily required to impose it, without taking into account the particularized circumstances of the crime and his criminal record.

Issue: Do the sentences the legislature enacts for noncapital crimes have to be proportionate to the offense and consider mitigating circumstances?

Reasoning: *** "... Severe, mandatory penalties may be cruel, but they are not unusual in the constitutional sense, having been employed in various forms throughout our Nation's history.... There can be no serious contention, then, that a sentence which is not otherwise cruel and unusual becomes so simple because it is 'mandatory.'

"Petitioner's 'required mitigation' claim, like his proportionality claim, does find support in our death-penalty jurisprudence. We have held that a capital sentence is cruel and unusual under the Eighth Amendment if it is imposed without an individualized determination that the punishment is 'appropriate'—whether or not the sentence is 'grossly disproportionate.' Petitioner asks us to extend this so-called 'individualized capital-sentencing doctrine,' to an 'individualized mandatory life in prison without parole sentencing doctrine.' We refuse to do so.

"Our cases creating and clarifying the 'individualized capital sentencing doctrine' have repeatedly suggested that there is no comparable requirement outside the capital context, because of the qualitative difference between death and all other penalties." ***

Disposition: Conviction affirmed; the defendant has no constitutional right to have the judge consider individualized factors when imposing a noncapital sentence or to determine that the sentence is proportionate to the severity of the crime.

12-11ac *United States v. Dunnigan:* 507 U.S. 87, 122 L.Ed. 2d 445, 113 S.Ct. 1111 (1993)

Facts: The defendant, Dunnigan, was charged in federal court with a single count of conspiracy to distribute cocaine. Five prosecution witnesses testified regarding her cocaine trafficking. Dunnigan took the stand as the sole defense witness. She denied all criminal acts attributed to her. On cross-examination, the defendant denied the truth of statements made by the prosecution witnesses and said she had not possessed or distributed cocaine during the summer in question or at any other time. At the sentencing hearing, the government requested an increase of two offense levels under United States Sentencing Guidelines Section 3C1.1 for "willfully obstructing or impeding proceedings." The judge concluded that false testimony at trial warranted the upward adjustment and sentenced her to 51 months incarceration.

Issue: Can the defendant's perjury at trial be used as grounds for increasing the sentence when there has been no conviction for perjury?

Reasoning: *** "[T]he enhancement provision is part of a sentencing scheme designed to determine the appropriate type and extent of punishment after the issue of guilt has been resolved. The commission of perjury is of obvious relevance in this regard, because it reflects on the defendant's criminal history, on her willingness to accept the commands of the law and the authority of the court, and on her character in general. * * *

"Of course, not every accused who testifies at trial and is convicted will incur an enhanced sentence under Section 3C1.1 for committing perjury. As we have just observed, an accused may give inaccurate testimony due to confusion, mistake or faulty memory. In other instances, an accused may testify to matters such as lack of capacity, insanity, duress or self-defense. Her testimony may be truthful, but the jury may nonetheless find the testimony insufficient to excuse criminal liability or prove lack of intent. For these reasons, if a defendant objects to a sentence enhancement resulting from her trial testimony, a district court must review the evidence and make independent findings necessary to establish a willful impediment to or obstruction of justice, or an attempt to do the same, under the perjury definition we have set out. When doing so, it is preferable for a district court to address each element of the alleged perjury in a separate and clear finding. * * *

"Respondent cannot contend that increasing her sentence because of her perjury interferes with her right to testify, for we have held on a number of occasions that a defendant's right to testify does not include a right to commit perjury. Nor can respondent contend Section 3C1.1 is unconstitutional on the simple basis that it distorts her decision whether to testify or remain silent. Our authorities do not impose a categorical ban on every governmental action affecting the strategic decisions of an accused, including decision whether or not to exercise constitutional rights. * * *

... "A sentence enhancement based on perjury does deter false testimony in much the same way as a separate prosecution for perjury. But the enhancement is more than a mere surrogate for a perjury prosecution. It furthers legitimate sentencing goals relating to the principal crime, including the goal of retribution and incapacitation. It is rational for a sentencing authority to conclude that a defendant who commits a crime and then perjures herself in an unlawful attempt to avoid responsibility is more threatening to society and less deserving of leniency than a defendant who does not so defy the trial process. The perjuring defendant's willingness to frustrate judicial proceedings to avoid criminal liability suggests that the need for incapacitation and retribution is heightened as compared with the defendant charged with the same crime who allows judicial proceedings to progress without resorting to perjury."

Disposition: Sentence affirmed; the fact that the defendant took the witness stand and committed perjury is a valid consideration at sentencing.

12-11ad *Kansas v. Crane:* 534 U.S. 407, 151 L.Ed. 2d 856, 122 S.Ct. 867 (2002)

Facts: Kansas sought civil commitment of Crane, a previously convicted sexual offender who, according to at least one of the state's psychiatric witnesses, suffers from both exhibitionism and antisocial personality disorder. After a jury trial, the Kansas District Court ordered Crane's civil commitment to a mental hospital. The Kansas Supreme Court reversed.

Issue: Can a person be held under civil commitment as a sexually violent predator if the state is unable to show that the person totally lacks control of his/her dangerous behavior?

Reasoning: "*Hendricks* [*Kansas v. Hendricks,* 521 U. S. 346 (1994)] referred to the Kansas Act as requiring a 'mental abnormality' or 'personality disorder' that makes it '*difficult,* if not impossible, for the [dangerous] person to control his dangerous behavior.' The word 'difficult' indicates that the lack of control to which this Court referred was not absolute. Indeed, as different *amici* on opposite sides of this case agree, an absolutist approach is unworkable. . . . Moreover, most severely ill people—even those commonly termed 'psychopaths'—retain some ability to control their behavior. Insistence upon absolute lack of control would risk barring the civil commitment of highly dangerous persons suffering severe mental abnormalities.

*** "*Hendricks* underscores the constitutional importance of distinguishing a dangerous sexual offender subject to civil commitment 'from other dangerous persons who are perhaps more properly dealt with exclusively through criminal proceedings.' That distinction is necessary lest 'civil commitment' become a 'mechanism for retribution or general deterrence'—functions properly those of criminal law, not civil commitment. . . .

". . . [W]e recognize that in cases where lack of control is at issue, 'inability to control behavior' will not be demonstrable with mathematical precision. It is enough to say that there must be proof of serious difficulty in controlling behavior. And this, when viewed in light of such features of the case as the nature of the psychiatric diagnosis, and the severity of the mental abnormality itself, must be sufficient to distinguish the dangerous sexual offender whose serious mental illness, abnormality, or disorder subjects him to civil commitment from the dangerous but typical recidivist convicted in an ordinary criminal case."

Disposition: Commitment to mental hospital upheld; prosecution did not have to show that Crane was totally unable to control his sexually violent conduct. He can be given an involuntary civil commitment.

Chapter Quiz

True/False

1. Determination of whether a defendant's Sixth Amendment right to a speedy trial has been denied is based solely on the length of time from arrest to beginning of the trial.
2. The prosecution must disclose exculpatory evidence to the defense prior to trial.
3. The defendant has the right to a trial without a jury.
4. The Sixth Amendment right to a jury trial is satisfied only if there are 12 people on the jury.
5. Due to the Sixth Amendment right to confront accusers, statements can be introduced at trial only if the person who made the statement takes the witness stand.
6. A person who has been acquitted can be tried again if serious errors by the judge caused the acquittal.
7. Civil forfeiture laws violate the Eighth Amendment if the person has already been convicted and given a fine as part of the sentence.
8. The death penalty can be imposed, at the discretion of the jury, for any murder that is considered heinous, atrocious, or cruel.
9. Due process mandates that a criminal defendant be mentally competent at all stages of the court proceedings.
10. Sexually violent predator laws are unconstitutional if they block the release of a defendant after the maximum sentence has been served for the crime.

Discussion Questions

1. Dan was indicted for murder. The prosecution was granted several continuances because the pathologist had not completed the autopsy report due to the breakdown of expensive laboratory equipment at the coroner's office. The county did not have money in the budget to repair it until the next fiscal year. The trial began 18 months after the indictment. During this delay, two witnesses Dan intended to call died of natural causes. Can Dan successfully have the charges dismissed due to a denial of his right to a speedy trial? Explain.

2. Mary was charged with robbery. Prior to trial, the defense counsel made a request for "all *Brady* material." The prosecutor quickly reviewed the file and responded that there was nothing in it that needed to be given to the defense. After trial, the defense attorney learned that the police had a statement in which Don claimed to have witnessed the robbery. Don had been at a lineup in which Mary participated and told the police that he wasn't sure, but he didn't think the robber was in the lineup. Can Mary have her conviction reversed for a constitutional violation of her due process right to discovery? Explain.
3. Sam was charged with DUI in a state where the maximum sentence is 12 months in county jail. During *voir dire* of the jury, the prosecutor used her peremptory challenges to exclude women from the jury. The defense made a timely objection. The prosecutor claimed that she was doing this because her experience has been that women are more likely to acquit in DUI cases. Can Sam have his conviction reversed because of a violation of equal protection? Explain.
4. Sally was on trial for grand theft. Donna was the only prosecution witness. During cross-examination, the defense sought to introduce the fact that Donna had been fired from a job due to dishonesty. The prosecution objected on the grounds that the events in question occurred when Donna was a minor. The judge ruled against the defense. Can Sally successfully appeal on the grounds that her right to confrontation was violated? Explain.
5. Dave entered a grocery store with the intent to rob Will, who had just cashed his paycheck. While in the store, he put a candy bar in his pocket. Based on double jeopardy, how many of the following can Dave be convicted of committing: burglary of the store, battery on Will, robbery of Will, and theft of the candy bar? Explain.
6. John killed Sue because she had been subpoenaed to be a witness against him in a robbery case. She died after he stabbed her 10 times and left her in the desert. The defense was able to show that John was being framed for the robbery but Sue was unaware the charges were false. Which of the following would be constitutionally permissible grounds for seeking the death sentence: mandatory death sentence for killing witnesses; killing was especially heinous; killing was done with intent to make victim suffer extreme pain? Explain. Write a jury instruction to explain to jurors how they should apply the aggravating and mitigating facts in this case.

Chapter 13

First Amendment Issues

Outline

The First Amendment encompasses freedoms of speech, assembly, press, and religion. In many cases, these various freedoms overlap. This chapter will address the freedoms m ost commonly encountered by law enforcement personnel.

13-1 Protecting Free Speech Rights

The essence of freedom of speech is freedom to communicate and express ideas. One of the main principles in this area is that government should not control the content of speech. Although highly protected, freedom of speech is not absolute. In 1918, Justice Holmes made the famous statement that freedom of speech would not protect a man falsely shouting "fire" in a theater and causing a panic [*Schenck v. United States,* 249 U.S.

47, 52 (1918)]. *Chaplinsky v. New Hampshire* [315 U.S. 568 at 572 (1941)], another landmark case, pointed out that free speech does not cover obscenity, libel, and slander, or insulting or "fighting" words—those that, by their very utterance, inflict injury or tend to incite an immediate breach of the peace.

Any statute that attempts to regulate speech must be content-neutral. The purpose for the regulation must be unrelated to the fact that the government approves, or does not approve, of what is said. Overbreadth, covering both protected and unprotected speech, is a common problem in this area. For example, an ordinance that made it a crime to "willfully or intentionally interrupt a city policeman * * * by verbal challenge during an investigation" was ruled overbroad because it covered both criminal conduct and "pure speech."

The Supreme Court held that New York's "Son of Sam" law was unconstitutional because it was content-based. The law required that the Crime Victims Board receive all income earned from publication of an accused or convicted person's "thoughts, feelings, opinions or emotions regarding such crime." The Court held:

> "The Son of Sam law is such a content-based statute. It singles out income derived from expressive activity for a burden the State places on no other income, and it is directed only at works with a specified content. Whether the First Amendment 'speaker' is considered to be Henry Hill [the convict who wrote *Wiseguy]*, whose income the statute places in escrow because of the story he has told, or Simon & Schuster, which can publish books about crime with the assistance of only those criminals willing to forgo remuneration for at least five years, the statute plainly imposes a financial disincentive only on speech of a particular content." [*Simon & Schuster v. Crime Victims Board,* 502 U.S. 105, 116 L.Ed. 2d 476, 112 S.Ct. 501 (1991)].

The press has the right to publish information of great public concern obtained in documents stolen by a third party. The Court also allowed the publication of material obtained by an illegal wiretap conducted by a third party (not a police officer). In both cases, the Court emphasized the public's need to know and noted that the press was free from responsibility for the illegal methods used to obtain the information. Had there been evidence that members of the press were involved in the illegal activity, the outcome of the decisions would have undoubtedly been different.

Freedom of speech is sometimes divided into "pure speech" and "symbolic speech." "Pure speech" refers to words (oral or written); "symbolic speech" includes actions designed to convey a message. In many situations, both "pure" and "symbolic" speech are involved.

"Symbolic speech" can be regulated more closely than can "pure speech." Examples of "symbolic speech" include wearing black armbands, burning draft cards, and burning the flag. *United States v. O'Brien,* [391 U.S. 367 (1968)], formulated a four-part test for regulation of symbolic acts: (1) the regulation must be within the government's constitutional power; (2) it must further an important or substantial government interest; (3) the government interest must be unrelated to suppression of free expression; and (4) the incidental restriction of the First Amendment must be no greater than essential to further the government's interest.

The First Amendment protects religious proselytizing, anonymous political speech, and the distribution of handbills. These activities cannot be prohibited. A city cannot mandate that individuals obtain a permit from the mayor's office and submit a signed registration form before going on private residential property to promote a "cause."

"Hate crime" statutes must pass scrutiny for their regulation of the content of speech. A statute that made it a misdemeanor to burn crosses, knowing that such conduct would arouse "anger, alarm or resentment in others on the basis of race, color, creed, religion or gender," was held unconstitutional [*R.A.V. v. City of St. Paul,* 505 U.S. 377, 120 L.Ed. 2d 305, 112 S.Ct. 2538 (1992)]. The state argued that the ordinance only applied to "fighting words," but the Court found that it violated the First Amendment because it applied only to speech on disfavored topics. Individuals who violate criminal laws forbidding cross burning could be punished for malicious mischief and arson, but not for expressing racial bias. On the other hand, imposing longer sentences for crimes because the victim was selected by race, religion, or any other factor does not violate the First Amendment.

Political expression is also covered. Once again, the rule is that the content of the speech cannot be censored. Any law that attempts to regulate political speech is reviewed under the "exacting scrutiny" standard and will be upheld only if it is narrowly tailored to serve an overriding state interest. States cannot prohibit anonymous political pamphlets; neither can they require that people involved in circulating initiative petitions be registered voters in the state or wear identification badges bearing their names. Groups that sponsor initiatives cannot be required to report the names and addresses of paid circulators or the amount paid to them. Fund-raising by political parties, charities, and activist groups is also protected by the First Amendment. Reasonable regulations can be placed on the size and location of signs, but cities cannot enact ordinances that totally prohibit signs on residential property.

Regulation of speech on government property has posed some unique problems. Three different approaches have been used: (1) Regulations on property traditionally available for public expression are subject to the highest scrutiny; (2) "public forums" (areas the government has opened for expressive activities of all or part of the public) can be regulated in the same manner as traditional public forums; and (3) restrictions imposed on speech on other government property are permitted so long as they are reasonable and content-neutral. Government-operated airports were found to be in the latter category; restrictions on solicitation of money inside the terminals were upheld [*International Society for Krishna Consciousness, Inc. v. Lee,* 505 U.S. 377, 120 L.Ed. 2d 541, 112 S.Ct. 2701 (1992)]. Dissemination of literature, without requesting money, could not be similarly curtailed.

It is important to note that the "content-neutral" requirement applies only to government activities. Granting permission to use the speaker's platform in a city park, for example, must be done without discrimination based on the viewpoints of the parties involved. This does not mean that groups using these public areas must give only neutral opinions. The key function of freedom of speech is to allow all sides of an issue to be expressed. The city must provide equal access to parks, parade routes, etc. for all groups requesting permission to stage demonstrations, no matter how controversial.

Commercial speech (advertising) can be regulated more carefully than can expression of personal views. The Court explained the permissible extent of these regulations:

> "... [T]he government may freely regulate commercial speech that concerns unlawful activity or is misleading. Commercial speech that falls into neither of those categories ... may be regulated if the government satisfies a test consisting of three related prongs: first, the government must assert a substantial interest in support of its regulation; second, the government must demonstrate that the restriction on commercial speech directly and materially advances that interest; and third, the regulation must be 'narrowly drawn.'" [*Florida v. Went for It, Inc.,* 515 U.S. 618, 132 L.Ed. 2d 541, 115 S.Ct. 2371 (1995)]

For example, advertisers can be required to be truthful, keep their ads off government property, and control the volume on sound trucks in residential neighborhoods. The Supreme Court has permitted regulations on the sale of drug paraphernalia by requiring dealers to purchase a license and record who makes purchases. The Court has also acknowledged the right of the government to prohibit public nudity, including nude dancing. Recent cases upheld a federal statute that prohibited broadcasting advertisements for a state-run lottery in adjoining states where such lotteries are illegal and State Bar rules that prohibited direct mail advertising by lawyers to victims during the first 30 days after a disaster but found a law unconstitutional that prohibited the listing of alcohol content on beer labels.

Even in the commercial speech arena, the regulations must be carefully tailored to meet the problem addressed. For example, prohibiting for-profit newspapers from placing newsracks on public streets was found to violate the First Amendment because the ordinance was overbroad. It distinguished between newspapers based on the amount of paid advertising, not on the basis of size, shape, appearance, or location of the newsracks. The city claimed the law was enacted in the interest of aesthetics, but it only applied to a very small percentage of newsracks in the city.

The Supreme Court has also been called upon to interpret the scope of the First Amendment in prisons and jails. While inmates retain their constitutional rights, regulations that serve a reasonable administrative purpose from a penological standpoint are allowed. Incoming mail can be checked for contraband and incoming books and magazines can be restricted if they pose a threat to security.

13-2 Freedom of Assembly

Although not specifically mentioned in the First Amendment, freedom of assembly is considered an integral part of free speech. The Supreme Court has required more than mere "social association" in order to invoke the First Amendment's protection—there must be some form of "expressive association."

Regulation of picketing and other demonstrations is permitted as long as the regulations are content-neutral and reasonably related to the government interest. Prohibiting public demonstrations late at night is clearly allowed; denying parade permits to unpopular causes is not. Ordinances governing the issuance of parade permits must contain explicit criteria for deciding whether to grant or deny them. When a permit is issued, the government cannot place restrictions on the viewpoints expressed by the participants; for example, the city of Boston could not mandate that the private group organizing the St. Patrick's Day parade allow a gay-rights group to march in the parade.

Occasionally, an injunction is issued to restrict demonstrations. This type of court order requires the parties to act as directed by the judge.

Injunctions must pass even stricter review than the laws regulating the time, place, and manner of demonstrations; they may burden speech no more than necessary to serve a significant government interest. Greater restrictions may be allowed if prior, less-restrictive injunctions have not solved the problem. Injunctions regulating picketing at abortion clinics are good examples. In *Madsen v. Women's Health Center, Inc* [512 U.S. 753, 129 L.Ed. 2d 593, 114 S.Ct. 2516 (1994)], the Court approved noise restrictions and a requirement that protesters stay off public property for a distance of 36 feet from the entrance. The size of the buffer zone was based on the width of the street in front of the clinic and other relevant facts. In another case, *Schenck v. Pro-Choice Network of Western New York* [519 U.S. 357, 137 L.Ed. 2d 1, 117 S.Ct. 855 (1997)], the Court approved an injunction that prevented protesters from going within 15 feet of doorways and driveways of the clinic; a "floating buffer zone," designed by the lower court to prevent demonstrators from approaching people as they walked up a sidewalk to the clinic, was overruled.

13-3 Media Access to Criminal Justice

Media access to criminal trials encompasses rights guaranteed under both the First and Sixth Amendments. The First Amendment gives the media a right to access; the Sixth Amendment gives the defendant the right to a fair trial. In some cases, these rights conflict because pretrial publicity may prejudice potential jurors. This chapter addresses the rights of the press. Sixth Amendment issues are covered in chapter 12.

The news media have claimed the right to publish any information that they deem fit. This does not mean that the Court cannot restrict their access to information in some circumstances. Carefully tailored, pretrial "gag orders" may be issued to prevent police, prosecutors, and defense attorneys from disclosing prejudicial information to the press. State laws also may prohibit disclosure of the names of juveniles to the press. Publication of information obtained in open court cannot be prohibited; neither can the publication of information legally obtained from non-government sources not covered by "gag orders." The Supreme Court has also ruled that the news media do not have the right to interview any inmate that they request or to have access to public facilities, such as jails, except areas otherwise open to the public.

Comments to the media by prosecutors and defense attorneys can prejudice a case. The Supreme Court recently approved a rule of professional conduct of the Nevada State Bar that prohibits lawyers from making statements that pose a "substantial likelihood of material prejudice." The Court rejected arguments that lawyers could be restricted only under circumstances in which a "gag order" could be issued.

The general rule is that court proceedings must be open to the press, with the exception of juvenile court. Specific cases have established the right of access to preliminary hearings, suppression hearings (except when publication of the proceedings would prejudice the case), *voir dire* of the jury, and trials. The defendant does not have the right to have the preliminary hearing or trial closed or to have cameras excluded from the courtroom. In order to close the courtroom, a judge must have specific facts that show a specialized need that outweighs the right to public access. Under some circumstances, a court can be closed when juvenile victims of sex crimes are testifying.

While the press has the right to obtain information for publication, it does not have a constitutional privilege to refuse to disclose the sources of its information to the court or a Grand Jury. Although the Supreme Court has not found a "news reporter" privilege, Congress and many state legislatures have statutorily enacted such a privilege.

13-4 Obscenity

Obscene material is unprotected by the First Amendment. *Miller v. California* [413 U.S. 15 (1973)] states the legal standard for determining obscenity: (1) "The average person, applying contemporary community standards" would find that the work, taken as a whole, appeals to the prurient interest; (2) the work depicts or describes, in a patently offensive way, sexual conduct specifically defined by the applicable state law; and (3) the work, taken as a whole, lacks serious literary, artistic, political, or scientific value. The older standard, which required a work to be "utterly without redeeming social value," has been abandoned.

Applying the *Miller* standard to individual works has been problematic. Items that are offensive and indecent, but not obscene, are protected by the First Amendment. The distinction is critical because the First Amendment forbids "prior restraint" of protected speech. To guard the free speech aspects of pornography, the courts have placed several restrictions on the police. The emergency exception to the warrant requirement cannot be used to seize allegedly obscene material if doing so would constitute "prior restraint." Affidavits in support of search warrants for allegedly obscene materials must give specific facts so that the issuing magistrate can determine if there is probable cause that each item to be seized is obscene.

Large-scale seizures under search warrants are also prohibited—only one copy per title can be seized prior to a judicial determination in an adversary hearing that the material is obscene. When items are seized under a search warrant there must be a prompt, post-seizure determination of the obscenity issue.

Possession of obscene materials in the privacy of one's home is protected by the First Amendment. Sending obscene matter through the mails or using other forms of transportation is not. More stringent regulations on the sale of pornography to minors may be adopted.

The Internet is increasingly being used by purveyors of pornography. The Communications Decency Act of 1996 was intended to restrict the access of minors to obscene material on the Internet. The Supreme Court ruled that the measures designed by Congress seriously infringed upon the free speech rights of adults and, therefore, violated the First Amendment. One of the major problems was the inability to design a system that could identify minors and restrict their access without imposing censorship on transmission of material to everyone else. The Court also noted that software was on the horizon that would allow parents to block their children's receipt of indecent programming on their home computers.

Child pornography presents a different problem. There is a compelling interest in protecting children from sexual exploitation. This interest in preventing the use of children in pornography gives states the right to make such actions criminal. Possession of pornographic pictures of children, even in the confines of the home, can be declared a crime. The same arguments do not hold for virtual child pornography. Since no children were used to make the images, this type of production cannot be totally banned. Attempts to ban child pornography on the Internet must comply with the "community standards" test and the evaluation of the work as a whole as required in *Miller v. California.* A tangential showing that pedophiles may use child pornography to lure children into participating in sexual acts, or that viewing child pornography may stimulate pedophiles and result in the molestation of children, is not enough.

The legal process to have individual items declared obscene is lengthy and difficult. Many cities have attempted other avenues, such as zoning and nuisance abatement procedures, to regulate "adult" bookstores and theaters. The Supreme Court has approved zoning laws that restrict the proximity of "adult bookstores" to residential areas and churches as long as the laws do not try to regulate free speech. Zoning cannot be so restrictive that it totally eliminates "adult" entertainment. The Court has also approved use of nuisance laws to close "adult bookstores" if it can be shown that the premises are used for prostitution and lewdness.

13-5 Regulation of Religious Practices

The First Amendment contains two separate protections for religion: the Establishment Clause and the Free Exercise Clause. The Establishment Clause forbids the government from establishing or endorsing religion. The Free Exercise Clause prohibits government interference with a person's exercise of religion. It must be remembered that freedom of religion includes the right to be an atheist or an agnostic. The courts have also recognized personal religious beliefs separate from organized religion.

The Supreme Court recently decided two cases dealing with the overlapping areas of freedom of religion and freedom of speech. It emphasized that the "content-neutral" approach to free speech prohibits restrictions on religious speech. If a "public forum" is open for groups to express their views, there cannot be restrictions prohibiting religious demonstrations. For example, a public park that normally allows displays at Christmas cannot prohibit the display of a cross. A similar approach was taken in a case involving the University of Virginia's policy of funding newspapers published by student organizations. Funding could not be denied for a religious-oriented student paper if student fees were used to support papers with secular agendas.

Most cases dealing with the freedom of religion that occur in criminal justice settings relate to custodial facilities, probation, and parole. A prisoner cannot be given "good time" credit or other incentives for participating in religious observances; nor can church attendance be made a condition of probation or parole. These would fall under the Establishment Clause.

The Free Exercise Clause has been the subject of much inmate litigation in the federal courts, although few cases have reached the Supreme Court. Some basic principles have been established: (1) Members of the clergy have access to custodial institutions but inmates cannot be forced to listen to them; (2) inmates have the right to use their own money to purchase religious books and materials; (3) inmates have the right to observe "holy days" that are significant to their religion; and (4) inmates may join a religious denomination while in prison. Other problem areas remain unresolved: special diets, clothing and rituals, and religious denomination not recognized outside the prison (e.g., the Church of the New Song [CONS]).

Freedom of religion, like freedom of speech, is not absolute. Religious belief is not a defense for violating a law enacted under a state's legitimate authority to control public conduct unless the motivation for enacting the law violated the Free Exercise Clause. For example, the use of peyote can be prosecuted as a felony, even though its use is a *bona fide* part of Native American religious ceremonies.

The Religious Freedom Restoration Act of 1993 prohibited all levels of government from placing a "substantial burden" on a person's exercise of religion unless the government could demonstrate that the law furthered a compelling governmental interest and was the least restrictive means of achieving that interest. The Supreme Court invalidated this law because Congress overstepped its power under the Fourteenth Amendment. Such substantive legislation can be passed to enforce provisions of the Bill of Rights only if there is a strong showing that remedial measures are necessary; the Court also questioned the appropriateness of the "strict scrutiny" standard in free exercise of religion cases.

Opponents of school vouchers have argued that the use of government money to pay for parochial school education is a violation of the First Amendment. In 2002, the Supreme Court rejected this argument and held that the vouchers promoted a valid secular purpose. Ohio enacted a voucher program as a way for low-income parents, in districts where public schools failed to provide adequate education, to transfer their children to better schools. The fact that 96 percent of the participating students enrolled in schools with religious affiliations was not seen as determinative on the issue of government support of religion. The Court found no government involvement because the individual parents, not the school district, made the decision to enroll their children in church schools.

13-6 Key Supreme Court Cases

13-6a *Texas v. Johnson:* 491 U.S. 397, 105 L.Ed. 2d 342, 109 S.Ct. 2533 (1989)

Facts: Johnson participated in a political demonstration dubbed the "Republican War Chest Tour" during the 1984 Republican National Convention in Dallas. The purpose of the demonstration was to protest policies of the Reagan administration and certain Dallas-based corporations. The demonstrators marched in the streets, chant political slogans, and stopped at several corporate locations to stage "die-ins," intended to dramatize the consequences of nuclear war. Other demonstrators spray-painted walls of buildings and overturned potted plants. Johnson was handed an American flag taken from one of the targeted buildings. The demonstration ended in front of the Dallas City Hall, where Johnson unfurled the American flag, doused it with kerosene, and set it on fire. While the flag burned, the protestors chanted, "America, the red, white, and blue, we spit on you." No one was physically injured or threatened with injury, although several witnesses testified that they had been seriously offended by the flag-burning. Johnson was charged with desecration of a venerated object in violation of Texas law; no one else involved in the demonstration was charged with a crime.

Issue: Does the First Amendment protect the act of burning a flag during a political protest rally?

Reasoning: * * * "In deciding whether particular conduct possesses sufficient communicative elements to bring the First Amendment into play, we have asked whether '[a]n intent to convey a particularized message was present, and [whether] the likelihood was great that the message would be understood by those who viewed it.' Hence, we have recognized the expressive nature of students' wearing of black armbands to protest American military involvement in Vietnam; of a sit-in by blacks in a 'whites only' area to protest segregation; of the wearing of American military uniforms in a dramatic presentation criticizing American involvement in Vietnam; and of picketing about a wide variety of causes.

"Especially pertinent to this case are our decisions recognizing the communicative nature of conduct relating to flags. Attaching a peace sign to the flag; saluting the flag; and displaying a red flag, we have held, all may find shelter under the First Amendment. That we have had little difficulty identifying an expressive element in conduct relating to flags should not be surprising. The very purpose of a national flag is to serve as a symbol of our country; it is, one might say, 'the one visible manifestation of two hundred years of nationhood.' * * * Pregnant with expressive content, the flag as readily signifies this Nation as does the combination of letters found in 'America.'

* * * "Johnson burned an American flag as part—indeed, as the culmination—of a political demonstration that coincided with the convening of the Republican Party and its renomination of Ronald Reagan for President. The expressive, overtly political nature of this conduct was both intentional and overwhelmingly apparent. * * * In these circumstances, Johnson's burning of the flag was conduct 'sufficiently imbued with elements of communication' to implicate the First Amendment.

"The Government generally has a freer hand in restricting expressive conduct than it has in restricting the written or spoken word. It may not, however, proscribe particular conduct because it has expressive elements. * * * It is, in short, not simply the verbal or nonverbal nature of the expression, but the governmental interest at stake, that helps to determine whether a restriction on that expression is valid.

* * * "Texas claims that its interest in preventing breaches of the peace justifies Johnson's conviction for flag desecration. However, no distur-

bance of the peace actually occurred or threatened to occur because of Johnson's burning of the flag. * * *

* * * "Thus, we have not permitted the Government to assume that every expression of a provocative idea will incite a riot, but have instead required careful consideration of the actual circumstances surrounding such expression, asking whether the expression 'is directed to inciting or producing imminent lawless action and is likely to incite or produce such action.' * * * To accept Texas' arguments that it need only demonstrate 'the potential for a breach of the peace' and that every flag-burning necessarily possesses that potential, would be to eviscerate our holding in *Brandenburg* [*Brandenburg v. Ohio,* 395 U.S. 444 (1969)]. This we decline to do.

"Nor does Johnson's expressive conduct fall within that small class of 'fighting words' that are 'likely to provoke the average person to retaliation, and thereby cause a breach of the peace.' No reasonable onlooker would have regarded Johnson's generalized expression of dissatisfaction with the policies of the Federal Government as a direct personal insult or an invitation to exchange fisticuffs.

* * * "We can imagine no more appropriate response to burning a flag than waving one's own, no better way to counter a flag-burner's message than by saluting the flag that burns, no surer means of preserving the dignity even of the flag that burned than by—as one witness here did—according its remains a respectful burial. We do not consecrate the flag by punishing its desecration, for in doing so we dilute the freedom that this cherished emblem represents."

Disposition: Conviction reversed; burning the flag in symbolic protest cannot be criminally punished.

13-6b *Wisconsin v. Mitchell:* 508 U.S. 47, 124 L.Ed. 2d 436, 113 S.Ct. 2194 (1993)

Facts: On the evening of October 7, 1989, a group of young black men and boys, including Mitchell, gathered at an apartment complex in Kenosha, Wisconsin. Several members of the group discussed a scene from the motion picture "Mississippi Burning," in which a white man beat a young black boy who was praying. The group moved outside and Mitchell asked them: "Do you all feel hyped up to move on some white people?" Shortly thereafter, a young white boy approached the group on the opposite side of the street from where they were standing. As the boy walked by, Mitchell said: "You all want to fuck somebody up? There goes a white boy; go get him." Mitchell counted to three and pointed in the boy's direction. The group ran toward the boy, beat him severely, and stole his tennis shoes. The boy was rendered unconscious and remained in a coma for four days. Mitchell was convicted of aggravated battery. That offense ordinarily carried a maximum sentence of two years' imprisonment; Mitchell's sentence was increased to a maximum of seven years based on a Wisconsin law that enhances the maximum penalty for an offense whenever the defendant "[i]ntentionally selects the person against whom the crime . . . is committed . . . because of the race, religion, color, disability, sexual orientation, national origin or ancestry of that person . . ." The Circuit Court sentenced Mitchell to four years' imprisonment for the aggravated battery.

Issue: Can a person be given a longer sentence because the victim was selected based on race, religion, or other protected status?

Reasoning: *** "[A] physical assault is not by any stretch of the imagination expressive conduct protected by the First Amendment.

"But the fact remains that under the Wisconsin statute the same criminal conduct may be more heavily punished if the victim is selected because of his race or other protected status than if no such motive obtained. Thus, although the statute punishes criminal conduct, it enhances the maximum penalty for conduct motivated by a discriminatory point of view more severely than the same conduct engaged in for some other reason or for no reason at all. Because the only reason for the enhancement is the defendant's discriminatory motive for selecting his victim, Mitchell argues (and the Wisconsin Supreme Court held) that the statute violates the First Amendment by punishing offenders' bigoted beliefs.

"Traditionally, sentencing judges have considered a wide variety of factors in addition to evidence bearing on guilt in determining what sentence to impose on a convicted defendant. The defendant's motive for committing the offense is one important factor. ***

"But it is equally true that a defendant's abstract beliefs, however obnoxious to most people, may not be taken into consideration by a sentencing judge. In *Dawson* [*Dawson v. Delaware,* 503 U.S. 159 (1992)], the State introduced evidence at a capital-sentencing hearing that the defendant was a member of a white supremacist prison gang. Because 'the evidence proved nothing more than [the defendant's] abstract beliefs,' we held that its admission violated the defendant's First Amendment rights. In so holding, however, we emphasized that 'the Constitution does not erect a per se barrier to the admission of evidence concerning one's beliefs and associations at sentencing simply because those beliefs and associations are protected by the First Amendment.' Thus, in *Barclay v. Florida,* 463 U.S. 939 (1983), (plurality opinion), we allowed the sentencing judge to take into account the defendant's racial animus towards his victim. . . .

Because 'the elements of racial hatred in [the] murder' were relevant to several aggravating factors, we held that the trial judge permissibly took this evidence into account in sentencing the defendant to death.

*** "Mitchell argues that the Wisconsin penalty-enhancement statute is invalid because it punishes the defendant's discriminatory motive, or reason, for acting. But motive plays the same role under the Wisconsin statutes as it does under federal and state antidiscrimination laws, which we have previously upheld against constitutional challenge. Title VII, for example, makes it unlawful for an employer to discriminate against an employee '*because of* such individual's race, color, religion, sex, or national origin.' 42 U.S.C. § 2000e-2(a)(1) (emphasis added by Court). In *Hishon* [*Hishon v. King & Spalding,* 467 U.S. 69 (1984)], we rejected the argument that Title VII infringed employers' first Amendment rights. And more recently, in *R.A.V. v. St. Paul,* 505 U.S. 377, 120 L.Ed. 2d 305, 112 S.Ct. 2538 (1992), we cited Title VII (as well as 18 U.S.C. § 242 and 42 U.S.C. §§ 1981 and 1982) as an example of a permissible content-neutral regulation of conduct.

"Nothing in our decision last Term in *R.A.V.* compels a different result here. That case involved a First Amendment challenge to a municipal ordinance prohibiting the use of '"fighting words" that insult, or provoke violence, "on the basis of race, color, creed, religion or gender."' Because the ordinance only proscribed a class of 'fighting words' deemed particularly offensive by the city—i.e., those 'that contain ... messages of "bias-motivated" hatred,'—we held that it violated the rule against content-based discrimination. But whereas the ordinance struck down in *R.A.V.* was explicitly directed at expression (i.e., 'speech' or 'messages'), the statute in this case is aimed at conduct unprotected by the First Amendment.

"Moreover, the Wisconsin statute singles out for enhancement bias-inspired conduct because this conduct is thought to inflict greater individual and societal harm. For example, according to the State and its *amici,* bias-motivated crimes are more likely to provoke retaliatory crimes, inflict distinct emotional harms on their victims, and incite community unrest. The State's desire to redress these perceived harms provides an adequate explanation for its penalty-enhancement provision over and above mere disagreement with offenders' beliefs or biases. As Blackstone said long ago, 'it is but reasonable that among crimes of different natures those should be most severely punished, which are the most destructive of the public safety and happiness.' ***

"The First Amendment, moreover, does not prohibit the evidentiary use of speech to establish the elements of a crime or to prove motive or intent. Evidence of a defendant's previous declarations or statements is commonly admitted in criminal trials subject to evidentiary rules dealing with relevancy, reliability, and the like. *** "

Disposition: Sentence affirmed; longer sentences for crimes motivated by racial hatred do not violate the First Amendment.

13-6c *Press-Enterprise Company v. Superior Court of California for the County of Riverside:* 478 U.S. 1, 92 L.Ed. 2d 1, 106 S.Ct. 2735 (1986)

Facts: Diaz, a nurse, was charged with 12 counts of capital murder for administering massive doses of the heart drug lidocaine to patients in a nursing home where he worked. At the preliminary hearing, the judge granted Diaz's unopposed motion to exclude the public from the hearing. At the conclusion of the 41-day hearing, the *Press-Enterprise*'s request that the transcript of the proceedings be released was denied and the record was sealed. The prosecution made a motion several months later for the release of the transcript but it was denied, upon defense request, because it contained information that might prejudice defendant's right to a fair trial. The *Press-Enterprise* then filed a peremptory writ of mandate for the release of the transcripts.

Issue: Does the press have a First Amendment right to be present at a preliminary hearing?

Reasoning: *** "In cases dealing with the claim of a First Amendment right of access to criminal proceedings, our decisions have emphasized two complementary considerations. First, because a 'tradition of accessibility implies the favorable judgment of experience,' we have considered whether the place and process has historically been open to the press and general public.

*** "Plainly the modern trial with jurors open to interrogation for possible bias is a far cry from the 'town meeting trial' of ancient English practice. Yet even our modern procedural protections have their origin in the ancient common law principle which provided not for closed proceedings, but rather for rules of conduct for those who attend trials.

"Second, in this setting the Court has traditionally considered whether public access plays a significant positive role in the functioning of the particular process in question. *** In *Press-Enterprise* [*Press-Enterprise Co. v. Superior Court,* 464 U.S. 501 (1984)], we summarized the holdings of prior cases, noting that openness in criminal trials, including the selection of jurors, 'enhances both the basic fairness of the criminal trial and the appearance of fairness so essential to public confidence in the system.'

*** "If the particular proceeding in question passes these tests of experience and logic, a qualified First Amendment right of public access attaches. But even when a right of access attaches, it is not absolute. While open criminal proceedings give assurances of fairness to both the public and the accused, there are some limited circumstances in which the right of the accused to a fair trial might be undermined by publicity. In such cases, the trial court must determine whether the situation is such that the rights of the accused override the qualified First Amendment right of access. In *Press-Enterprise* we stated:

> 'the presumption may be overcome only by an overriding interest based on findings that closure is essential to preserve higher values and is narrowly tailored to serve that interest. The interest is to be articulated along with findings specific enough that a reviewing court can determine whether the closure order was properly entered.'

"The considerations that led the Court to apply the First Amendment right of access to criminal trials in *Richmond Newspapers* [*Richmond Newspapers, Inc. v. Virginia,* 448 U.S. 555 (1980)] and *Globe* [*Globe Newspaper Co. v. Superior Court,* 457 U.S. 596 (1982)] and the selection of jurors in *Press Enterprise* lead us to conclude that the right of access applies to preliminary hearings as conducted in California.

"First, there has been a tradition of accessibility to preliminary hearings of the type conducted in California. ***

"The second question is whether public access to preliminary hearings as they are conducted in California plays a particularly significant positive role in the actual functioning of the process. ***

"It is true that unlike a criminal trial, the California preliminary hearing cannot result in the conviction of the accused and the adjudication is before a magistrate or other judicial officer without a jury. But these features, standing alone, do not make public access any less essential to the proper functioning of the proceedings in the overall criminal justice process. Because of its extensive scope, the preliminary hearing is often the final and most important step in the criminal proceedings. As the California Supreme Court stated in *San Jose Mercury-News v. Municipal Court,* 30 Cal. 3d 498 (1982), the preliminary hearing in many cases provides 'the sole occasion for public observation of the criminal justice system.'

"Similarly, the absence of a jury, long recognized as 'an inestimable safeguard against the corrupt or overzealous prosecutor and against the compliant, biased, or eccentric judge,' makes the importance of public access to a preliminary hearing even more significant. * * *

"Denying the transcripts of a 41-day preliminary hearing would frustrate what we have characterized as the 'community therapeutic value' of openness. * * *

"We therefore conclude that the qualified First Amendment right of access to criminal proceedings applies to preliminary hearings as they are conducted in California.

* * * "The First Amendment right of access cannot be overcome by a conclusory assertion that publicity might deprive the defendant of that right. And any limitation 'must be narrowly tailored to serve that interest.'"

Disposition: Writ granted; the press has the right to be present at a preliminary hearing unless there is an actual showing that closure is necessary to avoid prejudice at trial.

13-6d *Miller v. California:* 413 U.S. 15, 37 L.Ed. 2d 419, 93 S.Ct. 2607 (1973)

Facts: Miller conducted a mass-mailing campaign to advertise the sale of illustrated books, euphemistically called "adult" material. He was charged for causing five unsolicited, advertising brochures to be sent through the mail. The brochures advertised four books, entitled "Intercourse," "Man-Woman," "Sex Orgies Illustrated," and "An Illustrated History of Pornography," and a film, entitled "Marital Intercourse." The brochures contained some textual material but primarily consisted of very explicit drawings depicting men and women in groups of two or more engaging in a variety of sexual activities with genitals often prominently displayed. The recipient complained to the police. Miller was convicted of a misdemeanor for knowingly distributing obscene matter.

Issue: What is the First Amendment standard for judging obscenity?

Reasoning: * * * "This Court has recognized that the States have a legitimate interest in prohibiting dissemination or exhibition of obscene material when the mode of dissemination carries with it a significant danger of offending the sensibilities of unwilling recipients or of exposure to juveniles. * * *

"This much has been categorically settled by the Court, that obscene material is unprotected by the First Amendment. * * * We acknowledge, however, the inherent dangers of undertaking to regulate any form of expression. State statutes designed to regulate obscene materials must be carefully limited. As a result, we now confine the permissible scope of such regulation to works which depict or describe sexual conduct. That conduct must be specifically defined by the applicable state law, as written or authoritatively construed. A state offense must also be limited to works which, taken as a whole, appeal to the prurient interest in sex, which portray sexual conduct in a patently offensive way, and which, taken as a whole, do not have serious literary, artistic, political, or scientific value.

* * * "We emphasize that it is not our function to propose regulatory schemes for the States. That must await their concrete legislative efforts. It is possible, however, to give a few plain examples of what a state statute could define for regulation * * * (a) Patently offensive representations or descriptions of ultimate sexual acts, normal or perverted, actual or simulated (b) Patently offensive representations or descriptions of masturbation, excretory functions, and lewd exhibition of the genitals.

"Sex and nudity may not be exploited without limit by films or pictures exhibited or sold in places of public accommodation any more than live sex and nudity can be exhibited or sold without limit in such public places. At a minimum, prurient, patently offensive depiction or description of sexual conduct must have serious literary, artistic, political or scientific value to merit First Amendment protections. * * *

* * * "Under a national Constitution, fundamental First Amendment limitations on the powers of the States do not vary from community to community, but this does not mean that there are, or should or can be, fixed, uniform national standards of precisely what appeals to the 'prurient interest' or is 'patently offensive.' These are essentially questions of fact, and our nation is simply too big and too diverse for this Court to reasonably expect that such standards could be articulated for all 50 States in a single formulation, even assuming the prerequisite consensus exists. * * *

* * * "We hold that the requirement that the jury evaluate the materials with reference to 'contemporary standards of the State of California' serves this protective purpose and is constitutionally adequate."

Disposition: Conviction affirmed; a work is obscene if, taken as a whole, it appeals to the prurient interest in sex, portrays sexual conduct in a patently offensive way, and, taken as a whole, does not have serious literary, artistic, political, or scientific value.

13-7 Other Supreme Court Cases

13-7a *City of Houston v. Hill:* 482 U.S. 451, 96 L.Ed. 2d 398, 107 S.Ct. 2502 (1987)

Facts: Wayne Hill observed a friend, Charles Hill, intentionally stopping traffic on a busy street, evidently to enable a vehicle to enter traffic. Two Houston police officers approached Charles and began speaking with him.

Shortly thereafter, Wayne began shouting at the officers in an attempt to divert the officer's attention from Charles. He shouted, "Why don't you pick on somebody your own size?" The officer replied, "Are you interrupting me in my official capacity as a Houston police officer?" Wayne shouted back, "Yes, why don't you pick on somebody my size?" Wayne was arrested under a city ordinance for "willfully or intentionally interrupt[ing] a city policeman * * * by verbal challenge during an investigation." Charles was not arrested. Wayne was acquitted and brought this civil suit to have the ordinance declared unconstitutional. At trial, it was shown that the ordinance had been applied to "arguing," "talking," "interfering," "failing to remain quiet," "refusing to remain silent," "verbal abuse," "cursing," "verbally yelling," and "talking loudly, walking through scene."

Issue: Does the ordinance prohibiting verbal interruption of a police officer in the line of duty unconstitutionally interfere with freedom of speech?

Reasoning: * * * "The City's principal argument is that the ordinance does not inhibit the exposition of ideas, and that it bans 'core criminal conduct' not protected by the First Amendment. * * *

"We disagree with the City's characterization for several reasons. First, the enforceable portion of the ordinance deals not with core criminal conduct, but with speech. As the City has conceded, the language in the ordinance making it unlawful for any person to 'assault' or 'strike' a police officer is preempted by the Texas Penal Code * * * Accordingly, the enforceable portion of the ordinance makes it 'unlawful for any person to * * * in any manner oppose, molest, abuse or interrupt any policeman in the execution of his duty,' and thereby prohibits verbal interruptions of police officers.

"Second, contrary to the City's contention, the First Amendment protects a significant amount of verbal criticism and challenge directed at police officers. * * *

"The Houston ordinance * * * is not limited to fighting words nor even to obscene or opprobrious language, but prohibits speech that 'in any manner * * * interrupt[s]' an officer. The Constitution does not allow such speech to be made a crime. The freedom of individuals verbally to oppose or challenge police action without thereby risking arrest is one of the principal characteristics by which we distinguish a free nation from a police state.

* * * "Today's decision reflects the constitutional requirement that, in the face of verbal challenges to police action, officers and municipalities must respond with restraint. We are mindful that the preservation of liberty depends in part upon the maintenance of social order. But the First

Amendment recognizes, wisely we think, that a certain amount of expressive disorder not only is inevitable in a society committed to individual freedom, but must itself be protected if that freedom would survive."

Disposition: Statute held invalid; nonassaultive, verbal attacks on police officers are protected by the First Amendment.

13-7b *Brandenburg v. Ohio:* 395 U.S. 444, 23 L.Ed. 2d 430, 89 S.Ct. 1827 (1969)

Facts: Brandenburg telephoned an announcer-reporter on a Cincinnati TV station and invited him to a Ku Klux Klan rally. The reporter and cameraman were allowed to film the meeting. The film showed Brandenburg in Klan regalia carrying a gun and making a speech urging others to join the Klan's proposed march on Washington. In the film, he made the statement, "We're not a revengent organization, but if our President, our Congress, our Supreme Court, continues to suppress the white, Caucasian race, it's possible that there might have to be some revengeance taken." He was convicted under Ohio's Criminal Syndicalism Statute, which makes advocating violent means of political or economic change a crime.

Issue: Does a statute that makes it a crime to advocate violent overthrow of the government violate the First Amendment?

Reasoning: * * * "These later decisions have fashioned the principle that the constitutional guarantees of free speech and free press do not permit a State to forbid or proscribe advocacy of the use of force or of law violation except where such advocacy is directed to inciting or producing imminent lawless action and is likely to incite or produce such action. As we said in *Noto v. United States,* 367 U.S. 290, 297–298 (1961), 'the mere abstract teaching * * * of the moral propriety or even moral necessity for a resort to force and violence is not the same as preparing a group for violent action and steeling it to such action.' A statute which fails to draw this distinction impermissibly intrudes upon the freedoms guaranteed by the First and Fourteenth Amendments. It sweeps within its condemnation speech which our Constitution has immunized from governmental control.

"Measured by this test, Ohio's Criminal Syndicalism Act cannot be sustained. The Act punishes persons who 'advocate or teach the duty, necessity, or propriety' of violence 'as a means of accomplishing industrial or political reform'; or who publish or circulate or display any book or paper containing such advocacy; or who 'justify' the commission of violent acts 'with intent to exemplify, spread or advocate the propriety of the doctrines of criminal syndicalism'; or who 'voluntarily assemble' with a group formed 'to teach or advocate the doctrines of criminal syndicalism.' Neither the indictment nor the trial judge's instructions to the jury in any way refined the statute's bald definition of the crime in terms of mere advocacy not distinguished from incitement to imminent lawless action."

Disposition: Conviction reversed; advocacy of violence is protected by the First Amendment unless it is done in a manner likely to cause imminent lawless conduct.

13-7c *Barnes v. Glen Theatre, Inc.:* 501 U.S. 560, 115 L.Ed. 2d 504, 111 S.Ct. 2456 (1991)

Facts: Glen Theatre, Inc. owns two establishments in South Bend, Indiana, that wish to provide totally nude dancing as entertainment. Theater owners and employees filed this suit claiming the First Amendment's guarantee of freedom of expression prevents application of state laws prohibiting public nudity to this form of dancing.

Issue: Can nude dancing be prosecuted under statutes prohibiting public nudity?

Reasoning: * * * "Applying the four-part *O'Brien* [*United States v. O'Brien,* 391 U.S. 367 (1968)] test enunciated above, we find that Indiana's public indecency statute is justified despite its incidental limitations on some expressive activity. The public indecency statute is clearly within the constitutional power of the State and furthers substantial governmental interests. * * * [T]he statute's purpose of protecting societal order and morality is clear from its text and history. Public indecency statutes of this sort are of ancient origin, and presently exist in at least 47 States. Public indecency, including nudity, was a criminal offense at common law, and this Court recognized the common-law roots of the offense of 'gross and open indecency' * * * Public nudity was considered an act *malum en se.*

* * * "But we do not think that when Indiana applies its statute to the nude dancing in these nightclubs it is proscribing nudity because of the erotic message conveyed by the dancers. Presumably numerous other erotic performances are presented at these establishments and similar clubs without any interference from the state, so long as the performers wear a scant amount of clothing. Likewise, the requirement that the dancers don pasties and a G-string does not deprive the dance of whatever erotic message it conveys; it simply makes the message slightly less graphic. The perceived evil that Indiana seeks to address is not erotic dancing, but public nudity. The appearance of people of all shapes, sizes, and ages in the

nude at a beach, for example, would convey little if any erotic message, yet the state still seeks to prevent it. Public nudity is the evil the state seeks to prevent, whether or not it is combined with expressive activity.

* * * "The fourth part of the O'Brien test requires that the incidental restriction on First Amendment freedom be no greater than is essential to the furtherance of the governmental interest. * * * Indiana's requirement that the dancers wear at least pasties and a G-string is modest, and the bare minimum necessary to achieve the state's purpose."

Disposition: Civil suit has no merit; the state can prohibit nude dancing as part of a public indecency statute that punishes all public nudity.

13-7d *City of Newport v. Iacobucci:* 479 U.S. 92, 93 L.Ed. 2d 334, 107 S.Ct. 383 (1987)

Facts: The City Commission of Newport, Kentucky enacted an ordinance prohibiting nude or nearly nude dancing in local establishments licensed to sell liquor for consumption on the premises. Iacobucci, who owned a liquor establishment that offered nude or nearly nude entertainment, challenged the ordinance in federal court on First Amendment grounds. The District Court upheld the constitutionality of the ordinance.

Issue: Can states and/or cities regulate nude dancing at establishments that sell alcoholic beverages?

Reasoning: * * * "The Newport City Commission, in the preamble to the ordinance, determined that nude dancing in establishments serving liquor was 'injurious to the citizens' of the city. It found the ordinance necessary to a range of purposes, including 'prevent[ing] blight and the deterioration of the City's neighborhoods' and 'decreas[ing] the incidence of crime, disorderly conduct and juvenile delinquency.' Given 'the added presumption in favor of the validity of the * * * regulation in this area that the Twenty-first Amendment requires,' it is plain that, as in *Bellanca* [*New York State Liquor Authority v. Bellanca,* 452 U.S. 714 (1981)], the interest in maintaining order outweighs the interest in free expression by dancing nude. The fact that the Commonwealth of Kentucky has delegated one portion of its power under the Twenty-first Amendment to the electorate—the power to decide if liquor may be served in local establishments—does not differentiate this case from *Bellanca.*"

Disposition: Civil judgment for city affirmed; the right to regulate the sale of alcoholic beverages includes the right to regulate nude and nearly nude dancing where alcoholic beverages are sold.

13-7e *Village of Schaumburg v. Citizens for a Better Environment:* 444 U.S. 620, 63 L.Ed. 2d 73, 100 S.Ct. 826 (1980)

Facts: The Village of Schaumburg adopted an ordinance requiring charitable organizations that intended to solicit funds door-to-door or on public streets to obtain permits. Permits were only granted for organizations that spent at least 75 percent of receipts directly on charity. No more than 25 percent could be spent on salaries, benefits, and other overhead costs. Citizens for a Better Environment (CBE), which is registered with the state of Illinois as a charitable trust and has tax-exempt status from the U.S. Internal Revenue Service, was denied a permit because it failed to meet the 75 percent requirement. The Village of Schaumburg alleged that 60 percent of CBE's collections was spent for salaries and benefits for employees. CBE filed a civil suit to have the ordinance declared unconstitutional.

Issue: Can a city place restrictions on the fund-raising activities of charities?

Reasoning: * * * "Prior authorities, therefore, clearly establish that charitable appeals for funds, on the street or door-to-door, involve a variety of speech interests—communication of information, the dissemination and propagation of views and ideas, and the advocacy of causes—that are within the protection of the First Amendment. * * * Canvassers in such contexts are necessarily more than solicitors for money. Furthermore, because charitable solicitation does more than inform private economic decisions and is not primarily concerned with providing information about the characteristics and costs of goods and services, it has not been dealt with in our cases as a variety of purely commercial speech.

* * * "We agree with the Court of Appeals that the 75% limitation is a direct and substantial limitation on protected activity that cannot be sustained unless it serves a sufficiently strong, subordinating interest that the Village is entitled to protect. * * *

* * * "The Village's legitimate interest in preventing fraud can be better served by measures less intrusive than a direct prohibition on solicitation. Fraudulent misrepresentations can be prohibited and the penal laws used to punish such conduct directly. Efforts to promote disclosure of the finances of charitable organizations also may assist in preventing fraud by informing the public of the ways in which their contributions will be employed. Such measures may help make contribution decisions more informed, while leaving to individual choice the decision whether to contribute to organizations that spend large amounts on salaries and administrative expenses.

* * * "The 75% requirement is related to the protection of privacy only in the most indirect of ways. As the Village concedes, householders are equally disturbed by solicitations on behalf of organizations satisfying the 75% requirement as they are by solicitation of behalf of other organizations. The 75% requirement protects privacy only by reducing the total number of solicitors, as would any prohibition on solicitation."

Disposition: Civil judgment for CBE affirmed; the regulation on solicitation based on a percentage of receipts spent on charity violates the First Amendment.

13-7f *Members of Los Angeles City Council v. Taxpayers for Vincent:* 466 U.S. 789, 80 L.Ed. 2d 772, 104 S.Ct. 2118 (1984)

Facts: The Los Angeles City Municipal Code prohibits posting of signs on public property. Taxpayers for Vincent contracted with Candidate Outdoor Graphics Service (COGS) to make and post signs stating "Roland Vincent—City Council." COGS produced 15×44-inch cardboard signs and posted them on utility poles by draping them over cross-arms and stapling the cardboard pieces together at the bottom. City employees routinely removed all posters attached to utility poles. In the week of March 1, 1979, 1,207 signs were removed; 48 were Vincent's and the others were apparently commercial advertising. Taxpayers for Vincent filed a civil suit seeking an injunction to keep the city from removing the signs.

Issue: Does a city have the right to regulate placement of political signs on public property?

Reasoning: * * * "We turn to the question whether the scope of the restriction on appellees' expressive activity is substantially broader than necessary to protect the City's interest in eliminating visual clutter. The incidental restriction on expression which results from the City's attempt to accomplish such a purpose is considered justified as a reasonable regulation of the time, place, or manner of expression if it is narrowly tailored to serve that interest. * * *

"It is true that the esthetic interest in preventing the kind of litter that may result from the distribution of leaflets on the public streets and sidewalks cannot support a prophylactic prohibition against the citizen's exercise of that method of expressing his views. In *Schneider v. State*, 308 U.S. 147 (1939) the Court held that ordinances that absolutely prohibited handbilling on the streets were invalid. The Court explained that cities could adequately protect the esthetic interest in avoiding litter without abridging protected expression merely by penalizing those who actually litter. * * *

* * * "Here, the substantive evil—visual blight—is not merely a possible by-product of the activity, but is created by the medium of expression itself. In contrast to *Schneider*, therefore, the application of ordinance in this case responds precisely to the substantive problem which legitimately concerns the City. The ordinance curtails no more speech than is necessary to accomplish its purpose.

* * * "So here, the validity of the esthetic interest in the elimination of signs on public property is not compromised by failing to extend the ban to private property. The private citizen's interest in controlling the use of his own property justifies the disparate treatment. Moreover, by not extending the ban to all locations, a significant opportunity to communicate by means of temporary signs is preserved, and private property owners' esthetic concerns will keep the posting of signs on their property within reasonable bounds. Even if some visual blight remains, a partial, content-neutral ban may nevertheless enhance the City's appearance.

*** "While the First Amendment does not guarantee the right to employ every conceivable method of communication at all times and in all places, a restriction on expressive activity may be invalid if the remaining modes of communication are inadequate. The Los Angeles ordinance does not affect any individual's freedom to exercise the right to speak and to distribute literature in the same place where the posting of signs on public property is prohibited. To the extent that the posting of signs on public property has advantages over these forms of expression, there is no reason to believe that these same advantages cannot be obtained through other means."

Disposition: Civil judgment for the city affirmed; cities can regulate posting of signs on public property.

13-7g *Clark v. Community for Creative Non-Violence:* 468 U.S. 288, 82 L.Ed. 2d 221, 104 S.Ct. 3065 (1984)

Facts: In 1982, the Community for Creative Non-Violence (CCNV) received a permit from the National Park Service to conduct a winter-time demonstration in Lafayette Park and on the Capital Mall in Washington, D.C., for the purpose of demonstrating the plight of the homeless. They were allowed to construct two symbolic tent cities, but their request to sleep in the symbolic tents was rejected due to regulations that prohibit camping in the area. CCNV filed this suit to prevent application of the anticamping regulations to their proposed demonstration. The District Court ruled in favor of the National Park Service.

Issue: Can demonstrators be prohibited from sleeping overnight in a public park as part of a political protest?

Reasoning: * * * "[A] message may be delivered by conduct that is intended to be communicative and that, in context, would reasonably be understood by the viewer to be communicative. Symbolic expression of this kind may be forbidden or regulated if the conduct itself may constitutionally be regulated, if the regulation is narrowly drawn to further a substantial governmental interest, and if the interest is unrelated to the suppression of free speech.

* * * "The requirement that the regulation be content-neutral is clearly satisfied. The courts below accepted that view, and it is not disputed here that the prohibition on camping, and on sleeping specifically, is content neutral and is not being applied because of disagreement with the message presented. Neither was the regulation faulted, nor could it be, on the ground that without overnight sleeping the plight of the homeless could not be communicated in other ways. The regulation otherwise left the demonstration intact, with its symbolic city, signs, and the presence of those who were willing to take their turns in the day-and-night vigil. * * *

"It is also apparent to us that the regulation narrowly focuses on the Government's substantial interest in maintaining the parks in the heart of our capital in an attractive and intact condition, readily available to the millions of people who wish to see and enjoy them by their presence."

Disposition: Constitutionality of regulation affirmed; reasonable restrictions can be imposed on time, place, and manner of demonstrations.

13-7h *Hoffman Estates v. Flipside, Hoffman Estates, Inc.:* 455 U.S. 489, 71 L.Ed. 2d 362, 102 S.Ct. 2023 (1982)

Facts: The Village of Hoffman Estates enacted an ordinance regulating the sale of drug paraphernalia, that made it unlawful for any person "to sell any items, effect, paraphernalia, accessory or thing which is designed or marketed for use with illegal cannabis or drugs" without obtaining a license. To obtain a license, the business must file affidavits stating that the licensee and employees have not been convicted of a drug-related offense; keep records (including name and address of purchaser) on each sale; allow police to inspect records; and pay a $150 license fee. Flipside, an existing business in Hoffman Estates, filed a civil suit to have the ordinance declared unconstitutional.

Issue: Can local ordinances regulate the sales of drug paraphernalia?

Reasoning: * * * "First, the village has not directly infringed the noncommercial speech of Flipside or other parties. The ordinance licenses and regulates the sale of items displayed 'with' or 'within proximity of' 'literature encouraging illegal use of cannabis or illegal drugs,' but does not prohibit or otherwise regulate the sale of literature itself. Although drug-related designs or names on cigarette papers may subject those items to regulation, the village does not restrict speech as such, but simply regulates the commercial marketing of items that the labels reveal may be used for an illicit purpose. The scope of the ordinance therefore does not embrace noncommercial speech.

"Second, insofar as any commercial speech interest is implicated here, it is only the attenuated interest in displaying and marketing merchandise in the manner that the retailer desires. We doubt that the village's restriction on the manner of marketing appreciably limits Flipside's communication of information—with one obvious and telling exception. The ordinance is expressly directed at commercial activity promoting or encouraging illegal drug use. If that activity is deemed 'speech,' then it is speech proposing an illegal transaction, which a government may regulate or ban entirely. Finally, it is irrelevant whether the ordinance has an overbroad scope encompassing protected commercial speech of other persons, because the overbreadth doctrine does not apply to commercial speech.

* * * "Many American communities have recently enacted laws regulating or prohibiting the sale of drug paraphernalia. Whether these laws are wise or effective is not, of course, the province of this Court. We hold only that such legislation is not facially overbroad or vague if it does not reach constitutionally protected conduct and is reasonably clear in its application to the complainant."

Disposition: Civil judgment for Flipside reversed; local ordinances can regulate the sale of drug paraphernalia.

13-7i *Thornburgh v. Abbot:* 490 U.S. 401, 104 L.Ed. 2d 459, 109 S.Ct. 1874 (1989)

Facts: Regulations of the Federal Bureau of Prisons permit federal prisoners to receive publications from the "outside" unless authorized prison officials reject a specific issue of an incoming publication because it is detrimental to institutional security. Publications can be excluded if they describe procedures for constructing or using weapons, ammunition, bombs or incendiary devices; depict, encourage, or describe methods of escape from correctional facilities or contain blueprints or similar descriptions of specific institutions; describe procedures for brewing alcoholic beverages or manufacturing drugs; are written in code; depict, describe, or encourage activities that may lead to the use of physical violence or group disruption; encourage the commission of crimes; or have sexually explicit material involving homosexuality, sadomasochism, bestiality, or children. In this suit, a class action brought by a group of prisoners and publishers, the District Court upheld the regulation.

Issue: What restrictions can be placed on the First Amendment freedoms of prison inmates?

Reasoning: *** "*Martinez* [*Procunier v. Martinez*, 416 U.S. 396 (1974)] was our first significant decision regarding First Amendment rights in the prison context. There, the Court struck down California regulations concerning personal correspondence between inmates and noninmates, regulations that provided for censorship of [out-going] letters that 'unduly complain,' 'magnify grievances,' or 'expres[s] inflammatory political, racial, religious or other views or beliefs.' ***

*** "[W]e now hold that regulations affecting the sending of a 'publication' to a prisoner must be analyzed under the *Turner* [*Turner v. Safley*, 482 U.S. 78 (1987)] reasonableness standard. Such regulations are 'valid if [they are] reasonably related to legitimate penological interests.'

*** "The Court in *Turner* identified several factors that are relevant to, and that serve to channel, the reasonableness inquiry.

"The first *Turner* factor is multifold: We must determine whether the governmental objective underlying the regulations at issue is legitimate and neutral, and that the regulations are rationally related to that objective. ***

*** "Where, as here, prison administrators draw distinctions between publications solely on the basis of their potential implications for prison security, the regulations are 'neutral' in the technical sense in which we meant and used that term in *Turner*.

*** "A second factor the Court in *Turner* held to be 'relevant in determining the reasonableness of a prison restriction *** is whether there are alternative means of exercising the rights that remain open to prison inmates.' *** As the regulations at issue in the present case permit a broad range of publications to be sent, received, and read, this factor is clearly satisfied.

"The third factor to be addressed under the *Turner* analysis is the impact that accommodation of the asserted constitutional right will have on others (guards and inmates) in the prison. *** Where, as here, the right in question 'can be exercised only at the cost of significantly less liberty and safety for everyone else, guards and other prisoners alike,' the courts should defer to the 'informed discretion of correctional officials.'

"Finally, *Turner* held that 'the existence of obvious, easy alternatives may be evidence that the regulation is not reasonable, but is an "exaggerated response" to prison concerns. *** But if an inmate claimant can point to an alternative that fully accommodates the prisoner's rights at *de minimis* cost to valid penological interests, a court may consider that as evidence that the regulation does not satisfy the reasonable relationship standard.' We agree with the District Court that these regulations, on their face, are not an 'exaggerated response' to the problem at hand: No obvious, easy alternative has been established."

Disposition: Civil judgment for warden affirmed; reasonable regulations based on institutional safety may be imposed on incoming mail.

13-7j *City of Dallas v. Stanglin:* 490 U.S. 19, 104 L.Ed. 2d 18, 109 S.Ct. 1591 (1989)

Facts: The City of Dallas enacted an ordinance restricting admission to certain dance halls to persons between the ages of 14 and 18. The purpose of the ordinance was to provide places where teenagers could socialize with each other without the potentially detrimental influence of older teenagers and young adults. Stanglin operates a skating rink that was divided into two halves separated by plastic cones. One side was designated for dancing by persons age 14 to 18 while the other was open for anyone, regardless of age, who wanted to skate. No alcoholic beverages are served and security personnel are present. Stanglin filed a civil suit to prevent enforcement of the city ordinance. The trial court upheld the ordinance.

Issue: Do age restrictions imposed on public entertainment facilities infringe on freedom of association?

Reasoning: *** "[W]e do not think the Constitution recognizes a generalized right of 'social association' that includes chance encounters in dance halls. ***

*** "We hold that the Dallas ordinance does not infringe on any constitutionally protected right of association, and that a rational relationship exists between the age restriction for Class E dance halls and the city's interest in promoting the welfare of teenagers."

Disposition: Constitutionality of ordinance affirmed; city can regulate purely social contact if done in a rational manner.

13-7k *Thomas v. Chicago Park District:* 534 U.S. 316, 151 L.Ed. 2d 783, 122 S.Ct. 775 (2002)

Facts: A Chicago Park District ordinance requires that a permit be obtained in order to "conduct a public assembly, parade, picnic, or other event involving more than fifty individuals" or to engage in an activity such as "creat[ing] or emit[ting] any Amplified Sound." The ordinance provides that applications shall be processed in the order received and gives the Park District 14 days to grant or deny an application. The ordinance lists 13 specified grounds that can be used for rejecting applications. If it denies an application, it must clearly set forth in writing the grounds for denial and, where feasible, it must propose measures to cure defects in the application. This includes suggesting alternate times and places if the application is denied because a prior request has been granted to use the same facilities. Appeals can be taken to the General Superintendent of the Park District, who must rule on the appeal within seven days. Judicial review may be sought if the appealed ruling is affirmed.

Thomas and the Windy City Hemp Development Board applied for permits on several occasions: Some were granted; others denied. Thomas filed suit alleging denial of constitutional rights under 42 U.S.C. § 1983 because denials of permits were not automatically appealed to the court system. The trial court granted summary judgment in favor of the Chicago Park District.

Issue: Can a public entity utilize a system for granting permits to hold public meetings without including immediate judicial review of the denial of a request for a permit to use the park?

Reasoning: "Regulations of the use of a public forum that ensure the safety and convenience of the people are not 'inconsistent with civil liberties but . . . [are] one of the means of safeguarding the good order upon which [civil liberties] ultimately depend.' Such a traditional exercise of authority does not raise the censorship concerns that prompted us to impose the extraordinary procedural safeguards on the film licensing process in *Freedman* [*Freedman v. Maryland*, 380 U.S. 51 (1965)].

" . . . The Park District . . . may deny, for example, when the application is incomplete or contains a material falsehood or misrepresentation; when the applicant has damaged Park District property on prior occasions and has not paid for the damage; when a permit has been granted to an earlier applicant for the same time and place; when the intended use would present an unreasonable danger to the health or safety of park users or Park District employees, or when the applicant has violated the terms of a prior permit. Moreover, the Park District must process applications within 28 days, and must clearly explain its reasons for any denial. These grounds are reasonably specific and objective, and do not leave the decision 'to the whim of the administrator.' They provide '"narrowly drawn, reasonable and definite standards"' to guide the licensor's determination. And they are enforceable on review—first by appeal to the General Superintendent of the Park District, and then by writ of common-law certiorari in the Illinois courts . . .

*** "Granting waivers to favored speakers (or, more precisely, denying them to disfavored speakers) would of course be unconstitutional, but we think that this abuse must be dealt with if and when a pattern of unlawful favoritism appears, rather than by insisting upon a degree of rigidity that is found in few legal arrangements. . . . The prophylaxis achieved by insisting upon a rigid, no-waiver application of the ordinance requirements would be far outweighed, we think, by the accompanying senseless prohibition of speech (and other activity in the park) by organizations that fail to meet the technical requirements of the ordinance but for one reason or another pose no risk of the evils that those requirements are designed to avoid. On balance, we think the permissive nature of the ordinance furthers, rather than constricts, free speech."

Disposition: Lower court properly ruled in favor of the Park District; the regulations contained objective provisions for granting permits and an adequate appeals process.

13-7l *Frisby v. Schultz:* 487 U.S. 474, 101 L.Ed. 2d 420, 108 S.Ct. 2495 (1988)

Facts: Schultz, Braun, and other individuals who strongly oppose abortion expressed their views by picketing on a public street outside the home of a doctor who apparently performs abortions at two clinics in neighboring towns. Picketing occurred on at least six occasions for periods of less than two hours each. The size of the groups varied from 11 to more than 40 people. While the picketing was generally orderly and peaceful, it generated substantial controversy and numerous complaints. Brookfield, Wisconsin then adopted an ordinance that completely banned picketing "before or about" any residence. Faced with threat of arrest if they did not cease picketing, Schultz and Braun filed suit to have the ordinance declared unconstitutional.

Issue: Does a restriction on picketing focused on one individual house infringe on the First Amendment?

Reasoning: *** "The antipicketing ordinance operates at the core of the First Amendment by prohibiting appellees from engaging in picketing on an issue of public concern. Because of the importance of 'uninhibited, robust, and wide-open' debate on public issues, we have traditionally subjected restrictions on public issue picketing to careful scrutiny. ***

*** "In short, our decisions identifying public streets and sidewalks as traditional public fora are not accidental invocations of a 'cliche,' but recognition that '[w]herever the title of streets and parks may rest, they have immemorially been held in trust for the use of the public.' No particularized inquiry into the precise nature of a specific street is necessary; all public streets are held in the public trust and are properly considered traditional public fora. *** The residential character of those streets may well inform the application of the relevant test, but it does not lead to a different test; the antipicketing ordinance must be judged against the stringent standards we have established for restrictions on speech in traditional public fora. ***

*** "General marching through residential neighborhoods, or even walking a route in front of an entire block of houses, is not prohibited by this ordinance. Accordingly, we construe the ban to be a limited one; only focused picketing taking place solely in front of a particular residence is prohibited.

*** "The type of focused picketing prohibited by the Brookfield ordinance is fundamentally different from more generally directed means of communication that may not be completely banned in residential areas. *** The type of picketers banned by the Brookfield ordinance generally do not seek to disseminate a message to the general public, but to intrude upon the targeted resident, and to do so in an especially offensive way. Moreover, even if some such picketers have a broader communicative purpose, their activities nonetheless inherently and offensively intrudes on residential privacy. ***

*** "The First Amendment permits the government to prohibit offensive speech as intrusive when the 'captive' audience cannot avoid the objectionable speech. The target of the focused picketing banned by the Brookfield ordinance is just such a 'captive.' The resident is figuratively, and perhaps literally, trapped within the home and because of the unique and subtle impact of such picketing is left with no ready means of avoiding the unwanted speech."

Disposition: Constitutionality of ordinance affirmed; picketing focused on a single residence can be prohibited without violating the First Amendment.

13-7m *Shuttlesworth v. City of Birmingham, Alabama:* 394 U.S. 147, 22 L.Ed. 2d 162, 89 S.Ct. 935 (1969)

Facts: Shuttlesworth, a Negro minister, led a group of 52 Negroes on a march in Birmingham, Alabama on Good Friday in 1963. The participants walked two abreast for four blocks before being stopped by the police. They stayed on the sidewalks except at intersections and did not interfere with other pedestrians. No automobiles were obstructed; nor were traffic signals disobeyed. A crowd of spectators formed and followed the group. Shuttlesworth was convicted for organizing a parade without a permit. Evidence at trial showed that no permit had been sought because his group had previously applied for permits and had been categorically refused. He was sentenced to 90 days at hard labor with an additional 48 days at hard labor in default of payment of a $75 fine and $24 costs.

Issue: Can a city deny the right to hold parades based on the general welfare without infringing on First Amendment rights?

Reasoning: * * * "There can be no doubt that the Birmingham ordinance, as it was written, conferred upon the City Commission virtually unbridled and absolute power to prohibit any 'parade,' 'procession,' or 'demonstration' on the city's streets or public ways. For in deciding whether or not to withhold a permit, the members of the Commission were to be guided only by their own ideas of 'public welfare, peace, safety, health, decency, good order, morals or convenience.' This ordinance as it was written, therefore, fell squarely within the ambit of the many decisions of this Court over the last 30 years, holding that a law subjecting the exercise of First Amendment freedoms to the prior restraint of a license, without narrow, objective, and definite standards to guide the licensing authority, is unconstitutional * * *. And our decisions have made clear that a person faced with such an unconstitutional licensing law may ignore it and engage with impunity in the exercise of the right of free expression for which the law purports to require a license * * *.

* * * "Even when the use of its public streets and sidewalks is involved, therefore, a municipality may not empower its licensing officials to roam essentially at will, dispensing or withholding permission to speak, assem-

ble, picket, or parade, according to their own opinions regarding the potential effect of the activity in question on the 'welfare,' 'decency,' or 'morals' of the community."

Disposition: Conviction reversed; the ordinance requiring a parade permit must give very specific guidelines, based on valid constitutional reasons, for denying permits.

13-7n *Houchins v. KQED, Inc.:* 438 U.S. 1, 57 L.Ed. 2d 553, 98 S.Ct. 2588 (1978)

Facts: On March 31, 1975, KQED, which operated radio and television stations in the San Francisco Bay Area, ran a story on the suicide of a prisoner in the Greystone portion of the Santa Rita jail. This report included statements by a psychiatrist that jail conditions were responsible for the illness of the prisoner, and a denial by Houchins (the Sheriff). KQED requested permission to inspect the Greystone facility and take pictures. This civil suit was filed after the request was denied.

Issue: Does the press have a First Amendment right of access to custodial facilities?

Reasoning: *** "The public importance of conditions in penal facilities and the media's role of providing information afford no basis for reading into the Constitution a right of the public or the media to enter these institutions, with camera equipment, and take moving and still pictures of inmates for broadcast purposes. This Court has never intimated a First Amendment guarantee of a right of access to all sources of information within government control. ***

*** "The respondents' argument is flawed, not only because it lacks precedential support and is contrary to statements in this Court's opinions, but also because it invites the Court to involve itself in what is clearly a legislative task which the Constitution has left to the political process. Whether the government should open penal institutions in the manner sought by respondents is a question of policy which a legislative body might appropriately resolve one way or the other.

*** "Neither the First Amendment nor the Fourteenth Amendment mandates a right of access to government information or sources of information within the government's control. Under our holdings in *Pell v. Procunier* [417 U.S. 817 (1974)], and *Saxbe v. Washington Post* [417 U.S. 843 (1974)], until the political branches decree otherwise, as they are free to do, the media have no special right of access to the Alameda County Jail different from or greater than that accorded the public generally."

Disposition: Denial of access to jail affirmed; the media have no First Amendment right to access to jail facilities different from the rights of the general public.

13-7o *Nebraska Press Association v. Stuart:* 427 U.S. 539, 49 L.Ed. 2d 683, 96 S.Ct. 2791 (1976)

Facts: Six members of a family in Sutherland, Nebraska (a town of 850 people) were murdered. Simants was arrested and arraigned the next morning. Three days later, the local judge granted the prosecution's request for a "gag order" prohibiting those in attendance at the hearing from "releasing or authorizing the release for public dissemination in any form or manner whatsoever any testimony given or evidence adduced." The same "gag order" covered the preliminary hearing, which was open to the public. The Nebraska Press Association's petition for leave to intervene was granted and a new "gag order" was issued prohibiting reporting on five subjects: confessions Simants made to law enforcement, which had been introduced in open court at the arraignment; statements Simants made to other persons; contents of a note Simants wrote on the night of the crime; certain aspects of the medical testimony at the preliminary hearing; and the identity of victims of the alleged sexual assault and the nature of the assault. The media were also prohibited from reporting on the exact nature of the "gag order."

Issue: Can judges issue "gag orders" to prevent the press from reporting on cases prior to trial?

Reasoning: *** "We turn now to the record in this case to determine whether *** 'the gravity of the "evil," discounted by its improbability, justifies such invasion of free speech as is necessary to avoid the danger.' To do so, we must examine the evidence before the trial judge when the order was entered to determine (a) the nature and extent of pretrial news coverage; (b) whether other measures would be likely to mitigate the effects of unrestrained pretrial publicity; and (c) how effectively a restraining order would operate to prevent the threatened danger. The precise terms of the restraining order are also important. We must then consider whether the record supports the entry of a prior restraint on publication, one of the most extraordinary remedies known to our jurisprudence.

*** "Most of the alternatives to prior restraint of publication in these circumstances were discussed with obvious approval in *Sheppard v. Maxwell,* 384 U.S. 333, 357–362 (1966): (a) change of trial venue to a place less exposed to the intense publicity that seemed imminent in Lincoln

County; (b) postponement of the trial to allow public attention to subside; (c) searching questioning of prospective jurors *** to screen out those with fixed opinions as to guilt or innocence; (d) the use of emphatic and clear instructions on the sworn duty of each juror to decide the issues only on evidence presented in open court. Sequestration of jurors is, of course, always available. Although that measure insulates jurors only after they are sworn, it also enhances the likelihood of dissipating the impact of pretrial publicity and emphasizes the elements of the jurors' oath.

*** "We have noted earlier that pretrial publicity, even if pervasive and concentrated, cannot be regarded as leading automatically and in every kind of criminal case to an unfair trial. *** Appellate evaluations as to the impact of publicity take into account what other measures were used to mitigate the adverse effects of publicity. ***

*** "To the extent that this order prohibited the reporting of evidence adduced at the open preliminary hearing, it plainly violated settled principles: *** once a public hearing had been held, what transpired there could not be subject to prior restraint.

*** "Our analysis ends as it began, with a confrontation between prior restraint imposed to protect one vital constitutional guarantee and the explicit command of another that the freedom to speak and publish shall not be abridged. We reaffirm that the guarantees of freedom of expression are not an absolute prohibition under all circumstances, but the barriers to prior restraint remain high and the presumption against its use continues intact. We hold that, with respect to the order entered in this case prohibiting reporting or commentary on judicial proceedings held in public, the barriers have not been overcome; to the extent that this order restrained publication of such material, it is clearly invalid. To the extent that it prohibited publication based on information gained from other sources, we conclude that the heavy burden imposed as a condition to securing a prior restraint was not met and the judgment of the Nebraska Supreme Court is therefore reversed."

Disposition: Gag order reversed; prior restraint of the press is allowed only in special circumstances and must be very narrowly defined.

13-7p *Gentile v. State Bar of Nevada:* 501 U.S. 1030, 115 L.Ed. 2d 888, 111 S.Ct. 2720 (1991)

Facts: A few hours after his client was indicted, Gentile held a press conference at which he made a prepared statement and then responded to questions. In his statement, he alleged that: His client was innocent of stealing 4 kilograms of cocaine and $300,000 in traveler's checks from a deposit box police used at Western Vault Corporation, which the client owned; Detective Scholl was the guilty party; other alleged theft victims, who had deposit boxes at Western Vault Corporation, were convicted drug dealers and money launderers whom the police considered incredible liars until they needed their testimony in this case; four of the alleged victims made no police reports of the thefts until after the police publicly announced that the items were missing. Six months later, the client was acquitted and the State Bar of Nevada brought disciplinary charges against Gentile for violating State Bar Rule 177. The ruler, which Nevada enacted from Rule 3.6 of ABA Model Rules of Professional Conduct, prohibits attorneys from making "an extrajudicial statement that a reasonable person would expect to be disseminated by means of public communication if the lawyer knows or reasonably should know that it will have a substantial likelihood of materially prejudicing an adjudicative proceeding." Gentile appealed the "private reprimand" imposed by the State Bar for statements made at the press conference.

Issue: Can a lawyer be punished for holding news conferences and disclosing facts relevant to the defense's theory of the case?

Reasoning: *** "[T]he speech of lawyers representing clients in pending cases may be regulated under a less demanding standard than that established for regulation of the press in *Nebraska Press Assn. v. Stuart,* 427 U.S. 539 (1976), and the cases which preceded it. Lawyers representing clients in pending cases are key participants in the criminal justice system, and the State may demand some adherence to the precepts of that system in regulating their speech as well as their conduct. *** Because lawyers have special access to information through discovery and client communications, their extrajudicial statements pose a threat to the fairness of a pending proceeding since lawyers' statements are likely to be received as especially authoritative. We agree with the majority of the States that the 'substantial likelihood of material prejudice' standard constitutes a constitutionally permissible balance between the First Amendment rights of attorneys in pending cases and the state's interest in fair trials.

***"Few, if any, interests under the Constitution are more fundamental than the rights to a fair trial by 'impartial' jurors, and an outcome affected by extrajudicial statements would violate that fundamental right. Even if a fair trial can ultimately be ensured through *voir dire,* change of venue, or some other device, these measures entail serious costs to the system. *** The State has a substantial interest in preventing officers of the court, such as lawyers, from imposing such costs on the judicial system and on the litigants.

"The restraint of speech is narrowly tailored to achieve those objectives. The regulation of attorneys' speech is limited—it applies only to speech that is substantially likely to have a materially prejudicial effect; it is neutral as to points of view, applying equally to all attorneys participating in a pending case; and it merely postpones the attorney's comments until after the trial. While supported by the substantial state interest in preventing prejudice to an adjudicative proceeding by those who have a duty to protect its integrity, the rule is limited on its face to preventing only speech having a substantial likelihood of materially prejudicing the proceeding."

Disposition: Reprimand upheld; a lawyer's First Amendment freedom of speech is not violated by the restriction on holding news conferences under circumstances that pose is a "substantial likelihood of material prejudice" to the lawsuit.

NOTE: Application of Rule 177 in this case was not valid because other State Bar rules purporting to explain Rule 177 were void for vagueness.

13-7q *Globe Newspaper v. Superior Court for the County of Norfolk:* 457 U.S. 596, 73 L.Ed. 2d 248, 102 S.Ct. 2613 (1982)

Facts: Globe Newspaper Co. unsuccessfully attempted to gain access to a trial in which the defendant was charged with forcible rape of three minor girls. Both pretrial hearings and the trial were closed under a Massachusetts statute that requires closure to protect minor victims of sex crimes from further trauma and embarrassment. The defendant was acquitted. Globe appealed denial of its motion to open the courtroom.

Issue: Does an interest in protecting victims from publicity justify closing a courtroom to the public and the media?

Reasoning: *** "Although the right of access to criminal trials is of constitutional stature, it is not absolute. But the circumstances under which the press and public can be barred from a criminal trial are limited; the State's justification in denying access must be a weighty one. Where, as in the present case, the State attempts to deny the right of access in order to inhibit the disclosure of sensitive information, it must be shown that the denial is necessitated by a compelling governmental interest, and is narrowly tailored to serve that interest. ***

*** "We agree with respondent that the first interest—safeguarding the physical and psychological well-being of a minor—is a compelling one. But as compelling as that interest is, it does not justify a mandatory-closure rule, for it is clear that the circumstances of the particular case may affect the significance of the interest. A trial court can determine on a case-by-case basis whether closure is necessary to protect the welfare of a minor victim. Among the factors to be weighed are the minor victim's age, psychological maturity, and understanding the nature of the crime, the desires of the victim, and the interests of parents and relatives."

Disposition: Newspaper's appeal granted; the statute cannot make closing of a courtroom mandatory in cases of juvenile victims of sex crimes.

13-7r *New York v. P.J. Video:* 475 U.S. 868, 89 L.Ed. 2d 871, 106 S.Ct. 1610 (1986)

Facts: The police rented ten videocassette movies from P.J. Video. Investigator Groblewski viewed the movies in their entirety and executed affidavits summarizing the theme of, and conduct depicted in, each film. A magistrate issued a warrant for the search of the store and seizure of the 10 movies. Officers executed the warrant the next day and seized one or two copies of each movie. Obscenity charges were filed against P.J. Video on five of the movies. P.J. Video moved for suppression of the evidence because the issuing magistrate had not personally viewed the movies prior to signing the warrant. The motion was granted and the charges dismissed.

Issue: What is the correct standard for issuing a search warrant to seize allegedly obscene material?

Reasoning: * * * "We have long recognized that the seizure of films or books on the basis of their content implicates First Amendment concerns not raised by other kinds of seizures. For this reason, we have required that certain special conditions be met before such seizures may be carried out. In *Roaden v. Kentucky,* 413 U.S. 496 (1973), for example, we held that the police may not rely on the 'exigency' exception to the Fourth Amendment's warrant requirement in conducting a seizure of allegedly obscene materials, under circumstances where such a seizure would effectively constitute a 'prior restraint.' In A Quantity of *Books v. Kansas,* 378 U.S. 205 (1964), and M*arcus v. Search Warrant,* 367 U.S. 717 (1961), we had gone a step farther, ruling that the large-scale seizure of books or films constituting a 'prior restraint' must be preceded by an adversary hearing on the question of obscenity. In *Heller v. New York,* 413 U.S. 483 (1973), we emphasized that, even where a seizure of allegedly obscene materials would not constitute a 'prior restraint,' but instead would merely preserve evidence for trial, the seizure must be made pursuant to a warrant and there must be an opportunity for a prompt post-seizure judicial determination of obscenity. And in

Lee Art Theatre, Inc. v. Virginia, 392 U.S. 636 (1968), we held that a warrant authorizing the seizure of materials presumptively protected by the First Amendment may not issue based solely on the conclusory allegations of a police officer that the sought-after materials are obscene, but instead must be supported by affidavits setting forth specific facts in order that the issuing magistrate may 'focus searchingly on the question of obscenity.'

*** "In our view, the long-standing special protections described above, and enunciated in cases such as *Roaden, A Quantity of Books, Marcus, Heller,* and *Lee Art Theatre,* are adequate to ensure that First Amendment interests will not be impaired by the issuance and execution of warrants authorizing the seizure of books or films. We think, and accordingly hold, that an application for a warrant authorizing the seizure of materials presumptively protected by the First Amendment should be evaluated under the same standard of probable cause used to review warrant applications generally."

Disposition: Charges wrongly dismissed; a judge issuing a search warrant for obscene material may base his/her decision on the facts contained in an affidavit using same the probable cause standard used for other warrants.

13-7s *Reno v. American Civil Liberties Union:* 521 U.S. 844, 138 L.Ed. 2d 874, 117 S.Ct. 2329 (1997)

Facts: Congress passed the Communication Decency Act of 1996 (CDA) to limit exposure of minors to obscene material on the Internet. Two felonies found in Title 47 of the United States Code are challenged in this suit. Section 223(a) applies to "any comment, request, suggestion, proposal, image, or other communication which is obscene or indecent, knowing that the recipient of the communication is under 18 years of age." Section 223(d) applies to using an interactive computer service, such as the Internet, to send or display "any comment, request, suggestion, proposal, image, or other communication that, in context, depicts or describes, in terms patently offensive as measured by contemporary community standards, sexual or excretory activities or organs" in a manner available to a person under 18 years of age. Anyone who knowingly permits any telecommunications facility under his or her control to be used for these activities is also guilty of a federal felony.

Issue: Do the provisions of the Communication Decency Act that prohibit distribution of obscene and indecent material to persons under 18 years of age violate the First Amendment?

Reasoning: "It is true that we have repeatedly recognized the governmental interest in protecting children from harmful materials. But that interest does not justify an unnecessarily broad suppression of speech addressed to adults.

*** "The District Court found that at the time of trial existing technology did not include any effective method for a sender to prevent minors from obtaining access to its communications on the Internet without also denying access to adults. The Court found no effective way to determine the age of a user who is accessing material through e-mail, mail, explorers, news groups, or chat rooms. *** By contrast, the District Court found that '[d]espite its limitations, currently available *user-based* software suggests that a reasonably effective method by which *parents* can prevent their children from accessing sexually explicit and other material which *parents* may believe is inappropriate for their children will soon be widely available."

"The breadth of the CDA's coverage is wholly unprecedented. . . . CDA is not limited to commercial speech or commercial entities. Its open-ended prohibitions embrace all nonprofit entities and individuals posting indecent messages or displaying them on their own computers in the presence of minors. The general, undefined terms 'indecent' and 'patently offensive' cover large amounts of non-pornographic material with serious educational or other value. Moreover, the 'community standards' criterion as applied to the Internet means that any communication available to a nationwide audience will be judged by the standards of the community most likely to be offended by the message."

Disposition: Sections 223(a) and 223(d) of the Communications Decency Act violate the First Amendment; other portions of the Act are not affected by this decision.

13-7t *Osbourne v. Ohio:* 495 U.S. 103, 109 L.Ed. 2d 98, 110 S.Ct. 1691 (1990)

Facts: Osborne was convicted for possession of child pornography after a search of his home revealed four pictures of a naked boy, allegedly 14 years old, posed in sexually explicit positions.

Issue: Can the possession of child pornography be made a crime?

Reasoning: *** "In *Stanley* [*Stanley v. Georgia,* 394 U.S. 557 (1969)], Georgia primarily sought to proscribe the private possession of obscenity because it was concerned that obscenity would poison the minds of its viewers. We responded that '[w]hatever the power of the state to control public dissemination of ideas inimical to the public morality, it cannot constitutionally premise legislation on the desirability of controlling a person's private thoughts.' The difference here is obvious: The State does not rely on a paternalistic interest in regulating Osborne's mind. Rather, Ohio has enacted Section 2907.323(A)(3) in order to protect the victims of child pornography; it hopes to destroy a market for the exploitative use of children.

"'It is evident beyond the need for elaboration that a State's interest in "safeguarding the physical and psychological well-being of a minor" is "compelling." * * * The legislative judgment, as well as the judgment found in relevant literature, is that the use of children as subjects of pornographic materials is harmful to the physiological, emotional, and mental health of the child. That judgment, we think, easily passes muster under the First Amendment.' It is also surely reasonable for the State to conclude that it will decrease the production of child pornography if it penalizes those who possess and view the product, thereby decreasing demand.

* * * "Other interests also support the Ohio law. First, as *Ferber* [*New York v. Ferber,* 458 U.S. 747 (1982)] recognized, the materials produced by child pornographers permanently record the victim's abuse. The pornography's continued existence causes the child victims continuing harm by haunting the children in years to come. The State's ban on possession and viewing encourages the possessors of these materials to destroy them. Second, encouraging the destruction of these materials is also desirable because evidence suggests that pedophiles use child pornography to seduce other children into sexual activity.

"Given the gravity of the State's interests in this context, we find that Ohio may constitutionally proscribe the possession and viewing of child pornography."

Disposition: Conviction affirmed; the state has a compelling interest in protecting children that justifies criminalization of possession of child pornography.

13-7u *Arcara v. Cloud Books, Inc.:* 478 U.S. 697, 92 L.Ed. 2d 568, 106 S.Ct. 3172 (1986)

Facts: An undercover investigation of illicit sexual activities occurring at "Village Books and News Store" (owned and operated by Cloud Books) revealed that masturbation, fondling, and fellatio were being conducted by patrons on the premises within observation of the proprietor. Acts of solicitation of prostitution were also observed and undercover officers were solicited at least four times by male prostitutes. Based on this investigation, a civil complaint was filed seeking closure of the premises under the New York Public Health Law, which classified places of prostitution, lewdness, and assignation as public health nuisances. The trial court rejected claims that closure would violate First Amendment protections.

Issue: Can "adult bookstores" where prostitution and lewd conduct occur be closed as public nuisances without violating the First Amendment?

Reasoning: *** "It is true that the closure order in this case would require respondents to move their bookselling business to another location. Yet we have not traditionally subjected every criminal and civil sanction imposed through legal process to 'least restrictive means' scrutiny simply because each particular remedy will have some effect on the First Amendment activities of those subject to sanctions. Rather, we have subjected such restrictions to scrutiny only where it was conduct with a significant expressive element that drew the legal remedy in the first place, as in *O'Brien* [*United States v. O'Brien*, 391 U.S. 367 (1968)], or where a statute based on a nonexpressive activity has the inevitable effect of singling out those engaged in expressive activity, as in *Minneapolis Star* [*Minneapolis Star v. Minnesota Comm'r of Revenue*, 460 U.S. 575 (1983)]. This case involves neither situation, and we conclude the First Amendment is not implicated by the enforcement of a public health regulation of general application against the physical premises in which respondents happen to sell books."

Disposition: Civil judgment affirmed; premises are not exempt from public health laws merely because activities protected by the First Amendment are conducted on the premises.

13-7v *City of Renton v. Playtime Theaters, Inc.:* 475 U.S. 41, 89 L.Ed. 2d 29, 106 S.Ct. 925 (1986)

Facts: After holding public hearings and reviewing experiences of other cities, Renton, Washington adopted an ordinance prohibiting any "adult motion picture theater" from locating within 1,000 feet of any residential zone, single- or multiple-family dwelling, church, or park, and within one mile of any school. Playtime Theaters, which intended to convert two existing theaters to exhibit feature-length adult films, filed civil suit to have the ordinance declared unconstitutional.

Issue: Can a city control the location of "adult theaters" by zoning ordinances?

Reasoning: *** "In short, the Renton ordinance is completely consistent with our definition of 'content-neutral' speech regulations as those that 'are *justified* without reference to the content of the regulated speech.' The ordinance does not contravene the fundamental principle that underlies our concern about 'content-based' speech regulations: that 'government may not grant the use of a forum to people whose views it finds acceptable, but deny use to those wishing to express less favored or more controversial views.'

*** "The appropriate inquiry in this case, then, is whether the Renton ordinance is designed to serve a substantial governmental interest and allows for reasonable alternative avenues of communication. It is clear that the ordinance meets such a standard. As a majority of this Court recognized in *American Mini Theatres,* a city's 'interest in attempting to preserve a quality of urban life is one that must be accorded high respect.' Exactly the same vital governmental interests are at stake here.

*** "The First Amendment does not require a city, before enacting such an ordinance, to conduct new studies or produce evidence independent of that already generated by other cities, so long as whatever evidence the city relies upon is reasonably believed to be relevant to the problem that the city addresses. ***

"We also find no constitutional defect in the method chosen by Renton to further its substantial interests. Cities may regulate adult theaters by dispersing them, as in Detroit, or by effectively concentrating them, as in Renton. *** Moreover, the Renton ordinance is 'narrowly tailored' to affect only that category of theaters shown to produce the unwanted secondary effects, thus avoiding the flaw that proved fatal to the regulations in *Schad v. Mount Ephriam,* 452 U.S. 61 (1981) and *Erznoznik v. City of Jacksonville,* 422 U.S. 205 (1975).

*** "Finally, turning to the question whether the Renton ordinance allows for reasonable alternative avenues of communication, we note that the ordinance leaves some 520 acres, or more than five percent of the entire land area of Renton, open to use as adult theater sites. ***

*** "In our view, the First Amendment requires only that Renton refrain from effectively denying respondents a reasonable opportunity to open and operate an adult theater within the city, and the ordinance before us easily meets this requirement."

Disposition: Civil suit dismissed; a city has the right to use reasonable zoning ordinances to control the location of adult theaters.

13-7w *Employment Division, Department of Human Resources of Oregon v. Smith:* 494 U.S. 72, 108 L.Ed. 2d 876, 110 S.Ct. 1595 (1990)

Facts: Smith was fired from his job with a private drug rehabilitation organization because he ingested peyote for sacramental purposes at a ceremony of the Native American Church of which he is a member. He was also denied unemployment compensation. Possession of peyote is a Class B felony in Oregon unless its use is prescribed by a medical practitioner.

Issue: Can the state prohibit use of peyote in a religious ceremony?

Reasoning: *** "The Free Exercise Clause of the First Amendment, which has been made applicable to the States by incorporation into the Fourteenth Amendment, provides that '*Congress shall make no law respecting an establishment of religion, or prohibiting the free exercise thereof.* ***' The free exercise of religion means, first and foremost, the right to believe and profess whatever religious doctrine one desires. *** The government may not compel affirmation of religious belief, punish the expression of religious doctrines it believes to be false, impose special disabilities on the basis of religious view or religious status, or lend its power to one or the other side in controversies over religious authority or dogma.

"But the 'exercise of religion' often involves not only belief and profession but the performance of (or abstention from) physical acts: assembling with others for a worship service, participating in sacramental use of bread and wine, proselytizing, abstaining from certain foods or certain modes of transportation. It would be true, we think (though no case of ours has involved the point), that a state would be 'prohibiting the free exercise [of religion]' if it sought to ban such acts or abstentions only when they are engaged in for religious reasons, or only because of the religious belief that they display. It would doubtless be unconstitutional, for example, to ban the casting of 'statutes that are to be used for worship purposes,' or to prohibit bowing down before a golden calf.

"Respondents in the present case, however, seek to carry the meaning of 'prohibiting the free exercise [of religion]' one large step further. They contend that their religious motivation for using peyote places them beyond the reach of a criminal law that is not specifically directed at their religious practice, and that is concededly constitutional as applied to those who use the drug for other reasons. ***

*** "We have never held that an individual's religious beliefs excuse him from compliance with an otherwise valid law prohibiting conduct that the State is free to regulate.

*** "The government's ability to enforce generally applicable prohibitions of socially harmful conduct, like its ability to carry out other aspects of public policy, 'cannot depend on measuring the effects of a governmental action on a religious objector's spiritual development.' To make an individual's obligation to obey such a law contingent upon the law's coincidence with his religious beliefs, except where the State's interest is 'compelling'—

permitting him, by virtue of his beliefs, 'to become a law unto himself,'—contradicts both constitutional tradition and common sense.

*** "It is therefore not surprising that a number of States have made an exception to their drug laws for sacramental peyote use. But to say that a nondiscriminatory religious-practice exemption is permitted, or even that it is desirable, is not to say that it is constitutionally required, and that the appropriate occasions for its creation can be discerned by the courts. It may fairly be said that leaving accommodation to the political process will place at a relative disadvantage those religious practices that are not widely engaged in; but that unavoidable consequence of democratic government must be preferred to a system in which each conscience is a law unto itself or in which judges weigh the social importance of all laws against the centrality of all religious beliefs."

Disposition: Denial of unemployment benefits affirmed; use of peyote as part of a religious ceremony can be punished under the state's controlled substance laws.

Chapter Quiz

True/False

1. The First Amendment makes a law unconstitutional if it prohibits any form of speech.
2. Laws regulating speech must be content neutral.
3. The First Amendment only protects speech on government property.
4. Permits to use government property, such as a park, can be restricted to gatherings of groups that the government endorses.
5. States can legally enact "hate crime" laws that prohibit all forms of speech that are offensive to an ethnic group.
6. The press has access to trials but can be prohibited from attending pretrial hearings.
7. Judges are encouraged to grant "gag orders" to shield potential jurors from prejudicial pretrial publicity.
8. If a police officer enters an "adult bookstore" and sees magazines that he/she believes are obscene, the officer should seize all of the magazines and take them to a judge for a determination of their legal status.
9. When executing a search warrant in an "adult bookstore," the officer can only seize one copy of each book, film, or magazine listed in the warrant.
10. Proof that an activity is a *bona fide* part of a recognized religious group's doctrines is a complete defense for any criminal charges relating to that activity.

Discussion Questions

1. The local chapter of the Ku Klux Klan has requested a parade permit to march in a Negro neighborhood on Martin Luther King, Jr.'s birthday. The police fear that a violent confrontation will result. Should the parade permit be denied? Explain.
2. The local Kitty Kat Theatre is showing XXX-rated movies and every church in the city has protested. What can be done without violating the First Amendment?
3. A devout Muslim from the Middle East has moved into the city with his four wives. He has shown the district attorney passages out of the Koran that encourage men to have four wives. Can he be prosecuted for bigamy? Explain.

Chapter 14

The Exclusionary Rule

Outline

Although the U.S. Supreme Court has had the power to interpret the Constitution and the Bill of Rights since its inception, few cases involving the Fourth and Fifth Amendments were decided prior to 1914, when *Weeks v. United States* declared that evidence obtained by federal agents during an illegal search could not be used in federal court. The rule did not apply to state and local police. In fact, the rule was so narrow that the Silver Platter Doctrine emerged. This doctrine, which lasted until 1960, allowed evidence obtained unconstitutionally by local law enforcement officers to be used in federal court.

14-1 Basis for Exclusionary Rule

Mapp v. Ohio, decided in 1961, finally made the Exclusionary Rule binding on state courts. While *Mapp* made unconstitutionally obtained evidence inadmissible, it did not provide guidelines to help the police determine when the Fourth Amendment had been violated. The Court issued many decisions in the years following *Mapp* in an effort to clarify the application of the Fourth Amendment.

Over the years, the Supreme Court has followed two key rationales in applying the Exclusionary Rule: (1) deterrence of unconstitutional police conduct; and (2) judicial integrity. The deterrence rationale excludes evidence based on the belief that police officers will be more careful if they know their errors may mean they cannot convict the criminal. The reverse of this argument has been used in recent cases. If the Court believes that application of the rule would have little deterrent value in a specific situation, evidence can be used even though it was obtained in violation of the Fourth Amendment.

The judicial integrity approach excludes evidence because the courts should not be tainted by unconstitutional acts of the police. Very few cases have made judicial integrity the primary basis for their decision. Recent cases barely mention judicial integrity: The dominant rationale is now deterrence.

14-2 Fruit of the Poison Tree Doctrine

The Supreme Court's language in *Mapp* indicated that illegally seized evidence is totally inadmissible in court. Two years later in *Wong Sun*, the Court went even further and declared that evidence derived from illegally obtained evidence is also inadmissible. This is the Fruit of the Poison Tree Doctrine.

At some point, the taint of the original unconstitutional act dissipates. Various factors have caused this result: passage of time; exercise of free will by a person giving the police information; the fact a person has been released from police custody; a lengthy chain of events, etc. No one event automatically stops the Poison Tree Doctrine. The courts analyze all of the facts.

14-3 Exceptions to the Exclusionary Rule

Despite the broad language in *Mapp* and *Wong Sun*, there are many situations in which unconstitutionally seized evidence is admitted in court.

14-3a Good-Faith Exception

In 1984, the Supreme Court recognized a "good-faith" exception to the Exclusionary Rule. Officers must be acting under an objective, good-faith belief that what they are doing is constitutional. They must stay up-to-date on the law, and if they make a mistake, the facts must be such that a reasonable officer could have made the same mistake. If the officer has an ulterior motive, this exception does not apply.

To date, "good faith" has been very narrowly interpreted. It has been applied to the execution of search warrants that appeared to be valid on their face or that had very minor technical defects. An arrest made under a statute believed to be valid, but later ruled unconstitutional by the courts, was upheld. An arrest made in reliance on information in a computerized database that erroneously indicated that there was a warrant out for the suspect was also included in this exception; the Court noted that clerical personnel at the Court, and not law enforcement officers, caused the error. In all three types of cases, the initial arrest or search is not valid, but due to the "good-faith" exception, evidence discovered during the search incident to the arrest or found in plain view while executing the warrant is admissible.

14-3b Inevitable Discovery Exception

The inevitable discovery exception to the Exclusionary Rule is based on the idea that the police would have found the evidence even if they had not used unconstitutional procedures. In *Nix v. Williams,* which established this rule, the fact that hundreds of volunteers were searching for a missing child was used to show that the discovery of the body was inevitable. Each case will, of course, turn on its own facts. The prosecution must bear the burden of convincing the judge that the evidence would have been found by legal methods.

14-3c Independent Source Exception

To admit evidence under the independent source exception, the prosecution must be able to convince the judge that the police discovered the evidence independent of the unconstitutional procedures employed during the investigation. Only the evidence discovered by the legally authorized procedure is admissible. Unconstitutionally seized evidence remains tainted. In *Segura v. United States,* evidence had been illegally observed when the police entered the suspect's apartment immediately after arresting him. Later the police obtained a search warrant, based on legally obtained information, authorizing the search of the same apartment. Evidence not observed during the first search was seized. The Supreme Court found that the search warrant provided an independent source for the evidence seized during the second search. This would not have been so if the illegally seized evidence had been used to obtain the warrant.

The ultimate question is whether the second search or confession is genuinely independent of the prior unconstitutional activity. The credibility of the police officer(s) involved is the crucial factor in this analysis.

14-3d Public Safety Exception

The public safety exception is based on the idea that the police are justified in acting to protect the public from immediate danger even if it is necessary to violate someone's constitutional rights to do so. This exception was used to admit a gun that had been found when officers, immediately after making an arrest, asked where the weapon was hidden. Attempts to learn where a kidnap victim was being detained would have similar results. Only brief, urgent questions are permitted under this exception. Attempts to get a confession do not qualify.

14-3e Procedural Exceptions

A variety of situations have been found to be outside the scope of the exclusionary rule.

Harmless Error

The case will not automatically be reversed if the judge admitted unconstitutionally obtained evidence. The Harmless Error Rule applies to most constitutional violations. The conviction will be reversed if the judge is convinced beyond a reasonable doubt that the illegally obtained evidence influenced the jury's decision in the case.

Grand Jury

The Supreme Court has held that the right of the Grand Jury to investigate criminal cases is so deeply embedded in our legal history that it is stronger than the Exclusionary Rule. Unconstitutionally obtained evidence may be considered by the Grand Jury when deciding to return an indictment even though the same evidence will be inadmissible at trial.

Impeachment

While the Exclusionary Rule prevents the prosecution from using confessions obtained in violation of *Miranda* to establish its case, the rule is not a license to commit perjury. If a defendant takes the witness stand and testifies, statements made to the police can be used to impeach. The statements must relate to the same topics raised on direct examination. Confessions obtained by coercion cannot be used for this purpose. Where relevant, items seized in violation of the Fourth Amendment can also be used to impeach the defendant. The Court has restricted the use of illegally obtained evidence and confessions for impeachment to situations in which a defendant has testified; illegally obtained evidence and confessions cannot be used to impeach other defense witnesses.

Parole Revocation Hearings

The Supreme Court recently addressed the application of the Exclusionary Rule to parole revocation hearings. It balanced the need to search parolees and hold them accountable for their misconduct against the deterrent effect on law enforcement. The holding was that illegally seized evidence can be used at these hearings because the importance of parole supervision far exceeds any marginal effect that enforcement of the Exclusionary Rule might have on the behavior of the police.

Civil Cases

The Exclusionary Rule does not apply in civil cases. This is true even if the evidence was unconstitutionally seized by the police. The Court justified its decision on the grounds that police do not seize evidence for the purpose of civil suits; therefore, exclusion of the evidence would have no deterrent value.

Deportation

The Supreme Court also ruled that unconstitutionally obtained evidence can be used at hearings held by the Immigration and Naturalization Service to deport aliens.

Search by Private Person

The Bill of Rights was designed to protect people from an overbearing central government. Since *Mapp,* the Fourth Amendment has also been used to protect against actions by state and local governments. Under these principles the Exclusionary Rule applies to acts of law enforcement officers but not private citizens. The application of this rule depends on whether a private citizen is working as a "police agent" or functioning independently of the government.

Anyone who is acting at the direction of law enforcement officers is viewed as a "police agent" whether or not the person is paid by the police. For example, if a police officer told Sam, "Please sneak into John's house and bring me samples of the drugs you find," Sam would be acting as a police agent and the drugs would be inadmissible. The same result occurs when the police use highly suggestive, but indirect, comments to encourage someone to obtain evidence under circumstances that would violate the Fourth Amendment if done by the police. Suppose an officer told Sam, "You know, the Supreme Court has tied our hands so we cannot get the drugs. But if someone snuck into John's house and got them, we could make a good case against him." If Sam were to burglarize John's house and obtain the drugs, he would still be acting as a police agent and the drugs would be inadmissible. On the other hand, if Sam took drugs from John's house without prior contacts with the police and turned them over to the officer, the drugs would be admissible at John's criminal trial because Sam was acting as a private citizen and not as a police agent.

14-4 Who Can Utilize the Exclusionary Rule?

The term "standing" is used in a civil case to indicate who has the right to file a law suit. *Black's Law Dictionary* (1996) explains it: "Standing is a requirement that the plaintiffs have been injured or been threatened with injury by governmental action complained of, and focuses on the question of whether the litigant is the proper party to fight the lawsuit, not whether the issue itself is justiciable."

Older cases applied "standing" to Exclusionary Rule issues; the question was not whether there was an illegal search, but assuming there was, did the defendant have the right to have the evidence suppressed? For example, the police illegally searched Jill's apartment and found a stolen TV that Mary left there. Mary was arrested on the theft charge. If Mary filed a suppression motion, the court would first address the question of whether Mary had standing to object to the search of Jill's apartment. Most cases addressing this issue held that Mary did not; only Jill could object to the search of her apartment; therefore, the TV was admissible at Mary's trial.

The Supreme Court no longer uses the term "standing" when discussing the application of the Exclusionary Rule. Instead, it looks at the question of whose rights were violated. When Fourth Amendment issues are involved, the question becomes: Does the person who filed the suppression motion have a reasonable expectation of privacy that was violated by the police? If the person lived at the location that was searched, the answer is yes. This would give the resident the right to have the court proceed to the issue of whether the search was legal. The prosecution would then have the opportunity to introduce evidence showing that the search was legal, and the court would rule on whether the evidence was admissible.

In one case considered by the Supreme Court, a man at a party asked a friend to put a packet of drugs in her purse. The police illegally raided the party and searched the woman's purse. The Court ruled that the man had no expectation of privacy once he gave up possession of the drugs and placed them in the woman's purse; therefore, he could not object to the admission of the drugs at his trial even though they had been seized illegally. Another case involved the search of a car. Several men were riding in a car driven by the owner's brother; the owner of the car was not present. The car was stopped and illegally searched. The Court ruled that the passenger could not object to the search because he did not have an expectation of privacy in the car; he could object to an illegal search of his person.

The most recent case considered by the Supreme Court involved a drug arrest. An officer, acting on a tip, peaked through a gap in the blinds of an apartment window and observed three people packaging drugs. One lived there and the other two had come solely for the purpose of preparing the drugs for sale. The Court ruled that business visitors to a residence cannot object to an illegal search; only the resident's expectation of privacy had been violated. An earlier opinion that allowed overnight guests to challenge illegal searches was reaffirmed.

14-5 Key Supreme Court Cases

14-5a *Mapp v. Ohio:* 367 U.S. 643, 6 L.Ed. 2d 1081, 81 S.Ct. 1684 (1961)

Facts: On May 23, 1957, three Cleveland police officers arrived at Dollree Mapp's upstairs apartment looking for someone hiding out there who was wanted for questioning concerning a recent bombing. They also had information that there was a large amount of "policy paraphernalia" hidden in the home. When the police arrived, they knocked on the downstairs door and demanded to be let in. Mapp called her attorney and then refused to let them in without a search warrant. Officers kept the house under surveillance and three hours later, four additional officers arrived on the scene. When Mapp did not come to the door immediately the officers forced a door open and entered. Mapp's attorney arrived, but the officers would not permit him to see Mapp or enter the house. Mapp met the officers halfway down the stairs and demanded to see their search warrant. One of the officers help up a paper and claimed that it was a warrant. Mapp grabbed it and placed it in her bosom. A struggle ensued in which the officers recovered the paper. Mapp was then handcuffed for being belligerent in resisting their official rescue of the warrant. Mapp, still handcuffed, was forcibly taken to her bedroom where officers searched a dresser, a chest of drawers, a closet, and some suitcases. They also looked in a photo album and through her personal papers. They then searched the rest of the second floor including the child's bedroom, the living room, the kitchen, and the dinette. The basement of the building was also searched. No evidence that a search warrant ever existed was introduced at trial. Mapp was convicted of possession of obscene materials found during the search.

Issue: Is evidence obtained in violation of the Fourth Amendment admissible at trial?

Reasoning: "Seventy-five years ago, in *Boyd v. United States,* considering the Fourth and Fifth Amendments as running 'almost into each other' on the facts before it, this Court held that the doctrines of those Amendments 'apply to all invasions on the part of the government and its employees of the sanctity of a man's home and the privacies of life. It is not the breaking of his doors, and the rummaging of his drawers, that constitutes the essence of the offence; but it is the invasion of his indefeasible right of personal security, personal liberty and private property. * * * Breaking into a house and opening boxes and drawers are circumstances of aggravation; but any forcible and compulsory extortion of a man's own testimony or of his private papers to be used as evidence to convict him of crime or to forfeit his goods, is within the condemnation * * * [of those Amendments].' * * *

"Less than 30 years after *Boyd,* this Court, in *Weeks v. United States,* stated that 'the Fourth Amendment * * * put the courts of the United States and Federal officials, in the exercise of their power and authority, under limitations and restraints [and] * * * forever secure[d] the people, their persons, houses, papers and effects against all unreasonable searches and seizures under the guise of law * * * and the duty of giving to it force and effect is obligatory upon all entrusted under our Federal system with the enforcement of the laws.'

* * * " [T]he Court in that case clearly stated that use of the seized evidence involved 'a denial of the constitutional rights of the accused.' Thus, in the year 1914, in the *Weeks* Case, this Court 'for the first time' held that 'in a federal prosecution the Fourth Amendment barred the use of evidence secured through an illegal search and seizure.' * * *

"In 1949, 35 years after *Weeks* was announced, this Court, in *Wolf v. Colorado,* again for the first time, discussed the effect of the Fourth Amendment upon the States through the operation of the Due Process Clause of the Fourteenth Amendment.* * *

"Nevertheless, after declaring that the 'security of one's privacy against arbitrary intrusion by the police' is 'implicit in "the concept of ordered liberty" and as such enforceable against the States through the Due Process Clause,' and announcing that it 'stoutly adhere[d]' to the *Weeks* decision, the Court decided that the *Weeks* exclusionary rule would not then be imposed upon the States as 'an essential ingredient of the right.' * * *

"Today we once again examine *Wolf's* constitutional documentation of the right to privacy free from unreasonable state intrusion, and, after its dozen years on our books, are led by it to close the only courtroom door remaining open to evidence secured by official lawlessness in flagrant abuse of that basic right, reserved to all persons as a specific guarantee against that very same unlawful conduct. We hold that all evidence obtained by searches and seizures in violation of the Constitution is, by that same authority, inadmissible in a state court.

"Since the Fourth Amendment's right of privacy has been declared enforceable against the States through the Due Process Clause of the

Fourteenth, it is enforceable against them by the same sanction of exclusion as is used against the Federal Government. Were it otherwise, then just as without the *Weeks* rule the assurance against unreasonable federal searches and seizures would be 'a form of words,' valueless and undeserving of mention in a perpetual charter of inestimable human liberties, so too, without that rule the freedom from state invasions of privacy would be so ephemeral and so neatly severed from its conceptual nexus with the freedom from all brutish means of coercing evidence as not to merit this Court's high regard as a freedom 'implicit in the concept of ordered liberty.' * * *

"Moreover, our holding that the exclusionary rule is an essential part of both the Fourth and Fourteenth Amendments is not only the logical dictate of prior cases, but it also makes very good sense. There is no war between the Constitution and common sense. Presently, a federal prosecutor may make no use of evidence illegally seized, but a State's attorney across the street may, although he supposedly is operating under the enforceable prohibitions of the same Amendment. Thus the State, by admitting evidence unlawfully seized, serves to encourage disobedience to the Federal Constitution which it is bound to uphold. Moreover, as was said in *Elkins*, '[t]he very essence of a healthy federalism depends upon the avoidance of needless conflict between state and federal courts.' * * *

"There are those who say, as did Justice (then Judge) Cardozo, that under our constitutional exclusionary doctrine '[t]he criminal is to go free because the constable has blundered.' In some cases this will undoubtedly be the result. But, as was said in *Elkins*, 'there is another consideration—the imperative of judicial integrity.' The criminal goes free, if he must, but it is the law that sets him free. Nothing can destroy a government more quickly than its failure to observe its own laws, or worse, its disregard of the charter of its own existence. As Mr. Justice Brandeis, dissenting, said in *Olmstead v. United States:* 'Our Government is the potent, the omnipresent teacher. For good or for ill, it teaches the whole people by its example * * *. If the Government becomes a lawbreaker, it breeds contempt for law; it invites every man to become a law unto himself; it invites anarchy.' Nor can it lightly be assumed that, as a practical matter, adoption of the exclusionary rule fetters law enforcement. Only last year this Court expressly considered that contention and found that 'pragmatic evidence of a sort' to the contrary was not wanting. * * *

"The ignoble shortcut of conviction left open to the State tends to destroy the entire system of constitutional restraints on which the liberties of the people rest. Having once recognized that the right to privacy embodied in the Fourth Amendment is enforceable against the States, and that the right to be secure against rude invasions of privacy by state officers is, therefore, constitutional in origin, we can no longer permit that right to remain an empty promise. Because it is enforceable in the same manner and to like effect as other basic rights secured by the Due Process Clause, we can no longer permit it to be revocable at the whim of any police officer who, in the name of law enforcement itself, chooses to suspend its enjoyment. Our decision, founded on reason and truth, gives to the individual no more than that which the Constitution guarantees him, to the police officer no less than that to which honest law enforcement is entitled, and, to the courts, that judicial integrity so necessary in the true administration of justice."

Disposition: Conviction reversed; the obscene material found in Mapp's home is not admissible at trial because it was seized in violation of the Fourth Amendment.

14-5b *Wong Sun v. United States:* 371 U.S. 471, 9 L.Ed. 2d 441, 83 S.Ct. 407 (1963)

Facts: Federal agents arrested Hom Way at about 2 A.M. on June 4, 1959 in San Francisco for possession of heroin after six weeks of surveillance. Hom Way, who had never before acted as an informant, told the officers that he had purchased heroin from "Blackie Toy," the proprietor of a laundry facility on Leavenworth Street. At 6:00 A.M., several officers went to the Oye's Laundry on Leavenworth Street, which was owned by James Wah Toy (testimony at trial did not indicate why they assumed "Blackie Toy" and James Toy were the same person). Agent Alton Wong rang the bell and told Toy that he wanted to pick up laundry and dry cleaning. Toy replied that the laundry was not open until 8:00 A.M. As Toy tried to close the door, Agent Alton Wong produced his badge and identified himself as a federal agent. Toy immediately slammed the door and started running down the hallway toward his living quarters. Agent Alton Wong and the other agents broke open the door and followed Toy into his bedroom. As Toy reached into a nightstand drawer, Agent Alton Wong drew his gun and pulled Toy's hand out of the drawer. Toy was arrested and handcuffed. Officers found no narcotics when they searched the premises. When officers told Toy that Hom Way said he sold narcotics, Toy denied the allegation but stated that he knew someone who did. He then named "Johnny" and described the house on Eleventh Avenue where Johnny lived and kept heroin. The agents found Johnny Yee in the bedroom when they entered the house on Eleventh Avenue. Yee surrendered almost an ounce of heroin to the agents. Yee and Toy were taken to the office of the Bureau of Narcotics. Yee claimed that he had received the heroin four days earlier from "Sea Dog." Toy said that "Sea Dog" was Wong Sun and pointed out Wong Sun's house. Agent Alton Wong rang the bell and was admitted to the building by a buzzer. He met a woman on the landing who said Mr. Wong was in the back room sleeping. Officers arrested Wong Sun in his bedroom but found no narcotics when they searched the apartment. Toy, Wong Sun, and Yee were arraigned and each was released on his own recognizance. Within a few days, all three were interrogated at the office of the Narcotics Bureau by Agent William Wong. Each man was told of his right to withhold information that might be used against him and his right to advice of counsel but no attorney was present. After each interrogation, the agent prepared a statement, read it to the suspect, and asked him to make corrections and sign it. Toy refused to sign the statement. Wong Sun acknowledged the accuracy of the statement but refused to sign.

Issue: Can evidence that officers find as the result of information obtained during an illegal search be used at trial?

Reasoning: "The threshold question in this case, therefore, is whether the officers could, on the information which impelled them to act, have procured a warrant for the arrest of Toy. We think that no warrant would have issued on evidence then available. * * *

"It is conceded that Toy's declarations in his bedroom are to be excluded if they are held to be 'fruits' of the agents' unlawful action.

"In order to make effective the fundamental constitutional guarantees of sanctity of the home and inviolability of the person, this Court held nearly half a century ago that evidence seized during an unlawful search could not constitute proof against the victim of the search. The exclusionary prohibition extends as well to the indirect as the direct products of such invasions. * * *

"The exclusionary rule has traditionally barred from trial physical, tangible materials obtained either during or as a direct result of an unlawful invasion. It follows from our holding in *Silverman v. United States* that the Fourth Amendment may protect against the overhearing of verbal statements as well as against the more traditional seizure of 'papers and effects.' Similarly, testimony as to matters observed during an unlawful invasion has been excluded in order to enforce the basic constitutional policies. Thus, verbal evidence which derives so immediately from an unlawful entry and an unauthorized arrest as the officers' action in the present case is no less the 'fruit' of official illegality than the more common tangible fruits of the unwarranted intrusion. Nor do the policies underlying the exclusionary rule invite any logical distinction between physical and verbal evidence. Either in terms of deterring lawless conduct by federal officers, or of closing the doors of the federal courts to any use of evidence unconstitutionally obtained, the danger in relaxing the exclusionary rules in the case of verbal evidence would seem too great to warrant introducing such a distinction.

"The Government argues that Toy's statement to the officers in his bedroom, although closely consequent upon the invasion which we hold unlawful, were nevertheless admissible because they resulted from 'an intervening independent act of free will.' This contention, however, takes insufficient account of the circumstances. Six or seven officers had broken the door and followed on Toy's heels into the bedroom where his wife and child were sleeping. He had been almost immediately handcuffed and arrested. Under such circumstances it is unreasonable to infer that Toy's response was sufficiently an act of free will to purge the primary taint of the unlawful invasion. * * *

"We now consider whether the exclusion of Toy's declarations requires also the exclusion of the narcotics taken from Yee, to which those declarations led the police. The prosecutor candidly told the trial court that 'we wouldn't have found those drugs except that Mr. Toy helped us to.' * * * We need not hold that all evidence is 'fruit of the poisonous tree' simply because it would not have come to light but for the illegal actions of the police. Rather, the more apt question in such a case is 'whether, granting establishment of the primary illegality, the evidence to which instant objection is made has been come at by exploitation of that illegality or instead by means sufficiently distinguishable to be purged of the primary taint.' We think it clear that the narcotics were 'come at by the exploitation of that illegality' and hence that they may not be used against Toy. * * *

"We turn now to the case of the other petitioner, Wong Sun. We have no occasion to disagree with the finding of the Court of Appeals that his arrest, also, was without probable cause or reasonable grounds. At all events, no evidentiary consequences turn upon that question. For Wong Sun's unsigned confession was not the fruit of that arrest, and was therefore properly admitted at trial. On the evidence that Wong Sun had been released on his own recognizance after a lawful arraignment, and had returned voluntarily several days later to make the statement, we hold that the connection between the arrest and the statement had 'become so attenuated as to dissipate the taint.' * * * "

Disposition: Toy's conviction was reversed; statements made by Toy in his bedroom are inadmissible because officers entered the house in violation of the Fourth Amendment. Statements made by Wong Sun when he voluntarily returned to the Bureau of Narcotics after being released from custody are sufficiently unrelated to the illegal arrest to be admissible.

14-5c *United States v. Leon:* 468 U.S. 897, 82 L.Ed. 2d 677, 104 S.Ct. 3405 (1984)

Facts: In August 1981, a previously untested confidential informant told the Burbank Police Department that "Armando" and "Patsy" were selling large quantities of cocaine and methaqualone from their residence at 620 Price Drive. The informant claimed to have witnessed a sale by "Patsy" five months earlier and observed a shoebox containing a large amount of cash. The informant said that only small quantities of drugs were kept at the residence. An extensive investigation focused on the Price Drive residence and later on two other residences. Cars parked at the Price Drive residence were determined to be owned by Armando Sanchez, who had previously been arrested for possession of marijuana, and Patsy Stewart, who had no criminal record. During the surveillance, a car owned by Del Castillo, who had previously been arrested for possession of 50 pounds of marijuana, arrived at the Price Drive residence. A check of Del Castillo's probation records led the officers to Alberto Leon, whose telephone number Del Castillo had listed as his employer's. Leon had been arrested in 1980 on drug charges and an informant had told police Leon was heavily involved in importing drugs and stored a large quantity of methaqualone at his residence in Glendale.

Officers noted several people enter the Price Drive residence, stay a short time, and leave with small paper bags. They also observed Sanchez and Stewart board separate flights for Miami and later return to Los Angeles together. Upon their return, they consented to a search of their luggage at the airport, but officers found only a small quantity of marijuana.

An affidavit was prepared summarizing all the facts discovered during the investigation. A facially valid search warrant was issued and large quantities of drugs were found at two addresses and a small quantity at the Price Drive residence. Evidence was also found in Stewart's and Del Castillo's automobiles. The respondents were indicted for conspiracy to possess and distribute cocaine. The respondents' suppression motion was granted because the affidavit did not establish probable cause but the District Court did not suppress all of the evidence because some of the defendants lacked standing.

Issue: Does the Exclusionary Rule require the suppression of evidence discovered in good-faith reliance on a facially valid search warrant?

Reasoning: "Indiscriminate application of the exclusionary rule, therefore, may well 'generat[e] disrespect for the law and the administration of justice.' Accordingly, '[a]s with any remedial device, the application of the rule has been restricted to those areas where its remedial objectives are thought most efficaciously served.' * * *

* * * "[O]ur evaluation of the costs and benefits of suppressing reliable physical evidence seized by officers reasonably relying on a warrant issued by a detached and neutral magistrate leads to the conclusion that such evidence should be admissible in the prosecution's case-in-chief. * * *

"To the extent that proponents of exclusion rely on its behavioral effects on judges and magistrates in these areas, their reliance is misplaced. First, the exclusionary rule is designed to deter police misconduct rather than to punish the errors of judges and magistrates. Second, there exists no evidence suggesting that judges and magistrates are inclined to ignore or subvert the Fourth Amendment or that lawlessness among these actors requires application of the extreme sanction of exclusion.

"Third, and most important, we discern no basis, and are offered none, for believing that exclusion of evidence seized pursuant to a warrant will have a significant deterrent effect on the issuing judge or magistrate. * * *

"We conclude that the marginal or nonexistent benefits produced by suppressing evidence obtained in objectively reasonable reliance on a subsequently invalidated search warrant cannot justify the substantial costs of exclusion. * * * Nevertheless, the officer's reliance on the magistrate's probable-cause determination and on the technical sufficiency of the warrant he issues must be objectively reasonable. * * *

"Suppression therefore remains an appropriate remedy if the magistrate or judge in issuing a warrant was misled by information in an affidavit that the affiant knew was false or would have known was false except for his reckless disregard of the truth. The exception we recognized today will also not apply in cases were the issuing magistrate wholly abandoned his judicial role in the manner condemned in *Lo-Ji Sales, Inc. v. New York*, 442 U.S. 319; in such circumstances, no reasonably well-trained officer should rely on the warrant. Nor would an officer manifest objective good faith in relying on a warrant based on an affidavit 'so lacking in indicia of probable cause as to render official belief in its existence entirely unreasonable.' Finally, depending on the circumstances of the particular case, a warrant may be so facially deficient—i.e., in failing to particularize the place to be searched or the things to be seized—that the executing officers cannot reasonably presume it to be valid."

Disposition: Conviction affirmed; all evidence seized during the execution of the search warrant is admissible because of the officer's good-faith reliance on the validity of the warrant.

14-5d *Nix v. Williams:* 467 U.S. 431, 81 L.Ed. 2d 377, 104 S.Ct. 2501 (1984)

Facts: On December 24, 1968, 10-year-old Pamela Powers disappeared from a YMCA in Des Moines, Iowa. Shortly after she disappeared, Williams was seen leaving the YMCA carrying a large bundle wrapped in a blanket with two skinny, white legs protruding from the bundle. Williams's car was found near Davenport, Iowa (about 160 miles away) the next day. Clothing identified as belonging to Williams and Powers were found at a rest stop on Interstate 80 between Des Moines and Davenport. A warrant was issued for Williams's arrest. Surmising that the body had been left between Des Moines and the rest stop, officers began a large-scale search using 200 volunteers. Meanwhile, Williams was arrested and arraigned in Davenport. Des Moines officers who accompanied Williams on the return trip to Des Moines obtained statements from Williams that led to the discovery of the body. These statements were held to violate Williams's rights in *Brewer v. Williams,* 430 U.S. 387. Williams was retried without use of the incriminating statements and again convicted.

Issue: If there has been a violation of a defendant's rights, can evidence be used in court if it was inevitable that it would have been discovered by officers using constitutional means?

Reasoning: "It is clear that the cases implementing the exclusionary rule 'begin with the premise that the challenged evidence is in some sense the product of illegal governmental activity.' Of course, this does not end the inquiry. If the prosecution can establish by a preponderance of the evidence that the information ultimately or inevitably would have been discovered by lawful means—here the volunteers' search—then the deterrence rationale has so little basis that the evidence should be received. Anything less would reject logic, experience, and common sense.

*** "A police officer who is faced with the opportunity to obtain evidence illegally will rarely, if ever, be in a position to calculate whether the evidence sought would inevitably be discovered. *** On the other hand, when an officer is aware that the evidence will inevitably be discovered, he will try to avoid engaging in any questionable practice. In that situation, there will be little to gain from taking any dubious 'shortcuts' to obtain the evidence. Significant disincentives to obtaining evidence illegally—including the possibility of departmental discipline and civil liability—also lessen the likelihood that the ultimate or inevitable discovery exception will promote police misconduct. In these circumstances, the societal costs of the exclusionary rule far outweigh any possible benefits to deterrence that a good-faith requirement might produce.

"On this record it is clear that the search parties were approaching the actual location of the body and we are satisfied, along with three courts earlier, that the volunteer search teams would have resumed the search had Williams not earlier led the police to the body and the body inevitably would have been found."

Disposition: Williams's conviction at his second trial is affirmed; the victim's body is admissible in evidence because the search team would inevitably have found it without use of Williams's invalid confession.

14-5e *Segura v. United States:* 468 U.S. 796, 82 L.Ed. 2d 599, 104 S.Ct. 3380 (1984)

Facts: In January 1981, the New York Drug Enforcement Task Force received information that Segura and Colon were probably trafficking in cocaine from their New York apartment. Officers set up and observed a surveillance meeting between Segura and Rivudalla-Vidal. Three days later, they set up a meeting at a fast-food restaurant in Queens where a large quantity of cocaine would be delivered. Agents observed the transaction and followed Rivudalla-Vidal and Parra, stopping them as they were about to enter their apartment. A search produced cocaine and the two were immediately arrested. Rivudalla-Vidal agreed to cooperate with the agents and said that he had purchased the cocaine from Segura and that Colon had delivered it to the fast-food restaurant. Rivudalla-Vidal said that Segura was to call him at about 10:00 P.M. to learn if the cocaine had been sold; if so, Segura was to deliver more. About 6:30 P.M., agents discussed the case with an assistant United States attorney. Authorization to arrest Segura was obtained, but no search warrant was issued because the court was closed. Agents were told to make the arrest and secure the premises to prevent destruction of evidence.

Segura was arrested in the lobby of his apartment building about 11:15 P.M. Agents took him to his third-floor apartment; Colon answered when they knocked on the door. Agents then entered without consent and informed the four people present that Segura was under arrest and a search warrant was being sought. Agents conducted a limited security check of the apartment and saw items used for the packaging of drugs in the bedroom in plain view. The items were not seized. Colon was arrested; the search incident to her arrest revealed a loaded revolver and over $2,000 in cash. Agents took Colon, Segura, and the other occupants of the apartment to DEA headquarters. Agents remained in the apartment to secure it until a search warrant was issued about 5:00 P.M. the next day. Agents seized three pounds of cocaine, ammunition, over $50,000 in cash, and records of narcotics transactions during the execution of the search warrant along with the items previously seen.

Issues:

1. Can officers secure a premises during the time it takes to obtain a search warrant?
2. Are the drugs and other items discovered by the agents during the execution of a valid search warrant inadmissible because officers earlier made an illegal entry into the residence?

Reasoning: "The sanctity of the home is not to be disputed. But the home is sacred in Fourth Amendment terms not primarily because of the occupants' *possessory* interests in the premises, but because of their *privacy* interests in the activities that take place within. * * *

"As we have noted, however, a seizure affects only possessory interests, not privacy interests. Therefore, the heightened protection we accord privacy interests is simply not implicated where a seizure of the premises, not a search, is at issue. We hold, therefore, that securing a dwelling, on the basis of probable cause, to prevent the destruction or removal of evidence while a search warrant is being sought is not itself an unreasonable seizure of either the dwelling or its contents. We reaffirm at the same time, however, that, absent exigent circumstances, a warrantless search—such as that invalidated in *Vale v. Louisiana*—is illegal. * * *

* * *"Securing the premises from within, however, was no more an interference with the petitioners' possessory interests in the contents of the apartment than a perimeter 'stake-out.' In other words, the initial entry—legal or not—does not affect the reasonableness of the seizure. Under either method—entry and securing from within or a perimeter stakeout—agents control the apartment pending arrival of the warrant; both an internal securing and a perimeter stakeout interfere to the same extent with the possessory interests of the owners * * *. "None of the information on which the warrant was secured was derived from or related in any way to the initial entry into petitioners' apartment; the information came from sources wholly unconnected with the entry and was known to the agents well before the initial entry. No information obtained during the initial entry or occupation of the apartment was needed or used by the agents to secure the warrant. It is therefore beyond dispute that the information possessed by the agents before they entered the apartment constituted an independent source for the discovery and seizure of the evidence now challenged.

This evidence was discovered the day following the entry, during the search conducted under a valid warrant; it was the product of that search, wholly unrelated to the prior entry. The valid warrant search was a 'means sufficiently distinguishable' to purge the evidence of any 'taint' arising from the entry. Had police never entered the apartment but instead conducted a perimeter stakeout to prevent anyone from entering the apartment and destroying evidence, the contraband now challenged would have been discovered and seized precisely as it was here. The legality of the initial entry is, thus, wholly irrelevant under *Wong Sun* and *Silverthorne*."

Disposition: Conviction affirmed; (1) cocaine, cash, records, and ammunition were properly admitted into evidence because the search warrant was supported by untainted evidence; (2) officers have the right to secure the premises while seeking a search warrant if there is a reasonable fear that evidence will be destroyed if no action is taken.

14-5f *New York v. Quarles:* 467 U.S. 649, 81 L.Ed. 2d 550, 104 S.Ct. 2626 (1984)

Facts: On September 11, 1980, at approximately 12:30 A.M., Officers Kraft and Scarring were on patrol in Queens when a woman approached their car and told them that she had just been raped. The woman gave a description of the suspect and what he was wearing. She told the officers that the man had just entered the A & P supermarket located nearby and that he was carrying a gun. Officer Kraft entered the store while Officer Scarring radioed for assistance. Quarles, who matched the description given by the victim, was spotted approaching a check-out counter. Upon seeing the officer, Quarles turned and ran toward the rear of the store. Officer Kraft pursued him with a drawn gun but briefly lost sight of him when he turned a corner at the end of an aisle. When he regained sight of Quarles, Officer Kraft ordered Quarles to stop and put his hands over his head. By this time, more officers had arrived at the scene. Officer Kraft was the first to reach Quarles. He frisked him and discovered he was wearing an empty shoulder holster. After handcuffing him, Officer Kraft asked Quarles where the gun was. Quarles nodded in the direction of some empty cartons and said "the gun is over there." A loaded .38-caliber revolver was retrieved from one of the cartons. Quarles was formally arrested and given *Miranda* rights, which he waived. Quarles admitted owning the gun and was charged with criminal possession of a weapon.

Issue: Can statements obtained in violation of *Miranda* be used in court if they were obtained in order to protect public safety in an emergency?

Reasoning: "The Fifth Amendment guarantees that '[n]o person *** shall be compelled in any criminal case to be a witness against himself.' In *Miranda* this Court for the first time extended the Fifth Amendment privilege against compulsory self-incrimination to individuals subjected to custodial interrogation by the police. The Fifth Amendment itself does not prohibit all incriminating admissions; '[a]bsent some officially *coerced* self-accusation, the Fifth Amendment privilege is not violated by even the most damning admissions.' The *Miranda* Court, however, presumed that interrogation in certain custodial circumstances is inherently coercive and held that statements made under those circumstances are inadmissible unless the suspect is specifically informed of his *Miranda* rights and freely decides to forgo those rights. The prophylactic *Miranda* warnings therefore are 'not themselves rights protected by the Constitution but [are] instead measures to insure that the right against compulsory self-incrimination [is] protected.' Requiring *Miranda* warnings before custodial interrogation provides 'practical re-enforcement' for the Fifth Amendment. *** "We hold that on these facts there is a 'public safety' exception to the requirement that *Miranda* warnings be given before a suspect's answers may be admitted into evidence, and that the availability of that exception does not depend upon the motivation of the individual officers involved. ***

"Whatever the motivation of individual officers in such a situation, we do not believe that the doctrinal underpinnings of *Miranda* require that it be applied in all its rigor to a situation in which police officers ask questions reasonably prompted by a concern for the public safety. ***

*** "Procedural safeguards which deter a suspect from responding were deemed acceptable in *Miranda* in order to protect the Fifth Amendment privilege; when the primary social cost of those additional protections is the possibility of fewer convictions, the *Miranda* majority was willing to bear the cost. Here, had *Miranda* warnings deterred Quarles from responding to Officer Kraft's question about the whereabouts of the gun, the cost would have been something more than merely the failure to obtain evidence useful in convicting Quarles. Officer Kraft needed an answer to his question not simply to make his case against Quarles but to insure that further danger to the public did not result from the concealment of the gun in a public area.

"We conclude that the need for answers to questions in a situation posing a threat to the public safety outweighs the need for the prophylactic rule protecting the Fifth Amendment's privilege against self-incrimination."

Disposition: Conviction affirmed; the gun found as a result of the defendant's response to Officer Kraft's question is admissible because the purpose of the question was to protect the public's safety.

14-6 Other Supreme Court Cases

14-6a *Arizona v. Evans:* 514 U.S. 1, 131 L.Ed. 2d 34, 115 S.Ct. 1185 (1995)

Facts: Evans was stopped for driving the wrong way on a one-way street in front of the police station. A computer check indicated that there was an outstanding misdemeanor warrant for his arrest. While being handcuffed, Evans dropped a hand-rolled marijuana cigarette. A car search revealed a bag of marijuana under the passenger's seat. It was later determined that the outstanding warrant had been quashed 17 days prior to the arrest, but a court clerk failed to remove the warrant from the database. The trial court granted Evans's motion to suppress the marijuana.

Issue: Does the "good-faith" exception to the Exclusionary Rule apply to erroneous information in a computerized database maintained by the court?

Reasoning: * * * "'The question whether the exclusionary rule's remedy is appropriate in a particular context has long been regarded as an issue separate from the question whether the Fourth Amendment rights of the party seeking to invoke the rule were violated by police conduct.' * * * Where 'the exclusionary rule does not result in appreciable deterrence, then, clearly, its use . . . is unwarranted.'

* * * "If court employees were responsible for the erroneous computer record, the exclusion of evidence at trial would not sufficiently deter future errors so as to warrant such a severe sanction. First, as we noted in *Leon,* the exclusionary rule was historically designed as a means of deterring police misconduct, not mistakes by court employees. Second, respondent offers no evidence that court employees are inclined to ignore or subvert the Fourth Amendment or that lawlessness among these actors requires application of the extreme sanction of exclusion. * * *

"Finally, and most important, there is no basis for believing that application of the exclusionary rule in these circumstances will have a significant effect on court employees responsible for informing the police that a warrant has been quashed. Because court clerks are not adjuncts of the law enforcement team engaged in the often competitive enterprise of ferreting out crime, they have no stake in the outcome of particular criminal prosecutions. The threat of exclusion of evidence could not be expected to deter such individuals from failing to inform police officials that a warrant had been quashed.

"If it were indeed a court clerk who was responsible for the erroneous entry on the police computer, application of the exclusionary rule also could not be expected to alter the behavior of the arresting officer. *** There is no indication that the arresting officer was not acting objectively reasonably when he relied upon the police computer record. Application of the *Leon* framework supports a categorical exception to the exclusionary rule for clerical errors of court employees."

Disposition: Conviction affirmed; evidence obtained during a search incident to an arrest on a warrant erroneously included in a court-operated database is admissible in court.

14-6b *Murray v. United States:* 487 U.S. 533, 101 L.Ed. 2d 472, 108 S.Ct. 2529 (1988)

Facts: Based on information obtained from informants, federal agents set up surveillance on Murray and several co-conspirators. About 1:45 P.M. on April 6, 1983, they observed Murray drive a truck and Carter drive a green camper into a warehouse in South Boston. When Murray and Carter drove the vehicles out about 20 minutes later, the agents were able to see two individuals and a tractor-trailer rig bearing a long, dark container in the warehouse. Murray and Carter later turned over the car and camper to other drivers who were later arrested. Both vehicles contained marijuana. Several agents then converged on the South Boston warehouse and forced entry. No one was in the warehouse but the agents observed, in plain view, numerous burlap-wrapped bales later found to contain marijuana. They left without disturbing the bales, kept the warehouse under surveillance, and did not re-enter until they had a search warrant. Neither the entry into the warehouse nor the bales of marijuana were mentioned in the affidavit used to support the search warrant. Agents entered the warehouse immediately after the search warrant was issued and seized 270 bales of marijuana and customer lists.

Issue: Is evidence seized during plain view during the execution of a search warrant admissible in court if the same evidence was previously observed during an illegal entry into the location?

Reasoning: *** "Knowledge that the marijuana was in the warehouse was assuredly acquired at the time of the unlawful entry. But it was also acquired at the time of entry pursuant to the warrant, and if that later acquisition was not the result of the earlier entry there is no reason why the independent source doctrine should not apply. Invoking the exclusionary rule would put the police (and society) not in the same position they would have occupied if no violation occurred, but in a worse one.

"We think this is also true with respect to the tangible evidence, the bales of marijuana. It would make no more sense to exclude that then it would to exclude tangible evidence found upon the corpse in *Nix*, if the search in that case had not been abandoned and had in fact come upon the body. * * * The independent source doctrine does not rest upon such metaphysical analysis, but upon the policy that, while the government should not profit from its illegal activity, neither should it be placed in a worse position than it would otherwise have occupied. So long as a later, lawful seizure is genuinely independent of an earlier, tainted one (which may well be difficult to establish where the seized goods are kept in the police's possession) there is no reason why the independent source doctrine should not apply.

"The ultimate question, therefore, is whether the search pursuant to warrant was in fact a genuinely independent source of the information and tangible evidence at issue here. This would not have been the case if the agents' decision to seek the warrant was prompted by what they had seen during the initial entry, or if information obtained during that entry was presented to the Magistrate and affected his decision to issue the warrant."

Disposition: Case remanded to District Court to evaluate the facts; evidence seized while executing the warrant is admissible if the probable cause for the search warrant was based on facts independently obtained from the prior illegal entry.

14-6c *Harris v. New York:* 401 U.S. 222, 28 L.Ed. 2d 1, 91 S.Ct. 643 (1971)

Facts: Harris was charged with two counts of selling heroin to an undercover police officer. At the trial, the officer who testified to the details of the two sales was the state's chief witness. A second officer verified collateral details of the sales and a third testified about the chemical analysis of the heroin. Harris took the stand and denied making the first sale but admitted making the second one. He claimed he sold baking powder instead of heroin in an attempt to defraud the purchaser. On cross-examination, he was asked about specific statements he had made to police after his arrest that contradicted his trial testimony. He claimed he could not remember most of the alleged statements. The statements had been obtained after Harris's arrest without giving *Miranda* warnings. He was convicted on the second sale.

Issue: Can voluntary statements obtained in violation of *Miranda* be used to impeach a defendant who takes the witness stand in his own trial?

Reasoning: * * *"*Miranda* barred the prosecution from making its case with statements of an accused made while in custody prior to having or effectively waiving counsel. It does not follow from *Miranda* that evidence inadmissible against an accused in the prosecution's case in chief is barred for all purposes, provided of course that the trustworthiness of the evidence satisfies legal standards.

*** "Every criminal defendant is privileged to testify in his own defense, or to refuse to do so. But that privilege cannot be construed to include the right to commit perjury. Having voluntarily taken the stand, petitioner was under an obligation to speak truthfully and accurately, and the prosecution here did no more than utilize the traditional truth-testing devices of the adversary process. Had inconsistent statements been made by the accused to some third person, it could hardly be contended that the conflict could not be laid before the jury by way of cross-examination and impeachment.

"The shield provided by *Miranda* cannot be perverted into a license to use perjury by way of a defense, free from the risk of confrontation with prior inconsistent utterances. We hold, therefore, that petitioner's credibility was appropriately impeached by use of his earlier conflicting statements."

Disposition: Conviction affirmed; statements made without *Miranda* warnings can be used to impeach if the defendant takes the witness stand and testifies in a manner that is inconsistent with those statements.

14-6d *Pennsylvania Board of Probation & Parole v. Scott:* 524 U.S. 357, 141 L.Ed. 2d 344, 118 S.Ct. 2014 (1998)

Facts: Scott was on parole after being convicted of third-degree murder and serving the minimum sentence. He expressly consented to searches of his person, property, and residence as conditions of parole. An arrest warrant was issued for Scott based on violation of parole due to possession of firearms, consuming alcohol, and assaulting a co-worker. After the arrest, officers went to Scott's home and searched it—they found five firearms, a compound bow, and three arrows. The Board of Probation and Parole found sufficient evidence to support the alcohol and possession of weapons charges and revoked his parole.

Issue: Does the Exclusionary Rule apply at parole revocation hearings?

Reasoning: "In most cases, the State is willing to extend parole only because it is able to condition it upon compliance with certain requirements. The State thus has an 'overwhelming interest' in ensuring that a parolee complies with those requirements and is returned to prison if he fails to do so. The exclusion of evidence establishing a parole violation, however, hampers the

State's ability to ensure compliance with these conditions by permitting the parolee to avoid the consequences of his noncompliance. * * *

* * * " [A]pplication of the Exclusionary Rule to parole revocation proceedings would have little deterrent effect upon an officer who is unaware that the subject of his search is a parolee. * * * The likelihood that illegally obtained evidence will be excluded from trial provides deterrence against Fourth Amendment violations, and the remote possibility that the subject is a parolee and that the evidence may be admitted at a parole revocation proceeding surely has little, if any, effect on the officer's incentives."

Disposition: Parole revocation upheld; evidence seized in violation of the Fourth Amendment can be used at parole revocation hearings.

14-6e *United States v. Janis:* 428 U.S. 433, 49 L.Ed. 2d 1046, 96 S.Ct. 3021 (1976)

Facts: In November 1968, Los Angeles police obtained a warrant to search for bookmaking paraphernalia at two apartments and to search Levine and Janis. They seized wagering records and $4,940 in cash from Janis's property. The police contacted the U.S. Internal Revenue Service (IRS) with the information that Janis had been arrested for bookmaking. The police assisted the IRS in deciphering the coded wagering material and provided information gained during a 77-day surveillance. The IRS made an assessment against Janis and Levine for not paying $89,026 in wagering taxes based solely on information obtained from Los Angeles Police Department. Charges filed in state court were dismissed because the search warrant did not meet the standard set out in *Spinelli v. United States,* which had been decided after the warrant was issued. Eighteen months later Janis filed a civil suit to recover the money confiscated; the IRS filed a cross-complaint seeking the unpaid taxes.

Issue: Can evidence that is inadmissible in a criminal case because it was seized in violation of the Fourth Amendment be used in a civil case brought by a different government agency?

Reasoning: "In the present case we are asked to create judicially a deterrent sanction by holding that evidence obtained by a state criminal law enforcement officer in good-faith reliance on a warrant that later proved to be defective shall be inadmissible in a federal civil tax proceeding. Clearly, the enforcement of admittedly valid laws would be hampered by so extending the exclusionary rule, and, as is nearly always the case with the rule, concededly relevant and reliable evidence would be rendered unavailable. * * *

"If the exclusionary rule is the strong medicine that its proponents claim it to be, then its use in the situations in which it is now applied (resulting, for example, in this case in frustration of the Los Angeles police officers' good-faith duties as enforcers of the criminal laws) must be assumed to be a substantial and efficient deterrent. Assuming this efficacy, the additional marginal deterrence provided by forbidding a different sovereign from using the evidence in a civil proceeding surely does not outweigh the cost to society of extending the rule to that situation. If, on the other hand, the exclusionary rule does not result in appreciable deterrence, then, clearly, its use in the instant situation is unwarranted. Under either assumption, therefore, the extension of the rule is unjustified.

"In short, we conclude that exclusion from federal civil proceedings of evidence unlawfully seized by a state criminal enforcement officer has not been shown to have a sufficient likelihood of deterring the conduct of the state police so that it outweighs the societal costs imposed by the exclusion. This Court, therefore, is not justified in so extending the exclusionary rule."

Disposition: Civil proceedings to collect taxes may continue; the evidence that the state court excluded due to violation of the Fourth Amendment can be used in a federal civil case brought by the IRS.

14-6f *Immigration and Naturalization Service v. Lopez-Mendoza:* 468 U.S. 1032, 82 L.Ed. 2d 778, 104 S.Ct. 3479 (1984)

Facts:

Case 1: Immigration and Naturalization Service (INS) agents arrested Lopez-Mendoza at his place of employment, a transmission repair shop in San Mateo, California. Agents had responded to a tip and arrived at the shop about 8:00 A.M. without a warrant to search the premises. The proprietor of the shop refused permission for agents to interview employees during working hours. While one agent talked to the proprietor, another entered the shop and approached Lopez-Mendoza. In response to questions, Lopez-Mendoza told the agent his name, that he was from Mexico, and that he had no close relatives living in the area. Agents arrested him and took him to the INS office where, during additional questioning, he admitted that he was born in Mexico, was still a Mexican citizen, and had entered the United States illegally. Lopez-Mendoza was ruled deportable by an immigration judge in a civil proceeding.

Case 2: INS agents arrested Sandoval-Sanchez in 1977 at his place of employment, a potato processing plant in Pasco, Washington. Agents went to the plant with permission of the personnel manager to check for illegal aliens. During the change of shift, officers stationed themselves at the exists while Agent Bower and a uniformed Border Patrol agent entered the plant. They went to the lunchroom and identified themselves as immigration officers. Many people in the room rose and headed for the exits or milled around; others in the plant left their equipment and started running; still others who were entering the plant turned around and started walking back out. The two officers stationed themselves at the main entrance to the plant and looked for passing employees who averted their heads, avoided eye contact, or tried to hide themselves in a group. Those individuals were addressed with innocuous questions in English. Anyone who could not respond in English and who otherwise aroused Agent Bower's suspicions were questioned in Spanish regarding their right to be in the United States. Thirty-seven employees, including Sandoval-Sanchez, were briefly detained at the plant and then taken to the county jail. Agent Bower was uncertain about some of the facts surrounding the decision to question Sandoval-Sanchez. Sandoval-Sanchez exercised his right to a deportation hearing. Agent Bower questioned Sandoval-Sanchez further and recorded his admission of unlawful entry.

Issue: Can the INS use illegally seized evidence at a deportation hearing?

Reasoning: "A deportation proceeding is a purely civil action to determine eligibility to remain in this country, not to punish an unlawful entry though entering or remaining unlawfully in this country is itself a crime. * * *

"The deportation hearing is held before an immigration judge. The judge's sole power is to order deportation; the judge cannot adjudicate guilt or punish the respondent for any crime related to unlawful entry into or presence in this country. Consistent with the civil nature of the proceeding, various protections that apply in the context of a criminal trial do not apply in a deportation hearing. * * *

"The 'body' or identity of a defendant or respondent in a criminal or civil proceeding is never itself suppressible as a fruit of an unlawful arrest, even if it is conceded that an unlawful arrest, search, or interrogation occurred. * * *

"Respondent Sandoval has a more substantial claim. He objected not to his compelled presence at a deportation proceeding, but to evidence offered at that proceeding. * * *

"In these circumstances we are persuaded that the Janis balance between costs and benefits comes out against applying the exclusionary rule in civil deportation hearings held by the INS. By all appearances the INS has already taken sensible and reasonable steps to deter Fourth Amendment violations by its officers, and this makes the likely additional deterrent value of the exclusionary rule small. The costs of applying the exclusionary rule in the context of civil deportation hearings are high. In particular, application of the exclusionary rule in cases such as Sandoval's would compel the courts to release from custody persons who would then immediately resume their commission of a crime through their continuing, unlawful presence in this country. 'There comes a point at which courts, consistent with their duty to administer the law, cannot continue to create barriers to law enforcement in the pursuit of a supervisory role that is properly the duty of the Executive and Legislative Branches.'

"We do not condone any violations of the Fourth Amendment that may have occurred in the arrests of respondents Lopez or Sandoval. Moreover, no challenge is raised here to the INS's own internal regulations. Our conclusions concerning the exclusionary rule's value might change if there developed good reason to believe that Fourth Amendment violations by INS officers were widespread. Finally, we do not deal here with egregious violations of Fourth Amendment or other liberties that might transgress notions of fundamental fairness and undermine the probative value of the evidence obtained. At issue here is the exclusion of credible evidence gathered in connection with peaceful arrests by INS officers."

Disposition: Detention of Lopez-Mendoza and Sandoval-Sanchez violated the Fourth Amendment; however, the evidence can be used at the deportation hearing.

14-6g *United States v. Jacobsen:* 466 U.S. 109, 80 L.Ed. 2d 85, 104 S.Ct. 1652 (1984)

Facts: Early in the morning of May 1, 1981, a Federal Express supervisor at the Minneapolis-St.Paul airport asked the office manager to look at a package that had been damaged by a forklift. Following company policy on insurance claims, they opened the ordinary, cardboard box wrapped in brown paper to examine the contents. Inside, they found crumpled newspaper covering a tube about 10 inches long. The tube was made of silver duct tape. They cut open the tube and found four nested, zip-lock plastic bags. The innermost bag contained over six ounces of white powder. They notified Drug Enforcement Administration (DEA). The Federal Express employees returned the bags to the tube and put the tube back in the box before the DEA agents arrived. The first DEA agent to arrive reopened the box and subjected a small amount of the substance to chemical tests. It was determined to be cocaine. Using the results of the field test, DEA obtained a search warrant for the address to which the box was to be delivered. Bradley Jacobsen and Donna Jacobsen were arrested when the search warrant was executed. They were convicted on charges of possession of an illegal substance with intent to distribute.

Issue: Can evidence found due to a search by a private person be examined without a search warrant?

Reasoning: "The initial invasions of respondents' package were occasioned by private action. Those invasions revealed that the package contained only one significant item, a suspicious looking tape tube. Cutting the end of the tube and extracting its contents revealed a suspicious looking plastic bag of white powder. Whether those invasions were accidental or deliberate, and whether they were reasonable or unreasonable, they did not violate the Fourth Amendment because of their private character.

"The additional invasion of respondents' privacy by the government agent must be tested by the degree to which they exceeded the scope of the private search. * * *

"The Fourth Amendment is implicated only if the authorities use information with respect to which the expectation of privacy has not already been frustrated. In such a case the authorities have not relied on what is in effect a private search, and therefore presumptively violate the Fourth Amendment if they act without a warrant. * * *

"When the first federal agent on the scene initially saw the package, he knew it contained nothing of significance except a tube containing plastic bags and, ultimately, white powder. It is not entirely clear that the powder was visible to him before he removed the tube from the box. Even if the white powder was not itself in 'plain view' because it was still enclosed in so many containers and covered with papers, there was a virtual certainty that nothing else of significance was in the package and that a manual inspection of the tube and its contents would not tell him anything more than he already had been told. * * * Respondents could have no privacy interest in the contents of the package, since it remained unsealed and since the Federal Express employees had just examined the package and had, of their own accord, invited the federal agent to their offices for the express purpose of viewing its contents. The agent's viewing of what a private party had freely made available for his inspection did not violate the Fourth Amendment.

"Similarly, the removal of the plastic bags from the tube and the agent's visual inspection of their contents enabled the agent to learn nothing that had not previously been learned during the private search. It infringed no legitimate expectation of privacy and hence was not a 'search' within the meaning of the Fourth Amendment.

"While the agents' assertion of dominion and control over the package and its contents did constitute a 'seizure,' that seizure was not unreasonable.

The fact that, prior to the field test, respondents' privacy interest in the contents of the package had been largely compromised, is highly relevant to the reasonableness of the agents' conduct in this respect. *** The package itself, which had previously been opened, remained unsealed, and the Federal Express employees had invited the agents to examine its contents. Under these circumstances, the package could no longer support any expectation of privacy; *** Accordingly, since it was apparent that the tube and plastic bags contained contraband, and little else, this warrantless seizure was reasonable, for it is well-settled that it is constitutionally reasonable for law enforcement officials to seize 'effects' that cannot support a justifiable expectation of privacy without a warrant, based on probable cause to believe they contain contraband. ***

"A chemical test that merely discloses whether or not a particular substance is cocaine does not compromise any legitimate interest in privacy. This conclusion is not dependent on the result of any particular test. *** Congress has decided—and there is no question about its power to do so—to treat the interest in 'privately' possessing cocaine as illegitimate; thus governmental conduct that can reveal whether a substance is cocaine, and no other arguably 'private' fact, compromises no legitimate privacy interest. ***

"In sum, the federal agents did not infringe any constitutionally protected privacy interest that had not already been frustrated as the result of private conduct. To the extent that a protected possessory interest was infringed, the infringement was *de minimis* and constitutionally reasonable."

Disposition: Convictions affirmed; agents had the right to reopen the package, which was originally opened by a private freight company, and conduct a field test to determine if the substance within was cocaine.

14-6h *Minnesota v. Carter:* 525 U.S. 83, 142 L.Ed. 2d 373, 119 S.Ct. 469 (1998)

Facts: Officer Thielen went to an apartment building in Eagan, Minnesota to investigate a tip from a confidential informant. The officer looked through a gap in the closed blinds and observed several people putting white powder into bags. When Carter and Johns left the building in a previously identified Cadillac, the police stopped the car. As the police opened the door of the car to let Johns out, they observed a black, zippered pouch and a loaded handgun on the vehicle's floor; they then arrested Carter and Johns. The police searched the vehicle the next day and discovered pagers, a scale, and 47 grams of cocaine in plastic sandwich bags.

When a search warrant was executed in the apartment, police found cocaine residue on the kitchen table and plastic baggies similar to those found in the Cadillac. Officer Thielen identified Carter, Johns, and Thompson as the people he had observed placing powder into baggies. Thompson was the lessee of the apartment; Carter and Johns gave her one-eighth of an ounce of cocaine in return for the use of the apartment. Carter and Johns were in the apartment for approximately two and one-half hours for the sole purpose of packaging cocaine and had never been there before.

Issue: Can a person who is visiting a residence for business purposes at the time an illegal search is conducted have the evidence suppressed?

Reasoning: "The text of the [Fourth] Amendment suggests that its protections extend only to people in 'their' houses. But we have held that, in some circumstances, a person may have a legitimate expectation of privacy in the house of someone else. In *Minnesota v. Olson*, 495 U.S. 91 (1990), for example, we decided that an overnight guest in a house had the sort of expectation of privacy that the Fourth Amendment protects. * * *

* * * "If we regard the overnight guest in *Minnesota v. Olson* as typifying those who may claim the protection of the Fourth Amendment in the home of another, and one merely 'legitimately on the premises' as typifying those who may not do so, the present case is obviously somewhere in between. But the purely commercial nature of the transaction engaged in here, the relatively short period of time on the premises, and the lack of any previous connection between respondents and the householder all lead us to conclude that respondents' situation is closer to that of one simply permitted on the premises. We therefore hold that any search which may have occurred did not violate their Fourth Amendment rights."

Disposition: Conviction affirmed; the Fourth Amendment rights of a person who was visiting a residence for business purposes were not violated; therefore, he/she cannot have evidence suppressed.

Chapter Quiz

True/False

1. Since the enactment of the Fourth Amendment, the U. S. Supreme Court has insisted that evidence obtained in violation of this amendment is not admissible in a criminal trial.
2. The Exclusionary Rule originally applied in federal courts but not state courts.

3. The Fruit of the Poison Tree Doctrine applies to evidence discovered due to information obtained through unconstitutional means.
4. The "good-faith" exception to the Exclusionary Rule makes all evidence admissible at trial if it was seized by a police officer who had a good-faith belief that he/she was correctly complying with the Fourth Amendment.
5. The "inevitable discovery" exception to the Exclusionary Rule makes illegally obtained evidence admissible at trial if the judge concludes that it is inevitable that the police would have legally discovered the same piece of evidence.
6. The "public safety" exception to the Exclusionary Rule allows non-*Mirandazied* statements to be used at trial if they are responses to brief questioning done at the time of arrest in order to protect the public from eminent harm.
7. The Exclusionary Rule is not used during Grand Jury hearings.
8. Evidence seized in violation of the Fourth Amendment can be introduced at a probation revocation hearing.
9. Evidence illegally seized by the police can be introduced in civil cases.
10. Only criminal defendants whose personal expectation of privacy has been violated can utilize the Exclusionary Rule to block the introduction of evidence at their trials.

Discussion Questions

1. Officer Wilson entered Bob's house without a warrant. This was a clear violation of Bob's constitutional rights. While in the house, Officer Wilson saw a unique ring on the coffee table. He instantly knew the ring had been stolen during the burglary of Jane's house but had never thought of Bob as a suspect. When he returned to the police station, Officer Wilson asked the fingerprint analyst to compare Bob's fingerprints to those found at Jane's house after the burglary. The prints matched. Officer Wilson then arrested Bob and gave him the *Miranda* warnings. Bob confessed. Can Bob use the *Fruit of the Poison Tree Doctrine* to have the burglary case dismissed? Explain.
2. Officer Jones investigated a robbery and obtained a search warrant for Henry's house. The judge's secretary accidentally left out a paragraph when she typed the warrant. The gun used in the robbery and marked bills were found when the warrant was executed. Is this evidence admissible under the *good-faith exception* to the Exclusionary Rule? Explain.

3. Charles committed a burglary in City A and a robbery in City B. Officers in City A searched Charles's apartment illegally and copied information concerning the burglary from a notebook left on the table. Officers from City B arrested Charles for robbery two days later. During the legal search incident to that arrest, they recovered the same notebook. After reading it, they realized it was vital information regarding the burglary and gave it to detectives from City A. Is the information in the notebook regarding the burglary admissible under the *independent source exception* to the Exclusionary Rule? Explain.

4. Mike kidnapped Mary. Several hours later, police captured Mike, but did not find Mary. Immediately after the arrest, officers asked Mike where Mary was. He told them that she was locked in a closet at a nearby motel. Mike had not been given his *Miranda* warnings. Is this statement admissible under the *public safety exception* to the Exclusionary Rule? Explain.

Chapter 15

The Civil Rights Act

Outline

The Civil Rights Act of 1871 provides individuals redress for violations of constitutional rights by state and local officers; similar protections against violations by federal officers have been created by case law. The Act provides both civil and criminal penalties; Section 1983 of Title 42 of the United States Code, the most commonly used civil section, is the focus of this chapter.

15-1 History of the Civil Rights Act

The Civil Rights Act referred to in this chapter is found in Sections 1981 to 1988 of Title 42 of the United States Code. Corresponding criminal sections, requiring intentional misconduct, are found in Title 18. Since the mid-1960s, the civil statutes have become a major tool for individuals to redress their rights. In the 1960s and early 1970s the Supreme Court took an expansive approach to the coverage of the Civil Rights Act; since that time the trend has been toward a narrower construction.

Due to the historical context in which it was enacted, the Civil Rights Act was originally intended to protect former slaves against oppressive state action. Federal courts were given jurisdiction in order to avoid the hostility of some state courts toward minorities and abolitionists. Section 1983 of the Act specifically applies to: (1) deprivation of constitutional rights; (2) under color of state law. Since the statute makes no reference to racial discrimination, it can be used to vindicate any constitutional violation. Section 1985 covers conspiracies to violate civil rights.

15-2 Constitutional Torts

Congress never expanded the Civil Rights Act to cover actions taken by federal officers. In 1972, the Supreme Court created what is referred to as a "constitutional tort" to provide protection in these circumstances. *Bivens v. Six Unknown Named Agents of Federal Bureau of Narcotics* established the right to sue federal agents for violating Fourth Amendment rights. A wide variety of constitutional deprivations is now covered. There is no corresponding right to sue a federal agency unless sovereign immunity has been waived by statute. *Bivens* suits cannot be brought against private entities who provide services on behalf of the federal government. For example, Correctional Services Corporation (CSC), under contract with the Federal Bureau of Prisons, operates a number of prisons housing federal inmates but inmates cannot sue CSC based on a "constitutional tort."

The Supreme Court has also held that federal prisoners are not required to exhaust their administrative remedies before filing a *Bivens* suit for monetary damages. The decision rested heavily on two factors: Congress had not passed a law requiring such a procedure; and the administrative remedy made available by the Bureau of Prison was ill-defined and ineffective. Changes in either of these factors could result in a different conclusion by the Court.

Federal agents have qualified immunity for making arrests if a reasonable officer could have believed that the arrest was lawful in light of the established law and the evidence available at the time of the arrest. This form of immunity applies even though the officers had a reasonable, but mistaken, belief that probable cause existed. Correctional officers in the Federal Bureau of Prisons are liable for Eighth Amendment violations that create inhumane conditions of confinement only if they know that inmates face a substantial risk of serious harm and then disregard that risk by failing to take reasonable measures to protect the inmate. The question of immunity should normally be determined before trial by the judge and not submitted to the jury.

15-3 Actions Covered

The Civil Rights Act covers all forms of violations of constitutional rights. Suits against criminal justice personnel most commonly focus on violations of the Fourth, Fifth, Sixth, and Eighth Amendments, the Due Process Clause, and equal protection.

The Act imparts no rights itself: The person who files the suit (plaintiff) must show that a specific constitutional right has been violated. Actions taken by the police are covered whether done during a criminal investigation or while assisting in civil matters such as evictions.

The first step in the analysis is to look at the constitutional standard involved. For example, if the suit is based on the search of a home, the Fourth Amendment standards for such searches will be reviewed to determine if there was a constitutional violation.

The second step is to determine the standard of conduct that is covered by the Civil Rights Act. Generally, this will require intentional misconduct; negligence is not sufficient for recovery. In cases alleging the use of excessive force in prisons, the inquiry is whether the force was applied in a good-faith effort to maintain or restore discipline, or if it was done maliciously and sadistically to cause harm. An Eighth Amendment violation can be established even though no serious injuries were inflicted.

In cases regarding destruction of personal property, the Court has noted that the Due Process Clause is satisfied if the state provides adequate civil or administrative procedures to recover the value of the item lost. If such remedy exists, there is no violation of due process even if the property was destroyed intentionally.

The Doctrine of Abstention also comes into play in some civil rights suits. Under this doctrine, the federal courts abstain from interference in state matters if there is a state prosecution pending. The traditional rule of adjudicating only actual cases and controversies requires the Supreme Court to avoid giving advisory opinions; it will not hear a case involving only the possibility that someone's rights might be violated in the future.

Sometimes an inmate attempts to use a Civil Rights Act suit to challenge the constitutionality of a conviction as opposed to seeking damages for an illegal search or confession. To win this type of case, the inmate must show that the conviction has already been invalidated by one of the following procedures: reversed on direct appeal; expunged by executive order; declared invalid by a state tribunal; or called into question by a federal court's issuance of writ of *habeas corpus.* Prisoners must seek redress in state courts first, but even after these avenues have been exhausted, the federal courts will not accept a Civil Rights Act case challenging the constitutionality of a conviction unless one of the previous results was achieved. The same approach is applied to allegations of due process violations in the way prison disciplinary hearings were conducted: Relief is granted only if it is shown that the inmate's conduct did not merit discipline; procedural errors in cases in which the discipline would have been justified are not grounds for recovery.

Civil Rights Act suits have attempted to hold governmental agencies responsible for their employees' actions. The ability to successfully do so is very limited. For example, in a case in which the sheriff failed to seriously consider prior convictions when hiring a deputy, the court held that the county could be forced to pay damages based on inadequate pre-employment screening only if the plaintiffs were able to show that this officer was highly likely to inflict the particular injury suffered by the plaintiff.

15-4 Defenses

Civil rights suits range from flagrant violations of constitutional rights to frivolous suits filed for vexatious purposes. The main defense is usually that no constitutional violation occurred. This analysis is based on an objective review of the evidence. The fact that an officer had subjective bad faith does not alter the conclusion that no violation occurred.

The second line of defense is that the defendant is entitled to some form of immunity. A historical approach is used to determine who has immunity: Those who had tort immunity in 1871, when the legislation was passed, generally have immunity under Section 1983. The Supreme Court also uses this approach to decide whether the immunity is absolute or qualified.

A person with qualified immunity should not stand trial or face the other burdens of litigation. In effect, immunity from suit enables the government employee to have the case dismissed before trial rather than serving as a defense to civil liability. The issue should be ruled on as early in the litigation as possible. When deciding this issue, the trial should first consider whether a constitutional violation occurred: Taken in the light most favorable to the party asserting the injury, do the facts alleged show the conduct violated a constitutional right? If the answer is yes, the court must determine whether the right was clearly established. An officer will *not* be granted qualified immunity if the right was clearly established by prior law so that it would have been clear to a reasonable officer that his/her conduct was unlawful in the situation in question. This does not mean that there must be case law based on exactly the same facts; it is enough if there is precedent that fundamentally similar acts are unconstitutional.

Most actions of local, state, and federal law enforcement officers are covered by qualified immunity if they meet the following criteria: (1) the officer acted in good faith; (2) the officer made reasonable efforts to stay current on constitutional rights; and (3) a reasonable officer would have acted in a similar manner under the same circumstances. While testifying in court, however, officers enjoy the same absolute immunity as all other witnesses: They are not subject to suit under the Civil Rights Act even though they commit perjury.

Prison officials also have qualified immunity. This includes personnel assigned to the quasijudicial function of serving as hearing officers on disciplinary committees. Immunity does not extend to violations of rights clearly established by law at the time of their occurrence or to violations done maliciously. Employees of private corporations who operate prisons under contract with the state or county do not enjoy immunity in Civil Rights Act suits.

Judges have absolute immunity from monetary damage awards for their judicial actions even when acting in bad faith. This immunity does not prohibit issuing injunctions against a judge's prospective conduct nor does it extend to personnel decisions relating to courtroom employees. It also does not prohibit awarding the opposing party attorney's fees if a successful suit is brought against a judge.

Prosecutors have absolute immunity for actions taken within the scope of their duties. Qualified immunity applies when prosecutors give legal advice to police to assist them in an investigation. It is also applied if the prosecutor was involved in fabricating evidence during a preliminary investigation of the case or made false statements at a press conference that prejudiced the defendant's case. Prosecutors who step into the role of complaining witnesses—for example, by signing an affidavit included in the request for an arrest warrant—do not have absolute immunity for false statements in the affidavit.

Public defenders and court-appointed defense attorneys, on the other hand, have been held to have no immunity for intentional misconduct.

Local legislators, such as members of the city council, have absolute immunity for their legislative activities. State and regional legislators also have this type of immunity. For example, they cannot be sued for voting in favor of a law that was later determined to be unconstitutional. This rule applies regardless of the motive behind the actions.

Municipalities are no longer considered exempt from suits under the Civil Rights Act. To establish liability, a policy of disregard of constitutional rights must be shown. They were fact that the city employed the offending police officer, or the fact that a single act of misconduct occurred, is not enough. The city is responsible for failure to train if a pattern of conduct shows deliberate indifference to constitutional rights.

A city cannot be held liable for the actions of its officers unless the offending officer was named as a party to the suit and found to have violated a constitutional right. On the other hand, a city cannot claim qualified immunity for its unconstitutional policies by asserting the good faith of the individual police officer. Municipalities are immune from punitive damages. Release-dismissal agreements, in which a person agrees to forego civil suit if the criminal charges are dismissed, have been upheld.

States are immune from suits in federal court under the Eleventh Amendment. State officials can be sued, however, in their individual capacities. When an individual capacity suit is brought against a state official, the state cannot be required to pay the attorney's fees of the prevailing party.

15-5 Types of Recovery

Compensatory damages are the most common type of recovery in civil rights suits. They provide reimbursement for the plaintiff's expenses, such as medical bills and lost wages, while recovering from injuries. So called "general damages," which are intended to pay for pain and suffering or humiliation, are also allowed in Civil Rights Act suits.

Punitive damages are designed to punish the offender. The jury has discretion to award them in cases that show intentional, malicious conduct or reckless indifference to protected constitutional rights. The amount awarded is tied to the wrongfulness of the conduct and the ability of the defendant to pay, rather than the severity of the physical injury.

Defendants who establish immunity for the actions in question do not have to pay damages. Because officers acting in good faith have immunity, there is no monetary recovery in most suits filed under the Civil Rights Act. Flagrant violations cannot be said to have been done in "good faith," so immunity does not apply. Cases involving gross violations of constitutional rights frequently result in the award of punitive damages. The result of being able to raise immunity as a defense is that very few cases result in the plaintiff recovering money, but in the cases where damages in which awarded, the amount involved is usually large because it includes punitive damages.

An *injunction* (court order prohibiting specified future conduct) can be issued in civil rights cases only if there is an established pattern of disregard for constitutional rights that leads to the conclusion that violations will continue unless the court takes action. It is rare that a court finds that this standard has been met. When it does, the injunction usually orders an agency to change its policies; a monitor may be appointed to supervise compliance.

Section 1988 allows the prevailing party in a civil rights suit to recover attorney's fees but not the expenses incurred for expert witnesses who testified in the case. The judge reviews the bills submitted by the plaintiff's attorneys and determines what the defendant must pay. This statutory provision is contrary to the normal "American rule" that each party pays his/her own attorney. To qualify as a "prevailing party," the plaintiff must have received at least some relief on the merits of the claim. Monetary damages qualify; so do injunctions, declaratory judgments, consent decrees, and out-of-court settlements. Merely surviving a motion to dismiss is not enough nor is establishing the violation of a right when the defendant successfully pleads immunity as a defense.

The size of the monetary damages does not directly limit the recovery of attorneys' fees. The Supreme Court has rejected the theory that Section 1988 is a form of contingency fee agreement that limits the fee to a percentage of the amount recovered. Instead, the fee is based on the complexity of the case, the total hours devoted to the litigation, and the value to society. For this reason, sizable attorney's fees have been awarded for the vindication of constitutional rights that had limited financial impact on the individual plaintiff. Class actions, due to their complexity, frequently result in large awards of attorney's fees.

In some cases, defendants can recover attorney's fees from the plaintiff. To do so, the case must be shown to be frivolous. Successfully having the case dismissed is not enough. The courts have been reluctant to award fees to the defendant unless there is a showing that there is no possible basis for the suit. They have also hedged on making such awards when a *pro per* inmate drafted the pleadings because the lack of merit may be the result of poor draftsmanship rather than the facts of the case.

15-6 Key Supreme Court Cases

15-6a *Bivens v. Six Unknown Named Agents of Federal Bureau of Narcotics:* 403 U.S. 388, 29 L.Ed. 2d 619, 91 S.Ct. 1999 (1971)

Facts: On the morning of November 16, 1965, six agents of the Federal Bureau of Narcotics entered Bivens's apartment and arrested him for narcotics violations. The agents handcuffed him in front of his wife and children and threatened to arrest the entire family. They searched the apartment thoroughly. Bivens was taken to the federal courthouse in Brooklyn where he was interrogated, booked, and subjected to a visual strip search. Bivens filed a civil suit in federal court alleging excessive force in making a warrantless arrest and a search without probable cause. Bivens sought $15,000 from each agent for great humiliation, embarrassment, and mental suffering. The District Court dismissed the case.

Issue: Is there a right to recover civil damages for violations of constitutional rights by federal agents?

Reasoning: *** "The question is merely whether petitioner, if he can demonstrate an injury consequent upon the violation by federal agents of his Fourth Amendment rights, is entitled to redress his injury through a particular remedial mechanism normally available in the federal courts. 'The very essence of civil liberty certainly consists in the right of every individual to claim the protection of the laws, whenever he receives an injury.' Having concluded that petitioner's complaint states a cause of action under the Fourth Amendment, we hold that petitioner is entitled to recover money damages for any injuries he has suffered as a result of the agents' violation of the Amendment."

Disposition: Case dismissed in error; a person can sue a federal agent for violation of his/her constitutional rights.

15-6b *Graham v. Connor:* 490 U.S. 386, 104 L.Ed. 2d 443, 109 S.Ct. 1865 (1989)

Facts: On November 12, 1984, Graham, a diabetic, asked a friend to drive him to a nearby convenience store so he could purchase some orange juice to counteract an insulin reaction. He left the store because there were too many people in line, and asked his friend to drive him to a friend's house. Officer Connor, of the Charlotte, North Carolina Police Department, became suspicious after watching Graham's hasty entry and exit of the store. He stopped the car about one-half mile from the store. The driver explained Graham's problem with an insulin reaction but the officer ordered both men out of the car while he determined what had happened at the store. Due to the force used by the officers, Graham sustained a broken foot, cuts on his wrists, a bruised forehead, and an injured shoulder. Finally, Officer Connor received a report that Graham had done nothing wrong in the store. Graham was driven home and released. He brought a civil suit under the federal Civil Rights Act.

Issue: When can a suspect recover civil damages for the use of excessive force?

Reasoning: *** "We reject this notion that all excessive force claims brought under Section 1983 are governed by a single generic standard. As we have said many times, Section 1983 'is not itself a source of substantive rights,' but merely provides 'a method for vindicating federal rights elsewhere conferred.' In addressing the excessive force claim brought under

Section 1983, analysis begins by identifying the specific constitutional right allegedly infringed by the challenged application of force. In most instances, that will be either the Fourth Amendment's prohibition against unreasonable seizures of the person, or the Eighth Amendment's ban on cruel and unusual punishments, which are the two primary sources of constitutional protections against physically abusive governmental conduct. The validity of the claim must then be judged by reference to the specific constitutional standard which governs that right, rather than to some generalized 'excessive force' standard.

*** "Today we make explicit what was implicit in *Garner's* [*Tennessee v. Garner*, 471 U.S. 1 (1985)] analysis, and hold that *all* claims that law enforcement officers have used excessive force—deadly or not—in the course of an arrest, investigatory stop, or other 'seizure' of a free citizen would be analyzed under the Fourth Amendment and its 'reasonableness' standard, rather than under a 'substantive due process' approach. ***

*** "As in other Fourth Amendment contexts, however, the 'reasonableness' inquiry in an excessive force case is an objective one: The question is whether the officers' actions are 'objectively reasonable' in light of the facts and circumstances confronting them, without regard to their underlying intent or motivation. *** An officer's evil intentions will not make a Fourth Amendment violation out of an objectively reasonable use of force; nor will an officer's good intentions make an objectively unreasonable use of force constitutional."

Disposition: Case is sent back to the lower court; a person states a cause of action under 42 U.S.C. 1983 based on use of excessive force if the conduct was objectively unreasonable under the Fourth Amendment.

15-6c *Pierson v. Ray:* 386 U.S. 547, 18 L.Ed. 2d 288, 87 S.Ct. 1213 (1967)

Facts: Pierson was part of a group of 15 white and Negro Episcopal clergy who, in 1961, engaged in a "prayer pilgrimage" from New Orleans to Detroit. They entered the bus station waiting room in Jackson, Mississippi and disobeyed a sign that announced "White Waiting Room Only—By Order of the Police Department" and then attempted to enter the terminal's restaurant. Two Jackson police officers stopped them and ordered them to "move on." The ministers replied that they wanted to eat and refused to leave. Ray was one of the officers who arrested them for "congregating with others in a public place under circumstances such that a breach of the peace may be occasioned thereby and refusing to move on when ordered to do so by a police officer." Trial testimony indicated that they entered the waiting room peacefully and engaged in no boisterous or objectionable conduct; conflicting testimony characterized the crowd as either a small number of quiet onlookers or 30 people, some of whom were "in a very dissatisfied and ugly mood." A jury was waived and Spencer, a municipal police justice, presided over the trial. Each participant was sentenced to four months in jail and a fine of $200. On appeal, the charges were dropped. A civil rights suit was filed in federal court alleging false arrest and imprisonment. Jury verdicts were in favor of the police officers and judge.

Issues:

1. Do judges have absolute immunity from damages in Section 1983 suits?
2. Can police officers use qualified immunity if their actions were based on probable cause and good faith?

Reasoning: *** "We find no difficulty in agreeing with the Court of Appeals that Judge Spencer is immune from liability for damages for his role in these convictions. The record is barren of any proof or specific allegations that Judge Spencer played any role in these arrests and convictions other than to adjudge petitioners guilty when their cases came before his court. Few doctrines were more solidly established at common law than the immunity of judges from liability for damages for acts committed within their judicial jurisdiction. *** The immunity applies even when the judge is accused of acting maliciously and corruptly, and it 'is not for the protection or benefit of a malicious or corrupt judge, but for the benefit of the public, whose interest it is that the judges should be at liberty to exercise their functions with independence and without fear of consequences.' It is a judge's duty to decide all cases within his jurisdiction that are brought before him, including controversial cases that arouse the most intense feelings in the litigants. His errors may be corrected on appeal, but he should not have to fear that unsatisfied litigants may hound him with litigation charging malice or corruption. Imposing such a burden on judges would contribute not to principled and fearless decision making but to intimidation.

"We do not believe that this settled principle of law was abolished by Section 1983, which makes liable 'every person' who under color of law deprives another person of his civil rights. The legislative record gives no clear indication that Congress meant to abolish wholesale all common-law immunities. Accordingly, this Court held in *Tenney v. Brandhove*, 341 U.S. 367 (1951), that the immunity of legislators for acts within the legislative role was not abolished. The immunity of judges for acts within the judicial role is equally well established, and we presume that Congress would have specifically so provided had it wished to abolish the doctrine.

"The common law has never granted police officers an absolute and unqualified immunity, and the officers in this case do not claim that they are entitled to one. Their claim is rather that they should not be liable if they acted in good faith and with probable cause in making an arrest under a statute that they believed to be valid. Under the prevailing view in this country a peace officer who arrests someone with probable cause is not liable for false arrest simply because the innocence of the suspect is later proved. A policeman's lot is not so unhappy that he must choose between being charged with dereliction of duty if he does not arrest when he has probable cause, and being mulcted in damages if he does. Although the matter is not entirely free from doubt, the same consideration would seem to require excusing him from liability for acting under a statute that he reasonably believed to be valid but that was later held unconstitutional, on its face or as applied."

Disposition:

1. Case against judge correctly dismissed; the judge has absolute immunity for actions done in his/her judicial capacity.
2. Judgment in favor of police reversed and new trial ordered; police officers have qualified immunity if acting in good faith on probable cause that a valid statute has been violated.

15-6d *Buckley v. Fitzsimmons:* 509 U.S. 259, 125 L.Ed. 2d 209, 113 S.Ct. 2606 (1993)

Facts: Eleven-year-old Jeanine Nicarico was murdered on February 25, 1983 in DuPage County, Illinois. Fitzsimmons, the duly elected DuPage County State's Attorney, and the sheriff jointly supervised the investigation of the case. Testimony showed that numerous expert witnesses had been consulted and refused to make a "positive identification" of a boot-print found on the victim's door before an anthropologist from North Carolina was retained as an expert. Fitzsimmons convened a Special Grand Jury but, after an eight-month investigation and testimony from 100 witnesses, no indictment was returned. An indictment was obtained shortly before the primary election in which Fitzsimmons was facing opposition. He held a press conference during which he falsely asserted that numerous pieces of evidence, including the boot-print, tied Buckley to a burglary ring that committed the Nicarico murder. Mug shots of Buckley, which Fitzsimmons released to the media, were prominently displayed on television and in newspapers. Buckley's first trial ended with a hung jury. He was held in custody two more years awaiting retrial. During this period, another person confessed to the murder. The charges were dropped after the key expert witness died.

Issue: Does a prosecutor have absolute immunity for actions taken during the pre-indictment investigation of a case and for statements made to the press?

Reasoning: *** "In *Imbler v. Pachtman,* 424 U.S. 409 (1976), we held that a state prosecutor has absolute immunity for the initiation and pursuit of a criminal prosecution, including presentation of the state's case at trial. . . .

"We applied the *Imbler* analysis two Terms ago in *Burns v. Reed,* 500 U.S. 478 (1991). . . . We held . . . [i]mmunity for that action under Section 1983 accorded with the common-law absolute immunity of prosecutors and other attorneys for eliciting false or defamatory testimony from witnesses or for making false or defamatory statements during, and related to, judicial proceedings. Under that analysis, appearing before a judge and presenting evidence in support of a motion for a search warrant involved the prosecutor's "role as advocate for the State." Because issuance of a search warrant is a judicial act, appearance at the probable-cause hearing was "intimately associated with the judicial phase of the criminal process."

"We further decided, however, that prosecutors are not entitled to absolute immunity for their actions in giving legal advise to the police. We were unable to identify any historical or common-law support for absolute immunity in the performance of this function. We also noted that any threat to the judicial process from 'the harassment and intimidation associated with litigation' based on advise to the police was insufficient to overcome the '[a]bsen[ce] [of] a tradition of immunity comparable to the common-law immunity from malicious prosecution, which formed the basis for the decision in *Imbler.*' . . . In sum, we held that providing legal advice to the police was not a function 'closely associated with the judicial process.' ***

. . . "There is a difference between the advocate's role in evaluating evidence and interviewing witnesses as he prepares for trial, on the one hand, and the detective's role in searching for the clues and corroboration that might give him probable cause to recommend that a suspect be arrested, on the other hand. When a prosecutor performs the investigative functions normally performed by a detective or police officer, it is 'neither appropriate nor justifiable that, for the same act, immunity should protect the one and not the other.' Thus, if a prosecutor plans and executes a raid on a suspected weapons cache, he 'has no greater claim to complete immunity than activities of police officers allegedly acting under his direction.' ***

. . . "A prosecutor neither is, nor should consider himself to be, an advocate before he has probable cause to have anyone arrested.

. . . "A prosecutor may not shield his investigative work with the aegis of absolute immunity merely because, after a suspect is eventually arrested, indicted, and tried, that work may be retrospectively described as 'preparation' for a possible trial; every prosecutor might then shield himself from liability for any constitutional wrong against innocent citizens by ensuring that they go to trial. When the functions of prosecutors and detectives are the same, as they were here, the immunity that protects them is also the same.

"Fitzsimmons' statements to the media are not entitled to absolute immunity. . . . Indeed, while prosecutors, like all attorneys, were entitled to absolute immunity from defamation liability for statements made during the course of judicial proceedings and relevant to them, most statements made out-of-court received only good-faith immunity. . . .

"The functional approach of *Imbler,* which conforms to the common-law theory, leads us to the same conclusion. Comments to the media have no functional tie to the judicial process just because they are made by a prosecutor. . . . The conduct of a press conference does not involve the initiation of a prosecution, the presentation of the state's case in court, or actions preparatory for these functions. Statements to the press may be an integral part of a prosecutor's job, and they may serve a vital public function. But in these respects a prosecutor is in no different position than other executive officials who deal with the press and, as noted above, qualified immunity is the norm for them."

Disposition: Case remanded for trial; prosecutors have qualified immunity for actions taken during the pre-indictment investigation of the case and for statements made to the media.

15-6e *City of Canton, Ohio v. Harris:* 489 U.S. 378, 103 L.Ed. 2d 412, 109 S.Ct. 1197 (1989)

Facts: In April 1978, officers of the Canton Police Department arrested Harris and brought her to the police station. When she arrived at the station Harris was found sitting on the floor of the wagon. When asked if she needed medical attention, she responded with an incoherent remark. Twice after she was taken inside the station, she slumped to the floor. Officers finally left her lying on the floor to prevent her from falling again. No medical attention was ever given. About an hour after the arrest, she was released and taken to the hospital in an ambulance provided by her family. She was hospitalized for a week due to several emotional ailments and received outpatient treatment for about a year. The jury verdict in a suit under Section 1983 was in favor of the city.

Issue: When are governmental agencies liable under the Civil Rights Act for failure to properly train their personnel?

Reasoning: *** "In *Monell v. New York City Department of Social Services*, 436 U.S. 658 (1978), we decided that a municipality can be found liable under Section 1983 only where the municipality itself causes the constitutional violation at issue. Respondeat superior or vicarious liability will not attach under Section 1983. ***

*** "[A] municipality can be liable under Section 1983 only where its policies are the 'moving force [behind] the constitutional violation.' Only where a municipality's failure to train its employees in a relevant respect evidences a 'deliberate indifference' to the rights of its inhabitants can such a shortcoming be properly thought of as a city 'policy or custom' that is actionable under Section 1983. ***

*** "The issue in a case like this one, however, is whether that training program is adequate; and if it is not, the question becomes whether such inadequate training can justifiably be said to represent 'city policy.' *** But it may happen that in light of the duties assigned to specific officers or employees that need for more or different training is so obvious, and the inadequacy so likely to result in the violation of constitutional rights, that the policymakers of the city can reasonably be said to have been deliberately indifferent to the need. ***

"In resolving the issue of a city's liability, the focus must be on adequacy of the training program in relation to the tasks the particular officers must perform. That a particular officer may be unsatisfactorily trained will not alone suffice to fasten liability on the city, for the officer's shortcomings may have resulted from factors other than a faulty training program. It may be, for example, that an otherwise sound program has occasionally been negligently administered. Neither will it suffice to prove that an injury or accident could have been avoided if an officer had had better or more training, sufficient to equip him to avoid that *particular* injury-causing conduct. *** And plainly, adequately trained officers occasionally make mistakes; the fact that they do says little about the training program or the legal basis for holding the city liable.

"Moreover, for liability to attach in this circumstance the identified deficiency in a city's training program must be closely related to the ultimate injury. Thus in the case at hand, respondent must still prove that the deficiency in training actually caused the police officer's indifference to her medical needs."

Disposition: Verdict reversed; a city can be held responsible for failure to adequately train if the training program showed deliberate indifference to constitutional rights directly related to the injury sustained.

15-6f *City of Riverside v. Rivera:* 477 U.S. 561, 91 L.Ed. 2d 466, 106 S.Ct. 2686 (1986)

Facts: On August 1, 1975, a large number of unidentified police officers, acting without a warrant, used tear gas to break up a party at the home of Santos and Rivera. Many of the guests were arrested. Criminal charges were ultimately dropped for lack of probable cause. Rivera and others filed this Section 1983 suit against the city, the police chief, and 30 police officers. The District Court found that unnecessary physical force was used and that the party was not creating a disturbance. Rivera and the other plaintiffs were awarded $33,350 in compensatory damages and punitive damages of $13,300 on the federal claim. Attorneys' fees were awarded for 1,946.75 hours expended by two attorneys at $125 per hour and 84.5 hours by law clerks at $25 per hour, for a total of $245,456.25.

Issue: Must attorneys' fees be proportionate to the monetary recovery?

Reasoning: * * * "As an initial matter, we reject the notion that a civil rights action for damages constitutes nothing more than a private tort suit benefiting only the individual plaintiffs whose rights were violated. Unlike most private tort litigants, a civil rights plaintiff seeks to vindicate important civil and constitutional rights that cannot be valued solely in monetary terms. And, Congress has determined that 'the public as a whole has an interest in the vindication of the rights conferred by the statutes enumerated in Section 1988, over and above the value of a civil rights remedy to a particular plaintiff' * * * Regardless of the form of relief he actually obtains, a successful civil rights plaintiff often secures important social benefits that are not reflected in nominal or relatively small damages awards. In this case, for example, the District Court found that many of petitioners' unlawful acts were 'motivated by a general hostility to the Chicano community,' and that this litigation therefore served the public interest. * * * In addition, the damages a plaintiff recovers contributes significantly to the deterrence of civil rights violations in the future. This deterrent effect is particularly evident in the area of individual police misconduct, where injunctive relief generally is unavailable.

* * * "Congress made clear that it 'intended that the amount of fees awarded under [Section 1988] be governed by the same standards which prevail in other types of equally complex Federal litigation, such as

antitrust cases and *not be reduced because the rights involved may be non-pecuniary in nature.*' '[C]ounsel for prevailing parties should be paid, as is traditional with attorneys compensated by a fee-paying client, *for all time reasonably expended on a matter.*' Thus, Congress recognized that reasonable attorneys' fees under Section 1988 are not conditioned upon and need not be proportionate to an award of money damages.

*** "Congress enacted Section 1988 specifically because it found that the private market for legal services failed to provide many victims of civil rights violations with effective access to the judicial process. These victims ordinarily cannot afford to purchase legal services at the rates set by the private market."

Disposition: Award of attorneys' fees affirmed; the prevailing party is entitled to an award of attorney's fees for time reasonably expended on the case.

15-7 Other Supreme Court Cases

15-7a *Anderson v. Creighton:* 483 U.S. 635, 97 L.Ed. 2d 523, 107 S.Ct. 3034 (1987)

Facts: Anderson, an FBI agent, and other state and federal law enforcement officers conducted a warrantless search of the Creighton home. They sought a man suspected of a bank robbery committed earlier that day, but did not find him. The Creightons filed this suit in Minnesota state court and Anderson removed it to federal courts. The District Court granted summary judgment for Anderson.

Issue: Do federal officers in *Bivens* suits have qualified immunity if acting on probable cause?

Reasoning: *** "When government officials abuse their offices, 'action[s] for damages may offer the only realistic avenue for vindication of constitutional guarantees.' On the other hand, permitting damage suits against government officials can entail substantial social costs, including the risk that fear of personal monetary liability and harassing litigation will unduly inhibit officials in the discharge of their duties. *** [W]hether an official protected by qualified immunity may be held personally liable for an allegedly unlawful official action generally turns on the 'objective legal reasonableness' of the action. *** It should not be surprising, therefore, that our cases establish that the right the official is alleged to have violated must have been 'clearly established' in a more particularized, and hence more relevant, sense: The contours of the right must be sufficiently clear that a reasonable official would understand that what he is doing violated that right. This is not to say that an official action is protected by qualified immunity unless the very action in question has previously been held unlawful; but it is to say that in the light of preexisting law the unlawfulness must be apparent.

*** "It follows from what we have said that the determination whether it was objectively legally reasonable to conclude that a given search was supported by probable cause or exigent circumstances will often require examination of the information possessed by the searching official. *** The relevant question in this case, for example, is the objective (albeit fact-specific) question whether a reasonable officer could have believed Anderson's warrantless search to be lawful, in light of clearly established law and the information the searching officers possessed. Anderson's subjective beliefs about the search are irrelevant."

Disposition: Case remanded to trial court; federal agents have qualified immunity as long as they are acting in a reasonable belief that probable cause or exigent circumstances warrant their actions.

15-7b *Soldal v. Cook County, Illinois:* 506 U.S. 56, 121 L.Ed. 2d 450, 113 S.Ct. 538 (1992)

Facts: Soldal and his family resided in their trailer home at Willoway Terrace mobile home park in Elk Grove, Illinois, which was owned by Terrace Properties. Eviction proceedings were filed against Soldal. Under Illinois law, a tenant cannot be dispossessed absent a judgment of eviction. The first eviction suit was dismissed but a second action was filed in August 1987 claiming nonpayment of rent. Terrace Properties chose to forcibly evict the Soldals two weeks prior to the scheduled hearing on the eviction. Cook County's Sheriff's Department was notified that the trailer home was going to be removed and requested that for sheriff's deputies be present to forestall any possible resistance. The deputies knew that Terrace Properties did not have an eviction order. Terrace Properties employees began disconnecting utilities from the Soldal trailer and tore off the trailer's canopy and skirts. A tractor was hooked up to the trailer and towed it away. A deputy explained to Soldal that he was there to see that Soldal didn't interfere. Soldal unsuccessfully attempted to file criminal trespass complaints with other deputies that were present. Soldal filed a Section 1983 case. The trial judge granted summary judgment in favor of the defendant.

Issue: Can a Section 1983 suit be based on actions taken by police to assist in an eviction when there is no invasion of the privacy of the home?

Reasoning: *** "As a result of the state action in this case, the Soldal's domicile was not only seized, it literally was carried away, giving new meaning to the term 'mobile home.' We fail to see how being unceremoniously dispossessed of one's home in the manner alleged to have occurred here can be viewed as anything but a seizure invoking the protection of the Fourth Amendment. Whether the Amendment was in fact violated is, of course, a different question that requires determining if the seizure was reasonable. That inquiry entails the weighing of various factors and is not before us. ***

. . . "In our view, the reason why an officer might enter a house or effectuate a seizure is wholly irrelevant to the threshold question of whether the Amendment applies. What matters is the intrusion on the people's security from governmental interference. Therefore, the right against unreasonable seizures would be no less transgressed if the seizure of the house was undertaken to collect evidence, verify compliance with a housing regulation, effect an eviction by the police, or on a whim, for no reason at all. As we have observed on more than one occasion, it would be 'anomalous to say that the individual and his private property are fully protected by the Fourth Amendment only when the individual is suspected of criminal behavior.' ***

"The complaint here alleges that respondents, acting under color of state law, dispossessed the Soldals of their trailer home by physically tearing it from the foundation and towing it to another lot. Taking these allegations as true, this was no 'garden-variety' landlord-tenant dispute. The facts alleged suffice to constitute a 'seizure' within the meaning of the Fourth Amendment, for they plainly implicate the interests protected by that provision. . . ."

Disposition: Summary judgment reversed; a Section 1983 suit can be maintained for actions of law enforcement officers while assisting in an unlawful civil action even though there was no physical intrusion into the privacy of the home.

15-7c *Daniels v. Williams:* 474 U.S. 327, 88 L.Ed. 2d 662, 106 S.Ct. 662 (1986)

Facts: Daniels, an inmate in the Richmond, Virginia city jail, slipped and fell on a pillow left on a stairway. He filed a suit under Section 1983 to recover damages for back and ankle injuries based on a correctional officer's negligence. Motion for summary judgment was granted in favor of the correctional officer.

Issue: Can inmates recover under Section 1983 for negligent injuries?

Reasoning: * * * "The only tie between the facts of this case and anything governmental in nature is the fact that respondent was a sheriff's deputy at the Richmond city jail and petitioner was an inmate confined in that jail. But while the Due Process Clause of the Fourteenth Amendment obviously speaks to some facets of this relationship, we do not believe its protections are triggered by lack of due care by prison officials. * * * Where a government official's act causing injury to life, liberty or property is merely negligent, 'no procedure for compensation is required.'"

Disposition: Summary judgment correctly granted; an inmate has no right to sue under Section 1983 for negligently caused injuries.

15-7d *Hudson v. Palmer:* 468 U.S. 517, 82 L.Ed. 2d 393, 104 S.Ct. 3194 (1984)

Facts: During a "shakedown" of cells at the Bland Correctional Center in Virginia, a ripped pillowcase was found in a trash can near Palmer's cell. Disciplinary proceedings were instituted and Palmer was found guilty of destroying state property. He was given a written reprimand and ordered to reimburse the state for the cost of the pillowcase. Palmer filed a Section 1983 suit alleging that Hudson brought false charges against him with the intent to harass him and that Palmer had been deprived of his property without due process of law. Summary judgment was granted in favor of Hudson.

Issue: When can an inmate file a Section 1983 suit for deprivation of property?

Reasoning: * * * "Notwithstanding our caution in approaching claims that the Fourth Amendment is inapplicable in a given context, we hold that society is not prepared to recognize as legitimate any subjective expectation of privacy that a prisoner might have in his prison cell and that, accordingly, the Fourth Amendment proscription against unreasonable searches does not apply within the confines of the prison cell. The recognition of privacy rights for prisoners in their individual cells simply cannot be reconciled with the concept of incarceration and the needs and objectives of penal institutions.

* * * "Our holding that respondent does not have a reasonable expectation of privacy enabling him to invoke the protections of the Fourth Amendment does not mean that he is without a remedy for calculated harassment unrelated to prison needs. Nor does it mean that prison attendants can ride roughshod over inmates' property rights with impunity.

The Eighth Amendment always stands as a protection against 'cruel and unusual punishments.' By the same token, there are adequate state tort and common-law remedies available to respondent to redress the alleged destruction of his personal property.

*** "Accordingly, we hold that an unauthorized intentional deprivation of property by a state employee does not constitute a violation of the procedural requirements of the Due Process Clause of the Fourteenth Amendment if a meaningful post-deprivation remedy for the loss is available. For intentional, as for negligent deprivations of property by state employees, the State's action is not complete until and unless it provides or refused to provide a suitable post-deprivation remedy."

Disposition: Summary judgment properly granted; inmate cannot bring a Section 1983 suit for destruction of personal property if the state has provided an adequate means of civil redress.

15-7e *Moore v. Sims:* 442 U.S. 415, 60 L.Ed. 2d 994, 99 S.Ct. (1979)

Facts: On March 25, 1976, school authorities notified the Texas Department of Human Resources that Paul Sims was suffering from physical injuries apparently inflicted or aggravated by his father. The Department of Human Resources immediately took all three Sims children to a physician for examinations. All three children were found to be battered and Paul was hospitalized for 11 days. The Department of Human Services obtained an emergency *ex parte* order giving the department temporary custody of the children. Five days later, Mr. and Mrs. Sims appeared in court and moved to regain custody of their children. The judge was not available so the matter was not heard that day. Mr. and Mrs. Sims then filed *habeas corpus* to regain custody of the children. The judge hearing the petition found that jurisdiction was properly in another county and transferred the proceedings. Sims made no effort to have the case heard in the other county; instead this case was filed in federal court seeking a preliminary injunction declaring that the state laws on child abuse reporting and removal of children from the home were unconstitutional. Numerous procedural maneuvers followed. The District Court finally reviewed the statute.

Issue: When should federal courts abstain from proceedings involving state court actions?

Reasoning: *** "The *Younger* [*Younger v. Harris*, 401 U.S. 37 (1971)] doctrine, which counsels federal court abstention when there is a pending state proceeding, reflects a strong policy against federal intervention in state judicial processes in the absence of great and immediate irreparable injury to the federal plaintiff. * * *

* * * "In *Huffman* [*Huffman v. Pursue, Ltd.*, 420 U.S. 592 (1975)] we noted those well-established circumstances where the federal court need not stay its hand in the face of pending state proceedings. '*Younger*, and its civil counterpart which we apply today, do of course allow intervention in those cases where the District Court properly finds that the state proceeding is motivated by a desire to harass or is conducted in bad faith, or where the challenged statute is "flagrantly and patently violative of express constitutional prohibitions in every clause, sentence and paragraph, and in whatever manner and against whomever an effort might be made to apply it." * * *

* * * "Restated in the abstention context, the federal court should not exert jurisdiction if the plaintiffs 'had an *opportunity* to present their federal claims in the state proceedings.' * * * The question is whether that challenge can be raised in the pending state proceedings subject to conventional limits on justiciability. * * * Certainly abstention is appropriate unless state law clearly bars the interposition of the constitutional claims."

Disposition: Case dismissed; federal courts should not enter a case in which state prosecution is pending unless there is bad faith, harassment, or extraordinary circumstances.

15-7f *Heck v. Humphrey:* 512 U.S. 477, 129 L.Ed. 2d 383, 114 S.Ct. 2364 (1994)

Facts: Heck was convicted for voluntary manslaughter of his wife. While the direct appeal was pending, he filed a Civil Rights Act suit in federal court against two prosecutors and an Indiana State Police investigator alleging that they engaged in an "unlawful, unreasonable, and arbitrary investigation" leading to his arrest; they "knowingly destroyed" evidence "which was exculpatory in nature and could have proved [his] innocence," and they caused "an illegal and unlawful voice identification procedure" to be used at his trial. Heck sought compensatory and punitive damages; he did not request an injunction or release from custody. The Indiana Supreme Court later upheld his conviction; federal courts denied *habeas corpus* relief.

Issue: Can the Civil Rights Act be used to challenge the legality of a conviction?

Reasoning: "We hold that, in order to recover damages for allegedly unconstitutional conviction or imprisonment, or for other harm caused by actions whose unlawfulness would render a conviction or sentence invalid, a §1983 plaintiff must prove that the conviction or sentence has been reversed on direct appeal, expunged by executive order, declared invalid by a state tribunal authorized to make such determination, or called into question by a federal court's issuance of a writ of *habeas corpus.* A claim for damages bearing that relationship to a conviction or sentence that has not been so invalidated is not cognizable under §1983. Thus, when a state prisoner seeks damages in a §1983 suit, the district court must consider whether a judgment in favor of the plaintiff would necessarily imply the invalidity of his conviction or sentence; if it would, the complaint must be dismissed unless the plaintiff can demonstrate that the conviction or sentence has already been invalidated."

Disposition: Dismissal of the Civil Rights Act suit is affirmed; Heck cannot pursue the Civil Rights Act suit because his criminal conviction was affirmed and *habeas corpus* relief was denied.

15-7g *Saucier v. Katz:* 533 U.S. 194, 150 L.Ed. 2d 272, 121 S.Ct. 2151, (2001)

Facts: During a speech by Vice President Gore at the Presidio Army Base in San Francisco, Katz and other protesters rushed toward the speaker's platform in an attempt to unfurl a banner they had smuggled into the area. Saucier and another military police officer grabbed Katz from behind as he neared the speaker's platform. Katz was half-walked, half-dragged away and shoved into a waiting military van. He fell to the floor of the van but caught himself in time to avoid injury. He was held briefly at the military police station and released. Katz filed a *Bivens* action in federal court. Both the District Court and Court of Appeals refused to make a pre-trial ruling on Saucier's qualified immunity.

Issue: What standard should be used for a pre-trial determination of whether an officer has qualified immunity for the use of excessive force?

Reasoning: "In a suit against an officer for alleged violation of a constitutional right, the requisites of a qualified immunity defense must be considered in proper sequence. *** The privilege is an *immunity from suit* rather than a mere defense to liability; and like an absolute immunity, it is effectively lost if a case is erroneously permitted to go to trial. As a result, we repeatedly have stressed the importance of resolving immunity questions at the earliest possible stage in litigation.

"A court required to rule upon the qualified immunity issue must consider, then, this threshold question: Taken in the light most favorable to the party asserting the injury, do the facts alleged show the officers conduct violated a constitutional right? * * *

* * * "If no constitutional right would have been violated were the allegations established, there is no necessity for further inquiries concerning qualified immunity. On the other hand, if a violation could be made out on a favorable view of the parties' submissions, the next, sequential step is to ask whether the right was clearly established. This inquiry, it is vital to note, must be undertaken in light of the specific context of the case, not as a broad general proposition; and it too serves to advance understanding of the law and to allow officers to avoid the burden of trial if qualified immunity is applicable.

"In this litigation, for instance, there is no doubt that *Graham v. Connor* clearly establishes the general proposition that use of force is contrary to the Fourth Amendment if it is excessive under objective standards of reasonableness. Yet that is not enough. Rather, we emphasized in *Anderson* [*Anderson v. Creighton,* 483 U.S. 635 (1987)] that the right the official is alleged to have violated must have been clearly established in a more particularized, and hence more relevant, sense: The contours of the right must be sufficiently clear that a reasonable official would understand that what he is doing violates that right. The relevant, dispositive inquiry in determining whether a right is clearly established is whether it would be clear to a reasonable officer that his conduct was unlawful in the situation he confronted. * * *

* * * "In the circumstances presented to this officer, which included the duty to protect the safety and security of the Vice President of the United States from persons unknown in number, neither respondent nor the Court of Appeals has identified any case demonstrating a clearly established rule prohibiting the officer from acting as he did, nor are we aware of any such rule. Our conclusion is confirmed by the uncontested fact that the force was not so excessive that respondent suffered hurt or injury. On these premises, petitioner was entitled to qualified immunity, and the suit should have been dismissed at an early stage in the proceedings."

Disposition: The case should have been dismissed before trial; Saucier is entitled to qualified immunity.

15-7h *Malley v. Briggs:* 475 U.S. 335, 89 L.Ed. 2d 271, 106 S.Ct. 1092 (1986)

Facts: During a court-authorized wiretap, police intercepted a conversation was intercepted between Driscoll and "Dr. Shogun." Based on inferences from this conversation, the police concluded that a marijuana party had occurred at Briggs's home. A complaint was drawn up charging

Briggs and Driscoll with conspiring to violate the uniform controlled substance act. A judge signed arrest warrants for these two individuals and 20 others based on information obtained during the wiretap. Briggs was arrested, arraigned and released. Extensive news coverage resulted because Briggs was a prominent member of the community. The Grand Jury did not return an indictment and the charges were dropped. Briggs filed a civil rights suit against the officer in charge of the wiretap.

Issue: When are police entitled to qualified immunity from suit under Section 1983?

Reasoning: *** "Although we have previously held that police officers sued under Section 1983 for false arrest are qualifiedly immune, petitioner urges that he should be absolutely immune because his function in seeking an arrest warrant was similar to that of a complaining witness. The difficulty with this submission is that complaining witnesses were not absolutely immune at common law. In 1871, the generally accepted rule was that one who procured the issuance of an arrest warrant by submitting a complaint could be held liable if the complaint was made maliciously and without probable cause. ***

*** "Accordingly, we hold that the same standard of objective reasonableness that we applied in the context of a suppression hearing in *Leon* [*U.S. v. Leon,* 468 U.S. 897 (1984)], defines the qualified immunity accorded an officer whose request for a warrant allegedly caused an unconstitutional arrest. Only where the warrant application is so lacking in indicia of probable cause as to render official belief in its existence unreasonable will the shield of immunity be lost.

*** "In *Leon,* we stated that 'our good-faith inquiry is confined to the objectively ascertainable question whether a reasonable well-trained officer would have known that the search was illegal despite the magistrate's authorization.' The analogous question in this case is whether a reasonably well-trained officer in petitioner's position would have known that his affidavit failed to establish probable cause and that he should not have applied for the warrant. If such was the case, the officer's application for a warrant was not objectively reasonable, because it created the unnecessary danger of an unlawful arrest. It is true that in an ideal system an unreasonable request for a warrant would be harmless, because no judge would approve it. But ours is not an ideal system, and it is possible that a magistrate, working under docket pressures, will fail to perform as a magistrate should. We find it reasonable to require the officer applying for the warrant to minimize this danger by exercising reasonable professional judgment."

Disposition: New trial ordered; an officer is entitled to immunity if a reasonable officer acting in good faith would have believed that the action was constitutional.

15-7i *Briscoe v. LaHue:* 460 U.S. 325, 75 L.Ed. 2d 96, 103 S.Ct. 1108 (1983)

Facts: Briscoe, who was convicted of burglarizing a house trailer, brought a suit under Section 1983 against LaHue, a police officer in Bloomington, Indiana. LaHue testified at trial that Briscoe was one of 50 to 100 people in the area whose thumb print would match a partial print found at the scene. Briscoe claimed that the FBI had determined that the partial print was too incomplete to be of value in the investigation. The suit alleged that LaHue committed perjury and that this perjury led to Briscoe's conviction.

Issue: Does Section 1983 give a convicted person the right to sue an officer for giving perjured testimony at his/her trial?

Reasoning: * * * "In short, the common law provided absolute immunity from subsequent damages liability for all persons—governmental or otherwise—who were integral parts of the judicial process. It is equally clear that Section 1983 does not authorize a damages claim against private witnesses on the one hand, or against judges or prosecutors in the performance of their respective duties on the other. When a police officer appears as a witness, he may reasonably be viewed as acting like any other witness sworn to tell the truth—in which event he can make a strong claim to witness immunity; alternatively, he may be regarded as an official performing a critical role in the judicial process, in which event he may seek the benefit afforded to other governmental participants in the same proceeding. Nothing in the language of the statute suggests that such a witness belongs in a narrow, special category lacking protection against damage suits." * * *

* * * "The legislative history and statutory language indicate that Congress intended perjury leading to unjust acquittals of Klan conspirators to be prohibited by Section 2, the civil and criminal conspiracy section of the statute, now codified in relevant part at 42 U.S.C 1985(3) and 18 U.S.C. 241. But the language of Section 1—now codified as Section 1983—differs from that of Section 2 in essential respects, and we find no evidence that Congress intended to abrogate the traditional common-law witness immunity in Section 1983 actions."

Disposition: Suit dismissed; Section 1983 provides no right to sue a witness for committing perjury during a criminal trial.

15-7j *Procunier v. Navarette:* 434 U.S. 555, 55 L.Ed. 2d 24, 98 S.Ct. 855 (1978)

Facts: Navarette, an inmate at Soledad Prison in California, filed a civil rights suit against various prison officials alleging interference with outgoing mail. He claimed that various violations had occurred over a 15-month period in 1971 and 1972: failure to mail letters to legal assistance groups, the media, inmates at other prisons, and personal friends. Navarette alleged that these violations had been done in "bad-faith disregard" of his rights or by negligence or inadvertence of subordinate officers. Summary judgment was granted in favor of the prison officials.

Issue: Do prison officials have qualified immunity for good-faith violations of inmate's rights?

Reasoning: *** "We agree with petitioners that as prison officials and officers, they were not absolutely immune from liability in this Section 1983 damages suit and could rely only on the qualified immunity described in *Scheuer v. Rhodes,* 416 U.S. 232 (1974), and *Wood v. Strickland,* 420 U.S. 308 (1975). ***

"Under the first part of the *Wood v. Strickland* rule, the immunity defense would be unavailing to petitioners if the constitutional right allegedly infringed by them was clearly established at the time of their challenged conduct, if they knew or should have known that their conduct violated the constitutional norm. ***

*** "As a matter of law, therefore, there was no basis for rejecting the immunity defense on the ground that petitioners knew or should have known that their alleged conduct violated a constitutional right. Because they could not reasonably have been expected to be aware of a constitutional right that had not yet been declared, petitioners did not act with such disregard for the established law that their conduct 'cannot reasonably be characterized as in good faith.'

"Neither should petitioners' immunity defense be overruled under the second branch of the *Wood v. Strickland* standard, which would authorize liability where the official has acted with 'malicious intention' to deprive the plaintiff of a constitutional right or to cause him 'other injury.' This part of the rule speaks of 'intentional injury,' contemplating that the actor intends the consequences of his conduct."

Disposition: Case properly dismissed; prison officials are entitled to qualified immunity when acting in good-faith belief that their actions were constitutionally valid.

15-7k *Hope v. Pelzer:* 536 U.S. ___, 153 L.Ed. 2d 666, 122 S.Ct. 2508 (2002)

Facts: Hope was chained to a hitching post on two occasions. On May 11, 1995, while working on an Alabama chain gang, he got into an argument with another inmate. He was taken back to the prison and handcuffed to a hitching post. He was only slightly taller than the hitching post, so his arms were above shoulder height and grew tired. When he tried to move his arms to improve his circulation, the cuffs cut his wrists, causing pain. He was released after two hours when guards determined the altercation was caused by the other inmate. On June 7, 1995, he took a nap during the bus ride to the chain gang's worksite. When the bus arrived, he was slow in responding to an order to get off the bus. An exchange of vulgar remarks led to a wrestling match with a guard. Four other guards intervened, subdued Hope, handcuffed him, placed him in leg irons, and transported him back to the prison where he was cuffed to the hitching post. The guards made him take off his shirt, and he remained shirtless all day while the sun burned his skin. He remained attached to the post for approximately seven hours. He was given water only once or twice and was given no bathroom breaks despite Department of Corrections regulations to the contrary. A guard taunted him about his thirst as he gave water to some dogs.

Hope filed suit in federal court based on 42 U.S.C. § 1983 alleging a violation of his Eighth Amendment rights. The magistrate entered summary judgment in favor of the prison guards based on qualified immunity. The U. S. Court of Appeals made a similar ruling.

Issue: Were the prison guards entitled to have the case dismissed because they were acting in good faith?

Reasoning: "The threshold inquiry a court must undertake in a qualified immunity analysis is whether plaintiff's allegations, if true, establish a constitutional violation. * * *

"'[T]he unnecessary and wanton infliction of pain * * * constitutes cruel and unusual punishment forbidden by the Eighth Amendment.'" We have said that "[a]mong 'unnecessary and wanton' infliction of pain are those that are 'totally without penological justification.'" In making this determination in the context of prison conditions, we must ascertain whether the officials involved acted with "deliberate indifference" to the inmates' health or safety. We may infer the existence of this subjective state of mind from the fact that the risk of harm is obvious.

"As the facts are alleged by Hope, the Eighth Amendment violation is obvious. Any safety concerns had long since abated by the time petitioner was handcuffed to the hitching post because Hope had already been subdued, handcuffed, placed in leg irons, and transported back to the prison. . . . Despite the clear lack of emergency situation, the respondents knowingly subjected him to a substantial risk of physical harm, to unnecessary pain caused by the handcuffs and the restricted position of confinement for a 7-hour period, to unnecessary exposure to the heat of the sun, to prolonged thirst and taunting, and to a deprivation of bathroom breaks that created a risk of particular discomfort and humiliation. The use of the hitching post under these circumstances violated the 'basic concept underlying the Eighth Amendment [, which] is nothing less than the dignity of man.' This punitive treatment amounts to gratuitous infliction of 'wanton and unnecessary' pain that our precedent clearly prohibits.

"Despite their participation in this constitutionally impermissible conduct, the respondents may nevertheless be shielded from liability for civil damages if their actions did not violate 'clearly established statutory or constitutional rights of which a reasonable person would have known.' ***

. . . "For a constitutional right to be clearly established, its contours 'must be sufficiently clear that a reasonable official would understand that what he is doing violates that right. This is not to say that an official action is protected by qualified immunity unless the very action in question has previously been held unlawful; but it is to say that in the light of pre-existing law the unlawfulness must be apparent.'

*** "The obvious cruelty inherent in this practice should have provided respondents with some notice that their alleged conduct violated Hope's constitutional protection against cruel and unusual punishment. Hope was treated in a way antithetical to human dignity—he was hitched to a post for an extended period of time in a position that was painful, and under circumstances that were both degrading and dangerous. This wanton treatment was not done of necessity, but as punishment for prior conduct. Even if there might once have been a question regarding the constitutionality of this practice, the Eleventh Circuit precedent *Gates* [*Gates v. Collier,* 501 F. 2d 1290 (1974)] and *Ort* [*Ort v. White,* 813 F. 2e 318 (1987)], as well as the DOJ report condemning the practice, put a reasonable officer on notice that the use of the hitching post under the circumstances alleged by Hope was unlawful. The 'fair and clear warning' that these cases provided was sufficient to preclude the defense of qualified immunity at the summary judgment stage."

Disposition: Summary judgment vacated; officers do not have qualified immunity based on the facts alleged. Case should go back to the U. S. District Court for trial.

15-71 *Mireles v. Waco:* 502 U.S. 9, 116 L.Ed. 2d 9, 112 S.Ct. 286 (1991)

Facts: After Waco, a public defender, failed to appear at the initial calendar call in Judge Mireles's courtroom, Mireles became angry and instructed two police officers who were present to forcibly seize Waco and bring him into the courtroom. Waco alleged that the officer used excessive force to remove him from another courtroom, cursed at him, and called him vulgar and offensive names, and then slammed him through the doors and swinging gates of Judge Mireles's courtroom. Mireles allegedly "knowingly and deliberately approved and ratified" the officers' actions. Waco filed a civil rights suit, which Mireles succeeded in dismissing on grounds of judicial immunity.

Issue: Does a judge have absolute immunity for offensive conduct while on the bench?

Reasoning: *** "Like other forms of official immunity, judicial immunity is an immunity from suit, not just from ultimate assessment of damages. Accordingly, judicial immunity is not overcome by allegations of bad faith or malice, the existence of which ordinarily cannot be resolved without engaging in discovery and eventual trial.

"Rather, our cases make clear that the immunity is overcome in only two sets of circumstances. First, a judge is not immune from liability for nonjudicial actions, i.e., actions not taken in the judge's judicial capacity. Second, a judge is not immune for actions, though judicial in nature, taken in the complete absence of all jurisdiction.

*** "A judge's direction to court officers to bring a person who is in the courthouse before him is a function normally performed by a judge. Waco, who was called into the courtroom for purposes of a pending case, was dealing with Judge Mireles in the judge's judicial capacity.

"Of course, a judge's direction to police officers to carry out a judicial order with excessive force is not a 'function normally performed by a judge.' But if only the particular act in question were to be scrutinized, then any mistake of a judge in excess of his authority would become a 'nonjudicial' act, because an improper or erroneous act cannot be said to be normally performed by a judge. If judicial immunity means anything it means that a judge 'will not be deprived of immunity because the action he took was in error *** or was in excess of his authority.' Accordingly, as the language in *Stump* [*Stump v. Sparkman,* 435 U.S. 349 (1978)] indicates, the relevant inquiry is the 'nature' and 'function' of the act, not the 'act itself.' In other words, we look to the particular act's relation to a general function normally performed by a judge, in this case the function of directing police officers to bring counsel in a pending case before the court.

"Nor does the fact that Judge Mireles' order was carried out by police officers somehow transform his action from 'judicial' to 'executive' in character. A judge's direction to an executive officer to bring counsel before the court is no more executive in character than a judge's issuance of a warrant for an executive officer to search a home."

Disposition: Case correctly dismissed; a judge has absolute immunity for judicial acts even if done maliciously.

15-7m *Pulliam v. Allen:* 466 U.S. 522, 80 L.Ed. 2d 565, 104 S.Ct. 1970 (1984)

Facts: Allen was arrested in January 1980 for using abusive and insulting language, a Class 3 misdemeanor in Virginia, with a maximum penalty of a fine of $500. He was held in custody for 14 days pending trial because he could not post bond; when convicted, he was fined. He filed a Section 1983 case seeking declaratory and injunctive relief against the judge for incarcerating persons awaiting trial for nonincarcerable offenses. The District Court found it was Judge Pulliam's practice to require bond for nonincarcerable offenses and declared the practice to be a violation of due process and equal protection and issued an injunction against her. Allen was awarded $7,038 in attorney's fees and $653.09 in costs.

Issues:

1. Can an injunction be issued against a judge who is a defendant in a Section 1983 suit?
2. Can a judge who is a defendant in a Section 1983 suit be required to pay the plaintiff's attorney's fees?

Reasoning: *** "We conclude that judicial immunity is not a bar to prospective injunctive relief against a judicial officer acting in her judicial capacity. In so concluding, we express no opinion as to the propriety of the injunctive relief awarded in this case. Petitioner did not appeal the award of injunctive relief against her. ***

*** "Congress has made clear in Section 1988 its intent that attorney's fee be available in any action to enforce a provision of Section 1983. The legislative history of the statute confirms Congress' intent that an attorney's fee award be available even when damages would be barred or limited by 'immunity doctrines and special defenses, available only to public officials.' ***

"Congress' intent could hardly be more plain. Judicial immunity is no bar to the award of attorney's fees under 42 U.S.C. Section 1988."

Disposition: An injunction can be obtained against a judge under Section 1983; attorney's fees can be assessed against a defendant-judge if the plaintiff is the prevailing party.

15-7n *Tower v. Glover:* 467 U.S. 914, 81 L.Ed. 2d 758, 104 S.Ct. 2820 (1984)

Facts: Glover was arrested in California for an Oregon robbery; almost immediately he filed *habeas corpus* in federal court. Tower, a public defender, then represented Glover on different robbery charges; Babcock, a state public defender, represented Glover on an unsuccessful appeal in state court. After the conviction was affirmed, the *habeas corpus* petition was denied because state remedies had not been exhausted. Glover filed this suit and a similar state court suit alleging that the public defenders and other state officials had conspired to deprive him of his constitutional rights. The federal court dismissed the Section 1983 suit against Tower. Nearly two years later, the state court suit went to trial and the jury found that there had been no conspiracy.

Issue: Do public defenders have absolute immunity from civil rights suits for conspiracy to violate the rights of their clients?

Reasoning: *** "Indeed, few state supreme courts have addressed the question of public defender immunity; none to our knowledge has concluded that public defenders should enjoy immunity for intentional misconduct. It is true that at common law defense counsel would have benefited from immunity for defamatory statements made in the course of judicial proceedings, but this immunity would not have covered a conspiracy by defense counsel and other state officials to secure the defendant's conviction.

*** "We conclude that state public defenders are not immune from liability under Section 1983 for intentional misconduct 'under color of' state law, by virtue of alleged conspiratorial action with state officials that deprives their clients of federal rights."

Disposition: Suit improperly dismissed; public defenders do not have absolute immunity for intentional actions that violate their client's rights.

15-7o *City of Newport v. Fact Concerts, Inc.:* 453 U.S. 247, 69 L.Ed. 2d 616, 101 S.Ct. 2748 (1981)

Facts: In 1975, Fact Concerts, Inc. received permission from the Rhode Island Department of Natural Resources to present several summer jazz concerts at Fort Adams, a state park located in the city of Newport. They also obtained an entertainment license from Newport; the city retained the right to cancel the license without liability if "in the opinion of the City the interests of public safety demand." Shortly before the concert date, the group Blood, Sweat and Tears was hired as a replacement for an act that had canceled. The council, claiming that Blood, Sweat and Tears was a rock group that would attract an undesirable audience, voted to cancel the license unless the group was removed. At an emergency council meeting the day before the concert, the license was revoked because Fact Concerts had not complied with several minor safety procedures. The council then offered a new contract, which specifically prohibited Blood, Sweat and Tears from performing, for the same dates. Fact Concerts obtained a state court order prohibiting the city council from interfering with the concert. The two-day event, including a performance by Blood, Sweat and Tears, took place without incident. Fact Concerts filed a civil rights suit against the city council, the mayor, and the city alleging that the cancellation of the license amounted to content-based censorship and violated the right to free expression. The jury awarded Fact Concerts compensatory and punitive damages.

Issue: Is a municipality liable for punitive damages in a civil rights suit?

Reasoning: *** "In sum, we find that considerations of history and policy do not support exposing a municipality to punitive damages for the bad faith actions of its officials. Because absolute immunity from such damages obtained at common law and was undisturbed by the 42nd Congress, and because that immunity is compatible with both the purpose of Section 1983 and general principles of public policy, we hold that a municipality is immune from punitive damages under 42 U.S.C. 1983."

Disposition: Punitive damage award reversed; municipalities have absolute immunity from punitive damages for the bad-faith actions of their officials.

15-7p *Board of County Commissioners of Bryan County, Oklahoma v. Brown:* 520 U.S. 397, 137 L.Ed. 2d 626, 117 S.Ct. 1382 (1997)

Facts: When entering Oklahoma, Mr. Brown decided to avoid stopping at a checkpoint by making a U-turn and returning to Texas. Two sheriff's deputies pursued Brown's vehicle for about four miles at speeds up to 100 miles per hour. After the car stopped, Mrs. Brown did not exit as commanded. Deputy Burns used an "arm bar" technique, grabbed her arm at the wrist and elbow, pulled her from the vehicle, and spun her to the ground. Both of her knees were severely injured. She underwent corrective surgery and may ultimately need knee replacement surgery.

Issue: Is the county liable for damages in a Civil Rights Act suit based on negligence in pre-employment screening of employees?

Reasoning: "We assume that a jury could properly find in this case that Sheriff Moore's assessment of Burns' background was inadequate. Sheriff Moore's own testimony indicated that he did not inquire into the underlying conduct or the disposition of any of the misdemeanor charges reflected on Burns' record before hiring him. But this showing of an instance of inadequate screening is not enough to establish 'deliberate indifference.' *** Only where adequate scrutiny of an applicant's background would lead a reasonable policymaker to conclude that the plainly obvious consequence of the decision to hire the applicant would be the deprivation of a third party's federally protected right can the official's failure to adequately scrutinize the applicant's background constitute 'deliberate indifference.'

*** " [A] finding of culpability simply cannot depend on the mere probability that any officer inadequately screened will inflict any constitutional injury. Rather, it must depend on a finding that *this* officer was highly likely to inflict that *particular* injury suffered by the plaintiff. The connection between the background of the particular applicant and the specific constitutional violation alleged must be strong. ***

"Even assuming without deciding that proof of a single instance of inadequate screening could ever trigger municipal liability, the evidence in this case was insufficient to support a finding that, in hiring Burns, Sheriff Moore disregarded a known or obvious risk of injury. To test the link between respondent's injury, we must ask whether a full review of Burns' record reveals that Sheriff Moore should have concluded that Burns' use of excessive force would be a plainly obvious consequence of the hiring decision. On this point, respondent's showing was inadequate."

Disposition: Judgment reversed; the negligence in pre-employment screening of Burns did not amount to deliberate indifference to the constitutional rights of the citizens of the county.

15-7q *City of Los Angeles v. Heller:* 475 U.S. 796, 89 L.Ed. 2d 806, 106 S.Ct. 1571 (1986)

Facts: Heller sued the City of Los Angeles, individual members of the Police Commission, and two police officers alleging that he had been arrested without probable cause for DUI and the officers had used excessive force in making the arrest. The jury verdict indicated that Heller's rights had not been violated by the police officers; the District Court then dismissed the case against the remaining defendants.

Issue: Can a city be held liable for an officer's acts if the jury held the officer violated no constitutional right?

Reasoning: *** "They [the city and police commissioners] were sued only because they were thought legally responsible for Busley's actions; if the latter inflicted no constitutional injury on respondent, it is inconceivable that petitioners could be liable to respondent.

*** "[T]his was an action for damages, and neither *Monell v. New York City Department of Social Services,* 436 U.S. 658 (1978), nor any other of our cases authorizes the award of damages against a municipal corporation based on the actions of one of its officers when in fact the jury has concluded that the officer inflicted no constitutional harm. If a person has suffered no constitutional injury at the hands of the individual police officer, the fact that the departmental regulations might have authorized the use of constitutionally excessive force is quite beside the point."

Disposition: Case properly dismissed against city; a municipality is not liable for damages when a jury finds an officer violated no constitutional rights.

15-7r *Hafer v. Melo:* 502 U.S. 21, 116 L.Ed. 2d 301, 112 S.Ct. 358 (1991)

Facts: In 1988, Hafer successfully ran for election to the post of Auditor General of Pennsylvania. During the campaign, she promised to fire employees in the Auditor General's office who allegedly obtained their jobs by making payments to a former employee. Melo and seven other employees, whom Hafer fired because they "bought" their jobs, sued her.

Other plaintiffs in the case alleged that they were fired because of their political affiliation. All claims were dismissed on the basis of state immunity from suits.

Issue: Can state officials be sued in their personal capacity for violation of constitutional rights?

Reasoning: *** "In *Kentucky v. Graham,* 473 U.S. 159 (1985), the Court sought to eliminate lingering confusion about the distinction between personal- and official-capacity suits. We emphasized that official-capacity suits 'generally represent only another way of pleading an action against an entity of which an officer is an agent.' A suit against a state official in her official capacity therefore should be treated as a suit against the State. *** Because the real party in interest in an official-capacity suit is the governmental entity and not the named official, 'the entity's "policy or custom" must have played a part in the violation of federal law.' For the same reason, the only immunities available to the defendant in an official-capacity action are those that the governmental entity possesses.

"Personal-capacity suits, on the other hand, seek to impose individual liability upon a government officer for actions taken under color of state law. Thus, '[o]n the merits, to establish *personal* liability in a Section 1983 action, it is enough to show that the official, acting under color of state law, caused the deprivation of a federal right.' While the plaintiff in a personal-capacity suit need not establish a connection to governmental 'policy or custom,' officials sued in their personal capacity, unlike those sued in their official capacities, may assert personal immunity defenses such as objectively reasonable reliance on existing law.

*** "State executive officials are not entitled to absolute immunity for their official actions. In several instances, moreover, we have concluded that no more than a qualified immunity attaches to administrative employment decisions, even if the same official has absolute immunity when performing other functions.

*** "We hold that state officials, sued in their individual capacities, are 'persons' within the meaning of Section 1983. The Eleventh Amendment does not bar such suits nor are state officers absolutely immune from personal liability under Section 1983 solely by virtue of the 'official' nature of their acts."

Disposition: Case dismissed in error; state officials can be sued under Section 1983 for acts done in their individual capacities.

15-7s *Smith v. Wade:* 461 U.S. 30, 75 L.Ed. 2d 632, 103 S.Ct. 1625 (1983)

Facts: Wade brought this Section 1983 suit against Smith and four other guards in the administrative segregation unit of the Algoa Reformatory in Missouri. Evidence at trial showed that Smith added an inmate, sent to segregation for fighting, to Wade's cell. No efforts were made to find a less-crowded cell. The new inmate harassed, beat, and sexually assaulted Wade. Wade claimed Smith and the other defendants knew, or should have known, that he was likely to be assaulted under the circumstances. Only a few weeks earlier, another inmate had been beaten to death in the same dormitory while Smith was on duty. The jury awarded Wade $25,000 compensatory and $5,000 punitive damages against Smith.

Issue: What types of damages can be awarded against correctional officials for injuries to inmates?

Reasoning: * * * "Section 1983 was intended to create 'a species of tort liability' in favor of persons deprived of federally secured rights. * * *

* * * "As for punitive damages, however, in the absence of any persuasive argument to the contrary based on the policies of Section 1983, we are content to adopt the policy judgment of the common law—that reckless or callous disregard for the plaintiff's rights, as well as intentional violations of federal law, should be sufficient to trigger a jury's consideration of the appropriateness of punitive damages.

* * * "'If the plaintiff proves sufficiently serious misconduct on the defendant's part, the question whether to award punitive damages is left to the jury, which may or may not make such an award.' Compensatory damages, by contrast, are mandatory; once liability is found, the jury is required to award compensatory damages in an amount appropriate to compensate the plaintiff for his loss. Hence, it is not entirely accurate that punitive and compensatory damages were awarded in this case on the same standard. To make its punitive award, the jury was required to find not only that Smith's conduct met the recklessness threshold (a question of ultimate fact), but also that his conduct merited a punitive award of $5,000 in addition to the compensatory award (a discretionary moral judgment).

* * * "We hold that a jury may be permitted to assess punitive damages in an action under Section 1983 when the defendant's conduct is shown to be motivated by evil motive or intent, or when it involves reckless or callous indifference to the federally protected rights of others. We further

hold that this threshold applies even when the underlying standard of liability for compensatory damages is one of recklessness."

Disposition: Jury verdict affirmed; compensatory damages can be awarded when there is reckless or callous indifference to protected rights; punitive damages can also be awarded when there is reckless disregard of rights if the jury decides they are justified by the facts.

15-7t *Allee v. Medrano:* 416 U.S. 802, 40 L.Ed. 2d 566, 94 S.Ct. 2191 (1974)

Facts: In June 1966, Medrano and others began an effort to organize a union of the predominantly Mexican-American farmworkers on the lower Rio Grande Valley. These actions led to considerable local controversy. Nelson, one of the principal organizers, was arrested while attempting to persuade laborers from Mexico to support the strike. A union leader was arrested when he questioned a deputy's order to disperse a peaceful demonstration. Nelson was held on a $500 bond for an offense with a $200 fine; friends who came to post bond were verbally abused and told that if they did not leave, they would be jailed. Later that month, when several labor leaders were in the courthouse under arrest, they shouted "viva la huelga" in support of the strike. A deputy struck the union official and held a gun at his forehead, ordering him not to repeat those words in the courthouse. Texas Rangers were called in to assist local authorities. Many serious incidents followed. After arresting union members for picketing the railroad that carried produce out of the area, Rangers held two leaders so that their faces were only inches from a passing train. Officers made illegal arrests and charged union members with resisting arrest. Texas Rangers broke into a house and arrested Dumas in a violent and brutal fashion. As a result, Dumas was hospitalized for four days with a concussion; x-rays showed that he had been hit so hard that his spine was curved out of shape. When Nelson went to the sheriff's office to complain, he was arrested for threatening the life of certain Texas Rangers even though the captain in charge admitted that Nelson had not made a serious threat. Off-duty deputies in official cars regularly distributed an aggressive antiunion newspaper. Rangers told one union member that they had been called into the area to break the strike and would not leave until they had done so. Unlawful assembly laws were selectively enforced against the union organizers; unoffensive gatherings were treated as criminal. Persons with no knowledge of the events were solicited to file criminal complaints against the union. In June 1967, union efforts finally collapsed, largely due to official harassment. The union leaders filed Section 1983 and 1985 suits against local law enforcement and the Texas Rangers and obtained an injunction to prohibit police intimidation in the future.

Issue: When can an injunction be issued under Section 1983?

Reasoning: * * * "Nonetheless there remains the necessity of showing irreparable injury, 'the traditional prerequisite to obtaining an injunction' in any case.

"Such a showing was clearly made here as the unchallenged findings of the District Court show. The appellees sought to do no more than organize a lawful union to better the situation of one of the most economically oppressed classes of workers in the country. Because of the intimidation by state authorities, their lawful effort was crushed. The workers, and their leaders and organizers were placed in fear of exercising their constitutionally protected rights of free expression, assembly, and association. Potential supporters of their cause were placed in fear of lending their support. If they were to be able to regain those rights and continue furthering their cause by constitutional means, they required protection from appellants' concerted conduct. No remedy at law would be adequate to provide such protection.

"Isolated incidents of police misconduct under valid statutes would not, of course, be cause for the exercise of a federal court's equitable powers. * * * Where, as here, there is a persistent pattern of police misconduct, injunctive relief is appropriate. In *Hague v. Committee for Industrial Organization,* 307 U.S. 496 (1939), we affirmed the granting of such relief under strikingly similar facts. There also law enforcement officials set out to crush a nascent labor union. The police interfered with the lawful distribution of pamphlets, prevented the holding of public meetings, and ran some labor organizers out of town. The District Court declared some of the municipal ordinances unconstitutional. In addition, it enjoined the police from 'exercising personal restraint over [the plaintiffs] without warrant or confining them without lawful arrest and production of them for prompt judicial hearing * * * or interfering with their free access to the streets, parks, or public places of the city,' or from 'interfering with the right of the [plaintiffs], their agents and those acting with them, to communicate their views as individuals to others on the streets in an orderly and peaceable manner.'"

Disposition: Granting of injunction affirmed; a federal court can issue an injunction against police conduct if there is a persistent pattern of abuse of constitutional rights.

15-7u *Hewitt v. Helms:* 482 U.S. 755, 96 L.Ed. 2d 654, 107 S.Ct. 2672 (1987)

Facts: Helms was placed in administrative segregation pending investigation of his involvement in a prison riot at the Pennsylvania State Correctional Institution at Huntington. Over seven weeks later, a prison hearing committee, relying solely on an officer's report of testimony of an undisclosed informant, found Helms guilty of striking a correctional officer during the riot. Helms was sentenced to six months of disciplinary restrictive confinement. Helms filed the Section 1983 suit alleging undue delay in holding a hearing and reliance on uncorroborated hearsay violated due process. Summary judgment was entered against Helms on the merits; the judge did not reach the immunity issue. The U.S. Supreme Court granted *certiorari* and determined that the hearing process used met due process requirements. The Supreme Court did not address issue of whether the misconduct conviction violated constitutional rights; on remand, the Court of Appeals ordered the District Court to enter summary judgement for the plaintiff on this issue. Upon return to the District Court, summary judgment was granted in favor of the defendants on the issue of damages due to qualified immunity because the right involved was not "clearly established" at the time of the violation. Helms appealed but lost. The District Court granted Helms' request for attorney's fees.

Issue: When can attorney's fees be assessed against a defendant in a Section 1983 suit?

Reasoning: *** "In order to be eligible for attorney's fees under Section 1988, a litigant must be a 'prevailing party.' Whatever the outer boundaries of that term may be, Helms does not fit within them. Respect for ordinary language requires that a plaintiff receive at least some relief on the merits of his claim before he can be said to prevail. Helms obtained no relief. Because of the defendants' official immunity he received no damages award. No injunction or declaratory judgment was entered in his favor. Nor did Helms obtain relief without benefit of a formal judgment—for example, through a consent decree or settlement. The most that he obtained was an interlocutory ruling that his complaint should not have been dismissed for failure to state a constitutional claim. That is not the stuff of which legal victories are made.

*** "It is settled law, of course, that relief need not be judicially decreed in order to justify a fee award under Section 1988. A lawsuit sometimes produces voluntary action by the defendant that affords the plaintiff all or some of the relief he sought through a judgment—e.g., a monetary settlement or a change in conduct that redresses the plaintiff's grievances. When that occurs, the plaintiff is deemed to have prevailed despite the absence of a formal judgment in his favor. * * *The real value of the judicial pronouncement—what makes it a proper judicial resolution of a 'case or controversy' rather than an advisory opinion—is in the settling of some dispute *which affects the behavior of the defendant towards the plaintiff.* The 'equivalency' doctrine is simply an acknowledgment of the primacy of the redress over the means by which it is obtained. * * * As a consequence of the present lawsuit, Helms obtained nothing from the defendants. The only 'relief' he received was the moral satisfaction of knowing that a federal court concluded that his rights had been violated. * * *

* * * "We conclude that a favorable judicial statement of law in the course of litigation that results in judgment against the plaintiff does not suffice to render him a 'prevailing party.'"

Disposition: Attorney's fees granted in error; a plaintiff has the right to collect attorney's fees only if he/she receives a favorable judicial judgment, out-of-court settlement, or consent decree.

15-7v *Hughes v. Rowe:* 449 U.S. 5, 66 L.Ed. 2d 163, 101 S.Ct. 173 (1980)

Facts: Hughes and two other inmates at the Illinois State Penitentiary were charged with violating prison regulations by consuming homemade alcoholic beverages. He was placed in segregation and a disciplinary hearing was held two days later. At the hearing, Hughes admitted the violation and was given 10 days confinement in segregation, a demotion in class, and loss of 30 days; statutory good time. He filed a suit under Section 1983 alleging that there was no emergency to justify placing him in segregation prior to the disciplinary hearing and that the hearing officers at the disciplinary hearing were biased against him. After giving Hughes several opportunities to amend the suit, the District Court judge dismissed the case and awarded the state $400 in attorney's fees.

Issue: When can attorney's fees be assessed against the plaintiff in a Section 1983 suit?

Reasoning: * * * "Petitioner's complaint, like most prisoner complaints filed in the Northern District of Illinois, was not prepared by counsel. It is settled law that the allegations of such a complaint, 'however inartfully pleaded' are held 'to less stringent standards than formal pleadings drafted by lawyers.' Such a complaint should not be dismissed for failure to state a claim unless it appears beyond doubt that the plaintiff can prove no set of facts in support of his claim which would entitle him to relief. And of course, the allegations of the complaint are generally taken as true for purposes of a motion to dismiss.

"Applying these principles to petitioner's amended complaint, we conclude that all but one of its allegations were properly dismissed for failure to state a claim. * * *

"In *Christiansburg Garment Co. v. EEOC*, 434 U.S. 412 (1978), we held that the defendant in an action brought under Title VII of the Civil Rights Act of 1964 may recover attorney's fees from the plaintiff only if the District Court finds 'that the plaintiff's action was frivolous, unreasonable, or without foundation, even though not brought in subjective bad faith.' Although arguably a different standard might be applied in a civil rights action under 42 U.S.C. Section 1983, we can perceive no reason for applying a less stringent standard. The plaintiff's action must be meritless in the sense that it is groundless or without foundation. The fact that a plaintiff may ultimately lose his case is not in itself a sufficient justification for the assessment of fees. * * *

"These limitations apply with special force in actions initiated by uncounselled prisoners. Faithful adherence to the principles of *Haines v. Kerner* [404 U.S. 519 (1972)] dictates that attorney's fees should rarely be awarded against such plaintiffs. The fact that a prisoner's complaint, even when liberally construed, cannot survive a motion to dismiss does not, without more, entitle the defendant to attorney's fees. An unrepresented litigant should not be punished for his failure to recognize subtle factual or legal deficiencies in his claim. As the Court noted in *Christiansburg*, even if the law or the facts are somewhat questionable or unfavorable at the outset of litigation, a party may have an entirely reasonable ground for bringing suit."

Disposition: Award of attorney's fees reversed; attorney's fees should be awarded against a plaintiff in Section 1983 suits only if the suit is groundless or without foundation.

Chapter Quiz

True/False

1. The Civil Rights Act of 1871 applies to violations of constitutional rights that were done under the color of state law.
2. You can sue federal agents for a "constitutional tort" if they violate your constitutional rights.

3. A person can sue a police officer, but not other government employees, for violation of his/her constitutional rights.
4. A city can be successfully sued for a violation of civil rights if the plaintiff can prove that the city failed to sufficiently train its officers about constitutional issues.
5. Judges have absolute immunity from suit under the Civil Rights Act for actions done in their judicial capacity.
6. Prosecutors have absolute immunity from suit under the Civil Rights Act for all actions related to criminal cases.
7. Police officers have qualified immunity from suit under the Civil Rights Act.
8. A witness in a criminal trial has absolute immunity from civil suit under the Civil Rights Act relating to his/her testimony at trial.
9. If the plaintiff wins in a Civil Rights Act case, the defendant must pay the plaintiff's attorney fees.
10. If a Civil Rights Act suit is dismissed because it is frivolous, the plaintiff can be required to pay the defendant's attorney fees.

Discussion Questions

1. The police broke into Paul's home without probable cause and ransacked it while searching for a suspected drug dealer. What does Paul need to establish in order to win a Section 1983 suit? To overcome qualified immunity of the police officers? To hold the city liable for failure to train the officers? To receive attorney's fees?
2. Dan, a deputy district attorney, filed felony charges against Sam, fully knowing that the charges were based on false allegations by Sam's former business associate. Pat, a deputy public defender, was appointed to defend Sam. Pat made serious errors in handling the case and Sam was convicted. Can Sam win a Section 1983 suit against Dan? Can he win against Pat? Explain.
3. Inge was an inmate in the state prison when she was attacked by Kory, a correctional officer. Kory claims that he believed that Inge was attacking another correctional officer. What must Inge establish to win a Section 1983 suit? To overcome qualified immunity of the correctional officers? To hold the state liable for Kory's actions? To receive attorney's fees?
4. Miguel filed a Section 1983 suit alleging that the police in City X routinely arrest Chicanos without probable cause. At trial, he established that 50 percent of the people with Hispanic last names who are arrested for misdemeanors are released without filing charges. Can Miguel obtain an injunction against the police in City X? Explain.

Index

Key cases are in **bold**.

F

G

H

I

Y

Z